CW00486927

The Sunday Telegraph

GOOD
WINE
GUIDE
1999

ROBERT JOSEPH

DORLING KINDERSLEY
LONDON • NEW YORK • SYDNEY • MOSCOW
www.dk.com

A Dorling Kindersley Book

Visit us on the World Wide Web at
http://www.robert-joseph.com
and http://www.dk.com

Editor Robert Joseph
Deputy Editor Kitty Johnson
Senior Editorial Assistant Xenia Irwin
Editorial Assistants Lucy Barlow,
Marie-Pierre Eldon-Edington

Typeset by RJ Publishing Services
Film outputting bureau: Personality
Printed and bound in Italy by L.E.G.O.
First published in 1983 by The Sunday Telegraph

A CIP catalogue record is available from the British Library.

ISBN 0-7513-0616-9

CONTENTS

INTRODUCTION

As winemakers around the globe prepare to make their ultimate vintage of the 20th century, we would like to welcome you to the 14th – and biggest ever – edition of *The Sunday Telegraph Good Wine Guide*. As in the past, the Guide is really three books in one.

In the first section – the *Basics* – you will find all the grounding you need to get through a dinner party among wine buffs, as well as guidance on styles, flavours, vintages and the most compatible marriages between hundreds of wines and dishes.

The following section – the *A–Z* – is an encyclopedia of some 2,700 wines, terms, regions and producers that will enable you to find your way as easily through the intricacies of an auctioneer's catalogue as around the wine shelves of a supermarket. Unlike any other encyclopedia of its kind, the A–Z goes on to recommend currently available vintages and examples that show off specific wines and winemakers at their best.

The A–Z also uniquely tells you how to pronounce the names of all those wines. So, with the book to hand, you will never have to pause before ordering a bottle of Ngatarawa from New Zealand or Beaulieu Napa Valley Cabernet (it's *boh-lyoo* by the way, not *boh-lyuh* as a French-speaker might reasonably expect).

Having chosen your wine, you won't have to search to find a decent merchant from whom to buy it. Simply turn to the third section of the book – the *UK Merchants* – where you will find details of over 260 British stockists, ranging from quirky one-man-bands and City traditionalists to wine clubs, mail-order specialists, high street chains and supermarkets.

Taken as a whole, the **guide** should (as a reviewer wrote of a previous edition) be the 'only wine book you need' when choosing, buying or drinking wine in 1999.

This year's *Guide* particularly owes its existence to the efforts to Kitty Johnson, my deputy editor, and to editorial assistants Marie-Pierre Eldon-Edington, Xenia Irwin and Lucy Barlow. I also have to thank Piers Russell-Cobb and, at Dorling Kindersley, Ros Thiro, Vivien Crump, Ingrid Vienings, and Sue Jamieson who had the task of checking every dot and comma. Elfreda Pownell at the *Sunday Telegraph*; and Susan Vumbach Low, Chris Orr and Colin Bailey-Wood at *WINE* Magazine were as indulgent as ever. All of these people share any credit for this book; the criticism should fall on my shoulders alone.

THE
BASICS

NEWS

CHANGING TIMES

1998 was the year when Rolls Royce and Chrysler were bought by German motor manufacturers, and when the Californian Robert Mondavi winery launched the Seña and Luce wines it has 'co-produced' in Chile and Italy. Until now, every time I have tried to draw parallels between wine and cars or any other desirable item of modern life, I have been slapped down with the response that wine is different. It's not a manufactured item; it's the product of hundreds of years of tradition that lie behind the vineyards.

Well, maybe that's the way it used to be but, as the people at Mondavi and their competitors are now making abundantly clear, the styling, making and selling of a bottle of red or white wine now involves as much expertise in manufacturing, marketing and international brand-building as any four-door saloon.

As recently as 20 years ago, winemakers in the finest regions of France barely knew what their neighbours were doing on the other side of the cellar wall. Since then, wine has become a global industry. Bordeaux château-owners now make vintage port; Champagne houses produce Burgundy; Australians ferment wine in California; Spaniards reinvent Tokaji in Hungary. And so on, ad infinitum.

The shock to the old system is palpable. Early in 1998, the grandees of Bordeaux admitted as much by hosting a no-holds-barred round table at which a couple of dozen commentators from throughout the world (including myself) were invited to paint their own vision of 'Bordeaux, the brand'. Revealingly, though, while the visitors stressed the need to improve the quality of humble examples of the product, the Bordelais themselves appeared to be far more interested in matters of packaging and promotion.

Counting Sheep

Back in the New World, the impeccably packaged and promoted Mondavi joint-venture wines, like so many politicians' speeches and successful movies, left the appealing but oddly soulless impression of products that have been refined by focus groups and preview audiences. As these and far too many other wines demonstrate, the spirit of innovation which is outlawed by Europe's traditionalist appellation laws, is oddly just as hard to find among the supposedly pioneering winemakers of the New World.

Throughout the globe, grapegrowers and winemakers are treating a handful of French and Italian regions as though they, and they alone, invented the vinous wheel. There are scores of fascinating grapes and hundreds of delicious wine styles, but the focus in the new vineyards seems to be almost exclusively on replicating Bordeaux and Burgundy, with just a token glance at Tuscany and the Rhône.

Just look at the statistics. Fifteen years ago, California was producing some seven million 12-bottle cases of Chardonnay. In the Year 2000 that figure will have risen to 45,000,000 cases. On either side of the Andes mountains, Chile and Argentina have been busily indulging in their own orgy of Chardonnay planting – as have grapefarmers in Australia, South Africa, Southern France, Spain, Italy and Eastern Europe. No one knows just how much there is going to be; what we do know is that the acreage in California of the Riesling, for most wine experts by far the finer white grape variety, is actually going *down*.

Even more ludicrously, alongside the Chardonnay, the most keenly planted variety at the moment is the Merlot, a grape which only produces really good wine on very special sites and when given very careful handling. Despite this, the acreage of Merlot in California has grown from 2,500 in 1985 to at least 60,000 today.

The only good news about all the sheep-like planting is that the price of grapes in the vineyards is already plummeting – which has to be good news for the price of the stuff in the bottle.

Out of Reach

If decent basic wine will soon be as common as milk, 1998 brought the sad – for some – realisation that what auctioneers like to call 'fine and rare' wine is fast becoming the exclusive preserve of the seriously rich. Even today, a bottle of Château Margaux from a less than illustrious year can still be bought for around the price of a meal for two in a less than illustrious restaurant – and 15-20 times the cost of a pleasant ordinary red. But that differential is set to widen as a growing mass of new money globally continues to chase the strictly limited number of bottles of classic wine.

Once again, I'll unashamedly turn to the example of the motor industry. A few years ago, the idea of a £100,000 Mercedes would have been unthinkable – as would have been the notion of anyone paying £500 for a bottle of wine from Château le Pin, a château which didn't even exist when most of the classic books on Bordeaux were written.

In 1998 the price of le Pin dropped a little, following the temporary malady suffered by the tiger economies. But there was still no shortage of buyers for the 1997 vintage in Bordeaux, even though most experienced observers thought it woefully overpriced.

The Real McCoy, Margaux or Mouton...

Just as nature abhors a vacuum, dishonest minds find it impossible to pass up the chance to make a quick buck. Of all the world's more desirable items, bottles of fine wine are ludicrously easy to replicate and fake. If you want to check the authenticity of a questionable US $100 bill all you have to do is take it into a bank where the vaults will be full of genuine examples with which it can be compared. A doubtful painting can be set before an expert whose eye can analyse the skill, style, paint and brushwork.

Now, let's look at a bottle of Cheval Blanc 1947, Mouton-Rothschild 1945 or Pétrus 1982 – all frequent objects of the forger's art. Until the cork is removed, the only things to judge are the bottle – quite probably genuine, but possibly refilled – and an easily forgeable printed label and capsule. Convincing old corks are harder to mark and fake, though I understand there are processes that do age them up quite effectively. As for the wine, the trick lies in mixing vintages and/or regions. (California wine from the 1970s apparently stands in well for 50 year-old claret.) Done carefully, this kind of scam can yield quite extraordinary profits – and very little risk.

Experienced palates – auctioneers, merchants, skilled collectors – can spot a wine that is plainly out of character with what it claims to be, but many of the forgers' victims have no way of knowing whether the apparently venerable wine in their glass is the venerable wine they paid for. Besides, even the experts often surprisingly find the smell of rat a little too faint for anyone to cry foul. Technology is riding to the defence of winemakers and drinkers, in the shape of invisible identifying markers that can be placed in printed form on the label and even – in flavourless liquid form – within the wine itself. Using these to tag bottles of old claret will naturally be tricky, but if they are adopted for current vintages, they should go a long way to protecting us against future skulduggery.

What's Next?

As the last few drops drain out of the 20th century, I thought I might just make a little wish-list of the five things I'd most like to see happen in the world of wine over the next few years.

1) The belated disappearance of the natural cork.

What I am buying when I shell out for a bottle of wine is the content not the package – especially when the manufacturers of this particular piece of packaging conservatively admit that at least three in every hundred of their products will impart an unwelcome musty flavour to the liquid. (In my experience, a significantly larger proportion will insidiously flatten the flavour of the wine while going completely unblamed.)

Corks are part of a mystique that has nothing to do with the quality of the drink. Wine existed before the invention of the cork stopper and will continue to exist long after we have taken its replacement for granted. Metal screwcaps have been proven to keep all sorts of wine fresh for decades and should be introduced for inexpensive red and white forthwith. Producers of higher quality wine should test the long-term efficiency of plastic and traditional corks. And they should offer customers the choice between them.

2) The acceptance in the Old World that tradition, however admirable, should never be an excuse for laziness and a refusal to question whether there isn't a better way of doing things.

The smart châteaux of Bordeaux have had no compunction in introducing machines to concentrate the flavour of their grape juice, but their poorer neighbours are still forbidden from giving their vines a drink when they are dying of thirst. Bordeaux and Burgundy should be leading the way in experimenting with alternatives to cork (see above) rather than pretending that the problem doesn't concern them. And they should be experimenting with grape varieties and techniques that could raise the quality while maintaining the character of the humblest wines in both regions.

3) The acceptance in the New World that fashion, however seductive, should never be an excuse for laziness and a refusal to question whether there isn't a better way of doing things.

So, let's call a halt to blind follow-my-leader planting of Chardonnay and Merlot, and an immediate move towards the exploration of other grape varieties – and blends of them.

4) The disempowerment of over-influential gurus.

Robert Parker is an honest man with a very fine palate. But he is no more superhuman than any of a number of other honest men and women with very fine palates. Thankfully, wine has a butterfly-like tendency to avoid being pinned down precisely by any critic; all too often, it makes nonsense of our predictions and opinions and fools of us all. So, in the first years of the new century, maybe we'll all develop the courage to look beyond the gurus and their points out of 100 – and to learn to trust our own opinions and experience.

5) The renaissance of the individual wine merchant.

Throughout the world, wine has been inexorably sucked into supermarkets and discount stores where promotion, press comment, price and instant profit all hold sway. What a growing number of intelligent wine drinkers want now is a merchant with a limited range of varied, individual wines in which he or she personally believes – irrespective of the critics and the hype.

A PERSONAL SELECTION

An unashamedly quirky list of varied wines that, out of the thousands I have tasted this year, have caught my attention. Prices are rounded to the nearest pound. (For stockists, see page 252.)

RED WINES FOR DAILY DRINKING

1997 Deakin Estate Shiraz £5 (Oddbins, see page 261) Severe shortages of grapes Down Under have meant that inexpensive Australian reds have been less impressive recently. This is a tasty berryish exception to the rule.

1996 Fiuza Cabernet Sauvignon £5 (Bottoms Up, see page 254) Reliable modern winemaking in Portugal, from Australian-born, Portugal-based Peter Bright. Juicy blackcurranty value.

1997 Chiaro di Luna Montepulciano d'Abruzzo £5 (Fullers, see page 256) A fresh, young, modern version of what can be hefty over-ripe stuff. Herbs and crunchy berries.

1997 Pinotage Impala £5 (Waverley Direct, see page 254) Made from the grape that is to South Africa what the Zinfandel is to California. Youthful, spicy and delicious.

1997 Gouts et Couleurs Syrah-Mourvedre £4 (Somerfield, see page 263) 'Tastes and colours', is the name and this southern French blend of two Rhône grape varieties does indeed have far more spicy flavour than most at this price.

1997 Viña Armantes Tempranillo, Cooperativa San Gregorio £4 (Majestic, see page 259) Spain's wine revolution in a glass: good, youthful, strawberryish wine.

1997 Trio Merlot £6 (Wine Rack, see page 266) There are lots of good value Chilean reds around. This attractively plummy one has some really classy Merlot character.

1997 Terrasses de Guilhem Rouge £4 (Adnams, see page 252) A budget-priced red from the maker of Mas de Daumas Gassac, the cult Vin de Pays. At once fruity and richly gamey.

1996 Dom Pascual Tannat Roble £6 (Direct Wine Shipments, see page 255) The Tannat is an obscure grape that is used in South-West France and, to great effect, in this tasty, autumn-fruity, tobaccoey red from Uruguay.

1990 Domaine Boyar Special Reserve Cabernet Sauvignon £4 (Thresher, see page 264) A rare opportunity to drink an affordable, really mature wine. The kind of great, easy-drinking bargain that has won Bulgarian wines so many fans.

Red Wines for Special Occasions

1994 Wynn's John Riddoch Cabernet Sauvignon £31 (D. Byrne, Tel: 01200 423 152) A really great Australian red – full of typical Coonawarra blackcurrant and mint, with balanced oak.

1995 Manso de Velasco £12 (Portland Wine Co., see page 262) Miguel Torres' top-of-the-line wine from Chile is full of classy, complex, deep berry fruit flavours.

1996 Cullen Cabernet-Merlot £12 (Wine Cellars, see page 266) Vanya Cullen, one of the world's top female winemakers, is fast proving the Margaret River to be the source of some of Australia's subtlest, most complex wines.

1994 Meerlust Merlot £11 (James Nicholson, see page 261) Best known for its (less impressive) 'Rubicon' this South African estate regularly makes impressive plum and mulberry Merlots.

1995 Corton Clos des Cortons, Faiveley £40 (Direct Wine Shipments, see page 255) Sheer class Grand Cru red Burgundy at its best, with raspberry and licorice and just enough oak.

1994 Sitorey, Angelo Gaja £18 (Lay & Wheeler, see page 259) The wizard of Piedmont has produced a – relatively – early-drinking wine with lovely cherryish, tarry flavours.

1995 Sogrape Douro Reserva £8 (Booths, see page 253) Portugal's biggest wine company is proving with deep, dark, rich wines like this that the Douro can do more than just make port

1996 Qupé Bien Nacido Syrah £10 (Great Western, see page 257) Lovely spicy Rhône-style wine from southern California.

1996 Rivola Abadia Retuerta £7 (Victoria Wine, see page 265). Spain's answer to a Super Tuscan – at least that's the impression this impeccably-made complex wine made on me.

1995 Gallo Frei Ranch Zinfandel £9 (Asda, see page 254) I never thought I'd be praising a wine from E&J Gallo but, by any standards, this is top class, berryish Sonoma Zinfandel.

1995 Capitel Monte Olmi Amarone, Tedeschi £16 (Direct Wine Shipments, see page 255) Raisiny Amarone from a top class producer. Enjoy with a really good mature Parmesan.

1996 Fetzer Barrel Select Pinot Noir £9 (Oddbins, see page 261) Consistently the most impressive producer of fairly priced wines, Fetzer is right on target with this rich raspberryish example of what is still the trickiest red grape.

1994 Opus One £66 (D. Byrne, Tel: 01200 423 152) California's blackcurranty but complex answer to the best of Bordeaux.

1995 Ch. de Pez £20 (Bottoms Up, see page 254) Recently bought by Roederer and now making classic, stylish Bordeaux.

1990 Ch. Pontet-Canet £30 (Justerini & Brooks, see page 259) Surprisingly ready to drink now, but showing plenty of real cedary class and potential. Great wine, from a reliable chateau.

WHITE WINE FOR DAILY DRINKING

1997 Fox Wood Bruno's Block Chardonnay £5 (Noel Young Wines, see page 267) A subtle southern French wine made by the former owner of the Goundrey winery in Australia.

1997 Palo Alto Chardonnay £5 (Direct Wine Shipments, see page 255) From a new region in Chile, this is good medium-bodied wine with lovely pineapple flavour.

1997 Penfolds Rawson's Retreat Riesling £5 (Widely available) Yet more Australian proof that affordable wine that's made in huge quantities can outclass far pricier fare.

1996 Hugh Ryman Roussanne £5 (Waitrose, see page 265) A rich, spicy and floral wine made in southern France from a characterful grape variety rarely found outside the Rhône.

1997 Verdicchio Classico, Gioacchino Garofoli £4 (Tesco, see page 264) Verdicchio can be really dull stuff, but this is lovely, fresh and herby. A great antidote to oaky Chardonnay.

1997 Sacred Hill Oaked Semillon-Chardonnay £5 (Lea & Sandeman, see page 259) A tasty blend of peachy, buttery and vanilla flavours. Very Australian; very good.

1996 Alamos Ridge Chardonnay £5 (Fullers, see page 256) Great value wine from Argentina. Soft, fresh and very, very easy to drink. The kind of competition that ought to worry Chile.

1996 Marques de Griñon Durius Blanco £5 (Wine Cellars, see page 266) Fresh, unoaked white skilfully made in a modern style, using traditional Spanish grape varieties.

1997 Woodcutter's White £3 (Safeway, see page 262) A tasty unoaked bargain produced in Hungary from an indigenous grape,that is a mouthful to say, the Czerszegi Fuszeresa.

1997 Cortese Alto Monferrato, Araldica £5 (Valvona & Crolla, see page 265) Distinctive, dry, limey wine made in Piedmont from one of Italy's indigenous white grapes.

1997 Ponte Vecchio Oaked Soave £4 (Co-op, see page 255) A quietly revolutionary wine, at a very low price. Creamy, almondy and distinctly oaky. Unlike any Soave I've ever tasted before.

1997 Con Class Blanco £4 (Moreno, see page 260) Great value, delicious, tangy wine made from a blend of local grapes and Sauvignon in the little-known Spanish region of Rueda.

1997 Graves Blanc, Yvon Mau £5 (Fullers, see page 256) Peachy, young, dry white Bordeaux, with just enough oak.

1997 Montlouis Chapelle de Cray £6 (Victoria Wine, see page 265) Lovely rich, dry, appley, waxy Chenin Blanc from a good vintage in the Loire. Classic stuff.

1997 Schloss Schonborn Riesling Kabinett £6 (Somerfield, see page 263) Fresh, off-dry, appley wine with the perfumed subtlety that only German Riesling can achieve.

WHITE WINE FOR SPECIAL OCCASIONS

1996 Bernkasteler Badstube Riesling Kabinett £8 (James Nicholson, see page 261) Youthful, racy wine with ripe grapey fruit and zingy acidity. Great with spicy food.

Chablis Montée de Tonnerre Premier Cru 1996, Verget £18 (Lay & Wheeler, see page 259) Classic northern white Burgundy with pineapple, apple, cream and a steely backbone. Chardonnay whose complexity owes nothing to oak.

1996 Gewurztraminer Altenbourg Cuvée Laurence Dom. Weinbach-Faller £24 (Justerini & Brooks, see page 259) The Gewurztraminer grape at its least flashy and obvious. Lovely, subtle, yet concentrated wine with delicate lychee fruit.

1997 Mas de Daumas Gassac £16 (Adnams, see page 252) A brilliant spicy-creamy blend of Rhône grapes and Chardonnay, plus a touch of oaky vanilla. The classiest of all Vin de Pays whites.

1996 Tim Adams Semillon £9 (Tesco, see page 264) The flavours of peaches and oak combine beautifully in this rich, dry wine from Australia's Clare Valley.

1997 Sancerre Blanc les Caillottes, Pascal Jolivet £11 (D. Byrne, Tel: 01200 423 152) Clean, modern Sancerre from a top producer. Leafy, with flavours of gooseberry and elderflower.

1997 Chateau Tahbilk Marsanne £6 (Oddbins, see page 261) Distinctive, unoaked wine made in Australia from a grape variety more usually found in the Rhône.

1997 Shingle Peak Marlborough Sauvignon £8 (Christopher Piper, see page 261) Stylish New Zealand Sauvignon with just enough gooseberry and asparagus to reveal where it was made.

1997 Soave Classico Classico Pra £7 (Great Western, see page 257) Lovely creamy, almondy wine that shows just how good Soave can be – what a perfect accompaniment for food.

1997 Lagar de Cervena Albariño, Lagar De Forenelos £7 (Victoria Wine, see page 265) Wonderful, limey, licoricey unoaked wine from Galicia in the north-west of Spain.

1996 Jurançon Sec AC 1996, Domaine Castera £9 (Selfridges, see page 263) Distinctive, rich, perfumed, yet dry wine made from a little-known variety called the Gros Manseng.

1996 Byron Santa Maria Valley Chardonnay £15 (Sainsburys, see page 262) Very classy, melony, pineappley wine from a southern Californian subsidiary of Robert Mondavi.

1997 Dry Creek Chenin Blanc £8 (Great Northern, see page 257) One of the few really successful efforts with this grape from California. Fresh, rich, appley yet dry. Great with pork.

1995 Puligny-Montrachet les Folatières, G. Chavy £22 (Waitrose, see page 265) Impeccable white Burgundy with fresh fruit, biscuity richness and balanced oakiness. Stylish.

SPARKLING WINE AND ROSÉ

1994 Green Point £11 (Unwins, see page 265) Moët & Chandon's classy Australian wine, made from grapes grown in a range of very different regions and climates.

Yalumba Cuvée Two Sparkling Cabernet Sauvignon £9 (Oddbins, see page 261) An acquired taste perhaps, but one of the most enjoyably berryish wines I've drunk all year.

1993 Raventos i Blanc Cava Gran Reserva £10 (Waterloo Wine, see page 266) An unusually good example of traditional cava, with welcome reserves of freshness and flavour.

Seaview Pinot Noir-Chardonnay £8 (Widely available) The ideal choice for any wedding – or to keep in the fridge in readiness for an impromptu celebration. Lovely Champagne-like wine.

1993 Mambourg Pinot Gris Crémant d'Alsace £11 (Stevens Garnier, see page 264) Creamy sparkling wine with a hint of spice that comes from a blend that includes Pinot Gris.

1995 Miru Miru £13 (Majestic, see page 259) A great, fruity, yet subtle, Champagne-style sparkling wine from Marlborough in New Zealand that hit the middle of the target in its first vintage.

1990 Pol Roger Rosé £29 (D. Byrne, Tel: 01200 423 152) Serious rosé, with lovely deep raspberry and chocolate flavours.

Charles Heidsieck Non Vintage 'Mis en Cave 1993 £24 (Bottoms Up, see page 254) Revolutionary Non-vintage Champagne with a declared year of bottling. Easily outclasses many a Vintage in its clean but rich flavours and its complexity.

Champagne Drappier Grand Sendrée Brut 1985 £22 (D. Byrne, Tel: 01200 423 152) Great value Champagne of highly fragrant bouquet with spicy vanilla and citrus flavours.

1989 Lanson Noble Cuvée £53 (Thresher, see page 264) If you like Champagne with a touch of maturity, you will love this rich creamy wine. Very complex and great to drink with food.

Roederer Estate Quartet £14 (Wine Cellars, see page 266) The Californian offshoot of a great Champagne house. Classy and very Champagne-like, with raspberry fruit.

ROSÉ

1997 Familia Martinez Bujanda Rosado £6 (Bordeaux Direct, see page 253) Delicious, fresh, pink, strawberryish wine from one of the most reliable producers in Rioja.

1997 Ch. Minuty Prestige £9 (D. Byrne, Tel: 01200 423 152) A stylish rosé from vineyards near St. Tropez. Dry, peppery and serious enough to warrant that disconcertingly high price tag.

1997 l'Infinito Classico di Bardolino £7 (Direct Wine Shipments, see page 255) Distinctively cherryish, bright pink wine from vineyards close to Valpolicella.

SWEET AND FORTIFIED WINES

1995 Jurançon Ch. le Payral Cuvée Marie-Jeanne £12 (Noel Young, see page 246) Highly distinctive, complex, sweet and perfumed wine, with flavours of pears and apricots.

1994 Brown Brothers Family Reserve Late Harvested Noble Riesling £7 (Christopher Piper, see page 247) Intense sweet Australian at its best. Appley, fresh and lingering.

1995 Traminer No. 8 Nouvelle Vague Trockenbeeren-auslese, Alois Kracher £26 (Noel Young., see page 245) Lovely concentrated, raisiny wine from Austria's top producer of this style.

1991 Royal Tokaji Wine Company, Szt Tamas 5 Puttonyos £15 half-litre (Majestic see page 246) Liquid Old English Marmalade, with lovely intense, sweet yet tangy flavours.

FORTIFIED

Kourtaki Mavrodaphne de Patras £4 (Booths, see page 253) Lovely plummy-spicy, sweet red, made from a grape grown nowhere outside Greece.

Seppelt Rutherglen Show Muscat DP63 £8 (Wine Cellars, see page 266) Perfectliquid Christmas pudding with spice, hazelnuts and really subtle oak.

Elysium Black Muscat, Quady £7 (Lea & Sandeman, see page 259) Seductive, raisiny wine from warm vineyards in California's Central Valley. A great partner for ice cream.

Henriques & Henriques 10 Year Old Bual £16 (Hedley Wright, see page 258) Classic, nutty, orangey, plummy sweet Madeira to sip at with cake – or at the end of a meal.

Blandy's Duke of Sussex Special Dry Sercial £10 (Bennetts, see page 253) Limey, fresh, yet rich wine to serve cool with a bowl of salted almonds and some tender green olives.

Noval 40 Year Old Tawny £60 (Villeneuve, see page 265) A A rare chance to taste the extraordinary nutty-raisiny-woody flavours of really old barrel-aged port.

1980 Dow's Vintage Port £28 (Lay & Wheeler, see page 259) Good value vintage port from a decidedly underrated year. Ready to drink now, but should last a while yet.

Stanton & Killeen Rutherglen Muscadelle £7 (Selfridges, see page 263) Highly characterful fortified Australian, with a smell and flavour that combines currants with jasmine tea.

Osborne Rare India Solera Oloroso £30 (Gauntleys, see page 257) Wonderful, intense nutty sherry to sip slowly.

Apostoles Palo Cortado Superior Sherry £19 (D. Byrne, Tel: 01200 423 152) A deliciously unusual style that tastes rather like richer, fuller flavoured, nuttier Fino.

MILLENNIUM WINES

WINES FOR 2000

One of the more fascinating aspects of wine is the link a bottle can give both to the future and the past. You might, if you were lucky enough to lay your hands on one, drink a great Bordeaux made from grapes that were picked in 1949, half a century ago. Alternatively, this year you could lay down a case of the 1998 vintage with which to mark an anniversary sometime in the next century.

What makes the millennium rather different, though, is the excuse it gives people throughout the world more or less simultaneously to pull the cork from a few really special bottles – and the excuse it has given us to ask a few world famous wine experts what they'd like to be drinking as the 20th Century comes to a close.

AUTHOR'S SELECTION

My wines will be from producers that have meant something to me personally over the last 25 years. So, the Champagnes will have to include examples from Charles Heidsieck where I worked as a 16 year-old schoolboy in 1971, as well as some Billecart-Salmon and Dom Pérignon. A red and a white Burgundy would similarly recall the six – in wine terms – highly formative years I spent living there. The Bordeaux I'd choose, out of friendship for the people who make them and memories of the vintages would be from Châteaux Léoville-Barton and Margaux, while Cloudy Bay, Grange and Ridge would respectively recall my first experiences of New Zealand, Australia and California. Finally, there'll be a Chilean Carmenère – a grape variety I'm sure will be a star in the next century.

1985 Charles Heidsieck Blanc des Millénaires	*1983 Ch. Margaux*
	1990 Léoville-Barton
1970 Dom Pérignon	*1984 Ridge Geyserville*
1985 Billecart-Salmon	*1983 Penfolds Grange*
1985 Volnay Caillerets, Lafarge	*1998 Cloudy Bay Sauvignon Blanc*
1985 Meursault Perrières, Lafon	*1997 Santa Rita Carmenère*

MICHEL BETTANE

France's leading wine critic, Michel Bettane, is editorial advisor of *la Revue du Vin de France* and co-author of *Le Classement*, which, every year, draws up an authoritative hierarchy of French wines.

'My millennium will be spent in a group of around 12 in my house in the Beaujolais at Chénas. But I don't think we'll be drinking Beaujolais. There'll be plenty of Champagne – from Bollinger and the small estate of Jacques Selosse. Then there will be the 1982 Montrachet from the Domaine des Comtes Lafon, followed by some 1978 La Tâche, some 1982 Léoville-Lascases in magnums and, if we're up to it, some 1978 Hermitage from Sorrel. And for the end of the meal – which might include a *foie gras fait au Sauternes* – a little 1949 Château Gillette.'

1990 Champagne Jacques Selosse	*1978 La Tâche*
1985 Bollinger	*1982 Ch. Léoville-Lascases*
1982 Montrachet, Dom. des Comtes	*1978 Hermitage, Dom. Sorrel*
Lafon	*1949 Ch. Gillette, Sauternes*

MICHAEL BROADBENT MW

Former head of Christie's and author of seminal books on wine tasting and vintages, Michael Broadbent is unarguably the world's leading authority on the great wines of this and the last century.

'For breakfast there would be a traditional Buck's Fizz: Bollinger and fresh orange juice in a tankard. For mid-morning, Dr Loosen's Wehlener Sonnenuhr, and, with a light lunch, 1988 Pol Roger Cuvée Winston Churchill and the exquisite 1948 Ch. Léoville-Barton. For tea, we would sip my last bottle of Borges Terrantez 1862 Madeira with a slice of Madeira cake, and for dinner, I would enliven a 1923 Veuve Clicquot with some Veuve Clicquot Yellow Label Non vintage. With the fish, 1989 Ch. Laville Haut-Brion, and with the beef, 1900 Ch. Latour, followed by a magnum of 1870 Lafite. Finally we'd drink the 1929 Ch. Climens – with a nectarine.'

1995 Dr Loosen Wehlener	*1923 Veuve Clicquot*
Sonnenuhr Auslese Gold Kapsel	*1989 Ch. Laville Haut-Brion Blanc*
1988 Pol Roger Winston Churchill	*1900 Ch. Latour*
1948 Léoville-Barton	*1929 Ch. Climens*
1862 Terrantez Borges	*1870 Ch. Lafite*

ANTHONY DIAS BLUE

A syndicated wine columnist in over 300 newspapers across the United States, Anthony Dias Blue is also CBS Radio commentator and winner of the 1997 'IWSC Communicator of the Year' award.

'There will be 1928 Krug from the year my parents married, magnums of 1990 Roederer Cristal (full of the promise of the future), a 1996 Condrieu from Cuilleron (creamy, sensual and unencumbered by winemaker fiddling), a 1979 Trimbach Riesling (made in my first full year in California), a 1995 Williams-Selyem Pinot Noir (a rich, complex, upstart wine from a plucky winner), Joseph Phelps Insignia (America's best red?) and Penfolds Grange (the ultimate New World expression of power, fruit and complexity).'

1928 Krug	*1995 Williams-Selyem Pinot Noir,*
1990 Roederer Cristal	*Allen Vineyard*
1996 Condrieu, Cuilleron 'Les	*1995 Joseph Phelps Insignia*
Chaillets'	*1992 Penfolds Grange*
1979 Trimbach Clos Ste. Hune	

JAMES HALLIDAY

Australian-born former lawyer, James Halliday is not only an extraordinarily prolific wine writer and noted wine judge; he is also the creator of the award-winning Coldstream Hills winery.

'It will be virtually mandatory to become legless – with plenty of friends to share the experience. So the first requirement is that the bottles be large. I have already paid for six magnums of Dom Pérignon 1990, but may try to save one or two of them and keep the fire going with the Australian Green Point Millennium Cuvée. I have a solitary magnum of Domaine de la Romanée Conti 1990 Echézeaux, which I would not normally contemplate drinking so young, but it must surely be a lamb for the slaughter. As will my four magnums of 1988 St. Hallett Old Block Shiraz and one of 1961 Seppelt Great Western Special Claret MY17. And I do have something appropriate for the last gasp: several bottles of Henriques & Henriques Centenary Malmsey from its 1900 solera.'

1990 Dom Pérignon	*1961 Seppelt Great Western Special*
Green Point Millennium Cuvée	*Claret MY17*
1990 Echézeaux, DRC	*Henriques & Henriques Centenary*
1988 St. Hallett Old Block Shiraz	*Malmsey*

STEVEN SPURRIER

Wine writer and consultant, Steven Spurrier is known throughout the wine world as the creator of l'Academie du Vin, France's first private wine school and the organiser in 1973 of a now historic comparitive tasting of wines from France and California.

'I am assuming that my own celebration will take place in my house in Dorset, with around eight guests to dinner. The Champagnes would both be magnums: the Lanson being the prize I won for articles in Decanter Magazine, and the Krug a personal present from Remi Krug. The Meursault would mark my long friendship with the Lafon family, while the Grand-Puy-Lacoste and Bonnes Mares are, respectively, my best claret and Burgundy. As for the port, I simply love the richness of Graham's.'

1998 Lanson Noble Cuvée	1990 Bonnes Mares,
1985 Krug	Dom. Roumier
1990 Meursault Charmes,	1982 Ch. Grand-Puy-Lacoste
Comtes Lafon	1970 Graham's

SERENA SUTCLIFFE MW

One of only a few women with the title of *Master of Wine*, Serena Sutcliffe combines managing Sotheby's International Wine Department with being an award-winning writer, lecturer and broadcaster.

'My vinous plans for the Millennium are well under way, but the "venue" poses problems. Decanting and refrigeration could be a challenge on remote South Sea islands, so it may have to be the British countryside instead!

I'll drink Champagne non-stop as the new century dawns around the world, starting with a magnum of the glorious Dom Pérignon, before moving onto the exquisite Veuve Clicquot 1969. Then I'll have the Leflaive Chevalier Montrachet which is hedonistic heaven. Ensuite, as they say, La Tâche 1943, a dream of a wine: born before I was and in much better shape. Then La Tâche 1978 to compare. Finally d'Yquem 1975: dark amber and absolutely grandiose.'

1961 Dom Pérignon	1943 La Tâche
1969 Veuve Clicquot	1978 La Tâche
1992 Chevalier Montrachet,	1975 Ch. d'Yquem
Dom. Leflaive	

TASTING & BUYING

SPOILED FOR CHOICE

Buying wine today has become wonderfully – and horribly – like buying a gallon of paint. Just as the paint manufacturer's helpful chart can become daunting with its endless shades of subtly different white, the number of bottles and the information available on the supermarket shelves can make you want to give up and reach for the one that is most familiar, or most favourably priced.

If you're not a wine buff, why should you know the differences in flavour to be found in wines made from the same grape in Meursault in France, Mendocino in California and Maipo in Chile? Often, the merchant has helpfully provided descriptive terms to help you to imagine the flavour of the stuff in the bottle. But, these too can merely add to the confusion. Do you want the one that 'tastes of strawberries or raspberries', the 'refreshingly dry', or the 'crisp, lemony white'?

Over the next few pages, I can't promise to clear a six-lane highway through this jungle but, with luck, I shall give you a path to follow with rather more confidence when you are choosing a wine, and one from which you can stray to explore for yourself.

THE LABEL

Wine labels should reveal the country or region where the wine was produced (see page 30), and possibly the grape variety (see page 50) from which it was made. Both region and grape, however, offer only partial guidance as to what you are likely to find when you pull the cork.

Bear in mind the following:
1) Official terms such as Appellation Contrôlée, Grand or Premier Cru, Qualitätswein and Reserva are as trustworthy as official pronouncements by politicians.
2) Unofficial terms such as Reserve Personnel are, likewise, as trustworthy as unofficial pronouncements by the producer of any other commodity.
3) Knowing that a wine comes from a particular region is often like knowing nothing more about a person than where they were born; it provides no guarantee of how good the wine will be. Nor, how it will have been made (though there are often local rules). There will be nothing to tell you, for instance,

whether a Chablis is oaked or not; nor, more annoyingly, will an Alsace or a Vouvray always reveal its sweetness on the label.

4) Beware of falling into the trap of trusting a 'big name' region to make better wine than a supposedly lesser one. Rotten wines come out of Nuits-St-Georges, the Napa Valley, Margaux and Rioja – as well as just about every other region.

5) Don't expect wines from the same grape variety to taste the same wherever the grape is grown: a Chardonnay from South Africa might taste far drier than one from California and less fruity than one from Australia. The precise flavour and style will depend on the producer.

6) Just because a producer makes a good wine in one place, don't trust him to make others either there or elsewhere. For example, the team at Lafite Rothschild are responsible for the dire Los Vascos white in Chile; while some of Robert Mondavi's inexpensive Woodbridge wines bear no relation to the quality of his Reserve wines.

7) The fact that there is a château on a wine label has no bearing on the quality of the contents.

8) Nor does the boast that the wine is bottled at said château.

9) Nineteenth-century medals look pretty on a label; they say nothing about the quality of the 20th-century stuff in the bottle.

10) Price provides some guidance to a wine's quality: a very expensive bottle may be appalling, but it's unlikely that a very cheap one will be better than basic.

A WAY WITH WORDS

Before going any further, I'm afraid that there's no alternative to returning to the thorny question of the language you are going to use to describe your impressions.

You could of course dispense with descriptive words altogether, as one distinguished visitor did when he visited Bordeaux 170 years ago. Château Margaux was, he noted, 'a wine of fine flavour – but not of equal body'. Lafite, on the other hand, had 'less flavour than the former but more body – an equality of flavour and body'. As for Latour, well, that had 'more body than flavour', while Haut-Brion was merely 'a wine of fine flavour'. George Washington may have been a great president, but he was evidently not the ideal person from whom to learn the subtle differences in the way four of the world's most famous wines actually taste.

Michelangelo, on the other hand, was quite ready to apply his artistry to the white wine of San Gimignano in Tuscany, of which he said 'it kisses, licks, bites, thrusts and stings...'. Earlier still, in the 12th century, one Alexander Neckham described a wine he particularly liked as 'sweet-tasted as an almond, creeping like a squirrel, leaping like a roebuck, delicate as fine silk and colder than crystal', while contemporary pundits routinely refer to wines as having 'gobs of fruit' and tasting of 'kumquats and suede'.

So, there's nothing new in outlandish expressions for wine; each country and each generation simply comes up with its own vocabulary. Some descriptions, such as the likening to gooseberry and asparagus of wines made from the Sauvignon Blanc, are both historically and internationally well-established – and can be justified by scientific analysis, which confirms that the same aromatic chemical compound is found in the fruit, vegetable and wine.

No one knows why the Gewürztraminer should produce wines that smell and taste of lychees, or why reds made from the Grenache should be recognisably peppery, but they are. And recognising those hallmark smells and flavours can be very handy if ever you have to guess a wine's identity.

Then there are straightforward descriptions that could apply to almost anything we eat or drink. Wines can be fresh or stale, clean or dirty. If they are acidic, or overfull of tannin, they will be 'hard'; a 'soft' wine, by contrast might be easier to drink, but boring.

There are other less evocative terms. While a downright watery wine is 'dilute' or 'thin', subtle ones are called 'elegant'. A red or white whose flavour is hard to discern is described as 'dumb'.

Whatever the style of a wine, the quality it is supposed to have is 'balance'. A sweet white, for example, needs enough acidity to keep it from cloying. No one will ever enjoy a wine that is too fruity, too dry, too oaky or too *anything*.

The flavour that lingers in your mouth long after you have swallowed or spat it out is known as the 'finish'. Wines whose flavour – pleasant or unpleasant – hangs around, are described as 'long'; those whose flavour disappears quickly are 'short'.

Finally, there is 'complex', the word that is used to justify why one wine costs ten times more than another. A complex wine is like a well-scored symphony, while a simpler one could be compared to a melody picked out on a single instrument.

TASTING

Wine tasting is surrounded by mystery and mystique. And it shouldn't be – because all it really consists of is paying attention to the stuff in the glass, whether you're in the formal environment of a wine tasting, or taking a sip of the house white in your local wine bar. In fact, apart from spitting (which calls for unusually tolerant wine bars) there's really no difference in the way you actually do the tasting.

Every time you taste a wine, you will, above all, be deciding whether or not you like it. Beyond that, you may also be judging whether you reckon it to be a good example of what it claims to be.

A bottle of Champagne costs a lot more than basic Spanish fizz, so it should taste recognisably different. Some do, some don't.

See

The appearance of a wine can tell you quite a lot about it. Assuming that it isn't cloudy (in which case you should send it straight back), it will reveal its age and may give some hint of the grape and origin. Some grapes, like Burgundy's Pinot Noir, make naturally paler wines than, say, Bordeaux's Cabernet Sauvignon; wines from warmer regions tend to have deeper colours. Tilt the glass away from you over a piece of white paper and look at the rim of the liquid. The more watery and brown it is, the older the wine (Beaujolais Nouveau will be violet through and through).

Swirl

Vigorously swirl the wine around the glass for a moment or so to release any reluctant smells.

Sniff

You sniff a wine before tasting it for the same reason that you sniff a carton of milk before pouring its contents into your tea. The smell can tell you more about a wine than anything else. If you don't believe me, just try tasting anything while holding your nose, or while you've got a cold. When sniffing, concentrate on whether the wine seems fresh and clean, and on any particular smells that indicate how the wine is likely to taste.

What are your first impressions? Is the wine fruity, and, if so, which fruit does it remind you of? Does it have the characteristic vanilla smell of a wine that has been fermented and/or matured in new oak barrels? Is it spicy? Or herbaceous? Sweet or dry? Rich or lean?

Sip

Take a small mouthful and – this takes practice – suck air between your teeth and through the liquid. Look in a mirror while you're doing this: if your mouth looks like a cat's bottom and sounds like a child trying to suck the last few drops of Coca-Cola through a straw, then you're doing it right. Hold the wine in your mouth for a little longer to release as much of its flavour as possible.

Focus on the flavour. Ask yourself the same questions about whether it tastes sweet, dry, fruity, spicy, herbaceous. Is there just one flavour, or do several contribute to a 'complex' overall effect?

Apart from the flavour, concentrate on the texture of the wine. Some wines – Chardonnay, for example – are mouth-coatingly buttery, while others – eg Gewürztraminer – can seem to be almost oily. Muscadet is a good example of a wine with a texture that is closer to that of water.

Reds, too, vary in texture, some seeming tough and tannic enough to make the inside of one cheek want to kiss the inside of the other. Traditionalists were tolerant of that tannin, believing it necessary to a wine's longevity. More modern winemakers, including the men and women responsible for the best estates in Bordeaux and Burgundy, take a different view. For them, there is a difference between the harsh tannin and the 'fine' (non-aggressive) tannin to be found in wine carefully made from ripe grapes. A modern Bordeaux often has as much tannin as old-fashioned examples – but is far easier to taste and drink.

Spit

The only reason for spitting a wine out – unless it is actively repellent – is quite simply to maintain a measure of sobriety at the end of a lengthy tasting. I still have the notes I took during a long banquet in Burgundy at which there were dozens of great wines and not even the remotest chance to do anything but swallow. The descriptions of the first few are perfectly legible; the thirtieth apparently tasted 'very xgblorefjy'. If all you are interested in is the taste, not spitting is an indulgence; you ought to have got 90% of the flavour while the wine was in your mouth.

Pause for a moment or two after spitting the wine out. Is the flavour still there? How does what you are experiencing now compare with the taste you had in your mouth? Some wines have a surprisingly unpleasant aftertaste; others have flavours that linger deliciously in the mouth.

Should I Send it Back?

Wines are subject to all sorts of faults, though far less than they were even as recently as a decade ago.

Acid

All wines, like all fruit and vegetables, contain a certain amount of acidity. Without it they would go very stale very quickly. Wines made from unripe grapes will, however, taste unpalatably 'green' and like unripe apples or plums – or like chewing stalky leaves or grass.

Bitter

Bitterness is quite a different thing. On occasion, especially in Italy, a touch of bitterness may not only be forgivable, it may even be an integral part of a wine's character, as in the case of Amarone reds. Of course, the Italians like Campari too. Even so, a little bitterness goes a very long way.

Cloudy
Wine should be transparent. The only excuse for cloudiness is in a wine like an old Burgundy whose deposit has been shaken up.

Corked
People often complain that a wine is 'corked' when they find a few crumbs of cork floating on the surface. Genuinely corked wines have a musty smell and flavour that comes from a mould in the cork. Some corks are mouldier, and wines mustier, than others, but all corked wines become nastier the longer they are exposed to oxygen. Between 3–8% of wines – irrespective of their price – are corked. Screw caps and plastic corks are far better.

Crystals
Not a fault, but included because people often think there is something wrong with a white wine if there is a layer of fine white crystals in the bottom of the bottle. These are just tartrates that fall naturally.

Maderised/Oxidised
Madeira is fortified wine, from the island of the same name, that has been intentionally exposed to the air and heated in a special oven. Maderised wine is unfortified stuff from anywhere, which has been accidentally subjected to warmth and air. The difference between the two is that Madeira is delicious, extraordinary, nutty, tangy stuff, while maderised wine simply tastes like cheap, stale dry sherry.

Oxidised is a broader term, referring to wine that has been exposed to the air – or made from grapes that have cooked in the sun. The taste is reminiscent of poor sherry or vinegar – or both.

Sulphur (SO$_2$/H$_2$S)
Sulphur dioxide is almost universally used as a protection against the bacteria that would oxidise (qv) a wine. In excess, as sulphur dioxide, it will be smelled when you sniff the wine and may make you cough or sneeze. Even worse, though, is hydrogen sulphide and *mercaptans*, its associated sulphur compounds, which are created when sulphur dioxide combines with the wine. Wines with hydrogen sulphide smell of rotten eggs, while mercaptans reek of all sorts of nastiness, ranging from rancid garlic to burning rubber. If you think you have found these characteristics, pop a copper coin into your glass. It may clear up the problem completely.

Vinegary/Volatile
Volatile acidity is present in all wines, but only in small proportions. In excess – usually the result of careless winemaking – what can be a pleasant component (like a touch of balsamic vinegar in a sauce) tastes downright vinegary.

READING THE LABEL

INTRODUCTION

Labels – in all their different forms – are so much part of the business of wine that it may come as a surprsise that, even a century ago, they barely existed. Wine was sold by the barrel and served by the jug or decanter. Indeed, the original 'labels' were silver tags that hung on a chain around the neck of a decanter and were engraved with the word 'claret', 'hock', 'port' or whatever.

Today, however, printed wine labels include legally required information such as the amount of liquid in the bottle, its strength, the place where it was made and the name of the producer, brand-owner or importer. Confusingly, though, the rules governing what may be said on a label can vary between countries and between regions. Labels may also reveal a wine's style – the grape variety, oakiness or sweetness, for example. And lastly, they are part of the packaging that helps to persuade you to buy one wine rather than another. The following examples should help you through the maze.

CHAMPAGNE

The brand name

The producer

Volume of contents

The town were it was made

Alcoholic strength

The code that reveals the wine to be made by a 'négociant' (an NM)

WHITES

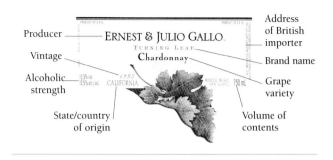

Producer — ERNEST & JULIO GALLO — Address of British importer

TURNING LEAF — Brand name

Vintage — Chardonnay

Alcoholic strength — 12.5% vol. 12.5% alc/vol. 1995 CALIFORNIA — WHITE WINE VIN BLANC 750 mL — Grape variety / Volume of contents

State/country of origin

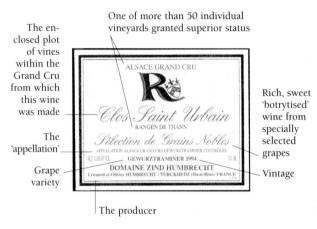

The enclosed plot of vines within the Grand Cru from which this wine was made

One of more than 50 individual vineyards granted superior status

ALSACE GRAND CRU

R

Clos Saint Urbain
RANGEN DE THANN

Sélection de Grains Nobles
APPELLATION ALSACE GRAND CRU GEWURZTRAMINER CONTRÔLÉE

ALC. 13.8% BY VOL. GEWURZTRAMINER 1994 75CL

DOMAINE ZIND HUMBRECHT
Léonard et Olivier HUMBRECHT - TURCKHEIM (Haut-Rhin) FRANCE

The 'appellation'

Rich, sweet 'botrytised' wine from specially selected grapes

Grape variety

Vintage

The producer

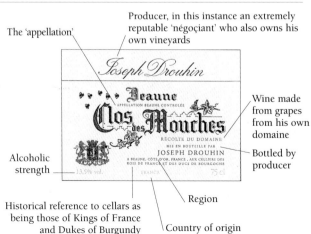

The 'appellation'

Producer, in this instance an extremely reputable 'négociant' who also owns his own vineyards

Joseph Drouhin

Beaune
APPELLATION BEAUNE CONTRÔLÉE

Clos des Mouches

RÉCOLTE DU DOMAINE
MIS EN BOUTEILLE PAR
JOSEPH DROUHIN
À BEAUNE, CÔTE-D'OR, FRANCE ; AUX CELLIERS DES
ROIS DE FRANCE ET DES DUCS DE BOURGOGNE
13.5% vol. FRANCE 75 cl

Wine made from grapes from his own domaine

Bottled by producer

Alcoholic strength

Region

Historical reference to cellars as being those of Kings of France and Dukes of Burgundy

Country of origin

27

REDS

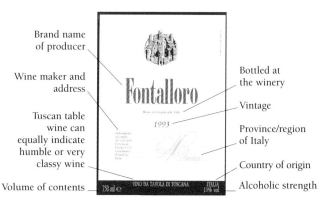

Brand name of producer

Wine maker and address

Tuscan table wine can equally indicate humble or very classy wine

Volume of contents

Bottled at the winery

Vintage

Province/region of Italy

Country of origin

Alcoholic strength

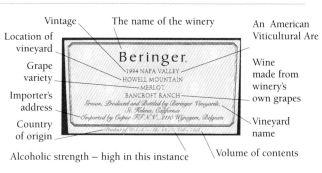

Vintage

The name of the winery

An American Viticultural Are

Location of vineyard

Grape variety

Importer's address

Country of origin

Wine made from winery's own grapes

Vineyard name

Alcoholic strength – high in this instance

Volume of contents

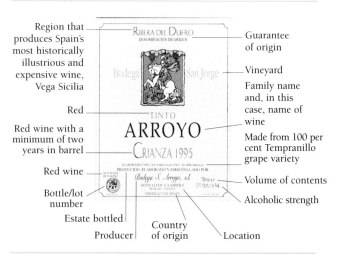

Region that produces Spain's most historically illustrious and expensive wine, Vega Sicilia

Red

Red wine with a minimum of two years in barrel

Red wine

Bottle/lot number

Estate bottled

Producer

Country of origin

Location

Guarantee of origin

Vineyard

Family name and, in this case, name of wine

Made from 100 per cent Tempranillo grape variety

Volume of contents

Alcoholic strength

DESSERTS/FORTIFIEDS

A puttonyo is the 'hod' of Aszú sweet grape paste used to sweeten Tokaji - the number of puttonyos indicates the wine's sweetness

The wine name

The producer

Paste made from 'nobly-rotten' grapes

First growth classification – dates back to 1700

Producer's crest

Volume of contents – smaller than standard wine bottle size

Alcoholic strength

Country of origin

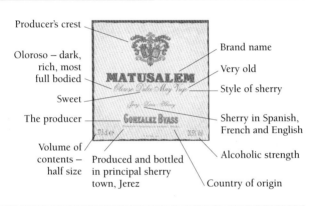

Producer's crest

Oloroso – dark, rich, most full bodied

Sweet

The producer

Volume of contents – half size

Produced and bottled in principal sherry town, Jerez

Brand name

Very old

Style of sherry

Sherry in Spanish, French and English

Alcoholic strength

Country of origin

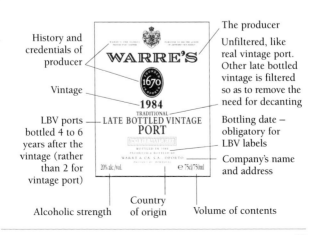

History and credentials of producer

Vintage

LBV ports bottled 4 to 6 years after the vintage (rather than 2 for vintage port)

The producer

Unfiltered, like real vintage port. Other late bottled vintage is filtered so as to remove the need for decanting

Bottling date – obligatory for LBV labels

Company's name and address

Alcoholic strength

Country of origin

Volume of contents

29

COUNTRIES

WHERE IN THE WORLD?

Despite the plethora of bottles whose labels bear the name of the same grape variety, the country and region in which a wine is made – with its climate, traditions and local taste – still largely dictate the style of the stuff that ends up in your glass. In the next few pages, we'll take a whirlwind tour of the wine world, which should give you a clearer idea of what to expect from all of the most significant winemaking nations. (For more information on grapes, terms and regions, see the A–Z, which starts on page 91.)

AUSTRALIA

> **Reading the label:** Late harvest/noble harvest – *sweet*. Show Reserve – *top-of-the-range wine, usually with more oak*. Tokay – *Australian name for the Muscadelle grape, used for rich liqueur wines*. Verdelho – *Madeira grape used for limey dry wines*. Mataro – *Mourvèdre*. Shiraz – *Syrah*. Tarrango – *local success story, fresh, fruity and Beaujolais-like*.

Twenty or so years ago, Australian wines were the butt of a Monty Python sketch. Today, these rich and often intensely fruity wines are the reliable vinous equivalent of Japanese hi-fi and cameras. It is hard to explain quite how this switch happened, but I would attribute much of the credit to the taste the Australians themselves have developed for wine. Having a populace that treats wine the way many Americans treat milk or beer has helped to provide the impetus for two of the best wine schools in the world – and for a circuit of fiercely fought competitions in which even the humblest wines battle to win medals.

Another strength has been the spirit of exploration which led to the establishment of regions like the Barossa and Hunter Valleys, and which is now fuelling the enthusiastic planting of vines in previously unknown places, such as Orange, Robe, Mount Benson, Young and Pemberton.

Remember these names; they are already appearing on a new generation of subtler Australian reds and whites that will make some of today's stars look like clod-hoppers. And look out too for unconventional blends of grape varieties, as well as delicious new

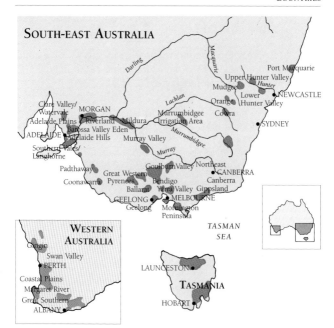

flavours none of us has ever tasted. Australia is the only region or country to have drawn up a master plan to dominate the world's premium wines within 25 years. Judging by what's been achieved so far, I think the Aussies may well be on track to achieving their ambitions.

AUSTRIA

> **Reading the label:** Ausbruch – *late harvested, between Beerenauslese and Trockenbeerenauslese*. Erzeugerabfüllung – *estate-bottled*. Morillon – *Chardonnay*. Schilfwein – *made from grapes dried on mats*.

Austrian winemakers are riding high, with brilliant, late harvest wines, dry whites and increasingly impressive reds. Names to look out for include Alois Lang, Kracher and Willi Opitz.

CANADA

> **Reading the label:** VQA (Vintners Quality Alliance) – *local designation seeking to guarantee quality and local provenance*.

The Icewines, made from grapes picked when frozen on the vine, are the stars here, though the Chardonnays are fast improving and progress is also being made with reds made from the Pinot Noir and Merlot.

EASTERN EUROPE

Some parts of Eastern Europe are coming to terms with life under capitalism a lot more successfully than others, but throughout the region, winemaking is improving by fits and starts.

BULGARIA

The pioneer of good Iron Curtain reds, Bulgaria remains a reliable source of inexpensive, ripe Cabernet Sauvignon and Merlot, as well as creditable examples of the earthy local Mavrud. Whites are getting better too, thanks largely to the efforts of visiting Australian winemakers.

HUNGARY

Still probably best known for its red Bull's Blood, Hungary's strongest card today lies in the rich Tokajis, the best of which are being made by foreign investors. Reds are improving, as are cheap and cheerful Australian-style Sauvignons and Chardonnays.

ROMANIA, MOLDOVA AND FORMER YUGOSLAVIA

It is too early to see whether the new Yugoslav republics can export as many bottles of wine as used to go out under the Laski Rizling label, but Romania produces decent if atypical Pinot Noir, while Moldova's strength lies in whites.

ENGLAND AND WALES

Despite an unhelpful climate and government, the vineyards of England and Wales are steadily developing a potential for using recently developed German grape varieties to make Loire-style whites, high-quality, late harvest wines and good fizz. There are reds too, but these are only really of curiosity value and are likely to remain so until global warming takes effect.

FRANCE

Reading the label: Appellation Contrôlée (or AOC) – *designation referring to the region and style of what are supposedly France's better wines.* Blanc de Blancs – *white wine made from white grapes.* Blanc de Noirs – *white wine made from black grapes.* Cave – *cellar.* Cave des Vignerons de – *usually a co-operative.* Cépage – *grape variety.* Château – *wine estate.* Chêne – *oak barrels, as in Fûts de Chêne.* Clos – (*historically*) *walled vineyard.* Côte(s)/Coteaux – *hillside.* Crémant – *sparkling.* Cuvée – *a specific blend.* Demi-sec – *medium sweet.* Domaine – *wine estate.* Doux – *sweet.* Grand Cru – *higher quality, or specific vineyards.* Gris – *pale rosé, as in Vin Gris.* Jeunes Vignes – *young vines (often ineligible to produce Appellation Contrôlée wine).* Méthode Classique – *used to* *indicate the Champagne method of making sparkling wine. Millésime – year or vintage. Mis en Bouteille au Château/Domaine – bottled at the estate. Moelleux – sweet. Monopole – a vineyard owned by a single producer. Mousseux – sparkling. Négociant (Eleveur) – a merchant who buys, matures, bottles and sells wine. Pétillant – lightly sparkling. Premier Cru – 'first growth', a quality designation that varies from area to area. Propriétaire (Récoltant) – vineyard owner/manager. Reserve (Personelle) – legally meaningless phrase. Sur Lie – aged on the lees (dead yeast). VDQS (Vin Délimité de Qualité Supérieur) – perpetually 'soon-to-be-abolished' official designation for wines which are better than Vin de Pays but not good enough for Appellation Contrôlée. Vieilles Vignes – old vines (could be any age from 20–80 years), should indicate higher quality. Villages – supposedly best part of a larger region, as in Beaujolais or Côtes du Rhône Villages. Vin de Pays – wine with regional character. Vin de Table – basic table wine. Stupid rules mean that these wines are banned from mentioning their provenance, grape varieties or vintage on their labels.*

Still the benchmark, or set of benchmarks, against which wine-makers in other countries test themselves. This is the place to find

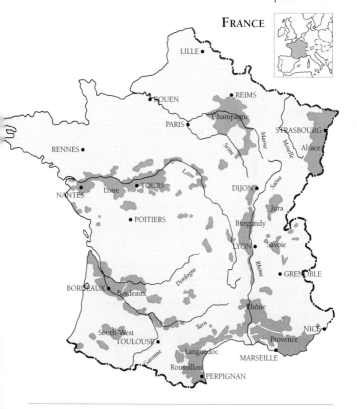

FRANCE

33

the Chardonnay in its finest oaked (white Burgundy) and unoaked (traditional Chablis) styles; the Sauvignon (from Sancerre and Pouilly Fumé in the Loire, and in blends with the Sémillon, Bordeaux); the Cabernet Sauvignon and Merlot (claret); the Pinot Noir (red Burgundy and Champagne); the Riesling, Gewurztraminer and Pinots Blanc and Gris (Alsace). The Chenin Blanc still fares better in the Loire than anywhere else and, despite their successes in Australia, the Syrah (aka Shiraz) and Grenache are still at their finest in the Rhône.

France's problem remains the unpredictability of the climate in most of its best regions, and the unreliability of far too many of its winemakers, who are often happy to coast along on the reputation of the region in which they happen to work.

ALSACE

> **Reading the label:** Sélection de Grains Nobles – *lusciously sweet wine made from grapes affected by Noble Rot.* Vendange Tardive – *late harvested.* Edelzwicker – *blend of white grapes, usually Pinot Blanc and Sylvaner.*

Often underrated, and confused with German wines from the other side of the Rhine, Alsace deserves to be more popular. Its odd assortment of grapes make wonderfully rich spicy wine, both in their customary dry and more unusual, late harvest styles. This is my bet to follow the success of its spicy red counterparts in the Rhône.

BORDEAUX

> **Reading the label:** Chai – *cellar.* Cru Bourgeois – *level beneath Cru Classé but possibly of similar quality.* Cru Classé – *'Classed Growth', a wine featured in the 1855 classification of the Médoc and Graves, provides no guarantee of current quality.* Grand Cru/Grand Cru Classé – *confusing terms, especially in St. Emilion, where the former is allocated annually on the basis of a sometimes less-than-arduous tasting, while the latter is reassessed every decade.*

For all but the keenest wine buff, Bordeaux is one big region (producing more wine than the whole of Australia) with a few dozen châteaux that have become internationally famous for their wine.

Visit the region, or take a look at the map, however, and you will find that this is essentially a collection of often quite diverse sub-regions, many of which are separated from each other by farm-land, forest or water.

Heading north from the city of Bordeaux, the Médoc is the region which includes the great communes of St. Estèphe, Pauillac, St. Julien and Margaux where some of the finest reds are made. Largely gravel soil suiting the Cabernet Sauvignon, though

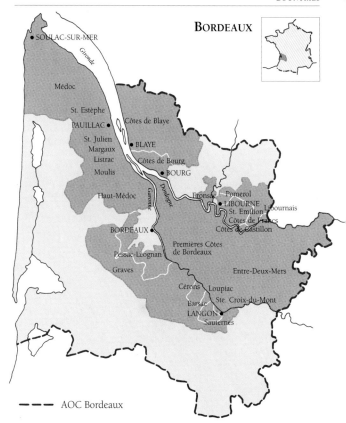

BORDEAUX

SOULAC-SUR-MER
Gironde
Médoc
St. Estèphe
PAUILLAC
Côtes de Blaye
St. Julien
Margaux
Listrac
Moulis
BLAYE
Côtes de Bourg
BOURG
Haut-Médoc
Garonne
Dordogne
Fronsac
Pomerol
LIBOURNE
Libournais
St. Emilion
Côtes de Francs
Côtes de Castillon
BORDEAUX
Premières Côtes
de Bordeaux
Pessac-Léognan
Graves
Entre-Deux-Mers
Cérons
Loupiac
Barsac
Ste. Croix-du-Mont
LANGON
Sauternes

– – – AOC Bordeaux

lesser Médoc wines, of which there are more than enough, tend to have a higher proportion of the Merlot. For the best examples of wines made principally from this variety, though, you have to head eastwards to St. Emilion and Pomerol where the Merlot is usually blended with the Cabernet Franc.

To the south of Bordeaux lie Pessac-Léognan and the Graves which produce some of Bordeaux's lighter, more delicate reds. This is also dry white country, where the Sémillon and Sauvignon Blanc hold sway. A little further to the south-east, the often misty climate provides the conditions required to make the great sweet whites of Sauternes and Barsac.

Each of these regions produces its own individual style of wine In some years, the climate suits one region and/or grape variety more than others. So, beware of vintage charts that seek to define the quality of an entire vintage across the whole of Bordeaux.

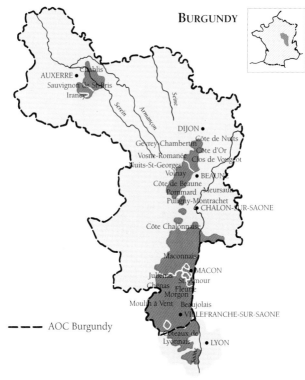

BURGUNDY

AUXERRE ● Chablis
Sauvignon de St-Bris
Irancy

DIJON ●

Gevrey-Chambertin Côte de Nuits
  Côte d'Or
Vosne-Romanée Clos de Vougeot
Nuits-St-Georges
  Volnay   ● BEAUNE
Côte de Beaune Meursault
  Pommard
  Puligny-Montrachet
  ● CHALON-SUR-SAONE

Côte Chalonnaise

Maconnais

  MACON
Julienas St-Amour
Chenas Fleurie
  Morgon
Moulin à Vent Beaujolais
  ● VILLEFRANCHE-SUR-SAONE

Coteaux de
Lyonnais ● LYON

– – – AOC Burgundy

BURGUNDY

Reading the label: Hospices de Beaune – *wines made and sold at auction by the charitable Hospices de Beaune.* Passetoutgrains – *a blend of Gamay and Pinot Noir.* Tasteviné – *a special label for wines that have passed a tasting by the Confrérie des Chevaliers de Tastevin.*

The heartland of the Pinot Noir and the Chardonnay, this is the region that produces such wines as Chablis, Nuits-St-Georges, Gevrey-Chambertin, Beaune, Meursault, Puligny-Montrachet, Mâcon Villages, Pouilly-Fuissé and Beaujolais. According to the official quality pyramid, the best wines come from the Grands Crus vineyards; next are the Premiers Crus, followed by plain village wines and, last of all, basic Bourgogne Rouge or Blanc.

Despite the simplicity of the system, however, it can be tough to find a good bottle. The region's many individual producers make their wines with varying measures of luck and expertise, generally selling in bulk to merchants who are just as variable in their skills and honesty. So, one producer's supposedly humble wine can be finer than another's pricier Premier or Grand Cru.

CHAMPAGNE

> **Reading the label:** Blanc de Blancs – *white wine from white grapes, ie pure Chardonnay*. Blancs de Noirs – *white wine made from black grapes*. Brut Sauvage/Zéro – *bone dry*. Extra-Dry – *(surprisingly) sweeter than Brut*. Grand Cru – *from a top-quality vineyard*. Négoçiant-manipulant (NM) – *buyer and blender of wines*. Non-Vintage – *a blend of wines usually based on wine of a single vintage*. Récoltant manipulant (RM) – *individual estate*.

Top-class Champagne has a unique blend of biscuity richness and subtle fruit. Beware cheap examples, however, and poor wine from big-name Champagne houses who should know better.

LOIRE

> **Reading the label:** Moelleux – *sweet*. Sur Lie – *on its lees (dead yeast), usually only applied to Muscadet*. Côt – *local name for the Malbec*.

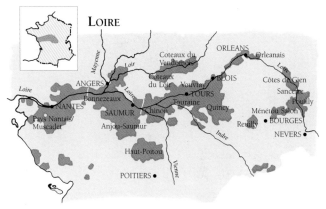

This is the heartland of fresh, dry Sauvignons as well as honeyed sweet wines from Vouvray, Quarts de Chaume and Bonnezeaux, fresh fizz in Saumur and Vouvray, and juicy blackcurrant reds in Chinon and Bourgeuil. Buy with care. Shoddy winemaking and sulphur dioxide abuse give far too many bottles – particularly late harvest, sweet ones – an unpleasantly 'woolly' character.

RHÔNE

> **Reading the label:** Vin Doux Naturel – *fortified wine, such as Muscat de Beaumes de Venise*. Côtes du Rhône Villages – *wine from one of a number of better sited villages in the overall Côtes du Rhône appellation, and thus, supposedly finer wine than plain Côtes du Rhône*.

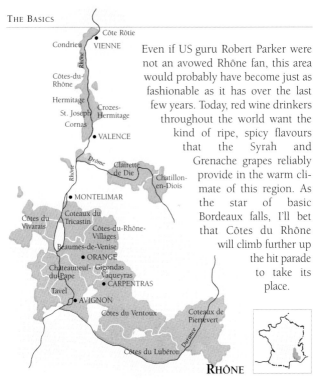

Even if US guru Robert Parker were not an avowed Rhône fan, this area would probably have become just as fashionable as it has over the last few years. Today, red wine drinkers throughout the world want the kind of ripe, spicy flavours that the Syrah and Grenache grapes reliably provide in the warm climate of this region. As the star of basic Bordeaux falls, I'll bet that Côtes du Rhône will climb further up the hit parade to take its place.

RHÔNE

THE SOUTH-WEST

Reading the label: Perlé or Perlant – *gently sparkling, used in one of the styles of Gaillac.*

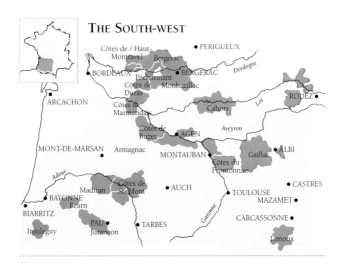

THE SOUTH-WEST

The conservative corner of France, heading inland from Bordeaux. This is the place to find wines like Jurançon, in its sweet and dry form, Gaillac, Cahors and Madiran. Once upon a time these wines, though famous among French wine buffs, were often quite old-fashioned in the worst sense of the term.

Today, a new wave of winemakers is learning how to extract unsuspected fruit flavours from grapes like the Gros and Petit Manseng, the Tannat, the Mauzac and the Malbec. These wines are worth the detour for anyone bored with the ubiquitous Cabernet Sauvignon and Chardonnay and dissatisfied with poor quality claret.

> **Reading the label:** Vin de Pays d'Oc – *country wine from the Languedoc region. Often some of the best stuff in the region.* Rancio – *woody, slightly volatile character in Banyuls and other fortified wines that have been aged in the barrel.*

LANGUEDOC-ROUSSILLON

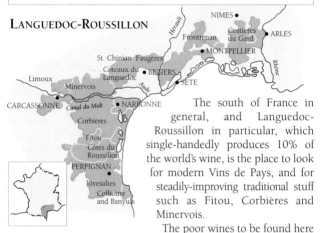

The south of France in general, and Languedoc-Roussillon in particular, which single-handedly produces 10% of the world's wine, is the place to look for modern Vins de Pays, and for steadily-improving traditional stuff such as Fitou, Corbières and Minervois.

The poor wines to be found here can be blamed on the conservatism of the producers. Even so, the combination of an ideal climate and increasingly dynamic winemaking (and substantial foreign investment) is raising the quality here, as well as in Provence to the east, where classics such as Cassis and Bandol now attract as much attention as the ubiquitous rosé.

EASTERN FRANCE

> **Reading the label:** Vin de Paille – *sweet, golden wine from grapes dried on straw mats.* Vin Jaune – *sherry-like, slightly oxidised wine.*

Savoie's zingy wines are often only thought of as skiing-fare but, like Arbois' nutty, sherry-style whites, they are characterfully different, and made from grape varieties that are grown nowhere else.

GERMANY

Reading the label: Amtliche Prüfungsnummer (AP number) – *official identification number*. Auslese – *sweet wine from selected grapes above a certain ripeness level*. Beerenauslese – *luscious, sweet wines from selected, ripe grapes (Beeren), hopefully affected by Botrytis*. Erzeugerabfüllung – *bottled by the grower/estate*. Halbtrocken – *off-dry*. Hock – *English name for Rhine wines*. Kabinett – *first step in German quality ladder, for wines which fulfil a certain natural sweetness*. Kellerei/kellerabfüllung – *cellar/producer/estate-bottled*. Landwein – *a relatively recent quality designation – the equivalent of a French Vin De Pays*. QbA (Qualitätswein bestimmter Anbaugebiete) – *basic quality German wine, meeting certain standards*. QmP (Qualitätswein mit Prädikat) – *QbA wine with 'special qualities' subject to (not very) rigorous testing. The QmP blanket designation is broken into five sweetness rungs, from Kabinett to Trockenbeerenauslese plus Eiswein*. Schloss – *literally 'castle', the equivalent of Château, designating a vineyard or estate*. Sekt – *very basic, sparkling wines*. Spätlese – *second step in the QmP scale, late harvested grapes, a notch drier than Auslese*. Staatsweingut – *state-owned wine estate*. Tafelwein – *table wine, only the prefix 'Deutscher' guarantees German origin*. Trocken – *dry*. Trockenbeerenauslese – *wine from selected dried grapes which are usually Botrytis-affected*. Weingut – *estate*. Weinkellerei – *cellar or winery*.

Ignore the oceans of sugar-water cynically exported by Germany under such labels as Liebfraumilch, Piesporter Michelsberg and Niersteiner Domtal. Ignore too, some of the big-name estates that still seem to get away with producing substandard fare. For real quality, look for Mosel Rieslings from producers like Dr Loosen and Richter, and new wave Rhine wines now being made by winemakers such as Künstler, Müller Catoir and Kurt Darting, not to mention the occasional successful red from Karl Lingenfelder. But, however convincing an explanation anyone might offer you for them, avoid dry 'Trocken' Kabinett wines from northern Germany unless you want the tartar and enamel removing from your teeth.

ITALY

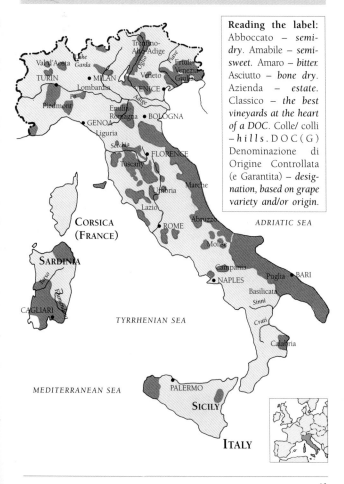

Reading the label: Abboccato – *semi-dry*. Amabile – *semi-sweet*. Amaro – *bitter*. Asciutto – *bone dry*. Azienda – *estate*. Classico – *the best vineyards at the heart of a DOC*. Colle/ colli – *hills*. D O C (G) Denominazione di Origine Controllata (e Garantita) – *designation, based on grape variety and/or origin*.

> Dolce – *sweet*. Frizzante – *semi-sparkling*. IGT, Indicazione Geografica
> Tipica – *questionable new designation for quality Vino da Tavola*.
> Imbottigliato nel'origine – *estate-bottled*. Liquoroso – *rich, sweet*.
> Passito – *raisiny wine made from sun-dried grapes*. Recioto – *strong,
> sweet (unless designated Amarone)*. Vino da Tavola – *table wine that
> does not fit into the DOC system. Includes basic stuff as well as some of
> Italy's top wines. To be replaced for the latter by* IGT.

Three facts about Italy. **1)** It is more a set of regions than a single
country. **2)** Few Italians comply for long with laws they find incon-
venient. **3)** Style is often valued more highly than content.
Taken together, these make for one of the world's most confusing
wine-producing countries. Individual producers all do their own
thing, using indigenous and imported grape varieties and designer
bottles and labels in ways that leave Euro-legislators – and humble
wine drinkers – exhilarated and exasperated in equal measure.

NEW ZEALAND

This New World country
has one of the most unpre-
dictable climates, but produces
some of the most intensely
flavoured wines. There are gooseberryish Sauvignon Blancs, Char
donnays and innovative Rieslings
and Gewürztraminers, as well as
some improving reds.

Hawke's Bay seems to be the most
consistent region for these, while
Gisborne, Marlborough, Auckland
and Martinborough share the
honours for white (though
the last has had some success
with the Pinot Noir).

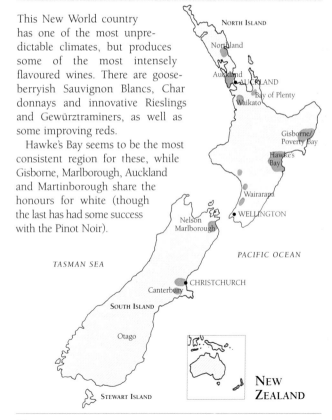

NORTH AFRICA

Islamic fundamentalism has done little to encourage winemaking of any description in North Africa. Even so, Algeria, Morocco and Tunisia can all offer full-flavoured, old-fashioned reds that will probably delight people who liked Burgundy when it routinely included a dollop of Algerian blackstrap.

PORTUGAL

Reading the label: Adega – *winery*. Branco – *white*. Colheita – *vintage*. Engarrafado na origem – *estate-bottled*. Garrafeira – *a vintage-dated wine with a little more alcohol and minimum ageing requirements*. Quinta – *vineyard or estate*. Reserva – *wine from a top-quality vintage, made from riper grapes than the standard requirement*. Velho – *old*. Vinho de Mesa – *table wine*.

Like Italy, Portugal has grapes grown nowhere else in the world. Unlike Italy, however, until recently the Portuguese had done little to persuade foreigners of the quality of these varieties.

But now, thanks to two Australian winemakers, Peter Bright and David Baverstock, and the efforts of dynamic, innovative Portuguese producers like Luis Pato in Bairrada, we are beginning to see what the native grapes can produce.

Try any of Pato's Bairradas, Bright's new-wave Douro reds and Baverstock's tasty Quinta do Crasto red wines from the Douro.

PORTUGAL

SOUTH AFRICA

Reading the label: Cap Classique – *South African term for Champagne method sparklers*. Cultivar – *grape variety*. Edel laat-oes – *noble late harvest*. Edelkeur – *'noble rot', a fungus affecting grapes and producing sweet wine*. Gekweek, gemaak en gebottel op – *estate-bottled*. Landgoedwyn – *estate wine*. Laat-oes – *late harvest*. Oesjaar – *vintage*. Steen – *local name for Chenin Blanc*.

At long last, South Africa's winemakers are beginning to live up to the promise that has always been claimed for their wines. Until recently, as visitors from Bordeaux, Britain and Australia have noticed, too many wines have had the 'green' flavour of over-cropped and under-ripe grapes. Wineries like Thelema, Saxenburg, Plaisir de Merle, Vergelegen and Fairview show what can be done, while Grangehurst, Kanonkop and Vriesenhof support the cause for South Africa's own spicy red grape, the Pinotage.

South Africa's late harvest and sparkling wines can also be of world class.

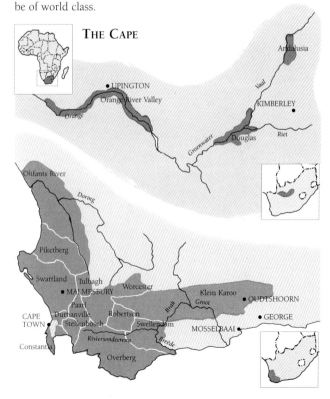

THE CAPE

44

SOUTH AMERICA

BOLIVIA

• LA PAZ

• BRASILIA

BRAZIL

PACIFIC
OCEAN

Parana

PARAGUAY

RIO DE JANEIRO

SAO PAULO

Salta   Teuco

Catamarca   Tucamán

Salado

ASUNCION

La Rioja

ATLANTIC
OCEAN

Aconcagua   San Juan   • CORDOBA   URUGUAY

Casablanca   Mendoza   • ROSARIO

Rapel   SANTIAGO   BUENOS

Curico   Maipo   AIRES

Maule   ARGENTINA   MONTEVIDEO

Itata   La Pampa

Bio Bio   Colorado

Rio
Negro   Negro

CHILE

Chico

SOUTH
AMERICA

ARGENTINA

> **Reading the label:** Malbec – *spicy red grape.* Torrontes – *unusual grapey white.*

As it chases Chile, this is a country to watch. The wines to look for now are the spicy reds made from the Malbec, a variety once widely grown in Bordeaux and still used in the Loire. Cabernets can be good too, as can the grapey but dry white Torrontes.

CHILE

> **Reading the label:** Envasado en Origen – *estate-bottled.* Carmenaire/Grand Vidure – *grape variety once used in Bordeaux but no longer found there.*

One of the most exciting wine-producing countries in the world, thanks to ideal conditions, skilled local winemaking and plentiful investment. The most successful grape at present is the Merlot, but the Cabernet, Chardonnay, Pinot Noir and Sauvignon can all display ripe fruit and subtlety often absent in the New World.

SOUTH EASTERN EUROPE

GREECE

Finally casting off its image as purveyor of Europe's worst wines, Greece is beginning to rediscover the potential of a set of highly characterful grape varieties. It will take time before many of the new-wave wines reach the outside world, but producers like Chateau Lazaridi, Gentilini and Hatzimichali are set for international success.

CYPRUS

Still associated with cheap sherry-substitute and dull wine, but things are changing. Look out for the traditional rich Commandaria.

TURKEY

Lurching out of the vinous dark ages, Turkey has yet to offer the world red or white wines that non-Turks are likely to relish.

LEBANON

Château Musar has survived all the tribulations of the last few years, keeping Lebanon on the map as a wine-producing country.

ISRAEL

Once a source of truly appalling wine, Israel can now boast world-class Cabernet and Muscat, from the Yarden winery in the Golan Heights. The big Carmel winery now produces acceptable wines too and has shrugged off the dismal offerings of the past.

SPAIN

Reading the label: Abocado – *semi-dry*. Año – *year*. Bodega – *winery or wine cellar*. Cava – *Champagne method sparkling wine*. Criado y Embotellado (por) – *grown and bottled (by)*. Crianza – *aged in wood*. DO(Ca) (Denominacion de Origen (Califacada)) – *Spain's quality designation, based on regional style, with a newly-introduced higher level* (Califacada) *to indicate superior quality*. Elaborado y Anejado Por – *made and aged for*. Gran Reserva – *a quality wine aged for a designated number of years in wood; more than for an ordinary Reserva*. Joven – *young wine, specially made for early consumption*. Reserva – *official designation for wine that has been aged for a specific period*. Sin Crianza – *not aged in wood*. Vendemia – *harvest or vintage*. Vino de Mesa – *table wine*. Vino de la Tierra – *new designation similar to the French 'Vin de Pays'*.

Spain used to be relied on for a certain style of highly predictable wine: soft, oaky reds with flavours of strawberry and vanilla, and whites that were either light, dry and unmemorable (Marqués de Cáceres Rioja Blanco), oaky and old-fashioned (traditional Marqués

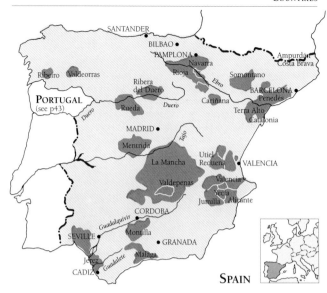

SPAIN

de Murrieta Rioja), or sweet and grapey (Moscatel de Valencia). Suddenly, however, like a car whose driver has just found an extra gear, Spanish wines have begun to leap ahead – into often largely uncharted territory. The first region to hail the revolution was Penedés, where winemaker Miguel Torres made a speciality of using both traditional and imported grape varieties.

Others have overtaken Torres, in regions like Somontano, Rueda and Navarra. In Rioja itself experiments are quietly going on to see whether the Cabernet Sauvignon can improve the flavour of this traditional wine. There are traditionalists who would prefer all this pioneering business to stop, but the wine genie is out of the Spanish bottle and there seems little chance of anyone forcing it back inside again.

SWITZERLAND

> **Reading the label:** Gutedel, Perlan, Fendant – *local names for the Chasselas*. Grand Cru – *top designation which varies from one canton to the next*. Süssdruck – *off-dry, red wine*.

Ferociously expensive for non-Swiss wine drinkers, but recommendable wines on their own terms. This is one of the only places the Chasselas produces anything even remotely memorable. (Incidentally, Switzerland is also the only country I know that has largely switched from corks to screw-caps, so you're unlikely to get a nasty, musty bottle.)

USA

> **Reading the label:** Blush – *rosé*. Champagne – *any sparkling wine*. Fumé – *oak-aged white wine, especially Sauvignon (Blanc Fumé)*. Meritage – *popular, if pretentious, name for a Bordeaux blend (white or red)*. Vinted – *made by (a vintner, or winemaker)*. White Grenache/Zinfandel, etc) – *refers to the unfashionable rosé, slightly pink wines, sometimes also referred to as 'blush'*.

CALIFORNIA

These are busy days for the best-known winemaking state of the Union. After 20 years of almost single-minded devotion to the Chardonnay and Cabernet Sauvignon and to the Napa Valley, the focus has broadened to take in a wider range of grapes (particularly Italian and Rhône varieties) and regions (Sonoma, Santa Barbara, especially for the Pinot Noir, plus San Luis Obispo, Santa Cruz, Mendocino and Monterey).

Within the Napa Valley too, where vineyards are being replanted in the wake of the damage caused by the phylloxera louse, there is growing acknowledgement that some sub-regions produce better wines than others. Carneros is already famous for its Pinot Noir, Oakville for its Chardonnay, while Rutherford and Stag's Leap are known for their Cabernet. But do try other worthwhile areas, such as Mount Veeder and Howell Mountain.

THE PACIFIC NORTH-WEST

Outside California, head north to Oregon for some of the best Pinot Noirs in the US (at a hefty price) and improving, but rarely earth-shattering Chardonnays, Rieslings and Pinot Gris. Washington State has some Pinot too, on the cooler, rainy west side of the Cascade mountains. On the east, the irrigated vineyards produce great Sauvignon and Riesling, as well as top-flight Chardonnay, Cabernet, Syrah and a very good Merlot.

NEW YORK AND OTHER STATES

Once the source of dire 'Chablis' and 'Champagne', New York State is now producing worthwhile wines, particularly in the micro-climate of Long Island, where the Merlot is thriving. The Finger Lakes are patchier but worth visiting, especially for the Rieslings and cool-climate Chardonnays. Elsewhere Virginia, Missouri, Texas, Maryland and even Arizona are all producing wines to compete with California and indeed some of the best that Europe can offer.

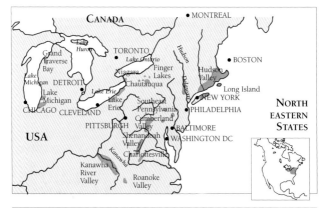

THE GRAPES

BLENDS OR SINGLE VARIETIES?

Some wines are made from single grape varieties – eg red or white Burgundy, Sancerre, German Riesling and Barolo – while others, such as red or white Bordeaux, California 'Meritage' wines, port and Châteauneuf-du-Pape, are blends of two or more types of grape. Champagne can fall into either camp, as can New World so-called 'varietal' wines which, though labelled as 'Chardonnay', 'Cabernet Sauvignon', etc, can contain up to 25% of other grape varieties, depending on local rules. Blends are not, per se, superior to single varietals – or vice versa.

WHITE WINE GRAPES

CHARDONNAY

Ubiquitous but hard to define. In Burgundy and the best California examples, (Kistler, Sonoma Cutrer) it tastes of butter and hazelnuts; lesser New World efforts are sweet and simple. Australians range from oaky tropical fruit juice to subtle buttery pineapple (Petaluma and Leeuwin). New Zealand's efforts are tropical too, but lighter and fresher (Te Mata, Cloudy Bay). Elsewhere, Chile is beginning to hit the mark, as is South Africa though some examples still taste unripe. In Europe, look around southern France, Italy, Spain and Eastern Europe, but beware of watery cheaper versions.

CHENIN BLANC

A Loire variety that produces fresh fizz, and both dry and lusciously sweet honeyed wines; also stuff that tastes like unripe apples and, when over-sulphured, old socks. Most California Chenins are semi-sweet and ordinary. South Africans call it the Steen, and make best use of it in sweet wines. The best Australians are made by Moondah Brook, and the New Zealanders by Millton.

GEWÜRZTRAMINER

Outrageous stuff that smells of parma violets and tastes of lychees. At its best in Alsace, dry and sweet, as a Vendange Tardive or Sélection de Grains Nobles (Zind Humbrecht, Schlumberger, Faller). Try examples from Germany, New Zealand and north-east Italy too.

MARSANNE

A classic flowery lemony variety used in the Rhône in wines like Hermitage (from producers like Guigal), and in Australia – especially in Goulburn in Victoria (Chateau Tahbilk and Mitchelton); in southern France (in Vin de Pays d'Oc blends such as La Pérousse and from Mas de Daumas Gassac) and in innovative wines from California. At its best young or after five or six years.

MUSCAT

The only variety whose wines actually taste as though they are made of grapes, rather than some other kind of fruit or vegetable. In Alsace, southern France and north-east Italy it is used to make dry wines. Generally, though, it performs best as fizz (Moscatos, and Asti Spumantes from Italy and Clairette de Die Tradition from France) and as sweet fortified wine. Look out for Beaumes de Venise and Rivesaltes in southern France, Moscatel de Setúbal in Portugal, Moscatel de Valencia in Spain, and Christmas puddingy Liqueur Muscat in Australia (Morris, Chambers, Yalumba).

PINOT BLANC/PINOT BIANCO

As rich as Chardonnay, but with less fruit. At its best in Alsace where it develops a lovely cashew nut flavour. When well handled it can also do well in Italy, where it is known as Pinot Bianco (Jermann), and in Germany, where it is called Weissburgunder. Most California Pinot Blancs are really made from the duller Melon de Bourgogne of Muscadet fame.

PINOT GRIS

An up-and-coming Alsace variety also known as Tokay but unrelated to any of the world's other Tokays. Its wines can be spicy, and appear in both sweet and dry versions. In Italy it is called Pinot Grigio and in Germany, Grauerburgunder. Look for New World examples from Oregon (Eyrie), California and New Zealand.

RIESLING

For purists this, not the Chardonnay, is the king of white varieties. Misunderstood – and often mispronounced as Rice-ling rather than Rees-ling – it carries the can for torrents of cheap German wine made from quite different grapes. At its best, it makes dry and sweet grapey, appley, limey wines that develop a spicy 'petrolly' character with age. The best examples come from Germany, in the Mosel (Dr Loosen) and Rhine (but beware of aggressively dry 'Trocken' tooth-enamel removers), Alsace (Zind-Humbrecht), Washington State (Kiona) and Australia (Grossett, Tim Adams). Don't confuse with the unrelated Laski, Lutomer, Welsch, Emerald or White Riesling.

SAUVIGNON/FUMÉ BLANC

The grape of Loire wines, such as Sancerre and Pouilly Fumé, and white Bordeaux, where it is often blended with the Sémillon. This gooseberryish variety now performs brilliantly in Marlborough in New Zealand (where the flavours can include asparagus and pea-pods), in South Africa (Thelema) and Australia (Shaw & Smith, Cullens). Chile has some good examples (from Casablanca) – and poor ones, made from a different variety called the Sauvignonasse. Washington State can get it right, but in California it is often horribly sweet or overburdened by the flavour of oak. (Oaked versions here and elsewhere are usually labelled Fumé Blanc.) Only the best ones improve after the first couple of years.

SÉMILLON

A distinctive peachy variety with only two successful homes. In Bordeaux, usually in blends with the Sauvignon Blanc, it produces sublime dry Graves and sweet Sauternes – and over-sulphured stuff that tastes like old dishcloths. In Australia there are brilliant, long-lived dry wines which are made purely from the Semillon in the Hunter Valley (often unoaked) and Barossa Valley (usually oaked). Good 'noble' late-harvest examples have also been produced (by de Bortoli) in Riverina. Elsewhere in Australia the grape is sometimes blended with the Chardonnay, a cocktail which has proved popular in California (in Geyser Peak's Semchard). Progress is being made in Washington State but most examples from California, New Zealand and Chile are disappointing.

SYLVANER

A characterful grape that is more or less restricted to Alsace and Franken in Germany, the Sylvaner has a recognisably 'earthy' character that is quite at odds with most modern wines. Crossing the Sylvaner with the Riesling, incidentally, produced the Müller-Thurgau, the 'catty' variety that is now common in Germany.

VIOGNIER

Now a cult grape, the Viognier was once more or less confined to the small appellations of Condrieu and Château Grillet in the Rhône, where good examples showed off its extraordinary perfumed, peach blossomy character, albeit at a high price. Today, however, it has been widely introduced to the Ardèche and Languedoc-Roussillon, California – where it is made with loving care (and over-generous exposure to oak barrels) – Eastern Europe, Argentina and Australia (Heggies Vineyard). While affordable examples are welcome, many are disappointing. This remains one of the world's trickier grape varieties to grow and make into wine. Buy with care.

RED WINE GRAPES

BARBERA

An Italian variety at its best in Piedmont. The keynote is a wild berryish flavour. Increasingly successful in blends with the Nebbiolo and Cabernet. Making inroads into California and Australia.

CABERNET SAUVIGNON

A remarkable success story, historically associated with the great red wines of the Médoc and Graves (where it is blended with the Merlot) and, more recently, with some of the best reds from the New World, especially California, Chile and Australia. Eastern Europe has good value examples (Bulgaria), as does southern France (Vin de Pays). Spain is rapidly climbing aboard (in the Penedès, Navarra and – though this is kept quiet – Rioja). The hallmark to look for is blackcurrant, though unripe versions (Bordeaux from poorer vintages and producers) taste like a blend of weeds and green peppers. There are some great Cabernets in Italy, though the 'Italian wine' flavour somehow always dominates the grape. Good New World Cabernets can smell and taste of fresh mint, but with time, like the best Bordeaux, they develop a rich, leathery 'cigar box' character.

GRENACHE/GARNACHA

Pepper – freshly ground black pepper – is the distinguishing flavour here, sometimes with the fruity tang of boiled sweets. At home in Côtes du Rhône and Châteauneuf-du-Pape, it is also used in Spain (as the Garnacha) in blends with the Tempranillo. Seek out 'Old Vine' or 'Bush' examples from Australia.

MERLOT

The most widely planted variety in Bordeaux and Languedoc-Roussillon and the subject of eager planting in California. In Bordeaux it is at its best in Pomerol, where wines can taste of ripe plums and spice, and in St. Emilion, where the least successful wines show the Merlot's less lovable dull and earthy character. Wherever it is made, the Merlot should produce softer wines than the Cabernet Sauvignon, though some California examples have been uncharacteristically tough. Elsewhere, Washington State and Chile are places to look, along with Italy and Eastern Europe.

NEBBIOLO/SPANNA

The red wine grape of Barolo and Barbaresco in Piedmont and now, thanks to modern winemaking, increasingly revealing a lovely cherry and rose-petally character, often with the sweet vanilla of new oak casks.

PINOT NOIR

The keynote flavours are of wild raspberry, plum and liquorice. The grape of all red Burgundy, and a major component of white and pink Champagne, the Pinot Noir has recently begun to perform well elsewhere. It is used to make pricy red and pink Sancerre, as well as light reds in Alsace and Germany (where it is called Spätburgunder). Italy makes a few good examples, but for the best modern efforts, look to California – especially Carneros (Saintsbury) and Santa Barbara (Au Bon Climat) – Oregon (Domaine Drouhin), Australia (Coldstream Hills), New Zealand (Martinborough), Chile (Cono Sur, Valdivieso) and South Africa.

PINOTAGE

Almost restricted to South Africa, this cross between the Pinot Noir and the Cinsaut can make berryish young wines that may develop rich gamey-spicy flavours. Sadly, far too few producers bring out these qualities. Try Kanonkop and Vriesenhof.

SANGIOVESE

The grape of Chianti, Brunello di Montalcino and of a host of popular Vino da Tavola wines in Italy, not to mention 'new wave' Italian-style wines in California. The recognisable flavour is of sweet tobacco, wild herbs and berries.

SYRAH/SHIRAZ

The extraordinary spicy brambly grape of the Northern Rhône (Hermitage, Cornas, etc) and the best reds of Australia (Henschke Hill of Grace and Penfolds Grange), where it is also blended with the Cabernet Sauvignon (just as it once was in Bordeaux). Elsewhere in Europe, the Marqués de Griñon has a great Spanish example, and Isole e Olena has made an unofficial one in Tuscany. Increasingly successful in California and Washington State.

TEMPRANILLO

Known under all sorts of names around Spain, including Cencibel (in Navarra) and Tinto Fino (in Ribeira del Duero), the grape gives Spanish reds their recognisable strawberry character. Often blended with the Garnacha, it works well with the Cabernet Sauvignon.

ZINFANDEL

California's 'own', related to the Italian Primitivo. In California, it makes rich spicy blueberryish reds (see Ridge Vineyards) and 'ports' and, when blended with sweet Muscat, sweet pink 'White Zinfandel'. Outside California, Cape Mentelle makes a good example in Western Australia and Delheim a floral one in South Africa.

OTHER GRAPES

WHITE

Albariño/Alvarinho Floral. Grown in Spain and Portugal.

Aligoté Lean Burgundy grape.

Arneis Perfumed variety in Piedmont.

Colombard Appley, basic; grown in S.W. France, US and Australia.

Furmint Limey variety, traditionally used for Tokaji.

Grüner Veltliner Limey. Restricted to Austria and Eastern Europe.

Kerner Dull German grape. Can taste leafy.

Müller-Thurgau/Rivaner Dull variety, grown in Germany and England. Can have a similar 'cat's pee' character to Sauvignon.

Roussanne Fascinating Rhône variety that deserves more attention.

Scheurebe Grapefruity grape grown in Germany.

Torrontes Grapey, Muscat-like variety of Argentina.

Ugni Blanc/Trebbiano Basic grape of S.W. France and Italy.

Verdejo Interesting Spanish variety of Rueda.

Verdelho Limey grape found in Madeira and Australian table wine.

Viura Widely planted, so-so Spanish variety.

Welschriesling Basic. Best in late harvest Austrians.

RED

Cabernet Franc Kid-brother of Cabernet Sauvignon, grown alongside it in Bordeaux and by itself in the Loire and Italy.

Carmenère/Grand Vidure Exciting spicy smoky variety once grown in Bordeaux; now limited to Chile.

Charbono Fun spicy-berryish grape only grown in California.

Cinsaut Spicy Rhône variety; best in blends.

Carignan Toffeeish non-aromatic variety widely used in S. France.

Concord US grape better used for grape juice or jelly.

Dolcetto Cherryish Piedmont grape.

Dornfelder Successful juicy variety grown in Germany.

Gamay The Beaujolais grape; less successful in the Loire and Gaillac.

Gamay Beaujolais/Valdiguié Mulberryish cousin of the Pinot Noir, grown in California. Confusingly unrelated to the Gamay.

Lemberger/Limberger/Blaufränkisch Berryish; successful in Washington State.

Malbec/Côt Once in Bordeaux blends; now Cahors, Loire, Argentina.

Mourvèdre (Mataro) Spicy Rhône grape; good in California and Australia, but can be hard and 'metallic'.

Petit Verdot Spicy ingredient of Bordeaux. Now being used neat.

Petite-Sirah Spicy; thrives in California and Mexico, and as Durif in Australia.

Ruby Cabernet Basic Carignan-Cabernet Sauvignon cross.

Tannat Tough variety of Madiran and Uruguay.

STYLES

STYLE COUNSEL

In simple terms, wine can be separated into one or more of a few easily recognisable styles: red, white and pink; still and sparkling; sweet and dry; light and fortified. To say that the contents of a bottle are red and dry does little, however, to convey the way a wine tastes. It could be a fruity Beaujolais, a mature Rioja with the sweet vanilla flavour of the oak barrels in which it was matured, a blueberryish California Zinfandel, or a tough young Bordeaux.

Knowing the geographic origin of a wine and the grape can of course give a clearer idea of what it is like, but it won't tell you everything. The human touch is as important in wine as it is in the kitchen. Some chefs like to assemble often quite eclectic flavours while others prefer a more conservative range of ingredients. The wine world is similarly riven between producers who focus on obvious fruit flavours, and winemakers, in France for example, who talk about the *goût de terroir* – the taste of the earth or soil.

In a world that is increasingly given to instant sensations, it is perhaps unsurprising that it is the fruit-lovers rather than the friends of the earthy flavour who are currently in the ascendant.

NEW WORLD/OLD WORLD

Until recently, these two winemaking philosophies could be broadly defined as belonging to the New and Old World. Places like California and Australia made wine that was approachably delicious when compared with the more serious wine being produced in Europe, which demanded time and food.

Life is never quite that cut-and-dried, however. Today, there are Bordeaux châteaux that are taking a decidedly New World approach and South Africans who take a pride in making wine as resolutely tough and old-fashioned as a Bordeaux of a hundred years ago.

Flying Winemakers

One phenomenon that has contributed to these changes in philosophy has been the 'flying winemakers' – mostly young Antipodeans who, like hired guns, are contracted to produce wine all over the world. Today, you can choose between a white Loire produced by a Frenchman – or one from the next vineyard that bears the evident fruity fingerprint of Australian-rules winemaking.

Fruit of Knowledge

European old-hands like to claim that the Australians use some kind of alchemy to obtain those fruity flavours. In fact, their secret lies in the care they take over every step in the winemaking process. Picking the grapes when they are ripe (rather than too early); preventing them from cooking beneath the midday sun (as often happens in Europe while work stops for lunch); pumping the juice through pipes that have been cleaned daily rather than at each end of a three-week harvest; fermenting at a cool temperature (overheated vats can cost a wine its freshness); and storing and bottling it carefully, will all help a wine made from even the dullest grape variety to taste fruitier.

COME HITHER

If the New Worlders want their wines to taste of fruit, they are – apart from some of those South Africans and a few diehard Californians – just as keen to make wine that can be drunk young. To achieve this, they take care not to squeeze the red grapes too hard, so as not to extract bitter, hard tannins, and they try to avoid their white wines being too evidently acidic.

Traditionalists claim that wines made this way do not age as well as their efforts. It is too early to say whether this is true in the long term, but there is no question that the newer wave red Bordeaux of, say 1985, have consistently given more people more pleasure since they were first released, than the supposedly greater 1970 vintage, whose wines remained dauntingly hard throughout their lifetime. A wine does not have to be undrinkable in its youth to develop into something that's good to drink later on; indeed wines that start out tasting unbalanced tend to go on tasting that way.

SPOTTING THE WOOD FROM THE TREES

Another thing that sets many new wave wines apart has nothing to do with grapes. Wines have been matured in oak barrels since Roman times, and traditionally new barrels were only bought to replace old ones that had begun to fall apart. Old casks have little to offer in the way of flavour but, for the first two or three years of their lives, new ones have a recognisable vanilla-caramel character which comes from the way the staves are bent over flames. It has taken winemakers a long time to discover the contribution the vanilla can make to the finished wine; indeed new casks were often rinsed out with dilute ammonia to remove it. Today, however, producers take the choice of forest, cooper and charring (light, medium or heavy 'toast') as seriously as the quality of their grapes.

Oak-mania began when top Bordeaux châteaux began to spend the income from the great vintages of the 1940s on replacements for their old barrels. In Burgundy in the 1970s, after an entire vintage was thought to have been spoiled by old barrels, the illustrious

Hospices de Beaune decreed that each harvest would go exclusively into new ones. Over the last 25 years, top producers and would-be top producers internationally have introduced at least a proportion of new oak, while even the makers of cheaper wine have found that dunking giant 'teabags' filled with small oak chips into wine vats could add some of that vanilla flavour too.

If you like oak, you should find it in top flight Bordeaux and Burgundy (red and white), Spanish wines labelled as Crianza, Reserva or Gran Reserva and Italians whose labels use the French term 'Barrique'. French wines that say they have been *'Elevé en fût de Chêne'* will generally taste oaky, but in some cases, this expression is merely used sneakily by a producer whose oak barrels are older than he is. Australian 'Show Reserve' will tend to be oaky, as will Reserve and 'Barrel Select' wines from anywhere in the New World, as well as wines describing themselves as 'Fumé Blanc'.

RED WINES – FRUITS, SPICE AND . . . COLD TEA

If you enjoy your red wines soft and juicily fruity, the styles to look for are Burgundy and other wines made from the Pinot Noir, Rioja and Navarra from Spain, inexpensive Australians, Pomerol, good St. Emilion from Bordeaux, and Merlots from almost anywhere. Look too for Nouveau, Novello and Joven (young wines).

The Kitchen Cupboard

Some grapes, such as the Sangiovese in Italy, are not so much fruity as herby, while the Syrah/Shiraz of the Rhône and Australia, the peppery Grenache and – sometimes – the Zinfandel and Pinotage can all be surprisingly spicy.

Some Like it Tough

Some places reliably produce traditional, cold tea tannic wine. Most basic recent Bordeaux and all but a few wines from St. Estèphe and Listrac in Bordeaux are a good bet, as are most older-style wines from Piedmont, reds from Duckhorn and Dunn in California and most South Africans. As a rule, the Cabernet Sauvignon will make tougher wines than the Merlot or Pinot Noir.

WHITE WINES – HONEY AND LEMON

If dry wines with unashamedly fruity flavours are what you want, try the Muscat, the Torrontes in Argentina, basic Riesling and Chardonnay and New World and Southern French Sauvignon Blanc.

Non-Fruit

For more neutral styles, go for Soave or Frascati from Italy, Muscadet, Grenache Blanc and most traditional wines from Spain and Southern France.

Riches Galore

The combination of richness and fruit is to be found in white Burgundy, better dry white Bordeaux and in Chardonnays, Sémillons and oaked Sauvignon (Fumé) wines from the New World.

Aromatherapy

Some perfumed, spicy grapes, like the Gewurztraminer, are frankly aromatic. The Tokay-Pinot Gris, the Gewurztraminer's neighbour in Alsace fits the bill, as do the Viognier in France, the Arneis in Italy, the Albariño in Spain and the Grüner Veltliner in Austria.

Middle of the Road

Today, people want wine that is – or says it is – either dry or positively sweet. The Loire can get honeyed semi-sweet wine right. Otherwise, head for Germany and Kabinett and Spätlese wines.

Pure Hedonism

Sweet wine is making a comeback as people rebel against the health fascism that sought to outlaw such pleasures. The first places to look are Bordeaux, the Loire (Moelleux), Alsace (Vendange Tardive or Sélection des Grains Nobles); Germany (Auslese, Beerenauslese Trockenbeerenauslese); Austria (Ausbruch); the New World (late harvest and noble late harvest); and Hungary (Tokaji 6 Puttonyos).

All of these wines should not only taste sweet, but have enough fresh acidity to prevent them from being in the least cloying. Also, they should have the additional, characteristic dried-apricot flavour that comes from grapes that have been allowed to be affected by a benevolent fungus known as *botrytis* or *noble rot*.

Other sweet wines such as Muscat de Beaumes de Venise are fortified with brandy to raise their strength to 15% or so. These wines can be luscious too, but they never have the flavour of *noble rot*.

PINK

Tread carefully. Provence and the Rhône should offer peppery-dry rosé just as the Loire and Bordeaux should have wines that taste deliciously of blackcurrant. Sadly, many taste dull and stale. Still, they are a better bet than California's dire sweet 'white' or 'blush' rosé. Look for the most recent vintage and the most vibrant colour.

SPARKLING

Fizz comes in various styles too. If you find Champagne too dry, but don't want a frankly sweet grapey fizz like Asti Spumante or France's Clairette de Die 'Tradition', try a fruity New World fizz like the Cuvée Napa from California or Seaview from Australia. If you don't like that fruitiness, try traditional Cava from Spain, Prosecco from Italy and Blanquette de Limoux from France.

STORING

STARTING A CELLAR

Not so long ago, when winemaking was less sophisticated and there were fewer ways to counter tricky vintages, there were two kinds of wines: the basic stuff to drink straight away, and the cream of the crop that was left in the barrel and/or bottle to age. So, a good wine was an old wine. And vice versa. Young wine and old wine had as much in common as hamburgers and *haute cuisine*.

Today, just as fast food now includes delicious sushi, there are brilliant wines that never improve beyond the first few years after the harvest, and are none the worse for that. On the other hand, some wines – German Riesling, fine claret and top Australian Shiraz, for example – by their very nature, still repay a few years' patience.

Unfortunately, identifying when each particular wine is likely to be at its best is very tricky. The 1947 Mouton Rothschild will last beyond the millennium – long after the 1987 has popped its vinous clogs. Like human beings, wines can evolve unpredictably. Some fail to live up to their early promise, others are late developers, while some go through odd phases when they temporarily seem to lose their appeal. On balance though, I would rather drink a wine that is a little too young, than one that has lost its fruit.

THE RESTING PLACE

While many of us – myself included – live in homes that are ill-suited for storing wine, one can often find an unused fireplace or a space beneath the stairs that offers wine what it wants: a constant temperature of around 7–10°C (never lower than 5°C nor more than 20°C), reasonable humidity (install a cheap humidifier or leave a sponge in a bowl of water), sufficient ventilation to avoid a musty atmosphere and, ideally, an absence of vibration (wines stored beneath railway arches – or beds – age faster). Alternatively, invest in a fridge-like Eurocave that guarantees perfect conditions (see page 253 for stockists) – or even adapt an old freezer.

RACKS

Purpose-built racks can be bought 'by the hole', and cut to fit awkwardly shaped bits of wall (see page 253 for stockists). Square chimney pots can be used too. If you have plenty of space, you could, for example, simply allocate a set of racks to red Burgundy, another to white, and a third to California wines. Unfortunately, though, even the best laid-out cellar plans tend to fall apart completely when a generous gift of two cases of Australian Shiraz suddenly has to be squeezed into a part of the cellar with space enough for just one.

CELLAR BOOKS

If the size of the cellar warrants it, give each hole in the rack a cross-referenced identity, from A1 at the top left to, say, Z100 at the bottom right. As bottles arrive, they can then be put in any available hole, and their address noted in a cellar book. Ideally, keep a regularly updated record of when and where you obtained each wine, what it cost and how each bottle tasted (is it improving or drying out?). Some people like leather-covered cellar books; I prefer my computer (Filemaker Pro or Microsoft Excel).

TO DRINK OR KEEP?

A guide to which corks to pop soon and which bottles to treasure for a few years in the rack:

Drink as Soon as Possible

Most wine at under £5, particularly Muscadet, Vins de Pays, white Bordeaux; Nouveau/Novello/Joven reds; Bardolino, Valpolicella; light Italian whites; most Sauvignon Blanc; almost all rosé.

Less than 5 Years

Most Petit-Château Bordeaux and Cru Bourgeois, and lesser Cru Classés clarets from poorer vintages; basic Alsace, Burgundy and better Beaujolais; Chianti, Barbera, basic Spanish reds; good mid-quality Germans; English wines; cheaper New World Chardonnays; all but the finest New and Old World Sauvignons; basic South African, Chilean and Australian reds.

5-10 Years

Most Cru Bourgeois Bordeaux from good years; better châteaux from lesser vintages; all but the best red and white Burgundy and Pinot and Chardonnay from elsewhere; middle-quality Rhônes; southern-French higher flyers; good German, Alsace, dry Loire and white Bordeaux; Portuguese reds; California and Washington State; South African, Chilean and New Zealand Merlots.

Over 10 Years

Top class Bordeaux, Rhône, Burgundy and sweet Loire from ripe years; top flight German late harvest, Italian Vino da Tavola and Barolo; best Australian Shiraz, Cabernet, Rieslings and Semillon, and California Cabernet.

SERVING

THE RULES OF THE GAME

'The art in using wine is to produce the greatest possible quantity of present gladness, without any future depression'.
The Gentleman's Table Guide, 1873

A century ago, the English used to add ice to claret and – in winter – a hint of spice. Today, Chinese wine drinkers apparently prefer their Mouton Cadet with a dash of Sprite. And why not? I'm sure the lemonade would do many a skinny Bordeaux a world of good. As with food and sex, it's worth questioning accepted rules – especially when they vary between cultures. Have no fear, the advice that follows is all based on common sense and experience – and offered only to help you to decide how you enjoy serving and drinking wine.

SOME LIKE IT HOT

Particular styles of wine, like types of food, taste better at particular temperatures. Warm Champagne is as appetising as warm strawberries. Outside British pubs, though, white wine and fizz are more often served too cold than too hot. Paradoxically, it is the reds that suffer most from being drunk too warm. Few of the people who serve wines at 'room temperature' recall that, when that term was coined, there wasn't a lot of central heating. Be ready to chill a fruity red by putting the bottle in a bucket of ice and water for five to ten minutes before serving.

Red Wine

When choosing the temperature for a red, focus on the flavour of the wine. Tough wines are best slightly warmer. This is a guide:
1) Beaujolais and other fruity reds: 10–13°C (an hour in the fridge).
2) Younger red Burgundy and Rhônes and older Bordeaux, Chianti, younger Rioja, New World Grenache and Pinotage: 14–16°C.
3) Older Burgundy, tannic young Bordeaux and Rhônes, Zinfandel, bigger Cabernet Sauvignon, Merlot and Shiraz, Barolo and other bigger Italian and Spanish reds: 16–18°C.

Rosé

Rosé should be chilled at 12–13°C, or for five to ten minutes in a bucket of ice and water.

White Wine

The cooler the wine, the less it will smell or taste. Subtler, richer wines deserve to be drunk a little warmer.

1) Lighter sweeter wines and everyday fizz: 4–8°C (two or three hours in the fridge or 10–15 minutes in ice and water).

2) Fuller-bodied, aromatic, drier, semi-dry, lusciously sweet whites; Champagne, simpler Sauvignons and Chardonnays: 8–11°C.

3) Richer dry wines: Burgundy, California Chardonnay: 12–13°C.

THE PERFECT OUTCOME

The Screwpull is still the most reliable way to get a cork out of a bottle. The 'waiter's friend' is the next best thing; otherwise choose a corkscrew that comes in the form of a wire spiral rather than one that looks like a large screw.

WHICH GLASSES?

On occasions when no other glass was available I have enjoyed great wine from a tooth mug. To be honest, though, I suspect I'd have got more out of the experience if something a little more stylish had come to hand. Glasses should be narrower across the rim than the bowl. Red ones should be bigger than white. If you like bubbles in your fizz, serve it in a flute rather than a saucer from which they will swiftly escape. Dartington Crystal, Schott and Riedel are among a number of companies that now produce attractive glasses that are specially designed to bring out the best in particular styles of wine.

TO BREATHE OR NOT TO BREATHE?

Some reds have an unwelcome gungy deposit; some red and white wines may benefit from the aeration of being poured into a decanter or another bottle. But don't decant every red wine you encounter. A tannic young claret, Cabernet or Italian red may soften to reveal unexpected flavours, but an old Burgundy or Rioja will have very little deposit and may be too light-bodied to gain from decanting.

Stand the bottle for up to a day before decanting it. Pour it very slowly, in front of a torch or candle, watching for the first signs of the deposit. Coffee filters suit those with less steady hands.

ORDER OF SERVICE

The rules say that white wines and youth respectively precede red wines and age; dry goes before sweet (most of us prefer our main course before pudding); the lighter the wine, the earlier. But what if the red Loire is lighter-bodied than the white Burgundy? Can the claret follow the Sauternes that you are offering with the foie gras? Ignore the absolutes but bear in mind the common sense that lies behind them. Work gently up the scale of fullness, 'flavour-someness' and quality, rather than swinging wildly between styles.

INVESTING

LIQUID ASSETS

In early 1998, a number of moderately wealthy British householders received unsolicited invitations to invest their money in claret. The value of red Bordeaux, those curious enough to enquire further were told, was rising dramatically – thanks to the explosion of enthusiasm for them in Asia.

The people who parted with their cash were the victims of a scam. As most reasonably well-informed people ought to have known, the economic state at the time left Asian wine enthusiasts in more of a mood to sell their claret than to invest in more. After huge price rises in 1997, early 1998 in fact saw the market fall.

Despite con-artists and temporary financial hiccups, however, buying the right wine from the right vintage at the right price is a good long term investment. And it's one that is likely to continue as such, given the limited production of top class wine and the ever growing number of people with a bit of spare cash to spend on it.

SUPPLY AND DEMAND

The United Kingdom alone currently produces some 200 *new* (pound) millionaires every week, or over 10,000 per year. Other countries, ranging from the Republic of Ireland to Russia are proving similarly productive. New money, whatever its nationality, tends to be attracted by the traditional trappings of wealth – like classic wine. And with just 20,000 dozen bottles made annually by an average Médoc château, let alone the 12,000 or so bottles on offer from a small Pomerol estate, it's hardly surprising that wines like these with established reputations, and critically approved new offerings are easy to sell. The only change in recent years has been the growing interest in wines - like the 'micro-wines' from Pomerol and St. Emilion and California that are produced in hundreds rather than thousands of cases.

THE RULES

1) The popularity and value of any wine can vary from one country to another. **2)** Wines are not like works of art; they don't last forever, so be ready to see their value fall. **3)** Tread carefully among wines like le Pin and Valandraud from Bordeaux and Screaming Eagle from California which have yet to prove their *long-term* potential. The prices of the new Bordeaux superstars began to fall during the first few months of 1998 and I wouldn't be surprised to them fall further over the next year or so. **4)** When buying *en primeur*, deal with financially solid merchants. **5)** At auction, favour wines that are known to have been carefully cellared. **6)** Store your wines carefully and securely – in your own cellar or elsewhere. **7)** Follow your wine's progress; read critics' comments and watch auction prices. **8)** Beware of falling reputations: the 1975 Bordeaux came after a series of poor vintages and sold at high prices; within a decade they had been eclipsed by the 1970 and 1982 vintages, and today are on few people's shopping lists. The 1974 Californian Cabernets, once heavily hyped, are now similarly questioned. The following wines are worth investing in:

FRANCE

Bordeaux

Châteaux l'Angélus, Ausone, Cheval Blanc, Cos d'Estournel, Ducru-Beaucaillou, Eglise-Clinet, Figeac, Grand-Puy-Lacoste, Gruaud-Larose, Haut-Brion, Lafite, Lafleur, Latour, Léoville Barton, Léoville Las Cases, Lynch Bages, Margaux, la Mission-Haut-Brion, la Mondotte, Montrose, Mouton-Rothschild, Palmer, Pétrus, Pichon Lalande, Pichon Longueville, le Pin, Rauzan Segla (recent vintages) Valandraud. Vintages: 1982, 1983 (for Margaux), 1985, 1986, 1988, 1989, 1990, 1995, 1996.

Burgundy

Drouhin Marquis de Laguiche, Gros Frères, Hospices de Beaune (from *négociants* such as Drouhin, or Jadot), Méo-Camuzet, Romanée-Conti (la Tâche, Romanée-Conti), Lafon, Leroy, de Vogüé.

Rhône

Chapoutier, Chave, Guigal (top wines), Jaboulet Aîné 'La Chapelle'.

PORTUGAL (PORT)

Cockburn's, Dow's, Fonseca, Graham's, Noval, Taylor's, Warre's.

CALIFORNIA

Beaulieu Private Reserve, Diamond Creek, Dominus, Duckhorn, Dunn Howell Mountain, Grace Family, Heitz Martha's Vineyard, (varied in the late 1980s and early 1990s), Matanzas Creek, Robert Mondavi Reserve, Opus One, Ridge, Spottswoode, Stag's Leap.

AUSTRALIA

Jim Barry 'The Armagh', Henschke Hill of Grace and Mount Edelstone, Leeuwin Chardonnay, Penfolds Grange and Bin 707, Petaluma Cabernet, Wynns 'John Riddoch', Virgin Hills, Yarra Yering.

VINTAGES

TIME WILL TELL

Twenty-five years ago, a vintage chart was as necessary for the enjoyment of wine as a corkscrew and a glass. But that was in the days when wine of any quality was only produced in a limited number of places, and in years when the climate was just right. Man had yet to develop ways – physical, chemical and organic – of combatting pests and disease that used to spoil wine with dreadful regularity.

Really disastrous vintages are a rarity now. Though frost can cut production, every year the most skilled and the luckiest producers in almost every region manage to make drinkable wines. Some places, however, are naturally more prone to tricky vintages than others. Northern Europe, for example, suffers more from unreliable sun and untimely rain than more southerly regions, let alone the warm, irrigated vineyards of Australia and the Americas.

A dependable climate does not necessarily make for better wine, however. Just as plants often bloom best in tough conditions, grapes develop more interesting flavours in what is known as a 'marginal' climate – which is why New World producers are busily seeking out cooler, higher altitude sites in which to plant their vines.

IT'S AN ILL WIND

Some producers can buck the trend of a climatically poor year – by luckily picking before the rainstorms, carefully discarding rotten grapes, or even using new techniques to concentrate the flavour of a rain-diluted crop. In years like these, well-situated areas within larger regions can, in any case, make better wines than their neighbours. So, *Grand* and *Premier Cru* vineyards in France, for example, owe their prestige partly to the way their grapes ripen. The difference in quality between regions can, however, also be attributed to the types of grapes that are grown. Bordeaux had a fair-to-good vintage for red wine in 1997, but a great one for Sauternes. Similarly, there are vintages where, for example, the St. Emilion and Pomerol châteaux have already picked their Merlot grapes in perfect conditions before rainstorms arrive to ruin the prospects of their counterparts' later-ripening Cabernet Sauvignon in the Médoc, only a few miles away.

The following pages suggest regions and wines for the most significant vintages of this century.

THE LAST FIVE YEARS

1998 (SOUTHERN HEMISPHERE)

Rain spoiled the normally ideal harvest conditions in Argentina, but New Zealand had a great vintage and there have been encouraging early reports from Australia, Chile and South Africa.

1997

Despite far less than ideal climatic conditions, Bordeaux's best châteaux used their skills to make surprisingly attractive red wines and some potentially brilliant sweet whites. There were good whites from Burgundy too; here, as elsewhere in Europe, though, the vintage was very variable, and rarely great. The exception to the rule was in Germany and Austria where terrific whites were made. South African reds will be slow to mature, and there were good wines from California, Washington, Australia and New Zealand.

1996

An unexpectedly classic vintage for the better châteaux of the Médoc, Graves and Sauternes (though less so in Pomerol) and for white Burgundy and the Loire. There were vintage-quality Champagnes, but Alsace and the Rhône were patchier. Germany made good but austere Kabinett and Spätlese wines, while Italy, Spain and Portugal had a fair quality vintage. California produced some top class reds and whites and it was a good year for New Zealand and Australia, though less so for South Africa.

1995

The best châteaux in Bordeaux made impressive, approachable wines, other efforts were very variable. White Burgundy, red Loire, Rhône, Alsace and Italy are worth buying, German wines and Spanish reds from Rioja and Ribera del Duero were excellent, as were many wines from Australia, New Zealand, South Africa, North and South America.

1994

Bordeaux made few really good reds. Alsace too was only average in quality, as was the Loire. The best Rhône reds came from the north of the region. Red Burgundy is good to drink now but generally not worth cellaring. Vintage port and Portuguese table wines were excellent. Italy's wines were average-to-good – and less impressive than the best from Austria and Germany. California had a great vintage, while the wines in Australia were good to very good – unlike the disappointing fare from South Africa and New Zealand.

1993

Bordeaux made light reds for early drinking. Elsewhere the quality was very patchy. There is excellent Tokaji, Alsace and Loires (red and white), good – if tough – red Burgundy and top class whites but only reasonable Rhônes. Wines were good in South Africa and New Zealand, but variable in Australia.

1992

A poor year in Bordeaux wines, but Champagne and white Burgundy were good. Red Burgundy is for early drinking. Taylor's and Fonseca produced great vintage port. Elsewhere this was a generally average vintage.

1991

Poor and uneven. Bordeaux are ready to drink, but reds from the Northern Rhône are a better bet. The best year for vintage port since 1985 and Spain, South Africa, California, New Zealand and Australia all had a good vintage.

1990

A great year for red and white Bordeaux, Champagne, German Rieslings and Alsace. Also Loire whites, red Rhônes, Burgundies Australians and Californians. Spain too had a good year for reds, especially from the Duero, and Italy had a great year for Barolo.

1985-1989

1989 Top-class, juicy ripe red and good white Bordeaux and Champagne. Stunning German wines (from Kabinett to TBA) and excellent Alsace. Outstanding Loires (especially red), good red and superb white Rhône, good red Burgundy. **1988** Slow-evolving claret, exquisite Sauternes, fine Champagne, long-lasting Italian reds, Tokaji, German, Alsace, Loire reds and sweet whites, good red and white Rhône and excellent red Burgundy. **1987** Fading Bordeaux and Burgundy. **1986** Powerful, long-lasting claret, good dry white and Sauternes, Australian reds, white Burgundy. **1985** California reds, claret, vintage port, Champagne, Spanish and Italian reds, Alsace, sweet Loire, red Rhône, Burgundy.

1980-1985

1984 South African reds, Australian reds and Rieslings. **1983** claret, red Rhône, Portuguese reds, Sauternes, Madeira, vintage port, Tokaji, sweet Austrians, Alsace. **1982** Claret, Champagne, Australian reds, Portuguese reds, Spanish reds, Italian reds, red and white Burgundy and Rhône. **1981** Champagne, Alsace. **1980** California and Australian Cabernets, Madeira, vintage port, Portuguese reds.

1970-1979

1979 Champagne, Sassicaia, sweet Austrians. **1978** Red and white Rhône, Portuguese reds, Bordeaux and Burgundy, Barolo, Tuscan and Loire reds. **1977** Port, sweet Austrians. **1976** Champagne, Loire reds and sweet whites, sweet Germans, Alsace, Sauternes. **1975** Top claret and port, Rioja, Eiswein, Sauternes, Penfolds Grange. **1974** California and Portuguese reds. **1973** Napa Cabernet, sweet Austrians. **1972** Tokaji. **1971** Bordeaux and Burgundy, Champagne, Portuguese reds, Barolo and Tuscan reds, sweet Austrians, Germans, red Rhône, Penfolds Grange. **1970** Port, Napa Cabernet, red Bordeaux, Champagne, Rioja, Chateau Musar.

1960-1969

1969 Sweet Austrians, red Rhône, Burgundy. **1968** Madeira, Rioja, Tokaji. **1967** Sauternes, Tuscan reds, Châteauneuf-du-Pape, German TBA. **1966** Port, red and white Burgundy, Champagne, Portuguese reds, claret, Australian Shiraz, **1965** Barca Velha. **1964** Claret, Tokaji, Champagne, Barca Velha, Vega Sicilia, Rioja, sweet Loire, red Rhône. **1963** Vintage port, Tokaji. **1962** Champagne, top Bordeaux and Burgundy, Rioja, Australian Cabernet and Shiraz. **1961** Claret, Sauternes, Champagne, Brunello, Barolo, sweet Austrians, Alsace, red Rhône. **1960** Port, top claret.

1950-1959

1959 Claret, Sauternes, Champagne, Tokaji, sweet Austrians, Germans, Loire and Alsace, red Rhône and Burgundy. **1958** Barolo. **1957** Madeira, Vega Sicilia, Chianti, Tokaji. **1956** Château Yquem. **1955** Claret, Sauternes, port, Champagne, Brunello, Penfolds Grange. **1954** Madeira. **1953** Claret, Tokaji, Champagne, Vega Sicilia, sweet Germans, Côte Rôtie, red and white Burgundy. **1952** Claret, Madeira, Champagne, Barolo, Tokaji, red Rhône, red and white Burgundy. **1951** Terrible everywhere. **1950** Madeira.

1940-1949

1949 Red and white Bordeaux, Champagne, Tokaji, sweet Germans; red Rhône and Burgundy. **1948** Port, Vega Sicilia. **1947** Bordeaux and Burgundy, port, Champagne, Tokaji, sweet Loire. **1946** Armagnac. **1945** Brunello, port, Bordeaux, Champagne, Chianti, sweet Germans, Alsace, red Rhônes and Burgundy. **1944** Madeira, port. **1943** Champagne, red Burgundy. **1942** Port, Rioja, Vega Sicilia. **1941** Madeira, Sauternes. **1940** Madeira.

ANNIVERSARY WINES

1939 Madeira. **1929** Claret, Sauternes, red Rhône, Burgundy. **1919** Red Burgundy. **1909** Sauternes. **1899** Claret, Sauternes. For examples, contact The Antique Wine Co (see Page 252).

WINE & HEALTH

WINE AND HEALTH

'Drink a glass of wine after your soup.
And you steal a rouble from your doctor.'

Russian proverb

Despite the efforts of the anti-alcohol lobbyists, scientists are steadily proving that the folklorists' belief in wine was not misplaced.

GREAT WHITE HOPE – OR GRAPE EXPECTATIONS?

After the flood of reports about the special 'healthful' qualities of red wine, the 1997 Allied Dunbar national fitness survey in Britain suggested that white wine can be just as good at reducing blood pressure and heart disease as red. In 1998 other studies also raised the possibility that many of the healthier qualities of wine are also to be found – though not as pleasurably – in grape juice. And a bright marketeer in Asia began selling pills made from red wine.

WINE AND HEART DISEASE

Wine seems to combat heart disease in two ways. People who daily drink up to half a litre of red wine have higher levels of HDL – 'good' cholesterol which escorts 'bad' cholesterol away from the artery walls and to the liver where it is destroyed. Resveratrol, an antifungal compound found in wine, lowers the cholesterol levels of rats.

WINE AND DIGESTION

Wine of both colours also helps to counter both constipation and diarrhoea, while white wine in particular stimulates the urinary functions. Wine has also been shown to kill cholera bacteria and to combat typhoid and trichinella, the poisonous compound in 'bad' pork. Surprisingly, leading researcher Dr Heinrich Kliewe actually recommends moderate amounts of wine as an accompaniment to some antibiotics. The wine apparently does not work against these drugs and can help to counteract some of their side effects.

WINE AND VITAMINS

According to Dr Heinrich Kliewe, red wine contains 'almost all the minerals and trace elements ... in two multivitamin preparations'.

WINE AND AGEING

Elderly, moderate drinkers are less prone to disability and are mentally fitter than both heavier and lighter drinkers. This may be due to the trace mineral boron, which helps older women maintain higher levels of oestrogen, in turn enabling them to absorb calcium. Wine is also believed to give some protection against Alzheimer's Disease.

WINE AND VIRUSES

According to Dr Jack Konowalchuk and Joan Speirs of Canada's Bureau of Microbial Hazards, the polyphenols in tannic red wine are effective against such viruses as cold sores and possibly even the supposedly incurable genital Herpes 2. Dr Konowalchuk's cold sore research was, it has to be said, carried out using wine concentrate.

WINE AND PREGNANCY

Despite the fears it arouses, Foetal Alcohol Syndrome is rare outside the poorest inner cities of the US. In 1997, the UK Royal College of Obstetricians and Gynaecologists reported that up to 15 units of alcohol per week should do no harm to a foetus.

WINE AND CALORIES

There is no difference in calories between a Muscadet or a claret. (around 110 per glass). Sweeter, but less alcoholic Liebfraumilch has about 79. A Stanford University survey suggests the action of the wine on the metabolism somehow makes its calories less fattening.

HANGOVERS

All alcohol – especially vintage port – is hangover-fare. The only way to avoid this fate is to drink plenty of water before going to bed.

WINE AND CANCER

Alcohol has been linked to rare occurrences of mouth and throat cancer – but only among smokers. Red wine is rich in gallic acid, an acknowledged anticarcinogenic, and wine's role in reducing stress has been associated with a lower incidence of certain forms of cancer.

WINE AND MIGRAINE

Red wine, like chocolate, can inhibit an enzyme called phenosulphotransferase-P, or PST-P, which naturally detoxifies all sorts of bacteria in the gut. An absence of PST-P is linked to migraine.

WINE AND ASTHMA

Wines that are heavily dosed with sulphur dioxide (used to combat bacteria in most dried, bottled and canned foods) can trigger asthma attacks. New World and organic wines have lower sulphur levels.

FOOD & WINE

MATCHMAKING FOR BEGINNERS

One of the most daunting aspects of wine has always been the traditional obsession with serving precisely the right wine with any particular dish – of only ever drinking red with meat and white with fish or shellfish.

It may be reassuring to learn that some of these time-honoured rules are just plain wrong. In Portugal, for example, the fishermen love to wash their sardines and salt cod down with a glass or two of harsh red wine. In Burgundy too, they not only drink local red wine with trout – they even poach the fish in it.

On the other hand, the idea that a platter of cheese is somehow incomplete without a bottle of red wine can be exploded in an instant. Just take a mouthful of claret immediately after eating a little goat's cheese or Brie. The wine will taste metallic and unpleasant, for the simple reason that the creaminess of the cheese reacts badly with the tannin – the toughness – in the wine. A fresh, dry white would be far more successful (its acidity would cut through the fat), while the claret would be shown to its best advantage alongside a harder, stronger cheese such as a Cheddar or a Parmesan. My advice for wine lovers – if you don't want to offer a range of wines to go with the platter – is to stick to one or two cheeses that really will complement the stuff in the glass.

Don't take anything for granted. Even such an obvious pairing as rare beef and Bordeaux surprisingly fails the test of an objective tasting. The protein of the meat somehow makes all but the fruitiest wines taste even tougher than they really are. If you're looking for a perfect partner for beef, uncork a Burgundy. If, on the other hand, it's the claret that takes precedence, you'd be far better off with lamb.

The difference between an ideal combination of food and wine and one that's just okay can be very subtle. Most of us have, after all, quite happily quaffed claret with our steak and found no reason to complain. But just as a keen cook will tinker with a recipe until it is just right, there's a lot to be said for making the occasional effort to find a pairing of dish and wine that really works. Like people who are happier in a couple than separately, some combinations of food and wine simply seem to bring out the best in each other.

A SENSE OF BALANCE

There is no real mystery about the business of matching food and wine. Some flavours and textures are compatible, and some are not. You might not want to eat strawberry mousse with your chicken casserole; on the other hand, apple sauce can do wonders for roast pork.

The key to spotting which relationships are marriages made in heaven and which have the fickleness of Hollywood romances, lies in identifying the dominant characteristics of what is on the plate and what is in the glass. And learning which are likely to complement each other, either through their similarities or through their differences.

LIKELY COMBINATIONS

It is not difficult to define particular types of food and wine, and to guess how they are likely to get on. A buttery sauce is happier with something tangily acidic, like a crisp Sauvignon Blanc, rather than a rich buttery Chardonnay. A subtly poached fish won't appreciate a fruit-packed New World white, and you won't do pheasant pie any favours by pulling the cork on a delicate red.

WHAT TO AVOID

Some foods and their characteristics, though, make life difficult for almost any drink. Sweetness, for example, in a fruity sauce served with a savoury dish seems to strip some of the fruitier flavours out of a wine. This may not matter if the stuff in your glass is a black-currant New World Cabernet Sauvignon, but it's bad news if it is a bone dry white or a tough red with no fruit to spare.

Cream is tricky too. Try fresh strawberries with Champagne – delicious; now add a little whipped cream to the equation and see what a nasty flavour you will have created. Creamy sauces can have the same effect on a wine.

Spices are problematical for most Western palates – due to the physical sensation of eating them rather than any particular flavour. A wine won't seem nasty after a mouthful of chilli sauce; it will simply lose its fruity flavour and taste of nothing at all. If it is a tannic red, the way it dries out the mouth will have the side effect of apparently accentuating the heat of the spice. For this reason, the ideal wine for most Westerners to drink with curry or a spicy Chinese or Thai dish would be a light, possibly slightly sweet, white.

As Simon Tam of the Wine Institute of Asia pointed out to me, however, Chinese palates react differently to these combinations. They like the burning effect of the chilli and see no point in trying to put out the fire with white wine.

ALWAYS WORTH A TRY

Some condiments actually bring out the best in wines. Sprinkling a little freshly ground pepper onto your meat or pasta can accentuate the flavour of a wine, just as it can with a sauce. Squeezing a fresh lemon onto your fish will reduce the apparent acidity of a white wine – a useful tip if you have inadvertently bought a case of tooth-strippingly dry German white or Muscadet. And, just as lemon can help to liven up a dull sauce, it will also help to make a dull white wine, such as a basic Burgundy or a Soave, taste more interesting – by neutralising the acidity in the wine, allowing its other flavours to make themselves apparent. Mustard performs a similar miracle when it is eaten with beef, somehow nullifying the effect of the meat protein on the wine.

MARRIAGE GUIDANCE

In the following pages, I have suggested wines to go with a wide range of dishes and ingredients, taking the dominant flavour as the keypoint. Don't treat any of this advice as gospel – use it instead as a launchpad for your own food and wine experiments.

And, if no wine seems to taste just right, don't be too surprised. Heretical as it may seem, some dishes are actually more enjoyable with all sorts of other drinks. The vinegar which is such a fundamental part of a British plate of fish and chips, for example, will do no wine a favour. Even keen wine lovers might well find a pot of tea a far more pleasurable accompaniment for it.

COOKING WITH WINE

Finally, a word or two about the often neglected business of how to make best use of wine in the kitchen (apart from its natural role as refreshment following a vigorous session of egg-beating, and as a tranquiliser for the moments when sauces curdle and soufflées refuse to rise). The first – and most often forgotten – rule to remember is that wine that's not good enough to drink is probably not good enough to pour into the frying pan or casserole. At least, not unless you take a perverse pleasure in using and eating sub-standard ingredients. On the other hand, despite the advice of classic French recipes, your 'coq au vin' won't be spoiled by your unwillingness to make it with a pricy bottle of Grand Cru Burgundy. A decent humbler red will do perfectly well, though it is worth trying to use a similar style to the one suggested.

Second – and just as important – remember that, with the exception of a few dishes such as sherry trifle or zabaglione, in which it is enjoyed in its natural state, wine, as an ingredient, needs to be cooked in order to remove the alcohol. So, add it early enough for the necessary evaporation to take place.

A

Almond   Liqueur Muscats or Beaumes de Venise.
Trout with Almonds   Bianco di Custoza, Pinot Blanc.
Anchovies
Salted Anchovies   Rioja red or white, Manzanilla or Fino sherry.
Fresh Anchovy (Boquerones)   Albariño, Vinho Verde, Aligoté.
Salade Niçoise   Muscadet, Vinho Verde or Beaujolais.
Tapenade   Dry sherry or Madeira.
Aniseed   Dry white.
Apple
Apple Pie or Strudel   Austrian off-dry white.
Apple Sauce   Riesling (dry or off-dry).
Blackberry and Apple Pie   Late harvest Riesling, Vouvray demi-sec.
Roast Pork with Apple Sauce   Off-dry Vouvray or Riesling.
Waldorf Salad   Dry Madeira.
Apricot   Late harvest Sémillon or Riesling, Jurançon Moelleux.
Artichoke   White Rhône.
Artichoke Soup   Loire white (dry), Pinot Gris.
Asparagus
Asparagus Soup   Fresh dry whites, Sauvignon Blanc.
Aubergine
Ratatouille   Bulgarian red, Chianti, simple Rhône or Provence red,
   Portuguese reds, New Zealand Sauvignon Blanc.
Stuffed Aubergines   Beefy spicy reds like Bandol, Zinfandel, a good
   Southern Rhône or a full-bodied Italian.
Avocado
Avocado with Prawns   Champagne, Riesling Kabinett, Sauvignon Blanc,
   Pinot Gris, Australian Chardonnay.
Avocado Vinaigrette   Unoaked Chardonnay, Chablis.

B

Bacon   Rich Pinot Gris or Alsace Riesling.
Bacon with Marinated Scallops   Fino sherry or mature Riesling,
   Shiraz-based Australians, Zinfandel from the States or a heavy Cape red.
Warm Bacon Salad   New World Sauvignon Blanc, California Fumé Blanc
   or a good Pouilly Fumé.
Banana
Flambéed Banana with Rum   Jurançon, Tokaji, Pedro Ximénez sherry, rum.
Banoffee Pie   Sweet Tokaji.
Barbecue Sauce   Inexpensive off-dry white or a simple fruity Cabernet.
Spare Ribs with Barbecue Sauce   Fruity Australian Shiraz, Grenache or
   Zinfandel, spicy Côtes du Rhône from a ripe vintage or an off-dry white.
Basil   Slightly sweet Chardonnay (ie California, commercial Australian).
Pasta in Pesto Sauce   New Zealand Sauvignon Blanc, Valpolicella.
Beans
Baked Beans   Light Zinfandel, Beaujolais, dry rosé or beer.
Bean Salad   Spanish reds such as Rioja Reserva and Rueda or New Zealand
   Sauvignon Blanc.
Bean Stew   Chunky Portuguese or Spanish reds.
Cassoulet   Serious white Rhône, Marsanne or Roussanne, or reds including
   Grenache and Syrah from the Rhône, crunchy Italian reds or Zinfandel.

Beef

Beef with Green Peppers in Black Bean Sauce Off-dry German Riesling or characterful dry white like white Rhône or Marsanne.

Beef with Spring Onions and Ginger Off-dry German Riesling or one of the more serious Beaujolais Crus.

Beef Stew Pomerol or St. Emilion, good Northern Rhône like Crozes-Hermitage, Shiraz or Pinot Noir from the New World.

Beef Stroganoff Tough beefy reds like Amarone, Brunello di Montalcino, Barolo, Côte Rotie or really ripe Zinfandel.

Beef Wellington Top Burgundy, Châteauneuf-du-Pape.

Beefburger Tasty country reds, from Italy or Southern France eg Corbières.

Boeuf Bourguignon Australian Bordeaux-style, Barolo or other robust reds with sweet fruit.

Boiled Beef and Carrots Bordeaux Rouge, Valpolicella Classico, Australian Shiraz.

Bresaola (Air Dried Beef) Beaujolais, Barbera and tasty reds from the Languedoc.

Carpaccio of Beef Chardonnay, Champagne, Cabernet Franc and other Loire reds, Pomerol.

Chilli Con Carne Robust fruity reds, Beaujolais Crus, Barbera or Valpolicella, spicy reds like Zinfandel or Pinotage.

Corned Beef Hash Characterful spicy reds from the Rhône or Southern France.

Daube of Beef Cheap Southern Rhône reds or Côtes du Rhône.

Goulash East European reds, Bulgarian Cabernet or Mavrud and Hungarian Kadarka or Australian Shiraz.

Meatballs Spicy rich reds from the Rhône, Zinfandel, Pinotage and Portuguese reds.

Panang Neuk (Beef in Peanut Curry) New World Chardonnay, New Zealand Sauvignon Blanc, or a spicy aromatic white Rhône.

Pastrami Zinfandel, good Bardolino, light Côtes du Rhône.

Rare Chargrilled Beef Something sweetly ripe and flavoursome, but not too tannic. Try Chilean Merlot.

Roast Beef Côte Rôtie, good Burgundy.

Salt Beef Loire reds from Gamay or Cabernet Franc.

Steak Pinot Noir and Merlot from the New World, Australian Shiraz, Châteauneuf-du-Pape, good ripe Burgundy.

Steak with Dijon Mustard Bordeaux, Cabernet Sauvignon from the New World or Australian Shiraz.

Steak and Kidney Pie/Pudding Bordeaux, Australian Cabernet Sauvignon, Southern Rhône reds or Rioja.

Steak au Poivre Cabernet Sauvignon, Chianti, Rhône reds, Shiraz or Rioja.

Steak Tartare Bourgogne Blanc, fruity reds, light on tannin; Beaujolais, Bardolino, etc, or traditionally vodka.

Thai Beef Salad New Zealand or South African Sauvignon Blanc, Gewürztraminer, Pinot Blanc.

Beer

Carbonnade à la Flamande Cheap Southern Rhône or Valpolicella.

Beetroot

Borscht Rich, dry Alsace Pinot Gris, Pinot Blanc or Italian Pinot Grigio.

Black Bean Sauce

Beef with Green Peppers in Black Bean Sauce Off-dry German Riesling or characterful dry white like white Rhône or Marsanne.

Blackberry

Blackberry and Apple Pie Late harvest Riesling, Vouvray demi-sec.

Black Cherry

Black Forest Gâteau Fortified Muscat, Schnapps or Kirsch.

Blackcurrant

Blackcurrant Cheesecake Sweet grapey dessert wines.

Blackcurrant Mousse Sweet sparkling wines.

Black Pudding

Chablis, New Zealand Chardonnay, Zinfandel or Barolo.

Brandy
    Christmas Pudding Australian Liqueur Muscat, tawny port, rich (sweet) Champagne, Tokaji.
    Crêpe Suzette Asti Spumante, Orange Muscat, Champagne cocktails.
Bream (freshwater) Chablis or other unoaked Chardonnay.
Bream (sea) White Rhône, Sancerre.
Brie Sancerre or New Zealand Sauvignon.
Brill Dry white, Soave, Albariño, Vinho Verde.
Broccoli
    Broccoli and Cheese Soup Slightly sweet sherry – Amontillado or Oloroso.
Butter
    Béarnaise Sauce Good dry Riesling.
    Beurre Blanc Champagne Blanc de Blancs, dry Vinho Verde.
Butternut Squash
    Butternut Soup Aromatic Alsace Gewürztraminer.

C

Cabbage
    Stuffed Cabbage East European Cabernet.
Cajun Spices Beaujolais Crus.
    Gumbo Zinfandel or maybe beer.
Camembert Dry Sauvignon Blanc or unoaked Chablis.
Capers Sauvignon Blanc.
    Skate with Black Butter Crisply acidic whites like Muscadet or Chablis.
    Tartare Sauce Crisply fresh whites like Sauvignon.
Caramel
    Caramelized Oranges Asti Spumante, Sauternes.
    Crème Caramel Aromatic sweet white – Muscat or Gewürztraminer Vendange Tardive.
Carp Franken Sylvaner, dry Jurançon, Hungarian Furmint.
Carrot
    Carrot and Orange Soup Madeira or perhaps an Amontillado sherry.
    Carrot and Coriander Soup Aromatic dry Muscat, Argentinian Torrontes.
Cashew Nuts Pinot Blanc.
    Chicken with Cashew Nuts Rich aromatic white, Pinot Gris or Muscat.
Cauliflower
    Cauliflower Cheese Fresh crisp Côtes de Gascogne white, Pinot Grigio, softly plummy Chilean Merlot or young unoaked Rioja.
Caviar Champagne or chilled vodka.
Celery
    Celery Soup Off-dry Riesling
Cheddar (mature) Good Bordeaux, South African Cabernet, port.
Cheese (general – see individual entries)
    Cheeseburger Sweetly fruity oaky reds – Aussie Shiraz, Rioja.
    Cheese Fondue Swiss white or Vin de Savoie.
    Cheese Platter Match wines to cheeses, taking care not to put too tannic a red with too creamy a cheese, and possibly even to offer white wines – which go well with all but the hardest cheese. Strong creamy cheeses demand fine Burgundy, blue cheese is made for late harvest wines, goat's cheese is ideal with Sancerre, Pouilly Fumé or other dry, unoaked Sauvignons. Munster is best paired with Alsace Gewürztraminer.
    Cheese Sauce (Mornay) Oaky Chardonnay.
    Cream Cheese, Crème Fraîche, Mozzarella, Mascarpone Fresh light dry whites – Frascati, Pinot Grigio.
    Raclette Swiss white or Vin de Savoie.

Cheesecake   Australian botrytised Semillon.
Cherry   Valpolicella, Recioto della Valpolicella, Dolcetto.
  Roast Duck with Cherry Sauce   Barbera, Dolcetto or Barolo.
Chestnut
  Roast Turkey with Chestnut Stuffing   Côtes du Rhône, Merlot or soft and mature Burgundy.
Chicken
  Chicken with Bamboo Shoots and Water Chestnuts   Dry German, New World Riesling.
  Barbecued Chicken   Rich and tasty white, Chardonnay.
  Chicken Casserole   Mid-weight Rhône such as Crozes-Hermitage or Lirac.
  Chicken Chasseur   Off-dry Riesling.
  Chicken & Ham Pie   Good Beaujolais.
  Chicken Kiev   Chablis, Aligoté or Italian dry white.
  Chicken Pie   White Bordeaux, simple Chardonnay or light Italian white.
  Chicken Soup   Soave, Orvieto or Pinot Blanc.
  Chicken Vol-au-Vents   White Bordeaux.
  Cock-a-Leekie   Dry New World white, simple red Rhône.
  Coq au Vin   Shiraz-based New World reds, red Burgundy.
  Coronation Chicken   Gewürztraminer, dry aromatic English, fresh Chinon.
  Cream of Chicken Soup   Big dry unoaked white (Chablis, Pinot Blanc).
  Devilled Chicken   Australian Shiraz.
  Fricassée   Unoaked Chardonnay.
  Lemon Chicken   Muscadet, Chablis or basic Bourgogne Blanc.
  Poached Chicken   Beaujolais, Valpolicella.
  Roast/Grilled Chicken   Reds or whites, though nothing too heavy – Burgundy is good, as is Barbera, though Soave will do just as well.
  Roast/Grilled Chicken with Bread Sauce   Côtes du Rhône or herby Provençal reds.
  Roast/Grilled Chicken with Sage and Onion Stuffing   Italian reds, especially Chianti, soft plummy Merlots and sweetly fruity Rioja.
  Roast/Grilled Chicken with Tarragon   Dry Chenin (Vouvray or perhaps a good South African).
  Saltimbocca (Escalope with Mozzarella and Ham)   Flavoursome dry Italian whites, Lugana, Bianco di Custoza, Orvieto.
  Smoked Chicken   Oaky Chardonnay, Australian Marsanne or Fumé Blanc.
  Southern Fried Chicken   White Bordeaux, Muscadet, Barbera, light Zinfandel.
  Tandoori Chicken   White Bordeaux, New Zealand Sauvignon Blanc.
Chicken Liver   Softly fruity, fairly light reds including Beaujolais, Italian Cabernet or Merlot, or perhaps an Oregon Pinot Noir.
  Chicken Liver Paté   Most of the above reds plus Vouvray Moelleux, Monbazillac or Amontillado sherry.
Chilli   Cheap wine or cold lager.
  Chilli Con Carne   Robust fruity reds, Beaujolais Crus, Barbera or Valpolicella, spicy reds like Zinfandel or Pinotage.
  Hot and Sour Soup   Crisply aromatic English white, Baden Dry.
  Szechuan-Style   Dry aromatic whites, Alsace Pinot Gris, Riesling, Grenache rosé, beer.
  Thai Beef Salad   New Zealand or South African Sauvignon Blanc, Gewürztraminer, Pinot Blanc.
Chinese (general)   Aromatic white (Gewürztraminer, Pinot Gris, English).
Chives   Sauvignon Blanc.
Chocolate   Orange Muscat, Moscatel de Valencia.
  Black Forest Gâteau   Fortified Muscat, Schnapps or Kirsch.
  Chocolate Cake   Beaumes de Venise, Bual or Malmsey Madeira, Orange Muscat, sweet German or fine Champagne.
  Chocolate Profiteroles with Cream   Muscat de Rivesaltes.
  Chocolate Roulade   German or Austrian Eiswein.
  Dark Chocolate Mousse   Sweet Black Muscat or other Muscat-based wines.
  Milk Chocolate Mousse   Moscato d'Asti.

Chorizo (Pork) Red or white Rioja, Navarra, Manzanilla sherry, Beaujolais or Zinfandel.

Cinnamon Riesling Spätlese, Muscat.

Clams Chablis or Sauvignon Blanc.

  Clam Chowder Dry white such as Côtes de Gascogne, Amontillado sherry or Madeira.

  Spaghetti Vongole Pinot Bianco or Lugana.

Cockles Muscadet, Gros Plant, Aligoté, dry Vinho Verde.

Coconut (milk) California Chardonnay.

  Green Curry Big-flavoured New World whites or Pinot Blanc from Alsace.

Cod Unoaked Chardonnay, good white Burgundy, dry Loire Chenin.

  Cod in Crumb Bake Lugana, Pinot Bianco, Pinot Blanc.

  Cod and Chips Any light crisp dry white, such as a Sauvignon from Bordeaux or Touraine. Alternatively, try dry rosé or Champagne. Remember, though, that heavy-handedness with the vinegar will do no favours for the wine. For vinegary chips, stick to tea.

  Salt Cod (Bacalhão de Gomes) Classically Portuguese red or white – Vinho Verde or Bairrada reds.

  Smoked Cod Vinho Verde.

Cod's Roe (smoked) Well-oaked New World Chardonnay.

Coffee

  Coffee Gâteau Asti Spumante.

  Coffee Mousse Asti Spumante, Liqueur Muscat.

  Tiramisu Sweet fortified Muscat, Vin Santo, Torcolato.

Cognac

  Steak au Poivre Cabernet Sauvignon, Chianti, Rhône reds, Shiraz, Rioja.

Coriander

  Carrot and Coriander Soup Aromatic dry Muscat.

  Coriander Leaf Dry or off-dry English white.

  Coriander Seed Dry herby Northern Italian whites.

Courgette

  Courgette Gratin Good dry Chenin from Vouvray or South Africa.

Couscous Spicy Shiraz, North African reds or earthy Southern French Minervois.

Crab Chablis, Sauvignon Blanc, New World Chardonnay.

  Crab Bisque Chablis, Pinot Gris or dry sherry.

  Crab Paté Crisp dry whites – Baden Dry or Soave.

  Crab and Sweetcorn Soup Sancerre, other Sauvignon Blanc.

  Dressed Crab Chablis or Mâcon Chardonnay

Cranberry

  Roast Turkey with Cranberry and Orange Stuffing Richly fruity reds like Shiraz from Australia, Zinfandel or modern Rioja.

Crayfish

  Freshwater Crayfish South African Sauvignon, Meursault.

  Salad of Crayfish Tails with Dill Rich South African Chenin blends or crisp Sauvignon, white Rhône.

Cream When dominant, not good with wine, particularly tannic reds.

Cucumber

  Cucumber Soup Dry Madeira.

Cumin Soave, Lugana.

Curry

  Beef in Peanut Curry New World Chardonnay, spicy aromatic white Rhône.

  Coronation Chicken Gewürztraminer, dry aromatic English wine or a fresh Chinon.

  Curried Turkey New World Chardonnay.

  Curried Beef Beefy, spicy reds; Barolo, Châteauneuf-du-Pape and Shiraz/Cabernet or off-dry aromatic whites – Gewürztraminer, Pinot Gris. Or try some Indian sparkling wine or cold Cobra lager.

  Tandoori Chicken White Bordeaux, New Zealand Sauvignon Blanc.

  Thai Green Chicken Curry Big New World whites or dry tasty Pinot Blanc from Alsace.

D

Dill Sauvignon Blanc.
  Gravadlax Ice cold vodka, Pinot Gris or Akvavit.
Dover Sole Sancerre, good Chablis, unoaked Chardonnay.
Dried Fruit Sweet sherry, tawny port.
  Bread and Butter Pudding Barsac or Sauternes, Monbazillac, Jurançon.
    Muscat de Beaumes de Venise or Australian Orange Muscat.
  Mince Pie Rich, late harvest wine or botrytis-affected Sémillon.
Duck Pinot Noir from Burgundy, California or Oregon, or perhaps an off-dry
    German Riesling.
  Cassoulet Serious white Rhônes, Marsanne or Roussanne, or try reds
    including Grenache and Syrah from the Rhône, berryish Italian reds or
    Zinfandel.
  Confit de Canard Alsace Pinot Gris or a crisp red like Barbera.
  Duck Paté Chianti or other juicy herby red, Amontillado sherry.
  Duck Paté with Orange Riesling or Rioja.
  Peking Duck Rice wine, Alsace Riesling, Pinot Gris.
  Roast Duck Big fruity reds like Aussie Cabernet, a ripe Nebbiolo or
    Zinfandel.
  Roast Duck with Cherry Sauce Barbera, Dolcetto or Barolo.
  Roast Duck with Orange Sauce Loire red or, surprisingly, a sweet white
    like Vouvray demi-sec.
  Smoked Duck California Chardonnay or Fumé Blanc.
Duck Liver
  Foie Gras de Canard Champagne, late harvest Gewürztraminer or
    Riesling, Sauternes.

E

Eel
  Jellied Eels A pint of stout.
  Smoked Eel Pale dry sherry, simple, fresh white Burgundy.
Egg
  Baked Eggs Bordeaux Blanc, Côtes de Gascogne or other simple white,
    young fruity red
  Crème Brulée Jurançon Moelleux, Tokaji.
  Eggs Benedict Unoaked Chardonnay, Blanc de Blancs fizz, Bucks Fizz or
    Bloody Mary.
  Eggs Florentine Unoaked Chardonnay, Pinot Blanc, Aligoté, Sémillon.
  Omelettes Cheap Beaujolais, Bardolino.
  Tortilla Young juicy Spanish reds and fresher whites from La Mancha or
    Rueda.

F

Fennel Sauvignon Blanc.
Fig Liqueur Muscat.
Frankfurter Côtes du Rhône or Budweiser beer.

Fish (general – see individual entries)
  Bouillabaisse Red or white Côtes du Rhône, dry rosé from Provence,
    California Fumé Blanc, Marsanne or Verdicchio.
  Cumberland Fish Pie California Chardonnay, Alsace Pinot Gris,
    Sauvignon Blanc.
  Fish and Chips Most fairly simple, crisply acidic dry whites (white
    Bordeaux, Sauvignon Blanc) or maybe a rosé. (See Cod.)
  Fish Cakes White Bordeaux, Chilean Chardonnay.
  Fish Soup Manzanilla, Chablis, Muscadet.
  Kedgeree Aligoté, crisp Sauvignon.
  Mediterranean Fish Soup Provençal reds and rosés, Tavel, Côtes du
    Rhône, Vin de Pays d'Oc.
  Seafood Salad Soave, Pinot Grigio, Muscadet or a lightly oaked
    Chardonnay.
  Sushi Saké.
Foie Gras (see Duck and Goose Liver)
Fruit (general – see individual entries)
  Fresh Fruit Salad Moscato d'Asti, Riesling Beerenauslese or Vouvray
    Moelleux.
  Fruit Flan Vouvray Moelleux, Alsace Riesling Vendange Tardive.
  Summer Pudding Late harvest Riesling, German or Alsace.

G

Game (general – see individual entries)
  Cold Game Fruity Northern Italian reds – Barbera or Dolcetto – good
    Beaujolais or light Burgundy.
  Roast Game Big reds, such as Brunello di Montalcino, old Barolo, good
    Burgundy.
  Well-hung Game Old Barolo or Barbaresco, mature Hermitage, Côte Rôtie
    or Châteauneuf-du-Pape, fine Burgundy.
  Game Pie Beefy reds, Southern French, Rhône, Australian Shiraz or South
    African Pinotage.
Garlic
  Aïoli A wide range of wines go well including white Rioja, Provence rosé,
    California Pinot Noir.
  Garlic Sausage Red Rioja, Bandol, Côtes du Rhône.
  Gazpacho Fino sherry, white Rioja.
  Raw Garlic Rosé.
  Roast/Grilled Chicken with Garlic Oaky Chardonnay or red Rioja.
  Roast Lamb with Garlic and Rosemary Earthy soft reds like California
    Petite Sirah, Rioja or Zinfandel.
  Snails with Garlic Butter Aligoté and light white Burgundy or perhaps a
    red Gamay de Touraine.
Ginger Gewürztraminer or Riesling.
  Beef with Onions and Ginger Off-dry German Riesling, one of the more
    serious Beaujolais Crus.
  Chicken with Ginger White Rhône, Gewürztraminer.
  Ginger Ice Cream Asti Spumante or late harvest Sémillon.
Goat's Cheese Sancerre, New World Sauvignon, Pinot Blanc.
  Grilled Goat's Cheese Loire reds.
Goose A good Rhône red like Hermitage, Côte Rôtie, or a crisp Barbera,
    Pinot Noir from Burgundy, California or Oregon, or perhaps an off-dry
    German Riesling.
  Confit d'Oie Best Sauternes, Monbazillac.
Goose Liver
  Foie Gras Best Sauternes, Monbazillac.

Gooseberry
    Gooseberry Fool Quarts de Chaume.
    Gooseberry Pie Sweet Madeira, Austrian Trockenbeerenauslese.
Grapefruit Sweet Madeira or sherry.
Grouse
    Roast Grouse Hermitage, Côte Rôtie, robust Burgundy or good mature
    claret.
Guinea Fowl Old Burgundy, Cornas, Gamay de Touraine, St. Emilion.

H

Haddock White Bordeaux, Chardonnay, Pinot Blanc.
    Mousse of Smoked Haddock Top white Burgundy.
    Smoked Haddock Fino sherry or oaky Chardonnay.
Hake Soave, Sauvignon Blanc.
Halibut White Bordeaux, Muscadet.
    Smoked Halibut Oaky Spanish white/Australian Chardonnay, white Bordeaux.
Ham
    Boiled/Roasted/Grilled/Fried Ham Beaujolais-Villages, Gamay de
    Touraine, slightly sweet German white, Tuscan red, lightish Cabernet
    (eg Chilean), Alsace Pinot Gris or Muscat.
    Braised Ham with Lentils Light, fruity Beaujolais, other Gamay, Côtes du
    Rhône.
    Honey-Roast Ham Riesling.
    Oak-Smoked Ham Oaky Spanish reds.
    Parma Ham Try a dry Lambrusco, Tempranillo Joven or Gamay de Touraine.
    Pea and Ham Soup Beaujolais.
Hare
    Hare Casserole Good Beaujolais Crus or, for a stronger flavour, try an
    Australian red.
    Jugged Hare Argentinian reds, tough Italians like Amarone, Barolo and
    Barbaresco, inky reds from Bandol or the Rhône.
Hazelnut Vin Santo, Liqueur Muscat.
    Warm Bacon, Hazelnut and Sorrel Salad New World Sauvignon Blanc,
    California Fumé Blanc or a good Pouilly Fumé.
Herbs (see individual entries)
Herring
    Fresh Herrings Sauvignon Blanc, Muscadet, Frascati or cider.
    Roll-Mop Herring Savoie, Vinho Verde, Akvavit, cold lager.
    Salt Herring White Portuguese.
    Sprats Muscadet, Vinho Verde.
Honey Tokaji.
    Baklava Moscatel de Setúbal.
Horseradish
    Roast Beef with Horseradish California Pinot Noir or mature
    Burgundy.
Houmous French dry whites, Retsina, Vinho Verde.

I

Ice Cream Try Marsala or Pedro Ximénez sherry.
Indian (general) Gewürztraminer (spicy dishes); New World Chardonnay
    (creamy/yoghurt dishes); New Zealand Sauvignon Blanc (Tandoori).

J

Japanese Barbecue Sauce
  Teriyaki Spicy reds like Zinfandel or Portuguese reds.
John Dory Good white Burgundy or Aussie Chardonnay.

K

Kedgeree New World Sauvignon Blanc or Sauvignon.
Kidney
  Lambs' Kidneys Rich spicy reds; Barolo, Cabernet Sauvignon, Rioja reserva.
  Steak and Kidney Pie/Pudding Bordeaux, Australian Cabernet Sauvignon, Southern Rhône reds or Rioja.
Kipper New World Chardonnay or a good fino sherry. Or, if you are having it for breakfast, Champagne, a nice cup of tea or Dutch gin.

L

Lamb
  Cassoulet Serious white Rhône, Marsanne or Roussanne, or reds including Grenache and Syrah from the Rhône, berryish Italian reds or Zinfandel.
  Casserole Rich and warm Cabernet-based reds from France or California Zinfandel.
  Cutlets or Chops Cru Bourgeois Bordeaux, Chilean Cabernet.
  Haggis Beaujolais, Côtes du Rhône, Côtes du Roussillon, Spanish reds, malt whisky.
  Irish Stew A good simple South American or Eastern European Cabernet works best.
  Kebabs Modern (fruity) Greek reds or sweetly ripe Australian Cabernet/Shiraz.
  Kleftiko (Lamb Shanks Baked with Thyme) Greek red from Nemea, Beaujolais, light Cabernet Sauvignon.
  Lancashire Hotpot Robust country red – Cahors, Fitou.
  Moussaka Brambly Northern Italian reds (Barbera, Dolcetto, etc), Beaujolais, Pinotage, Zinfandel, or try some good Greek wine from a modern producer.
  Roast Lamb Bordeaux, New Zealand Cabernet Sauvignon, Cahors, Rioja reserva, reds from Chile.
  Roast Lamb with Thyme Try a New Zealand Cabernet Sauvignon or Bourgeuil.
  Shepherd's Pie Barbera, Cabernet Sauvignon, Minervois, Zinfandel, Beaujolais, Southern French red.
Langoustine Muscadet, Soave, South African Sauvignon.
Leek
  Cock-a-Leekie Dry New World white, simple red Rhône.
  Leek and Potato Soup Dry whites, Côtes de Gascogne.
  Leek in Cheese Sauce Dry white Bordeaux, Sancerre or Australian Semillon.
  Vichysoisse Dry whites, Chablis, Bordeaux Blanc.

Lemon
  Lemon Cheesecake Moscato d'Asti.
  Lemon Meringue Pie Malmsey Madeira.
  Lemon Sorbet Late harvest Sémillon or sweet Tokaji.
  Lemon Tart Sweet Austrian and German wines.
  Lemon Zest Sweet fortified Muscats.
Lemon Grass New Zealand Sauvignon, Sancerre, Viognier.
Lemon Sole Chardonnay.
Lentils Earthy country wines, Côtes du Rhône.
  Chicken Dhansak Sémillon or New Zealand Sauvignon.
  Dhal Soup Try Soave or Pinot Bianco.
Lime Australian Verdelho, Grüner Veltliner, Furmint.
  Kaffir Lime Leaves (in Thai Green Curry, etc.) Big-flavoured New World
    whites or Pinot Blanc from Alsace.
  Thai Beef Salad New Zealand or South African Sauvignon Blanc,
    Gewürztraminer, Pinot Blanc.
Liver
  Calves' Liver Good Italian Cabernet, Merlot or mature Chianti.
  Fegato alla Veneziana Nebbiolo, Zinfandel or Petite Sirah.
  Lambs' Liver Chianti, Aussie Shiraz or Merlot.
  Liver and Bacon Côtes du Rhône, Zinfandel, Pinotage.
Lobster Good white Burgundy.
  Lobster Bisque Grenache rosé, fresh German white, Chassagne-
    Montrachet, dry Amontillado sherry.
  Lobster in a Rich Sauce Champagne, Chablis, fine white Burgundy, good
    white Bordeaux.
  Lobster Salad Champagne, Chablis, German or Alsace Riesling.
  Lobster Thermidor Rich beefy Côtes du Rhône, oaky Chardonnay or a
    good deep-coloured rosé from Southern France.

M

Mackerel Best with Vinho Verde, Albariño, Sancerre and New Zealand
    Sauvignon.
  Smoked Mackerel Bourgogne Aligoté, Alsace Pinot Gris.
  Smoked Mackerel Paté Sparkling Vouvray, Muscadet.
Mallard Côte Rôtie, Ribera del Duero or Zinfandel.
Mango Best eaten in the bath with a friend and a bottle of Champagne.
    Otherwise, go for Asti Spumante or Moscato.
Marjoram Provençal reds.
Marsala
  Chops in Marsala Sauce Australian Marsanne or Verdelho.
Mascarpone
  Tiramisu Sweet fortified Muscat, Vin Santo, Torcolato.
Meat (general – see individual entries)
  Cold Meats Juicy, fruity reds, low in tannin ie Beaujolais, Côtes du
    Rhône, etc.
  Consommé Medium/Amontillado sherry.
  Meat Paté Beaujolais, Fumé Blanc, lesser white Burgundy.
  Mixed Grill Versatile uncomplicated red – Aussie Shiraz, Rioja, Bulgarian
    Cabernet.
Melon Despite its apparently innocent juicy sweetness, melon can be very
    unfriendly to most wines. Try tawny port, sweet Madeira or sherry,
    Quarts de Chaume, late harvest Riesling.
Mincemeat
  Mince Pie Complemented by rich, sweet late harvest wine or botrytis-
    affected Sémillon.

Mint Beaujolais, young Pinot Noir, or try a New Zealand or Australian Riesling.
  Thai Beef Salad New Zealand or South African Sauvignon Blanc, Gewürztraminer, Pinot Blanc.
Monkfish A light fruity red such as Bardolino, Valpolicella, La Mancha Joven or most Chardonnays.
Mushroom Merlot-based reds, good Northern Rhône, top Piedmontese reds.
  Mushroom Soup Bordeaux Blanc, Côtes de Gasgogne.
  Mushrooms à la Greque Sauvignon Blanc or fresh modern Greek white.
  Risotto with Fungi Porcini Top-notch Piedmontese reds – mature Barbera, Barbaresco or earthy Southern French reds.
  Stuffed Mushrooms Chenin Blanc, Sylvaner.
  Wild Mushrooms Nebbiolo, red Bordeaux.
Mussels Sauvignon Blanc, light Chardonnay, Muscadet Sur Lie.
  Moules Marinières Bordeaux Blanc or Muscadet Sur Lie.
  New Zealand Green-Lipped Mussels New Zealand Sauvignon Blanc.
Mustard Surprisingly, can help red Bordeaux and other tannic reds to go with beef which might otherwise accentuate their tough, tannic character.
  Dijon Mustard Beaujolais.
  English Wholegrain Mustard Beaujolais, Valpolicella.
  French Mustard White Bordeaux.
  Steak with Dijon Mustard Cabernet Sauvignon from the New World or Australian Shiraz.

N

Nectarine Sweet German Riesling.
Nutmeg Rioja, Aussie Shiraz or, for sweet dishes, Australian late harvest Semillon.
Nuts Amontillado sherry, Vin Santo and Tokaji.

O

Octopus Rueda white or a fresh modern Greek white.
Olives Dry sherry, Muscadet, Retsina.
  Salade Niçoise Muscadet, Vinho Verde or Beaujolais.
  Tapenade Dry sherry or Madeira.
Onion
  Caramelized Onions Shiraz-based Australians, Zinfandel from the States or a good Pinotage.
  French Onion Soup Sancerre or dry, unoaked Sauvignon Blanc, Aligoté, white Bordeaux.
  Onion/Leek Tart Alsace Gewürztraminer, New World Riesling or a good unoaked Chablis.
Orange
  Caramelized Oranges Asti Spumante, Sauternes or Muscat de Beaumes de Venise.
  Crêpe Suzette Sweet Champagne, Moscato d'Asti.
  Orange Sorbet Moscato or sweet Tokaji.
  Orange Zest Dry Muscat, Amontillado sherry.
Oregano Provençal reds, red Lambrusco, more serious Chianti or lightish Zinfandel.
Oxtail Australian Cabernet, good Bordeaux.

Oyster Sauce
Beef and Mangetout in Oyster Sauce Crisp dry whites like Muscadet or a Northern Italian Lugana or Pinot Bianco, white Rhône, Gewürztraminer.

Oysters Champagne, Chablis or other crisp dry white.

P

Paprika
Goulash Eastern European red like Bulgarian Cabernet or Mavrud, Hungarian Kadarka or Aussie Shiraz.

Parmesan Salice Salentino, Valpolicella.
Baked Chicken Parmesan with Basil Chenin Blanc, Riesling.

Parsley Dry Italian whites – Bianco di Custoza, Nebbiolo or Barbera.
Parsley Sauce Pinot Grigio, Hungarian Furmint, lightly oaked Chardonnay.

Partridge
Roast Partridge Australian Shiraz, Gevrey-Chambertin, Pomerol or St. Emilion.

Pasta
Lasagne Valpolicella, Barbera, Teroldego, Australian Verdelho or Sauvignon.
Pasta with Meat Sauce Chianti, Bordeaux Rouge.
Pasta with Pesto Sauce New Zealand Sauvignon Blanc, Valpolicella.
Pasta with Seafood Sauce Soave, Sancerre.
Ravioli with Spinach and Ricotta Pinot Bianco/Grigio, Cabernet d'Anjou.
Spaghetti with Tomato Sauce California Cabernet, Zinfandel, Chianti.
Spaghetti Vongole Pinot Bianco, Lugano.
Tagliatelle Carbonara Pinot Grigio or a fresh red Bardolino or Beaujolais.

Peach Sweet German Riesling.
Peaches in Wine Riesling Auslese, Riesling Gewürztraminer Vendange Tardive, sweet Vouvray.

Peanuts
Beef in Peanut Curry New World Chardonnay, an aromatic white Rhône.
Satay Gewürztraminer.

Pepper (corns)
Steak au Poivre Cabernet Sauvignon, Chianti, Rhône reds, Shiraz or Rioja.

Peppers (fresh green, red) New Zealand Cabernet, Loire reds, crisp Sauvignon Blanc, Beaujolais, Tuscan red.

Peppers (yellow) Fruity Italian reds, Valpolicella, etc.
Stuffed Peppers Hungarian red – Bull's Blood, Chianti or spicy Rhône reds.

Pheasant Top-class red Burgundy, good American Pinot Noir, mature Hermitage.
Pheasant Casserole Top class red Burgundy, mature Hermitage.
Pheasant Paté Côtes du Rhône, Alsace Pinot Blanc.

Pigeon Good red Burgundy, rich Southern Rhône. Chianti also goes well.
Warm Pigeon Breasts on Salad Merlot-based Bordeaux or Cabernet Rosé.

Pike Eastern European white.

Pine Nuts
Pesto Sauce New Zealand Sauvignon Blanc, Valpolicella.

Pizza
Fiorentina Pinot Bianco, Pinot Grigio, Vinho Verde, Sauvignon Blanc.
Napoletana Verdicchio, Vernaccia de San Gimignano, white Rhône.
Quattro Formagi Pinot Grigio, Frascati, Bianco di Custoza.
Quattro Stagioni Valpolicella, Bardolino, light Chianti, good Soave.

Plaice White Burgundy, South American Chardonnay, Sauvignon Blanc.

Plum
Plum Pie Trockenbeerenauslese, Côteaux du Layon.

Pork

Cassoulet Serious white Rhône, Marsanne or Roussanne, or reds including Grenache and Syrah from the Rhône, berryish Italian reds or Zinfandel.

Pork Casserole Mid-weight, earthy reds like Minervois, Navarra or Montepulciano d'Abruzzo.

Pork Pie Spicy reds, Shiraz, Grenache.

Pork with Prunes Cahors, mature Chinon or other Loire red or rich southern French wine such as Corbières, Minervois or Faugères.

Pork Rillettes Pinot Blanc d'Alsace, Menetou-Salon Rouge.

Pork Sausages Spicy Rhône reds, Barbera.

Pork and Sage Sausages Barbera, Côtes du Rhône.

Pork Spare Ribs Zinfandel, Aussie Shiraz.

Roast Pork Rioja reserva, New World Pinot Noir, dry Vouvray.

Roast Pork with Apple Sauce Off-dry Vouvray or Riesling.

Saucisson Sec Barbera, Cabernet Franc, Alsace Pinot Blanc or Beaujolais (Villages or Crus).

Spare Ribs with Barbecue Sauce Fruity Australian Shiraz, Grenache or Zinfandel, spicy Côtes du Rhône from a ripe vintage or an off-dry white.

Szechuan-Style Pork Dry aromatic whites, Alsace Pinot Gris, Riesling, Grenache rosé, beer.

Prawns
White Bordeaux, dry Australian Riesling, Gavi.

Prawn Cocktail Light fruity whites – German Riesling.

Prawns in Garlic Vinho Verde, Pinot Bianco.

Prawn Vol-au-Vents White Bordeaux, Muscadet.

Thai Prawns Gewürztraminer, dry aromatic Riesling or New Zealand Sauvignon Blanc.

Prunes
Australian late harvest Semillon.

Pork with Prunes and Cream Sweet Chenin-based wines or good Mosel Spätlese.

Prune Ice Cream Muscat de Beaumes de Venise.

Q

Quail Light red Burgundy, full-flavoured white Spanish wines.

Quince Lugana.

Braised Venison with Quince Jelly Rich and fruity Australian or Chilean reds, good ripe Spanish Rioja or a Southern French red.

R

Rabbit

Rabbit Casserole New World Pinot Noir or mature Châteauneuf-du-Pape.

Rabbit in Cider Muscadet, demi-sec Vouvray, cider or Calvados.

Rabbit with Mustard Franken wine or Czech Pilsner beer.

Rabbit in Red Wine with Prunes Good mature Chinon or other Loire red.

Roast Rabbit Tasty, simple young Rhône, red, white or rosé.

Raspberries
New World late harvest Riesling or Champagne, Beaujolais, demi-sec Champagne.

Raspberry Fool Vouvray Moelleux.

Raspberry Vinegar
Full-bodied Pinot Noir.

Warm Bacon and Sorrel Salad New World Sauvignon Blanc, California Fumé Blanc or a good Pouilly Fumé.

Redcurrant
    Cumberland Sauce Rioja, Australian Shiraz.
Red Mullet Dry rosé, New World Chardonnay, Sauvignon Blanc.
Rhubarb
    Rhubarb Pie Moscato d'Asti, Alsace, German or Austrian late harvest Riesling.
Rice
    Rice Pudding Monbazillac, sweet Muscat, Asti Spumante or California Orange Muscat.
Rocket Lugana, Pinot Blanc.
Roquefort The classic match is Sauternes or Barsac, but almost any full-flavoured, botrytised sweet wine will be a good partner for strong, creamy blue cheese.
Rosemary Light red Burgundy or Pinot Noir.
    Roast Lamb with Garlic and Rosemary Earthy soft reds like California Petite Sirah, Rioja or Zinfandel.
Rum
    Flambéed Banana with Rum Jurançon, Tokaji, Pedro Ximénez sherry, rum.

S

Saffron Dry whites especially Chardonnay.
    Bass in Saffron Sauce Riesling (German, Australian or Austrian), Viognier.
    Paella with Seafood White Penedés, unoaked Rioja, Navarra, Provence rosé.
Sage Chianti, or country reds from the Languedoc. Otherwise Sauvignon Blancs are great, especially Chilean.
    Roast Chicken, Goose or Turkey with Sage and Onion Stuffing Italian reds, especially Chianti, soft, plummy Merlots, sweetly fruity Rioja and brambly Zinfandel.
Salami Good beefy Mediterranean rosé, Sardinian red, Rhône red, Zinfandel, dry aromatic Hungarian white.
Salmon
    Carpaccio of Salmon Cabernet Franc, Chardonnay, Australian reds, red Loire, Portuguese reds, Puligny-Montrachet.
    Grilled Salmon White Rhône (especially Viognier).
    Poached Salmon Chablis, good white Burgundy, other Chardonnay, Alsace Muscat, white Bordeaux.
    Poached Salmon with Hollandaise Muscat, Riesling, good Chardonnay.
    Salmon Paté Best white Burgundy.
Salmon Trout Light Pinot Noir from the Loire, New Zealand, good dry unoaked Chardonnay, Chablis, etc.
Sardines Fresh Muscadet, Vinho Verde, very light and fruity reds such as Loire, Gamay.
Scallops Chablis and other unoaked Chardonnay.
    Coquilles St-Jacques White Burgundy.
    Marinated Scallops with Bacon Fino sherry or mature Riesling.
    Scallops Mornay White Burgundy, Riesling Spätlese.
Sea Bass Good white Burgundy.
    Bass in Saffron Sauce Riesling (German, Austrian or Australian), Viognier.
Seafood (general – see individual entries)
    Paella with Seafood White Penedés, unoaked Rioja, Navarra, Provence rosé.
    Platter of Seafood Sancerre, Muscadet.
    Seafood Salad Soave, Pinot Grigio, Muscadet, lightly oaked Chardonnay.
Sesame Seeds Oaked Chardonnay.
Shrimps Albariño, Sancerre, New World Sauvignon, Arneis.
    Potted Shrimps New World Chardonnay, Marsanne.

Skate Bordeaux white, Côtes de Gascogne, Pinot Bianco.
Smoked Salmon Chablis, Alsace Pinot Gris, white Bordeaux.
  Avocado and Smoked Salmon Lightly oaked Chardonnay.
  Smoked Salmon Paté English oaked Fumé Blanc, New Zealand Chardonnay.
Smoked Trout
  Smoked Trout Paté Good white Burgundy.
Snapper Australian or South African dry white.
Sorbet Like ice cream, can be too cold/sweet for most wines. Try fortified
    Muscats or see under individual entries (orange, lemon, etc).
Sorrel Dry Loire Chenin or Sauvignon Blanc.
Soy Sauce Zinfandel or Australian Verdelho.
Spinach Pinot Grigio, Lugana.
  Eggs Florentine Chablis or unoaked Chardonnay, Pinot Blanc, Aligoté,
    Sémillon.
  Spinach/Pasta Bakes Soft fruity Italian reds (Bardolino, Lambrusco) rich
    whites.
Spring Rolls Pinot Gris, Gewürztraminer or other aromatic whites.
Squid Gamay de Touraine, Greek or Spanish white.
  Squid in Batter Crisp and neutral dry white – Muscadet.
  Squid in Ink Nebbiolo or Barbera.
Stilton Tawny port.
Strawberry – No Cream Surprisingly, red Rioja, Burgundy (or other young
    Pinot Noir), especially if the berries are marinaded. More conventionally,
    sweet Muscats or fizzy Moscato.
  Strawberries and Cream Vouvray Moelleux, Monbazillac.
  Strawberry Meringue Late harvest Riesling.
  Strawberry Mousse Sweet or fortified Muscat.
Sweet and Sour Dishes (general) Gewürztraminer or beer.
Sweetbreads Lightly oaked Chardonnay, Chablis, Pouilly-Fuissé or light
    red Bordeaux.
  Sweetbreads in Mushroom, Butter and Cream sauce Southern French
    whites, Vin de Pays Chardonnay.
Sweetcorn Rich and ripe whites – California Chardonnay.
  Corn on the Cob Light fruity whites – German Riesling.
  Sweetcorn Soup with Chicken Chilean Sauvignon, Southern French
    whites, Soave, Chilean Merlot.
  Sweetcorn Soup with Crab Sancerre, other Sauvignon Blanc.

T

Taramasalata Oaked Chardonnay or English Fumé Blanc.
Tarragon White Menetou-Salon or South African Sauvignon Blanc.
  Roast/Grilled Chicken with Tarragon Dry Chenin Blanc, Vouvray, South
    African whites.
Thyme Ripe and fruity Provençal reds, Rioja, Northern Italian whites.
  Roast Lamb with Thyme New Zealand Cabernet Sauvignon, Bourgeuil.
Toffee Moscatel de Setúbal, Eiswein.
  Banoffee Pie Sweet Tokaji.
Tomato
  Gazpacho Fino sherry, white Rioja.
  Pasta in a Tomato Sauce California Cabernet, Zinfandel, Chianti.
  Tomato Soup Sauvignon Blanc.
Tripe Earthy French country red, Minervois, Cahors, Fitou.
Trout Pinot Blanc, Chablis.
  Smoked Trout Bourgogne Aligoté, Gewürztraminer, Pinot Gris.
  Trout with Almonds Bianco di Custoza, Pinot Blanc.
Truffles Red Burgundy, old Rioja, Barolo, Hermitage.

Tuna
  Carpaccio of Tuna Australian Chardonnay, red Loire, Beaujolais.
  Fresh Tuna Alsace Pinot Gris, Australian Chardonnay, Beaujolais.
  Tinned Tuna New World dry, fruity whites, Côtes de Gascogne.
Turbot Best white Burgundy, top California or Australian Chardonnay.
Turkey
  Roast Turkey Beaujolais, light Burgundy and quite rich or off-dry whites.
  Roast Turkey with Chestnut Stuffing Rhône, Merlot or mature Burgundy.

V

Vanilla Liqueur Muscat.
  Crème Brulée Jurançon Moelleux, Tokaji.
  Custard Monbazillac, sweet Vouvray.
Veal
  Blanquette de Veau Aromatic, spicy whites from Alsace.
  Roast veal Light Italian whites or fairly light reds – Spanish or Loire.
  Wienerschnitzel Austrian Grüner Veltliner or Hungarian Pinot Blanc.
Vegetables
  Roasted and Grilled Light juicy reds, Beaujolais, Sancerre and Sauvignon
    Blanc. Unoaked and lightly oaked Chardonnay.
  Vegetable Soup Pinot Blanc or rustic reds such as Corbières.
  Vegetable Terrine Good New World Chardonnay.
Venison Pinotage, rich red Rhône, mature Burgundy, earthy Italian reds.
  Venison Casserole Shiraz-based Australians, American Zinfandel, Cape red.
Vinegar
  Choucroute Garnie White Alsace, Italian Pinot Grigio or Beaujolais.
  Sauerkraut Pilsner beer.

W

Walnut Tawny port, sweet Madeira.
Watercress
  Watercress Soup Aromatic dry Riesling (Alsace or Australia).
Whitebait Fino sherry, Spanish red/white (Garnacha, Tempranillo), Soave.

Y

Yams Depends on the sauce. When subtly prepared, try Pinot Blanc.
Yoghurt Needs full-flavoured wines, such as Sémillon.

Z

Zabaglione Marsala, Australian Liqueur Muscat or a French Muscat such as
  Muscat de Beaumes de Venise.

A–Z

of

WINE

HOW TO READ THE ENTRIES

Names of wines are accompanied by a glass symbol (♼); grape varieties by a bunch of grapes (❦). Wine regions appear in a purple band.

Words that have their own entry elsewhere in the A–Z appear in italics. Recommended wines may also be cross-referenced.

Poor vintages are not listed. Particularly good years that are ready to drink now are featured in bold; vintages that will improve with keeping are in purple.

♼ **Ch. l'Angélus** [lon jay-loos] (*St. Emilion Grand Cru Classé, Bordeaux*, France) Flying high since the late 1980s, this is a lovely, plummy *St. Emilion* to watch. The *second label* Carillon d'Angélus is also well worth seeking out. 79 **82 83 85 86 87** 88 89 90 92 93 94 95 96 97 ☆☆☆☆☆ **1990 ££££**; ☆☆☆ 1991 **£££**

Throughout this section, examples are given of recommended vintages, producers or wines which represent good examples of the region, style or maker.

Recommended wines are accompanied by stars.
☆☆☆☆☆ = *outstanding in their style.*
☆☆☆☆ = *excellent in their style.*
☆☆☆ = *good in their style.*

Prices are indicated, using the following symbols:

£	Under £5
££	£5–10
£££	£10–20
££££	Over £20

PRONUNCIATION GUIDE

All but the most common words are followed by square [ ] brackets, which enclose pronunciation guides. These use the 'sounding-out' phonetic method, with the accented syllable (if there is one) indicated by capital letters. For example, **Spätlese** is pronounced as *SHPAYT-Lay-Zuh*. The basic sounds employed in this book's pronunciations are as follows:

a as in can	ah as in father	ay as in day	ur as in turn
ch as in church	kh as in loch	y as in yes	zh as in vision
ee as in see	eh as in get	g as in game	i as in pie
ih as in if	j as in gin	k as in cat	o as in hot
oh as in soap	oo as in food	ow as in cow	uh as in up

Foreign sounds: eu is like a cross between oo and a; an italicised *n* or *m* is silent and the preceding vowel sounds nasal; an ñ is like an n, followed by a y (as in Bourgogne); an italicised *r* sounds like a cross between r and w; rr sounds like a rolled r.

A

Abboccato [ah-boh-kah-toh] (Italy) Semi-dry.
Abfüller/Abfüllung [ab-few-ler/ ab-few-lerng] (Germany) Bottler/bottled by.
Abocado [ah-boh-KAH-doh] (Spain) Semi-dry.

Abruzzi/zzo [ah-broot-zee/zoh] (Italy) Region on the east coast, with often dull *Trebbiano* whites and fast-improving *Montepulciano* reds.
Barone Cornacchia; Castello di Salle; *Cantina Tollo*; Edoardo Valentini.

AC (France) See *Appellation Contrôlée*.
♼ **Acacia** [a-kay-shah] (*Carneros*, California) One of California's best producers of *Chardonnay* and *Pinot Noir*. Under the same ownership as the similarly excellent *Chalone*, *Edna Valley* and *Carmenet*. ☆☆☆☆ 1995 Marina Vineyard Chardonnay £££
Acetic acid [ah-see-tihk] This volatile acid (CH3COOH) features in tiny proportions in all wines. Careless winemaking can result in wine being turned into acetic acid, a substance most people know as vinegar.

Acidity Naturally occuring (*tartaric* and malic) acids in the grapes are vital to contributing freshness, and also help to preserve the wine while it ages. In cool regions, the malic is often converted to lactic by a natural process known as *malolactic fermentation*, which gives the wines a buttery texture and flavour. In hotter countries (and sometimes cooler ones) the acid level may (not always legally) be adjusted by adding *tartaric* and citric acid.

Aconcagua Valley [ah-kon-kar-gwah] (*Central Valley*, Chile) Region noted for blackcurranty *Cabernet Sauvignon*. The sub-region is *Casablanca*. Grapes from both are used by many Chilean producers. *Errazuriz.*

☆ **Tim Adams** (*Clare Valley*, Australia) Highly successful producer of *Riesling*, rich peachy *Semillon* and deep-flavoured *Shiraz* and now the intense peppery Fergus *Grenache*. ☆☆☆☆☆ **1996 The Fergus £££**
Adega [ah-day-gah] (Portugal) Winery – equivalent to Spanish *bodega*.

Adelaide Hills [ah-dur-layd] (*South Australia*) Cool, high-altitude region, long known for top-class, lean *Riesling* and *Semillon*; now more famous for *Sauvignon Blanc* and *Chardonnay* from *Ashton Hills*, *Petaluma* and *Shaw & Smith*, *Pinot Noir*, and sparkling wine such as *Croser*. See also the new region of *Lenswood*. **Henschke; Mountadam; Heggies.**

☆ **Weingut Graf Adelmann** [graf-eh-del-man] (*Wurttemberg*, Germany) One of the region's best estates, making good red wines from grapes such as the *Trollinger,* Lemberger and Urban. Look for Brüssele'r Spitze wines.
☆ **Age** [ah-khay] (*Rioja*, Spain) Big, modern, highly commercial winery.
🍇 **Aglianico** [ah-lee-AH-nee-koh] (Italy) Thick-skinned grape grown by the Ancient Greeks but now more or less restricted to Southern Italy, where it produces dark hefty *Taurasi* and *Aglianico del Vulture*.

☆ **Aglianico del Vulture** [ah-lee-AH-nee-koh del vool-TOO-reh] (*Basilicata*, Italy) Tannic liquoricey-chocolatey blockbusters made on the hills of an extinct volcano. **D'Angelo; Basilium; Casele.**

Agricola vitivinicola (Italy) Wine estate.
☆ **Aguja** [ah-khoo-ha] (*Leon*, Spain) Rare, so-called 'needle' wines, whose slight spritz comes from adding ripe grapes to the fermented wine.

Ahr [ahr] (Germany) Northernmost *anbaugebiet*, making light-bodied reds.

🍇 **Airén** [i-REHN] (Spain) The world's most planted variety. Dull and fortunately more or less restricted to the region of *La Mancha*.

Ajaccio [ah-JAK-see-yoh] (*Corsica*, France) One of *Corsica's* many questionable *appellations*. The tangily intense reds and oaked whites from *Comte Peraldi* are better than mere holiday fare. **Gie Les Rameaux.**

🍇 **Albana di Romagna** [ahl-BAH-nah dee roh-MAN-yah] (*Emilia-Romagna*, Italy) Improving but traditionally dull white wine which, for political reasons, was made Italy's first white *DOCG*, thus making a mockery of the whole Italian system of denominations.
🍇 **Albariño** [ahl-BAH-ree-nyoh] (*Galicia*, Spain) The Spanish name for the Portuguese *Alvarinho* grape variety, and the peachy-spicy wine that is made from it in *Rias Baixas*, *Galicia*. Arguably Spain's best, most interesting, white. **Lagar de Cervera; Martin Codex; Pazo de Barrantes; Valdamor.**
Alcohol The magic ingredient that first encouraged man to muck around with fizzy grape juice. This simple compound, technically known as ethanol, is formed by the action of yeast on sugar during fermentation, and is responsible for wine's popularity, its balance, preservation and ageability.

🌢 **Aleatico** [ah-lay-AH-tee-koh] (Italy) Red grape producing sweet, *Muscat*-style, often fortified wines. Gives name to *DOCs* A. di Puglia and A. di Gradoli.

Alella [ah-LEH-yah] (*Catalonia*, Spain) *DO* district producing better whites (from grapes including the *Xarel-lo*) than reds. ☆☆☆☆ **1996 Marqués de Alella Clássico £££**

Alenquer [ah-lehn-KEHR] (*Oeste*, Portugal) Coolish region producing good reds from the *Periquita* grape and *Muscat*-style whites from the *Fernão Pires*. There are also increasingly successful efforts from some of France's familiar varietals.

Alentejo [ah-lehn-TAY-joh] (Portugal) Up-and-coming province north of the Algarve, with good red *Borba*. Australian-born *David Baverstock* produces juicy *Esperão; JM da Fonseca* makes Morgado de Reguengo; and *Peter Bright*, another Aussie, produces the award-winning Tinta da Anfora plus other good examples at *JP Vinhos*. **Borba; Cartuxa; Redondo.**

Alexander Valley (*Sonoma*, California) *Appellation* in which *Simi, Jordan, Murphy Goode* and *Geyser Peak* are based. Good for approachable reds. Red: 86 89 **90** 91 92 **94** 95 96 97 White: **92** 94 95 96 97

Algeria Old-fashioned, mostly red wines made by state-run cooperatives.

🍷 **Caves Aliança** [ah-lee-an-sah] (Portugal) Modern *Bairrada, Douro* and better-than-average *Dão*. ☆☆☆ **1992 Garrafeira Particular ££**

Alicante (*Valencia*, Spain) Hot region producing generally dull stuff apart from the sweetly honeyed *Moscatels* that appreciate the heat.

🌢**Alicante-Bouschet** [al-ee-KONT- boo-SHAY] Unusual dark-skinned and fleshed grapes traditionally used (usually illegally) for dyeing pallid reds made from nobler fare. *Rockford* in Australia uses it to make a good rosé.

🌢**Aligoté** [Al-lee-GOH-tay] (*Burgundy*, France) The region's lesser white grape, making dry, sometimes sharp wine that is traditionally mixed with *cassis* for *Kir*. With loving care and a touch of oak it can imitate basic *Bourgogne* Blanc, especially in the village of *Bouzeron*. Highly-regarded in Eastern Europe. **La Digoine; Domaine Dujac; Aubert de Vilaine.**

🍷 **Alion** [ah-lee-yon] (*Ribera del Duero*, Spain) Instantly successful new venture by the owners of *Vega Sicilia*, with oakier, fruitier, more modern wines. ☆☆☆☆☆ **1991 Reserva £££**

🍷 **All Saints** (*Rutherglen*, Australia) Good producer of *Liqueur Muscat, Tokay* and *late harvest* wines.

🍷 **Allegrini** [ah-leh-GREE-nee] (*Veneto*, Italy) Go-ahead top-class producer of single-vineyard *Valpolicella* and *Soave*. ☆☆☆☆ **1990 Amarone della Valpolicella £££**

🍷 **Thierry Allemand** [al-mon] (*Rhône*, France) Producer of classic, concentrated, single-vineyard *Cornas* from a tiny 2.5-hectare (6-acre) estate. ☆☆☆☆☆ **1995 Cornas Cuvée les Reynards £££**

Allier [a-lee-yay] (France) Spicy oak favoured by makers of white wine.

Almacenista [al-mah-theh-nee-stah] (*Jerez*, Spain) Fine old unblended *sherry* from a single *solera* – the *sherry* equivalent of a single malt whisky. **Lustau.**

Almansa [ahl-MAN-suh] (Spain) Warm region noted for softish reds which can be almost black, thanks to the red juice of the grapes used.

☲ **Aloxe-Corton** [a-loss kawr-ton] (*Burgundy*, France) *Côte de Beaune commune* with slow-maturing, majestic, sometimes tough, uninspiring reds (including the *Grand Cru Corton*) and potentially sublime whites (including *Corton-Charlemagne*). Invariably pricy *Louis Latour's* whites can be fine.
White: 79 85 86 87 88 89 90 92 95 Red: 78 85 86 87 **88 89 90** 92 95 96
Arnoux; Bonneau du Martray; Drouhin; Jadot; Leflaive; Tollot-Beaut.

Alsace [al-sas] (France) Northerly region whose warm micro-climate enables producers to make riper-tasting wines than their counterparts across the Rhine. Wines are named after the grapes – *Pinot Noir, Gewurztraminer, Riesling, Tokay/Pinot Gris, Pinot Blanc* (known as Pinot d'Alsace), *Sylvaner* and (rarely) *Muscat*. In the right hands, the 50 or so *Grand Cru* vineyards should yield better wines. *Late harvest* off-dry wines are labelled *Vendange Tardive* and *Sélection des Grains Nobles*. References to *Reserve* and Sélection Personnelle often mean nothing.
White: 76 79 81 83 85 86 88 89 90 93 94 95 Paul Blanck; Albert Boxler; Ernest J & F Burn; Jean-Pierre Dirler; Dopff au Moulin; Faller; Hugel; Josmeyer; André Kientzler; Marc Kreydenweiss; Albert Mann; Mittnacht-Klack; René Muré; Ostertag; Schlumberger; Schoffit; Trimbach; Weinbach; Zind Humbrecht.

☲ **Elio Altare** [Ehl-lee-yoh al-TAh-ray] (*Piedmont*, Italy) The genial Svengali-like leader of the *Barolo* revolution and inspirer of *Clerico* and *Roberto Voerzio,* who now run him a very close race. ☆☆☆☆ **1993 Barolo la Morra £££**

☲ **Altesino** [al-TEH-see-noh] (*Tuscany*, Italy) First class producers of *Brunello di Montalcino,* oaky *Vino da Tavola Cabernet* ('Palazzo') and *Sangiovese* ('Altesi').

Alto-Adige [ahl-toh ah-dee-jay] (Italy) Aka Italian Tyrol and Sudtirol. *DOC* for a range of mainly white wines, often from Germanic grape varieties; also light and fruity reds from the *Lagrein* and Vernatsch. Not living up to its promise of the early 1980s, when it was considered one of the most exciting regions in Europe. Gaierhof; Alois Lageder; Pojer & Sandri; Tiefenbrunner; Viticoltori Alto Adige.

❧ **Alvarinho** [ahl-vah-reen-yoh] (Portugal) White grape aka *Albariño*; at its lemony best in *Vinho Verde* and in the *DO* Alvarinho de Monção. *Amabile* [am-MAH-bee-lay] (Italy) Semi-sweet.

☲ **Castello di Ama** [ah-mah] (*Tuscany*, Italy) Fine, small *Chianti* estate. Look out for the single vineyard Vigna l'Apparita wines. ☆☆☆☆ **1994 Chianti Classico**

Amador County [am-uh-dor] (*California*,) Intensely-flavoured, old-fashioned *Zinfandel*. Look for Amador Foothills Winery's old-vine *Zinfandels* and top-of-the-range stuff from *Sutter Home* and *Monteviña.*
Red: 86 87 **88** 89 **90** 91 92 94 95 96 White: 94 95 96 97

☲ *Amarone* [ah-mah-ROH-neh] (*Veneto*, Italy) Literally 'bitter'; used particularly to describe *Recioto*. Best known as *Amarone della Valpolicella. Allegrini; Quintarelli; Tedeschi.*

☲ **Amberley Estate** [am-buhr-lee] (*Western Australia*) Young estate with a fair *Semillon* and *Cabernet-Merlot* blend.

☲ **Bodegas Amézola de la Mora** [ah-meh-THOH-lah deh lah MAW-rah] (*Rioja*, Spain) Eight-year-old estate producing unusually classy red *Rioja*. ☆☆☆☆ **1991 Crianza**

☲ **Amiral de Beychevelle** [beh-shuh-vel] (*Bordeaux*, France) *Second label* of Ch. *Beychevelle.*

☲ **Amity** [am-mi-tee] (*Oregon*, US) Producer of quality berryish *Pinot Noir* and good dry *Gewurztraminer.* ☆☆☆☆ **1995 Pinot Noir**

🍷 **Guy Amiot** [am-mee-yoh] (*Burgundy*, France) Small, first class *Chassagne-Montrachet* estate with great examples of tasty red. ☆☆☆☆ **1996 1er Cru Chassagne St Jean Rouge**

Amontillado [am-mon-tee-yah-doh] (*Jerez*, Spain) Literally 'like Montilla'. In Britain, this is traditionally a pretty basic medium-sweet *sherry*; in Spain, however, it is a fascinating dry, nutty wine. ***Gonzalez Byass; Lustau;* Sanchez Romate.**

Amtliche Prüfungsnummer [am-tlish-eh proof-oong-znoomer] (Germany) Official identification number supposedly relating to quality. (In fact, to earn one, wines merely have to have scored 1.5 out of 5 in a blind tasting.) Appears on all *QbA/QmP* wines.

Anbaugebiet [ahn-bow-geh-beet] (Germany) Term for 11 large regions (e.g. *Rheingau*). *QbA* and *QmP* wines must include the name of their *anbaugebiet* on their labels.

Anderson Valley (*Mendocino*, California) Small, cool area, good for white and sparkling wines including the excellent *Scharffenberger* and *Roederer.* Do not confuse with the less impressive Anderson Valley, *New Mexico*. Red: 86 87 **88** 89 **90** 91 **94** 95 White: 91 92 **94** 95 96 97

🍷 **Pierre André** [on-dray] (*Rhône*, France) Good, little-known producer of organic *Châteauneuf-du-Pape*.

🍷 **Ch. l'Angélus** [lo*n* jay-loos] (*St. Emilion Grand Cru Classé, Bordeaux*, France) Flying high since the late 1980s, this is a lovely plummy *St. Emilion* to watch. The *second label* Carillon d'Angélus is also well worth seeking out. 79 81 82 83 **85 86 87** 88 89 90 92 **93 94** 95 96 ☆☆☆☆☆ **1990 ££££**

🍷 **Marquis d'Angerville** [don-jehr-veel] (*Burgundy*, France) Long-established *Volnay* estate with rich, long-lived traditional wines from here and from the neighbouring village of *Pommard*. ☆☆☆☆ **1995 Volnay Champans ££££**

🍷 **Anghelu Ruju** [an-jeh-loo roo-yoo] (*Sardinia*, Italy) Intensely nutty-raisiny, port'n-lemony wine made by *Sella & Mosca* from dried *Cannonau* grapes. ☆☆☆☆ **1981 Sella & Mosca ££**

🍷 **Ch. d' Angludet** [don gloo-day] (*Cru Bourgeois, Margaux, Bordeaux*, France) Made by the late *Peter Sichel*, classy cassis-flavoured, if slightly earthy, wine that can generally be drunk young but is worth waiting for. 78 79 81 82 83 85 86 88 89 90 91 92 93 94 95 96

🍷 **Angoves** [an-gohvs] (*Padthaway*, Australia) *Murray River* producer with improving, inexpensive *Chardonnay* and *Cabernet*.

🍷 **Weingut Paul Anheuser** [an-hoy-zur] (*Nahe*, Germany) One of the most stalwart and credible supporters of the *Trocken* movement, and a strong proponent of the *Riesling*, this excellent estate is also unusually successful with its *Ruländer* and *Pinot Noir*. ☆☆☆☆ **1993 Kreuznacher Monchberg ££**

🍷 **Anjou** [o*n*-joo] (*Loire*, France) Dry and *Demi-Sec* whites, mostly from *Chenin Blanc*, with up to 20 per cent *Chardonnay* or *Sauvignon Blanc*. The rosé is almost always awful but there are good, light reds. Look for Anjou-Villages in which *Gamay* is not permitted. Within Anjou, there are smaller, more specific *ACs*, most importantly *Savennières* and *Coteaux du Layon*. Red: **88** 89 90 95 96 97 White: 88 89 **90 94** 95 96 97 Sweet White: **76 83 85 88 89** 90 94 95 96 97 ***Ch. du Breuil*; Dom. du Closel; V de V Leberton; Richou; Ch. la Varière.**

Annata [ahn-NAH-tah] (Italy) *Vintage*.

Año [An-Yoh] (Spain) Year, preceded by a figure – e.g. 5 – which indicates the wine's age at the time of bottling. Banned by the EU since 1986.

🍷 **Roberto Anselmi** [an-sehl-mee] (*Veneto*, Italy) Source of *Soave Classico* wines that are exceptions to the generally dismal rule, as well as some extremely serious sweet examples. ☆☆☆☆ **1995 I Capitelli Recioto di Soave £££**

🍷 **Antinori** [an-tee-NOR-ree] (*Tuscany*, Italy) Pioneer merchant-producer who has improved the quality of *Chianti*, with examples such as Villa Antinori and Pèppoli, while spearheading the *Super-Tuscan* revolution with superb wines like *Tignanello, Sassicaia* and *Solaia*. ☆☆☆☆☆ **1994 Castello della Sala Cervaro ££; ☆☆☆☆☆ 1994 Solaia ££££**

AOC (France) See *Appellation Contrôlée*.

AP (Germany) See *Amtliche Prüfungsnummer*.

Appellation Contrôlée (AC/AOC) [AH-pehl-lah-see-o*n* ko*n* TROH-lay] (France) Increasingly questioned designation for 'top quality' wine: guarantees origin, grape varieties and method of production – and in theory, quality, though tradition and vested interest combine to allow some pretty appalling wines to receive the rubber stamp.

Aprémont [ah-pray-mo*n*] (Eastern France) Floral, slightly *petillant* white from skiing region. **Cave Cooperative 'le Vigneron Savoyard'. ☆☆☆ 1997 Ch. d'Aprémont ££**

Apulia [ah-pool-ee-yah] (Italy) See *Puglia*.

Aquileia [ah-kwee-LAY-ah] (*Friuli-Venezia Giulia*, Italy) *DOC* for easy-going, single-variety wines. The *Refosco* can be plummily refreshing. **Ca'Bolani and Corvignano Cooperatives.**

🍷 **Ararimu** [ah-rah-REE-moo] (*Auckland*, New Zealand) See *Matua Valley*.

Arbin [ahr-ba*n*] (*Savoie*, France) Red wine made from Mondeuse grapes. Somehow tastes better after a day's skiing than after work in the city.

Arbois [ahr-bwah] (Eastern France) *AC* region with light reds from the *Trousseau* and *Pinot Noir* and dry whites from the Sauvignon and *Chardonnay*. Look out for the *sherry*-like *Vin Jaune* and fizz. ☆☆☆☆ **1992 Savagnin, Fruitière Vinicole d'Arbois ££**

🍷 **Ch. d' Arche** [dahrsh] (*Sauternes 2ème Cru Classé, Bordeaux*, France) Greatly improved, but still slightly patchy. 83 **86 88 89** 90 93 94 95 97

🍷 **Viña Ardanza** [veen-yah ahr-dan-thah] (*Rioja*, Spain) Highly reliable, fairly full-bodied red wines made with a high proportion (40 per cent) of *Grenache*; good, *oaky* white, too. ☆☆☆☆ **1990 Rioja Tinto Reserva ££**

🍷 **d'Arenberg** [dar-ren-burg] (*McLaren Vale*, Australia) Excellent up-and-coming producer with memorably named, impressive sweet and dry table wines and unusually dazzling fortifieds. ☆☆☆☆☆ **1996 The Footbolt, Old Vine, Shiraz £££; ☆☆☆☆ 1997 The Noble Riesling £££**

Argentina Fast up-and-coming nation whose strongest suit lies in its *Malbec*. *Cabernet* and *Merlot* have a touch more backbone than many efforts from Chile and there are interesting wines made from Italian red varieties. *Chardonnays* and grapey whites from the *Muscat*-like *Torrontes* are worthwhile too. **Luigi Bosca; Canale; *Catena; Etchart; Morande; Norton;* Torino; *Trapiche; Weinert.***

🍷 **Tenuta di Argiano** [teh-noo-tah dee ahr-zhee-ahn-noh] (*Tuscany*, Italy) Instant success story, with top-class vineyards, and lovely juicy reds. ☆☆☆☆☆ **1991 Brunello di Montalcino Reserva ££££**

🍷 **Argyle** (*Oregon*, US) Classy fizz and still wines from *Brian Croser* (of *Petaluma*). ☆☆☆☆ **1994 Argyle Brut £££**

🍷 **Ch. d'Arlay** [dahr-lay] (*Jura*, France) Reliable producer of nutty *Vin Jaune* and light, earthy-raspberry *Pinot Noir*.

☙ Dom. de l'Arlot [dur-lahr-loh] (*Burgundy*, France) Brilliant, award-winning, recently constituted *Nuits-St.-Georges* estate under the same – insurance company – ownership as *Ch. Pichon-Longueville*. Delicate modern reds (including an increasingly impressive *Vosne-Romanée*) and a rare example of white *Nuits-St.-Georges*. ✩✩✩✩ 1994 Nuits-St.-Georges Clos de l'Arlot £££; ✩✩✩✩ 1995 Vosne-Romanée 1er Cru les Suchots. £££

☙ Ch. d'Armailhac [darh-MI-yak] (*Pauillac 5ème Cru Classé, Bordeaux*, France) Same stable as *Mouton-Rothschild*, and increasingly showing similar rich flavours. 78 81 **82** 83 85 86 **88** 89 90 92 93 **94** 95 96 97 ✩✩✩✩ 1990 ££££

☙ Dom. du Comte Armand [komt-arh-mon] (*Burgundy*, France) Only one wine – the exceptional *Pommard* Clos des Epeneaux. ✩✩✩✩ 1995 Pommard 1er Cru Clos des Epeneaux £££

☙ Arneis [ahr-nay-ees] (*Piedmont*, Italy) Spicy white; makes good, young, unoaked wine. *Voerzio; Bava*.

☙ Ch. l' Arrosée [lah-roh-say] (*St. Emilion Grand Cru Classé, Bordeaux*, France) Small, well-sited property with fruity intense wines. 79 81 **82** 83 **85** 86 87 88 89 90 92 93 94 95 97 ✩✩✩✩ 1990 ££££

☙ Arrowfield (*Hunter Valley*, Australia) Producer of ripe, full-flavoured *Chardonnay* and some good young *tawny port*-style wine.

☙ Arrowood (*Sonoma Valley*, California) Excellent *Chardonnay* and *Cabernet* from the former winemaker of *Ch. St. Jean*. ✩✩✩✩ 1995 Sonoma County Chardonnay, ££££

☙ Ismael Arroyo [uh-ROY-oh] (*Ribera del Duero*, Spain) A name to watch for flavoursome reds. ✩✩✩✩ 1990 Mesoneros de Castilla ££

☙ Arruda [ahr-ROO-dah] (*Oeste*, Portugal) Inexpensive *Beaujolais*-style reds.

☙ Artadi [ahr-tah-dee] (*Rioja*, Spain) Up-and-coming producer with particularly good *Crianza* wines. ✩✩✩✩ 1995 Viñas de Gain £££

☙ Giacomo Ascheri [ash-SHEH-ree] (*Piedmont*, Italy) New-wave producer. Impressive single-vineyard, tobacco 'n' berry wines, also *Nebbiolo* and Freisa del Langhe. ✩✩✩✩ 1993 Barolo Vigna Farina £££

Asciutto [ah-shoo-toh] (Italy) Dry.

Asenovgrad [ass-seh-nov-grad] (Bulgaria) Demarcated northern wine region with rich plummy reds from *Cabernet Sauvignon, Merlot* and *Mavrud*.

☙ Ashton Hills (*Adelaide Hills*, Australia) Small up-and-coming winery producing good reds as well as subtle, increasingly creditable *Chardonnay* and *Riesling*. ✩✩✩✩ 1996 Riesling ££

Assemblage [ah-sehm-blahj] (France) The art of blending wine from different grape varieties. Associated with *Bordeaux* and *Champagne*.

Assmanhausen [ass-mahn-how-zehn] (*Rheingau*, Germany) If you like sweet *Pinot Noir*, this is the place to come looking for it.

☙ Asti (*Piedmont*, Italy) Town famous for sparkling *Spumante*, lighter *Moscato d'Asti* and red *Barbera d'Asti*. Red: 82 **85 88** 89 90 **93 94** 95 96 White: 97 Bersano; Fontanafredda; Martini.

Astringent Mouth-puckering. Associated with young red wine. See *tannin*.

Aszu [ah-soo] (*Hungary*) The sweet syrup made from dried and (about 10–15 per cent) 'nobly rotten' grapes (see *botrytis*) used to sweeten *Tokaji*.

☙ Ata Rangi [ah-tah ran-gee] (*Martinborough*, New Zealand) Inspiring small estate with high-quality *Pinot Noir* and New Zealand's only successful *Shiraz*. ✩✩✩✩ 1996 Pinot Noir £££

☙ Au Bon Climat [oh bon klee-Mat] (*Santa Barbara*, California) Top-quality producer of characterful and flavoursome *Pinot Noir* and classy *Chardonnay*. ✩✩✩✩ 1995 Bien Nacido Vineyard Chardonnay £££

♊ Dom. des Aubuisières [day Soh-bwee-see-yehr] (*Loire*, France) Bernard Fouquet's *Vouvray domaine* produces impeccable wines, which range all the way from richly dry to lusciously sweet. ☆☆☆☆ 1995 **Vouvray Moelleux le Marigny £££**

Auckland (New Zealand) An all-embracing designation which once comprised over a quarter of the country's vineyards. Auckland is often wrongly derided by outsiders who have failed to notice that some vintages favour this region over other better-known areas such as Marlborough. *Collards; Goldwater Estate; Kumeu River; Matua Valley.*

Aude [ohd] (South-West France) Prolific *département* traditionally producing much ordinary wine. Now *Corbières* and *Fitou* are improving as are the *Vins de Pays*, thanks to plantings of new grapes (such as the *Viognier*) and the efforts of firms like *Skalli Fortant de France, Val d'Orbieu and Domaine Virginie.*

Ausbruch [ows-brook] (Austria) Term for rich *botrytis* wine which is sweeter than *Beerenauslese* but less sweet than *Trockenbeerenauslese.*

Auslese [ows-lay-zuh] (Germany) Mostly sweet wine from selected ripe grapes, usually affected by *botrytis*. Third rung on the *QmP* ladder.

♊ Ch. Ausone [oh-zohn] (*St. Emilion Premier Grand Cru Classé, Bordeaux*, France) Pretender to the crown of top *St. Emilion*, this old estate, which owes its name to the Roman occupation, can produce fine complex *claret*. Until the winemaking was taken over by *Michel Rolland* in 1995, however, the wine lacked the intensity demanded by the critics of the 1990s. 76 78 79 81 **82 83** 85 **86** 88 89 90 92 93 94 95 96 97 ☆☆☆☆☆ 1990 **££££**

Austria Home of all sorts of whites, ranging from dry *Sauvignon Blancs,* greengagey *Grüner Veltliners* and ripe *Rieslings* to especially luscious *late harvest* wines. Reds are increasingly successful too – particularly the *Pinot-Noir*-like *St Laurents*. *Juris; Alois Kracher; Willi Opitz;* Johan Tschida; Umathum.

♣ Auxerrois [oh-sehr-wah] (France) Named after the main town in northern *Burgundy*, this is the Alsatians' term for a fairly dull local variety that may be related to the *Sylvaner Melon de Bourgogne* or *Chardonnay*. South Africa's winemakers learned about it involuntarily when cuttings were smuggled into the *Cape* and planted there under the misapprehension that they were *Chardonnay*. (Were they intentionally sold a pup? I wonder.) In *Luxembourg* it is called the *Luxembourg Pinot Gris.*

♊ Auxey-Duresses [oh-say doo-ress] (*Burgundy*, France) Beautiful *Côtes de Beaune* village best known for its buttery whites, but producing greater quantities of raspberryish, if often quite rustic, reds. A slow developer. *Robert Ampeau;* Jean-Pierre Diconne; *Olivier Leflaive; Michel Prunier;* Vincent Prunier; Guy Roulot.

AVA (US) Acronym for American Viticultural Areas, a recent and somewhat controversial attempt to develop an American *appellation* system. It makes sense in smaller *appellations* like *Mount Veeder;* less so in larger, more heterogenous ones like *Napa.*

♊ Quinta da Aveleda (*Vinho Verde*, Portugal) Famous estate producing disappointing dry *Vinho Verde.*

Avelsbach [ahr-vel-sarkh] (*Mosel*, Germany) *Ruwer* village producing delicate, light-bodied wines. Qba/Kab/Spät: 85 87 **88** 89 90 **91** 92 **93 94** 95 96 97 Aus/Beeren/Tba: **83** 85 **88 89** 90 91 92 **93 94** 95 97

Avignonesi [ahr-veen-yon-nay-see] (*Tuscany*, Italy) Ultra-classy producer of *Vino Nobile di Montepulciano*, *Super-Tuscans* such as Grifi, a pure *Merlot* described by an American critic as Italy's *Pétrus*. There are also serious *Chardonnay* and *Sauvignon* whites – plus an unusually good *Vin Santo*. ☆☆☆☆☆ 1993 Merlot £££; ☆☆☆☆☆ 1994 Grifi £££

Ayala [ay-yah-lah] (*Champagne*, France) Underrated producer which takes its name from the village of Ay. ☆☆☆☆ 1988 Blanc de Blancs £££

Ayl [ihl] (*Mosel*, Germany) Distinguished *Saar* village producing steely wines. Qba/Kab/Spät: 86 88 **89** 90 **91** 92 **93** 94 95 96 97
Aus/Beeren/Tba: **83** 85 88 **89** 90 91 92 **93** 94 95 97

Azienda [a-see-en-dah] (Italy) Estate.

B

Babich [ba-bitch] (*Henderson*, New Zealand) The rich 'Irongate' *Chardonnay* is the prize wine here, but the *Sauvignon Blanc* is good too. The reds improve with every vintage. ☆☆☆☆ 1997 Hawke's Bay Sauvignon Blanc £££

Quinta da Bacalhôa [dah ba-keh-yow] (*Setúbal*, Portugal) The good and innovative *Cabernet-Merlot* made by Peter Bright at JP Vinhos. ☆☆☆☆ 1995 ££

Bacchus [ba-kuhs] White grape. A *Müller-Thurgau-Riesling* cross, making light, flowery wine. **Denbies; Tenterden.**

Dom. Denis Bachelet [dur-nee bash-lay] (*Burgundy*, France) Classy, small *Gevrey-Chambertin* estate with cherryish wines that are great young – and with five or six years of age. ☆☆☆☆☆ 1995 Charmes-Chambertin ££££; ☆☆☆☆ 1995 Gevrey-Chambertin Vieilles Vignes ££££

Backsberg Estate [bax-burg] (*Paarl*, South Africa) *Chardonnay* pioneer, with good, quite Burgundian versions. ☆☆☆ 1995 Chardonnay ££

Bad Durkheim [baht duhr-kime] (*Pfalz*, Germany) Chief *Pfalz* town, producing some of the region's finest whites, plus some reds. Qba/Kab/Spät: **85** 86 88 **89** 90 91 92 **93** 94 95 96 97
Aus/Beeren/Tba: **83** 85 88 **89** 90 91 92 **93** 94 95 96 97 *Kurt Darting.*

Bad Kreuznach [baht kroyts-nahkh] (*Nahe*, Germany) This is the chief and finest wine town of the region, giving its name to the entire lower *Nahe*. **75** 76 83 85 86 88 **89** 90 91 92 93 94 95 96 97 *Paul Anheuser.*

Badacsony [bah-dah-chaw-nyih] (*Hungary*) Wine region renowned for full-flavoured whites.

Baden [bah-duhn] (Germany) Warm southern region of Germany, with ripe grapes to make dry (*Trocken*) wines. Some of these – including the ubiquitous 'Baden Dry' – are good, as are some of the *Pinot Noirs*.

Baden Winzerkeller (ZBW) [bah-den vin-zehr-keh-luhr-rih] (*Baden*, Germany) Huge co-op whose reliability has done much to set *Baden* apart from the rest of Germany.

Badia a Coltibuono [bah-dee-yah ah kohl-tee-bwoh-noh] (*Tuscany*, Italy) One of Italy's most reliable producers of *Chianti*, pure *Sangiovese* and *Chardonnay*. Renowned for mature releases. ☆☆☆☆ 1995 Chianti Classico ££; ☆☆☆☆☆ 1990 Chianti Classico Cetamura ££

🌱**Baga** [bah-gah] (*Bairrada*, Portugal) Spicily fruity red grape variety – used in *Bairrada*.

🍷 **Ch. Bahans-Haut-Brion** [bah-on oh-bree-on] (*Graves, Bordeaux,* France) The *second label* of *Ch. Haut Brion*. Red: 82 83 85 **86** 87 88 **89** 90 92 93 94 95 96 ☆☆☆☆ **1990 ££££**

🍷 **Bailey's** (*Victoria*, Australia) Traditional, good *Liqueur Muscat* and hefty, old-fashioned *Shiraz*. Current wines are a little more subtle but still pack a punch. ☆☆☆☆ **1994: 1920's Block Shiraz £££**

🍷 **Bairrada** [bi-rah-dah] (Portugal) *DO* region south of Oporto, traditionally making dull whites and tough reds. Revolutionary producers like *Sogrape, Luis Pato* and *Alianca* are proving what can be done. Look for spicy blackberryish reds; creamy whites. **Red: 85 86 87 88 90 91 92 94** 95 96

Baja California [bah-hah] (*Mexico*) The part of *Mexico* abutting the Californian border, probably best known for exporting illegal aliens and importing adventurous Californians and hippies in search of a good time. Also a successful, though little known, wine region; home to the Santo Tomas and *LA Cetto* wineries.

Balance Harmony of fruitiness, *acidity, alcohol* and *tannin*. Balance can develop with age but should be evident in youth, even when, through *acidity* or *tannin* for example, wines may appear difficult to taste.

Balaton [bah-la-ton] (*Hungary*) Wine region frequented by *flying wine-makers*, and producing fair-quality reds and whites.

🍷 **Anton Balbach** [an-ton bahl-barkh] (*Rheinhessen*, Germany) Potentially one of the best producers in the *Erden* region – especially for *late harvest* wines. ☆☆☆☆☆ **1996 Nierstein Hipping Auslese Riesling ££££**

🍷 **Bodegas Balbás** [bal-bash] (*Ribera del Duero*, Spain) Small producer of juicy *Tempranillo* reds, using uncrushed grapes and also *Bordeaux*-style *Cabernet* blends and a lively rosé.

🍷 **Balbi** [bal-bee] (*Mendoza*, Argentina) Producer of good, inexpensive modern wines, including particularly appealing dry rosés.

🍷 **Ch. Balestard-la-Tonnelle** [bah-les-star lah ton-nell] (*St. Emilion Grand Cru Classé, Bordeaux*, France) Good, quite traditional *St. Emilion* built to last. 81 83 85 **86** 87 **88** 89 90 92 93 94 95 96 97

🍷 **Balgownie Estate** [bal-GOW-nee] (*Geelong*, Australia) One of Victoria's most reliable producers of lovely, intense, blackcurranty *Cabernet* in *Bendigo*. *Chardonnays* are big and old-fashioned and *Pinot Noirs* are improving. ☆☆☆☆ **1994 Cabernet Sauvignon, Bendigo £££**

🍷 **Bandol** [bon-dohl] (*Provence*, France) *Mourvèdre*-influenced plummy, herby reds, and improving whites. **Ch. de Pibarnon; Dom. Tempier; Ch. Vannières.**

🍷 **Villa Banfi** [veel-lah ban-fee] (*Tuscany*, Italy) US-owned producer with a range of improving *Brunello* and *Vini da Tavola*. ☆☆☆☆☆ **1991 Brunello di Montalcino Castello Banfi ££££**

🍷 **Bannockburn** (*Geelong*, Australia) Gary Farr uses his experience of making wines at *Dom. Dujac* in *Burgundy* to produce concentrated, toughish *Pinot Noir* at home. The *Chardonnay* is also pretty good, if slightly big for its boots, and the *Bordeaux* blends are impressive too. ☆☆☆☆ **1994 Pinot Noir ££**

🍷 **Banyuls** [bon-yools] (*Provence*, France) France's answer to *tawny port*. Fortified, *Grenache*-based, *Vin Doux Naturel,* ranging from off-dry to lusciously sweet. The *Rancio* style is rather more like *Madeira*. **L'Etoile; Dom. du Mas Blanc; Clos de Paulilles; Dom. de la Rectorie; Dom. la Tour Vieille; Vial Magnères.**

Antonio Barbadillo [bahr-bah-deel-yoh] (*Jerez*, Spain) Great producer of *Fino* and *Manzanilla*. ☆☆☆☆ Solera Manzanilla ££

Barbaresco [bahr-bah-ress-koh] (*Piedmont*, Italy) *DOCG* red from the *Nebbiolo* grape, with spicy fruit plus depth and complexity. Traditionally approachable earlier (three to five years) than neighbouring *Barolo* but, in the hands of *Angelo Gaja* – and in the best vineyards – potentially of almost as high a quality. 78 79 82 **85 88 89** 90 **93 94** 95. *Gaja*, **Castello di Neive; Alfredo Prunotto**.

🐝**Barbera** [Bar-Beh-Rah] (*Piedmont*, Italy) Grape making fruity, spicy, characterful wine (e.g. B. d'Alba and B. d'Asti), usually with a flavour reminiscent of cheesecake with raisins. Now in *California*, *Mexico* and (at *Brown Bros.*) Australia.

René Barbier [Ren-nay Bah-Bee-Yay] (*Penedès*, Spain) Dynamic producer of commercial wines and an unusually impressive *Priorato*. ☆☆☆☆ 1994 **Priorato Clos Mogador ££**

Barca Velha [bahr-kah vayl-yah] (*Douro*, Portugal) Portugal's most famous red, made from port varieties by *Ferreira*. It's tough stuff this, but plummy enough to be worth keeping – and paying for. Also look out for Reserva Especial released in more difficult years. ☆☆☆☆ 1983 **Ferreirinha ££££**

Bardolino [bar-doh-lee-noh] (*Veneto*, Italy) Light and unusually approachable for a traditional *DOC* Italian red. Also comes as Chiaretto Rosé. Commercial versions are often dull but at best are Italy's answer to *Beaujolais*. Best drunk young unless from an exceptional producer. *Boscaini; Masi;* **Portalupi**.

Gilles Barge [bahzh] (*Rhône*, France) Son of Pierre who won an international reputation for his fine, classic *Côte Rôtie*. Gilles, who now runs the estate, has also shown his skill with *St. Joseph*.

Guy de Barjac [gee dur bar-jak] (*Rhône*, France) A master of the *Syrah* grape, producing some of the best – and most stylish – *Cornas* around.

Barolo [bah-ROH-loh] (*Piedmont*, Italy) Noblest of *DOCG* reds, made from *Nebbiolo*. Old-fashioned versions are undrinkably dry and tannic when young but, from a good producer and year, can last and develop extraordinary complexity. Modern versions are ready earlier. 78 79 82 **85 88 89** 90 **93** 95 *Aldo Conterno; Borgogno; Clerico; Elio Altare; Fontanafredda; Mascarello; Roberto Voerzio*.

Baron de Ley [Bah-Rohn Duh Lay] (*Rioja*, Spain) Small *Rioja* estate whose wines, partly aged in French oak, take several years to 'come round' but are worth waiting for. ☆☆☆☆ 1994 Reserva ££; ☆☆☆☆ 1994 **Rioja Reserva ££**

Barossa Valley [bah-ros suh] (Australia) Big, warm region north-east of Adelaide which is famous for traditional, old vine *Shiraz* and *Grenache*, 'ports' and *Rieslings* which age to oily richness. *Chardonnay* and *Cabernet* have moved in more recently, and the former makes subtler, classier wines along with *Riesling* in the increasingly popular higher altitude vineyards of the *Eden Valley* and *Adelaide Hills*. *Barossa Valley Estate; Basedow; Bethany; Wolf Blass; Grant Burge; Hardy's; Henschke; Krondorf; Peter Lehmann; Melton; Orlando; Penfolds; Rockford; Yalumba*.

Barossa Valley Estate (*Barossa Valley*, Australia) Top end of BRL *Hardy's* wine portfolio with good old-vine *Barossa* reds. ☆☆☆☆☆ 1995 **Ebeneezer Shiraz £££**

Daniel Barraud [Bah-roh] (*Burgundy*, France) Dynamic producer of single-*cuvée* Pouilly-Fuissé.

Barrique [ba-reek] (France) French barrel, particularly in *Bordeaux*, holding 225 litres. Term used in Italy to denote (new) barrel ageing.

🍷 **Jim Barry** (*Clare Valley*, Australia) Producer of the dazzling, spicy, mulberryish Armagh *Shiraz*. ☆☆☆☆☆ **1992 The Armagh ££££**

🍷 **Barsac** [bahr-sak] (*Bordeaux*, France) *AC* neighbour of *Sauternes* with similar, though not quite so rich, *Sauvignon/Sémillon* dessert wines. 70 **71** **73** 76 78 79 81 83 85 86 88 89 90 95 97 ***Ch. Climens; Doisy-Dubroca; Ch. Coutet; Doisy-Daëne.***

🍷 **Ghislaine Barthod-Noëllat** [jee-lenn Bar-Toh Noh-Way-Lah] (*Burgundy*, France) Top class Chambolle-Musigny estate. ☆☆☆☆ **1995 Chambolle-Musigny les Charmes £££**

🍷 **De Bartoli** [day bahr-toh-lee] (*Sicily*, Italy) If you want to drink *Marsala* rather than use it in cooking, this is the name to remember. The raisiny Bukkuram, made from *Passito Muscat* grapes, is an alternative delight. ☆☆☆☆ **1990 Josephine Doré ££**

🍷 **Barton & Guestier** [bahr-ton ay geht-tee-yay] (*Bordeaux*, France) Highly commercial *Bordeaux* shipper. ☆☆☆ **1994 Ch. Magnol ££**

🍷 **Barwang** [bahr-wang] (*New South Wales*, Australia) Label for exciting cool-climate wines produced in newly-planted vineyards near Young in eastern *New South Wales*. ☆☆☆☆ **1995 Cabernet Sauvignon ££**

🍷 **Basedows** [baz-zeh-dohs] (South Australia) Producer of big, concentrated *Shiraz* and *Cabernet* and ultra-rich *Semillon* and *Chardonnays*. ☆☆☆☆ **1996 Barossa Shiraz ££**

Basilicata [bah-see-lee-kah-tah] (Italy) Southern wine region chiefly known for *Aglianico del Vulture* and some improving *Vini da Tavola*. ☆☆☆☆ **1995 Aglianico Terre al Monte, Rivera ££**

🍷 **Bass Philip** (*Victoria*, Australia) South *Gippsland* pioneer who is arguably making Australia's best, most *Burgundy*-like *Pinot Noir*. ☆☆☆☆ **1995 Pinot Noir £££**

🍷 **Von Bassermann-Jordan** [fon bas-suhr-man johr-dun] (*Pfalz*, Germany) A highly traditional producer often using the fruit of its brilliant vineyards to produce *Trocken Rieslings* with far more ripeness than is often to be found in this style. ☆☆☆☆ **1996 Forster Jesuitengarten Spätlese £££**

🍇 **Bastardo** [bas-tahr-doh] (Portugal) Red grape traditionally used widely in *port* and previously in *Madeira*, where there are a few wonderful old bottles still to be found. Shakespeare refers to a wine called 'Brown Bastard'.

🍷 **Ch. Bastor-Lamontagne** [bas-tohr-lam-mon-tañ] (*Sauternes*, *Bordeaux*, France) Remarkably reliable classy *Sauternes*; surprisingly inexpensive alternative to the big-name properties. 82 **83** 85 86 88 89 90 94 95 97

🍷 **Ch. Batailley** [bat-tih-yay] (*Pauillac 5ème Cru Classé, Bordeaux*, France) Approachable, quite modern tobacco-cassis-cedar *claret* with more class than its price might lead one to expect. 70 78 79 **82** **83** **85** 86 87 **88** 89 90 94 **95** 96 97

🍷 **Bâtard-Montrachet** [bat-tahr mon-rah-shay] (*Burgundy*, France) Biscuity-rich white *Grand Cru* shared between *Chassagne-* and *Puligny-Montrachet*. Wines are often very fine; always expensive. ***J-N Gagnard; Vincent Leflaive; Michel Niellon; Ramonet; Etienne Sauzet.***

🍷 **Beni di Batasiolo** [bay-nee dee bat-tah-see-oh-loh] (*Piedmont*, Italy) Producer of top-class *Barolo*, impressive cherryish *Dolcetto*, intense berryish *Brachetto*, and a subtle *Chardonnay*. ☆☆☆☆☆ **1993 Barolo £££**

🍷 **Dom. des Baumard** [day boh-marh] (*Loire*, France) Best producer of *Quarts de Chaume* and source of top class *Savennières*. ☆☆☆☆☆ **1995 Quarts de Chaume ££££**

� **Bava** [bah-vah] (*Piedmont*, Italy) Innovative producer making good *Moscato Barbera*, reviving indigenous grapes such as the rarely grown raspberryish *Ruche* and even producing a rather wonderful curious herb-infused *Nebbiolo*. ☆☆☆☆ 1990 Stradivario Barbera d'Asti Superiore ££

� **Ch. Beau-Séjour (-Bécot)** [boh-say-zhoor bay-koh] (*St. Emilion Grand Cru Classé, Bordeaux*, France) Reinstated in 1996 after a decade of demotion. Now making fairly priced, greatly improved wine. 75 82 83 85 **86** 88 89 90 92 93 94 95 96 97

� **Ch. Beau-Site** [boh-seet] (*St. Estèphe Cru Bourgeois, Bordeaux*, France) Benchmark *St. Estèphe* in the same stable as *Ch. Batailley*. 75 78 **82** 83 85 **86** 87 88 89 90 92 93 94 95 96

� **Ch. de Beaucastel** [boh-kas-tel] (*Rhône*, France) The top estate in *Châteauneuf-du-Pape* using organic methods to produce richly gamey, long-lived, spicy reds, and rare but fine creamy-spicy whites. ☆☆☆☆ 1995 Côtes du Rhône Coudoulet ££; ☆☆☆☆ 1994 Châteauneuf-du-Pape Homage Jacques Perrin ££££

� **Beaujolais** [boh-zhuh-lay] (*Burgundy*, France) Light fruity red from the *Gamay*, good chilled and for early drinking. *Beaujolais-Villages* is better, and the 10 *Crus* better still. With age, these can taste like (fairly ordinary) *Burgundy*. The *Crus*: *Morgon; Chénas; Brouilly; Côte de Brouilly; Juliénas; Fleurie; Regnié; St. Amour; Chiroubles, Moulin-à-Vent*.

� **Beaujolais Blanc** (*Burgundy*, France) *Chardonnay* whites, rarely seen under this name. Commonly sold as *St. Véran*. Charmet; Tête.

� **Beaujolais-Villages** (*Burgundy*, France) From the north of the region, fuller-flavoured and more alcoholic than plain *Beaujolais*, though not necessarily from one of the named *Cru* villages. *Duboeuf; Pivot; Large*.

� **Beaulieu Vineyard** [bohl-yoo] (*Napa Valley*, California) Historic winery that has suffered at the hands of its multinational owners. The Georges de Latour Private Reserve *Cabernet* can be impressive and keeps well, and recent vintages of *Beautour* have improved. Other wines are memorably and unworthily ordinary. ☆☆☆☆ 1994 Cabernet Sauvignon Napa Valley Georges de Latour Private Reserve ££

� **Beaumes de Venise** [bohm duh vuh-neez] (*Rhône*, France) *Côtes du Rhône* village producing spicy dry reds and better-known sweet, grapey, fortified *Vin Doux Naturel* from the *Muscat*. Dom. des Bernardins; Chapoutier; Dom de Coyeux.

� **Ch. Beaumont** [boh-mon] (*Haut-Médoc Cru Bourgeois, Bordeaux*, France) High-flying estate whose most recent wines have seemed slightly disappointing. **82** 85 **86** 88 **89 90** 92 **93** 94 95 96

� **Beaumont des Crayères** [boh-mon day cray-yair] (*Champagne*, France) Quality-conscious cooperative with fizz to match some of the biggest names in *Champagne*.

� **Beaune** [bohn] (*Burgundy*, France) Large commune that gives its name to the *Côte de Beaune* and produces soft, raspberry-and-rose-petal *Pinot Noir*. As in *Nuits-St.-Georges*, there are plenty of *Premier Crus*, but no *Grands Crus*. The walled city is the site of the famous *Hospices* charity auction. Reds are best from *Michel Prunier, Louis Jadot, Bouchard Père et Fils* (since 1996), Ch. de Chorey; Albert Morot and *Joseph Drouhin* who also make a very successful example of the ultra-rare white.

� **Ch. Beauregard** [boh-ruh-gahr] (*Pomerol, Bordeaux*, France) Estate that has recently begun to follow the trend towards juicy oaky (perhaps slightly straightforward) *Pomerol*. **82** 85 **86** 88 **89 90** 92 93 **94** 95 96

Ch. Beauséjour-Duffau-Lagarosse [boh-say-zhoor doo-foh lag-gahr-ros] (*St. Emilion Premier Grand Cru Classé, Bordeaux*, France) Traditional wine for those who like their St. *Emilions* to be quite tough and *tannic*. 82 83 85 86 88 89 90 92 93 94 95 96
☆☆☆☆ **1989 ££££**

Cave de Beblenheim [beb-len-hihm] (*Alsace*, France) Reliable across-the-board cooperative.

Graham Beck (*Robertson*, South Africa) Producer of some of South Africa's best fizz.

Beerenauslese [behr-ren-ows-lay-zuh] (Austria/Germany) Sweet wines from selected, ripe grapes (Beeren), hopefully affected by *botrytis*.

Bekaa Valley [bik-kahr] (Lebanon) War-torn region in which *Serge Hochar* grows the grapes for his *Ch. Musar* wines.

Ch. de Bel-Air [Bel-Ehr] (*Lalande-de-Pomerol, Bordeaux*, France) Impressive property making wines to make some *Pomerols* blush. 82 85 86 88 **89** 90 92 93 **94** 95 96 97

Ch. Bel-Orme-Tronquoy-de-Lalande [bel-orm-tron-kwah-duh-la-lond] (*Haut-Médoc Grand Bourgeois, Bordeaux*, France) Traditional estate with generally old-fashioned wines. **82** 83 85 86 88 89 **90** 92 93 94 95 96 97

Ch. Belair [bel-lehr] (*St. Emilion Premier Grand Cru Classé, Bordeaux*, France) *Ch. Ausone*'s stablemate – much lighter in style, but still a classy, long-lived, traditional *St. Emilion*. (Don't confuse with the Lalande-de-Pomerol Ch. de Bel-Air – or any of the countless lesser Belairs scattered around Bordeaux). 78 **79 82 83 85 86** 88 89 90 92 93 94 95 96 97

Albert Belle [bel] (*Rhône*, France) An estate that has only just begun to bottle its own excellent red and – oaky – white Hermitage.

Bellet [bel-lay] (*Provence*, France) Tiny *AC* behind Nice producing fairly good red, white and rosé from local grapes including the Rolle, the *Braquet* and the *Folle Noir*. Pricey and rarely seen outside France. **Ch. de Bellet.**

Bellingham (South Africa) Improving commercial winery.
☆☆☆☆ **1996 Pinotage ££**

Bendigo [ben-dig-goh] (*Victoria*, Australia) Warm region producing big-boned, long-lasting reds with intense berry fruit. *Balgownie;* **Heathcote; *Jasper Hill; Mount Ida; Passing Clouds;* Water Wheels.**

Bentonite [ben-ton-nite] Type of clay used as a clarifying agent to remove proteins from wine before bottling to avoid the subsequent development of a protein haze in the bottle. Popular as a non-animal-derived *fining* material.

Benziger [ben-zig-ger] (*Sonoma*, California) Classy wines at the top end of the *Glen Ellen* range. ☆☆☆☆ **1995 Cabernet Sauvignon ££**

Berberana [behr-behr-rah nah] (*Rioja*, Spain) Increasingly dynamic producer of a range of fruitier young-drinking styles, as well as the improving Carta de Plata and Carta de Oro and Lagunilla *Riojas*, plus sparkling Marquès de Monistrol and the excellent Marquès de Griñon range.
☆☆☆☆ **1994 Berberana Reserva ££**

Bereich [beh-ri-kh] (Germany) Vineyard area, subdivision of an *anbaugebiet*. On its own indicates simple *QbA* wine, e.g. *Niersteiner.* Finer wines are followed by the name of a (smaller) *grosslage;* better ones by that of an individual vineyard.

Bergerac [behr-jur-rak] (France) Traditionally treated as 'lesser' neighbour of Bordeaux, but possibly soon to be assimilated into that regional *appellation*. The red and dry whites here, though often pretty mediocre, can still be better value than much basic *claret* and dry white *Bordeaux*, while the sweet *Monbazillac* often outclasses standard-quality *Sauternes*.
Ch. Court-les-Muts; la Jaubertie; Tour des Gendres.

Bergkelder [berg-kel-dur] (*Cape*, South Africa) Huge firm that still matures and bottles wines for such top-class *Cape* estates as *Meerlust*, which, like its counterparts in *Bordeaux* and *California*, really ought to bottle their own. Even so, the Bergkelder's own *Stellenryck* wines are worth watching out for; the cheaper Fleur du Cap range is likeable enough and *Pongracz* fizz is first class.

Beringer Vineyards [ber-rin-jer] (*Napa Valley*, California) Big Swiss-owned producer, increasingly notable for its single-vineyard *Cabernet Sauvignons* (Knights Valley, *Howell Mountain, Spring Mountain* and Private Reserve), *Cabernet Francs*, Burgundy-like *Chardonnays* and *late harvest* wines. ☆☆☆☆☆ 1996 Howell Mountain Terre Rouge Cabernet £££

Bernkastel [berhrn-kah-stel] (*Mosel*, Germany) Town and area on the *Mittelmosel* and source of some of the finest *Riesling* (like the famous Bernkasteler Doktor), and a lake of poor-quality stuff. QbA/Kab/Spät: **85** 86 **88 89 90** 91 **92 93 94** 95 96 97 Aus/Beeren/Tba: **83 85** 88 89 90 91 92 93 94 95 96 97 ***Dr Loosen; JJ Prum; Von Kesselstadt; Wegeler Deinhard.***

Bernardus (*Monterey*, California) Producer of rich, unsubtle, unashamedly New World-style *Sauvignon Blanc, Chardonnay* and *Pinot Noir.* ☆☆☆☆ Pinot Noir Santa Maria Valley Bien Nacido Vineyard ££

Berri Renmano [ber-ree ren-mah-noh] (*Riverland*, Australia) The controlling force behind the giant *BRL Hardy*, controlling quality brands like *Thomas Hardy*, *Barossa Valley Estates, Château Reynella* and *Houghton*. Under its own name, though, it is better known for inexpensive reds and whites.

Dom Bertagna [behr-tan-ya] (*Vougeot,* France) Recently improved estate notable for offering the rare (relatively) affordable *Premier Cru Vougeot* alongside its own version of the easier-to-find *Clos Vougeot Grand Cru*. ☆☆☆☆ 1995 Chambertin £££

Bertani [behr-tah-nee] (*Veneto*, Italy) Producer of good *Valpolicella*. ☆☆☆☆ 1995 Recioto della Valpolicella Amarone Classico Superiore ££

Best's Great Western (*Victoria*, Australia) Under-appreciated winery in *Great Western* making delicious concentrated *Shiraz* from old vines, attractive *Cabernet*, *Dolcetto*, *Colombard* and rich *Chardonnay* and *Riesling*. ☆☆☆☆☆ 1996 Great Western Riesling ££

Bethany [beth-than-nee] (*Barossa Valley,* Australia) Impressive small producer of knockout *Shiraz*. ☆☆☆☆☆ 1995 Shiraz £££

Dom. Henri Beurdin [bur-dan] (*Loire*, France) White and rosé from *Reuilly*. ☆☆☆ 1995 Reuilly Blanc ££

Ch. Beychevelle [bay-shur-vel] (*St. Julien 4ème Cru Classé*, *Bordeaux*, France) A fourth growth that achieves the typical cigar-box character of *St. Julien* but somehow fails to excite. The *second label Amiral de Beychevelle* can be a worthwhile buy. **70** 78 **82** 83 85 86 87 88 89 90 91 92 **94** 95 96 ☆☆☆☆☆ 1990 ££££

Léon Beyer [bay-ur] (*Alsace*, France) Serious producer of lean long-lived wines. ☆☆☆ 1996 Gewurztraminer Comtes d'Eguisheim ££

Beyerskloof [bay-yurs-kloof] (*Stellenbosch*, South Africa) Newish venture, with Beyers Truter (of *Kanonkop)* on its way to producing South Africa's top *Cabernet* and *Stellenbosch Pinotage*. ☆☆☆☆ 1995 Cabernet ££

Bianco di Custoza [bee-yan-koh dee koos-toh-zah] (*Veneto*, Italy) Widely exported *DOC*. A reliable, crisp, light white from a blend of grapes. A better-value alternative to most basic *Soave*. **Gorgo; Portalupi; *Tedeschi;* le Vigne di San Pietro; *Zenato.***

Maison Albert Bichot [bee-shoh] (*Burgundy,* France) Big *négoçiant* in *Beaune* with excellent *Chablis* and *Vosne-Romanée,* plus a range of perfectly adequate wines sold under a plethora of other labels. ☆☆☆☆ 1995 Chablis Grand Cru Vaudésir £££

Biddenden [bid-den-den] (Kent, England) Maker of wines from the usual range of Germanic grapes, but showing impressive mastery of the peachy *Ortega*. ☆☆☆ 1995 Ortega £

Bienvenue-Batard-Montrachet [bee-yen-veh-noo bat-tahr mon ra-rhay] (*Burgundy*, France) Fine white *Burgundy* vineyard with potential-ly gorgeous *biscuity* wines – at a price. ☆☆☆☆ 1995 Domaine Leflaive ££££

Weingut Josef Biffar [bif-fah] (*Pfalz*, Germany). *Deidesheim* estate that is on a roll at the moment with its richly spicy wines. ☆☆☆☆ 1996 Deidesheimer Kieselberg Riesling Auslese ££

Billecart-Salmon [beel-kahr sal-mon] (*Champagne*, France) Wine drinkers' fizz: light but great with food. Possibly the region's best all-rounder for quality and value. The one *Champagne* house whose subtle but decidedly ageable *non-vintage*, *vintage* and rosé I buy without hesita-tion. Superlative. ☆☆☆☆☆ Champagne Brut £££; ☆☆☆☆☆ Cuvée Elisabeth Salmon Brut ££££

Billiot [bil-lee-yoh] (*Champagne*, France) Impressive small producer with classy rich fizz. ☆☆☆☆ Cuvée de Reserve NV £££

Bingen [bing-urn] (*Rheinhessen*, Germany) Village giving its name to a *Rheinhessen bereich* that includes a number of well-known *grosslage*. QbA/Kab/Spät: 85 86 **88 89 90** 91 92 **93** 94 95 96 97
Aus/Beeren/Tba: **83 85** 88 89 90 91 92 **93 94** 95 96 97

Binissalem [bin-nee-sah-lem] (*Mallorca*, Spain) The holiday island is proud of its demarcated region, though why, it's hard to say. José Ferrer's and Jaime Mesquida's wines are the best of the bunch.

Biondi-Santi [bee-yon-dee san-tee] (*Tuscany*, Italy) Big-name property making absurdly expensive and often disappointing *Brunello di Montalcino* that can also be bought – after a period of vertical storage at room temperature – at the local trattoria. ☆☆☆ 1977 Brunello Di Montalcino ££££

Biscuity Flavour of biscuits (e.g. Digestive or Rich Tea) often associated with the *Chardonnay* grape, particularly in *Champagne* and top-class mature *Burgundy*, or with the yeast that fermented the wine.

Bitouzet-Prieur [bee-too-zay pree-yur] (*Burgundy*, France) If you like classic *Meursault* that's built to last rather than seduce instantly with ripe fruit and oak, try this estate's 1995 *Meursault Perrières*. The *Volnays* are good too.

Dom. Simon Bize [beez] (*Burgundy*, France) Intense, long-lived and good-value wines produced in *Savigny-lès-Beaune*. ☆☆☆☆ 1993 Savigny-lès-Beaune les Vergelesses £££

Blaauwklippen [blow-klip-pen] (*Stellenbosch*, South Africa) Large estate, veering between commercial and top quality. The *Cabernet* and *Zinfandel* are the strong cards. ☆☆☆ 1995 Zinfandel ££

Black Muscat Grown chiefly as a table grape; also produces very mediocre wine – except that made at the *Quady* winery in California. ☆☆☆☆ Elysium ££

Blagny [blan-yee] (*Burgundy*, France) Tiny source of good unsubtle red (sold as Blagny) and potentially top-class white (sold as *Meursault, Puligny-Montrachet*, Blagny, Hameau de Blagny or la Pièce sous le Bois).Red: 78 80 **83 85** 86 **88 89 90** 92 95 96 *Robert Ampeau; Jobard; Thierry Matrot.*

Blain-Gagnard [blan gan-yahr] (*Burgundy*, France) Excellent producer of creamy modern *Chassagne-Montrachet*. ☆☆☆☆ 1995 Chassagne-Montrachet ££££

Blanc de Blancs [blon dur blon] A white wine, made from white grapes – hardly worth mentioning except in the case of *Champagne*, where *Pinot Noir*, a black grape, usually makes up 30–70 per cent of the blend. In this case, Blanc de Blancs is pure *Chardonnay*.

Blanc de Noirs [blon dur nwahrr] A white (or frequently very slightly pink-tinged wine) made from red grapes by taking off the free-run juice, before pressing to minimise the uptake of red pigments from the skin. ☆☆☆☆☆ Duval-Leroy Fleur de Champagne £££

☘ **Paul Blanck** [blank] (*Alsace*, France) Top-class *Alsace domaine*, specialising in single *Cru* wines. ☆☆☆☆ 1996 Riesling Furstentum £££

☘ **Blandy's** [blan-deez] (*Madeira*, Portugal) Brand owned by the Madeira Wine Company and named after the sailor who began the production of fortified wine here. Brilliant old wines. ☆☆☆☆☆ 15 Year Old Malmsey £££

☘ **Blanquette de Limoux** [blon ket dur lee-moo] (*Midi*, France) *Méthode Champenoise* fizz, which, when good, is appley and clean. Best when made with a generous dose of *Chardonnay*, as the local *Mauzac* tends to give it an earthy flavour with age. ☆☆☆☆ Domaine de l'Aigle ££

☘ **Wolf Blass** (*Barossa Valley*, Australia) German immigrant who prides himself on producing immediately attractive 'sexy' (his term) reds and whites, by blending wines from different regions of *South Australia* and allowing them plentiful contact with new oak. ☆☆☆☆ 1995 President's Selection Shiraz £££

🍇 **Blauburgunder** [blow-boor-goon-durh] (Austria) The name the Austrians give their light, often sharp, *Pinot Noir*.

🍇 **Blauer Portugieser** [blow-urh por-too-gay-suhr] (Germany) Red grape used in Germany and Austria to make light, pale wine.

☘ **Blaufränkisch** [blow-fran-kish] (Austria) Berryish grape used to make wines that compete with the red wines of the Loire.

Bocksbeutel [box-boy-tuhl] (*Franken*, Germany) The famous flask-shaped bottle of *Franken,* adopted by the makers of *Mateus* Rosé.

Bockstein [bok-stihn] (*Mosel*, Germany) A vineyard in the village of *Ockfen*.

Bodega [bod-day-gah] (Spain) Winery or wine cellar; producer.

☘ **Bodegas y Bebidas** [bod-day-gas ee beh-bee-das] (Spain) One of Spain's most dynamic wine companies, and maker of *Campo Viejo*.

Body Usually used as 'full-bodied', meaning a wine with mouth-filling flavours and probably a fairly high alcohol content.

☘ **Jean-Marc Boillot** [bwah-yoh] (*Burgundy*, France) Small *Pommard domaine* run by the son of the winemaker at *Olivier Leflaive* with good examples from neighbouring villages. ☆☆☆☆☆ 1995 Volnay £££

☘ **Jean-Claude Boisset** [bwah-say] (*Burgundy*, France) Fast-growing *négociant* which now owns a long list of Burgundy *négociants*, including the excellent *Jaffelin* and the much improved *Bouchard Aîné*. Boisset also makes passable wines in *Languedoc-Roussillon*. ☆☆☆ 1996 Merlot Vin de Pays d'Oc ££

☘ **Boisson-Vadot** [bwah-son va-doh] (*Burgundy*, France) Classy, small *Meursault domaine*. ☆☆☆☆☆ 1992 Meursault Genevrières £££

☘ **Bolla** [bol-lah] (*Veneto*, Italy) Producer of plentiful, adequate *Valpolicella* and *Soave*, and of smaller quantities of impressive single vineyard wines like its Jago and Creso. ☆☆☆☆ 1990 Amarone Classico della Valpolicella £££

☘ **Bollinger** [bol-an-jay] (*Champagne*, France) Great family-owned firm at *Ay*, whose wines need age. The luscious and rare *Vieilles Vignes* is made from pre-*phylloxera* vines, while the nutty *RD* was the first late-disgorged *Champagne* to hit the market. ☆☆☆☆ 1990 Grande Année ££££

Bommes [bom] (*Bordeaux*, France) *Sauternes commune* and village containing several *Premiers Crus* such as la Tour Blanche, Lafaurie-Peyrauguey, Rabaud-Promis and Rayne Vigneau. 70 **71 75** 76 83 85 86 88 89 90 95 96 97

🍷 **Ch. le Bon-Pasteur** [bon-pas-stuhr] (*Pomerol, Bordeaux*, France) The impressive private estate of *Michel Rolland*, who acts as consultant – and helps to make fruit-driven wines – for half his neighbours, as well as producers in almost every other wine-growing region in the universe. 70 75 76 **82 83 85 86** 87 **88** 89 90 92 93 94 95 96 97

🍷 **Domaine de la Bongran** [bon-grah] See *Jean Thevenet*.

🍷 **Henri Bonneau** [bon-noh] (*Rhône*, France) *Châteauneuf-du-Pape* producer with two special *cuvées* – 'Marie Beurrier' and 'des Celestins' – and a cult following. ☆☆☆☆☆ **1992 Réserve des Celestins ££££**

🍷 **Dom. Bonneau du Martray** [bon-noh doo mahr-tray] (*Burgundy*, France) Largest grower of *Corton-Charlemagne* and a recently dynamically-improved producer thereof. Also produces a classy red *Grand Cru Corton*. ☆☆☆☆☆ **1995 Corton ££££**

🍷 **Ch. Bonnet** [bon-nay] (*Bordeaux*, France) Top-quality *Entre-Deux-Mers* château whose wines are made by *Jacques Lurton*.

🍷 **F. Bonnet** [bon-nay] (*Champagne*, France) Reliable, little-known producer with good wines under its own and customers' names. ☆☆☆☆ **Blanc de Blancs Champagne Brut £££**

🍷 **Bonnezeaux** [bonn-zoh] (*Loire*, France) Within the *Coteaux du Layon*, this is one of the world's greatest sweet wine producing areas, though the wines are often over-sulphured. 76 83 85 86 **88 89** 90 93 94 95 René Renou; Dom Godineau ☆☆☆☆ **Ch. de Fesles 'La Chapelle' £££**

🍷 **Bonny Doon Vineyard** (*Santa Cruz*, California) Randall Grahm, sorceror's apprentice, experimentor; and original '*Rhône* Ranger' also has an affection for unfashionable French and Italian varieties, which is increasingly evident in a range of characterful red, dry and *late harvest* whites. The sheep-like Californian wine industry needs more mavericks like Grahm. ☆☆☆☆☆ **1995 Old Telegram £££**

Borba [Bohr-Bah] (*Alentejo*, Portugal) See *Alentejo*.

🍷 **Bordeaux** [bor-doh] (France) Largest (supposedly) quality wine region in France, producing reds, rosés and deep pink *Clairets* from *Cabernet Sauvignon, Cabernet Franc, Petit Verdot*, and *Merlot*, and dry and sweet whites from (principally) blends of *Sémillon* and *Sauvignon*. *Bordeaux Supérieur* denotes (relatively) riper grapes. Dry whites from regions like the *Médoc* and *Sauternes*, where they are not part of the mainstream activity, are (for no good reason) sold as *Bordeaux Blanc*, so even the efforts by *Châteaux d'Yquem, Margaux*, and *Lynch-Bages* are sold under the same label as the most basic supermarket blended white. See *Graves, Médoc, Pomerol, St. Emilion* etc.

🍷 **Borgogno** [baw-gon-yoh] (*Piedmont*, Italy) Resolutely old-fashioned *Barolo* producer whose wines can develop a sweet tobaccoey richness with age. In their youth, though, they're often not a lot of fun. ☆☆☆☆ **1985 Barolo ££££**

🍷 **De Bortoli** [baw-tol-lee] (*Riverina*, Australia) Fast-developing firm (following its move into the *Yarra Valley*) which startled the world by making a *botrytised*, peachy, honeyed 'Noble One' *Semillon* in the unfashionable *Riverina* which (undeservingly) beats *Ch. d'Yquem* in blind tastings. ☆☆☆☆ **1997 Deen de Bortoli Yarra Valley Chardonnay ££**

🍷 **Bodega Luigi Bosca** [bos-kah] (*Mendoza*, Argentina) Top-class producer with good *Sauvignons* and *Cabernets*.

🍷 **Boscaini** [bos-kah-yee-nee] (*Veneto*, Italy) Innovative producer linked to *Masi* and making better-than-average *Valpolicella* and *Soave*. ☆☆☆☆ **1993 Valpolicella Amarone Classico Marone ££**

🍷 **Boschendal Estate** [bosh-shen-dahl] (*Cape*, South Africa) Modern winery producing some of the *Cape's* best fizz and fast-improving whites. ☆☆☆ **1996 Reserve Chardonnay ££**

�>️ **Ca' del Bosco** [kah-del-bos-koh] (*Lombardy*, Italy) Classic, if pricy *barrique*-aged *Cabernet/Merlot* blends, fine *Chardonnay* and good *Pinot Bianco/Pinot Noir/Chardonnay Méthode Champenoise Franciacorta*, from perfectionist producer Maurizio Zanella.
☆☆☆☆☆ 1995 Maurizio Zanella ££££

�>️ **Ch. le Boscq** [bosk] (*St. Estèphe Cru Bourgeois, Bordeaux*, France) Improving property that excels in good vintages, but tends to make tough wines in lesser ones. 82 83 85 86 87 88 **89** 90 92 **93** 95 96

�>️ **Les Bosquet des Papes** [bos-kay day pap] (*Rhône*, France) Serious *Châteauneuf-du-Pape* producer, making wines that last.

Botrytis [boh-tri-tiss] Botrytis cinerea, a fungal infection that attacks and shrivels grapes, evaporating their water and concentrating their sweetness. Vital to *Sauternes* and the finer German and Austrian sweet wines. See *Sauternes, Trockenbeerenauslese, Tokaji*.

�>️ **Bott-Geyl** [bott-gihl] (*Alsace*, France) Young producer, whose impressive *Grand Cru* wines suit those who like their *Alsace* big and rich.
☆☆☆☆ 1995 Gewurztraminer Sonnenglanz ££

Bottle-fermented Commonly found on the labels of US sparkling wines to indicate the *Méthode Champenoise*, and gaining wider currency. Beware, though – it can indicate inferior *'transfer method'* wines.

�>️ **Bouchard Aîné** [boo-shahrr day-nay] (*Burgundy*, France) For a long time, an unimpressive merchant, now taken over by *Boisset* and now under the winemaking control of the excellent Bernard Repolt of *Jaffelin*.

�>️ **Bouchard-Finlayson** [boo-shard] (*Walker Bay*, South Africa) Serious small-scale joint venture between Peter Finlayson (brother of Walter at *Glen Carlou*) and Paul Bouchard, formerly of *Bouchard Aîné* in France. Wines are made from some of South Africa's best cool-climate fruit (including grapes from *Elgin*). ☆☆☆☆ 1996 Chardonnay ££

�>️ **Bouchard Père & Fils** [boo-shahrr pehrr ay fees] (*Burgundy*, France) Traditional merchant with some great vineyards. Bought in 1996 by the *Champagne* house of *Henriot*, who are evidently much more quality-conscious than the Bouchard family. The best wines are the *Beaunes*, especially the Beaune de l'Enfant Jésus, as well as the La Romanée from *Vosne-Romanée*. ☆☆☆☆ 1995 Beaune Vigne de l'Enfant Jésus £££

�>️ **Pascal Bouley** [boo-lay] (*Burgundy*, France) Producer of good, if not always refined *Volnay*. ☆☆☆☆ 1995 Volnay Champans £££

Bouquet Overall smell, often made up of several separate aromas. Used by Anglo-Saxon enthusiasts more often than by professionals.

�>️ **Ch. Bourgneuf** [boor-nurf] (*Pomerol, Bordeaux*, France) Rising star with rich plummy *Merlot* fruit. 81 82 83 **85** 86 88 **89** 90 92 **95 96**
☆☆☆☆☆ 1990 £££

Bourgogne [boorr-goyñ] (*Burgundy*, France) French for *Burgundy*.

�>️ **Bourgueil** [boorr-goyy] (*Loire*, France) Red *AC* in the *Touraine*, producing crisp grassy-blackcurranty 100 per cent *Cabernet Franc* wines that can age well in good years like 1995. *Caslot-Galbrun; Druet.*

�>️ **Ch. Bouscassé** [boo-ska-say] (*Madiran*, France) See *Ch. Montus*

�>️ **Ch. Bouscaut** [boos-koh] (*Pessac-Léognan, Bordeaux*, France) Good, rather than great *Graves* property; better white than red.

�>️ **J. Boutari** [boo-tah-ree] (*Greece*) One of the most reliable names in Greece, producing good traditional red wines in Nemea and Naoussa.

�>️ **Bouvet-Ladubay** [boo-vay lad-doo-bay] (*Loire*, France) Producer of good *Loire* fizz and better *Saumur-Champigny* reds. ☆☆☆ 1995 Saumur Rubis Rouge £££

🌿 **Bouvier** [boo-vee-yay] (Austria) Characterless variety used to produce tasty but mostly simple *late harvest* wines.

Bouzeron [booz-rron] (*Burgundy*, France) Village in the *Côte Chalonnaise*, principally known for *Aligoté* which is supposedly at its best here. ☆☆☆☆☆ 1996 Aligoté Aubert de Villaine ££

♀ **Bouzy Rouge** [boo-zee roozh] (*Champagne*, France) Sideline of a black grape village: an often thin-bodied, rare and overpriced red wine which, despite what they say, rarely ages. 89 90 94 ✰✰✰ *Gosset* ££££

♀ **Bowen Estate** [boh-wen] (*Coonawarra*, Australia) An early *Coonawarra* pioneer proving that the region can be as good for *Shiraz* as for *Cabernet*. ✰✰✰✰ 1994 Cabernet Sauvignon £££

♀ **Domaines Boyar** [boy-yahr] (*Bulgaria*) Privatised producers, especially in the *Suhindol* region, selling increasingly worthwhile 'Reserve' reds under the Lovico label. Other wines are less reliably recommendable. ✰✰✰✰ 1990 Lambol Special Reserve Cabernet Sauvignon ££

♀ **Ch. Boyd-Cantenac** [boyd-kon-teh-nak] (*Margaux 3ème Cru Classé*, *Bordeaux*, France) A third growth generally performing at the level of a fifth – or less. 78 **82 83 85 86** 88 89 90 93 94 96 97

🍇 **Brachetto d'Acqui** [brah-KET-toh dak-wee] (*Piedmont,* Italy) Eccentric Muscatty red grape. Often *frizzante*. *Beni di Batasiolo.*

♀ **Ch. Branaire-Ducru** [brah-nehr doo-kroo] (*St.-Julien 4ème Cru Classé*, *Bordeaux*, France) New owners are doing wonders for this fourth growth *St. Julien* estate. Red: 75 79 81 **82** 83 85 86 87 88 89 90 91 92 93 95 ✰✰✰✰ 1985 ££££

♀ **Brand's Laira** [lay-rah] (*Coonawarra*, Australia) Traditional producer, much improved since its purchase by *McWilliams*. Delving into the world of *Pinot Noir* and sparkling *Grenache* rosé.

♀ **Ch. Brane-Cantenac** [brahn kon teh-nak] (*Margaux 2ème Cru Classé*, *Bordeaux*, France) Perennial under-achieving *Margaux*, whose *second label*, the discouragingly named Ch. Notton, can be a worthwhile buy. 75 78 79 81 82 83 85 86 87 88 89 90 95 96 ✰✰✰ 1985 ££££

🍇 **Braquet** [brah-ket] (*Midi*, France) Grape variety used in *Bellet*.

Brauneberg [brow-nuh-behrg] (*Mosel*, Germany) Village best known in the UK for the *Juffer* vineyard. ✰✰✰✰ 1993 Brauneberger Juffer Kabinett, Weingut Max Ferd Richter ££££

Brazil Country in which large quantities of fairly light-bodied wines are produced in a region close to Puerto Allegre, where it tends to rain at harvest time. Large amounts of (unexceptional) *Zinfandel* have been shipped north to the US, however. The Palomas vineyard on the *Uruguayan* border has a state-of-the-art winery and a good climate. The wines have yet to reflect those advantages, however.

♀ **Breaky Bottom** (Sussex, England) One of Britain's best, whose *Seyval Blanc* rivals dry wines made in the *Loire* from supposedly finer grapes.

♀ **Marc Bredif** [bray-deef] (*Loire*, France) Big, and quite variable *Loire* producer, with still and sparkling wine, including some good *Vouvray*. ✰✰✰ Bredif Brut NV ££

♀ **Ch. du Breuil** [doo breuh-yee] (*Loire*, France) Source of good *Coteaux de Layon*, and relatively ordinary examples of other *appellations*. ✰✰✰✰ 1995 Coteaux de Layon, Beaulieu ££.

♀ **Weingut Georg Breuer** [broy-yer] (*Rheingau*, Germany) Innovative producer with classy *Rieslings* and high quality *Rülander.*

♀ **Bricco Manzoni** [bree-koh man-tzoh-nee] (*Piedmont*, Italy) Non-*DOC* oaky red blend of *Nebbiolo* and *Barbera* grapes grown on vines which could produce *Barolo* from *Monforte* vineyards. A wine that is drinkable young. ✰✰✰✰ 1990 Valentino Migliorini £££

♀ **Bridgehampton** (*Long Island*, US) Producer of first class *Merlot* and *Chardonnay* to worry a Californian.

♀ **Bridgewater Mill** (*Adelaide Hills*, Australia) More modest sister winery to the highly regarded *Petaluma*, using grapes from other sources as well as their own. ✰✰✰✰ 1996 Chardonnay ££

Peter Bright Australian-born Peter Bright of the *JP Vinhos* winery produces top-class Portuguese wines, including Tinta da Anfora and Quinta da Bacalhoa, plus a growing range in countries such as Spain and Chile, under the Bright Brothers label. ☆☆☆☆ **1997 Bright Brothers Atlantic Vines ££**

Bristol Cream (*Jerez*, Spain) See *Harvey's*.

Jean-Marc Brocard [broh-kah*rr*] (*Burgundy*, France) Very classy *Chablis* producer with well-defined individual vineyard wines, also producing unusually good *Aligoté*.
☆☆☆☆ **1995 Chablis Bougros £££**

Brokenwood (*Hunter Valley*, Australia) Long-established, first class source of great *Semillon*, *Shiraz* and even (unusually for the *Hunter Valley*) *Cabernet*. Look out for the 'Cricket Pitch' bottlings. ☆☆☆☆ **1996 Shiraz ££**

Brouilly [broo-yee] (*Burgundy*, France) Largest of the ten *Beaujolais Crus* producing pure fruity *Gamay*. 94 95 96 97 **Pierre Cotton; *Sylvain Fessy*; Laurent Martray; Ch. des Tours.**

Ch. Broustet [broo-stay] (*Barsac 2ème Cru Classé*, *Bordeaux*, France) Rich, quite old-fashioned, well-oaked *Barsac* second growth. 70 **71 75** 76 83 85 86 88 89 90 95 96 97

Brown Brothers (*Victoria*, Australia) Family-owned and *Victoria*-focused winery with a penchant for exploring new wine regions and grapes. The wines are reliably good, though for real excitement, you should look to the *Shiraz* and the *Liqueur Muscat* (following the purchase of the old All Saints winery in *Rutherglen*). The *Orange Muscat* and *Flora* remains a delicious mouthful of liquid marmalade, the *Tarrango* is a good alternative to *Beaujolais*, and the sparkling wine is a new success. ☆☆☆☆☆ **1994 Family Reserve Late Harvest Noble Riesling £££**

David Bruce (*Santa Cruz*, California) Long established *Zinfandel* specialist whose wines can be tougher than they ought to be. The 1996 *Petite Sirah* is approachably attractive.

Bruisyard Vineyard [broos-syard] (Suffolk, England) High-quality vineyard. ☆☆☆ **1990 Müller-Thurgau ££**

Alain Brumont [broo-mon] (*South-West* France) *Madiran* modernist with top-class reds under the Montus and Bouscassé labels, plus stunning banana-ish *late harvest Pacherenc de Vic Bilh* called Brumaire. ☆☆☆ **1995 Ch. Bouscassé ££**

Le Brun de Neuville [bruhn duh nuh-veel] (*Champagne*, France) Good little-known producer with classy *vintage* and excellent rosé and *Blanc de Blancs*. ☆☆☆ **Champagne Rosé Brut £££**

Willi Bründlmayer [broodl-mi-yurh] (Austria) Oaked *Chardonnay* and *Pinots* of every kind, *Grüner Veltliner* and even a fairish shot at *Cabernet*. This is one of Austria's rising stars.

Lucien & André Brunel [broo-nel] (*Rhône*, France) The Brunels' 'Les Caillous' produces good, traditional, built-to-last *Châteauneuf-du-Pape*.

Brunello di Montalcino [broo-nell-oh dee mon-tahl-chee-noh] (*Tuscany*, Italy) Prestigious *DOCG* red from a *Sangiovese* clone. 78 79 81 **82 85 88 90 94 95 97 *Altesino*; *Argiano*; Villa Banfi; Tenuta Caparzo; Costanti; Lambardi; Talenti; Val di Suga.**

Brut [broot] Dry, particularly of *Champagne* and sparkling wines. Brut nature/sauvage/zéro are even drier, while '*Extra-Sec*' is perversely applied to (slightly) sweeter fizz.

Bual [bwahl] (*Madeira*) Grape producing softnutty wine – wonderful with cheese. ***Blandy's; Cossart Gordon; Henriques & Henriques.***

Buçaco Palace Hotel [boo-sah-koh] (Portugal) Red and white wines made from grapes grown in *Bairrada* and *Dão*, which last forever but cannot be bought outside the Disneyesque Hotel itself.

Bucelas [boo-sel-las] (Portugal) *DO* area near Lisbon, best known for its intensely coloured, aromatic, bone-dry white wines. **Caves Velhas.**

🍷 **Buena Vista** [bway-nah vihs-tah] (*Carneros*, California) One of the biggest estates in *Carneros*, this is an improving producer of California *Chardonnay, Pinot Noir* and *Cabernet*. Look out for Reserve wines.

Bugey [boo-jay] (*Savoie*, France) *Savoie* district producing a variety of wines, including spicy white Roussette de Bugey, from the grape of that name.

🍷 **Reichsrat von Buhl** [rihk-srat fon bool] (*Pfalz*, Germany) One of the area's best estates, due partly to vineyards like the *Forster Jesuitengarten*. ☆☆☆☆ **1996 Forster Ungeheuer Riesling Auslese 'Classic' £££**

🍷 **Buitenverwachting** [biht-turn-fur-vak-turng] (*Constantia*, South Africa) Enjoying a revival since the early 1980s, this show-piece organic winery of *Constantia* is making particularly tasty organic whites. ☆☆☆ **1996 Chardonnay ££**

Bulgaria Developing slowly since the advent of privatisation and *flying winemakers*. Bulgaria's reputation still relies on its country wines, *Cabernet Sauvignons* and *Merlots*; there are no real examples of wines worth pulling out for a special occasion. *Mavrud* is the traditional red variety and Lovico, *Rousse*, Iambol, *Suhindol* and Haskovo the names to look out for.

🍷 ***Bull's Blood*** (*Eger*, Hungary) The gutsy red wine, aka Egri Bikaver, which gave defenders the strength to fight off Turkish invaders, is mostly anaemic stuff now, but privatisation has brought some improvement. ☆☆☆ **1996 Eger Bikaver Reserve, Tibor Gal Gia. ££**

🍷 **Buller** (*Rutherglen*, Australia) Makers of sometimes excellent fortified wines.

🍷 **Burdon** (*Jerez*, Spain) The brand used by *Luis Caballero* for his top-class range of *sherries*. ***Lustau*.**

🍷 **Bernard Burgaud** [boor-goh] (*Rhône*, France) Serious producer of *Côte Rôtie*. ☆☆☆☆ **1995 Côte Rôtie £££**

🍷 **Grant Burge** (*Barossa Valley*, Australia) Dynamic producer and – since 1993 – owner of *Basedows*. ☆☆☆☆ **1993 Meshach Shiraz £££**

Burgenland [boor-gen-lund] (Austria) Wine region bordering *Hungary*, climatically ideal for fine sweet *Auslese* and *Beerenauslese*. ***Feiler-Artinger*; Helmut Lang; *Kracher*.**

🍷 **Weinkellerei Burgenland** [vihn-kel-ler-rih boor-gen-lund] (*Neusiedlersee*, Austria) Cooperative with highly commercial *late harvest* wines.

🍷 **Alain Burguet** [al-lan boor-gay] (*Burgundy*, France) One-man *domaine* which proves how good plain *Gevrey-Chambertin* can be without heavy doses of new oak. Look for his *Vieilles Vignes*. ☆☆☆☆ **1995 Bourgogne Vieilles Vignes £££**

🍷 **Burgundy** (France) Home to *Pinot Noir* and *Chardonnay*; wines range from banal to sublime, but are never cheap. See *Chablis, Côte de Nuits, Côte de Beaune, Mâconnais, Beaujolais* and individual villages.

🍷 **Leo Buring** [byoo-ring] (*South Australia*) One of the many labels used by the *Penfolds* group, specialising in whites and mature *Shiraz's*.

🍷 **Weingut Dr Bürklin-Wolf** [boor-klin-volf] (*Pfalz*, Germany) Impressive estate with great organic *Riesling* vineyards and fine dry wines.

🍷 **Ernest J&F Burn** [boorn] (*Alsace*, France) Classy estate with vines in the Goldert *Grand Cru*. Great traditional *Gewurztraminer, Riesling* and *Muscat*. ☆☆☆☆ **1994 Gewurztraminer Goldert Clos St. Imer £££**

Buttery Rich fat smell often found in good *Chardonnay* (often as a result of *malolactic fermentation)* or in wine that has been left on its *lees*.

Buxy (Cave des Vignerons de) [book-see] (*Burgundy*, France) Cooperative with fair-value oaked Bourgogne Rouge and *Montagny*.

Buzbag [buz-bag] (*Turkey*) Rich, dry red wine. Rarely well-made and often *oxidised*.

Byron Vineyard [bih-ron] (*Santa Barbara*, California) Impressive *Santa Barbara* winery with investment from *Mondavi*, and a fine line in *Pinots* and *Chardonnays*. ☆☆☆☆ 1995 Pinot Noir Santa Barbara Reserve £££

C

Luis Caballero [loo-is cab-ih-yer-roh] (*Jerez*, Spain) Quality *sherry* producer responsible for the *Burdon* range; also owns *Lustau*.

Château La Cabanne [la ca-ban] (*Pomerol*, *Bordeaux*, France) Up-and-coming *Pomerol* property. 79 81 **82** 83 85 86 88 89 90 92 93 94 95 96

Cabardès [cab-bahr-des] (*South-West* France) Up-and-coming region north of Carcassonne using traditional Southern and *Bordeaux* varieties to produce good if rustic reds.

Cabernet d'Anjou/de Saumur [cab-behr-nay don-joo / dur soh-moor] (*Loire*, France) Light, fresh, grassy, blackcurranty rosés, typical of their grape, the *Cabernet Franc*. 78 81 83 **85** 86 **88 89 90** 95

Cabernet Franc [ka-behr-nay fron] Kid brother of *Cabernet Sauvignon*; blackcurranty but more leafy. Best in the *Loire*, Italy, and increasingly in Australia and California and, of course, as a partner of the *Cabernet Sauvignon* and particularly *Merlot* in *Bordeaux*. See *Chinon* and *Trentino*.

Cabernet Sauvignon [ka-ber-nay soh-vin-yon] The great red, blackcurranty, cedary, green peppery grape of *Bordeaux*, where it is blended with *Merlot* and other varieties. Despite increasing competition from the Merlot, this is still by far the most successful red varietal, grown in every reasonably warm winemaking country on the planet. See *Bordeaux, Coonawarra, Chile, Napa,* etc.

Marqués de Cáceres [mahr-kehs day cath-thay-res] (*Rioja*, Spain) Modern French-influenced *bodega* making fresh-tasting wines. A good, if anonymous, new-style white has been joined by a promising oak-fermented version and a recommendable rosé (*rosado*), plus a grapey *Muscat*-style white. ☆☆☆☆ 1994 Rioja Tinto ££

Ch. Cadet-Piola [ka-day pee-yoh-lah] (*St. Emilion Grand Cru Classé*, *Bordeaux*, France) Not always the producer of the classiest wines, but most are made to last, with concentrated fruit and *tannin* to spare. 75 79 82 **83 85** 86 88 89 90 92 93 95 96

Cadillac [kad-dee-yak] (*Bordeaux*, France) Sweet but rarely luscious (non-*botrytis*) old-fashioned *Sémillon* and *Sauvignon* whites for drinking young and well-chilled. Ch. Fayau is the only really recommendable wine. Its *d'Yquem*-style label is pretty smart too. **83** 86 **88 89 90** 94 95 96 97

Cafayate [ka-fah-yeh-tay] (Argentina) See *Etchart*.

Cahors [kah-orr] (*South-West*, France) 'Rustic' *Bordeaux*-like reds produced mainly from the local *Tannat* and the *Cot* (*Malbec*). Some examples are frankly *Beaujolais*-like while others are *tannic* and quite full-bodied, though far lighter than they were in the days when people spoke of 'the black wines of Cahors'. **Ch. du Cèdre; Ch. Lamartine; Clos Triguedina.**

Ch. Caillou [kih-yoo] (*Barsac 2ème Cru Classé, Bordeaux*, France) Fair, but rather simple wine – at its best in 1988 and 1990. 75 76 78 81 82 83 85 86 87 88 89 90 94 95 96

Cain Cellars (*Napa*, California) Spectacular *Napa* hillside vineyards devoted to producing a classic *Bordeaux* blend of five varieties – hence the name of the wine. ☆☆☆☆ **1994 Cain Five £££**

Cairanne [keh-ran] (*Rhône*, France) Named *Côtes du Rhône* village known for good peppery reds. **82 83 85 88** 89 90 92 93 95 96 ☆☆☆☆ **1996 Domaine Richaud ££**

Cakebread (*Napa*, California) Long-established producer of rich reds, *Sauvignon Blanc, Chardonnay* and improving *Pinot Noir.* ☆☆☆☆ **1994 Cabernet Sauvignon ££**

Calabria [kah-lah-bree-ah] (Italy) The 'toe' of the Italian boot, making Cirò from the local Gaglioppo reds and *Greco* whites. *Cabernet* and *Chardonnay* are promising, too, especially those made by Librandi.

Calem [kah-lin] (*Douro*, Portugal) Quality-conscious, small *port* producer. The speciality *Colheita tawnies* are among the best of their kind. ☆☆☆☆ **1987 Quinta da Foz Vintage ££££**

Calera Wine Co. [ka-lehr-uh] (*Santa Benito*, California) Maker of some of California's best *Pinot Noir* from individual vineyards such as Jensen, Mills, Reed and Selleck. The *Chardonnay* and *Viognier* are pretty special, too. ☆☆☆☆ **1994 Pinot Noir Selleck £££**

California (US) Major wine-producing area of the US. See *Napa, Sonoma, Santa Barbara, Amador, Mendocino*, etc, plus individual wineries. Red: 84 **85** 86 87 **90 91** 92 93 95 96 White: **85 90 91** 92 95 96 97

Viña Caliterra [kal-lee-tay-rah] (*Curico*, Chile) Sister company of *Errazuriz*, founded as a joint venture with *Franciscan*, which is now doing their own thing at *Veramonte*. Now a 50-50 partner with *Mondavi* and co-producer of *Seña*. ☆☆☆**1996 Cabernet Sauvignon Riserva ££**

Ch. Calon-Segur [kal-lon say-goor] (*St. Estèphe 3ème Cru Classé, Bordeaux*, France) Traditional *St. Estèphe* that has recently – with the 1995 and 1996 vintages – begun to surpass its third growth status. 78 **82** 83 **85** 86 **88** 89 90 91 93 94 95 96 ☆☆☆☆ **1993 £££**

Quinta da Camarate [kin-tah dah kam-mah-rah-tay] (*Estremadura*, Portugal) Attractive *Cabernet Sauvignon*-based red from *JM da Fonseca*. 89 90

Ch. Camensac [kam-mon-sak] (*Haut-Médoc 5ème Cru Classé, Bordeaux*, France) Improving property following investment in 1994. **82** 85 **86** 88 89 90 91 92 93 94 95 96 ☆☆☆☆ **1993 £££**

Campania [kahm-pan-nyah] (Italy) Region surrounding Naples, known for *Taurasi, Lacryma Christi* and *Greco di Tufo* and wines from *Mastroberadino*.

Campbells (*Rutherglen*, Australia) Classic producer of fortified *Muscat* and rich concentrated reds under the Bobbie Burns label. ☆☆☆☆ **1996 Bobbie Burns Rutherglen Shiraz ££**

Campillo [kam-pee-yoh] (*Rioja*, Spain) A small estate producing *Rioja* made purely from *Tempranillo*, showing what this grape can do. The white is less impressive. ☆☆☆☆ **1988 Gran Riserva ££**

☙ **Bodegas Campo Viejo** [kam-poh vyay-hoh] (*Rioja*, Spain) A go-ahead, often underrated *bodega* whose *Reserva* and *Gran Reserva* are full of rich fruit. Albor, the unoaked red (pure *Tempranillo*) and white (*Viura*) are first-class examples of modern Spanish winemaking.
☆☆☆☆1989 Gran Reserva ££

Canada Surprising friends and foes alike, British Columbia and, more specifically, *Ontario* are producing good *Chardonnay, Riesling*, improving *Pinot Noirs* and intense *Icewines*, usually from the *Vidal* grape.

☙ **Canard Duchêne** [kan-nah doo-shayn] (*Champagne*, France) Improving subsidiary of *Veuve Clicquot*. ☆☆☆☆ 1990 Brut £££

☙ **Canépa** [can-nay-pah] (Chile) Good rather than great winery, making progress with *Chardonnays* and *Rieslings* as well as reds.
☆☆☆☆ 1997 Chardonnay ££

❦ **Cannonau** [kan-non-now] (*Sardinia*, Italy) An Italian red *clone* of the *Grenache*, producing a variety of wine styles from sweet to dry, mostly in *Sardinia*.

☙ **Cannonau di Sardegna** [kan-non-now dee sahr-den-yah] (*Sardinia*, Italy) Heady, robust, dry-to-sweet, *DOC* red made from the *Cannonau* grape. ☆☆☆☆ 1994 Sella & Mosca ££

☙ **Ch. Canon** [kan-non] (*St. Emilion Premier Grand Cru Classé, Bordeaux*, France) Greatly improved since its takeover and heavy investment prior to the 1997 harvest. 82 83 **85 86** 87 88 89 90 92 93 94 95 96 97

☙ **Ch. Canon** [kan-non] (*Canon-Fronsac, Bordeaux*, France) Small property in *Canon-Fronsac* owned by Christian *Moueix*. 82 83 85 **86** 88 89 90 92 93 95 97 ☆☆☆ **1993** £££

☙ **Ch. Canon de Brem** [kan-non dur brem] (*Canon-Fronsac, Bordeaux*, France) A very good *Moueix*-run *Fronsac* property. 81 **82** 83 85 86 88 89 90 92 93 95 ☆☆☆ **1993** ££

☙ **Canon-Fronsac** [kah-non fron-sak] (*Bordeaux*, France) Small *AC* bordering on *Pomerol*, with attractive plummy, *Merlot*-based reds from increasingly good value, if rustic, *petits châteaux*. **82 83 85** 86 **88 89** 90 94 95 96 *Ch. Canon-Moueix; Ch. Moulin Pey-Labrie.*

☙ **Ch. Canon-la-Gaffelière** [kan-non lah gaf-fel-yehr] (*St. Emilion Grand Cru Classé, Bordeaux*, France) High-flying estate following a purchase by an innovative, quality-conscious Austrian who, in 1996, created the instant superstar *la Mondotte*. 82 83 85 **86** 87 88 89 90 92 93 94 95 96 97

☙ **Ch. Canon-Moueix** [kan-non mwex] (*Canon-Fronsac, Bordeaux*, France) A stylish addition to the *Moueix* empire in *Canon-Fronsac*. 82 83 85 86 87 88 89 90 92 93 94 95 ☆☆☆ **1995** ££

☙ **Ch. Cantemerle** [kont-mehrl] (*Haut-Médoc 5ème Cru Classé, Bordeaux*, France) A *Cru Classé* situated outside the main villages of the *Médoc*. Classy, perfumed wine with bags of blackcurrant fruit. 61 78 81 82 **83** 85 88 89 90 92 93 95 96 ☆☆☆☆ 1992 ££

Cantenac [kont-nak] (*Bordeaux*, France) *Commune* within the *appellation* of *Margaux* whose *châteaux* include *Palmer*. 78 79 81 **82** 83 85 **86** 88 89 90 94 95 96

☙ **Ch. Cantenac-Brown** [kont-nak brown] (*Margaux 3ème Cru Classé, Bordeaux*, France) Finally – in 1997 – improving from its disappointing state. 70 81 82 83 85 **86** 87 88 89 90 93 94 95 97

Canterbury (New Zealand) Following its early success with *Pinot Noir* by *St. Helena*, Waipara in this region of the South Island has produced highly aromatic *Riesling, Pinot Blanc* and *Chablis*-like *Chardonnay*. *Giesen; St. Helena; Pegasus Bay; Melness; Waipara Springs.*

Cantina (Sociale) [kan-tee-nuh soh-chee-yah-lay] (Italy) Winery (cooperative).

Cap Classique [kap-klas-seek] (South Africa) Now that the term '_Méthode Champenoise_' has unreasonably been outlawed, this is the phrase developed by the South Africans to describe their _Champagne_-method sparklers.

☒ **Ch. Cap-de-Mourlin** [kap-dur-mer-lan] (_St. Emilion Grand Cru Classé, Bordeaux_, France) Until 1983 when they were amalgamated, there were, confusingly, two different _châteaux_ with this name. Good mid-range stuff. 79 81 **82 83** 85 86 88 89 90 93 94 95 96 ☆☆☆☆ **1988 ££**

☒ **Caparzo** [ka-pahrt-zoh] (_Tuscany_, Italy) Classy, _Brunello di Montalcino_ estate producing wines that age well. ☆☆☆☆ **1988 £££**

Cape (South Africa) All of the vineyard areas of South Africa are located in the Western Cape, most of them within an hour or two from Capetown. See under _Stellenbosch, Paarl, Franschhoek, Walker Bay, Robertson, Tulbagh, Worcester_ etc. Red: 86 **87** 89 **91 92** 93 94 95 96 97 White: **87 91** 92 93 94 95 96 97

☒ **Cape Mentelle** [men-tel] (_Margaret River_, Western Australia) Brilliant French-owned winery, founded, like _Cloudy Bay_, by David Hoehnen. Impressive _Semillon-Sauvignon_, _Shiraz_, _Cabernet_ and, remarkably, a wild berryish _Zinfandel_, to shame many a Californian. ☆☆☆☆ **1996 Semillon-Sauvignon Blanc ££**

☒ **Capel Vale** [kay-puhl vayl] (_Swan Valley_, Western Australia) Just to the north of the borders of _Margaret River._ A good source of _Riesling, Gewurztraminer_ and improving reds such as the Baudin blend. ☆☆☆☆ **1997 Unwooded Chardonnay ££**

☒ **Villa di Capezzana** [kap-pay-tzah-nah] (_Tuscany_, Italy) Conte Ugo Contini Bonacossi not only deserves credit for getting _Carmignano_ its _DOCG,_ he also helped to promote the notion of _Cabernet_ and _Sangiovese_ as compatible bedfellows, helping to open the door for all those priceless – and pricy – _Super-Tuscans_. ☆☆☆ **1993 Ghiaie della Furba £££**

Capsule The sheath covering the cork. Once lead, now plastic, or a type of tin. In the case of new-wave 'flanged' bottles, however, it is noticeable by its transparency or absence.

☒ **Caramany** [kah-ram-man-nee] (_Midi_, France) New _AC_ for an old section of the _Côtes du Roussillon-Villages_, near the _Pyreneés._ **Vignerons Catalans.**

Carbonic Maceration See _Macération Carbonique._

☒ **Ch. Carbonnieux** [kar-bon-nyeuh] (_Graves Cru Classé, Bordeaux_, France) Until recently, the whites here aged well, but lacked fresh appeal in their youth. Since 1991, however, they have greatly improved and the raspberryish reds are becoming some of the most reliable in the region. Red: 82 83 85 **86** 88 89 90 91 92 94 95 White: 88 89 90 92 93 94 95 ☆☆☆☆ **1992 Red £££**

☒ **Carcavelos** [kar-kah-veh-losh] (Portugal) _DO_ region producing usually disappointing fortified wines close to Lisbon. Vineyards are giving way to suburban sprawl.

☒ **Cantina dei Produttori Nebbiolo Carema** [proh-doo-tohr-ree nay-bee-yoh-loh kah-ray-mah] (_Piedmont_, Italy) Wonderful perfumed _Nebbiolo_ produced in limited quantities.

🍇 **Carignan** [kah-ree-nyon] Prolific red grape making usually dull, coarse wine for blending, but classier fare in _Corbières_ and _Fitou._ In Spain it is known as _Cariñena_ and Mazuelo, while Italians call it Carignano. ☆☆☆☆ **1994 La Tour Boisee ££;** ☆☆☆☆ **1993 Terre Brune £££**

☒ **Louis Carillon & Fils** [ka-ree-yon] (_Burgundy_, France) Great modern _Puligny_ estate. ☆☆☆☆ **1995 Puligny-Montrachet Perrières ££££**

Cariñena [kah-ree-nyeh-nah] (Spain) Important *DO* of Aragon for rustic reds, high in alcohol and, confusingly, made not from the *Cariñena* (or *Carignan)* grape, but mostly from the *Garnacha Tinta.* Also some whites. ☆☆☆☆ **1996 Bodegas San Valero Santero ££**

Cariñena [kah-ree-nyeh-nah] (Spain) The Spanish name for *Carignan.*

Viña Carmen [veen-yah kahr-men] (*Maipo,* Chile) Quietly developing a reputation as one of the best red wine producers in Chile. Seek out the Grand Vidure Carmenère. ☆☆☆☆ **1996 Merlot Reserve ££**

Carmenère [kahr-meh-nehr] (Chile) Smoky-spicily distinctive grape that although almost extinct in Bordeaux is still a permitted variety for *claret.* Widely planted in Chile where it is usually sold as *Merlot.* Look for examples like the Santa Inès Carmenère or Carmen Grand Vidure.

Carmenet Vineyard [kahr-men-nay] (*Sonoma Valley,* California) Excellent and unusual when tucked away in the hills and producing long-lived, very *Bordeaux*-like but approachable reds, *Chardonnay,* and also (even more unusually for California) good *Semillon-Sauvignon* and *Cabernet Franc.* ☆☆☆☆ **1993 Sangiacomo Carneros Chardonnay ££**

Les Carmes-Haut-Brion [lay kahrm oh bree-yon] (*Bordeaux,* France) Small property neighbouring *Ch. Haut-Brion* in Pessac-Léognan.

Carmignano [kahr-mee-nyah-noh] (*Tuscany,* Italy) Exciting alternative to *Chianti,* in the same style but with the addition of *Cabernet* grapes. See *Villa di Capezzana.* 82 85 88 90 91 93 94 95 97

Carneros [kahr-neh-ros] (California) Small, fog-cooled, high-quality region shared between the *Napa* and *Sonoma* Valleys. Producing top-class *Chardonnay* and *Pinot Noir.* Red: 84 **85** 86 87 **90 91** 92 93 95. White: **85 90 91** 92 95 *Acacia; Carneros Creek; Domaine Carneros; Domaine Chandon; Mondavi; Mumm Cuvée Napa; Saintsbury; Swanson.*

Dom. Carneros (*Napa Valley,* California) *Taittinger's* US fizz – produced in a perfect and thus ludicrously incongruous replica of their French HQ. The wine, however, is one of the best New World efforts by the Champenois. ☆☆☆☆**1990 Brut Blanc de Blancs ££££**

Carneros Creek (*Carneros,* California) Producer of ambitious but disappointing *Pinot Noir* under this name and the far better (and cheaper) berryish Fleur de Carneros.

Ch. Caronne-Ste-Gemme [ka-ron sant jem] (*Haut-Médoc Grand Bourgeois Exceptionnel, Bordeaux,* France) A reliable but not overly showy *Cru Bourgeois.* 81 **82** 83 85 86 88 **89** 90 92 93 94 95 96 ☆☆☆☆ **1990 £££**

Carpineto [Kah-pi-neh-toh] (*Tuscany,* Italy) High quality producer of *Chianti,* and *Chardonnay* and *Cabernet* that are sold under the Farnito label. ☆☆☆☆ **1994 Chianti Riserva ££**

Carr Taylor (Sussex, England) One of England's more business-like estates. ☆☆☆ **1994 Sparkling Wine.££**

Ch. Carras [kar-ras] (*Macedonia,* Greece) Until recently the only internationally visible Hellenic effort at modern winemaking. Disappointing when compared with *Hatzimichalis.*

Les Carruades de Lafite [kah-roo-ahd-dur la-feet] (*Pauillac, Bordeaux,* France) The *second label* of *Ch. Lafite.* Rarely (quite) as good as its counterpart *les Forts de Latour,* nor *Ch. Margaux's Pavillon Rouge.* ☆☆☆☆ **1995 ££**

Ch. Carsin [kahr-san] (*Entre-Deux-Mers, Bordeaux,* France) Finnish-owned, Aussie-style winery proving that this *appellation* is capable of producing wines of class and complexity. Australian-born Mandy Jones makes particularly tasty whites. 93 94 95 96 97 ☆☆☆ **1995 Cuvee Prestige Blanc ££**

Casa [kah-sah] (Italy, Spain, Portugal) Firm or company.

Casablanca [kas-sab-lan-ka] (*Aconcagua*, Chile) New region in *Aconcagua*; a magnet for quality conscious winemakers and producing especially impressive *Sauvignons, Chardonnays* and *Gewurztraminers*. ***Caliterra; Viña Casablanca; Concha y Toro; Santa Carolina; Santa Emiliana; Santa Rita; Veramonte; Villard.***

Viña Casablanca [veen-yah kas-sab-lan-ka] (*Casablanca*, Chile) Go-ahead winery in the region of the same name. A showcase for the talents of winemaker *Ignacio Recabarren*. ☆☆☆☆ **1997 Casablanca Valley White Label Sauvignon Blanc ££**

Caslot-Galbrun [kah-loh gal-bruhn] (*Loire*, France) Top-class producer of serious, long-lived red *Loires*.

Cassegrain [kas-grayn] (*New South Wales*, Australia) Tucked away in the Hastings Valley on the East Coast, but also drawing grapes from elsewhere. The wines can be variable, but are often impressive. ☆☆☆☆ **1994 Semillon Hastings Valley ££**

Cassis [ka-sees] (*Provence*, France) Tiny coastal *appellation* producing (unreliable) red, (often dull) white and (good) rosé. **Clos Ste. Magdeleine; la Ferme Blanche.**

Castelgiocondo [kas-tel-jee-yah-kon-doh] (*Tuscany*, Italy) High-quality *Brunello* estate owned by *Frescobaldi*.

Castell'in Villa [kas-tel-lin-veel-lah] (*Tuscany*, Italy) Producer of powerful *Chianti Classico Riserva* and a *Vino da Tavola* called Santa Croche.

Castellare [kas-tel-lah-ray] (*Tuscany*, Italy) Innovative small *Chianti Classico* estate whose *Sangiovese-Malvasia* blend, Nera I Sodi di San Niccoló, *Vino da Tavola*, is worth seeking out.

Castellblanch [kas-tel-blantch] (*Catalonia*, Spain) Producer of better-than-most *Cava* – provided that you catch it very young. ☆☆☆ **Cava Brut Zero ££**

Casteller [kas-teh-ler] (*Trentino-Alto-Adige*, Italy) Pale red, creamy-fruity wines for early drinking, made from *Schiava*. See *Ca'Vit*.

Cat's pee Describes the tangy smell frequently found in typical – and often delicious – *Müller-Thurgau* and *Sauvignon*.

Vignerons Catalans [veen-yehr-ron kah-tak-lon] (*Midi*, France) Dynamic cooperative with decent inexpensive wines.

Catalonia [kat-tal-loh-nee-yah] (Spain) The semi-autonomous region in which are found the *Penedés, Priorato, Conca de Barberá, Terra Alta* and *Costers del Segre*.

Catena Estate [kat-tay-nah] (Argentina) Quality-focused part of the giant Catena-Esmeralda concern, helped by the expertise of ex-*Simi* Californian winemaker Paul Hobbs. ☆☆☆☆ **1996 Chardonnay ££**

Cattier [Kat-ee-yay] (*Champagne*, France) Up-and-coming producer with good non-vintage wines.

Dom. Cauhapé [koh-ap-pay] (*South-West* France) Extraordinary *Jurançon* producer of excellent *Vendange Tardive* and dry wines from the *Manseng* grape. ☆☆☆☆ **1996 Jurançon Sec Chant des Vignes ££**

Cava [kah-vah] (*Catalonia*, Spain) Fizz produced in *Penedés* by the *Methode Champenoise*, but handicapped by innately dull local grapes and ageing, which deprives it of freshness. Avoid *vintage* versions and look instead for Anna de *Codorníu* and *Raimat* Cava – both made from *Chardonnay* – or such well-made exceptions to the earthy rule as *Juvé y Camps, Conde de Caralt, Cava Chandon* and *Segura Viudas*.

Cava (Greece) Legal term for wood and bottle-aged wine.

Cave [kahv] (France) Cellar.

♀ **Caymus Vineyards** [kay-muhs] (*Napa Valley*, California) Traditional producer of concentrated Italianate reds (including a forceful *Zinfandel*) and a characterful *Cabernet Franc*. Liberty School is the *second label*.
☆☆☆☆ **1994 Cabernet Sauvignon £££**

♀ **Dom. Cazes** [kahrs] (*Midi*, France) Maker of great *Muscat de Rivesaltes*, rich marmaladey stuff which makes most *Beaumes de Venise* seem very dull. ☆☆☆☆ **1996 Muscat de Rivesaltes ££**

♀ **Cellier le Brun** [sel-yay luh-bruhn] (*Marlborough*, New Zealand) Specialist producer of *Méthode Champenoise* sparkling wine under the expert supervision of Daniel Le Brun, an expatriate Frenchman.
☆☆☆☆ **Brut NV £££**

♣ **Cencibel** [sen-thee-bel] (*Valdepeñas*, Spain) An alternative name for *Tempranillo*.

Central Coast (California) Increasingly interesting, varied set of regions south of San Francisco, including *Santa Barbara, Monterey, Santa Cruz* and *San Luis Obispo*. Red: 84 85 86 87 **90 91** 92 93 94 95 96 White: **85 90 91** 92 95 96 97

Central Valley (California) Huge irrigated region controlled by winemaking giants who annually make nearly three-quarters of the state's wines without, so far, producing much to compete with the fruit of similar regions Down Under. Newly planted vineyards and a concentration on the most climatically advantaged parts of the region are beginning to pay off for grape varieties like the *Sauvignon Blanc* but I'd question the potential of the increasingly widely planted *Merlot* here. Better, smaller-scale winemaking would probably help too (this is wine-factory country). *Quady*'s fortified and sweet wines are still by far the best wines here. Red: **85** 86 87 **90 91** 92 93 95 96 97 White: **90 91** 92 95 96 97

Central Valley (Chile) The region in which most of *Chile*'s wines are made. It includes *Maipo, Rapel, Maule* and *Curico*, but not the new cool-climate region of *Casablanca*, which is in *Aconcagua*, further north.

Cépage [say-pahzh] (France) Grape variety.

♀ **Cepparello** [chep-par-rel-loh] (*Tuscany*, Italy) The brilliant pure *Sangiovese Vino da Tavola* made by Paolo de Marchi of *Isole e Olena*.
☆☆☆☆ **1994 £££**

♀ **Ceretto** [cher-ret-toh] (*Piedmont*, Italy) Big producer of mid-quality *Barolo*s and more impressive single-vineyard examples. ☆☆☆☆ **1993 Barolo Brunate ££££**

♀ **Ch. de Cérons** [say-roń] (*Bordeaux*, France) One of the best properties in *Cérons*. White: 83 86 **88** 89 90 ☆☆☆☆ **1990 Château de Cerons £££**

♀ **Ch. Certan de May** [sehr-toń dur may] (*Pomerol, Bordeaux*, France) Top-class *Pomerol* estate with subtly plummy wine. 70 75 78 **79 81 82** 83 85 86 87 88 89 90 94 95 96 ☆☆☆☆ **1990 ££££**

♀ **Ch. Certan-Giraud** [sehr-toń zhee-roh] (*Pomerol, Bordeaux*, France) *Pomerol* at its most overtly plummy. Good vintages last well. 75 78 79 82 **83** 85 86 87 88 89 90 93 94 95 96

♣ **César** [say-zahr] (*Burgundy*, France) The forgotten plummy-raspberryish red grape of *Burgundy*, still vinified near *Chablis* by Simonnet-Fèvre.

♀ **LA Cetto** [chet-toh] (*Baja California*, Mexico) With wines like LA Cetto's tasty *Cabernet* and spicy-soft *Petite Sirah*, it's hardly surprising that *Baja California* is now beginning to compete with a more northerly region across the US frontier. ☆☆☆ **1993 Nebbiolo ££**

Chablais [shab-lay] (*Vaud*, Switzerland) A good place to find *Pinot Noir* rosé and young *Chasselas* (sold as *Dorin*).

🍷 **Chablis** [shab-lee] (*Burgundy*, France) When not overpriced Chablis offers a steely European finesse that New World *Chardonnays* rarely capture. *Grands Crus* should show extra complexity. 85 **86** 88 89 **90** 92 94 95 96 97 *William Fèvre; Laroche; Raveneau; La Chablisienne; Durup; Louis Michel; J-M Brocard; René Dauvissat; Servin; Vocoret.*

🍷 **La Chablisienne** [shab-lees-yen] (*Burgundy*, France) Cooperative making wines from *Petit Chablis* to *Grands Crus* under a host of labels. Rivals the best estates in the *appellation*. ☆☆☆☆ 1996 Champagne £££
Chai [shay] (France) Cellar/winery.

🍷 **Chalk Hill** (*Sonoma*, California) Classy producer of rich *Chardonnay*, stylish *Sauvignon Blanc* and lovely berryish *Cabernet*. ☆☆☆☆ 1994 Cabernet Sauvignon £££

🍷 **Ch. Chalon** [shal-lon] (*Jura*, France) Speciality Jura AC for a *Vin Jaune* which should keep almost indefinitely. 1979 Arbois £££££

🍷 **Chalone** [shal-lohn] (*Monterey*, California) Under the same ownership as *Acacia*, *Edna Valley* and *Carmenet*, this 25-year old winery is one of the big names for *Pinot Noir* and *Chardonnay*. Unusually *Burgundian*, long-lived. ☆☆☆☆ 1994 Chardonnay £££

Chalonnais/Côte Chalonnaise [shal-lohn-nay] (*Burgundy*, France) Source of lesser-known, less complex *Burgundies* – *Givry*, *Montagny*, *Rully* and *Mercurey*. Potentially (rather than always actually) good-value. Red: 85 87 **88** 89 90 91 92 95 96 White: 85 **86** 87 **88** 89 **90 92** 95 96

🍷 **Chambers Rosewood** (*Rutherglen*, Australia) Competes with *Morris* for the crown of best *Liqueur Muscat* maker. The Rosewood is worth seeking out. ☆☆☆☆ Old Vine Muscadelle ££

🍷 **Ch. Chambert-Marbuzet** [shom-behr mahr-boo-zay] (*St. Estèphe Cru Bourgeois*, *Bordeaux*, France) Characterful *Cabernet*-based *St. Estèphe*. 70 76 78 79 81 82 83 85 86 87 88 89 90 91 92 93 94 95

🍷 **Chambertin** [shom-behr-tan] (*Burgundy*, France) Ultra-cherryish, damsony *Grand Cru* whose name was adopted by the village of Gevrey. Famous in the 14th century, and Napoleon's favourite. Chambertin Clos-de-Bèze, Charmes-Chambertin, Griottes-Chambertin, Latricières-Chambertin, Mazis-Chambertin and Ruchottes-Chambertin are neighbouring *Grands Crus*. 76 78 79 83 85 **87 88** 89 90 92 95 96 *Armand Rousseau; Bachelet; B Clair; Drouhin; Dujac; Faiveley; Denis Mortet; J Roty; A Burguet; Engel; Pierre Amiot; Bernard Meaume; B Dugat-Py.*

🍷 **Chambolle-Musigny** [shom-bol moo-see-nyee] (*Burgundy*, France) *Côte de Nuits* village whose wines are sometimes more like perfumed examples from the *Côte de Beaune*. Criticism of quality drove producers to tighten up the *appellation* tastings in 1993. Others may follow. *Georges Roumier* is the local star, and *Drouhin*, *Dujac* and *Ponsot* are all reliable, as are *Ghislaine Barthod, Mugnier, de Vogüe* and *Leroy*. Red: 76 78 79 **80** 82 83 **85** 86 87 **88 89 90** 92 95 96

🍷 **Champagne** [sham-payn] (France) Source of potentially the greatest sparkling wines, from *Pinot Noir*, *Pinot Meunier* and *Chardonnay* grapes. See individual listings. **81** 82 83 85 86 88 89 90 91 92

🍷 **Didier Champalou** [dee-dee-yay shom-pah-loo] (*Loire*, France) Young estate with serious sweet, dry and sparkling *Vouvray*. ☆☆☆☆ 1995 Vouvray Sec ££

Champigny [shom-pee-nyee] (*Loire*, France) See *Saumur*.

☲ **Ch. Champy** [shom-pee] (*Burgundy*, France) Long-established, recently much-improved *Beaune négociant*. ☆☆☆☆1993 Volnay Premier Cru Les Caillerets **££££**

☲ **Dom. Chandon** [doh-mayn shahn-dahn] (*Napa Valley*, California) *Moët & Chandon*'s Californian winery, until recently under-performing, has finally been allowed to compete with its counterpart at *Dom. Chandon* in Australia. Wines are sold in the UK as Shadow Creek. ☆☆☆☆ Napa County Reserve **£££**

☲ **Dom. Chandon** [doh-mihn shon-don] (*Yarra Valley*, Australia) Sold as *Green Point* in the UK. Winemaker Tony Jordan proved to its owners, *Moët & Chandon,* that Aussie grapes, grown in a variety of cool climates, compete with *Champagne*. Now joined by a creditable, *Chablis*-like, still Colonades *Chardonnay*. ☆☆☆☆ 1995 **£££**

☲ **Dom. Chandon de Briailles** [shon-don dur bree-iy] (*Burgundy*, France) Good *Savigny-lès-Beaune* estate whose owner is related to the *Chandon* of *Champagne*. ☆☆☆☆ 1994 Savigny-lès-Beaune **££££**

☲ **Chanson** [shon-son] (*Burgundy*, France) Improving *Beaune* merchant. Go for the *domaine* wines. ☆☆☆ 1996 Beaune Clos des Fèves **£££**

☲ **Ch. de Chantegrive** [shont-greev] (*Graves, Bordeaux*, France) Large modern *Graves* estate with excellent modern reds and whites. Red: 82 83 85 87 88 93 94 **95 96** White: 89 90 92 93 **94 95 96**

☲ **Chapel Down** (Kent, England) David Cowdroy's impressive winery-only operation uses grapes sourced from vineyards throughout southern England. ☆☆☆☆ 1997 Bacchus **£££**

☲ **Chapel Hill Winery** (*McLaren Vale*, Australia) Pam Dunsford's impressively rich – some say too rich – reds and whites have recently been joined by a similarly leaner, unoaked *Chardonnay*. ☆☆☆☆☆ 1996 Cabernet Sauvignon **£££**

☲ **Chapoutier** [shah-poo-tyay] (*Rhône*, France) Family-owned merchant rescued from its faded laurels by a new generation who are using more or less organic methods. Not all wines live up to their early promise but credit is deserved for the initiative of printing labels in braille. Watch out for Chapoutier's upcoming Australian venture too. ☆☆☆☆ 1995 Châteauneuf-du-Pape **££**

Chaptalisation [shap-tal-lih-zay-shuhn] The legal (in some regions) addition of sugar during fermentation to boost a wine's *alcohol* content.

🌢 **Charbono** [shar-boh-noh] (California) Obscure grape variety grown in California but thought to come from France. Makes interesting, very spicy, full-bodied reds at *Inglenook, Duxoup* and *Bonny Doon*.

🌢 **Chardonnay** [shar-don-nay] The great white grape of *Burgundy, Champagne* and now the New World. Capable of fresh simple charm in *Bulgaria* and buttery hazelnutty richness in *Meursault*. See producers.

Charmat [shar-mat] The inventor of the *Cuve Close* method of producing cheap sparkling wines. See *Cuve Close*.

☲ **Ch. des Charmes** [day sharm] (Canada) Good *Ontario* maker of *Chardonnay, Pinot* and *Icewine*. ☆☆☆☆ 1994 Paul Bosc Estate Icewine **££££**

Charta [kahr-tah] (*Rheingau*, Germany) *Rheingau* syndicate using an arch as a symbol to indicate dry (*Trocken*) styles designed to be suitable for drinking with food – although often apparently acidic enough to remove enamel from teeth. *Spätlese* and preferably *Auslese* versions are made from riper grapes. *Kabinetts* are for keen lemon-suckers.

☲ **Chartron & Trébuchet** [shar-tron ay tray-boo-shay] (*Burgundy*, France) Good small merchant specialising in white *Burgundies*.

☲ **Chassagne-Montrachet** [shah-san mon-rash-shay] (*Burgundy*, France) *Côte de Beaune commune* making grassy, *biscuity*, fresh yet rich whites and mid-weight often rustic-tasting wild fruit reds. Pricy but sometimes less so than neighbouring *Puligny* and as recommendable. White: 78 84 **85 86** 87 **88** 89 **90 92 93 94 95**. Red: 78 83 **85** 86 87 **88 89 90** 92 93 94 **95** *Michel Niellon; Marc Colin; Jean-Noël Gagnard; M Morey; Colin-Déleger; L. Carillon; Roux; Ramonet; J. Pillot.*

DOM. DE CHEVALIER

Ch. Chasse-Spleen [shas spleen] (*Moulis Cru Bourgeois, Bordeaux,* France) *Cru Bourgeois château* whose wines can, in good years, rival those of many a *Cru Classé*, but which have shone a little less brightly of late. 70 78 79 **81** 82 **83 85 86** 87 88 89 90 94 95 96 97 ☆☆☆☆ **1990 £££**

🍇**Chasselas** [shas-slah] Widely grown, prolific white grape making light often dull wine principally in Switzerland, eastern France and Germany. Good examples are rare. ☆☆☆☆ **1995 Vieilles Vignes, Reserve Pierre Sparr ££**

Dom. du Chasseloir [shas-slwah] (*Loire*, France) Makers of good *domaine Muscadets*. ☆☆☆☆ **1997 Cuvée de Ceps Centenaires ££**

Château [sha-toh] (*Bordeaux*, France) Literally means 'castle'. Some châteaux are extremely grand, many are merely farmhouses. A building is not required; the term applies to a vineyard or wine estate. Château names cannot be invented, but there are plenty of defunct titles that are used unashamedly by large cooperative wineries to market their members' wines.

Châteauneuf-du-Pape [shah-toh-nurf-doo-pap] (*Rhône*, France) Traditionally the best reds (rich and spicy) and whites (rich and floral) of the southern *Rhône*. Thirteen varieties can be used for the red, though purists still favour *Grenache*. 78 81 83 85 88 89 90 93 94 95 96 *Ch. de Beaucastel; Chapoutier; Font de Michelle; Guigal; Rayas; Clos des Papes; Clos des Mont-Olivet; Lucien & André Brunel; Les Bosquet des Papes; Dom. de Beaurenard; Pierre André; Henri Bonneau; Ch. La Nerthe; Vieux Télégraphe.*

Jean-Claude Chatelain [shat-lan] (*Loire*, France) Classy *Pouilly-Fumé* producer. ☆☆☆☆ **1995 Pouilly-Fumé £££**

Gérard Chave [sharv] (*Rhône*, France) The best estate in *Hermitage*. Wines demand patience. NB: labels read JL Chave; the eldest son in alternate generations is thus named, so it is thought unnecessary to print anything else in between times. ☆☆☆☆☆ **1994 Hermitage ££££**

Chavignol [sha-veen-yol] (*Loire*, France) Village within the *commune* of *Sancerre*.

Dom Gérard Chavy [shah-vee] (*Burgundy*, France) High-quality estate. ☆☆☆☆☆ **1995 Puligny-Montrachet les Folatières ££££**

Chénas [shay-nass] (*Burgundy*, France) Good but least-well-known of the *Beaujolais Crus*. Daniel Robin and *Duboeuf* are worthy examples.

Dom. du Chêne [doo-shehn] (*Rhône*, France) Small estate producing rich ripe *Condrieu* and top class *St. Joseph*, the best *cuvée* of which is sold as 'Anais'.

Chêne [shehn] (France) Oak, as in *Fûts de Chêne* (oak barrels).

🍇**Chenin Blanc** [shur-nan-blon for France, shen nin blonk for elsewhere] Honeyed white grape of the *Loire*. Wines vary from bone-dry to sweet and long-lived. High acidity makes it ideal for fizz, while sweet versions benefit from *noble rot*. French examples are often marred by green unripe flavours and heavy handedness with *sulphur dioxide*. Grown successfully in South Africa (where it is known as *Steen*) and, though less frequently, New Zealand and Australia. It is generally disappointing in California. See *Vouvray, Quarts de Chaumes, Bonnezeaux, Saumur.*

Ch. Cheval Blanc [shuh-vahl blon] (*St. Emilion Premier Grand Cru Classé, Bordeaux*, France) Supreme *St. Emilion* property, unusual in using more *Cabernet Franc* than *Merlot*. 75 76 78 79 80 **81 82 83 85 86** 87 88 89 90 92 93 94 95 96 ☆☆☆☆ **1995 ££££**

Dom. de Chevalier [shuh-val-yay] (*Graves Cru Classé, Bordeaux*, France) Great *Pessac-Léognan* estate which proves itself in difficult years for both red and white. Red: 70 78 79 **81 83** 85 86 87 88 89 90 92 93 94 95 96 White: 83 85 87 88 89 90 92 93 94 95 96 ☆☆☆☆☆ **1992 Blanc, Pessac-Léognan ££££**

Chevaliers de Tastevin [shuh-val-yay duh tast-van] (*Burgundy*, France) A *confrérie* based in *Clos de Vougeot*, famed for grand dinners and fancy robes. Wines approved at an annual tasting may carry a special 'tasteviné' label.

☰ **Cheverny** [shuh-vehr-nee] (*Loire*, France) Light floral whites from *Sauvignon* and *Chenin Blanc* and now, under the new 'Cour Cheverny' *appellation*, wines made from the limey local *Romarantin* grape. 83 85 86 88 89 90 94 95 96 ☆☆☆☆ **1996 Dom. des Huards ££**

☰ **Robert Chevillon** [roh-behr shuh-vee-yon] (*Burgundy*, France) Produces long-lived wines. ☆☆☆☆ **1992 Nuits-St.-Georges les Vaucrains £££**

☰ **Chianti** [kee-an-tee] (*Tuscany*, Italy) (*Classico/Putto/Rufina*) Sangiovese-dominant *DOCG*. Generally better than pre-1984, when it was customary to add wine from further south, and mandatory to put dull white grapes into the vat with the black ones. Wines labelled with the insignia of the *Classico*, *Putto* or the *Rufina* areas are supposed to be better. Trusting good producers, however, is a far safer bet. 79 **82 85 88 90 94** 95 96 97 *Antinori; Isole e Olena; Castell'in Villa; Castellare; Ruffino; Castello dei Rampolla; Castello di Volpaia; Frescobaldi; Selvapiana; Rocca di Castagnoli.*

☰ **Chiaretto di Bardolino** [kee-ahr-reh-toh dee bahr-doh-lee-noh] (*Lombardy*, Italy) Potentially refreshing, berryish, light reds and rosés from around Lake Garda. Rarely exported.

☰ **Michele Chiarlo** [Mee-Kay-Leh Kee-Ahr-Loh] (*Piedmont*, Italy) Increasingly impressive modern producer. ☆☆☆☆ **1993 Barolo ££££**

Chile Rising source of juicy blackcurranty *Cabernet* and (potentially even better) *Merlot, Semillon, Chardonnay* and *Sauvignon*. *Santa Rita; Casa-blanca; Concha y Toro; Errazuriz; Caliterra; Casa Lapostolle; Montes.*

☰ **Chiltern Valley Vineyards** (Oxfordshire, England) Excellent Oxfordshire estate with a growing reputation, especially for its *late harvest* wines. ☆☆☆ **1992 Old Luxters ££**

☰ **Chimney Rock** (*Stag's Leap District*, California) Producer of serious *Cabernet*. ☆☆☆☆ **1992 Reserve Stag's Leap District £££**

☰ **Chinon** [shee-non] (*Loire*, France) An *AC* within *Touraine* for (mostly) red wines from the *Cabernet Franc* grape. Excellent in ripe years; otherwise potentially thin and green. *Olga Raffault* makes one of the best, or try *Couly-Dutheil*. Red: 78 83 **85** 86 **88 89 90** 95 96

☰ **Chiroubles** [shee-roo-bl] (*Burgundy*, France) Fragrant and early-maturing *Beaujolais Cru*, best expressed by the likes of Bernard Méziat. 85 87 **88 89 90 91** 93 94 95 ☆☆☆☆ **1996 Dom. Emile Cheyson ££**

☰ **Chivite** [shee-vee-tay] (*Navarra*, Spain) Innovative producer whose reds and rosés easily outclass many of those from big name *Rioja bodegas*. ☆☆☆☆ **1994 Gran Feudo £££**

☰ **Chorey-lès-Beaune** [shaw-ray lay bohn] (*Burgundy*, France) Modest raspberry and damson reds once sold as *Côte de Beaune Villages*, and now appreciated in their own right. 85 87 **88 89 90** 92 93 94 95 96 *Tollot-Beaut; Ch. de Chorey* ☆☆☆☆ **1995 Tollot-Beaut £££**

☰ **Churchill** (*Douro*, Portugal) Small, dynamic young firm founded by Johnny Graham, whose family once owned a rather bigger *port* house. 82 85 91 92 96 ☆☆☆☆☆ **1992 Vintage ££££**

Chusclan [shoos-klon] (*Rhône*, France) Named village of *Côtes du Rhône* with maybe the best rosé of the area. ☆☆☆ **1997 Caves de Chusclan Roux ££**

Cinsaut/Cinsault [san-soh] Fruity-spicy red grape with high acidity, often blended with *Grenache*. One of 13 permitted varieties of *Châteauneuf-du-Pape*, and also in the blend of *Ch. Musar* in the *Lebanon*. Widely grown in South Africa and Australia.

Ch. Cissac [see-sak] (*Haut-Médoc Cru Bourgeois*, *Bordeaux*, France) Traditional *Cru Bourgeois*, close to *St. Estèphe*, making tough wines that last. Those who dislike *tannin* should stick to ripe vintages. **70 75 78** 81 **82** 83 85 86 88 89 90 **92 93 94** 95 96 ☆☆☆☆ **1990 £££**

Ch. Citran [see-tron] (*Haut-Médoc Cru Bourgeois*, *Bordeaux*, France) Improving – though still not dazzling – *Cru Bourgeois*, thanks to major investment by the Japanese. 82 85 86 87 88 **89 90** 91 92 93 **94 95 96**

Bruno Clair [klehr] (*Burgundy*, France) *Marsannay* estate with good *Fixin*, *Gevrey-Chambertin*, *Morey-St.-Denis* and *Savigny*. ☆☆☆☆ **1995 Gevrey-Chambertin Clos St. Jacques ££££**

Clairet [klehr-ray] (*Bordeaux*, France) The word from which we derived *claret* – originally a very pale-coloured red from *Bordeaux*. Seldom used.

Clairette [klehr-ret] (*Midi*, France) Dull white grape of southern France.

Clairette de Die [klehr-rheht duh dee] (*Rhône*, France) Unexciting sparkling wine normally, however, the Cuvée Tradition, made with *Muscat* is invariably far better; grapey and fresh – like a top-class French *Asti Spumante*. ☆☆☆ **Clairette de Die Tradition, Cave Diose ££**

Auguste Clape [klap] (*Rhône*, France) Probably the supreme master of *Cornas*. Great, intense, long-lived wines. ☆☆☆☆☆ **1995 Cornas ££££**

La Clape [la klap] (*Languedoc-Roussillon*, France) Little-known *cru* within the *Coteaux de Languedoc* with tasty *Carignan* reds and soft creamy whites.

Clare Valley [klehr] (South Australia) Well-established slatey soil region enjoying a renaissance with high-quality *Rieslings* that age well, and deep-flavoured *Shiraz*, *Cabernet* and *Malbec*. ***Petaluma; Penfolds; Mitchells; Leasingham; Tim Adams; Tim Knappstein; Pikes; Lindemans.***

Clarendon Hills (*Blewitt Springs*, South Australia) Fairly young, very self-confident estate which has scored highly with US critics who like the intensity of ripe flavour of the wines here. Like some Australian observers, I'm impressed but not *that* impressed. ☆☆☆☆☆ **1996 Merlot ££££**

Claret [klar-ret] English term for red *Bordeaux*.

Clarete [klah-reh-Tay] (Spain) Term for light red – frowned on by the EU.

Classed Growth (France) Literal translation of *Cru Classé*, commonly used when referring to the status of *Bordeaux châteaux*.

Classico [kla-sih-koh] (Italy) A defined area within a *DOC* identifying what are supposed to be the best vineyards, e.g. *Chianti* Classico, *Valpolicella* Classico.

Henri Clerc et fils [Klehr] (*Burgundy*, France) Top class white *Burgundy* estate. ☆☆☆☆ **1992 Puligny-Montrachet Folatières ££££**

Ch. Clerc-Milon [klehr mee-lon] (*Pauillac 5ème Cru Classé*, *Bordeaux*, France) Juicy member of the *Mouton-Rothschild* stable. **78** 81 **82** 83 85 **86** 87 88 89 90 92 93 94 95 ☆☆☆☆ **1993 £££**

Domenico Clerico [doh-meh-nee-koh Klay-ree-koh] (*Piedmont*, Italy) Makes great *Barolo* and *Dolcetto* and Arte, a *Nebbiolo, Barbera* blend. ☆☆☆☆ **1993 Barolo Pajana £££**

Climat [klee-mah] (*Burgundy*, France) An individual named vineyard.

Ⅹ Ch. Climens [klee-mons] (*Barsac Premier Cru Classé, Bordeaux*, France) Gorgeous, quite delicate *Barsac* which easily outlasts many heftier *Sauternes*. 71 75 76 78 79 **80** 81 82 **83 85 86** 88 89 90 95 96 97 ☆☆☆☆☆ **1990 £££**

Ⅹ Ch. Clinet [klee-nay] (*Pomerol, Bordeaux*, France) Starry property with lovely, complex, intense wines. 82 83 85 **86** 87 88 89 90 91 92 93 95 96

Clone [klohn] Specific strain of a given grape variety. For example, more than 300 clones of *Pinot Noir* have been identified.

Clos [kloh] (France) Literally, a walled vineyard.

Ⅹ Clos de la Roche [kloh duh lah rosh] (*Burgundy*, France) One of the most reliable *Côte d'Or Grands Crus*. ☆☆☆☆ **1993 Ponsot ££££**

Ⅹ Clos de Mesnil [kloh duh may-neel] (*Champagne*, France) *Krug's* single vineyard *Champagne* made entirely from *Chardonnay* grown in the Clos de Mesnil vineyard. ☆☆☆☆☆ **1985 ££££**

Ⅹ Clos de Tart [kloh duh tahr] (*Burgundy*, France) *Grand Cru* vineyard in *Morey-St.-Denis*, exclusive to Mommessin. Others might make the wine better, but it does age well. ☆☆☆☆ **1990 ££££**

Ⅹ Clos de Vougeot [kloh duh voo-joh] (*Burgundy*, France) *Grand Cru* vineyard, once a single monastic estate but now divided among more than 70 owners, some of whom are decidedly uncommitted to quality. **Dom. Rion; Joseph Drouhin; Jean Gros; Leroy; Méo Camuzet; Faiveley; Arnoux; Confuron.**

Ⅹ Ch. Clos des Jacobins [kloh day zha-koh-Ban] (*St. Emilion Grand Cru Classé, Bordeaux*, France) Generally rich and ripe, if not always the most complex of wines. 75 78 79 81 **82 83** 85 86 87 88 89 90 92 93 **95 96** 97

Ⅹ Clos des Mont-Olivet [kloh day mon-to-lee-vay] (*Rhône*, France) *Châteauneuf-du-Pape* estate with a rare mastery of white wine. The top red is called 'Cuvée du Papet'.

Ⅹ Clos des Papes [kloh day pap] (*Rhône*, France) Producer of serious *Châteauneuf-du-Pape* which – in top vintages – rewards a few years cel-laring.

Ⅹ Clos du Bois [kloh doo bwah] (*Sonoma Valley*, California) Top-flight producer whose 'Calcaire' *Chardonnay* and Marlstone *Cabernet Merlot* are particularly fine. ☆☆☆☆ **1996 Calcaire Chardonnay £££**

Ⅹ Clos du Ciel [kloh doo see-yel] (*Stellenbosch*, South Africa) Inspiring *Chardonnay* from South African wine critic John Platter.

Ⅹ Clos du Clocher [kloh doo klosh-shay] (*Pomerol, Bordeaux*, France) Reliably rich plummy wine. 93 **94** 95 96 ☆☆☆☆ **1995 £££**

Ⅹ Clos du Marquis [kloh doo mahr-kee] (*St. Julien, Bordeaux*, France) The *second label* of *Léoville-Las-Cases*. 93 94 95 96

Ⅹ Clos du Roi [kloh doo rwah] (*Burgundy*, France) *Beaune Premier Cru* that is also part of *Corton Grand Cru*.

Ⅹ Clos du Val [kloh doo vahl] (*Napa Valley*, California) Bernard Portet, brother of Dominique who runs *Taltarni* in Australia, makes generally good, if sometimes disappointing *Stag's Leap* reds – including *Cabernet* and *Merlot*. They develop with time. ☆☆☆☆ **1994 Merlot £££**

Ⅹ Clos l'Eglise [klos lay-gleez] (*Pomerol, Bordeaux*, France) Attractive spicy wines from a consistent small *Pomerol* Estate. 75 81 83 85 86 88 89 90 92 93 94 95 96

Ⅹ Clos Floridène [kloh floh-ree-dehn] (*Graves, Bordeaux*, France) Classy, oaked, white *Graves* made by superstar *Denis Dubourdieu*. 90 92 93 **94** 95 96 ☆☆☆☆ **1995 £££**

Ⅹ Clos Fourtet [kloh foor-tay] (*St. Emilion Premier Grand Cru, Bordeaux*, France) Traditional *St. Emilion* for those who don't like too much fruit. **82** 83 85 86 88 89 90 92 93 95 96 ☆☆☆ **1995 £££**

Ⅹ Clos René [kloh ruh-nay] (*Pomerol, Bordeaux*, France) Estate making increasingly concentrated though approachable wines. **82 83** 85 86 87 88 89 90 91 92 93 94 95 96

☨ **Clos St.-Landelin** [kloh San lon-duhr-lan] (*Alsace*, France) Long-lived wines; the sister label to *Muré*.

☨ **Ch. La Clotte** [lah klot] (*St. Emilion Grand Cru Classé, Bordeaux*, France) Variable; potentially very good. 82 **83** 85 86 88 89 90 92 93 94 **95** 96

☨ **Cloudy Bay** (*Marlborough*, New Zealand) Under the same French ownership as *Cape Mentelle,* this cult winery has a waiting list for every vintage of its *Sauvignon* (despite an uncharacteristically disappointing 1997). The *Chardonnay* is reliably impressive, as are the rare *late harvest* wines. The *Pelorus* fizz, made by an American winemaker, is – thankfully – less of a buttery mouthful than it used to be.

☨ **Clusel-Roch** [kloo-se rosh] (*Rhône*, France) Good, traditional *Côte Rôtie* and *Condrieu* producer. ✰✰✰✰ **1995 Côte Rôtie Les Grandes Places £££**
   Cave Co-operative (France) Cooperative winery.

☨ **JF Coche-Dury** [kosh doo-ree] (*Burgundy*, France) A superstar *Meursault* producer whose basic reds and whites outclass his neighbours' supposedly finer fare. ✰✰✰✰✰ **1995 Meursault £££**

☨ **Cockburn-Smithes** [koh burn] (*Douro*, Portugal) Unexceptional Special Reserve but producer of great *vintage* and superlative *tawny port*. 55 60 **63** 67 **70** 75 83 **85** 91 94 ✰✰✰✰ **10 Year Old Tawny £££**

☨ **Codorníu** [kod-dor-nyoo] (*Catalonia*, Spain) Humungous fizz maker whose Anna de Codorníu is a good *Chardonnay*-based *Cava*. The Californian effort tastes, well, *Cava*-ish, despite using *Champagne* varieties. ✰✰✰ **1996 Vintage ££**

Colchagua Valley [kohl-shah-gwah] (*Central Valley*, Chile) Up-and-coming sub-region. **Los Vascos; Lapostolle; Undurraga.**

☨ **Coldstream Hills** (*Yarra Valley*, Australia) Founded by lawyer-turned winemaker and wine writer *James Halliday* and recently bought by *Penfolds*, this is the source of stunning *Pinot Noir,* great *Chardonnay* and increasingly impressive *Cabernets* and *Merlots*. Proof that critics can make as well as break a wine! ✰✰✰✰ **1997 Reserve Pinot Noir £££**
   Colheita [kol-yay-tah] (Portugal) Harvest or vintage – particularly used to describe *tawny port* of a specific year.

☨ **Marc Colin** [mahrk koh-lan] (*Burgundy*, France) Family estate with a small chunk of *Le Montrachet*. ✰✰✰✰ **1995 Chassagne-Montrachet £££**

☨ **Michel Colin-Deleger** [koh-lah day-day-jay] (*Burgundy*, France) Up-and-coming *Chassagne-Montrachet* estate. ✰✰✰✰ **1995 Chassagne-Montrachet les Chénevottes ££££**

☨ **Collards** [kol-lards] (*Auckland*, New Zealand) Small producer of lovely pineappley *Chardonnay* and appley *Chenin Blanc*.

☨ **Collegiata** [koh-lay-jee jah-tah] (*Toro,* Spain) Rich red wine from the *Tempranillo* produced in a little known region.
   Colle/colli [kol-lay/kol-lee] (Italy) Hill/hills.

☨ **Colli Berici** [kol-lee bay-ree-chee] (*Veneto*, Italy) Red and white *DOC*.

☨ **Colli Orientali del Friuli** [kol-lee oh-ree yehn-tah-lee del free-yoo-lee] (*Friuli-Venezia Giulia*, Italy) Lively single-variety whites and reds from near the *Slovenian* border. Subtle, honeyed and very pricy *Picolit*, too.

☨ **Collio** [kol-lee-yoh] (*Friuli-Venezia Giulia*, Italy) High-altitude region with a basketful of white varieties, plus those of *Bordeaux* and red *Burgundy*. Refreshing and often unshowy.

☨ **Collioure** [kol-yoor] (*Midi*, France) Intense *Rhône*-style red from *Languedoc-Roussillon*, often marked by the *Mourvèdre* in the blend. ✰✰✰✰ **1995 Clos de Paulilles ££**

❦ **Colombard** [kol-om-bahrd] White grape grown in *South-West* France for making into Armagnac and good, light, modern whites by *Yves Grassa* and *Plaimont*. Also planted in Australia (*Primo Estate* and *Best's*) and the US, where it is known as French Colombard.

❦ **Jean-Luc Colombo** [kol-lom-boh] (*Rhône*, France) Oenologist guru to an impressive number of *Rhône* estates – and producer of his own good, modern *Côtes du Rhône* and *Cornas*. People who feel new oak has no home in the *Rhône* may prefer to buy elsewhere; I like these wines.
☆☆☆☆ 1995 Cornas Les Ruchets £££

❦ **Columbia Crest** (*Washington State*, US) *Second label* of *Ch. Ste. Michelle*. ☆☆☆ 1994 Columbia Crest Valley Estate Merlot £££

❦ **Columbia Winery** (*Washington State*, US) Producer of good *Chablis*–style *Chardonnay* and *Graves*-like *Semillon*; subtle single-vineyard *Cabernet*, especially good *Merlot*, *Syrah* and Burgundian *Pinot Noir*. ☆☆☆☆ 1991 Red Willow Vineyard £££

Commandaria [com-man-dah-ree-yah] (Cyprus) Traditional dessert wine with rich raisiny fruit.

Commune [kom-moon] (France) Small demarcated plot of land named after its principal town or village. Equivalent to an English parish.

Conca de Barberá [kon-kah deh bahr-beh-rah] (*Catalonia*, Spain) Cool region where *Torres's* impressive but pricy *Milmanda* is produced, as is *Hugh Ryman's* rather cheaper Santara. ☆☆☆☆ 1995 Santara Chabonell Cabernet Sauvignon ££; ☆☆☆☆ 1995 Torres Milmanda Chardonnay £££

❦ **Viña Concha y Toro** [veen-yah kon-chah ee tohr-roh] (*Maipo*, Chile) Steadily improving, thanks to the efforts of winemaker *Ignacio Recabarren* and investment in *Casablanca*. Best wines are sold under Don Melchior, Marques de Casa Concha, Trio and Casillero del Diablo labels.
☆☆☆☆☆ 1997 Trio Merlot ££

❦ **Conde de Caralt** [kon-day day kah-ralt] (*Catalonia*, Spain) One of the best names in *Cava*. Catch it young.

❦ **Conde de Valdemar** [kon-day day val-day-mahr] (*Rioja*, Spain) Label used by the excellent *Martinez Bujanda*. ☆☆☆ 1995 Rioja Crianza £££

❦ **Condrieu** [kon-dree-yuhh] (*Rhône*, France) One of the places where actor Gerard Dépardieu owns vines. Fabulous, pricy, pure *Viognier*: a cross between dry white wine and perfume. Far better than the hyped and high-priced *Ch. Grillet* next door. 82 85 87 **88 89 90** 91 94 95 96 *Georges Vernay; Etienne Guigal; Yves Cuilleron; Patrick & Christophe Bonneford; Antoine Montez; Robert Niero; Alain Parent & Gerard Dépardieu; Phillipe & Christophe Pichon; Hervé Richard; Francois Villand; Gerard Villano.* ☆☆☆☆ 1996 les Ceps du Nebadon, Perret £££

Confréries [kon-fray-ree] (France) Promotional brotherhoods of those with some link to a particular wine or a specific area. Many, however, are nowadays more about pomp and pageantry, kudos and backslapping, than active promotion.

❦ **Jean-Jacques Confuron** [con-foor-ron] (*Burgundy*, France) Go-ahead producer with good *Nuits-St.-Georges*, *Vosne-Romanée* and *Clos Vougeot*. ☆☆☆☆☆ 1995 Romanée St. Vivant ££££

❦ **Conn Creek** (*Napa Valley*, California) Maker of attractively fruity *Cabernet* blends and rich *Chardonnay*. ☆☆☆☆ 1990 Cabernet Sauvignon £££

❦ **Cono Sur** [kon-noh soor] (Chile) *Concha y Toro* subsidiary with a range of varietals including a classy *Pinot Noir* from *Casablanca*. Returning to form after the arrival of a new winemaker (in 1998). ☆☆☆ 1996 Casablanca Reserve Pinot Noir ££

❦ **Ch. la Conseillante** [lah kon-say-yont] (*Pomerol*, *Bordeaux*, France) Brilliant property with lovely, complex, perfumed wines. 70 75 76 79 **81 82** 83 84 **85** 86 87 88 89 90 91 93 94 95 96

Consejo Regulador [kon-say-hoh ray-goo-lah-dohr] (Spain) Administrative body responsible for *DO* laws.

Consorzio [kon-sohr-zee-yoh] (Italy) Producers' syndicate, often with its own seal of quality.

Constantia [kon-stan-tee-yah] (South Africa) The first New World wine region. Until recently, the big name was *Groot Constantia*. Now *Klein Constantia, Buitenverwachting* and *Steenberg* explain the enduring reputation. Red: **82 84 86 87 89 91 92** 93 94 95 White: **87 91** 92 93 94 95 96

☰ **Aldo Conterno** [al-doh kon-tehr-noh] (*Piedmont*, Italy) Truly top-class *Barolo* estate with similarly top-class *Barbera*. Nobody does it better.
☆☆☆☆☆ **1990 Barolo Bricco Bussia Soprana £££££**

☰ **Conterno Fantino** [kon-tehr-noh fan-tee-noh] (*Piedmont*, Italy) The other worthwhile Conterno. ☆☆☆☆ **1994 Barolo Sori Ginestra £££**

☰ **Viñedos del Contino** [veen-yay-dos del con-tee-no] (*Rioja,* Spain) *CVNE*-owned *Rioja* Alavesa estate whose wines can have more fruit and structure than most. ☆☆☆☆ **1989 Rioja Reserva ££**

Coonawarra [koon-nah-wah-rah] (South Australia) Internationally acknowledged top-class mini-region, stuck in the middle of nowhere, with cool(ish) climate and terra rossa soil. Great blackcurranty-minty *Cabernet*, underrated *Shiraz*, big *Chardonnays* and full-bodied *Riesling*. *Petaluma; Penfolds; Wynns; Rouge Homme; Parker Estate; Lindemans; Katnook.*

☰ **Coopers Creek** (*Auckland*, New Zealand) Good individualistic whites including a *Chenin-Semillon* blend, *Chardonnay, Sauvignon* and *Riesling*.

☰ **Copertino** [kop-per-tee-noh] (*Apulia*, Italy) Fascinating berryish wine made from the *Negroamaro*. ☆☆☆☆ **1994 Riserva Cantina Sociale ££**

☰ **Corbans** (*Henderson*, New Zealand) Big winery (encompassing *Cooks*). Good rich *Merlot* reds (even, occasionally, from *Marlborough*). ☆☆☆☆ **1997 Marlborough Sauvignon Blanc ££**

☰ **Corbières** [kawr-byayr] (*Languedoc-Roussillon*, France) Region where a growing number of small estates are now making tasty red wines, despite the shortcomings of the *Carignan*. *Ch. Lastours; Mont Tauch.*

☰ **Cordon Negro** [kawr-don nay-groh] (*Catalonia*, Spain) Brand name for *Freixenet's* successful *Cava*. The recognisable matt black bottle and generous marketing must account for sales. This is not a fizz I voluntarily drink.

☰ **Coriole** [koh-ree-ohl] (*McLaren Vale*, Australia) *Shiraz* specialist that has diversified into *Sangiovese*. The *Semillons* and *Rieslings* are pretty good too. ☆☆☆☆ **1994 Lloyd Shiraz ££**

☰ **Corison** [kaw-ree-son] (*Napa*, California) Winery specialising in juicy Cabernet. ☆☆☆☆ **1994 Cabernet Sauvignon Napa Valley £££**

Corked Unpleasant, musty smell and flavour, caused by fungus attacking the cork. Almost always gets worse on contact with oxygen.

☰ **Cornas** [kawr-nas] (*Rhône*, France) Smoky spicy *Syrah; tannic* when young but worth keeping. 76 78 82 83 85 88 89 90 91 95 96 *Clape; Tain Cooperative; Juge; de Barjac; Colombo; Thierry Allemand; Durvieu Serette; Jacques Lemercier; Robert Michel; Noël Verset; Alain Voge.*

Corsica (France) Mediterranean island making robust reds, whites and rosés under a raft of *appellations* (doled out to assuage rebellious islanders). *Vins de Pays* (*de l'Ile de Beauté*) are often more interesting. ☆☆☆ **1995 Dom. du Mont St. Jean Oak Aged Chardonnay ££**

☧ **Dom. Corsin** [kawr-san] (*Burgundy*, France) Reliable *Pouilly-Fuissé* and *St. Véran* estate. ☆☆☆ **1995 St. Véran ££**

❧ **Cortese** [kawr-tay-seh] (*Piedmont*, Italy) Herby grape used in *Piedmont* and to make *Gavi*. Drink young.

☧ **Corton** [kawr-ton] (*Burgundy*, France) *Grand Cru* hill potentially making great, intense, long-lived reds and – as *Corton-Charlemagne* – whites. The supposed uniformly great vineyards seem to run a suspiciously long way round the hill. Reds can be very difficult to taste young; many never develop. White: **78 85 87 88** 89 **90 92** 95 96 Red: **78** 83 **85** 86 87 **88 89 90 92** 95 96 *Bonneau du Martray; Chandon de Briailles; Dubreuil-Fontaine; Nudant; Faiveley; Laleur-Piot; Maillard; Tollot-Beaut.*

☧ **Corvo** [kawr-voh] (*Sicily*, Italy) Ubiquitous producer of pleasant reds and whites. ☆☆☆ **1994 Corvo, Duca di Salaparuta ££**

☧ **Ch. Cos d'Estournel** [koss-des-tawr-nel] (*St. Estèphe 2ème Cru Classé Bordeaux*, France) In *St. Estèphe*, but making wines with *Pauillac* richness and fruit, this is top-class *Bordeaux*. Spice is the hallmark. **61 70 75 76 78** 79 **82 83 85** 86 88 **89** 90 91 92 93 94 95 96 97

☧ **Ch. Cos Labory** [koss la-baw-ree] (*St. Estèphe 5ème Cru Classé, Bordeaux*, France) Good traditional, if tough, wines. 89 90 92 93 95 96
Cosecha [coh-seh-chah] (Spain) Harvest or *vintage*.

☧ **Cosentino** (*Napa*, California) Producer of serious long-lived reds. ☆☆☆☆ **1995 Napa Reserve Merlot ££££**

☧ **Cossart Gordon** (*Madeira*, Portugal) High-quality brand used by the Madeira Wine Co. ☆☆☆☆☆ **5 year Old Sercial £££**

Costers del Segre [kos-tehrs del say-greh] (*Catalonia*, Spain) *DO* created for *Raimat,* which unlike their competitors elsewhere in Spain, is allowed to irrigate its vineyards. ☆☆☆ **1989 Raimat Abadia Reserva ££**

☧ **Costières de Nîmes** [kos-tee-yehr duh neem] (*Midi*, France) An up-and-coming region which can make reds to match the northern *Rhône*. ☆☆☆☆ **1995 Mas de Bressades ££**

☧ **Costières du Gard** [kos-tee-yehr doo gahr] (*South-West*, France) Fruity reds, rarer whites and rosés.

❧ **Cot** [koh] (France) The grape of *Cahors* and the *Loire* (aka *Malbec*).

☧ **Paul Cotat** [koh-tah] (*Loire*, France) The *Sauvignon's* relative lack of popularity in the US has made superstar *Sancerre* producers there something of a rarity. But Cotat's wines repay ageing and deserve their success. ☆☆☆☆☆ **1995 La Grande Côte £££**

Côte d'Or [koht dor] (*Burgundy*, France) Geographical designation for the finest slopes, encompassing the *Côte de Nuits* and *Côte de Beaune*.

☧ **Côte de Beaune (Villages)** [koht duh bohn] (*Burgundy*, France) The southern half of the *Côte d'Or*. With the suffix '*Villages*', indicates red wines from one or more of the specified *communes*. Confusingly, wine labelled simply '*Côte de Beaune*' comes from a small area around *Beaune* itself and often tastes like wines of that *appellation*. White: **82 85 86** 87 **88** 89 **90 92** 95 **96** Red: **78** 83 **85 88 89 90 91** 92 95 96

☧ **Côte de Brouilly** [koht duh broo-yee] (*Burgundy*, France) *Beaujolais Cru*: distinct from *Brouilly* – often finer. Floral and ripely fruity; will keep for a few years. 88 89 **90 91** 94 95 96 97 Bernillon; Ch. Thivin.

Côte de Nuits (Villages) [koht duh nwee] (*Burgundy*, France)
Northern, and principally 'red' end of the *Côte d'Or*. The suffix '*Villages*'
indicates wine from one or more specified *communes*. 78 **80** 82 83 **85** 86
87 **88 89 90** 92 93 94 95 96

Côte des Blancs [koht day blon] (*Champagne*, France) Principal
Chardonnay-growing area.

Côte Rôtie [koh troh tee] (*Rhône*, France) Powerful, smoky yet refined
Syrah (possibly with a touch of white *Viognier*) from the northern
Rhône, divided into two principal hillsides, the 'Brune' and 'Blonde'.
Most need at least six years. 76 78 80 **82** 83 **85** 86 **88** 89 90 91 95 96
Barge; Burgaud; Champet; Clusel-Roch; Gallet; *Gasse;* Gentaz-
Dervieuz; Gerin; *Guigal; Jamet; Jasmin; Ogier; Rostaing;* Saugère;
L. de Vallouit.

Côte(s), Coteaux [koht] (France) Hillsides.

Coteaux Champenois [koh-toh shom-puh-nwah] (*Champagne*,
France) Madly over-priced, mostly thin, light and acidic, still wine of
the area. *Laurent Perrier's* is better than most, but it's still only worth
buying in the ripest vintages. 82 83 85 86 88 89 90 91 92 ☆☆☆
Laurent Perrier £££

Coteaux d'Aix-en-Provence [koh-toh dayks on prov vons] (*Provence*,
France) A recent *AC* region producing light floral whites, fruity reds and
dry rosés using *Bordeaux* and *Rhône* varieties. ☆☆☆ 1992 Château
Pigoudet Rouge Grand Reserve ££

Coteaux d'Ancenis [koh-toh don-suh-nee] (*Loire*, France) So far,
only *VDQS* status for this region near Nantes, producing light reds
and deep pinks from the *Cabernet Franc* and *Gamay*, and also
Muscadet-style whites.

Coteaux d'Ardèche [koh-toh dahr-desh] (*Rhône*, France) Light
country wines, mainly from the *Syrah* and *Chardonnay*. A popular place
with Burgundians who need to produce affordable alternatives to their
own region's white wine.

Coteaux de l'Aubance [koh-toh duh loh bons] (*Loire*, France) Light
wines (often semi-sweet) grown on the banks of a *Loire* tributary. Quite
rare outside the region. White: 83 **85 86 88** 89 90 94 95 96

Coteaux des Baux-en-Provence [koh-toh day boh on pro-vonss]
(*Provence*, France) Inexpensive fruity reds, whites and rosés, plus the cult
Dom. de Trévallon, which impressively demonstrates what can be done
round here. ☆☆☆☆ 1994 Chapelle de Romanin ££

Coteaux du Languedoc [koh-toh doo long-dok] (*Midi*, France) A big
appellation, and a popular source of fast-improving rich reds from *Rhône*
and southern grapes. 91 93 94 95 ☆☆☆☆ 1994 Domaine de L'Hortus,
Grande Cuvée ££

Ⅎ **Coteaux du Layon** [koh-toh doo lay-yon] (*Loire*, France) Whites from the *Chenin Blanc* grape that are slow to develop and long lived. Lots of lean dry wine but the sweet *Bonnezeaux* and *Quarts de Chaume* are superior. The wines of *Moulin Touchais* and Clos Ste. Catherine are worth seeking out, as are Pierre Bise, *Ch. du Breuil* and Dom. des Sablonettes. Sweet White: **76** 83 **85** 86 **88 89** 90 **94 95** 96

Ⅎ **Coteaux du Loir** [koh-toh doo lwahr] (*Loire*, France) Clean vigorous whites from a *Loire* tributary. 83 **85** 86 **88 89 90** 94 95 96 97

Ⅎ **Coteaux du Lyonnais** [koh-toh doo lee-ohn-nay] (*Rhône*, France) Just to the south of *Beaujolais*, making some very acceptable good value wines from the same grapes. **Descottes**; *Duboeuf*; Fayolle.

Ⅎ **Coteaux du Tricastin** [koh-toh doo tris-kass-tan] (*Rhône*, France) Southern *Rhône appellation*, emerging as a source of good value, soft, peppery/blackcurranty reds. **85 88** 89 **90 92 94 95 96** 97

Ⅎ **Côtes de Bourg** [koht duh boor] (*Bordeaux*, France) Clay-soil region just across the water from the *Médoc* and an increasingly reliable source of good value, if somewhat fast-maturing, *Merlot*-dominated plummy reds. Whites are much less impressive. Red: 83 85 86 **88 89** 90 94 95 96

Ⅎ **Côtes de Buzet** [koht duh boo-zay] (*Bordeaux*, France) *AC* region adjoining *Bordeaux*, producing light *clarety* reds, and duller whites from *Sauvignon*. **Les Vignerons de Buzet.**

Ⅎ **Côtes de Castillon** [koht duh kass-tee-yon] (*Bordeaux*, France) Region where the *Merlot* is often a lot more lovingly handled than in nearby *St. Emilion*. **Ch. d'Aiguilhe; de Belcier; Côte Montpezat; Lapeyronie; Poupille.**

Ⅎ **Côtes de Duras** [koht duh doo-rahs] (*Bordeaux*, France) Inexpensive whites from the *Sauvignon*, often better value than basic *Bordeaux* Blanc (but that's not saying much).

Ⅎ **Côtes de Francs** [koht duh fron] (*Bordeaux*, France) Up-and-coming region close to *St. Emilion* where pioneering producers such as *Ch. de Francs* and *Puygeraud* are making increasingly good reds.

Ⅎ **Côtes de Montravel** [koht duh mon-Rah-vel] (*South-West*, France) Source of dry and sweet whites and reds which are comparable to neighbouring *Bergerac*.

Ⅎ **Côtes de/Premières Côtes de Blaye** [koht duh/pruh-myerh koht duh blih] (*Bordeaux*, France) A ferry-ride across the river from *St. Julien*, the limestone soils found here make for good *Merlot*. Sadly, so far, poor winemaking has prevented many estates from living up to this potential. 82 85 86 **88 89** 90 94 95 96 **Ch. Bertinerie; les Jonqueyres; des Tourtes.**

☧ **Côtes de Provence** [koht dur prov-vonss] (*Provence*, France)
Improving, good value, fruity whites and ripe spicy reds. However the
rosés, for which the region is best known, are often carelessly made and
stored, before being served to holidaymakers who rarely notice the so-
called pink wine is a deep shade of bronze and decidedly unrefreshing. A
region, incidentally, with as much appeal to organic winemakers as to fans
of Mr Mayle's rural tales. ☆☆☆☆ **1993 Dom Rabiega Clos d'Ière ££**

☧ **Côtes de Quenelle** [koht duh kuhr-nel] (*South-West*, France) Suzanne
Brochet's efforts here still show a distinctly Chilean influence but they
are much more approachable and confident than they used to be.

☧ **Côtes de St. Mont** [koht duh san-mon] (*South-West*, France) Large
VDQS area encompassing the whole of the Armagnac region. *Plaimont* is
the largest and best-known producer.

☧ **Côtes du Frontonnais** [koht doo fron-ton-nay] (*South-West*, France)
Up-and-coming inexpensive red (and some rosé); fruitily characterful.

☧ **Côtes du Marmandais** [koht doo mahr-mon-day] (South-West
France) Uses the *Bordeaux* red grapes plus *Gamay*, *Syrah* and others to
make pleasant, fruity, inexpensive wines. ☆☆☆ **1995 Les Vignerons de
Beaupuy £**

☧ **Côtes du Rhône (Villages)** [koht doo rohn] (*Rhône*, France) Spicy
reds produced mostly in the southern part of the *Rhône* Valley. The best
supposedly come from a set of better *Villages* (and are sold as *CdR
Villages*), though some single *domaine* 'simple' *Côtes du Rhônes* outclass
many *Villages* wines. *Grenache* is the key red wine grape, though
recent years have seen a growing use of the *Syrah*. Whites which can
include new-wave *Viogniers* are improving. Red: 85 88 89 90 93 94 95
96 Dom. de Cabasse; *Grand Moulas*; *Guigal*; Richaud; la Soumade;
Ste. Anne.

☧ **Côtes du Roussillon (Villages)** [koht doo roo-see-yon] (*Midi*, France)
Up-and-coming for red, white and rosé, but not always worthy of its *AC*.
Côtes du Roussillon Villages is better. **Gauby; de Jau; *Vignerons Catalans*.**

☧ **Côtes du Ventoux** [koht doo von-too] (*Rhône*, France) Improving
everyday country reds that are similar to *Côtes du Rhône*. 85 88 89 90 94
95 96 *Jaboulet Aîné*; la Vieille Ferme

☧ **Côtes du Vivarais** [koht doo vee-vah-ray] (*Provence*, France) Light
southern *Rhône*-like reds, fruity rosé and fragrant light whites.

Cotesti [kot tesh-tee] (Romania) Easterly vineyards growing varieties such
as *Pinots Noir*, *Blanc*, *Gris* and *Merlot*.

☧ **Cotnari** [kot nah-ree] (Romania) Traditional and now very rare white
dessert wine. Has potential.

Bodegas el Coto [el kot-toh] (*Rioja*, Spain) Small estate producing good medium-bodied El Coto and Coto de Imaz reds. ☆☆☆☆☆ 1987 Rioja Coto de Imaz Gran Réserva £££

Cottin Frères [cot-tah] (*Burgundy*, France) A new name that has been adopted by the Cottin Brothers who run the dynamic *Nuits-St.-Georges* négoçiant firm of *Labouré Roi*. Fairly priced wines. ☆☆☆☆ 1996 Chassagne-Montrachet £££

Ch. Coufran [koo-fron] (*Haut-Médoc Cru Bourgeois*, *Bordeaux*, France) Maker of soft, often rather dull, wine. **82** 83 85 **86** 88 **89** 90 94 95 96

Coulée de Serrant [koo-lay duh seh-ron] (*Loire*, France) Great dry *Chenin* from a top property in *Savennières* run by *Nicolas Joly*, a leading champion of 'biodynamique' winemaking. The Becherelle vineyard is great too. ☆☆☆☆ 1996 ££££

Paul Coulon et Fils [Koo-lon] (*Rhône*, France) Serious *Rhône* producer. ☆☆☆☆ 1995 Dom. de Beaurenard, Boisrenard Châteauneuf-du-Pape ££££

Coulure [koo-loor] Climate-related wine disorder which causes reduced yields (and possibly higher quality) as grapes shrivel and fall off the vine.

Couly-Dutheil [koo-lee doo-tay] (*Loire*, France) High-quality *Chinon* estate using single vineyards from land just behind the *château* in which Henry II imprisoned his wife, Eleanor of Aquitaine. ☆☆☆☆ 1992 Clos de L'Echo £££

Viña Cousiño Macul [koo-sin-yoh mah-kool] (*Maipo*, Chile) The most traditional producer in Chile. Reds are more successful than whites. ☆☆☆ 1995 Finis Terrae ££

Ch. Coutet [koo-tay] (*Barsac Premier Cru Classé*, *Bordeaux*, France) Delicate neighbour to *Ch. Climens*, often making comparable wines: Cuvée Madame is top flight. **71 75** 76 **81** 82 **83** 85 **86** 87 **88 89** 90 95 97

Ch. Couvent-des-Jacobins [koo-von day zhah-koh-ban] (*St. Emilion Grand Cru Classé*, *Bordeaux*, France) Producer of juicy plummy-spicy wines. **82** 83 85 86 88 89 90 **92 93** 94 95 96 ☆☆☆ 1993 £££

Cowra [kow-rah] (*New South Wales*, Australia) Up-and-coming region, making a name for itself with *Chardonnay*, for which it will one day eclipse its better known but less viticulturally ideal neighbour, the *Hunter Valley*.

Dom. de Coyeux [duh cwah-yuh] (*Rhône*, France) One of the best producers of *Côtes du Rhône* and *Muscat de Beaumes de Venise*.

Cranswick Estate (*South-East*, Australia) Successful *Riverina* producer making reliable inexpensive wines, widely available under the Barramundi label. ☆☆☆☆ 1997 Nine Pines Cabernet Sauvignon ££

Quinta do Crasto [kin-tah doh cras-toh] (*Douro*, Portugal) An up-and-coming small *port* producer with lovely red table wines made by Australian-born *David Baverstock*, who is also responsible for *Esperão* and *Quinta de la Rosa*. ☆☆☆☆☆ 1997 Douro Red ££

Cream Sherry (*Jerez*, Spain) Popular style (though not in Spain) produced by sweetening an *oloroso*. A visitor to *Harvey's* apparently preferred one of the company's *sherries* to the then popular 'Bristol Milk'. 'If that's the milk', she joked, 'this must be the Cream'.

Crémant [kray-mon] (France) Term used in *Champagne*, denoting a slightly sparkling style due to a lower pressure of gas in the bottle. Elsewhere, a term to indicate sparkling wine, e.g. Crémant de *Bourgogne*, de *Loire* and d'*Alsace*.

Créme de Cassis [kraym duh kas-seess] (*Burgundy*, France) Fortified fruit essence perfected in *Burgundy* using blackcurrants from around Dijon. Commonly drunk mixed with sharp local *Aligoté* as *Kir*, or sparkling wine, as *Kir* Royale. Crème de Mûre (blackberries), Framboise (raspberries), Fraise (strawberries) and Pèche (peaches) are also delicious.

Crépy [kray-pee] (*Savoie*, France) Crisp floral white from *Savoie*.

Criado y Embotellado (por) [kree-yah-doh ee em-bot-tay-yah-doh] (Spain) Grown and bottled (by).

Crianza [kree-yan-thah] (Spain) Literally keeping 'con Crianza' means aged in wood – often preferable to the *Reservas* and *Gran Reservas,* which are highly prized by Britons but can taste dull and dried-out.

♀ **Crichton Hall** [krih-ton] (*Rutherford*, California) Small winery specialising in top class *Chardonnay.* ☆☆☆☆ 1995 Chardonnay £££

Crisp Fresh, with good *acidity.*

♀ **Ch. le Crock** [lur krok] (*St. Estèphe Cru Bourgeois, Bordeaux,* France) Traditional property which like *Léoville-Poyferré,* its stablemate, has shown great recent improvement. 82 83 85 86 88 **89** 90 92 93 95 96

♀ **Croft** (Spain/Portugal) *Port* and *sherry* producer making highly commercial but rarely memorable wines. The *vintage port* is back on form. 55 60 **63** 66 67 **70** 75 77 82 85 94 ☆☆☆☆ 1990 LBV £££

♀ **Ch. La Croix** [la crwah] (*Pomerol, Bordeaux,* France) Producer of long-lasting traditional wines. 75 76 79 81 82 83 **85** 86 88 89 90 92 93 94 95 96 ☆☆☆☆ 1992 ££££

♀ **Ch. la Croix-de-Gay** [la crwah duh gay] (*Pomerol, Bordeaux,* France) Classy estate whose complex wines have good, blackcurranty-plummy fruit. 81 **82 83** 85 86 **88** 89 90 91 **92** 93 94 95 96

♀ **Ch. Croizet-Bages** [krwah-zay bahzh] (*Pauillac 5ème Cru Classé, Bordeaux,* France) Underperformer showing some signs of improvement. **82** 83 85 86 87 88 **90** 92 93 94 95 96

♀ **Croser** [kroh-sur] (*Adelaide Hills,* Australia) Made by *Brian Croser* of *Petaluma* in the Piccadilly Valley, this is one of the New World's most *Champagne*-like fizzes. Has become less lean as the proportion of *Pinot Noir* has increased. ☆☆☆☆ 1993 Brut £££

🍇 **Crouchen** [kroo-shen] (France) Obscure white grape known as Clare Riesling in Australia and Paarl Riesling in South Africa.

♀ **Crozes-Hermitage** [krohz ehr-mee-tahzh] (*Rhône,* France) Up-and-coming *appellation* on the hills behind supposedly greater *Hermitage.* Smoky blackberryish reds are pure *Syrah.* Whites (made from *Marsanne* and *Roussanne*) are creamy but less impressive. And they rarely keep. Red: **76** 78 82 83 85 **88** 89 90 91 95 White: **88 89 90** 91 94 95 *Alain Graillot; Dom Combier; Paul Jaboulet Aîné;* Dom. du Pavilion-Mercure.

Cru Bourgeois [kroo boor-zhwah] (*Bordeaux,* France) Wines beneath the *Crus Classés,* satisfying certain requirements, which can be good value for money and, in certain cases, better than more prestigious *classed growths.*

Cru Classé [kroo klas-say] (*Bordeaux,* France) The best wines of the *Médoc* are crus classés, split into five categories from first (top) to fifth growth (or *Cru*) for the Great Exhibition in 1855. The *Graves, St. Emilion* and *Sauternes* have their own classifications.

Cru Grand Bourgeois/Exceptionnel [kroo gron boor-jwah/ek-sep-see-yoh-nel] (*Bordeaux,* France) An estate-bottled *Haut-Médoc Cru Bourgeois,* which is supposedly aged in oak barrels. Term is the same as Cru Bourgeois *Supérieur,* though *Exceptionnel* is a now defunct term for wines from the area encompassing the *Crus Classés.*

♀ **Weingut Hans Crusius** (*hans skroos-yuhs*) (*Nahe,* Germany) Family-run estate prized for the quality of its highly traditional wines. Some of the best, ripest *Trocken* wines around.

Crusted Port (*Douro,* Portugal) An affordable alternative to *vintage port* – a blend of different years, bottled young and allowed to throw a deposit. *Churchill's; Graham's; Dow's.*

♀ **Yves Cuilleron** [Kwee-yehr-ron] (*Rhône,* France) Rising young star with individual vineyards in *Condrieu* and *St. Joseph.* ☆☆☆☆☆ 1995 St. Joseph les Serines ££££

♀ **Cullen** (*Margaret River,* Australia) Brilliant pioneering estate showing off the sensitive winemaking skills of Vanya Cullen. Source of stunning *Sauvignon-Semillon* blends, *claret*-like reds, a highly individual *Pinot Noir* and a Burgundian-style *Chardonnay.* ☆☆☆☆☆ 1996 Cabernet-Merlot ££

Cultivar [kul-tee-vahr] (South Africa) South African for grape variety.

🍷 **Ch. Curé-Bon-la-Madelaine** [koo-ray bon lah mad-layn] (*St. Emilion Grand Cru Classé, Bordeaux*, France) Very small *St. Emilion* estate next to *Ausone*. 75 78 81 **82** 83 85 86 88 89 90 94 95 96

Curico [koo-ree-koh] (Chile) Region in which *Torres, San Pedro* and *Caliterra* have vineyards. Being eclipsed by *Casablanca* as a source for cool-climate whites, but still one of Chile's best wine areas for red and white. ***Caliterra*; Echeverria; la Fortuna; *Montes; Torres; Valdivieso.***

🍷 **Cuvaison Winery** [koo-vay-san] (*Napa Valley*, California) Swiss-owned winery with high-quality *Carneros Chardonnay*, increasingly approachable *Merlot* and now good *Pinot Noir.* Calistoga Vineyards is a *second label*.

Cuve close [koov klohs] The third-best way of making sparkling wine, in which the wine undergoes secondary fermentation in a tank and is then bottled. Also called the *Charmat* or *Tank method*.

Cuvée (de Prestige) [koo-vay] Most frequently a blend put together in a process called *assemblage*. *Prestige Cuvées* are (particularly in *Champagne*) supposed to be the cream of a producer's production.

🍷 **Cuvée Napa** (*Napa*, California) The Californian venture by *Mumm Champagne*, and still offering better quality and value for money than the mother-ship back in France.

🍷 **CVNE** [koo-nay] (*Rioja*, Spain) Compania Vinicola del Norte de Espana, a large high-quality operation, run by the owners of *Contino*, producing the excellent Viña Real in *Crianza, Reserva, Imperial* or *Gran Reserva* in the best years, and a light CVNE *Tinto*. Some recent releases have been slightly less dazzling. ☆☆☆☆ **1994 Monopole Rioja Blanco ££**

Cyprus Shifting its focus away from making ersatz *'sherry'*. Even so, the best wine is still the fortified *Commandaria*.

Czech Republic A region to watch for is *St. Laurents*. The best wines are *Pinot Blanc* and the local *Irsay Oliver*. Try also the funky sparkling reds.

D

🍷 **Didier Dagueneau** [dee-dee-yay dag-guhn-noh] (*Loire*, France) The iconoclastic producer of some of the best, steeliest *Pouilly-Fumé*, and even the occasional *late harvest* effort that upsets the authorities. Look out for the 'Pur Sang' and 'Silex' bottlings.

🍷 **Ch. Dalem** [dah-lem] (*Fronsac, Bordeaux*, France) Maker of rich full-bodied *Fronsac*. 82 83 **85** 86 88 89 90 91 92 93 94 95 96

🍷 **Dalwhinnie** [dal-win-nee] (*Pyrenees, Victoria*, Australia) Quietly classy producer close to *Taltarni*. Reds made to last. ☆☆☆☆ **1996 Shiraz £££**

🍷 **Dão** [downg] (Portugal) Once Portugal's best-known region – despite the traditional dullness of its wines. Thanks to pioneering producers like *Sogrape* and *Aliança* both reds and whites are improving. Red: **80 85 88 90 91 93** 94 95 96 ☆☆☆☆ **1996 Quinta dos Roques ££**

🍷 **Ch. Dassault** [das-soh] (*St. Emilion Grand Cru Classé, Bordeaux*, France) Good juicy *St. Emilion*. 82 83 **85** 86 88 89 **90** 92 93 94 95

🍷 **Kurt Darting** [koort dahr-ting] (*Pfalz*, Germany) New-wave producer who cares more about ripe flavour than making the tooth-scouringly dry wine favoured by some of his neighbours. ☆☆☆☆ **1996 Ungsteiner Bettelhaus Riesling Kabinett ££££**

✗ **Ch. de la Dauphine** [duh lah doh-feen] (*Fronsac*, *Bordeaux*, France) Proof that *Fronsac* deserved its reputation in the days when it was better-regarded than *St. Emilion*. 85 86 87 88 89 90 92 93 94 95

✗ **Domaine d'Auvenay** [Dohv-nay] (*Burgundy*, France) Estate belonging to Lalou Bize Leroy, former co-owner of the *Dom. de la Romanée-Conti,* and now also at *Dom. Leroy*. Great, long-lived, hard-to-obtain examples of *Auxey-Duresses, Meursault, Puligny-Montrachet* and *Grands Crus* of the *Côtes de Nuits*.

✗ **Réné and Vincent Dauvissat** [doh-vee-sah] (*Burgundy*, France) One of the best estates in *Chablis*. Watch out for other Dauvissats – the name is also one of several used by the *La Chablisienne* cooperative. ☆☆☆☆ 1996 Chablis les Clos **££**

✗ **Ch. Dauzac** [doh-zak] (*Margaux 5ème Cru Classé, Bordeaux*, France) Rejuvenated, following its purchase in 1993 by André Lurton of *Ch. la Louvière*. That year's wine was unusually successful for the vintage. 82 83 85 86 **88 89 90** 93 94 95 96

✗ **Dealul Mare** [day-al-ool mah-ray] (Romania) Carpathian region once known for whites, now producing surprisingly good *Pinot Noir.* ☆☆☆ 1996 Idlerock Merlot Reserve **£**

✗ **Etienne & Daniel Defaix** [duh-fay] (*Burgundy*, France) Classy traditional *Chablis* producer, making long-lived wines with a steely bite. ☆☆☆☆ 1996 Chablis 'Vieilles Vignes' **££**
  Dégorgée (dégorgement) [day-gor-jay] The removal of the deposit of inert yeasts from *Champagne* after maturation.

✗ **Dehlinger** (*Sonoma*, California) *Russian River Pinot Noir* and *Chardonnay* specialist that is proving highly successful with *Syrah.*

Deidesheim [di-dess-hime] (*Pfalz*, Germany) Distinguished wine town noted for flavoursome *Rieslings*. QbA/Kab/Spät: **85 86 88 89 90** 91 92 93 94 95 96 97 Aus/Beeren/Tba: **83 85** 88 89 90 91 92 93 94 95 96 97

✗ **Deinhard** [dine-hard] (*Mosel*, Germany) See *Wegeler Deinhard.*

✗ **Marcel Deiss** [dise] (*Alsace*, France) A tiny property producing some of the best wine in the region, including some unusually good *Pinot Noir*. ☆☆☆☆☆ 1995 Riesling Burg de Bergheim **££££**

✗ **Delaforce** [del-lah-forss] (*Douro*, Portugal) Small *port* house with lightish but good *vintage* and *tawny*. 55 58 60 **63 66** 70 74 75 77 85 94 ☆☆☆ His Eminence's Choice **£££**

✗ **Delas Frères** [del-las] (*Rhône*, France) *Négociant* with great *Hermitage* vineyards and now promising much since its purchase by *Louis Roederer*. ☆☆☆ 1994 Hermitage Les Bessards **£££**

✗ **Delatite** [del-la-tite] (*Victoria*, Australia) Producer of lean-structured, long-lived wines. ☆☆☆☆ 1995 Limited Release Chardonnay **££**

✗ **Delegats** [del-leg-gats] (*Auckland*, New Zealand) Family firm which has hit its stride recently with impressively (for New Zealand) ripe reds, especially plummy *Merlots*. The *second label* is 'Oyster Bay'. ☆☆☆☆ 1996 Reserve Hawke's Bay Chardonnay **£££**

✗ **Philippe Delesvaux** [Dels-voh] (*Loire*, France) Quality-conscious *Coteaux de Layon* estate with some good red too.

✗ **Delheim Wines** [del-hihm] (*Stellenbosch*, South Africa) A commercial estate with lean, quite traditional reds and white.
  Demi-sec [duh-mee sek] (France) Medium-dry.

✗ **Demoiselle** [duh-mwah-zel] (*Champagne*, France). A new *Champagne* name to watch with attractive, light, creamy wines.

✗ **Denbies Wine Estate** [den-bees] (Surrey, England) Part tourist attraction, part winery, the largest wine estate England has so far produced. Sweet wines can be good, but a clear sense of winemaking direction is needed here.

✗ **Peter Dennis** (*McLaren Vale*, Australia) Reliable producer with rich ripe whites and notable *Merlot*. ☆☆☆☆ 1996 Chardonnay **££**

Deutsches Weinsiegel [doyt-shur vihn-see-gel] (Germany) Seals of various colours – usually neck labels – awarded for merit to German wines. Treat with circumspection.

Deutscher Tafelwein [doyt-shur tah-fuhl-vihn] (Germany) Table wine, guaranteed German as opposed to Germanic-style EC *Tafelwein*. Can be good value – and often no worse than *Qualitätswein*, the supposedly 'quality' wine designation that includes every bottle of *Liebfraumilch*.

⟂ Deutz [duhtz] (*Champagne*, France, and also Spain, New Zealand, California) Reliable small but dynamic producer at home and abroad, now owned by *Roederer*. The *Montana Marlborough* Cuvée from New Zealand was created with the assistance of Deutz, as was the *Yalumba 'D'* in Australia. 1990 Cuvée William Deutz ££££

⟂ Maison Deutz [may-zon duhtz] (*Arroyo Grande*, California) A 150-acre cool-climate vineyard joint venture between Nestlé and *Deutz* with, unusually, a bit of *Pinot Blanc* in the – generally – excellent blend.

⟂ Devaux [duh-voh] (*Champagne*, France) Small producer with a knack of producing fairly-priced wine and unusually good rosé.
☆☆☆☆ Champagne Rosé Brut £££

Diabetiker Wein [dee-ah-beh-ti-ker vihn] (Germany) Very dry wine with most of the sugar fermented out (as in a Diat lager); suitable for diabetics.

⟂ Diamond Creek (*Napa Valley*, California) Big Name producer with a set of very good vineyards (Gravelly Meadow, Red Rock Terrace and Volcanic Hill) that produce toughly intense red wines which demand, but do not always repay, patience. ☆☆☆☆ 1994 Volcanic Hill Cabernet ££££

⟂ Dieu Donné Vineyards [dyur don-nay] (*Franschhoek*, South Africa) Variable producer of quality varietals in the *Franschhoek* valley. The 1992 *Chardonnay* was legendary.

⟂ Dom. Disznókó [diss-noh-koh] (*Tokaji*, Hungary) Newly-constituted estate belonging to AXA and run by Jean-Michel Cazes of *Ch. Lynch-Bages*. Top-class modern sweet *Tokaji* and dry lemony *Furmint*. ☆☆☆☆ 1995 Tokaji Dry Furmint £££; ☆☆☆☆☆ 1993 Tokaji Aszu 6 Puttonyos £££

DLG (Deutsche Landwirtschaft Gesellschaft) (Germany) Body awarding medals for excellence to German wines – far too generously.

DO Denominac/ion/ão de Origen (Spain, Portugal) Demarcated quality area, guaranteeing origin, grape varieties and production standards (everything, in other words except the quality of the stuff in the bottle).

DOC Denominacion de Origen Califacada (Spain) Ludicrously, and confusingly, Spain's newly launched higher quality equivalent to Italy's *DOCG* shares the same initials as Italy's lower quality *DOC* wines. So far, restricted to *Rioja* – good, bad and indifferent. In other words, this official designation should be treated – like Italy's *DOCs* and *DOCGs* and France's *Appellation Contrôlée* – with something less than total respect.

DOC(G) Denominazione di Origine Controllata (e Garantita) (Italy) Quality control designation based on grape variety and/or origin. 'Garantita' is supposed to imply a higher quality level, in much the same way that Italy's politicians and businessmen are supposed to be incorruptible. It is worth noting, that while the generally dull wines of *Albana di Romagna* received the first white DOCG (ahead of all sorts of more worthy candidates) the new efforts to bring *Vini da Tavola* into the system left such internationally applauded wines as *Tignanello* out in the cold among the most basic *DOCs*.

⟂ Ch. Doisy-Daëne [dwah-zee di-yen] (*Barsac 2ème Cru Classé*, *Bordeaux*, France) Fine *Barsac* property whose wines are typically more restrained than many a *Sauternes*. The top wine is L'Extravagance. 76 78 79 81 82 83 85 86 **88 89** 90 91 94 95 96 97

⟂ Ch. Doisy-Dubroca [dwah-zee doo-brohkah] (*Barsac 2ème Cru Classé*, *Bordeaux*, France) Underrated estate producing ultra-rich wines at often attractively low prices. **75** 76 78 79 **81 83** 85 86 87 88 89 90 95 96 97

Ch. Doisy-Védrines [dwah-zee vay-dreen] (*Barsac 2ème Cru Classé*, *Bordeaux*, France) Reliable *Barsac* property which made a stunningly concentrated 1989 (and a less impressive 1990). 70 **75 76** 78 79 81 **82 83** 85 86 **88** 89 90 92 93 95 96 97

Dolcetto (d'Alba, di Ovada) [dohl-cheh-toh] (*Piedmont*, Italy) Grape producing anything from soft everyday red to very robust and long-lasting examples. Generally worth catching quite young though. *Bava; Vajra.*

> **Dôle** [Dohl] (Switzerland) *Appellation* of *Valais* producing attractive reds from the *Pinot Noir* and/or *Gamay* grapes. Best bought by people who have plenty of Swiss currency and who like light wines to knock back after a day on the piste.

Dom Pérignon [dom peh-reen-yon] (*Champagne*, France) *Moët et Chandon's Prestige Cuvée*, named after the cellarmaster who is erroneously said to have invented the *Champagne* method. Impeccable white and (very rare) rosé. (Moët will disgorge older vintages to order. Write and ask.) ☆☆☆☆☆ **1990 ££££**

Domaine (Dom.) [doh-mayn] (France) Wine estate.

Domecq [doh-mek] (*Jerez/Rioja*, Spain) Producer of La Ina *fino* and the rare, wonderful 511A *amontillado*.

Ch. la Dominique [lah doh-mee-neek] (*St. Emilion Grand Cru Classé*, *Bordeaux*, France) High-flying property; one of the finest in *St. Emilion*. 70 **71** 78 79 81 **82 83 86** 88 89 90 93 94 95 96

Dominus [dahm-ih-nuhs] (*Napa Valley*, California) *Christian Moueix* of *Ch. Petrus's* modestly named competitor to *Opus One* has now developed an accessibility that was lacking in early years. Even so, it is concentrated stuff that is built to last. ☆☆☆☆☆ **1994 Napa Valley Napanook Vineyard ££££**

Doonkuna [doon-koo-nah] (*New South Wales*, Australia) Small winery making decent red wine close to the capital. ☆☆☆☆ **1992 Shiraz ££**

Dopff 'Au Moulin' [dop-foh-moo-lan] (*Alsace*, France) Underrated *négociant* with concentrated *Grand Cru* wines.

Dopff & Irion [dop-fay-ee-ree-yon] (*Alsace*, France) Improving, but not to be confused with Dopff 'Au Moulin', its more recommendable namesake. ☆☆☆ **1994 Riesling Les Sorcières ££**

Dorin [doh-ran] (*Vaud*, Switzerland) The Swiss name for *Chasselas* in the *Vaud* region.

Dornfelder [dorn-fel-duh] (Germany) Juicy berryish grape.

Dosage [doh-sazh] The addition of sweetening syrup to naturally dry *Champagne* after *dégorgement* to replace the wine lost with the yeast, and to set the sugar to the desired level (even *Brut Champagne* requires up to 4 grammes per litre of sugar to make it palatable).

> **Douro** [doo-roh] (Portugal) The *port* region and river, producing increasingly good table wines thanks partly to the efforts of *Sogrape*, and Australians *David Baverstock* (at *Quinta de la Rosa* and *Crasto*) and *Peter Bright*. *Barca Velha; Sogrape.*

Doux [doo] (France) Sweet.

Dow's [dows] (*Douro*, Portugal) One of the big two (with *Taylor's*) and under the same family ownership as *Warre's*, *Smith Woodhouse* and *Graham's*. Great *vintage port* and similarly impressive *tawny*. The *single-quinta* Quinta do Bomfim wines offer a chance to taste the Dow's style affordably. 55 60 **63 66 70** 72 75 77 85 91 94 ☆☆☆☆ **20 Year Old Tawny ££**

Drappier [drap-pee-yay] (*Champagne*, France) Small, recommendable producer. ☆☆☆☆☆ **Champagne Carte d'Or Brut £££**

Jean-Paul Droin [drwan] (*Burgundy*, France) Good small *Chablis* producer with approachable 'modern' wines. ☆☆☆☆ **1996 Chablis Montée de Tonnerre £££**

🍷 **Dromana Estate** [droh-mah-nah] (*Mornington Peninsula*, Australia) Viticulturalist Gary Crittenden makes good *Chardonnay* and raspberryish *Pinot Noir*, which might benefit from less of the expertise he unashamedly uses to achieve high yields per vine. ☆☆☆☆ **1996 Chardonnay £££**

🍷 **Dom. Drouhin** [droo-an] (*Oregon*, US) Top *Burgundy* producer's highly expensive investment in the US that's increasingly producing world-beating reds – thanks to Veronique Drouhin's skill and commitment and some of *Oregon's* best vineyards. ☆☆☆☆ **1995 Pinot Noir ££££**

🍷 **Joseph Drouhin** [droo-an] (*Burgundy*, France) Probably *Burgundy's* best *négoçiant*, with first class red and white wines that are unusually representative of their particular *appellations*. Also look out for the rare white *Beaune* from its own Clos des Mouches, top-class *Clos de Vougeot* and unusually (for a *négoçiant*) high-quality *Chablis*. The Marquis de Laguiche *Montrachet* is sublime. ☆☆☆☆☆ **1995 Chambertin Clos de Bèze ££££**

🍷 **Pierre-Jacques Druet** [droo-ay] (*Loire*, France) Most reliable *Bourgueil* producer making characterful individual *cuvées*. ☆☆☆☆ **1995 Vaumoreau £££**

Dry Creek (*Sonoma*, California) A rare example of a Californian *AVA* region whose wines have an identifiable quality and style. Look out for *Sauvignon Blanc* and *Zinfandel*. Red: 84 **85** 86 87 **90 91** 92 93 95 96 White: **85 90 91** 92 95 96. ***Dry Creek; Duxoup; Quivira; Nalle; Rafanelli.***

🍷 **Dry Creek Vineyard** (*Sonoma*, California) Eponymous vineyard within the *Dry Creek AVA* making well-known *Fumé Blanc*, great *Chenin Blanc* and impressive reds. ☆☆☆☆ **1995 Zinfandel £££**

🍷 **Dry River** (*Martinborough*, New Zealand) Small estate with a particularly impressive *Pinot Gris*. ☆☆☆ **1997 Sauvignon Blanc £££**

🍷 **Duboeuf** [doo-burf] (*Burgundy*, France) The 'King of *Beaujolais*', who introduced the world to the boiled sweet flavour of young *Gamay* when most versions tasted like *Châteauneuf-du-Pape*. A range of good examples from individual growers, vineyards and villages. Reliable *nouveau*, good straightforward *Mâconnais* white, single domaine *Rhônes* and now the world's biggest plantation of *Viognier*. ☆☆☆☆ **1997 Morgon ££**

Denis Dubordieu [doo-bor-dyuh] *Bordeaux* white wine guru.

🍷 **Dubreuil-Fontaine** [doo-broy fon-tayn] (*Burgundy*, France) Quite traditional estate, producing full-flavoured red and white wines from the *Corton* hillsides. ☆☆☆☆☆ **1995 Corton-Charlemagne ££££**

🍷 **Duckhorn** (*Napa Valley*, California) Vaunted producer now moving away from the intentionally impenetrable style of his highly priced *Merlot*. This may dismay collectors and wine snobs but I'll open a bottle to celebrate. ☆☆☆☆ **1995 Napa Valley Merlot £££**

🍷 **Ch. Ducru-Beaucaillou** [doo-kroo boh-ki-yoo] (*St.Julien 2ème Cru Classé*, *Bordeaux*, France) '*Super Second*' with a less obvious style than peers such as *Léoville-Las-Cases* and *Pichon-Lalande*. Especially back on form in 1996 and 1997 after a disappointing patch in the late 1980s. Second wine is Croix-Beaucaillou. **70 75** 76 **78** 79 80 **81** 82 **83 85** 86 87 88 89 90 91 92 93 94 95 96 97

🍷 **Dom. Bernard Dugat-Py** [doo-gah pee] (*Burgundy*, France) Superstar *Gevrey-Chambertin* estate with great *Grand Cru* vineyards. ☆☆☆☆☆ **1995 Charmes-Chambertin ££££**

🍷 **Ch. Duhart-Milon-Rothschild** [doo-ahr mee-lon rot-sheeld] (*Pauillac 4ème Cru Classé*, *Bordeaux*, France) Under the same management as *Lafite* and benefiting from heavy investment. 78 79 80 81 **82** 83 **85** 86 87 88 89 90 91 92 93 95 96

🍷 **Dom. Dujac** [doo-zhak] (*Burgundy*, France) Cult *Burgundy* producer with fine, long-lived, if sometimes rather light-coloured, wines from *Morey-St.-Denis*, (including a particularly good *Clos de la Roche*) that are packed with intense *Pinot Noir* flavour. Now helped by Gary Farr of the excellent *Bannockburn* in Australia and busily investing time and effort into vineyards in southern France. ☆☆☆☆ **1995 Bonnes Mares ££££**

Dumb As in dumb nose, meaning without smell.

♟ **Dunn Vineyards** (*Napa Valley*, California) Tough, forbidding *Cabernets* from *Howell Mountain* for the very, very patient collectors. ☆☆☆☆ **1994 Cabernet Sauvignon Howell Mountain £££**

Durbach [door-bahk] (*Baden*, Germany) Top vineyard area of this *anbaugebiet*.

🍇**Durif** [dyoor-if] See *Petite Sirah*.

♟ **Jean Durup** [doo-roop] (*Burgundy*, France) Modern estate whose owner controversially believes in extending vineyards of *Chablis* into what some claim to be less distinguished soil, and not using new oak. The best wines are sold as Ch. de Maligny. ☆☆☆☆ **1996 Château de Maligny Vieilles Vignes ££**

🍇**Dusty Miller** (England) Local name for *Pinot Meunier*.

♟ **Duxoup Wine Works** [duk-soop] (*Sonoma Valley*, California) Inspired winery-in-a-shed, producing very good characterful *Charbono* and fine *Syrah* from bought-in grapes. The curious name – which is incidentally not one to drop among collectors who prefer tougher fare from *château*-like edifices – has nothing to do with the Marx Brothers movie. It refers to the owners' belief that starting a winery and planting a vineyard would – in the US expression – be as 'easy as duck soup'. ☆☆☆ **1993 Charbono £££**

E

♟ **E&E** (*Barossa*, South Australia) One of the jewels of the *BRL Hardy* crown, producing rich, full-flavoured reds and whites. ☆☆☆☆ **1994 Black Pepper Shiraz £££**

♟ **Maurice Ecard** [Ay-car] (*Burgundy*, France) Very recommendable *Savigny-lès-Beaune* estate with good *Premier Cru* vineyards. ☆☆☆☆ **1995 Savigny-lès-Beaune les Serpentières £££**

♟ **Echézeaux** [ay-shuh-zoh] (*Burgundy*, France) *Grand Cru* vineyard between *Clos de Vougeot* and *Vosne-Romanée* and more or less an extension of the latter commune. *Flagey-Echézeaux*, a village on the relatively vine-less side of the Route Nationale, takes its name from the 'flagellation' used by the peasants to gather corn in the 6th century. Grands-Echézeaux should be finer. ***Dom. de la Romanée-Conti; Henri Jayer; Dom. Dujac; Dom. Thierry Vigst.***

♟ **L' Ecole No. 41** [ay-kohl] (*Washington State*, US) Stylish producer of classy *Chardonnay* and *Merlot*. Also supplies rich *Semillon*. ☆☆☆☆ **1991 Cabernet Sauvignon ££££**

Edelfäule [ay-del-fow-luh] (Germany) *Botrytis cinerea*, or 'noble rot'.

Edelzwicker [ay-del-zwik-kur] (*Alsace*, France) Generic name for a blend of grape varieties. The idea of blends is coming back – but not the name (see *Hugel*).

♟ **Edmunds St. John** (*Alameda*, California) Producer with his heart in the *Rhône* – and a taste for rich spicy *Syrah* and *Zinfandel* reds. ☆☆☆☆☆ **1995 Durell Vineyard Syrah ££££**

♟ **Edna Valley Vineyard** (California) Long-standing maker of rich buttery *Chardonnay* in the *AVA* of the same name. In the same stable as *Chalone*, *Carmenet* and *Acacia* and now in an ambitious joint Californian venture called Paragon with *Penfolds*. ☆☆☆ **1995 Brock Chardonnay ££**

Eger [eg-gur] (Hungary) Region of Hungary where *Bull's Blood* is made.

Dom. de l'Eglise [duh lay glees] (*Pomerol, Bordeaux,* France) Fairly priced, middle-of-the-range, wines. 79 82 83 85 86 88 89 90 92 95 96

Ch. l'Eglise-Clinet [Lay gleez klee-nay] (*Pomerol, Bordeaux,* France) A terrific château that's fast getting even better. 70 71 75 76 78 79 81 82 83 85 86 **88** 89 **90** 91 92 93 **94** 95 96 ☆☆☆☆☆ **1993 ££££**

Egri Bikaver [eh-grih bih-kah vehr] (*Eger,* Hungary) See *Bull's Blood.*

Einzellage/n [ine-tseh-lah-gur/gehn] (Germany) Single vineyard; most precise and often the last part of a wine name, finer by definition than a *grosslage.*

Eiswein [ihs-vihn] (Germany/Austria) The ultimate ultra-concentrated *late harvest* wine, made from grapes naturally frozen on the vine. Rare and hard to make (and consequently very pricy) in Germany but more affordable in Austria and, increasingly, Canada. Intensely delicious but often with worryingly high levels of *acidity.*

Eitelsbach [ih-tel-sbahk] (*Mosel,* Germany) One of the top two *Ruwer* wine towns, and the site of the famed Karthäuserhofberg vineyard.

Elaborado y Anejado Por [ay-lah-boh-rah-doh ee anay-hahdo pohr] (Spain) 'Made and aged for'.

Elba [el-bah] (Italy) Island off the *Tuscan* coast where they make full dry reds and whites.

🍇**Elbling** [el-bling] Inferior Germanic white grape.

Elderton (*Barossa Valley,* Australia) Maker of big, rich, competition-winning wines, especially *Shiraz and Cabernet.* ☆☆☆☆ **1994 Barossa Valley Command Shiraz £££**

Eléver/éléveur [ay-leh-vay/vay-leh-vuhr] To mature or 'nurture' wine, especially in the cellars of the *Burgundy négociants,* who act as éléveurs after traditionally buying in wine made by small estates.

Elgin [el-gin] (South Africa) Coolish – *Burgundy*-like – apple-growing country which is rapidly attracting the interest of big wine producers. Watch out for the Paul Cluver reds and whites from *Neil Ellis.* May eventually overshadow all but the best parts of *Stellenbosch* and *Paarl.*

Neil Ellis (*Stellenbosch,* South Africa) One of the *Cape's* best new-wave winemakers and a pioneer of the new region of *Elgin.* ☆☆☆☆ **1997 Sauvignon Blanc ££**

Eltville [elt-vil] (*Rheingau,* Germany) Town housing the *Rheingau* state cellars and the German Wine Academy, producing good *Riesling* with backbone. QbA/Kab/Spät: **85** 86 **88 89 90** 91 92 93 94 95 96 97 Aus/Beeren/Tba: **83** 85 **88 89 90** 91 92 93 94 95 96 97

Elyse Wine Cellars (*Napa,* California) *Zinfandel* specialist with vineyards on *Howell Mountain.* Look out too for the Nero Misto spicy *Zinfandel, Petite Sirah* blend. ☆☆☆☆☆ **1995 Morisoli Zinfandel**

🍇**Emerald Riesling** [rees-ling] (California) Bottom of the range white cross grape (*Riesling* x *Muscadelle*). At its best it is fresh and fruity but decidedly undistinguished.

Emilia-Romagna [eh-mee-lee-yah roh-ma-nya] (Italy) Region around Bologna best known for *Lambrusco;* also the source of *Albana, Sangiovese* di Romagna and *Pagadebit.*

En primeur [on pree-muh] New wine, usually *Bordeaux.* Specialist merchants buy and offer wine *en primeur* before it has been released; customers rely on their merchant's judgement – and gurus' verdicts – to make a good buy. In the US and Australia, where producers like *Mondavi* and *Petaluma* are selling their wine in this way, the process is known as buying 'futures'.

� **Ch. l'Enclos** [lon kloh] (*Pomerol, Bordeaux*, France) Gorgeously rich, fairly priced wines. 79 **82** 83 85 86 88 **89** 90 91 92 93 94 95 96

� **René Engel** [On-jel] (*Burgundy*, France) Producer of rich, long-lived wines in *Vosne-Romanée* and *Clos Vougeot*. ☆☆☆☆☆ **1995 Echézeaux ££££**

English wine Produced from grapes grown in England (or Wales), as opposed to the now-to-be-phased-out British wine, which is made from imported concentrate. Quality has improved in recent years, as winemakers have developed their own personality, changing from semi-sweet, mock-Germanic to dry mock-*Loire* and now, increasingly, to aromatic-but-dry and *late harvest*. ***Breaky Bottom; Thames Valley Vineyards; Bruisyard; Three Choirs; Carr Taylor; Chiltern Valley.***

Enoteca [ee-noh-teh-kah] (Italy) Literally wine library or, now, wine shop.

� **Entre-Deux-Mers** [on-truh duh mehr] (*Bordeaux*, France) Once a region of appalling sweet wine from vineyards between the cities of *Bordeaux* and Libourne. Now a source of basic *Bordeaux* Blanc and principally dry *Sauvignon*. Reds are sold as *Bordeaux* Rouge. Both reds and whites suffer from the difficulty grapes can have in ripening here in cool years. *Ch. Bonnet* is the star.

Erbach [ayr-bahkh] (*Rheingau*, Germany) Town noted for fine full *Riesling*, particularly from the Marcobrunn vineyard. QbA/Kab/Spät: **85** 86 **88 89 90** 91 92 93 94 95 96 Aus/Beeren/Tba: **83** 85 **88** 89 90 91 92 93 94 95 96 97 *Schloss Reinhartshausen; Schloss Schönborn.*

🍇 **Erbaluce** [ehr-bah-loo-chay] (*Piedmont*, Italy) White grape responsible for the light dry wines of the *Caluso*, and also the sweet sun-dried *Caluso Passito*.

� **Erbaluce di Caluso** [ehr-bah-loo-chay dee kah-loo-soh] (*Piedmont*, Italy) Dry quite herby white wine made from the *Erbaluce* grape (*Bava* makes a good one, blending in a little *Chardonnay*). ☆☆☆ **1996 Ferrando £**

Erden [ehr-durn] (*Mosel-Saar-Ruwer*, Germany) In the *Bernkastel bereich*, this northerly village produces full, crisp, dry *Riesling* and includes the famous Treppchen vineyard. QbA/Kab/Spät: **85** 86 **88 89 90** 91 92 93 94 95 96 Aus/Beeren/Tba: **83** 85 **88** 89 90 91 92 93 94 95 96 ☆☆☆☆ **1996 Erdener Prälat Riesling Kabinett, Dr Loosen ££££**

� **Errazuriz** [ehr-raz-zoo-riz] (*Aconcagua Valley*, Chile) One of Chile's big name producers and owner of *Caliterra*. Wines have been improved by input from *Mondavi*. Look out for the 'Wild Ferment' *Chardonnay* and recently launched *Syrah*. ☆☆☆☆ **1997 Syrah Reserve £££**

Erzeugerabfüllung [ayr-tsoy-guhr-ab-foo-loong] (Germany) Bottled by the grower/estate.

� **Esk Valley** (*Hawke's Bay*, New Zealand) Under the same ownership as *Vidal* and *Villa Maria*. Successful with *Bordeaux*-style reds and juicy rosé. ☆☆☆☆☆ **1997 Estate Chardonnay ££**

� **Frederic Esmonin** [Ehs-moh-na'] (*Burgundy*, France) Estate with good vineyards in *Nuits-St.-Georges*, *Gevrey-Chambertin* and *Chambolle-Musigny*. ☆☆☆☆☆ **1991 Mazis-Chambertin ££££**

� **Esparão** [esp-per-row] (*Alentejo*, Portugal) Revolutionary wines made by Australian-born David Baverstock.

Espum/oso/ante [es-poom-mo-soh/san-tay] (Spain/Portugal) Sparkling.

� **Estancia** (*Napa/Monterey*, California) *Second label* of *Franciscan* producing highly commercial wines which – for some reason – sometimes seem to be better received by US critics than *Franciscan's* finer and more serious efforts.

Esters Chemical components in wine responsible for all those extraordinary odours of fruits, vegetables, hamster cages and trainers.

Estufa [esh-too-fah] (*Madeira*, Portugal) The vats in which *Madeira* is heated, speeding maturity and imparting its familiar 'cooked' flavour.

Eszencia [es-sen-tsee-yah] (*Tokaji*, Hungary) Incredibly sweet and concentrated syrup made by piling around 100kg of *late-harvested*, *botrytised* grapes into *puttonyos* and letting as little as three litres of incredibly sticky treacle dribble out of the bottom. This will only ferment up to about 4 per cent alcohol, over several weeks, before stopping completely. It is then stored and used periodically to sweeten normal *Aszú* wines. The Tzars of Russia discovered the joys of Eszencia, and it has long been prized for its effects on the male libido. It is incredibly hard to find, even by those who can see the point in doing anything with the outrageously expensive syrup other than pouring it on ice-cream. The easier-to-find *Aszú Essencia* (one step sweeter than *Aszú* 6 *puttonyos*) is far better value.

🍷 **Arnaldo Etchart** [et-shaht] (*Cafayate*, Argentina) Dynamic producer, benefiting from advice by *Michel Rolland* of *Pomerol* fame, and also investment by its new owners Pernod Ricard. The key wine here, though, is the grapey white *Torrontes*. ☆☆☆ **1994 Cafayate Cabernet Sauvignon £**

Etna [eht-nuh] (*Sicily*, Italy) From the Sicilian volcanic slopes; hot-climate, soft, fruity *DOC* reds, whites and rosés. Can be flabby.

🍷 **Etude** [ay-tewd] (*Napa*, California) Thoughtful superstar consultant Tony Soter experiments by marrying specific sites and clones of *Pinot Noir*. Apart from these wines, there are good rich *Napa* reds and *Carneros Chardonnay*. ☆☆☆☆☆ **1996 Pinot Noir Napa Valley £££**

🍷 **Ch. l' Evangile** [lay-van-zheel] (*Pomerol*, *Bordeaux*, France) A classy and increasingly sought-after property that can, in great vintages like 1988, 1989 and 1990, sometimes rival its neighbour *Pétrus*, but in a more *tannic* style. **75** 78 79 **82 83 85** 86 87 **88 89 90** 92 93 **95 96** ☆☆☆☆ **1990 ££££**

🍷 **Evans Family/Evans Wine Co** (*Hunter Valley*, Australia) Len Evans' (founder, ex-chairman of *Rothbury Vineyards*) own estate and company. Good rich *Chardonnay* and *Semillon* as characterful and generous as their maker. Set for expansion following the sale of *Rothbury* to *Mildara-Blass*.

🍷 **Evans & Tate** (*Margaret River*, Australia) Much improved producer following its move from the hot *Swan Valley* into the cooler *Margaret River*. ☆☆☆☆ **1996 Margaret River Chardonnay £££**

🍷 **Eventail de Vignerons Producteurs** [ay-van-tih] (*Burgundy*, France) Reliable source of *Beaujolais*.

🍷 **Eyrie Vineyards** [ih-ree] (*Oregon*, US) Pioneering *Pinot Noir* producer in the *Willamette Valley*, whose success in a blind tasting of *Burgundies* helped to attract *Joseph Drouhin* to invest his francs in a vineyard here. ☆☆☆☆ **1996 Pinot Gris £££**

F

🍷 **Fairview Estate** (*Paarl*, South Africa) Go-ahead estate where Charles Back – both under his own name and under that of Fairview – makes good-value wines more open-mindedly than some of his neighbours. One of the few South Africans responsible for genuine innovation. ☆☆☆☆ **1997 Pinotage.**

🍷 **Joseph Faiveley** [fay-vlay] (*Burgundy*, France) Impressive modern *négoçiant* with particular strength in vineyards in the *Côte de Nuits* and *Nuits-St.-Georges*. ☆☆☆☆ **1995 Corton Clos des Cortons ££££**

🍷 **Far Niente** [fah nee-yen-tay] (*Napa Valley*, California) Well regarded producer of sometimes over-showy *Chardonnay* and *Cabernet*.

Ch. de Fargues [duh-fahrg] (*Sauternes, Bordeaux*, France) Elegant wines made by the winemaker at *Ch. d'Yquem* – and a good alternative. 70 71 75 76 78 79 80 83 85 86 88 89 90 95 96 97 ☆☆☆☆ 1990 ££££

Gary Farrell (*Sonoma*, California) A *Russian River Pinot Noir* maker to watch. ☆☆☆☆ 1994 Pinot Noir ££££

Fat Has a silky texture which fills the mouth. More fleshy than meaty.

Fattoria [fah-tor-ree-ah] (Italy) Estate, particularly in *Tuscany*.

Faugères [foh-zhehr] (*Midi*, France) With neighbouring *St. Chinian*, this gently hilly region is a major cut above the surrounding *Coteaux du Languedoc*, and potentially the source of really exciting red, whites and rosés. For the moment, however, most still taste pretty rustic. G. Alquier; Ch. des Estanilles.

Bernard Faurie [fow-ree] (*Rhône*, France) Tournon-based producer who makes intense perfumed wines with great longevity.

Bodegas Faustino Martinez [fows-tee-noh mahr-tee-nehth] (*Rioja*, Spain) Dependable *Rioja* producer with excellent (*Gran*) *Reservas*, fair whites and a decent *cava*. ☆☆☆☆ 1988 Tinto Gran Reserva £££

Favorita [fahvoh-ree-tah] (*Piedmont*, Italy) Traditional variety from *Piedmont* transformed by modern winemaking into delicate floral whites. Conterno; Villa Lanata; Bava.

Weingut Feiler-Artinger [fih-luh arh-ting-guh] (*Rust*, Austria) Superlative innovative producer of dry and, especially, *late harvest* wines. ☆☆☆ 1995 Ausbruch Essenz Pinot Noir £££

Fattoria di Felsina Berardenga [fah-toh-ree-ah dee fehl-see-nah beh-rah-den-gah] (*Tuscany*, Italy) Very high quality *Chianti* estate. ☆☆☆☆☆ 1994 Chianti Riserva £££

Fendant [fon-don] (Switzerland) See *Chasselas*.

Fer [fehr] (South-West France) Grape used to make *Marcillac*. *Fermentazione naturale* [fehr-men-tat-zee-oh-nay] (Italy) 'Naturally sparkling' but, in fact, indicates the *cuve close* method.

Fernão Pires [fehr-now pee-rehsh] (Portugal) Muscatty grape, used to great effect by *Peter Bright* of the *João Pires* winery.

Ch. Ferrand Lartique [feh-ron lah-teek] (*St. Emilion Grand Cru, Bordeaux*, France) Tiny 5-acre estate producing full-bodied rich wines from 40-year-old vines.

Luigi Ferrando (*Piedmont* Italy) Producer in the Carema *DOC* of good *Nebbiolo*-based wines that are surprisingly light and elegant in style.

Ferrari-Carano [fuh-rah-ree kah-rah-noh] (*Sonoma*, California) Some US critics take these wines seriously; I find the *Chardonnays* too sweet. ☆☆☆☆ 1994 Fumé Blanc Sonoma County Reserve £££

AA Ferreira [feh-ray-rah] (*Douro*, Portugal) Traditional Portuguese *port* producer, equally famous for its excellent *tawnies* as for its *Barca Velha*, Portugal's best traditional unfortified red. ☆☆☆☆ Duque de Braganca 20 Year Old Tawny ££; ☆☆☆☆ 1987 Vintage Port £££

Gloria Ferrer (*Sonoma*, California) Unmemorable fizz from the firm that owns *Freixenet* (the people behind *Cordon Negro*).

Ch. Ferrière [feh-ree-yehr] (*Margaux 3ème Cru Classé, Bordeaux*, France) Once tiny, now rather bigger, thanks to the convenience of belonging to the same owners as the *Margaux Cru Bourgeois, Ch. la Gurgue*. 89 90 91 92 93 94 95 96 ☆☆☆☆ 1995 £££

Ch. de Fesles [dur fel] (*Loire*, France) Classic *Bonnezeaux*. ☆☆☆☆☆ 1996 Bonnezeaux ££££

Sylvain Fessy [seel-van fes-see] (*Burgundy*, France) Reliable small *Beaujolais* producer with wide range of *crus*.

Henry Fessy [on-ree fes-see] (*Burgundy*, France) Consistent *négociant*, vineyard owner and producer of *Beaujolais*. ☆☆☆ 1996 Cote-de-Brouilly Dom. de l'Heronde ££

Fête des Fleurs [fayt day fluh] (*Bordeaux*, France) Annual social event where the Bordelais gather to party and the *château* chosen to host the affair tries to outdo the previous year's extravaganza.

Fetzer [fet-zuh] (*Mendocino*, California) The best of the bigger Californian wineries. One of the few which really tries to make good wine at (relatively) lower prices and a laudable pioneering producer of 'Bonterra' organic wines. Recently taken over but still run by the family. ☆☆☆☆ 1996 Barrel Select Pinot Noir ££; ☆☆☆☆ 1995 Bonterra Chardonnay ££

Nicolas Feuillatte [fuh-yet] (*Champagne*, France) Quietly rising star with good value wine. ☆☆☆ 1989 Cuvée Speciale £££

William Fèvre [weel-yum feh-vr] (*Burgundy*, France) Quality *Chablis* producer who has been a revolutionary in his use of new oak. His efforts in Chile have been improving with each vintage. ☆☆☆☆ 1994 Chablis Grand Cru Bougros ££££

Ch. Feytit-Clinet [fay-tee klee-nay] (*Pomerol*, *Bordeaux*, France) A *Moueix* property with good, delicate wines. 79 81 **82** 83 **85** 86 87 88 89 90 94 95 96

Les Fiefs-de-Lagrange [fee-ef duh lag-ronzh] (*St. Julien*, *Bordeaux*, France) Recommendable *second label* of *Ch. Lagrange*.

Ch. de Fieuzal [duh fyuh-zahl] (*Pessac-Léognan Grand Cru Classé*, *Bordeaux*, France) Recently sold *Pessac-Léognan* property which has made great whites and lovely raspberryish reds. Abeille de Fieuzal is the (excellent) *second label*. Red: 75 79 81 **82** 83 **85** 86 88 89 90 91 92 93 94 95 96 White: **85** 88 **89** 90 91 **92** 93 **96** 97

Ch. Figeac [fee-zhak] (*St. Emilion Premier Grand Cru*, *Bordeaux*, France) Forever in the shadow of its neighbour, *Cheval Blanc*, but still one of the most characterful *St. Emilions*. 64 70 78 **82** 83 84 **85** 86 88 89 90 92 93 94 95 96 97 ☆☆☆☆ 1994 ££££

Finger Lakes (*New York State*, US) Cold region whose producers struggle (sometimes effectively) to produce good *vinifera*, including *late harvest Riesling*. *Hybrids* such as *Seyval Blanc* are more reliable. **Wagner.**

Fining The clarifying of young wine before bottling to remove impurities, using a number of agents including *isinglass* and *bentonite*.
Finish What you can still taste after swallowing.

Fino [fee-noh] (*Jerez*, Spain) Dry, delicate *sherry* which gains its distinctive flavour from the *flor* or yeast which grows on the surface of the wine during maturation. Drink chilled, with tapas, preferably within two weeks of opening. **Lustau; Barbadillo; Hidalgo; Gonzalez Byass.**

Firestone (*Santa Ynez*, California) Good producer – particularly of good value *Chardonnay*, *Merlot* and *Sauvignon* and *late harvest Riesling* – in southern California. ☆☆☆☆ 1996 Barrel Fermented Chardonnay ££

Fisher (*Sonoma*, California) Top class producer of limited-production, single-vineyard *Cabernets* and *Chardonnays* from hillside vineyards. ☆☆☆☆☆ 1994 Wedding Vineyard Cabernet Sauvignon ££££

Fitou [fee-too] (*Midi*, France) Long considered to be an up-market *Corbières* but actually rather a basic southern *AC*, making reds largely from the *Carignan* grape. The wines here may have become more refined, with a woody warmth, but they never quite shake off their rustic air. **Mont Tauch.**

Fixin [fee-san] (*Burgundy*, France) Northerly village of the *Côte de Nuits*, producing lean, tough, uncommercial reds which can mature well. *Faiveley* makes a good one. 76 **78** 79 **80** 82 83 **85** 86 87 **88 89** 90 92 95 96 ☆☆☆☆ 1995 Jaffelin £££

Flabby Lacking balancing *acidity*.

Flagey-Echézeaux [flah-jay ay-shuh-zoh] (*Burgundy*, France) Village on the wrong (non-vine) side of the Route National 74 that lends its name to the *appellations* of *Echézeaux* and *Grands Echézeaux*.

Ch. La Fleur [flur] (*St. Emilion*, *Bordeaux*, France) Small *St. Emilion* property producing softly fruity wines. 82 83 85 86 88 **89** 90 92 94 95 96

Ch. la Fleur-de Gay [flur duh gay] (*Pomerol*, *Bordeaux*, France) *Ch. Croix de Gay*'s best wine and thus heavily sought after. Due for improvement in 1998. 82 **86** 88 89 90 94 95 96

Ch. la Fleur-Pétrus [flur pay-trooss] (*Pomerol*, *Bordeaux*, France) For those who find *Pétrus* a touch too hefty, not to mention a touch unaffordable, this next-door neighbour offers gorgeously accessible *Pomerol* flavour for (in *Pétrus* terms) a bargain price. 70 **75** 78 79 **81** 82 **83** 85 86 87 88 89 90 92 93 95 96

Fleurie [fluh-ree] (*Burgundy*, France) One of the 10 *Beaujolais Crus*, ideally fresh and fragrant, as its name suggests. Best vineyards include La Madonne and Pointe du Jour. Dom. Bachelard and Guy Depardon are names to watch. 90 95 96 96 97 Berrod; Chignard; Déprés; Métrat.

Flor [flawr] Yeast which grows naturally on the surface of some maturing sherries, making them potential *finos*.

⚘**Flora** [flor-rah] A cross between *Semillon* and *Gewürztraminer*, best known in *Brown Brothers Orange Muscat* and Flora.

Flora Springs (*Napa Valley*, California) Good, unusual *Sauvignon Blanc* (Soliloquy) and classy *Merlot*, *Cabernet Sauvignon* & *Cabernet Franc* blend (Trilogy). ☆☆☆☆ 1994 Rutherford Cabernet £££

Emile Florentin [floh-ron-tan] (*Rhône*, France) Maker of ultra-traditional, ultra-*tannic*, chewy *St. Joseph*.

Flying winemakers Young (usually) Antipodeans who have, since the 1980s, been despatched like vinous mercenaries to wineries worldwide to make better and more reliable wine than the home teams can manage. Often, as they have proved, all it has taken to improve the standards of a European cooperative has been a more scrupulous attitude towards picking ripe grapes (rather than impatiently harvesting unripe ones) and keeping tanks and pipes clean. The best-known include *Jacques Lurton*, *Hugh Ryman*, *Kym Milne*, *Peter Bright*, John Worontschak and Nick Butler.

⚘**Folle Noir** [fol nwah] (France) Traditional grape used to make *Bellet*.

Ch. Fombrauge [fom-brohzh] (*St. Emilion*, *Bordeaux*, France) Middling *St. Emilion*. 82 83 85 86 88 89 90 92 93 94 95 96 ☆☆☆ 1994 £££

Ch. Fonplégade [fon-pleh-gahd] (*St. Emilion Grand Cru Classé*, *Bordeaux*, France) If you like your *St. Emilion* tough, this is for you. 78 **82** 83 85 86 87 88 89 90 94 95 96 ☆☆☆ 1989 ££££

Ch. Fonroque [fon-rok] (*St. Emilion Grand Cru Classé*, *Bordeaux*, France) Property with concentrated wines, but not always one of *Moueix*'s finest. 70 **75** 78 79 82 **83 85** 86 88 89 90 92 93 94 95 96

Fonseca Guimaraens [fon-say-ka gih-mah-rans] (*Douro*, Portugal) Now a subsidiary of *Taylor*'s but still independently making great *port*. In blind tastings the 1976 and 1978 beat supposedly classier houses' supposedly finer vintages. See also *Guimaraens*. Fonseca: 60 **63 66 70** 75 77 80 83 **85** 95 Fonseca Guimaraens: **76 78** 82 84 88 92 94 ☆☆☆☆☆ 1984 Fonseca Guimaraens Vintage Port ££££

JM da Fonseca Internacional [fon-say-ka in-tuhr-nah-soh-nahl] (*Setúbal* Peninsula, Portugal) Highly commercial firm whose wines include Lancers, the *Mateus*-lookalike, semi-fizzy, semi-sweet pinks, whites sold in mock-crocks and fairly basic fizz made by a process known as the *Russian Continuous*.

JM da Fonseca Successores [fon-say-ka suk-ses-saw-rays] (*Estremadura*, Portugal) Unrelated to the *port* house of the same name and no longer connected to *JM da Fonseca Internacional*. Family-run firm, which with *Aliança* and *Sogrape* is one of Portugal's big three dynamic wine companies. Top reds include Pasmados, *Periquita* (from the grape of the same name), *Quinta da Camarate*, Terras Altas Dão and the *Cabernet*-influenced 'TE' *Garrafeiras*. Dry whites are less impressive, but the sweet old *Moscatel de Setúbals* are luscious classics. ☆☆☆☆ 1992 Quinta da Camarate, Terras do Sado ££££

♈ **Dom. Font de Michelle** [fon-duh-mee-shel] (*Rhône*, France) Reliable producer of medium-bodied red *Châteauneuf-du-Pape* and tiny quantities of brilliant, almost unobtainable, white. ☆☆☆ 1995 Châteauneuf-du-Pape £££

♈ **Fontana Candida** [fon-tah-nah kan-dee-dah] (*Lazio*, Italy) Good producer, especially for *Frascati*. The top wine is Colle Gaio which is good enough to prove the disappointing nature of most other wines from this area. ☆☆☆ 1996 Frascati Superiore Terre dei Grifi ££

♈ **Fontanafredda** [fon-tah-nah-freh-dah] (*Piedmont*, Italy) Big producer with impressive *Asti Spumante* and very approachable (especially single-vineyard) *Barolo*. ☆☆☆☆ 1993 Barolo Derralunga di Alba ££££

♈ **Domaine de Font Sane** [fon-sen] (*Rhône*, France) Producer of fine *Gigondas* in a very underrated *AC*. Very traditional and full-bodied.

♈ **Fontodi** [Fon-Toh-Dee] (*Tuscany*, Italy) Classy *Tuscan* producer with Flaccianello, a good *Vino da Tavola*. ☆☆☆☆ 1996 Chianti Classico ££££

♈ **Forman** (*Napa Valley*, California) Rick Forman makes good *Cabernet* and *Merlot* and refreshingly non-buttery *Chardonnay*. ☆☆☆☆ 1995 Cabernet Sauvignon ££££

Forst [Fawrst] (*Pfalz*, Germany) Wine town producing great concentrated *Riesling*. Famous for the *Jesuitengarten* vineyard. QbA/Kab/Spät: 85 86 88 89 90 91 92 93 94 95 Aus/Beeren/Tba: 83 85 88 89 90 91 92 93 94 95 96 97 ☆☆☆☆ 1996 Forster Jesuitengarten, Dr V Basserman-Jordan £££

♈ **Fortant de France** [faw-tan duh frons] (*Languedoc-Roussillon*, France) Good-quality revolutionary brand owned by *Skalli* and specialising in varietal *Vin de Pays d'Oc*. ☆☆☆☆ 1997 Syrah £

♈ **Les Forts de Latour** [lay faw duh lah-toor] (*Pauillac, Bordeaux*, France) *Second label* of *Ch. Latour*. Not, as is often suggested, made exclusively from the fruit of young vines and wine which might otherwise have ended up in *Ch. Latour* – there are vineyards whose grapes are grown specially for Les Forts – but still often better than other *classed growth châteaux*. 82 83 85 86 88 90 91 92 93 94 95 96

♈ **Bernard Fouquet** [Foo-kay] (*Loire*, France) A name to watch in *Vouvray*, with modern examples of sweet, medium ('tendre') and dry, sold under the Dom. des Aubuisières label. ☆☆☆☆☆ 1995 Moelleux Marigny £££

♈ **Ch. Fourcas-Dupré** [faw-kass doo-pray] (*Listrac Cru Bourgeois*, *Bordeaux*, France) Tough, very traditional *Listrac*. 70 75 78 81 82 83 85 86 87 88 89 90 91 92 95 96

♈ **Ch. Fourcas-Hosten** [faw-kass hos-ten] (*Listrac Cru Bourgeois*, *Bordeaux*, France) Firm, old-fashioned wine with plenty of 'grip' for *tannin* fans. 75 78 81 82 83 85 86 87 88 89 90 91 92 95 96

♈ **Foxen** (*Santa Ynez*, California) *Pinot* producer now moving successfully into *Syrah*. ☆☆☆☆ 1995 Syrah £££

♈ **Ch. Franc-Mayne** [fron-mayn] (*St. Emilion Grand Cru Classé*, *Bordeaux*, France) Dry, austere, traditional wines for those who like them that way. 85 86 87 88 89 90 94 95 96 ☆☆☆ 1990 £££

♈ **Franciacorta** [fran-chee yah-kor-tah] (*Lombardy*, Italy) *DOC* for good, light, French-influenced reds but better noted for sparklers made to sell at the same price as *Champagne*, if not more than. See *Ca Del Bosco*.

♈ **Franciscan Vineyards** [fran-sis-kan] (*Napa Valley*, California) Reliable *Napa* winery whose Chilean owner, Agustin Huneeus, has pioneered natural yeast wines with his *Burgundy*-like 'Cuvée Sauvage' *Chardonnay* and has punctured the pretentious balloons of some of his neighbours – including the supporters of a '*Rutherford Bench*' appellation. Now also making wine in Chile – at *Veramonte*. ☆☆☆☆ 1994 Chardonnay Sauvage.

♈ **Ch. de Francs** [day fron] (*Côtes de Francs, Bordeaux*, France) Well-run estate which makes great-value crunchy, blackcurrenty wine and, with *Ch. Puygeraud*, helps to prove the worth of this little-known region.

Franken [fran-ken] (Germany) *Anbaugebiet* making characterful, sometimes earthy, dry whites, traditionally presented in the squat flagon-shaped '*bocksbeutel*' on which the *Mateus* bottle was modelled. One of the key varieties is the *Sylvaner* which helps explain the earthiness of many of the wines. The weather here does make it easier to make dry wine than in many other regions, however.

Franschhoek [fran-shook] (South Africa) Valley leading into the mountains away from *Paarl* (and thus cooler). The soil is a little suspect, however, and the best producers are mostly clustered at the top of the valley, around the picturesque eponymous town. Red: **84 86 87** 89 **91 92** 93 94 95 96 White: **87 91** 92 93 94 95 96

☒ **Frascati** [fras-kah-tee] (*Latium*, Italy) Clichéd dry or semi-dry white from *Latium*. At its best it is soft and clean with a fascinating 'sour cream' flavour. Drink within 12 months of *vintage*. **Fontana Candida; Colli di Catone.**

☒ **Ca' dei Frati** [kah day-yee frah-tee] (*Lombardy*, Italy) Fine producers, both of *Lugana* and *Chardonnay*-based fizz.
☒ **Freemark Abbey** (*Napa Valley*, California) Producer of good, rather than great *Cabernet*. ☆☆☆ **1992 Cabernet Sauvignon ££££**
☒ **Frei Weingartener Wachau** [fri-vine-gahrt-nur vah-kow] (*Wachau*, Austria) Fine cooperative with great vineyards, dry and sweet versions of the indigenous *Grüner Veltliner* and concentrated *Rieslings* that outclass the efforts of many a big-name estate in Germany. ☆☆☆☆ **1993 Riesling Burgerspitalstiftung Spitz Smaragd £££**
☒ **Freixenet** [fresh-net] (*Catalonia*, Spain) Giant in the *cava* field and proponent of traditional *Catalonian* grapes in fizz. Its dull, big-selling *Cordon Negro* is a perfect justification for adding *Chardonnay* to the blend.
☒ **Marchesi de' Frescobaldi** [mah-kay-see day fres-koh-bal-dee] (*Tuscany*, Italy) Family estate with classy wines including *Castelgiocondo,* Mormoreto, a *Cabernet Sauvignon* based wine, the rich white *Pomino* Il Benefizio *Chardonnay*, *Pomino* Rosso using *Merlot* and *Cabernet Sauvignon*, and Nippozano in *Chianti*. Now in joint venture to make *Luce* with *Mondavi*. ☆☆☆☆ **1996 Pomino Bianco £££**
☒ **Freycinet** [fres-sih-net] (*Tasmania*, Australia) Small East Coast winery with some of Australia's best *Pinot Noir*. ☆☆☆☆ **1995 Pinot Noir £££**

☒ **Friuli-Venezia Giulia** [free-yoo-lee veh-neht-zee-yah zhee-yoo-lee-yah] (Italy) Northerly region containing a number of *DOCs* which focus on single-variety wines like *Merlot, Cabernet Franc, Pinot Bianco, Pinot Grigio* and *Tocai*. **Jermann; Bidoli; Puiatti; Zonin.**

Frizzante [freet-zan-tay] (Italy) Semi-sparkling especially *Lambrusco*.
☒ **Frog's Leap** (*Napa Valley*, California) Winery whose owners combine organic winemaking skill with a fine sense of humour (their slogan is 'Time's fun when you're having flies'). Tasty *Zinfandel*, 'wild yeast' *Chardonnay* and unusually good *Sauvignon Blanc*. ☆☆☆ **1995 Chardonnay £££**

☒ **Fronsac/Canon Fronsac** [fron-sak] (*Bordeaux*, France) *Pomerol* neighbours, who regularly produce rich, intense, affordable wines. They are rarely subtle; however, with some good winemaking from men like *Christian Moueix* of *Ch. Pétrus* (he is a great believer in these regions), they can often represent some of the best buys in *Bordeaux*. Canon Fronsac is supposedly the better of the pair. **83 85** 86 **88 89** 90 94 95 96 *Ch. Canon; Dalem;* Fontenil; Moulin Haut Laroque; Vieille Cure.

Ch. de Fuissé [duh fwee-say] (*Burgundy*, France) Jean-Jacques Vincent is probably the best producer in this *commune*, making wines comparable to some of the best of the *Côte d'Or*. The *Vieilles Vignes* can last as long as a good *Chassagne-Montrachet;* the other *cuvées* run it a close race.

Fumé Blanc [fyoo-may blahnk] The name originally adapted from *Pouilly Blanc Fumé* by *Robert Mondavi* to describe his California oaked *Sauvignon*. Now widely used for this style.

Furmint [foor-mint] (*Tokaji*, Hungary) Lemony white grape, used in Hungary for *Tokaji* and, given modern winemaking, good dry wines. See *Royal Tokaji Wine Co* and *Disznókö*. ☆☆☆ 1995 Disznókö Fürmint £

Fürstlich Castell'sches Domanenamt [foorst-likh kas-tel-shes doh-man-nehn-nahmt] (*Franken*, Germany) Prestigious producer of typically full-bodied dry whites from the German *anbaugebiet* of *Franken*.

Fûts de Chêne (élévé en) [foo duh shayne] (France) Oak barrels (matured in).

G

Ch. la Gaffelière [gaf-fuh-lyehr] (*St. Emilion Premier Grand Cru*, *Bordeaux*, France) Lightish-bodied but well-made wines. Not to be confused with *Ch. Canon la Gaffelière*. **82 83** 85 **86** 88 89 90 92 93 94 95 96

Dom. Jean-Noël Gagnard [jon noh-wel gan-yahr] (*Burgundy*, France) A reliable *domaine* with vineyards which spread across *Chassagne-Montrachet*. There is also some *Santenay*. ☆☆☆☆ 1995 Chassagne-Montrachet Clos de la Maltroye ££££

Jacques Gagnard-Delagrange [gan-yahr duh lag-ronzh] (*Burgundy*, France) A top-class producer to follow for those traditionalists who like their white *Burgundies* delicately oaked. ☆☆☆☆ 1992 Chassagne-Montrachet ££££

Gaillac [gih-yak] (South-West France) Light, fresh, good-value reds and (sweet, dry and slightly sparkling) whites, produced using *Gamay* and *Sauvignon* grapes, as well as the indigenous *Mauzac*. The reds can rival *Beaujolais*. Ch. Clement Ternes; Labastide de Levis; Robert Plageoles.

Pierre Gaillard [gi-yahr] (*Rhône*, France) A good producer of *Côte Rôtie*, *St. Joseph* and *Condrieu*. ☆☆☆☆ 1995 Côte Rôtie ££££

Gainey Vineyard [gay-nee] (*Santa Barbara*, California) Classy reds and whites, especially *Pinot* and *Chardonnay*. ☆☆☆☆ 1995 Chardonnay £££

Gaja [gi-yah] (*Piedmont*, Italy) The man who proved that wines from the previously modest region of *Barbaresco* could sell for higher prices than top-class *clarets*, let alone the supposedly classier neighbours *Barolo* (an example of which he now makes too). Individual vineyard reds are of great quality and the *Chardonnay* is the best in Italy. Asking whether they're worth these prices is like questioning the cost of a Ferrari.

Galestro [gah-less-troh] (*Tuscany*, Italy) There is no such thing as *Chianti* Bianco – the light, grapey stuff that is made in the *Chianti* region is sold as Galestro. *Antinori; Frescobaldi.*

E & J Gallo [gal-loh] (*Central Valley*, California) The world's biggest wine producer; annual production is around 60 per cent of the total Californian harvest and more than the whole of Australia or *Champagne*. At the top end, there is now some pretty good but pricy *Cabernet* and *Chardonnay* from Gallo's own huge 'Northern *Sonoma* Estate', a piece of land which was physically re-contoured by their bulldozers. The new Turning Leaf wines are good too, at their level; with the exception of the *French Colombard*, the rest of the basic range, though much improved and very widely stocked, is still pretty ordinary. ☆☆☆☆☆ 1994 Frei Ranch Zinfandel £££; ☆☆☆☆ 1995 Laguna Ranch Chardonnay £££

❦**Gamay** [ga-may] (*Beaujolais*, France) Light-skinned grape traditional to *Beaujolais* where it is used to make fresh and fruity reds for early drinking, usually by the *carbonic maceration* method, and more serious *cru* wines that resemble light *Burgundy*. Also successful in California (*J Lohr*), Australia (*Brown Bros.*) and South Africa (*Fairview*).

Gamey Smell or taste distinctly, if oddly, reminiscent of hung game. Particularly associated with old *Pinot Noirs* and *Syrahs*. Sometimes at least partly attributable to the combination of those grapes' natural characteristics with overly generous doses of **sulphur dioxide** by winemakers. Modern examples of both styles seem to be distinctly less gamey than in the past.

� **Gancia** [gan-chee-yah] (*Piedmont*, Italy) Reliable producer of *Asti Spumante* and good dry Pinot di Pinot, as well as *Pinot Blanc* fizz.

☓ **Ch. de la Gardine** [Gar-Deen] (*Rhône*, France) A good large *Châteauneuf-du-Pape* estate. 'Les Générations' is the top *cuvée*. ☆☆☆☆☆ 1995 'Les Générations' ££££

❦**Garnacha Blanca** [gahr-na-cha blan-ka] (Spain) The *Grenache* Blanc, with which *Miguel Torres* has chosen to make his white Coronas. Peppery but sometimes short of fruit.

❦**Garnacha Tinta** [gahr-na-cha tin-ta] (Spain) The Spanish name for *Grenache*. Rarely as intense as in France, but can be attractively peppery.

Garrafeira [gah-rah-fay-rah] (Portugal) Indicates a producer's *'reserve'* wine, which has been selected and given extra time in cask (minimum 2 years) and bottle (minimum 1 year).

☓ **Vincent Gasse** [gass] (*Rhône,* France) Next to La Landonne. Tiny production of superb, concentrated, inky black wines. ☆☆☆☆ 1991 Côte Rôtie Brune.££££

☓ **Gattinara** [Gat-tee-nah-rah] (*Piedmont*, Italy) Red *DOC* from the *Nebbiolo* – varying in quality but generally full-flavoured and dry. 78 79 82 **85 88** 89 90 93 94 95 96 **Travaglini.**

☓ **Domaine Gauby** [Goh-Bee] (*Côtes de Roussillon*, France) Serious *Roussillon* reds and (*Muscat*) whites. The Muntada *Syrah* is the top *cuvée*. ☆☆☆☆☆ 1995 Côtes de Roussillon Muntada ££££

☓ **Gavi** [gah-vee] (*Piedmont*, Italy) Generally unexceptional dry white wine from the *Cortese* grape. Compared by Italians to white *Burgundy* with which it and the creamily pleasant Gavi di Gavi share a propensity for high prices.

☓ **Ch. le Gay** [luh gay] (*Pomerol*, *Bordeaux*, France) Good *Moueix* property with intense complex wine. 70 **75 76** 78 79 **82 83 85** 86 88 89 90 94 95 96 ☆☆☆☆ 1990 £££

☓ **Ch. Gazin** [Ga-zan] (*Pomerol*, *Bordeaux*, France) Has become far more polished since the mid 1980s. 85 86 **87** 88 89 90 92 93 94 95 96 ☆☆☆☆ 1995 ££££

Geelong [zhee-long] (*Victoria*, Australia) Cool region pioneered by Idyll Vineyards (makers of old-fashioned reds) and rapidly attracting notice with *Bannockburn's* and Scotchman Hill's *Pinot Noirs*.

Geisenheim [gi-zen-hime] (*Rheingau*, Germany) Home of the German Wine Institute wine school, once one of the best in the world, but now overtaken by more go-ahead seats of learning in France, California and Australia. Qba/Kab/Spät: **85** 86 **88 89 90** 91 92 93 94 95 96 97 Aus/Beeren/Tba: **83 85** 88 89 90 91 92 93 94 95 96 97

☓ **Ch. de la Genaiserie** [Jeh-Nay-Seh-Ree] (*Loire*, France) Classy, lusciously honeyed, single-vineyard wines from *Coteaux du Layon*. ☆☆☆☆☆ 1995 Coteaux du Layon Chaume ££££

Generoso [zheh-neh-roh-soh] (Spain) Fortified or dessert wine.

🍷 **Gentilini** [zhen-tee-lee-nee] (*Cephalonia*, Greece) Nick Cosmetatos's modern white wines, made using classic Greek grapes and French varieties, should be an example to all his countrymen who are still happily making and drinking stuff which tastes as fresh as an old election manifesto.

🍷 **JM Gerin** [ger-an] (*Rhône*, France) A producer of good modern *Côte Rotie* and *Condrieu*; uses new oak to make powerful, long-lived wines. ☆☆☆☆ **1995 Côte Rôtie Les Grandes Places ££££**

🍷 **Gevrey-Chambertin** [zheh-vray shom-behr-tan] (*Burgundy*, France) Best-known big red *Côte de Nuits commune*; very variable, but still capable of superb, plummy cherryish wine. The top *Grand Cru* is *Le Chambertin* but, in the right hands, *Premiers Crus* like Les Cazetiers can beat this and the other *Grands Crus*. 78 83 **85 88 89 90** 92 95 96 *Vallet Frères; Alain Burguet; Denis Bachelet; Roty; Rossignol-Trapet; Armand Rousseau; Dujac.*

🌳**Gewurztraminer** [geh-voort-strah-mee-nehr] White (well, slightly pink) grape, making dry-to-sweet, full, oily-textured, spicy wine. Best in *Alsace*, but also grown in Australasia, Italy, the US and Eastern Europe. Instantly recognisable by its parma-violets-and-lychees character. **Zind Humbrecht; Scherer; Schoffit (in *Alsace*); Casablanca (in Chile); Stonecroft (in New Zealand).**

🍷 **Geyser Peak** [Gih-Suhr] (*Alexander Valley*, California) Australian wine-maker Darryl Groom revolutionised Californian thinking in this once Australian-owned winery with his *Semillon-Chardonnay* blend ('You mean *Chardonnay*'s not the only white grape?'), and with reds which show an Aussie attitude towards ripe *tannin*. A name to watch. Canyon Creek is the good value *second label*. ☆☆☆☆ **1994 Marietta Cellars Shiraz ££**

🍷 **Ghiaie della Furba** [gee-yah del-lah foor-bah] (*Tuscany*, Italy) Great *Cabernet*-based *Super Tuscan* from *Villa di Capezzana*.

🍷 **Giaconda** [zhee-ya-kon-dah] (*Victoria*, Australia) Small producer hidden away high in the hills. Impressive *Pinot Noir* and *Chardonnay*.

🍷 **Bruno Giacosa** [zhee-yah-koh-sah] (*Piedmont*, Italy) Stunning wine-maker with a large range, including *Barolos* (Vigna Rionda in best years) and *Barbarescos* (Santo Stefano, again, in best years). Recent success with whites, including a *Spumante*. ☆☆☆☆ **1993 Barolo ££**

🍷 **Gie les Rameaux** [lay ram-moh] (*Corsica*, France) One of this island's top producers.

🍷 **Giesen** [gee-sen] (*Canterbury*, New Zealand) Small estate, with particularly appley *Riesling* from *Canterbury*, and *Sauvignon* from *Marlborough*. ☆☆☆☆ **1997 Marlborough Sauvignon Blanc ££**

🍷 **Gigondas** [zhee gon-dass] (*Rhône*, France) *Côtes du Rhône commune*, with good-value, spicy/peppery, blackcurranty reds which show the *Grenache* at its best. A good competitor for nearby *Châteauneuf*. 78 79 **83 85 88** 89 90 93 94 95 96 *Font-Sane; Guigal.*

🍷 **Ch. Gilette** [gil-lette] (*Sauternes*, *Bordeaux*, France) Eccentric, unclassified but of classed-growth quality *Sauternes* kept in tank (rather than cask) for 20 or 30 years. Rare, expensive, worth it. 49 53 59 **61 62 67 70**

Gippsland [gip-sland] (*Victoria*, Australia) Up-and-coming coastal region where *Bass Philip* and *Nicholson River* are producing fascinating and quite European-style wines. Watch out for some of Australia's finest *Pinot Noirs*.

🍷 **Vincent Girardin** [van-son zhee-rahr-dan] (*Burgundy*, France) Reliable *Santenay* producer with vines in several other *communes*. ☆☆☆ **1995 Beaune Clos des Vignes Franches ££££**

♈ Casa Girelli [zhee-reh-lee] (*Veneto*, Italy) Big, but generally uneven, producer.

Giropalette [zhee-roh-pal-let] Large machine which, in *méthode champenoise,* automatically and highly efficiently replaces the human beings who used to perform the task of *remuage.* Used by almost all the bigger *Champagne* houses which, needless to say, prefer to conceal them from visiting tourists.

♈ Camille Giroud [kah-mee zhee-roo] (*Burgundy*, France) Laudably old-fashioned family-owned *négociant* with no love of new oak and small stocks of great mature wine that go a long way to prove that good *Burgundy* really doesn't need it to taste good. ☆☆☆☆ 1993 Santenay ££££

Gisborne [giz-bawn] (New Zealand) North Island vine-growing area since the 1920s. Cool, wettish climate, mainly used for New Zealand's best *Chardonnay.* An ideal partner for *Marlborough* in blends. White: 89 91 94 95 96 *Coopers Creek;* Matawhero; *Millton; Corbans;* Montana; Judd.

♈ Ch. Giscours [zhees-koor] (*Margaux 3ème Cru Classé, Bordeaux,* France) *Margaux* property which, despite the lovely blackcurranty wines it produced in the late 1970s and early 1980s, today remains on the threshold of competition with the best. 71 75 76 78 79 81 82 85 86 88 89 90 91 92 96 ☆☆☆ 1982 ££££

♈ Givry [zheev-ree] (*Burgundy*, France) *Côte Chalonnaise* commune, making typical and affordable, if rather jammily rustic, reds and creamy whites. French wine snobs recall that this was one of King Henri IV's favourite wines, forgetting the fact that a) he had many such favourites dotted all over France and b) his mistress – of whom he also probably had several – happened to live here. Red: 78 80 85 86 87 88 89 90 92 93 94 95 96 Steinmaier; *Joblot; Ragot;* Thénard; Mouton.

♈ Glen Carlou [kah-loo] (*Paarl*, South Africa) Small-scale winery with rich, oily, *oaky Chardonnay* and less convincing reds. ☆☆☆ 1996 Chardonnay ££

♈ Glen Ellen (*Sonoma Valley*, California) Dynamic firm producing large amounts of commercial tropical fruit juice-like *Chardonnay* under its 'Proprietor's Reserve' label. Reds are good value. The *Benziger* range is better. ☆☆☆ 1996 Proprietor's Reserve Chardonnay ££

Glenrowan [glen-roh-wan] (*Victoria*, Australia) Area near *Rutherglen* with a similar range of excellent *liqueur Muscats* and *Tokays.*

♈ Ch. Gloria [glaw-ree-yah] (*St. Julien Cru Bourgeois, Bordeaux*, France) One of the first of the super *Crus Bourgeois.* Now back on form after a disappointing patch. 70 75 82 83 85 86 88 89 90 92 93 94 95 96

♈ Golan Heights Winery [goh-lan] (Israel) Until recently almost the only non-sacramental wines in Israel were made by *Carmel,* who produced one of the least palatable *Sauvignons* I have ever encountered. Today, *Carmel* wines are greatly improved, thanks to competition from this enterprise at which Californian expertise is used to produce good *Kosher Cabernet* and *Muscat.* ☆☆☆ 1996 Chardonnay ££

♈ Goldwater Estate (*Auckland*, New Zealand) *Bordeaux*-like red wine specialist on *Waiheke Island* whose wines are expensive but every bit as good as many similarly-priced French offerings. ☆☆☆ 1996 Chardonnay £££

♈ Gonzalez Byass [gon-zah-lez bih-yas] (*Jerez*, Spain) If *sherry* is beginning to enjoy a long awaited comeback, this is the company that should take much of the credit. While competitors were scurrying around telling people to add ice to their *sherry,* or inventing spurious styles like 'pale *cream',* Gonzalez Byass stuck to its guns making the world's best-selling *fino, Tío Pepe* – and a supporting cast of the finest, most complex, traditional *sherries* available to mankind. ☆☆☆☆☆ Matusálem Oloroso ££££

♀ **Gosset** [gos-say] (*Champagne*, France) The oldest house in *Champagne* producing some marvellous *cuvées*, particularly the Grand Millésime. ☆☆☆☆ **Brut Excellence NV ££££**

♀ **Henri Gouges** [Gooj] (*Burgundy*, France) Long-established estate, producing truly classic long-lived wines. ☆☆☆☆☆ **1995 Nuits-St.-Georges Vaucrains ££££**

Goulburn Valley [gohl-boorn] (*Victoria*, Australia) Small, long-established region reigned over by the respectively ancient and modern *Ch. Tahbilk* and *Mitchelton,* both of whom make great *Marsanne*, though in very different styles.

♀ **Gould Campbell** [goold] (*Douro*, Portugal) Underrated member of the same stable as *Dow's, Graham's and Warre's*. 60 63 66 70 75 77 80 83 85 91 94 ☆☆☆ **1985 Vintage Port £££**

♀ **Goundrey** [gown-dree] (*Western Australia*) Young winery in the up-and-coming region of *Mount Barker,* bought by an American millionaire who has continued the founder's policy of making impressively fruity but not overstated *Chardonnay* and *Cabernet*. ☆☆☆☆ **1995 Reserve Cabernet Sauvignon £££**

Graach [grahkh] (*Mosel-Saar-Ruwer*, Germany) *Mittelmosel* village producing fine wines. Best known for its *Himmelreich* vineyard. QbA/Kab/Spät: **85 86 88 89 90** 91 92 93 94 95 96 Aus/Beeren/Tba: **83 85** 88 89 90 91 92 93 94 95 96 *Deinhard; JJ Prum; Max Ferd Richter; Von Kesselstadt.*

♀ **Graham** [gray-yam] (*Douro*, Portugal) Sweetly delicate wines, sometimes outclassing the same stable's supposedly finer but heftier *Dow's*. Malvedos is the Single *Quinta*. **55** 60 **63 66 70** 75 77 85 91 94 ☆☆☆ **1977 Vintage Port ££££**

♀ **Alain Graillot** [al-lan grih-yoh] (*Rhône*, France) Producer who should be applauded for shaking up the sleepy, largely undistinguished *appellation* of *Crozes-Hermitage,* using grapes from rented vineyards. All the reds are excellent, and La Guiraude is the wine from the top vineyard. ☆☆☆☆ **1995 Crozes Hermitage £££**

Gran Reserva [gran rays-sehr-vah] (Spain) Quality wine aged for a designated number of years in wood and, in theory, only produced in the best vintages. Can be dried out and less worthwhile than *Crianza* or *Reserva*.

Grand Cru [gron kroo] (France) The finest vineyards and – supposedly – the equally fine wine made in them. Official designation in *Bordeaux, Burgundy* and *Alsace*. Vague in *Bordeaux* (especially in *St. Emilion* which can be described as either *Grand Cru, Grand Cru Classé* – or both – or *Premier Grand Cru Classé*) and somewhat unreliable in *Alsace*. In *Burgundy* single vineyards with their own *ACs*, e.g. *Montrachet*, do not need to carry the name of the village (e.g. *Chassagne-Montrachet*) on their label.

♀ **Ch. Grand Mayne** [Gron-Mayn] (*St. Emilion Grand Cru, Bordeaux,* France) Producer of rich, deeply flavoursome, modern *St. Emilion*. Not for traditionalists perhaps, but still due for promotion to *Premier Grand Cru* status. 82 83 85 86 87 88 89 90 92 93 94 95 96

♀ **Ch. du Grand Moulas** [gron moo-lahs] (*Rhône*, France) Very classy *Côtes du Rhône* property with unusually complex wines. ☆☆☆☆ **1995 ££**

Grand Vin [gron van] (*Bordeaux*, France) The first (quality) wine of an estate – as opposed to its *second label*.

♀ **Ch. Grand-Pontet** [gron pon-tay] (*St. Emilion Grand Cru Classé, Bordeaux,* France) Rising star with showy wines. 82 83 85 **86** 88 89 90 92 93 94 95

♀ **Ch. Grand-Puy-Ducasse** [gron pwee doo-kass] (*Pauillac 5ème Cru Classé, Bordeaux,* France) Excellent wines from fifth growth *Pauillac* property. 79 81 **82** 83 85 86 88 89 90 91 92 93 94 95 96

☰ **Ch. Grand-Puy-Lacoste** [gron pwee lah-kost] (*Pauillac 5ème Cru Classé, Bordeaux*, France) Top-class fifth growth owned by the Borie family of *Ducru-Beaucaillou* and right up there among the *Super Seconds*. One of the best-value wines in the region. 61 70 75 78 79 81 82 83 85 86 88 89 90 91 92 93 94 95 96 ☆☆☆ **1990 ££££**

☰ **Grande Rue** [grond-roo] (*Burgundy*, France) Recently promoted *Grand Cru* in *Vosne-Romanée*, across the way from *Romanée-Conti* (hence the promotion). Sadly, the Dom. Lamarche to which this *monopole* belongs is a long-term under-performer.

Grandes Marques [grond mahrk] (*Champagne*, France) Once-official designation for 'big name' *Champagne* houses.

☰ **Grands-Echézeaux** [grons AY-sheh-zoh] (*Burgundy*, France) One of the best *Grand Crus* in *Burgundy*; see *Echézeaux*.

☰ **Grange** [graynzh] (South Australia) *Penfolds*' and Australia's greatest wine – 'The Southern Hemisphere's only first growth' – pioneered by Max Schubert in the early 1950s and made from *Shiraz* produced by 70-year-old vines sited in several South Australian regions. Recently discovered in the US and thus a collector's item that sells out as soon as each vintage hits the streets. ☆☆☆☆☆ **1990 ££££**

☰ **Grangehurst** [graynzh-huhrst] (*Stellenbosch*, South Africa) Exceptionally concentrated modern reds from a tiny winery converted from the family squash court! Expanding. Good *Cabernet* and *Pinotage*. ☆☆☆☆ **1994 Pinotage ££**

☰ **Ch. Grangeneuve de Figeac** [gronzh-nuhv duh fee-zhak] (*St. Emilion, Bordeaux*, France) *Second label* of Ch. *Figeac*.

☰ **Weingut Grans-Fassian** [grans-fass-yan] (*Mosel*, Germany) Improving estate with some really fine, classic wine – especially at a supposedly basic level. ☆☆☆☆ **1995 Riesling ££**

☰ **Yves Grassa** [gras-sah] (Sout-West France) Pioneering producer of *Vin de Pays des Côtes de Gascogne* – now moving from *Colombard* and *Ugni Blanc* into *Sauvignon Blanc*. ☆☆☆ **1996 Ch. Tariquet Sauvignon Blanc ££**

☰ **Alfred Gratien** [gras-see-yen] (*Champagne*, France) Good *Champagne* house, using traditional methods. Also owner of *Loire* sparkling winemaker, Gratien et Meyer, based in *Saumur*. ☆☆☆ **1989 Vintage Champagne ££££**

🍇 **Grauerburgunder** [grow-urh-buhr-goon-duhr] (Germany) Another name for *Pinot Gris*. *Müller-Cattoir*.

☰ **Dom. la Grave** [lah grahv] (*Graves, Bordeaux*, France) Small property in the *Graves* with a growing reputation for 100 per cent *Sémillon* whites. Red: **89 90** 91 94 95 96 White: **89** 91 93 96 97

☰ **Grave del Friuli** [grah-veh del free-yoo-lee] (*Friuli-Venezia Giulia*, Italy) *DOC* for young-drinking reds and whites. *Cabernet, Merlot* and *Chardonnay* are increasingly successful.

☰ **Graves** [grahv] (*Bordeaux*, France) Large region producing vast quantities of white, from good to indifferent. The best whites come from the northern part of the Graves and are sold as *Pessac-Léognan*. Reds can have a lovely raspberryish character. Red: **70** 75 78 79 81 82 83 85 86 88 89 90 94 95 96 White: 71 75 78 79 82 **83 85 86** 88 **89** *90 93 94 95 96 Haut-Brion; Ch. de Chantegrive; Dom. de Chevalier; Dom. la Grave; Smith-Haut-Lafitte; du Seuil; Clos Floridène.*

Great Western (*Victoria*, Australia) Region noted for *Seppelt's* fizzes including the astonishing 'Sparkling *Burgundy*' *Shirazes*, for *Best's* and for the wines of *Mount Langi Ghiran*.

🍷 **Greco di Tufo** [greh-koh dee too-foh] (*Campania*, Italy) From *Campania*, best-known white from the ancient Greco grape; dry, characterfully herby southern wine. **Librandi; Botomagno.**

Greece Finally, if belatedly, beginning to modernise its wine industry – and to exploit the potential of a set of grapes grown nowhere else. Unfortunately, as Greece begins to rid itself of its taste for the stewed, oxidised styles of the past, the modern wines are so popular in the smart restaurants in Athens that they appear to be both expensive and hard to find overseas. ***Boutari; Ch. Carras; Gentilini; Hatzimichalis;* Lazarides.**

🍷 **Green Point** (*Yarra Valley*, Australia) See *Dom. Chandon*.

🍷 **Green & Red** (*Napa Valley*, California) Fast-rising star with impressive *Zinfandel*. ☆☆☆☆ **1993 Chiles Mill Vineyard Unfiltered Zinfandel £££**

🍇 **Grenache** [greh-nash] Red grape of the *Rhône* (aka *Garnacha* in Spain) making spicy, peppery, full-bodied wine, provided yields are kept low. Also increasingly used to make rosés across Southern France, Australia and California.

🍷 **Marchesi de Gresy** [mah-kay-see day greh-see] (*Piedmont*, Italy) Good producer of single vineyard *Barbaresco*. ☆☆☆☆ **1990 Martinenga Camp Gros ££££**

🍷 **Grgich Hills** [guhr-gich] (*Napa Valley*, California) Pioneering producer of *Cabernet Sauvignon, Chardonnay* and *Fumé Blanc*. The name is a concatenation of the two founders – Mike Grgich and Austin Hills, rather than a topographical feature.

🍇 **Grignolino** [green-yoh-lee-noh] (*Piedmont*, Italy) Red grape and modest but refreshing cherryish wine, e.g. the *DOC* Grignolino d'Asti. Drink young.

🍷 **Ch. Grillet** [gree-yay] (*Rhône*, France) *Appellation* consisting of a single estate and producer of slowly improving *Viognier* white. Neighbouring *Condrieu* is better value. ☆☆☆ **1993 Ch. Grillet ££££**

🍷 **Marqués de Griñon** [green-yon] (*La Mancha, Rioja, Ribera del Duero*, Spain/Argentina) Dynamic exception to the dull *La Mancha* rule, making wines, with the help of *Michel Rolland*, which can outclass *Rioja*. The juicy *Cabernet Merlot* and fresh white *Rueda* have been joined by Durius, a blend from *Ribera del Duero*, an exceptional new *Syrah* and an extraordinary *Petit Verdot*. Look out too for new wines from Argentina. ☆☆☆☆ **1996 Durius Tinto ££**

🍷 **Bernard Gripa** [gree-pah] (*Rhône*, France) Maker of top-notch *St. Joseph* – ripe, thick, *tarry* wine that could age forever. ☆☆☆☆ **1994 St. Joseph Le Berceau £££**

🍷 **Jean-Louis Grippat** [gree-pah] (*Rhône*, France) An unusually great white *Rhône* producer in *Hermitage* and *St. Joseph*. His reds in both *appellations* are less stunning, but still worth buying in their subtler-than-most way. Look out too for his ultra-rare Cuvée des Hospices, *St. Joseph* Rouge. ☆☆☆☆ **1994 Hermitage Blanc ££££**

🍷 **Dom. Jean Grivot** [gree-voh] (*Burgundy*, France) Top-class *Vosne-Romanée* estate whose winemaker Etienne has recently escaped from the spell of Lebanese guru oenologist Guy Accad, whose advice made for some curious wines in the 1980s. ☆☆☆☆ **1992 Vosne-Romanée Beaux Monts ££££**

🍷 **Robert Groffier** [grof-fee-yay] (*Burgundy*, France) Up-and-coming estate, with top class wines from *Chambolle-Musigny*. ☆☆☆☆☆ **1995 Bonnes Mares ££££**

🍷 **Groot Constantia** [khroot-kon-stan-tee-yah] (*Constantia*, South Africa) Government-run, 300-year-old wine estate and national monument – that is finally making worthwhile wines. ☆☆☆ **1995 Cabernet Sauvignon £££**

☨ **Dom. Anne Gros** [groh] (*Burgundy*, France) Unfortunately for one's wallet, the best wines from this *Vosne-Romanée domaine* are as expensive as they are delicious – but they are worth every penny. ☆☆☆☆ **1993 Richebourg ££££**

☨ **Jean Gros** [groh] (*Burgundy*, France) Slightly less impressive *Vosne-Romanée* producer, but the *Clos Vougeot*s are good. ☆☆☆☆ **1990 Clos du Vougeot ££££**

🍇 **Gros Lot/Grolleau** [groh-loh] (*Loire*, France) The workhorse black grape of the *Loire*, particularly in *Anjou*, used to make white, rosé and sparkling *Saumur.*

🍇 **Gros Plant (du Pays Nantais)** [groh-plon doo pay-yee non-tay] (*Loire*, France) Light, sharp white *VDQS* wine from the western *Loire*. In all but the best hands, serves to make even a poor *Muscadet* look good.

☨ **Grosset** [gros-set] (*South Australia*) Terrific white wine (*Chardonnay, Riesling, Semillon*) specialist in the *Clare* Valley. Give them time to develop. Also try the Gaia red *Bordeaux*-blend. ☆☆☆☆ **1996 Jeremy Grosset Riesling £££**

Grosslage [gross-lah-guh] (Germany) Wine district, the third subdivision after *anbaugebiet* (e.g. *Rheingau*) and *bereich* (e.g. *Nierstein*). For example, *Michelsberg* is a *grosslage* of the *bereich* Piesport.

☨ **Groth** [grahth] (*Napa Valley*, California) Serious producer of quality *Cabernet* and *Chardonnay*. ☆☆☆☆ **1992 Cabernet Sauvignon Napa Valley £££**

☨ **Grove Mill** (New Zealand) Relatively new winery specialising in more aromatic styles such as *Riesling*. ☆☆☆ **1996 Lansdowne Chardonnay £££**

☨ **Ch. Gruaud-Larose** [groo-oh lah-rohz] (*St. Julien 2ème Cru Classé*, *Bordeaux*, France) One of the stars of the *Cordier* stable. Rich but potentially slightly unsubtle. The second wine is 'Le Sarget'. **61** 70 75 76 **78** 79 **82 83 85 86** 88 89 90 91 92 93 94 95 96

🍇 **Grüner Veltliner** [groo-nuhr felt-lee-nuhr] Spicy white grape of Austria and Eastern Europe, producing light, fresh, aromatic wine – and for *Willi Opitz* an extraordinary *late harvest* version. *Kracher;* Lang; Schuster; Steininger.

☨ **Bodegas Guelbenzu** [guhl-bent-zoo] (*Navarra*, Spain) Starry new-wave producer of rich red wines using local grapes and *Cabernet*. ☆☆☆☆ **1994 Merlot ££**; ☆☆☆ **1994 Guelbenzu Evo ££**

☨ **Guenoc** [gwen-nahk] (*Lake County*, California) Lillie Langtry's winery. Sadly, not a source of superstar wines. ☆☆☆ **1996 Chardonnay Genevieve Magoon Vineyard ££££**

☨ **Guerrieri-Rizzardi** [gwer-reh-ree rit-zar-dee] (*Veneto*, Italy) Solid organic producer, with good *Amarone* and single vineyard *Soave Classico*. ☆☆☆☆ **1995 Fontis Vineale Minus £££**

☨ **Guffens-Heynen** [goof-fens ay-na(n)] (*Burgundy*, France) Rising star in *Pouilly-Fuissé*. ☆☆☆☆ **1995 Pouilly-Fuissé £££**

☨ **E Guigal** [gee-gahl] (*Rhône*, France) Still the yardstick for *Rhône* reds, despite increased competition from *Chapoutier*. His extraordinarily pricy single-vineyard La Mouline, La Landonne and La Turque wines from *Côte Rôtie* are still ahead of the young turks and the 'Brune et Blonde' blend of grapes from two hillsides remains a benchmark for this *appellation*. The basic red and white *Côtes du Rhône* are also well worth looking out for. ☆☆☆☆☆ **1995 Condrieu la Doriane £££**; ☆☆☆☆ **1994 Côte Rôtie Brune et Blonde ££**

☨ **Guimaraens** [gee-mah-rens] (*Douro*, Portugal) Associated with *Fonseca*; under-rated *port*-house making good wines. ☆☆☆☆☆ **1984 Fonseca Guimaraens Vintage Port ££££**

☨ **Ch. Guiraud** [gee-roh] (*Sauternes Premier Cru Classé*, *Bordeaux*, France) *Sauternes classed-growth*, recently restored to original quality. Good wines but rarely among the most complex sweet *Bordeaux*. 67 79 81 82 **83** 85 **86** 87 88 89 90 92 93 94 95 96 97 ☆☆☆☆ **1990 ££££**

☨ **Weingut Gunderloch** [goon-duhr-lokh] (*Rheinhessen*, Germany) One of the few estates to make *Rheinhessen* wines of truly reliable quality. ☆☆☆☆ **1996 Niersteiner Rothenbergl Riesling Auslese £££**

�₸ **Gundlach-Bundschu** [guhnd-lakh buhnd-shoo] (*Sonoma Valley*, California) Good, well-made, juicy *Merlot* and spicy *Zinfandel*. ☆☆☆☆ **1991 Rhinefarm Vineyard Zinfandel £££**

�₸ **Louis Guntrum** [goon-troom] (*Rheinhessen*, Germany) Family-run estate with a penchant for *Sylvaner*. ☆☆☆☆ **1996 Oppenheimer Herrenberg Silvaner Eiswein ££££**

☰ **Ch. la Gurgue** [lah guhrg] (*Margaux Cru Bourgeois*, *Bordeaux*, France) *Cru Bourgeois* across the track from *Ch. Margaux*. Less impressive since the same owner's *Ch. Ferrière* has both improved and increased its production. Coincidence presumably. 83 85 86 88 89 90 94 95 96

🍇 **Gutedel** [goot-edel] (Germany) German name for the *Chasselas* grape.

☰ **Friedrich-Wilhelm Gymnasium** [free-drikh vil-helm-gim-nahz-yuhm] (*Mosel*, Germany) Big-name estate that ought to be making better wine. ☆☆☆☆ **1996 Graacher Himmelreich Riesling Spätlese £££**

☰ **Gyöngyös Estate** [zhon-zhosh] (*Eger*, Hungary) Ground-breaking winery in which *Hugh Ryman* first produced drinkable Eastern European *Sauvignon* and *Chardonnay*. ☆☆☆ **1996 Sauvignon £**

H

☰ **Weingut Fritz Haag** [hahg] (*Mosel-Saar-Ruwer*, Germany) Superlative small estate with classic *Rieslings*. ☆☆☆☆ **1996 Brauneberger Juffer Sonnenuhr Riesling Auslese ££££**

☰ **Weingut Reinhold Haart** [rihn-hohld hahrt] (*Mosel*, Germany) Fast rising *Piesport* star. ☆☆☆☆ **1996 Piesporter Goldtröpfchen Riesling Auslese £££**

Halbtrocken [hahlb-trok-en] (Germany) Off-dry. Usually a safer buy than *Trocken* in regions like the *Mosel, Rheingau* and *Rheinhessen,* but still often aggressively acidic. Look for *QbA* or *Auslese* versions.

Hallgarten [hal-gahr-ten] (*Rheingau*, Germany) Important town near *Hattenheim* producing robust wines including the (in Germany) well-regarded produce from *Schloss Vollrads*. QbA/Kab/Spät: 85 86 **88 89 90** 91 92 93 95 96 97 Aus/Beeren/Tba: 83 85 88 89 90 92 93 94 95 96 97

☰ **Hamilton Russell Vineyards** (*Walker Bay*, South Africa) Pioneer of impressive *Pinot Noir* and *Chardonnay* at a winery in Hermanus at the southernmost tip of the *Cape*. Now expanded to include a *second label* – Southern Right – to produce a varietal *Pinotage*, and a *Chenin*-based white. ☆☆☆☆ **1997 Pinot Noir £££**

☰ **Hanging Rock** (*Victoria*, Australia) As in the movie, 'Picnic at....' this winery makes Australia's biggest, butteriest fizz and some good reds and whites. ☆☆☆☆ **1996 Cabernet-Merlot £££**

☰ **Hardy's** (*South Australia*) The second biggest wine producer in Australia, encompassing *Houghton* and *Moondah Brook* in *Western Australia*, *Leasingham* in the *Clare Valley*, *Redman* in *Coonawarra*, Hardy's itself and *Ch. Reynella*. Hardy's range is reliable throughout, including the commercial Nottage Hill, new Bankside, and multi-regional blends, though the wines to look for are the top-of-the-range Eileen and Thomas Hardy. The *Ch. Reynella* wines made from *McLaren Vale* fruit (and, in the case of the reds, using basket presses) are good, quite lean examples of the region. Look out for Hardy's non-Australian ventures in Italy (d'Istinto) and France (la Baume). ☆☆☆☆☆ **1995 Eileen Hardy Shiraz £££**

☰ **Harlan Estate** (*Napa Valley*, California) Small quantities of *Bordeaux*-style reds, made with input from *Michel Rolland*, using grapes from hillside vineyards. ☆☆☆☆ **1993 Proprietory Red £££**

🍇 **Hárslevelü** [harsh-leh-veh-loo] (Hungary) White grape used in *Tokaji* and for light table wines.

 Harvees (*Jerez*, Spain) Maker of the ubiquitous *Bristol Cream*. Other styles are unimpressive.

 Hatzimichalis [hat-zee-mikh-ahlis] (Atalanti, Greece) The face of future Greek winemaking? Hopefully. This self-taught producer's small estate makes top-notch *Cabernet Sauvignon, Merlot, Chardonnay* and fresh dry Atalanti white. ☆☆☆ **1994 Cava Red ££**

 Ch. Haut-Bages-Averous [oh-bahj-aveh-roo] (*Pauillac Cru Bourgeois*, *Bordeaux*, France) *Second label* of *Ch. Lynch-Bages*. Good-value black-curranty *Pauillac*. 82 83 **85** 86 88 89 90 93 94 95 96

 Ch. Haut-Bages-Libéral [oh-bahj-lib-ay-ral] (*Pauillac 5ème Cru Classé*, *Bordeaux*, France) Classy small property in the same stable as *Chasse-Spleen*. 75 78 **82** 83 85 **86** 87 88 89 90 91 93 94 95 96

 Ch. Haut-Bailly [oh bih-yee] (*Pessac-Léognan Cru Classé*, *Bordeaux*, France) Recently sold: brilliant *Pessac-Léognan* property consistently making reliable, excellent quality, long-lived red wines. **61** 64 **70** 78 **79** 81 83 **85** 86 87 88 89 90 92 93 94 95 96

 Ch. Haut-Batailley [oh-ba-tih-yee] (*Pauillac 5ème Cru Classé*, *Bordeaux*, France) Subtly-styled wine from the same stable as *Ducru-Beaucaillou* and *Grand-Puy-Lacoste* 85 86 88 89 90 91 92 93 **95 96** 97

 Ch. Haut-Brion [oh bree-yon] (*Pessac-Léognan Premier Cru Classé*, *Bordeaux*, France) Pepys' favourite and still the only non-*Médoc* first growth. Situated in the *Graves* on the outskirts of *Bordeaux* in the shadow of the gasworks. Wines can be tough and hard to judge when young but, at their best they develop a rich, fruity, perfumed character which sets them apart from their peers. 1989 and 1996 were both especially good, as – comparatively – were 1993, 1994 and 1995.The white is rare and often sublime. Red: **61 70 71 75 78 79 82** 85 86 88 89 90 91 92 93 94 95 96 White: 85 87 88 89 90 91 92 93 94 95 96

 Ch. Haut-Marbuzet [oh-mahr-boo-zay] (*St. Estèphe Cru Bourgeois*, *Bordeaux*, France) A *cru bourgeois* which thinks it's a *cru classé*. Well-made, immediately imposing wine with bags of oak. Decidedly new-wave *St. Estèphe*. 70 **75** 76 **78** 81 **82 83 85** 86 88 89 90 92 93 94 95 96

 Haut-Médoc [oh-may-dok] (*Bordeaux*, France) Large *appellation* which includes nearly all of the well-known *crus classés*. Basic Haut-Médoc should be better than plain *Médoc*. **82** 83 **85 86** 88 89 90 94 95 96

 Haut-Poitou [oh-pwa-too] (*Loire*, France) A source of basic inexpensive *Sauvignon*. A team of Australians from *BRL Hardy* has recently shown that a dose of skilful winemaking pays dividends here.

 Hautes Côtes de Beaune [oht-coht-duh-bohn] (*Burgundy*, France) Rustic wines from a group of villages situated in the hills above the big-name *communes*. Worth buying in good vintages; in poorer ones the grapes have problems ripening. Much of the wine seen outside the region is made by one of *Burgundy*'s improving cooperatives. Red: 83 **85 88 89 90** 92 94 95 96 White: **85** 86 88 89 **90** 92 95 96 97

 Hautes Côtes de Nuits [oht-coht-duh-nwee] (*Burgundy*, France) Slightly tougher than *Hautes Côtes de Beaune*, particularly when young. White wines are very rare. Red: **80** 82 83 **85** 86 87 **88 89 90** 92 95 96

 Hawke's Bay (New Zealand) Major North Island vineyard area which is finally beginning to live up to the promise of producing top-class reds. Whites can be fine too, though rarely achieving the bite of *Marlborough*. *Te Mata; Delegats; Morton Estate; Esk Valley; CJ Pask; Vidal; Villa Maria;* Sacred Hill; *Ngatarawa; Montana;* Church Road; *Babich*.

✴ **Hedges** (*Washington State*, US) Producer of good, rich, berryish reds.
☆☆☆ **1994 Red Mountain Cabernet £££**

✴ **Heemskerk** [heems-kuhrk] (*Tasmania*, Australia) Until recently associated with *Roederer* in the making of *Jansz*, this is a producer of (good) Aussie fizz and also the source of some sturdy reds. ☆☆☆☆ **1993 Jansz Sparkling Brut £££**

✴ **Heggies** [heg-gees] (South Australia) *Yalumba's* impressive estate in the *Adelaide Hills*, making good *Riesling* and improving *Viognier, Merlot* and *Pinot Noir*. Also marvellous *botrytis*-affected stickies. ☆☆☆☆ **1997 Botrytis-Affected Riesling ££**

✴ **Charles Heidsieck** [hihd-seek] (*Champagne*, France) Go-ahead producer which has recently introduced the clever notion of labelling its non-*vintage* wine with its 'mis en cave' – bottling date. Wines are all recommendable. ☆☆☆☆☆ **Brut Réserve Mis en Cave 1993 ££££**

✴ **Heidsieck Dry Monopole** [hihd-seek] (*Champagne*, France) A subsidiary of *Mumm* and thus now controlled by Seagrams. Wines have improved recently. ☆☆☆ **Diamont Bleu ££££**

✴ **Heitz Cellars** [hihtz] (*Napa Valley*, California) One of the great names of California and the source of stunning reds in the 1970s. Recent releases of the flagship Martha's Vineyard *Cabernet* have tasted unacceptably musty, however, as have the traditionally almost-as-good Bella Oaks. At the winery and among some critics, such criticisms are apparently treated as lèse-majesté. ☆☆☆☆ **1990 Cabernet Sauvignon Napa Valley £££**

✴ **Joseph Henriot** [on-ree-yoh] (*Champagne*, France) Modern *Champagne* house producing soft rich wines. Now also shaking things up and improving wines at its recently purchased *Bouchard Père et Fils négociant* in *Burgundy*. ☆☆☆☆ **Champagne Blanc de Blancs ££££**

✴ **Henriques & Henriques** [hen-reeks] (*Madeira*, Portugal) One of the few independent producers still active in *Madeira*. Top quality. ☆☆☆☆☆ **10 Year Old Bual £££**

✴ **Henschke** [hench-kee] (*Adelaide Hills*, Australia) One of the world's best. From the long-established Hill of Grace with its 130-year-old vines and (slightly less intense) Mount Edelstone *Shirazes* to the new Abbott's Prayer *Merlot-Cabernet* from *Lenswood*, the *Riesling* and Tilly's Vineyard white blend, there's not a duff wine here; the reds last forever. Compare and contrast with *Heitz*. ☆☆☆☆☆ **1992 Hill of Grace Shiraz ££££**

✴ **Hermitage** [ayr-mee-tazh] (*Rhône*, France) Supreme Northern *Rhône* appellation for long-lived pure *Syrah*. Whites are less reliable. Red: 76 78 82 83 85 88 89 90 91 95 White: 82 85 87 88 89 90 91 94 95 *Chave; Guigal; Jaboulet Aîné; Delas;* Bernard Faurie; *Chapoutier.*

✴ **The Hess Collection** (*Napa Valley*, California) High-class *Cabernet* producer, high in the *Mount Veeder* hills. The lower-priced Hess Select *Monterey* wines are worth buying too. ☆☆☆☆☆ **1995 Napa Valley Chardonnay £££**

Hessische Bergstrasse [hess-ishuh behrg-strah-suh] (Germany) Smallest *anbaugebiet* capable of fine *Eisweins* and dry *Sylvaners* which can surpass those of nearby *Franken*. QbA/Kab/Spät: **85 88 89 90** 91 92 93 94 95 96 97 Aus/Beeren/Tba: **83 85 88 89 90 91 92 93 94 95 97**

✴ **Vinicola Hidalgo y Cia** [hid-algoh ee-thia] (*Jerez*, Spain) Specialist producer of impeccable dry 'La Gitana' *sherry* and a great many own-label offerings. ☆☆☆☆ **La Gitana Manzanilla ££**

✴ **Hill Smith Wines** (South Australia) A classy firm, under the same family ownership as *Yalumba* and *Heggies* Vineyard, and now active in New Zealand and California (where its *Voss* wines are made). ☆☆☆ **1997 Estate Chardonnay ££;** ☆☆☆☆☆ **1996 Pewsey Vale Cabernet ££**

Hillstowe [hil-stoh] (*South Australia*) Up-and-coming producer in the *McLaren Vale*, using grapes from various parts of the region to produce unusually stylish *Chardonnay, Sauvignon Blanc* and *Cabernet-Merlot*. ☆☆☆☆ 1994 Buxton Cabernet Merlot £££; ☆☆☆☆ 1997 Buxton Sauvignon ££

Himmelreich [him-mel-rihkh] (*Mosel*, Germany) One of the finest vineyards in *Graach*. QbA/Kab/Spät: **85 86 88 89** 90 **91** 92 93 94 95 96 97 Aus/Beeren/Tba: **83** 85 88 89 90 91 92 93 94 95 97

Paul Hobbs (*Sonoma*, California) Former winemaker at *Simi*, and now a consultant at *Catena* and *Valdivieso* in South America, Paul Hobbs makes fine *Pinot Noir*, *Cabernet* and rich *Chardonnay* from the memorably-named 'Dinner Vineyard'.

Serge Hochar [hosh-ah] see *Ch. Musar.*

Hochfeinste [hokh-fihn-stuh] (Germany) 'Very finest'.

Hochgewächs QbA [hokh-geh-fex] (Germany) Recent official designation for *Rieslings* which are as ripe as a *QmP* but can still only call themselves *QbA*. This from a nation supposedly dedicated to simplifying what are acknowledged to be the most complicated labels in the world.

Hochheim [hokh-hihm] (*Rheingau*, Germany) Village whose fine *Rieslings* gave the English word *'Hock'*. QbA/Kab/Spät: **85** 86 **88 89 90** 91 92 93 94 95 96 Aus/Beeren/Tba: **83 85** 88 89 90 91 92 93 94 95 96 Geh'rat Aschrott; Konigen Victoria Berg.

Hogue Cellars [hohg] (*Washington State*, US) Highly dynamic, family-owned *Yakima Valley* producer of good *Chardonnay*, *Riesling*, *Merlot* and *Cabernet*. ☆☆☆☆ 1996 Late Harvest Riesling £££

Hollick (*Coonawarra*, Australia) A good, traditional producer; the *Ravenswood* is particularly worth seeking out. ☆☆☆☆ 1994 Coonawarra Cabernet-Merlot £££

Ch. Hortevie [awt-uhr-vee] (*St. Julien*, *Bordeaux*, France) Not really a château at all – the wine (which is excellent, if a touch rustic) is made at *Ch. Terrey-Gros-Caillou*. 82 83 **85** 86 88 89 90 92 94 95 96

Dom. de l'Hortus [Or-Toos] (*Languedoc-Roussillon*, France) Exciting spicy reds from *Pic St. Loup* in the *Coteaux de Languedoc* that easily out-class many an effort from big name producers in the *Rhône*. ☆☆☆☆ 1994 Grande Cuvée £££

Hospices de Beaune [os-peess duh bohn] (*Burgundy*, France) Hospital whose wines (often *cuvées* or blends of different vineyards) are sold at an annual charity auction, the prices of which are erroneously thought to set the tone for the *Côte d'Or* year. In the early 1990s, wines were generally sub-standard, improving instantly in 1994 with the welcome return of winemaker André Porcheret who has since proved controversial by (in 1997) making wines that struck some critics (not this one) as too big and rich. In any case, be aware that although price lists often merely indicate 'Hospices de Beaune' as a producer, all of the wines bought at the auction are matured and bottled by local merchants, some of whom are more scrupulous than others.

Houghton [haw-ton] (*Swan Valley*, Australia) Long-established sub-sidiary of *Hardy's*. Best known for its *Chenin*-based rich white blend tra-ditionally sold Down Under as 'White *Burgundy*' and sold in Europe as 'HWB'. The Wildflower Ridge commercial wines are good, as are the ones from the *Moondah Brook* vineyard. Look out too for the new *Cabernet-Shiraz-Malbec* 'Jack Mann', named after one of *Western Australia's* pio-neering winemakers. ☆☆☆☆ 1996 Wildflower Ridge Shiraz ££; ☆☆☆ 1995 Wildflower Ridge Chenin Blanc £

Weingut von Hovel [fon huh-vel] (*Mosel-Saar-Ruwer*, Germany) A 200-year-old estate with fine *Rieslings* from great vineyards. These repay the patience that they demand. ☆☆☆☆ 1996 Oberemmeler Hutte Riesling Kabinett £££

Howard Park (*Western Australia*) John Wade is one of the best wine-makers in *Western Australia*. ☆☆☆☆ **1995 Cabernet-Merlot £££;** ☆☆☆☆ **1996 Chardonnay £££**

Howell Mountain [how-wel] (*Napa Valley*, California) Increasingly well respected hillside region in the north of the *Napa Valley*, capable of fine whites and reds that justify its *AVA*. Red: **85 86 87 90 91** 92 93 95 96 White: **85 90 91** 92 95 96 Beringer; la Jota; Dunn.

Alain Hudelot-Noëllat [ood-uh-loh noh-el-lah] (*Burgundy*, France) A great winemaker whose generosity with oak is matched, especially in his *Grand Cru Richebourg* and *Romanée St.Vivant*, by intense fruit flavours. ☆☆☆☆☆ **1995 Vosne-Romanée les Suchots ££££**

Huelva [wel-vah] (*Extremadura*, Spain) *DO* of the *Extremadura* region, producing rather heavy whites and fortified wines.

Gaston Huët [oo-wet] (*Loire*, France) Winemaker Noël Pinguet produces top-quality individual vineyard examples of *Sec*, *Demi-Sec* and *Moëlleux* wines. The non-vintage fizz, though only made occasionally, is top class too. ☆☆☆☆ **1990 Vouvray Moelleux Le Haut Lieu Premier Trie ££££**

Hugel et Fils [oo-gel] (*Alsace*, France) Reliable *négociant*. Best are the *late harvest* and Jubilee wines. The wine 'Gentil' revives the tradition of blending different grape varieties. ☆☆☆☆ **1993 Riesling 'Jubilee' £££**

Hungary Country too long known for its infamous *Bull's Blood*, and *Olasz Rizling* rather than the far more interesting sweet wines. *Royal Tokaji; Hugh Ryman; Kym Milne; Disznókö; Egervin; Nagyrede; Nezmely.*

Hunter Valley (*New South Wales*, Australia) The best-known wine region in Australia is ironically one of the least suitable parts in which to make wine. When the vines are not dying of heat and thirst they are drowning beneath the torrential rains which like to fall at harvest time. Even so, the *Shirazes* and *Semillons* – traditionally sold as 'Hermitage', 'Claret', 'Burgundy', 'Chablis' and 'Hunter Valley Riesling' – develop remarkably. *Lake's Folly; Brokenwood; Rothbury Estate; Rosemount; Tyrrells; McWilliams; Lindemans; Reynolds; Evans Family; Petersons.*

Hunter's (*Marlborough*, New Zealand) One of *Marlborough*'s most consistent producers of ripe fruity *Sauvignon Blancs* and now a quality fizz. ☆☆☆☆☆ **1995 Miru Miru Brut £££**

Huxelrebe [huk-sel-ray-buh] Minor white grape, often grown in England but proving what it can do when harvested late in Germany. **Anselmann (Germany); Nutbourne Manor; Barkham Manor (England).**

Hybrid [hih-brid] Cross-bred grape Vitis *vinifera* (European) x Vitis *labrusca* (North American) – an example is *Seyval Blanc*.

Hydrogen sulphide Naturally occurring rotten egg-like gas produced by yeasts as a by-product of fermentation, or by *reductive* conditions. Before bottling, may be cured by *racking*. If left untreated, hydrogen sulphide will react with other components in the wine to form *mercaptans*. Stinky bottled wines may be 'cleaned up' by the addition of a copper coin.

I

Icewine Increasingly popular Anglicisation of the German term *Eiswein*, used particularly by Canadian producers making luscious, spicily exotic wines from the frozen grapes of varieties like *Vidal*.

Il Podere dell'Olivos [eel poh-deh-reh del-oh-lee-vohs] (California) Pioneering producer of Italian varietals. ☆☆☆ **1995 Tocai Fruiliano ££**

Imbottigliato nel'origine [im-bot-til-yah-toh neh-loh-ree-zhee-nay] (Italy) Estate-bottled.

Immich Batterieberg [Ih-mikh bat-teh-ree-burg] (*Mosel*, Germany) Source of long lasting, good, rather than great wines. ☆☆☆☆ **1996 Enkircher Batterieberg Riesling Auslese £££**

Imperial(e) [am-pay-ray-ahl] (*Bordeaux*, France) Bottle containing almost six and a half litres of wine (eight and a half bottles). Cherished by collectors partly through rarity, partly through the greater longevity that large bottles give their contents.

India Source of generally execrable table wine and surprisingly reliable fizz, labelled as Marquis de Pompadour or *Omar Khayam*.

Inferno [een-fehr-noh] (*Lombardy*, Italy) *Lombardy DOC*. Chiefly red from the *Nebbiolo,* needing ageing for at least five years. ☆☆☆ **1994 Nino Negri ££**

Inglenook Vineyards [ing-gel-nook] (*Napa Valley*, California) Once-great winery which, like *Beaulieu,* fell into the hands of the giant Grand Metropolitan. The Gothic building and vineyards now belong appropriately to Francis Ford-Coppola. The brand has been sold to a firm with little evident love of fine wine.

Inniskillin (*Ontario*, Canada) Long-established, pioneering winery with good *Icewines* (from the *Vidal* grape), highly successful *Chardonnay,* improving *Pinot Noir* and a rare example of a good *Maréchal Foch*. ☆☆☆☆ **1995 Chardonnay Klose Vineyard ££££**

Institut National des Appellations d'Origine (INAO) (France) French official body which designates and (half-heartedly) polices quality, and outlaws sensible techniques like irrigation and the blending of *vintages* which are permitted elsewhere. Maybe this is why *Appellation Contrôlée* wines are often inferior to the newer *Vins de Pays* over which this body has no authority.

International Wine Challenge (England) International wine competition, held each May in London. (The author is founder chairman.)

Irancy [ee-ron-see] (*Burgundy*, France) Little-known light reds and rosés made near *Chablis* from a blend of grapes including the *Pinot Noir* and the little-known *César.* Curiously, Irancy has *AC* status whereas *Sauvignon de St. Bris,* a nearby source of superior whites, is merely a *VDQS* region.

Iron Horse Vineyards (*Sonoma Valley*, California) One of the best sparkling wine producers in the New World, thanks to cool climate vineyards. Reds and still whites are increasingly impressive too. ☆☆☆ **1993 Chardonnay Estate Cuvée Joy £££**

Irouléguy [ee-roo-lay-gee] (South-West France) Earthy spicy reds and rosés, improving whites. The local co-op makes the best wines.

Isinglass [Ih-sing-glahs] *Fining* agent derived from sturgeon bladders.

Isole e Olena [ee-soh-lay ay oh-lay-nah] (*Tuscany*, Italy) Brilliant small *Chianti* estate with a pure *Sangiovese Super-Tuscan, Cepparello* and Italy's first (technically illegal) *Syrah*. ☆☆☆☆ **1995 Cepparello £££**

Israel Once the source of appalling stuff, but the new-style varietal wines are improving. **Golan Heights; Carmel.**

Ch. d'Issan [dee-son] (*Margaux 3ème Cru Classé*, *Bordeaux*, France) Recently revived *Margaux* third growth with lovely, recognisable blackcurranty *Cabernet Sauvignon* intensity. 70 **75** 78 79 81 **82 83** 85 86 88 89 90 93 94 95 96

🍷**Italian Riesling/Riesling Italico** [ee-tah-lee-koh] Not the great *Rhine Riesling*, but another name for an unrelated variety, which also goes by the names *Welschriesling, Lutomer* and *Laski Rizling,* and is widely grown in Northern and Eastern Europe. At its best in Austria.

Italy Tantalising, seductive, infuriating. In many ways the most exciting wine nation in the world, though, as ever, in a state of change as it reorganises its wine laws. See individual regions.

J

🍷 **JP Vinhos** (Portugal) See *Peter Bright*.

🍷 **Paul Jaboulet Aîné** [zha-boo-lay ay-nay] (*Rhône*, France) The wine world was saddened to learn of the death this year from a heart attack of Gérard Jaboulet, the highly popular international face of this family *négociant* which owns the illustrious *Hermitage* La Chapelle vineyard. Despite being overshadowed nowadays by *Guigal*, this remains a reliable producer of a wide range of wines apart from the La Chapelle, including white *Hermitage*, chunky *St. Joseph*, good *Côtes du Rhône* and *Châteauneuf-du-Pape*. ☆☆☆☆ **1995 Crozes Hermitage Dom. de Thalabert ££**

🍷 **Jackson Estate** (*Marlborough*, New Zealand) Next-door neighbour to *Cloudy Bay* and producer of *Sauvignon*, which is giving that superstar estate a run for its money. The sparkling wine is good too. ☆☆☆☆ **1997 Sauvignon Blanc ££**

🍷 **Jacob's Creek** (*South Australia*) Brilliantly commercial South Australian wines made by *Orlando*.

🍷 **Jacquart** [zha-kahr] (*Champagne*, France) Large cooperative with some very passable wines. ☆☆☆☆ **1990 Blanc de Blancs ££££**

🍷**Jacquère** [zha-kehr] The slightly citrusy grape of *Savoie*.

🍷 **Jacquesson et Fils** [jak-son] (*Champagne*, France) A small *Champagne* house that deserves to be better known, particularly for its exceptional, delicately stylish *Blanc de Blancs*. ☆☆☆☆ **1990 Blanc de Blancs ££££**

🍷 **Louis Jadot** [zha-doh] (*Burgundy*, France) Good, sometimes great, *Beaune négociant* with a growing number of its own top-class vineyards in *Beaune, Chassagne-* and *Puligny-Montrachet*. Jadot has also been a pioneering producer of *Rully* in the *Côte Châlonnais*. Whites are most impressive. ☆☆☆☆ **1995 Bonnes Mares ££££**

🍷 **Jaffelin** [zhaf-lan] (*Burgundy*, France) Small *négociant* recently bought from *Drouhin* by *Boisset*. Particularly good at supposedly 'lesser' *appellations* – *Rully Blanc* and *Monthélie* are particularly good – but winemaker Bernard Repolt (who is now also responsible for the improving wines at *Bouchard Aîné*) is now showing his skills across the board. ☆☆☆☆ **1995 Fixin ££££**

🍷 **Joseph Jamet** [zha-may] (*Rhône*, France) Top-class *Côte Rôtie* estate, making unusually stylish wines for this often high-profile *appellation*. ☆☆☆☆ **1994 Côte Rôtie ££££**

🍷 **Jamieson's Run** (*Coonawarra*, Australia) *Mildara's* pair of prize winning, good-value red and white wines. ☆☆☆☆☆ **1996 Jamieson's Run Reserve ££**

🍷 **Dom. de la Janasse** [ja-nass] (*Rhône*, France) High quality *Châteauneuf-du-Pape* estate, producing three individual wines under this *appellation*, plus a good *Côtes du Rhône* les Garrigues. ☆☆☆☆ **1995 Châteauneuf-du-Pape Vieilles Vignes £££**

🍷 **Jansz** [yantz] (*Tasmania*, Australia) See *Heemskirk*.

🍷 **Robert Jasmin** [zhas-man] (*Rhône*, France) Traditionalist *Côte Rôtie* estate, eschewing new oak. ☆☆☆☆☆ **1994 Côte Rôtie ££££**

Jasnières [zhan-yehr] (*Loire*, France) On rare occasions bone-dry and – even rarer – *Moelleux*, sweet *Chenin Blanc* wines from *Touraine*. Buy carefully. Poorly made, over-sulphured efforts offer a pricy chance to taste the *Chenin* at its worst. White: **86 88 89 90** 94 95 Sweet White: **76** 83 **85** 86 **88 89** 90 94 95 96

🍷 **Jasper Hill** (*Bendigo*, Australia) Winery in Heathcote with a cult following for both reds and whites – especially those from the Georgia's Paddock vineyard. ☆☆☆☆ **1995 Georgia's Paddock Riesling, Heathcote ££**

🍷 **Jaume Serra** [how-may seh-rah] (*Penedès*, Spain) Privately owned company which recently relocated from *Alella* to *Penedès*, and is doing good things with *Xarel-lo*.

🍷 **Patrick Javillier** [zha-vil-yay] (*Burgundy*, France) Reliable, small merchant making meticulous village *Meursault* and good reds. ☆☆☆☆ **1995 Meursault Clos Cronin ££££**

🍷 **Henri Jayer** [zha-yay] (*Burgundy*, France) Cult winemaker whose top *Côte de Nuits* reds rival those of the *Dom. de la Romanée-Conti*. Now retired but still represented on labels referring to Georges et Henri. Also an influence on the wines of *Meo Camuzet*.

🍷 **Robert Jayer-Gilles** [zhah-yay-zheel] (*Burgundy*, France) *Henri Jayer*'s cousin, whose top wines – including an *Echézeaux* – bear comparison with those of his more famous relative. (His whites – particularly the *Aligoté* – are good too.) ☆☆☆☆ **1995 Echézeaux du Dessus £££**

🍷 **Jekel Vineyards** [jeh-kel] (*Arroyo Seco*, California) After a spell under other owners, and a more recent takeover taking it into the same camp as *Fetzer* – it is once again run by its founder Bill Jekel, a famous critic of *terroir*. *Cabernets* and *Chardonnays* are better nowadays than the very commercial *Riesling* and are worth following if you accept their slightly herbaceous style. ☆☆☆☆ **1996 Cabernet Sauvignon £££**

Jerez (de la Frontera) [hay-reth] (Spain) Centre of the *sherry* trade, giving its name to entire *DO* area. ***Gonzalez Byass; Lustau; Hidalgo; Barbadillo.***

🍷 **Jermann** [zhehr-man] (*Friuli-Venezia Giulia*, Italy) Brilliant winemaker who gets outrageous flavours – and prices – out of every white grape variety he touches. Look out for the Vintage Tunina blend of *Tocai, Picolit* and *Malvasia*, and the 'Dreams' white blend plus the single-vineyard Capo Martino. Also good at *Chardonnay, Pinot Gris* and *Pinot Blanc*. ☆☆☆☆ **1996 Dreams £££**

Jeroboam [zhe-roh-bohm] Large bottle; in *Champagne* holding three litres (four bottles); in *Bordeaux*, four and a half (six bottles). Best to check before writing your cheque.

Jesuitengarten [zhes-yoo-wi-ten-gahr-ten] (*Rheingau*, Germany) One of Germany's top vineyards – well-handled by *Bassermann-Jordan*. QbA/Kab/Spät: **85** 86 **88 89 90** 91 92 93 94 95 96 97 Aus/Beeren/Tba: **83 85** 88 89 90 91 92 93 94 95 96 97

Jeunes Vignes [zhuhn veen] Denotes vines too young for their crop to be sold as an *Appellation Controlée* wine.

🍷 **Dom. François Jobard** [fron-swah joh-bahr] (*Burgundy*, France) Small, great white wine estate in *Meursault*. ☆☆☆☆ **1995 Meursault Genevrières £££**

🍷 **Dom. Joblot** [zhob-loh] (*Burgundy*, France) One of the top *domaines* in *Givry*. ☆☆☆ **1995 Cellier Aux Moines ££££**

🍷 **Charles Joguet** [zho-gay] (*Loire*, France) One of the finest producers of red *Loire*, making *Chinon* wines that can last. He is also notable in having some of the only quality vines in France that have not been grafted onto *phylloxera*-resistant American rootstock. ☆☆☆☆ **1996 Chinon, Clos de la Cure ££**

Johannisberg [zho-han-is-buhrg.] (*Rheingau*, Germany) Village making superb *Riesling*, which has lent its name to a *bereich* covering all the *Rheingau*. QbA/Kab/Spät: **85** 86 **88 89 90** 91 92 93 94 95 96 97
Aus/Beeren/Tba: **83 85** 88 89 90 91 92 93 94 95 96 97

🍷 **Johannisberg Riesling** [rees-ling] Californian name for *Rhine Riesling*.
🍷 **Weingut Karl-Heinz Johner** [karl-hihntz yoh-nuh] (*Baden*, Germany) Former winemaker at *Lamberhurst*, now making good *oaky Pinot Noir* in southern Germany.
🍷 **Pascal Jolivet** [zhol-lee-vay] (*Loire*, France) Superstar producer of modern *Sancerre* and *Pouilly-Fumé*. ☆☆☆☆ **1996 Sancerre Chêne Marchand £££**
🍷 **Nicolas Joly** [Zhoh-lee] (*Loire*, France) The biodynamic owner-wine-maker behind the *Coulée de Serrant* in *Savennières*.
🍷 **Jordan** (*Stellenbosch*, South Africa) Young winery whose Californian-trained winemakers are hitting the mark with their *Sauvignon* and *Chardonnay*. ☆☆☆☆ **1997 Jordan Estate Chardonnay £££**
🍷 **Jordan** (*Sonoma Valley*, California) *Sonoma* winery surrounded by the kind of hype more usually associated with *Napa*. Table wines – from the *Alexander Valley* – are mostly good rather than great, though the fizz is of *Champagne* quality. ☆☆☆☆☆ **1991 'J', Sonoma County ££££**
🍷 **Joseph** (*South Australia*) Label used by *Primo Estate* for its wines.
🍷 **Josmeyer** [jos-mi-yur] (*Alsace*, France) Estate producing wines that are more delicate and restrained than those of some of its neighbours. ☆☆☆☆ **1996 'H' Vieilles Vignes Pinot Auxerrois £££**
🍷 **Weingut Toni Jost** [toh-nee yohst] (*Mittelrhein*, Germany) A new-wave producer with (well-sited) vines in Bacharach, good reds and a penchant for experimenting (often successfully) with new oak barrels. ☆☆☆☆☆ **1996 Martinsthaler Rödchen Riesling Trocken £££**
🍷 **La Jota** [lah hoh-tah] (*Napa Valley*, California) Small *Howell Mountain* producer with stylish reds, including an unusually good *Cabernet Franc*. ☆☆☆ **1995 Cabernet Franc £££**
🍷 **Judd's Hill** (*Napa Valley*, California) Young winery with dazzling *Cabernets*. ☆☆☆☆ **1994 Cabernet Sauvignon Napa Valley.**

Juffer [yoof-fuh] (*Mosel*, Germany) Famous vineyard in the village of *Brauneberg*. QbA/Kab/Spät: **85** 86 **88 89 90** 91 92 93 94 95 96 97
Aus/Beeren/Tba: **83 85** 88 89 90 91 92 93 94 95 96 97

Jug wine (California) American term for quaffable *Vin Ordinaire*, mainly originating from the *Central Valley* in California.
🍷 **Marcel Juge** [zhoozh] (*Rhône*, France) Producer of one of the subtlest classiest examples of *Cornas*. ☆☆☆☆ **1993 Cornas £££**

🍷 **Juliénas** [joo-lee-yay-nas] (*Burgundy*, France) One of the ten *Beaujolais Crus*, producing classic vigorous wine which often benefits from a few years in bottle. 85 87 88 89 90 **91** 93 94 95 96 97 **Ch. de Juliénas; Dom. Michel Tête;** *Eventail des Producteurs.*

🍷 **Weingut Juliusspital** [yoo-lee-yoos-shpit-ahl] (*Franken*, Germany) Top-class estate whose profits benefit the poor and sick. A good source of *Riesling* and *Sylvaner*.

Jumilla [hoo-mee-yah] (Spain) Improving *DO* region, traditionally known for heavy high-alcohol wines but increasingly making lighter *Beaujolais*-style ones. **87** 89 90 **91 94** 95 96

🍷 **Côtes de Jura** [koht duh zhoo-rah] (Eastern France) Region containing *Arbois* and *Savoie*, home of the *Savagnin* (not *Sauvignon*) grape and best known for specialities such as *Vin Gris*, *Vin Jaune* and *Vin de Paille*.

🍷 **Cave de Jurançon** [kahv duh zhoo-*ron*-*son*] (South-West France) Good co-operative cellar making rich, dry, apricoty white and excellent long-living sweet wines. ☆☆☆☆ **1995 Jurançon Grains Sauvage ££**

🍷 **Jurançon** [zhoo-*ron*-*son*] (South-West France) Rich, dry apricoty white and excellent sweet wines made from the *Gros* and *Petit Manseng* found almost nowhere else. **83** 85 86 **89 90** 92 93 95 96 **Dom. J-P Bousquet; Castera; Cauhapé.**

🍷 **Justin** (*San Luis Obispo*, California) A winery to watch, with stunning reds, including a great *Cabernet Franc* and Isosceles, a *Bordeaux* blend. ☆☆☆☆ **1994 Isosceles San Luis Obispo County Reserve.**

🍷 **Juvé y Camps** [hoo-vay ee kamps] (*Catalonia*, Spain) The exception which proves the rule – by making and maturing decent *cava* from traditional grapes and excellent vintage *Brut*.

K

Kabinett (Germany) First step in German quality ladder, for wines which achieve a certain natural sweetness.

🍷 **Ch. Kefraya** [keh-frah-ya] (Lebanon) *Ch. Musar* is not the only Lebanese winery; this is the other one that's worth taking seriously. ☆☆☆ **1996 Ch. Kefraya £££**

Kaiserstuhl-Tuniberg [kih-sehr shtool too-nee-burg] (*Baden*, Germany) Supposedly finest *Baden bereich* (actually it covers a third of *Baden's* vineyards) with top villages producing rich spicy *Riesling* and *Sylvaner* from volcanic slopes. QbA/Kab/Spät: **85 88 89 90** 91 92 93 94 95 96 97 Aus/Beeren/Tba: **83 85** 88 89 90 91 92 93 94 95 96 97

Kallstadt [kahl-shtaht] (*Pfalz*, Germany) Village containing the best-known and finest vineyard of Annaberg, making luscious full *Riesling*. QbA/Kab/Spät: **85** 86 **88 89 90** 91 92 93 94 95 96 97 Aus/Beeren/Tba: **83 85** 88 89 90 91 92 93 94 95 96 97

🍷 **Kanonkop Estate** [ka-NON kop] (*Stellenbosch*, South Africa) Estate with largely traditional equipment, but a modern approach to its unusually classy *Pinotage*. The light red blend, 'Kadette', is good too, and *Bordeaux*-style 'Paul Sauer' is one of the *Cape's* best. ☆☆☆☆ **1995 Pinotage ££**

🍷 **Katnook Estate** (*Coonawarra*, Australia) Small estate making the highly commercial Deakin Estate wines as well as plenty of such innovative stuff as a *late harvest Coonawarra Chardonnay* and top-class *Coonawarra Merlot* and *Cabernet*. ☆☆☆☆☆ **1995 Riddoch Merlot £££**

Kellerei/kellerabfüllung [kel-luh-rih/kel-luh-rab-foo-loong] (Germany) Cellar/producer/estate-bottled.

🍷 **Kendall-Jackson** (*Clear Lake*, California) High-profile, fast-growing producer with supposedly classy *Chardonnay* and *Sauvignon* which are decidedly off-dry. Reds are better. ☆☆☆☆ **1995 Pinot Noir Vintners Reserve ££**

🍷 **Kenwood Vineyards** (*Sonoma Valley*, California) Classy *Sonoma* winery with good single-vineyard *Chardonnays* and impressive, if sometimes rather tough, *Cabernets* (including one made from the author Jack London's vineyard). The star is the brilliant *Zinfandel*. ☆☆☆☆☆ **1994 Zinfandel ££**

🍇 **Kerner** [kuh-nuh] A white grape variety. A *Riesling*-cross that is grown in Germany and also widely in England. ***Anselmann.***

Weingut Reichsgraf von Kesselstatt [rihkh-sgraf fon kes-sel-shtat] (*Mosel-Saar-Ruwer*, Germany) Large, impressive collection of four *Riesling* estates spread between the *Mosel*, *Saar* and *Ruwer*. ✩✩✩✩ Piesporter Goldtröpfchen Riesling Spätlese £££

Kiedrich [kee-drikh] (*Rheingau*, Germany) Top village high in the hills whose vineyards can produce great intense *Rieslings*. QbA/Kab/Spät: 85 86 **88 89 90** 91 92 93 94 95 96 97 Aus/Beeren/Tba: **83 85** 88 89 90 91 92 93 94 95 **96** 97

Kientzheim [keents-him] (*Alsace*, France) Village noted for its *Riesling*. 71 75 **76 83 85 86** 88 **89 90** 92 93 95 96 97

André Kientzler [keent-zluh] (*Alsace*, France) Classy producer with better-than-average *Pinot Blanc*. ✩✩✩✩ 1995 Pinot Blanc d'Alsace ££

JF Kimich [kih-mikh] (*Pfalz*, Germany) Fast-rising star making rich spicy wines typical of the *Pfalz*. *Gewurztraminers* are as good as *Rieslings* ✩✩✩✩ 1992 Forster Elster Riesling Kabinett ££££

Kiona [kih-yoh-nah] (*Washington State*, US) Small producer in the middle of nowhere with a penchant for berryish reds and intensely flavoured *late harvest* wines. ✩✩✩✩ 1995 Cabernet Sauvignon ££££

Kir (*Burgundy*, France) A mixture of sweet fortified *Crème de Cassis* (regional speciality of *Burgundy*) with simple and often rather *acidic* local white wine (*Aligoté*, or basic *Bourgogne* Blanc) to produce a delicious summertime drink. Try it with *Crème de Mûre* or *Crème de Framboise* instead.

Ch. Kirwan [keer-wahn] (*Margaux 3ème Cru Classé*, *Bordeaux*, France) Rejuvenated property belatedly coming out of prolonged doldrums. Still doesn't warrant its third growth status. 70 78 81 **82 83** 85 86 87 88 89 90 92 93 94 95 96

Kistler [kist-luh] (*Sonoma Valley*, California) Probably California's top *Chardonnay* producer, with a really dazzling range of uncompromising complex single-vineyard wines and fast-improving *Pinot Noirs*. *Burgundy* quality at *Burgundy* prices. ✩✩✩✩✩ 1996 Chardonnay McCrea Vineyard ££££

Klein Constantia [klihn kon-stan-tee-yah] (*Constantia*, South Africa) Small go-ahead estate on the site of the great 17th-century *Constantia* vineyard. Wines, especially the *Sauvignon*, do not always quite live up to the hype the estate has received, nor the enduring historic prestige of the *Constantia* region. The star wine is the sweet 'Vin de Constance' which is sadly hard to find outside South Africa. ✩✩✩ 1997 Sauvignon Blanc ££

Klusserath [kloo-seh-raht] (*Mosel-Saar-Ruwer*, Germany) Small village best known in UK for *Sonnenuhr* and Konigsberg vineyards. QbA/Kab/Spät: 85 86 **88 89 90** 91 92 93 94 95 96 97 Aus/Beeren/Tba: **83 85** 88 89 90 91 92 93 94 95 96 97

Tim Knappstein [nap-steen] (*Clare Valley, Lenswood*, Australia) Long-time master of *Riesling* from the *Clare Valley*. Apart from *Clare* wines, look out for the brilliant *Sauvignon* and promising *Pinot Noirs* all of which are sold under the *Lenswood* label. (The Knappstein label itself now belongs to *Mildara* and is unconnected to Tim Knappstein.) ✩✩✩✩ 1996 Lenswood Chardonnay £££

Knudsen-Erath [noos-den ee-rath] (*Oregon*, US) One of the better pioneers of this region, but still far from earth-shattering.

Konocti Cellars [ko-nok-tih] (*Lake County*, California) Dynamic producer with good straightforward wines.

Kosher (Israel) Wine made under complex rules. Every seventh vintage is left unharvested and non-Jews are barred from the winemaking process.

Korbel [Kor-BEL] (*Sonoma*, California) Producer of basic California fizz.

☲ **Kourtakis** [koor-tah-kis] (Greece) One of Greece's growing number of dynamic wine companies with unusually recommendable whites and good examples of the characterful native *Mavrodaphne*. ☆☆☆☆ Mavrodaphne £££

☲ **Weinlaubenhof Weingut Alois Kracher** [Ah-loys krah-kuh] (*Neusiedlersee*, Austria) Source of world-class, (very) *late harvest* wines including a very unusual effort which blends the *Chardonnay* with the *Welschriesling*. ☆☆☆☆☆ 1995 Traminer No. 8 Nouvelle Vague Trockenbeerenauslese ££££

Krems [krems] (*Wachau*, Austria) Town and *Wachau* vineyard area producing Austria's most stylish *Rieslings* from terraced vineyards.

Kreuznach [kroyt-znahkh] (*Nahe*, Germany) Northern *bereich*, boasting fine vineyards situated around the town of *Bad Kreuznach*. QbA/Kab/Spät: 85 86 **88 89 90** 91 92 93 94 95 96 97 Aus/Beeren/Tba: **83 85** 88 89 90 91 92 93 94 95 96 97

☲ **Dom. Kreydenweiss** [krih-den-vihs] (*Alsace*, France) Top-class organic producer with particularly good *Pinot Gris* and *Riesling*.

☲ **Krondorf** [kron-dorf] (*Barossa Valley*, Australia) Winery specialising in traditional, big *Barossa* style wines. ☆☆☆☆ 1995 Chardonnay Show Reserve £££

☲ **Krug** [kroog] (*Champagne*, France) The *Ch. Latour* of *Champagne*. Great vintage wine, extraordinary rosé and pure *Chardonnay* from the *Clos de Mesnil* vineyard. Theoretically the best non-vintage, thanks to the greater proportions of aged Reserve wine. ☆☆☆☆☆ 1989 Vintage ££££

☲ **Kruger-Rumpf** [kroo-gur roompf] (*Nahe*, Germany) Nahe estate, demonstrating the potential of varieties like the *Scheurebe*. ☆☆☆☆☆ 1996 Munsterer Dautenpflänzer Riesling Spätlese Halbtrocken ££££

☲ **Kuentz-Bas** [koontz bah] (*Alsace*, France) Reliable producer for *Pinot Gris* and *Gewurztraminer*. ☆☆☆ 1996 Gewurztraminer Cuvée Tradition £££

☲ **Kuhling-Gillot** [koo-ling gil-lot] (*Rheinhessen*, Germany) Hitherto a little-known producer, now fast developing a reputation for his rich concentrated wines. ☆☆☆☆ 1996 Oppenheimer Sackträger Riesling Spätlese ££££

☲ **Kumeu River** [koo-myoo] (*Auckland*, New Zealand) One of the best winemakers in New Zealand, Michael Brajkovich is successful with a wide range of wines, including a very unusual dry *botrytis Sauvignon* which easily outclasses many a dry wine from *Sauternes*. ☆☆☆☆☆ 1996 Chardonnay £££

☲ **Kunde** [koon-day] (*Sonoma*, California) Producer of good *Chardonnay* and *Zinfandel*.

☲ **Weingut Franz Künstler** [koont-sluh] (*Rheingau*, Germany) A new superstar producer who is showing the big name estates of the *Rheingau* what they ought to be doing with their *Riesling*. ☆☆☆☆ 1992 Hochheimer Holle Riesling Auslese ££

☲ **KWV** (*Cape*, South Africa) Huge cooperative formed by the South African government at a time when surplus wine seemed set to flood the industry and, for a long time, maintained by the National Party when it needed to keep the members of the big wine cooperatives, well, cooperative. Now facing privatisation and accusations of having been involved in the sale of fake *Champagne*, the KWV is a fascinating example of the way in which old Afrikaans establishment is having to come to terms with the advent of a free market at home and an outside world whose taste in wine has little in common with many of the traditional favourites in the *Cape*. Winemaking has improved recently – especially the wines sold under the Cathedral Cellars label. ☆☆☆☆ 1994 Cathedral Cellars Merlot £££; ☆☆☆☆ 1994 Cathedral Cellars Pinotage £££

L

Ch. Labégorce [la-bay-gors] (*Bordeaux*, France) Good traditional *Margaux*. 75 79 81 **82 83 85** 86 88 **89** 90 94 95 96

Ch. Labégorce-Zédé [la-bay-gors zay-day] (*Margaux Cru Bourgeois*, *Bordeaux*, France). An estate that belongs to the same Thienpont family as *Vieux Château Certan* and *le Pin*. A name to remember for wine beyond its Bourgeois class. 81 82 **83 85 86** 88 **89** 90 92 94 95 96

Labouré-Roi [la-boo-ray rwah] (*Burgundy*, France) A highly successful and very commercial *négociant*, responsible for some quite impressive wines. See *Cottin Frères*. ☆☆☆ **1995 Meursault Clos de la Baronne £££**

🍇**Labrusca** [la-broo-skah] *Vitis labrusca*, the North American species of vine, making wine which is often referred to as 'foxy'. All *vinifera* vine stocks are grafted on to *phylloxera*-resistant *labrusca* roots, though the vine itself is banned in Europe and its wines, thankfully, are almost unfindable.

Ch. Lacoste-Borie [la-cost-bo-ree] (*Pauillac*, *Bordeaux*, France) The reliable *second label* of *Grand-Puy-Lacoste*. ☆☆☆ **1995 Ch. Lacoste-Borie £££**

Lacryma Christi [la-kree-mah kris-tee] (*Campania*, Italy) Literally, 'tears of Christ', the melancholy name for some amiable, light, rather rustic reds and whites. Those from Vesuvio are *DOC*. ☆☆☆ **1996 Mastroberardino Rosso £££**

Ladoix-Serrigny [la-dwah-seh-reen-yee] (*Burgundy*, France) Village including parts of *Corton* and *Corton-Charlemagne*. The village wines are not well known and some bargains are still to be found. White: 79 **85 86** **88** 89 **90 92** 95 96 Red: 78 83 **85** 87 **88 89 90** 92 **94** 95 96 **Capitain-Gagnerot; *Dubreuil-Fontaine; Maréchale.***

Patrick de Ladoucette [duh la-doo-set] (*Loire*, France) Fine intense *Pouilly-Fumé*, sold as 'Baron de L'. Other wines are greatly improved in recent years. ☆☆☆☆ **1996 Baron de 'L' ££££**

Michel Lafarge [la-farzh] (*Burgundy*, France) One of the very best producers in *Volnay* – and indeed *Burgundy*. Fine, long-lived, modern wine. ☆☆☆☆ **1995 Volnay Clos des Chênes £££**

Ch. Lafaurie-Peyraguey [la-foh-ree pay-rah-gee] (*Sauternes Premier Cru Classé*, *Bordeaux*, France) Much-improved *Sauternes* estate that has produced creamy, long-lived wines in the 1980s and in the 1990s. 78 80 **81** 82 **83** 85 **86** 88 **89 90** 96 95 ☆☆☆☆ **1990 ££££**

Ch. Lafite-Rothschild [la-feet roh-chihld] (*Pauillac Premier Cru Classé*, *Bordeaux*, France) Often almost impossible to taste young, this *Pauillac* first growth is still one of the monuments of the wine world – especially since the early 1980s. **61** 75 76 78 79 **81 82** 83 84 85 86 87 88 89 90 91 92 93 94 95 96 ☆☆☆☆ **1994 ££££**

Ch. Lafleur [la-flur] (*Pomerol*, *Bordeaux*, France) *Christian Moueix*'s pet *Pomerol*, often on a par with the wine *Moueix* makes at *Pétrus*. **61 62 66** 70 75 78 79 **82 83 85 86** 88 **89** 90 **92 93** 94 95 96 ☆☆☆☆ **1994 ££££**

Ch. Lafleur-Gazin [la-flur-ga-zan] (*Pomerol*, *Bordeaux*, France) Another good *Moueix* wine. **82** 83 85 86 88 89 90 92 93 94 95 96

Dom. des Comtes Lafon [day comt la-fon] (*Burgundy*, France) The best domaine in *Meursault*, with great vineyards in *Volnay* and a small slice of *Montrachet*. Wines last forever. ☆☆☆☆ **1995 Meursault Les Charmes ££££**

Ch. Lafon-Rochet [la-fon-ro-shay] (*St. Estèphe 4ème Cru Classé*, *Bordeaux*, France) Increasingly modern *St. Estèphe*. 70 79 81 82 **83** 85 86 88 89 90 91 92 93 94 95 96 97 ☆☆☆☆ **1994 £££**

Alois Lageder [la-GAY-duh] (*Trentino-Alto-Adige*, Italy) New-wave producer of the kind of [wine the *Alto-Adige* ought to make.

Lago di Caldaro [LA-goh dah KAHL-deh-roh] (*Trentino-Alto-Adige*, Italy) Also known as the *Kalterersee*, using the local *Schiava* grape to make cool light reds with slightly unripe, though pleasant fruit.

⬩ **Ch. Lagrange** [la-gronzh] (*St. Julien 3ème Cru Classé, Bordeaux*, France) A once under-performing third growth rejuvenated by Japanese cash and local know-how (for a while from Michel Delon of *Léoville-Las-Cases*). Look out for *Les Fiefs de Lagrange*, the impressive *second label*. 70 82 83 84 **85 86** 88 89 90 91 92 93 94 95 96

⬩ **Ch. Lagrange** [la-gronzh] (*Pomerol, Bordeaux*, France) Yet another *Moueix* property – and yet another good wine. **70 75** 78 81 **82** 83 **85** 86 87 88 89 90 92 93 94 95 96 ☆☆☆ **1993 £££**

🍾**Lagrein** [la-grayn] (Italy) Cherryish red grape of north east Italy.

⬩ **Ch. la Lagune** [la-goon] (*Haut-Médoc 3ème Cru Classé, Bordeaux*, France) Lovely accessible wines which last well and are worth buying even in poorer years. **70 75 78** 79 **82** 85 86 88 89 90 92 93 94 95 96

Lake County (California) Vineyard district salvaged by improved irrigation techniques and now capable of some fine wines as well as *Kendall Jackson's* highly commercial efforts. Red: 84 **85** 86 87 **90 91** 92 93 95 White: **85 90 91** 92 95 96 *Guenoc*.

⬩ **Lake's Folly** (*Hunter Valley*, Australia) Meet Max Lake, surgeon-turned-winemaker-cum writer/researcher who has great theories about the sexual effects of sniffing various kinds of wine. He is also a leading Australian pioneer of *Chardonnay*, with an unusually successful *Hunter Valley Cabernet Sauvignon*. Wines now made by Max's son, Stephen. ☆☆☆☆ **1994 Cabernet Sauvignon, Hunter Valley £££**

⬩ **Lalande de Pomerol** [la-LOND duh po-meh-rol] (*Bordeaux*, France) Bordering on *Pomerol* with similar, but less fine wines. Still generally better than similarly priced *St. Emilions*. Some good-value *Petits-Châteaux*. 70 82 83 85 86 **88 89** 90 92 93 94 95 96

Ch. Lalande-Borie [la-LOND bo-ree] (*St. Julien, Bordeaux*, France) In the same stable as *Ch. Ducru-Beaucaillou*. Reliable wines. 82 85 86 88 89 90 91 92 93 94 95 96 ☆☆☆ **1989 £££**

⬩ **Ch. Lamarque** [la-mahrk] (*Haut-Médoc Cru Bourgeois, Bordeaux*, France) Spectacular *château* with good traditional wines. 82 **83** 85 **86** 88 89 90 91 92 93 94 95 96 ☆☆☆ **1992 £££;** ☆☆☆ **1993 ££**

⬩ **Lamberhurst** (*Kent*, England) One of the first English vineyards and still one of the more reliable, though rarely the most innovative. (Other non-English wines sold by Lamberhurst are not recommendable.)

⬩ **Lamborn Family** (*Napa Valley*, California) Tiny *Howell Mountain* producer, focussing on rich concentrated long-lived *Zinfandel*.

⬩ **Dom. des Lambrays** [lom-bray] (*Burgundy*, California) Under new ownership and promising further improvements in quality. Already very worthwhile, though. ☆☆☆ **1994 Clos des Lambrays £££**

⬩ **Lambrusco** [lam-broos-koh] (*Emilia-Romagna*, Italy) Famous/infamous low-strength (7.5 per cent) sweet, fizzy UK and North American version of the fizzy dry red wine favoured in Italy. The real thing – fascinating with its dry, unripe, cherry flavour – comes with a cork rather than a screw-cap. ☆☆☆ **Secco Sorbara Cavicchioli £**

⬩ **Ch. de Landiras** [lon-dee-ras] (*Bordeaux*, France) An out-of-the-way corner of the *Graves* that has been reclaimed from the forest by Peter Vinding-Diers and also serves as the winery for the *Dom. La Grave* property a few miles away. Red: 88 89 **90** 94 95 96 White: 90 91 **93** 95 96

⬩ **Landmark** (*Sonoma*, California) Small *Chardonnay* specialist with rich, fruity, buttery wines from individual 'Damaris' and 'Overlook' vineyards. Not the subtlest fare, but very seductive. ☆☆☆☆ **1993 Chardonnay Damaris Reserve £££**

Landskroon Estate [land-skroon] (*Paarl*, South Africa) Good traditional '*port*', *Shiraz* and a rare solo outing for *Cabernet Franc*.
Landwein [land-vihn] (Germany) The equivalent of a French *Vin De Pays* from one of 11 named regions (*anbaugebiet*). Often dry.

Ch. Lanessan [la-neh-son] (*Haut-Médoc Cru Bourgeois, Bordeaux*, France) Old-fashioned *Cru Bourgeois* largely untouched by new oak. A long-lived argument for the way things used to be done. **79 82 83 85 86** 88 89 90 **93** 94 95 96 **97** ☆☆☆☆ **1993 £££**

Langhe [lang-gay] (*Piedmont*, Italy) A range of hills; when preceded by '*Nebbiolo delle*', indicates declassified *Barolo* and *Barbaresco*.

Ch. Langoa-Barton [lon-goh-wah-bahr-ton] (*St. Julien 3ème Cru Classé, Bordeaux*, France) *Léoville-Barton*'s (slightly) less complex kid brother. Often one of the best bargain *classed growths* in *Bordeaux*. Well made in poor years. **70 75** 76 **78 79 82** 83 85 **86** 88 89 90 91 92 93 94 95 96 97 ☆☆☆☆ **1993 £££**

Languedoc-Roussillon [long-dok roo-see-yon] (*Midi*, France) One of the world's largest wine regions and, until recently, a major source of the wine lake. But a combination of government-sponsored up-rooting and keen activity by *flying winemakers* and (a few) dynamic producers is beginning to turn this into a worrying competitor for the New World. The region includes *appellations* like *Fitou, Corbières* and *Minervois, Faugères, St. Chinian, Coteaux de Languedoc, Côtes de Roussillon* and a torrent of *Vin De Pays d'Oc*. Sadly, many of the best, more ambitious, wines are hard to find outside France.

Lanson [lon-son] (*Champagne*, France) Much improved *Champagne* house with decent non-vintage 'Black Label', good *Demi-Sec* and sublime *vintage* fizz. ☆☆☆☆ **1988 Noble Cuvée Vintage ££££**

Casa Lapostolle [la-pos-tol] (*Colchagua Valley*, Chile) One of Chile's newest stars. Belongs to the owners of Grand Marnier and benefiting from the expertise of *Michel Rolland*. Classy *Merlot* reds; whites need more work. ☆☆☆☆ **1996 Merlot Cuvée Alexandre ££**

Ch. Larcis-Ducasse [lahr-see doo-kass] (*St. Emilion Grand Cru Classé, Bordeaux*, France) Property whose lightish wines rarely live up to the potential of its hillside site. 66 78 79 81 **82** 83 85 86 88 89 90 94 95 96 ☆☆☆☆ **1990 £££**

Ch. Larmande [lahr-mond] (*St. Emilion Grand Cru Classé, Bordeaux*, France) A property to watch for well-made ripe-tasting wines. 85 86 **88 89** 90 92 93 94 95 96

Dom. Laroche [la-rosh] (*Burgundy*, France) Good *Chablis négociant* with some enviable vineyards of its own, including *Premiers* and *Grands Crus*. Reliable southern French *Chardonnay Vin De Pays d'Oc* and innovative wines from *Corsica*. ☆☆☆☆ **1997 Chablis Saint-Martin £££**

Ch. Lascombes [las-komb] (*Margaux 2ème Cru Classé, Bordeaux*, France) Much improved, subtle second growth *Margaux* which often exemplifies the perfumed character of this *appellation*, but could still do better. 70 75 82 83 85 **86 88** 89 90 91 92 93 94 95 96 ☆☆☆☆ **1994 ££££**

Laski Riesling/Rizling [lash-kee riz-ling] (Former Yugoslavia) Yugoslav name for white grape, unrelated to the *Rhine Riesling*, aka *Welsch, Olasz* and *Italico*.

Ch. de Lastours [duh las-toor] (*Languedoc-Roussillon*, France) Combined winery and home for people with mental disabilities and frequently providing ample proof that *Corbières* can rival *Bordeaux*. Look out for the *cuvée* Simone Descamps. ☆☆☆ **1994 Cuvée Fûts de Chêne ££**
Late harvest Made from (riper) grapes picked after the main vintage. Should have at least some *botrytis*.

Late-Bottled Vintage (Port) (LBV) (*Douro*, Portugal) Officially, bottled four or six years after a specific (usually non-declared) *vintage*. Until the late 1970s, this made for a *vintage port*-style wine that matured earlier, was a little lighter and easier to drink, but still needed to be decanted. Until recently, the only houses to persevere with this style were *Warres* and *Smith Woodhouse* who labelled their efforts 'Traditional' LBV. Almost every other LBV around, however, was of the filtered, 'modern' style pioneered by *Taylors*. These taste pretty much like up-market *ruby* and *vintage character ports,* need no decanting and bear very little resemblance to real *vintage* or even *crusted port*. Belatedly, a growing number of producers are now confusingly offering 'Traditional' as well as modern LBV. Under their self-imposed laws, the port shippers infuriatingly allow themselves to use the same name for these two very different styles of wine. Which is not very surprising really, as one very prominent retired *port* maker admitted, he and his competitors have always done well out of confusing their customers.

Latium/Lazio [lah-tee-yoom] (Italy) The vineyard area surrounding Rome, including *Frascati* and *Marino*. **Fontana Candida; Colli di Catone.**

⚊ **Louis Latour** [loo-wee lah-toor] (*Burgundy*, France) Under-performing *négociant* who still pasteurises his – consequently muddy-tasting – reds, treating them in a way no quality-conscious New World producer would contemplate. Some whites, including *Corton-Charlemagne*, can be sublime. ☆☆☆☆ **1993 Montrachet ££££;** ☆☆☆☆ **1992 Corton-Charlemagne ££££**

⚊ **Ch. Latour** [lah-toor] (*Pauillac Premier Cru Classé*, *Bordeaux*, France) Recently bought – from its British owners, Allied Domecq – by the same self-made French millionaire who this year bought Christie's. First growth *Pauillac* which can be very tricky to judge when young, but which develops majestically. *Les Forts de Latour* is the – often worthwhile – *second label.* **61** 62 64 **66** 67 **70** 73 **75** 76 **78** 79 80 81 82 83 85 86 88 89 90 91 92 93 94 95 96 ☆☆☆☆ **1994 ££££**

⚊ **Ch. Latour-à-Pomerol** [lah-toor ah po-meh-rol] (*Pomerol*, *Bordeaux*, France) A great value, tiny (3,500-case) *Pomerol* under the same ownership as *Ch. Pétrus* and the same *Moueix* winemaking team. It is a little less concentrated than its big brother, but then it is around a quarter of the price, too. 76 78 79 81 **82** 83 **85** 86 88 89 90 92 93 94 95 96 ☆☆☆☆ **1990 ££££**

⚊ **Ch. Latour-Martillac** [la-toor mah-tee-yak] (*Graves Cru Classé*, *Bordeaux*, France) Good, if sometimes overlooked reds and whites. Red: **82** 83 **85** 86 88 89 90 91 92 93 94 95 96 White: 86 88 **89** 90 91 **92** 93 94 96

Laudun [loh-duhn] (*Rhône*, France) Named village of *Côtes du Rhône,* with peppery reds and attractive rosés.

⚊ **Laurel Glen** (*Sonoma* Mountain, California) Small hillside-estate with ripe-flavoured *Bordeaux*-style reds that are well respected by true Californian wine lovers. Terra Rosa is the accessible *second label.* ☆☆☆☆ **1994 Terra Rosa Cabernet Merlot ££**

⚊ **Dominique Laurent** [Loh-ron] (*Burgundy*, France) A new name to watch, this young *négociant* was founded a few years ago by a former patissier who has rapidly shown his skills at buying and maturing top class wines from several *appellations*. Wines are hard to find.

⚊ **Laurent-Perrier** [law-ron pay-ree-yay] (*Champagne*, France) One of the more reliable larger houses with particularly recommendable rosé. ☆☆☆☆ **1990 Vintage Brut ££££**

⚊ **Ch. Laville Haut-Brion** [la-veel oh-bree-yon] (*Graves Cru Classé*, *Bordeaux*, France) Exquisite white *Graves* that lasts for 20 years or more. 62 **66** 75 82 **83** 85 86 88 89 90 92 93 94 95 96

Lazio [lat-zee-yoh] (Italy) See *Latium*.

LBV (*Douro*, Portugal) See *Late-Bottled Vintage*.
Lean Lacking body.

Leasingham (South Australia) *BRL Hardy* subsidiary in the *Clare Valley* that makes top flight reds and whites, including great *Shiraz* and *Chardonnay*. ☆☆☆☆ **1996 Cabernet-Malbec £££**

Lebanon Best known for the remarkable *Ch. Musar* from the *Bekaa Valley*. See also *Ch. Kefraya*.

Leconfield [leh-kon-feeld] (South Australia) Reliable producer of highly impressive intense *Coonawarra* reds that improve with every vintage. ☆☆☆☆☆ **1996 Cabernet Sauvignon £££**

Lees or lie(s) The sediment of dead yeasts that fall in the barrel or vat as a wine develops. See *Sur Lie*.

Leeuwin Estate [loo-win] (*Margaret River*, Western Australia) Showcase winery (and concert venue) whose genuinely world-class ('art label') *Chardonnay* is one of Australia's priciest and longest-lived. Other wines are less dazzling. ☆☆☆☆☆ **1994 Art Series Chardonnay £££**

Dom. Leflaive [luh-flayv] (*Burgundy*, France) A new generation of Leflaives is using organic methods – and making better wines than ever. ☆☆☆☆☆ **1995 Bienvenue-Bâtard-Montrachet ££££**

Olivier Leflaive [luh-flayv] (*Burgundy*, France) The *négoçiant* business launched by Vincent Leflaive's nephew. High-class white wines. ☆☆☆☆ **1995 Meursault £££**

Peter Lehmann [lee-man] (*Barossa Valley*, Australia) The grand (not so) old man of the *Barossa Valley*, Peter Lehmann and his son Doug make intensely concentrated *Shirazes*, *Cabernets*, *Semillons* and *Chardonnays* which make up in character (and value for money) what they lack in subtlety. Stonewell is the best red. ☆☆☆☆☆ **1992 Stonewell Shiraz £££**

Length How long the taste lingers in the mouth.

Lenswood (South Australia) New high-altitude region near *Adelaide*, proving its potential with *Sauvignon*, *Chardonnay*, *Pinot Noir* and even (in the case of *Henschke*'s Abbott's Prayer), *Merlot* and *Cabernet Sauvignon*. Pioneers include *Stafford Ridge* and *Knappstein*'s Lenswood who also makes good *Pinot Noir*. White: **86 87** 88 **90 91 94 95** Red: **80 82 84 85 86 87** 88 **90 91 94** 95 ***Tim Knappstein; Stafford Ridge.***

Lenswood (South Australia) See Knappstein

Léognan [lay-ohn-yon] (*Bordeaux*, France) Leading village of *Graves* with its own *AC*, *Pessac-Léognan*. ***Lurton***.

León [lay-on] (Spain) North-western region producing acceptable dry, fruity reds and whites.

Jean León [zhon lay-ON] (*Catalonia*, Spain) American pioneer of *Chardonnay* and *Cabernet*, recently bought by *Torres*. ☆☆☆☆ **1991 Cabernet Sauvignon £££**

Leonetti Cellars [lee-oh-net-tee] (*Washington State*, US) One of the best red wine producers in the US. Now showing its skills with *Sangiovese*. ☆☆☆☆ **1994 Cabernet Sauvignon Columbia Valley ££**

Ch. Léoville-Barton [lay-oh-veel bahr-ton] (*St. Julien 2ème Cru Classé*, *Bordeaux*, France) The charming Anthony Barton produces one of the classiest wines in *Bordeaux*. A fairly priced, reliably stylish *St. Julien* second growth, whose wines are among the best in the *Médoc*. *Langoa Barton* is the sister property. **61 70 75** 76 **78** 81 **82** 83 85 86 87 88 89 90 91 92 93 94 95 ☆☆☆☆☆ **1993 ££££**

Ch. Léoville-Las-Cases [lay-oh-veel kas-kahz] (*St. Julien 2ème Cru Classé*, *Bordeaux*, France) Impeccably made *St. Julien* Super Second which now often matches its neighbour *Ch. Latour*, partly through the severity of the selection process that decides how much of each year's wine will go into the Grand Vin and how much into the *Clos du Marquis 'second label'*. Michel Delon, the owner, knows just how good his wine is, however, and now does everything possible to raise its price to the level of his first growth neighbours. 76 **78** 81 **82 83 85** 86 88 89 90 91 92 93 94 95 96

Ch. Léoville-Poyferré [lay-pwah-feh-ray] (*St. Julien 2ème Cru Classé*, *Bordeaux*, France) 1995, 1996 and 1997 showed the touch of *Michel Rolland* here. A rising star. The *second label* is Moulin Riche. **82 83** 84 85 86 87 88 89 90 91 93 94 95 96 ☆☆☆☆ **1991 ££££**

Dom. Leroy [luh-rwah] (*Burgundy*, France) Organic *domaine* in *Vosne-Romanée* founded by the former co-owner of the *Dom. de la Romanée-Conti* and making wines as good as those of that estate. ☆☆☆☆☆ **1995 Chambertin ££££**

🍷**Lexia** [lex-ee-yah] See *Muscat d'Alexandrie*.

Lie(s) See *Lees/Sur Lie*.

Liebfraumilch [leeb-frow-mihlkh] (Germany) Seditious exploitation of the *QbA* system. Good examples are pleasant; most are alcoholic sugar-water bought on price alone.

Lievland [leev-land] (*Stellenbosch*, South Africa) Estate which has emerged as a high quality specialist producer of *Shiraz* and *late harvest* wines. ☆☆☆☆ **1995 Shiraz ££**

Hubert Lignier [Lee-nee-yay] (*Burgundy*, France) *Morey-St.-Denis* estate that produces classic long-lived wines. ☆☆☆☆☆ **1995 Morey-St.-Denis £££**

Ch. Lilian-Ladouys [la-dwees] (*St. Estèphe Cru Bourgeois*, *Bordeaux*, France) Young estate which has failed to live up to its promising start. 89 90 91 92 93 94 95 96

Limestone Ridge (South Australia) *Lindemans'* often excellent *Coonawarra* red blend. ☆☆☆☆ **1994 Shiraz Cabernet £££**

Limousin [lee-moo-zan] (France) Oak forest that provides barrels that are high in wood *tannin*. Better, therefore, for red wine than for white.

Limoux [lee-moo] (*Midi*, France) New *appellation* for *Chardonnays* which were previously sold as *Vin De Pays d'Oc*. See *Blanquette*.

Lindauer [lin-dowr] (*Marlborough*, New Zealand) Good-value *Montana* fizz. ☆☆☆☆ **Special Reserve ££**

Lindemans (South Australia) Once *Penfolds'* greatest rival, now (like so many other once-independent Aussie producers) its subsidiary. Noted for long-lived *Hunter Valley Semillon* and *Shiraz*, *Coonawarra* reds and good-value multi-region blends, such as the internationally successful Bin 65 *Chardonnay* and Bin 45 *Cabernet*.

Weingut Karl Lingenfelder [lin-gen-fel-duh] (*Pfalz*, Germany) Great new-wave *Rheinpfalz* producer of a special *Riesling*, *Dornfelder*, *Scheurebe* and an unusually successful *Pinot Noir*. ☆☆☆☆ **1994 Freisenheimer Riesling Halbtrocken Spätlese ££**

Jean Lionnet [lee-oh-nay] (*Rhône*, France) Classy *Cornas* producer whose Rochepertuis is a worthwhile buy. The *St. Péray* is an unusually good example of its *appellation* too. ☆☆☆☆ **1995 Cornas Dom. de Rochepertuis £££**

Ch. Liot [lee-yoh] (*Barsac*, *Bordeaux*, France) Good light and elegant *Barsac*. 75 76 82 83 86 88 89 90 92 94 96 97 ☆☆☆☆ **1992 £££**

Liqueur Muscat (*Rutherglen*, Australia) A wine style unique to Australia. Other countries make fortified *Muscats*, but none achieve the caramelised marmalade and Christmas pudding flavours that *Rutherglen* can achieve. **Mick Morris; Campbell's.**

Liqueur d'Expedition [lee-kuhr dex-pay-dees-see-yon] (*Champagne*, France) Sweetening syrup for *dosage*.

Liqueur de Tirage [lee-kuhr duh tee-rahzh] (*Champagne*, France) The yeast and sugar added to base wine to induce secondary fermentation (and hence the bubbles) in bottle.

Liquoreux [lee-koh-ruh] (France) Rich and sweet.

Liquoroso [lee-koh-roh-soh] (Italy) Rich and sweet.

Lirac [lee-rak] (*Rhône*, France) Peppery, *Tavel*-like rosés, and increasingly impressive, deep berry-fruit reds. Red: **82 83 85 88** 89 90 95 96 97 **Perrin; Delorme; Ch. D'Aqueria; André Méjan; Ch. Mayne Lalande; Bouchassy.**

Listel [lees-tel] (*Languedoc-Roussillon*, France) Recently taken over, improving pioneer with vineyards on beaches close to Sète. Best wines: rosé ('Grain de Gris') and sparkling *Muscat* (Pétillant de Raisin).

Listrac [lees-trak] (*Bordeaux*, France) Small *commune* in the *Haut-Médoc*, near *Moulis*, though quite different in style. Clay makes this *Merlot* country, though this isn't always reflected in the vineyards. Most wines are toughly unripe. 70 75 76 **78** 79 81 **82** 83 **85 86** 88 89 90 94 95 96 **Ch. Clarke; *Fourcas-Hosten; Ch. Poujeaux.***

Livermore (Valley) [liv-uhr-mohr] (California) Warm climate vineyard area with fertile soil producing full rounded whites, including increasingly fine *Chardonnay*. Red: 84 **85** 86 87 **90 91** 92 93 95 White: **85 90 91 92** 95 96 ***Wente*; Concannon; Livermore Cellars.**

Los Llanos [los yah-nos] (*Valdepeñas*, Spain) Commendable modern exception to the tradition of dull *Valdepeñas*, with quality mature reds.

De Loach [duh lohch] (*Sonoma*, California) Look for the letters OFS – Our Finest Selection – on the *Chardonnay* and *Cabernet*. But even these rarely surpass the stunning individual vineyard *Zinfandels*.

J Lohr [lohr] (Santa Clara, California) Winery noted for its well-made affordable wines, particularly the Wildflower and now more classic noble styles. ☆☆☆☆ **1996 Riverstone Chardonnay ££**

Loire [lwahr] (France) An extraordinary variety of wines come from this area – dry whites such as *Muscadet* and the classier *Savennières, Sancerre* and *Pouilly-Fumé*; grassy summery reds; – *Chinon* and *Bourgeuil;* buckets of rosé – some good, most dreadful; glorious sweet whites – *Vouvray* etc – and very acceptable sparkling wines (also *Vouvray* plus *Crémant de Loire*). Stick to growers and *domaines*. White: 83 **85 86 88 89 90** 94 95 Sweet White: **76** 83 **85** 86 **88 89** 90 94 95 **96 97**. Red: **78** 83 **85** 86 **88 89 90** 95 **96 97**

Lombardy [lom-bahr-dee] (Italy) Region (and vineyards) around Milan, known mostly for sparkling wine but also for increasingly interesting reds, such as Valcalepio and *Oltrepò Pavese* and the whites of *Lugana*. Red: **78** 79 81 **82 85 88 90** 94 95 **96** 97

Long Island (*New York State*, US) A unique micro-climate where fields once full of potatoes are now yielding classy *Merlot* and *Chardonnay*. See *Bridgehampton, Hargrave and Palmer Vineyards*.

Longridge (*Stellenbosch*, South Africa) Designer winery tailoring three ranges (Longridge, Bay View and Capelands) to the export market. ☆☆☆☆ **1996 Chardonnay £**

Lontue [lon-too-way] (Chile) Region where some of Chile's best *Merlots* are being made. ***Santa Carolina; Valdevieso; San Pedro.***

❖ **Weingut Dr. Loosen** [loh-sen] (*Mosel-Saar-Ruwer*, Germany) New-Wave *Riesling* producer. Probably the best and most reliable in the *Mosel* (I only wish he'd use a little less *sulphur dioxide*). ☆☆☆☆ **1997 Urziger Würzgarten Riesling Auslese Gold ££££**

❖ **Lopez de Heredia** [loh-peth day hay-ray-dee-yah] (*Rioja*, Spain) Ultra-traditional winery producing old-fashioned Viña Tondonia white and *Gran Reserva* reds. ☆☆☆ **1993 Vina Tondonia Tinto Crianza £££**

❖ **Louisvale** [loo-wis-vayl] (*Stellenbosch*, South Africa) Once avowed *Chardonnay* specialists, Louisvale's range has expanded to include some *Cabernet*-based reds. ☆☆☆ **1995 Cabernet Merlot ££**

❖ **Loupiac** [loo-peeyak] (*Bordeaux*, France) *Sauternes* neighbour with similar but less fine wines. **83 85 86 88 89 90 95 97 *Ch. Loupiac-Gaudiet.***

❖ **Ch. Loupiac-Gaudiet** [loo-pee-yak goh-dee-yay] (*Loupiac, Bordeaux*, France) A good producer of *Loupiac*. **83 85 86 88 89 90 95 96 97**

❖ **Ch. la Louvière** [lah loo-vee-yehr] (*Graves, Bordeaux*, France) André Lurton's best known *Graves* property. Reliable, rich, modern whites and reds. The second wine is called 'L de Louvière. Red: 81 **82** 83 **85 86** 88 89 90 91 92 93 94 95 96 White: 86 88 **89 90** 91 92 93 94 95 96 ☆☆☆☆ **1993 Red £££**

❖ **Van Loveren** [van loh-veh-ren] (*Robertson*, South Africa) Large family-owned estate producing excellent value for money wine. Concentrating primarily on classic fresh whites and also soft reds. ☆☆☆ **1996 Late harvest Gewurztraminer £**

Côtes du Lubéron [koht doo LOO-bay-ron] (*Rhône*, France) Reds like light *Côtes du Rhône*, pink and sparkling wines and *Chardonnay*-influenced whites. A new *appellation* and still good value.

❖ **Luce** [loo-chay] (*Tuscany*, Italy) Co-production between *Mondavi* and *Frescobaldi* who have combined forces to produce a perfectly pleasant but overpriced red.

❖ **Lugana** [loo-gah-nah] (*Lombardy*, Italy) Potentially appley almondy whites made from the *Trebbiano*, grown on the shores of Lake Garda. ☆☆☆☆ **1996 Villa Flora, Zenato ££**

Lugny [loo-nee] (*Burgundy*, France) See *Mâcon*.

❖ **Pierre Luneau** [loo-noh] (*Loire*, France) A rare beast: a top-class *Muscadet* producer. M. Luneau likes to try out wacky ideas with his wines like keeping juice under nitrogen for a few years to see what happens. ☆☆☆ **1996 Muscadet Sur Lie 'L' d'Or ££**

❖ **Cantine Lungarotti** [kan-tee-nah loon-gah-roh-tee] (*Umbria*, Italy) Innovative producer who more or less created the *Torgiano* denomination. ☆☆☆☆ **1986 Rubesco Riserva Monticchio ££££**

❖ **Jacques Lurton** [loor-ton] Son of the owner of *Ch. la Louvière* and *Ch. Bonnet* in *Entre-Deux-Mers* who, having made a success there (especially with his whites), now makes wine all over the world. Look out for Hermanos Lurton wines from Spain and Bodega Lurton wines from Argentina. ☆☆☆☆ **1996 'Les Bateaux' Syrah, Vin de Pays d'Oc ££**

❖ **Ch. de Lussac** [loo-sak] (*Lussac St. Emilion, Bordeaux*, France) A name to watch out for in *Lussac St. Emilion.* **86 89 90 94 95 96**

❖ **Lussac-St. Emilion** [loo-sak sant-ay-mee-yon] (*Bordeaux*, France) Potentially worthwhile satellite of *St. Emilion.* **82** 83 **85** 86 **88** 89 90 94 95 96

❖ **Emilio Lustau** [loos-tow] (*Jerez*, Spain) Great *sherry* producer, particularly noted for individual *almacanista* wines. ☆☆☆☆ **Almacanista Dry Oloroso ££**

Lutomer [loo-toh-muh] (Slovenia) Wine-producing area still known mostly for its (very basic) Lutomer *Laski Riesling*. Now doing better things with *Chardonnay*.

Luxembourg [luk-sehm-burg] Source of some pleasant, fresh, white wines from *Alsace*-like grape varieties, and generally dire fizz.

🍷 **Ch. Lynch-Bages** [lansh bazh] (*Pauillac 5ème Cru Classé, Bordeaux*, France) Reliably over-performing fifth growth *Pauillac* belonging to Jean-Michel Cazes of *Ch. Pichon-Longueville*. The (very rare) white is worth seeking out too. **70** 75 78 **82 83 85** 86 88 89 90 91 92 93 94 95 96

🍷 **Ch. Lynch-Moussas** [lansh moo-sahs] (*Pauillac 5ème Cru Classé, Bordeaux*, France) Slowly improving. **85** 86 88 89 **90** 91 **94 95 96**

M

🍷 ***Macération carbonique*** [ma-say-ra-see-yon kahr-bon-eek] Technique of fermenting uncrushed grapes under pressure of a blanket of carbon dioxide gas to produce fresh fruity wine. Used in *Beaujolais*, southern France and, increasingly, the New World.

🍷 **Machard de Gramant** [ma-shahr duh gra-mon] (*Burgundy*, France) Producer of superb *Nuits-St.-Georges, Vosne-Romanée* and *Savigny-lès Beaune*. ☆☆☆☆ 1994 Vosne-Romanée Clos des Réas £££

Mâcon/Mâconnais [ma-kon/nay] (*Burgundy*, France) Avoid unidentified 'rouge' or 'blanc' on wine lists. Mâcons with the suffix *Villages, Superieur* or Prissé, *Viré, Lugny* or Clessé should be better. The region contains the *appellations St.-Véran* and *Pouilly-Fuissé*. For straight Mâcon try *Jadot* or *Duboeuf*, but the *Dom. Thevenet Dom. de la Bongran* from Clessé is of *Côte d'Or* quality. Red: **78** 80 **85** 86 87 88 89 90 92 95 96 White: 84 **85 86** 87 **88** 89 **90 92** 95 96 Caves de Lugny; Cave de Prissé; Roger Lasserat.

🍷 **Maculan** [mah-koo-lahn] (*Veneto*, Italy) A superstar producer of black-curranty *Cabernet* Breganze, an oaked *Pinot Bianco-Pinot Grigio-Chardonnay* blend called Prato di Canzio and the lusciously sweet *Torcolato*. ☆☆☆☆ 1994 Ferrata Cabernet ££

🍷 **Madeira** [ma-dee-ruh] (Portugal) Atlantic island producing fortified wines, usually identified by style: *Bual, Sercial, Verdelho* or *Malmsey*. Most is ordinary stuff for use by mainland European cooks and, more rarely, finer fare for those who appreciate the unique marmaladey character of good Madeira. *Henriques & Henriques;* Barros e Souza.

Maderisation [mad-uhr-ih-zay-shon] Deliberate procedure in *Madeira*, produced by the warming of wine in *estufas*. Otherwise undesired effect, commonly produced by high temperatures during storage, resulting in a dull flat flavour, tinged with a *sherry* taste and colour.

🍷 **Madiran** [ma-dee-ron] (*South West*, France) Robust country reds made from the *Tannat* grape; *tannic* when young, but worth ageing. *Producteurs de Plaimont; Ch. Montus; Bouscassé;* Dom. du Crampilh.

🍷 **Ch. Magdelaine** [Mag-duh-layn] (*St. Emilion Premier Grand Cru, Bordeaux*, France) *St. Emilion* estate owned by JP *Moueix* and neighbour to *Ch. Ausone*, producing reliable rich wines. **61 70 71** 75 78 79 81 **82 83** 85 86 88 89 90 92 93 94 95 96 ☆☆☆☆ 1993 £££

Magnum Large bottle containing the equivalent of two bottles of wine (one and a half litres in capacity).

Maipo [mih-poh] (Chile) Historic region in which are found many gooproducers. Reds are most successful, especially *Cabernet*, *Merlot* and softer *Chardonnays* are also made.Watch out for new varieties and enterprising organic vineyards. **Aquitania (Paul Bruno);** ***Canepa; Concha y Toro; Cousino Macul;*** **Peteroa;** ***Santa Carolina;*** **Santa Inés;** ***Santa Rita; Undurraga; Viña Carmen.***

Maître de Chai [may-tr duh chay] (France) Cellar master.

Malaga [ma-la-gah] (Spain) A semi-moribund Andalusian *DO* producing raisiny dessert wines of varying degrees of sweetness, immensely popular in the 19th century. **Lopez Hermanos.**

Ch. Malartic-Lagravière [mah-lahr-teek lah-gra-vee-yehr] (*Pessac-Léognan Cru Classé, Bordeaux*, France) Previously slumbering estate, bought in 1994 by *Laurent Perrier*, improving new-wave whites; reds need time. Red: 81 **82** 83 85 **86** 88 89 90 91 92 93 94 95 96 White: 85 **87** 88 89 90 91 92 94 95 96

Malbec [mal-bek] Red grape, now rare in *Bordeaux* but widely planted in Argentina, the *Loire* (where it is known as the *Côt*), *Cahors* and also in Australia. Producing rich, plummy, silky wines.

Ch. Malescasse [ma-les-kas] (*Haut-Médoc Cru Bourgeois, Bordeaux*, France) Watch this space; since 1993, wines have been made by the former cellarmaster of *Pichon-Lalande*. 82 83 85 86 88 89 90 93 94 95 96

Ch. Malescot-St-Exupéry [ma-les-koh san tek-soo-peh-ree] (*Margaux 3ème Cru Classé, Bordeaux*, France) Understated but sometimes quite classy wines. 70 **82** 83 86 87 88 89 90 91 92 94 95 96 ☆☆☆ **1993 £££**

Ch. de Malle [duh mal] (*Sauternes 2ème Cru Classé, Bordeaux*, France) Good *Sauternes* property near Preignac, famous for its beautiful *château*. 76 78 **81** 82 **83** 85 **86** 88 89 90 91 94 95 96 97 ☆☆☆☆ **1990 ££££**

Mallorca [ma-yor-kah] (Spain) See *Binissalem*.

Malolactic fermentation [ma-loh-lak-tik] Secondary 'fermentation' in which appley *malic acid* is converted into the 'softer' creamier *lactic* acid by naturally present or added strains of bacteria. Almost all red wines undergo a malolactic fermentation. For whites, it is common practice in *Burgundy*. It is varyingly used in the New World, where natural acid levels are often low. Recognisable in excess in wine, as a buttermilky flavour.

Ch. de la Maltroye [mal-trwah] (*Burgundy*, France) Classy modern *Chassagne*-based estate with fingers in fourteen *AC* pies around *Burgundy*, all of whose wines are made by *Dom. Parent*. ☆☆☆☆ **1996 Chassagne-Montrachet les Grandes Ruchottes ££££**

Malvasia [mal-vah-see-ah] *Muscatty* white grape vinified dry in Italy (as a component in *Frascati* for example), but far more successfully as good, sweet, traditional *Madeira*, where it is known as *Malmsey*. It is not the same grape as *Malvoisie* (see below).

Malvoisie (*Loire*, France) Local name for the *Pinot Gris;* used in dessert wines.

La Mancha [lah man-cha] (Spain) Huge region known for mostly dull and old-fashioned wines, but in recent times producing increasingly clean modern examples. Also the place where the *Marquès de Griñon* is succeeding in his experiments with new vine-growing techniques and grapes, especially *Syrah*.

Albert Mann (*Alsace*, France) Top grower who always manages to express true varietal character without overblown alcohol flavours. ☆☆☆☆ **1995 Tokay Pinot Gris Grand Cru Fürstentum £££**

🍾**Manseng (Gros M. & Petit M.)** [man-seng] (*South-West*, France)
Two varieties of white grape grown in south-western France. The Gros M.
is a flavoursome workhorse for much of the dry white of the Armagnac
region, whereas Petit M. is capable of extraordinary apricot-and-cream
concentration in the great *vendange tardive* wines of *Jurançon*. The
Manseng is one of the few noble varieties not to have found wide favour
across the globe, possibly because it is low-yielding and hard to grow.
Dom. Cauhapé; Grassa; Producteurs de Plaimont.

Manzanilla [man-zah-nee-yah] (*Jerez*, Spain) Dry tangy *sherry* – a *fino*
style widely (though possibly mistakenly) thought to take on a salty tang
from the coastal *bodegas* of Sanlucar de Barrameda. *Don Zoilo; Barbadillo;
Hidalgo.*

🍷 **Maranges** [mah-ronzh] (*Burgundy*, France) A new hillside *appellation*
promising potentially affordable, if a little rustic, *Côte d'Or* wines. White:
90 92 95 96 Red: 90 92 95 96 ☆☆☆☆ 1996 Dom. Chevrot £££

Marc [mahr] (France) The residue of pips, stalks and skins left after the
grapes are pressed – and often distilled into a fiery brandy of the same
name, e.g. Marc de Bourgogne.

🍷 **Marcassin** (*Sonoma*, California) Helen Turley produces *Côte d'Or Grand
Cru* quality *Chardonnays* in tiny quantities from a trio of vineyards.
Almost unobtainable.

Marches [MAHR-kay] (Italy) Central wine region on the Adriatic coast,
below Venice. Best known for *Rosso Conero* and good, dry, fruity
Verdicchio whites. *Umani Ronchi; Garofoli; Fazi Battaglia.*

🍷 **Marcillac** [mah-see-yak] (*South-West*, France) Full-flavoured country
reds, made principally from the *Fer* grape – they may also contain some
Cabernet and *Gamay.*

🍾**Maréchal Foch** [mah-ray-shahl fohsh] A *hybrid* vine producing red
grapes in Canada and Eastern North America. *Inniskillin.*

Margaret River (*Western Australia*) Cool(ish) vineyard area on the coast of
Western Australia, gaining notice for *Cabernet Sauvignon* and *Chardonnay*.
Also Australia's only *Zinfandel*. White: 85 86 87 88 90 91 93 94 95 96
Red: 80 82 83 85 86 87 88 90 91 92 93 94 95 96 *Cape Mentelle;
Moss Wood; Leeuwin; Cullen; Pierro; Vasse Felix; Ch. Xanadu.*

🍷 **Margaux** [mahr-goh] (*Bordeaux*, France) Large *commune* with a concentration of *Crus Classés* including Ch. *Margaux, Palmer, Lascombes.* Sadly,
other wines which should be deliciously blackberryish are variable,
partly thanks to the diverse nature of the soil, and partly through the producers' readiness to sacrifice quality for the sake of yields. Curiously,
though, if you want a good 1983, this vintage succeeded better here than
elsewhere in the *Médoc*; 1995s are good too. Also worth hunting out are
generic Margaux from reputable *négociants*. 70 75 78 81 82 83 85 86 88
89 90 94 95

🍷 **Ch. Margaux** [mahr-goh] (*Margaux Premier Cru Classé, Bordeaux*,
France) Peerless *first growth*, back on form since the dull 1970s, and
producing intense wines with cedary perfume and velvet softness when
mature. The second wine, *Pavillon Rouge* (red and matching white), is
worth buying too. 61 78 79 81 82 83 84 85 86 87 88 89 90 91 92 93
94 95 96 97 ☆☆☆☆☆ 1990 ££££

🍷 **Markham** (*Napa Valley*, California) A producer to watch for both reds
and whites. ☆☆☆☆ 1995 Barrel Fermented Napa Valley Chardonnay
£££; ☆☆☆☆ 1993 Petite Sirah £££

Marlborough [morl-buh-ruh] (New Zealand) An important wine area with cool climate in the South Island producing excellent *Sauvignon*, *Chardonnay* and improving *Merlot* and *Pinot Noir*, as well as a number of impressive sparkling wines. White: **89 91** 92 96 97 ***Cloudy Bay; Hunter's; Vavasour; Jackson Estate; Cellier le Brun; Montana.***

Marne et Champagne [mahr-nay-shom-pan-y] (*Champagne*, France) Huge cooperative which owns the Besserat de Bellefon, *Lanson* and Alfred Rothschild labels, and seems to be able to provide really good own-label wines for UK merchant and supermarket buyers who are prepared to pay the price!

Ch. Marquis-de-Terme [mahr-kee duh tehrm] (*Margaux 4ème Cru Classé*, *Bordeaux*, France) Traditional property with quite tough wines. **81** 82 **83** 85 **86** 87 88 89 90 93 95 96 ☆☆☆ **1990 £££**

Marsala [mahr-sah-lah] (*Sicily*, Italy) Dark, rich, fortified wine from *Sicily* essential for use in recipes such as Zabaglione. ***De Bartoli;*** **Pellegrino; Cantine Florio.**

Marsannay [mahr-sah-nay] (*Burgundy*, France) Northernmost village of the *Côte de Nuits* with a range of largely undistinguished but, for *Burgundy*, affordable *Chardonnay* and *Pinot Noir* (red and rosé). White: **79** 84 **85 86** 87 **88** 89 **90 92** 95 Red: 76 **78** 79 **80** 83 **85** 86 87 **88 89 90** 92 95 96 ***Bruno Clair; Louis Jadot.***

Marsanne [mahr-san] (*Rhône*, France) The grape usually responsible (in blends with *Roussanne*) for most of the northern *Rhône* white wines. Also successful in the *Goulburn Valley* in *Victoria* for *Ch. Tahbilk* and *Mitchelton* and in California for *Bonny Doon*. It has a delicate perfumed intensity when young and fattens out with age. Look out for un-oaked versions from Australia. ***Tahbilk; Mitchelton; Bonny Doon; Guigal.***

Martinborough (New Zealand) Up-and-coming North Island region for *Pinot Noir* and *Chardonnay*. White: 87 88 **89 91** 92 **94** 96 Red: **83 85 87** 89 90 **91 92** 93 94 95 96 ***Martinborough Vineyard; Dry River; Ata Rangi; Palliser Estate.***

Martinborough Vineyard (*Martinborough*, New Zealand) Producer of the best Kiwi *Pinot Noir* and one of the best *Chardonnays*. Wines can be so *Burgundian* in style that the 1991 *Pinot Noir* was refused an export licence for being untypically 'farmyardy' until a delegation of wine-loving politicians intervened. ☆☆☆☆ **1995 Chardonnay £££**

Martinelli (*Sonoma*, California) Century-old *Zinfandel* specialists, making rich intense reds from this variety and juicy *Pinot Noirs*.

Bodegas Martinez Bujanda [mahr-tee-neth boo-han-dah] (*Rioja*, Spain) New-wave producer of fruit-driven wines sold as *Conde de Valdemar*. Probably the most consistently recommendable producer in *Rioja*. ☆☆☆☆**1995 Rioja Crianza £££**

Martini (*Piedmont*, Italy) Good *Asti Spumante* from the producer of the vermouth house which invented 'lifestyle' advertising – still we're all guilty of something. ☆☆☆ **Asti Fratelli Martini ££**

Louis Martini (*Napa Valley*, California) Grand old name right on form at the moment. Superlative long-lived *Cabernet* from the Monte Rosso vineyard. ☆☆☆☆ **1995 Chardonnay Reserve £££;** ☆☆☆☆☆ **1994 Merlot Reserve £££**

Marzemino [mahrt-zeh-mee-noh] (Italy) Spicy red grape producing black plummy wines.

Mas Amiel [mahs ah-mee-yel] (*Provence*, France) The producer of wonderful rich almost *port*-like wine in the tiny *appellation* of Maury in the west of *Provence*. ☆☆☆☆ **Maury 15 Ans d'Age £££**

☉ **Mas de Daumas Gassac** [mas duh doh-mas gas-sac] (*Midi*, France) Ground-breaking *Hérault vin de pays* red, compared by some to top *claret*. Its flavours come from an eclectic blend of upto half a dozen varieties, including *Pinot Noir, Syrah, Mourvèdre* and *Cabernet* – and a unique *'terroir'*. Approachable when young, but lasts for ages. *The* white blend including *Viognier* is similarly impressive. ☆☆☆☆ 1996 Rouge £££

☉ **Bartolo Mascarello** [mas-kah-reh-loh] (*Piedmont*, Italy) Great ultra-traditional *Barolo* specialist whose rose-petally wine proves that the old ways can compete with the new.

☉ **Giuseppe Mascarello** [mas-kah-reh-loh] (*Piedmont*, Italy) Top-class *Barolo* estate (unconnected with that of *Bartolo Mascarello*), producing characterful wine from individual vineyards. Great *Dolcetto*. ☆☆☆☆ 1993 Monprivato ££££

☉ **Masi** [mah-see] (*Veneto*, Italy) Producer with reliable, affordable reds and whites and single-vineyard wines which serve as a justification for *Valpolicella's* denomination. ☆☆☆☆ 1993 Campo Fiorin £££

☉ **Massandra** [mahsan-drah] (*Crimea*, CIS) Famous as the source of great, historic, dessert wines which were sold at a memorable Sotheby's auction in 1991, this is now the place to find good but not great *Cabernet*.

Master of Wine (MW) One of a small number of people (around 250) internationally who have passed a gruelling set of wine exams.

☉ **Mastroberardino** [maas tro be rah dino] (*Campania*, Italy) Top producer of rich wines from Italy's south. ☆☆☆☆ 1996 Lacryma Christi Rosso £££

☉ **Matanzas Creek** [muh-tan-zuhs] (*Sonoma Valley*, California) Top-class complex *Chardonnay*, good *Sauvignon* and high-quality accessible *Merlot*. ☆☆☆☆ 1994 Merlot ££££

🍇 **Mataro** [muh-tah-roh] See *Mourvèdre*.

☉ **Mateus** [ma-tay-oos] (Portugal) Highly commercial pink and white off-dry *frizzante* wine made by *Sogrape*, Portugal's biggest producer, sold in bottles traditional in *Franken*, Germany, and with a label depicting a palace with which the wine has no connection. A 50-year-old marketing masterpiece. The name is now being used for *Sogrape's* more serious reds.

☉ **Thierry Matrot** [tee-yer-ree ma-troh] (*Burgundy*, France) Top-class white producer with great white and recommendable red *Blagny*. ☆☆☆☆ 1992 Meursault Les Charmes ££££

☉ **Matua Valley** [ma-tyoo-wah] (*Auckland*, New Zealand) Reliable maker of great (*Marlborough*) *Sauvignon*, (Judd Estate) *Chardonnay* and *Merlot*. Also producer of the even better *Ararimu* red and white. Shingle Peak is the *second label*. ☆☆☆☆ 1997 Judd Estate Chardonnay £££

☉ **Yvon Mau** [ee-von moh] (*Bordeaux & South-West*, France) Highly commercial producer of *Bordeaux* and other, mostly white, wines from *South-West* France. Occasionally good.

☉ **Ch. Maucaillou** [mow-kih-yoo] (*Moulis Cru Bourgeois*, *Bordeaux*, France) *Cru Bourgeois* in the *commune* of *Moulis* producing approachable wines to beat some *Crus Classés*. 75 82 83 **85 86** 88 **89 90 92 93** 94 95 96

Maule [mow-lay] (Chile) Up-and-coming *Central Valley* region especially for white wines (*Sauvignon* in particular) but warm enough for red. *Santa Carolina*; Carta Vieja

☉ **Bernard Maume** [Mohm] (*Burgundy*, France) Small *Gevrey-Chambertin* estate run by a biology professor and his son. ☆☆☆☆ 1995 Mazis-Chambertin £££

Bodegas Mauro [mow-roh] (Spain) Just outside the *Ribera del Duero DO*, but making very similar rich red wines.

🍇 **Mauzac** [moh-zak] (France) White grape used in southern France for *vin de pays* and *Gaillac*. Can be characterful and floral or dull and earthy.

🍇 **Mavrodaphne** [mav-roh-daf-nee] (Greece) Characterful indigenous Greek red grape, and the wine made from it. Dark and strong, it needs ageing to be truly worth drinking. ☆☆☆☆ Kourtakis Mavrodaphne of Patras ££

🍷**Mavrud** [mah-vrood] (Bulgaria) Traditional red grape and the character-ful, if rustic, wine made from it.

🍷 **Maximin Grünhaus** [mak-siee min groon-hows] (*Mosel-Saar-Ruwer*, Germany) Dr. Carl von Schubert's 1,000-year-old estate producing intense *Rieslings*. ☆☆☆☆ **1996 Abtsberg Riesling Spätlese ££££**

🍷 **Maxwell** (*McLaren Vale*, Australia) Reliable producer of intense *Shiraz, Merlot* and *Semillon*. ☆☆☆☆ **1992 Ellen Street Shiraz £££**

🍷 **Mayacamas** [mih-yah-kah-mas] (*Napa Valley*, California) Long-estab-lished winery on *Mount Veeder* with *tannic* but good old-fashioned *Cabernet* and long-lived rich *Chardonnay*. ☆☆☆☆ **1994 Cabernet Sauvignon ££££**

🍷 **McGuigan Brothers** (*Hunter Valley*, Australia) Commercial and occasion-ally quite impressive stuff from the former owners of *Wyndham Estate*. ☆☆☆☆ **1996 Shareholders' Cabernet Merlot ££**

McLaren Vale (South Australia) Region close to Adelaide renowned for European-style wines, but possibly too varied in topography, soil and climate to create its own identity. White: 86 87 88 **90 91 94** 95 Red: 80 82 84 85 86 87 88 **90 91** 94 95 96 *Geoff Merrill; Ch. Reynella; d'Arenberg; Maxwell.*

🍷 **McWilliams** (*Hunter Valley*, Australia) *Hunter Valley*-based, evidently non-republican firm with great traditional ('Elizabeth') *Semillon* and ('Philip') *Shiraz* which are now sold younger than previously and so may need time. Fortified wines can be good, too, as are the pioneering *Barwang* and improved *Brand's* wines. Surprisingly good at 'Bag-in-box' wines! ☆☆☆☆ **1992 Elizabeth Semillon £££**

🍷 **Médoc** [may-dok] (*Bordeaux*, France) Area encompassing the region of *Bordeaux* south of the *Gironde* and north of the town of *Bordeaux* in which the *Cru Classés* as well as far more ordinary fare are made. Should be bet-ter than basic *Bordeaux* and less good than *Haut-Médoc*, which tend to have more flavour: experience however suggests that this is not always the case. 82 83 85 86 88 89 90 92 93 94 95 96

🍷 **Meerlust Estate** [meer-loost] (*Stellenbosch*, South Africa) One of the *Cape's* best estates. Classy *Merlots* and a highly rated *Bordeaux*-blend called 'Rubicon', both of which will hopefully one day, some time in the future, benefit from being bottled on the estate rather than by the *Bergkelder*. ☆☆☆☆ **1994 Merlot £££**

🍷 **Gabriel Meffre** [mef-fr] (*Rhône*, France) Sound commercial *Rhône* and, now, southern French producer under the Galet Vineyards label. However still maintains a tradition of producing reliable more classy wines. ☆☆☆ **1995 Châteauneuf-du-Pape Laurus ££**

🍷 **Ch. Megyer** [meg-yer] (*Tokaji*, Hungary) French-owned pioneer of *Tokaji* and *Furmint*.

🍷**Melon de Bourgogne** [muh-lon duh boor-goyn] (France) Tricky grape imported from *Burgundy* (where it is no longer grown) to *Muscadet*, where some producers are still trying to comprehend why it can be so difficult to work with!

🍷 **Charles Melton** (*Barossa Valley*, Australia) Small-scale producer of lovely still and sparkling *Shiraz* and world-class rosé called 'Rose of Virginia', as well as Nine Popes, a wine based on, and mistakenly named after, *Châteauneuf-du-Pape*. ☆☆☆☆ **1995 Shiraz Barossa Valley £££**

Mendocino [men-doh-see-noh] (California) Northern, coastal wine county known for unofficial marijuana farming and for its laid back wine-makers who successfully exploit cool microclimates to make 'European-style' wines. Red: 84 **85** 86 87 **90 91** 92 93 95 White: **85 90 91** 92 95 *Fetzer; Scharffenberger.*

Mendoza [men-doh-zah] (Argentina) Capital of a now up-and-coming principal wine region. Source of good rich reds from firms producing traditional style reds but with more uplifting fruit.. **La Agricola; *Etchart; Trapiche;* Bianchi; *Catena;* Finca Flichman; *Norton;* San Telmo; Lurton; la Rural; *Morande.***

Menetou-Salon [men-too sah-lon] (*Loire*, France) Bordering on *Sancerre*, making similar if earthier, less pricy *Sauvignon*, as well as some decent *Pinot Noir. Henri Pellé* makes the best. White: 94 95 96 97 Red: **90** 91 92 93 94 95 96 97 ☆☆☆☆ **1996 Menetou Salon Blanc, Morogues Les Cris ££**

Dom. Méo-Camuzet [may-oh-ka-moo-zay] (*Burgundy*, France) Brilliant *Côte de Nuits* estate with top-class vineyards and intense, oaky wines, made, until his retirement, by the great *Henri Jayer.* ☆☆☆☆ **1994 Vosne-Romanée aux Brûlées ££££**

Mercaptans [mehr-kap-ton] See *hydrogen sulphide*.

Mercier [mehr-see-yay] (*Champagne*, France) Subsidiary, or is it sister company, of *Moët & Chandon* and producer of improving but pretty commercial fizz which, according to the advertisements, is the biggest seller in France. ☆☆☆☆ **Champagne Mercier Demi-Sec £££**

Mercurey [mehr-koo-ray] (*Burgundy*, France) Village in the *Côte Chalonnaise*, where *Faiveley* makes high quality wine. Red: **78** 80 **85** 86 87 88 89 90 92 95 White: 84 **85 86** 87 **88** 89 **90 92** 95 96 **Ch. de Chamilly; de Chamirey; *Dom. Faiveley;* Michel Juillot; Meix-Foulot; *Pillot.***

Meridian (*San Luis Obispo*, California) Good value *Pinot Noir* from *Santa Barbara*.

Merlot [mehr-loh] 'Flavour of the Month', if the ludicrous orgy of planting in California's *Central Valley* is anything to go by. Soon to be everyone's unloved child, when grapegrowers and winemakers discover that this red variety only produces appealing soft, honeyed, even toffee-ish wine with plummy fruit when it is planted in the right (ideally clay) soil, and kept to very moderate yields. In other words, quite the opposite of what it will get in the *Central Valley*. It is traditionally used to balance the more tannic *Cabernet Sauvignon* throughout the *Médoc*, where it is actually the most widely planted grape; as it is in *Pomerol* and *St. Emilion*, where clay also prevails. Also increasingly – though not spectacularly – successful in the *Languedoc* in southern France. California's best efforts include *Newton, Matanzas Creek* and (recently) *Duckhorn*. Australia, South Africa and New Zealand have had few real successes, but there are impressive efforts from *Washington State* and Chile.

Merricks Estate (*Mornington Peninsula*, Australia) Small estate specialising in *Shiraz*. ☆☆☆☆ **1994 Shiraz**

Geoff Merrill (*McLaren Vale*, Australia) The ebullient moustachioed winemaker who has nicknamed himself 'The Wizard of Oz'. Impressive if restrained *Semillon, Chardonnay* and *Cabernet* in *McLaren Vale* under his own label, plus easier-going Mount Hurtle wines (especially the rosé). ☆☆☆☆ **1995 Reserve Chardonnay £££**

Merryvale (*Napa Valley*, California) Starry winery with especially good Reserve and Silhouette *Chardonnay* and Profile *Cabernet*. ☆☆☆☆ **1995 Reserve Chardonnay £££**

Méthode Champenoise [may-tohd shom-puh-nwahz] Term restricted to *Champagne* – and method used for all quality sparkling wines. Labour-intensive, because bubbles are made by secondary fermentation in bottle, rather than in a vat or by the introduction of gas. Bottles are individually given the '*dégorgémont* process', topped up and recorked!

Methuselah Same size bottle as an *Imperiale* (six litres). Used in *Champagne*.

♆ Meursault [muhr-soh] (*Burgundy*, France) Superb white *Burgundy*; the *Chardonnay* ideally showing off its nutty, buttery richness in full-bodied dry wine. Like *Nuits-St.-Georges* and *Beaune* it has no *Grands Crus* but great *Premiers Crus* such as Charmes, Perrières and Genevrières. There is a little red here too, some of which is sold as *Volnay-Santenots*. White: **79 85 86 87 88 89 90 92 95 96 *Comtes Lafon; Coche-Dury; Drouhin; Ropiteau; Michelot; Ampeau; Jobard; Roulot; Pierre Morey; Prieur.***

♆ Ch. de Meursault [muhr-soh] (*Burgundy*, France) If on a trip to *Beaune* worth a visit. See *Patriarche.* ☆☆☆☆☆ **1993 Meursault £££**

Mexico See *Baja California.*

♆ Ch. Meyney [may-nay] (*St. Estèphe Cru Bourgeois*, *Bordeaux*, France) Improving *St. Estèphe* property, with wines that are richer in flavour than some of its neighbours. 81 **82** 83 85 86 87 88 89 90 91 92 93 94 95 96

♆ Peter Michael (*Sonoma*, California) UK-born Sir Peter Michael produces stunning *Sonoma*, *Burgundy*-like *Chardonnays*, *Sauvignons* and *Cabernets.* ☆☆☆☆ **1993 Cabernet Sauvignon 'Les Pavots', Knights Valley £££**

♆ Louis Michel et Fils [mee-shel] (*Burgundy*, France) Top-class *Chablis* producer. ☆☆☆☆ **1996 Chablis Montée de Tonnerre ££££**

♆ Robert Michel (*Rhône*, France) Produces softer *Cornas* than most from this sometimes tough *appellation*: beautiful strong yet silky wines. ☆☆☆☆ **1995 Cornas la Geynale £££**

♆ Alain Michelot [mee-shloh] (*Burgundy*, France) Producer of exceptionally perfumed elegant *Nuits-St.-Georges* that can be enjoyed young – but this doesn't mean that they aren't worth keeping. ☆☆☆☆ **1993 Nuits-St.-Georges Les Chaignots ££££**

♆ Dom. Michelot-Buisson [mee-shloh bwee-son] (*Burgundy*, France) One of the great old *Meursault* properties. A pioneer of estate bottling – and of the use of new oak. Wines are rarely subtle, but then they never lack typical *Meursault* flavour either. ☆☆☆☆ **1993 Meursault Les Genevrières ££££**

Michelsberg [mikh-kels-buhrg] (*Mosel*, Germany) One of the largest *grosslage,* known for the quantity of its production rather than the quality. A great deal of dull *Müller-Thurgau* is sold as *Piesporter Michelsberg.*

♆ Mildara Blass [mil-dah-rah] (*South Australia*) A highly dynamic company that recently bought *Rothbury,* having been itself acquired by Fosters. *Coonawarra* wines, including the very commercial *Jamieson's Run,* are best. Sometimes labels seem to resemble those of competitors' wines. Other labels/subsidiaries include *Yarra Ridge, Stonyfell, Annie's Lane, Robertson's Well, Wolf Blass, Saltram, Yellowglen* and *Balgownie.* All in all an enormous, varied portfolio of styles. ☆☆☆☆ **1995 Mildara Coonawarra Cabernet Sauvignon £££**

♆ Millton Estate (*Auckland*, New Zealand) James Millton is an obsessive, not to say a masochist. He loves the hard-to-make *Chenin Blanc* and uses it to make first-class organic wine in *Gisborne.* Sadly, it seems, most people would rather buy his *Chardonnay.* ☆☆☆☆ **1997 Barrel-Fermented Chenin Blanc ££**

♆ Milmanda [mil-man-dah] (*Conca de Barbera*, Spain) *Torres'* top label *Chardonnay.* Classy by any standards. ☆☆☆☆☆ **1996 £££**

♆ Kym Milne Antipodean *flying winemaker* who has been quietly expanding his empire with great success, particularly with Vinfruco in *South Africa*; at Le Trulle in southern *Italy* and at *Nagyrede* in Hungary. ☆☆☆☆ **Primavera Four Seasons Spring Italian White ££**

🍷 **Minervois** [mee-nehr-vwah] (*South-West*, France) *Corbières*' supposedly (slightly) classier cousin, producing firm, sometimes fruity, sometimes dull suppertime reds. Most wines are *Carignan*-based, but an enterprising Australian called Nerida Abbott has discovered that it is legal to produce a pure *Syrah* – and even to label it as '*Shiraz*' (a term that is apparently not recognised in France as a synonym for this variety). Whites and rosés are considerably less interesting. **Abbott's Cumulus; Clos Centeilles; Gourgazaud; Piccinini; Ste. Eulalie; la Tour Boisée; Villerambert-Julien.**

Mis en Bouteille au Ch./Dom. [mee on boo-tay] (France) Bottled at the estate.

🍷 **Ch. la Mission-Haut-Brion** [lah mee-see-yon oh-bree-yon] (*Pessac-Léognan Cru Classé, Bordeaux*, France) Tough but rich reds which rival, and occasionally overtake, its supposedly classier neighbour *Haut-Brion*. **61 64 66** 75 **78 79 81 82 83** 84 **85** 86 **87** 88 89 90 91 92 93 94 95 96

🍷 **Mitchell** (*Clare Valley*, Australia) Good producer of *Riesling* and of the Peppertree *Shiraz*, one of the *Clare Valley's* best reds. Also good for *Riesling, Semillon* and one of those very Australian style wines, a sparkling *Shiraz*. ☆☆☆☆ **1996 Riesling ££**

🍷 **Mitchelton** (*Goulburn Valley*, Australia) A modern producer of *Marsanne* and *Semillon* which now belongs to *Petaluma*. *Late harvest Rieslings* are also good, as is a *Beaujolais*-style red, known as Cab Mac. The Preece range – named after the former winemaker – is also well worth seeking out owing to its French style. ☆☆☆☆ **1996 Viognier/Roussanne £££**

Mittelhaardt [mit-tel-hahrt] (*Pfalz*, Germany) Central and best *bereich* of the *Rheinpfalz*. QbA/Kab/Spät: **85** 86 **88 89 90** 91 92 93 94 95 96 Aus/Beeren/Tba: **83 85** 88 89 90 91 92 93 94 95 96 97

Mittelmosel [mit-tel-moh-zuh] (*Mosel-Saar-Ruwer*, Germany) Middle and best section of the *Mosel*, including the *Bernkastel bereich*. QbA/Kab/Spät: **85** 86 **88 89 90** 91 92 93 94 95 96 Aus/Beeren/Tba: **83 85** 88 89 90 91 92 93 94 95 96 97

Mittelrhein [mit-tel-rihne] (Germany) Small, northern section of the *Rhine*. Good *Rieslings* that are sadly rarely seen outside Germany. QbA/Kab/Spät: **85** 86 **88 89 90** 91 92 93 94 95 Aus/Beeren/Tba: **83 85** 88 89 90 91 92 93 94 95 96 97

🍷 **Mittnacht-Klack** [mit-nakt-clack] (*Alsace*, France) Seriously high-quality wines with particular accent on '*vendage tardive*' and *late havest* wines. ☆☆☆☆ **1995 Gewurztraminer ££££**

Moelleux [mwah-luh] (France) Sweet.

🍷 **Moët & Chandon** [moh-wet ay shon-don] (*Champagne*, France) The biggest producer in *Champagne*. *Dom Pérignon*, the top wine, and *vintage* Moët are reliably good and new *cuvées* of 'Brut Imperial Non-Vintage' though not always brilliant, show a welcome reaction to recent criticism. Watch out too for a good *Brut* Rosé. ☆☆☆☆☆ **1992 Vintage £££**

🍷 **Clos Mogador** [kloh MOH-gah-dor] (*Priorato*, Spain) Juicy, modern, and more importantly, stylish red wine from the once ultra-traditional and rustic region of *Priorato*. The shape of things to come. ☆☆☆ **1992 Clos Mogador £££**

🍷 **Moillard** [mwah-yar] (*Burgundy*, France) Middle-of-the-road *négoçiant* whose best wines are sold under the 'Dom. Thomas Moillard' label.

Moldova Young republic next to Romania whose as yet uncertain potential is being tested by *Hugh Ryman* at the Hincesti winery.

☥ **Monbazillac** [mon-ba-zee-yak] (*South-West*, France) *Bergerac AC* using the grapes of sweet *Bordeaux* to make improving alternatives to *Sauternes*. 88 89 90 95 97

☥ **Ch. Monbousquet** [mon-boo-skay] (*St. Emilion Grand Cru Classé*, *Bordeaux*, France) Newly taken over and now producing rich concentrated wines. The 1994 was specially successful. 78 79 82 **85** 86 88 89 90 92 93 94 95 96 ☆☆☆ 1993 Ch. Monbousquet, St. Emilion £££

☥ **Ch. Monbrison** [mon-bree-son] (*Margaux*, *Bordeaux*, France) Reliable constant overperformer in this often disappointing *appellation*. 78 79 82 **85** 86 88 89 90 92 94 95 96 97 ☆☆☆☆ 1990 ££££

☥ **Mönchof** [moon-chof] (*Mosel*, Germany) Top *Mosel* producer with vineyards in *Urzig*.

☥ **Ch. de Moncontour** [mon-con-toor] (*Loire*, France) One of the more recommendable – and affordable – sources of still and sparkling *Vouvray*. ☆☆☆ 1993 Vouvray Demi-Sec ££

☥ **Robert Mondavi** [mawn-dah-vee] (*Napa Valley*, California) Pioneering producer of great Reserve *Cabernet* and *Pinot Noir*, and back-on-form *Chardonnay*, and inventor of *oaky Blanc Fumé Sauvignon*. The Coastal wines are good but the Woodbridge wines, though pleasant, are far less interesting. Co-owner of *Opus One* and now in a joint venture with *Caliterra* in Chile and *Frescobaldi* in Tuscany. ☆☆☆☆ 1994 Cabernet Sauvignon Reserve £££

☥ **Mongeard-Mugneret** [mon-zhahr moon-yeh-ray] (*Burgundy*, France) A source of invariably excellent and sometimes stunningly exotic red *Burgundy*. ☆☆☆☆ 1993 Vosne-Romanée Suchots ££££

🍇**Monica (di Cagliari/Sardegna)** [moh-nee-kah] (*Sardinia*, Italy) Red grape and wine of *Sardinia* producing drily tasty and fortified spicy wine.

☥ **Marqués de Monistrol** [moh-nee-strol] (*Catalonia*, Spain) Single-estate *cava*. Also producing noble varietals. ☆☆☆☆ 1994 Merlot ££

Monopole [mo-noh-pohl] (France) Literally, exclusive – in *Burgundy* denotes single ownership of an entire vineyard.

☥ **Mont Gras** [mon gra] (*Colchagua*, Chile) Fast-improving winery. ☆☆☆☆ Merlot Reserva 1996 ££

☥ **Clos du Mont Olivet** [Mo(n)-toh-lee-vay] (*Rhône*, France) Good *Châteauneuf-du-Pape* producer. Cuvée du Papet is the top wine. ☆☆☆☆ 1995 Châteauneuf-du-Pape £££

☥ **Les Producteurs du Mont Tauch** [mon-tohsh] (*Midi*, France) Southern cooperative with surprisingly good, top-of-the-range wines. ☆☆☆☆ Fitou Ch. de Segure ££

☥ **Montagne St. Emilion** [mon-tan-yuh san tay-mee-yon] (*Bordeaux*, France) A 'satellite' of *St. Emilion*. Often good-value reds which can outclass supposedly finer fare from *St. Emilion* itself. Drink young. 82 83 **85** 86 88 89 90 94 95 96

☥ **Montagny** [mon-tan-yee] (*Burgundy*, France) Tiny hillside *Côte Chalonnaise commune* producing good lean *Chardonnay* that can be a match for many *Pouilly-Fuissés*. *Premier Crus* are not from better vineyards; they're just made from riper grapes. White: 84 **85** 86 87 **88** 89 90 92 95 *Antonin Rodet; Olivier Leflaive; Caves de Buxy; Louis Latour; Michel; Vachet.*

☥ **Montalcino** [mon-tal-chee-noh] (*Tuscany*, Italy) Village near Sienna known for *Brunello di Montalcino*, *Chianti's* big brother, whose reputation was largely created by *Biondi Santi*, whose wines no longer deserve the prices they command. *Rosso di Montalcino* is lighter. 78 79 81 **82** **85** 88 90 94 95 *Altesino; Costanti; Frescobaldi; Banfi; Poggio Antico.*

Y Montana (*Marlborough*, New Zealand) Impressively consistent, huge firm with tremendous *Sauvignons,* improving *Chardonnays* and good-value *Lindauer* and *Deutz Marlborough Cuvée* fizz. Reds still tend to be on the green side. Look out for the smartly packaged single-estate wines such as the Brancott *Sauvignon.* ☆☆☆☆ **1996 Renwick Estate Chardonnay £££**

Y Monte Real [mon-tay ray-al] (*Rioja*, Spain) Made by Bodegas Riojanos; generally decent, richly flavoured and tannic *Rioja.*

Y Bodegas Montecillo [mon-tay-thee-yoh] (*Rioja*, Spain) Classy wines including the oddly named Viña Monty. The Cumbrero Blanco white is good, too. ☆☆☆ **1989 Viña Monty Gran Reserva ££**

Y Montée de Tonnerre [mon-tay duh ton-nehr] (*Burgundy*, France) Excellent *Chablis Premier Cru.*

Y Montefalco Sagrantino [mon-teh-fal-koh sag-ran-tee-noh] (*Umbria*, Italy) Intense cherryish red made from the local Sagrantino grape.

Y Ch. Montelena [mon-teh-lay-nah] (*Napa Valley*, California) Its two long-lived *Chardonnays* (from *Napa* and the rather better *Alexander Valley*) make this one of the more impressive producers in the state. The vanilla-and-blackcurrancy *Cabernet* is too impenetrable, however.

❦Montepulciano [mon-tay-pool-chee-yah-noh] (Italy) Confusingly, both a red grape used to make red wines in central and South-East Italy (Montepulciano *d'Abruzzi*, etc) and the name of a town in *Tuscany* (see *Vino Nobile di Montepulciano*). **Poliziano.**

Monterey [mon-teh-ray] (California) Underrated region south of San Francisco, producing potentially good if sometimes rather grassy wines. Red: 84 **85** 86 87 **90 91** 92 93 95 White: **85 90 91** 92 95 *Jekel; Sterling Redwood Trail; Estancia.*

Y The Monterey Vineyard (*Monterey*, California) Reliable inexpensive varietal wines now under the Redwood Trail label. Go for the 'Classic' range. Beware of some of their wines, the small print of whose labels reveal them to have been made in the *Languedoc* region in France.

Y Viña Montes [mon-tehs] (*Curico*, Chile) Go-ahead winery with improving reds (including the flagship Alpha M) and improved *Sauvignon.* ☆☆☆☆ **1996 Montes Alpha M Reserve Red ££;** ☆☆☆ **1995 Reserve Oak-aged Sauvignon ££**

Y Monteviña [mon-tay-veen-yah] (*Amador County*, California) Exceptionally good *Zinfandel* from *Amador County,* reliable *Cabernet, Chardonnay* and a *Fumé Blanc* to make *Robert Mondavi* weep. ☆☆☆ **1995 Chardonnay ££**

Y Monthélie [mon-tay-lee] (*Burgundy*, France) Often overlooked *Côte de Beaune* village producing potentially stylish reds and whites. The appropriately named Dom. Monthélie-Douhairet is the most reliable estate. White: 79 84 **85 86** 87 **88** 89 **90** 92 95 96 Red: 78 80 83 **85** 86 87 **88 89 90** 92 95 96 *Dom. Monthélie-Douhairet; Jaffelin.*

Montilla-Moriles [mon-tee-yah maw-ree-lehs] (Spain) *DO* region producing *sherry*-type wines in *solera* systems, often so high in alcohol that fortification is unnecessary. Good examples easily match basic *sherry,* offering better value for money. Occasional successes, though, achieve far more. **Bodegas Toro Albala.**

Y Dom. de Montille [duh mon-tee] (*Burgundy*, France) A lawyer-cum-winemaker whose *Volnays* and *Pommards*, if rather tough and astringent when young, are unusually fine and long-lived. Classy stuff. ☆☆☆☆ **1995 Volnay Taillepieds £££**

♀ Montlouis [mon-lwee] (*Loire*, France) Neighbour of *Vouvray* making similar, lighter-bodied, dry, sweet and sparkling wines. White: 83 **85 86 88 89 90** 94 95 Sweet White: 76 83 **85** 86 **88 89** 90 94 95 **96 Berger; Delétang; Levasseur; Moyer; la Taille aux Loups.**

♀ Le Montrachet [luh mon-ra-shay] (*Burgundy*, France) Shared between the villages of *Chassagne-* and *Puligny-Montrachet*, with its equally good neighbours *Bâtard-M.*, *Chevalier-M.*, *Bienvenue-Bâtard-M.*, *Criots-Bâtard-M.*, potentially the greatest, biscuitiest white *Burgundy* – and thus dry white wine – in the world. *Drouhin;* **Marquis de Laguiche,** *Domaine de la Romanée-Conti, Sauzet, Comtes Lafon.*

♀ Ch. Montrose [mon-rohz] (*St. Estèphe 2ème Cru Classé, Bordeaux,* France) Back-on-form *St. Estèphe* renowned for its longevity. More typical of the *appellation* than *Cos d'Estournel* but often less approachable in its youth. However, still maintains a rich, tarry, inky style. Especially good in 1994, though less so in 1995 and 1996. **61 64** 66 **70 75** 76 78 79 81 **82** 83 84 85 86 88 89 90 91 92 93 94 95 96 97

♀ Ch. Montus [mon-toos] (*South-West,* France) Ambitious producer in *Madiran* with carefully oaked examples of *Tannat* and *Pacherenc de Vic Bilh. Bouscassé* is a cheaper more approachable label.

♙ Moondah Brook (*Swan Valley*, Australia) An atypically (for the baking *Swan*) cool vineyard belonging to *Houghtons* (and thus *Hardys*). The stars are the wonderful tangy *Verdelho* and richly oaky *Chenin Blanc.* The *Chardonnay* and reds are less impressive.

♙ Moorilla Estate [moo-rillah] (*Tasmania*, Australia) Long-established, recently reconstituted estate with particularly good *Riesling.*

Mór [mohr] (Hungary) Hungarian town making clean aromatic white wines from a blend including the *Traminer.*

♙ Morande [moh-ran-day] (Argentina/Chile) Impressive winemaker, producing wine often from pioneering varieties on both sides of the Andes. ☆☆☆☆ **1997 Aventura Carignan ££**

♟ Morellino di Scansano [moh-ray-lee-noh dee skan-sah-noh] (*Tuscany*, Italy) Amazing cherry and raspberry, young-drinking red made from a clone of *Sangiovese.* **Le Pupile.**

♀ Dom. Marc Morey [maw-ray] (*Burgundy*, France) Estate producing stylish white *Burgundy.* ☆☆☆☆ **1996 Chassagne-Montrachet Morgeot £££**

♀ Dom. Pierre Morey [maw-ray] (*Burgundy*, France) Top-class *Meursault* producer known for concentrated wines in good vintages. ☆☆☆☆ **1995 Meursault Perrières £££**

♀ Bernard Morey et Fils [maw-ray] (*Burgundy*, France) Top-class producer in *Chassagne-Montrachet* with good vineyards here and in *St. Aubin.* ☆☆☆☆ **1993 Chassagne-Montrachet 1er Cru Morgeot ££££**

Morey-St.;-Denis [maw-ray san duh-nee] (*Burgundy*, France) *Côtes de Nuits* village which produces deeply fruity, richly smooth reds, especially the *Grand Cru* 'Clos de la Roche'. Best producer is *Domaine Dujac*, which virtually makes this *appellation* its own. 76 **78** 79 **80** 82 83 **85** 86 87 **88** 89 90 92 95 96 *Dujac; Lignier.*

♀ Morgon [mohr-gon] (*Burgundy*, France) One of the ten *Beaujolais Crus.* Worth maturing, as it can take on a delightful chocolate/cherry character. **88 89** 90 91 93 94 95 96 *Sylvain Fessy; Georges Duboeuf (aka Marc Dudet);* Jean Descombes; Jean Foillard; Lapierre; Piron.

♟ Morio Muskat [maw-ree-yoh moos-kat] White grape grown in Germany and Eastern Europe and making simple grapey wine.

Mornington Peninsula (*Victoria*, Australia) Some of Australia's newest and most southerly vineyards on a perpetual upward crescent. Close to Melbourne and under threat from housing developers. Good *Pinot Noir*, minty *Cabernet* and juicy *Chardonnay*, though the innovative T'Galant is leading the way with other varieties. **T'Galant; *Stoniers; Dromana.***

🍷 **Morris of Rutherglen** (*Rutherglen*, Australia) Despite the takeover by *Orlando* and the retirement of local hero and champion winemaker Mick Morris, this is still an extraordinarily successful producer of delicious *Liqueur Muscat* and *Tokay* (seek out the Show Reserve). Also worth buying is a weird and wonderful sparkling red made from the *Durif*. ☆☆☆☆ **Liqueur Muscat £££**

🍷 **Denis Mortet** [mor-tay] (*Burgundy*, France) Fast up-and-coming producer with straight *Gevrey-Chambertin* that is every bit as good as some of his neighbours *Grands Crus*. ☆☆☆☆ **1995 Gevrey-Chambertin £££**

🍷 **Morton Estate** (Waikato, New Zealand) Top-class producer of *Sauvignon*, *Chardonnay* and *Loire* and *Bordeaux*-styles. The wines across the board are now reaching a far more appreciative audience. ☆☆☆☆ **1996 Hawke's Bay Chardonnay ££**

🍷 **Moscatel de Setúbal** [mos-kah-tel day say-too-bahl] (Portugal) See *Setúbal*.

🍇 **Moscato** [mos-kah-toh] (Italy) The Italian name for *Muscat*, widely used across Italy in all styles of white wine from *Moscato d'Asti*, through the more serious *Asti Spumante*, to dessert wines like Moscato di Pantelleria.

🍷 **Moscato d'Asti** [mos-kah-toh das-tee] (Italy) Delightfully grapey, sweet and fizzy low alcohol wine from the *Muscat*, or *Moscato* grape. Far better (and cheaper) than designer alcoholic lemonade; it's more flavoursome. Drink young.

Mosel-Saar-Ruwer [moh-zuhl sahr roo-vuhr] (Germany) Region surrounding the rivers of its name.

🍷 **Mosel/Moselle** [moh-zuhl] (Germany) River and loose term for *Mosel-Saar-Ruwer* wines, equivalent to the '*Hock*' of the Rhine. Not to be confused with the uninspiring *Vins de Moselle* produced on the French side of the river. The wines tend have flavours of green fruits when young but develop a wonderful ripeness as they fill out with age. Arguably, the best wine region in Germany today. QbA/Kab/Spät: **85** 86 **88 89 90** 91 92 93 94 95 96 Aus/Beeren/Tba: **83 85** 88 89 90 91 92 93 94 95 96 97 ***Dr Loosen;* JJ Chriastobel; E. Jakoby-Mathy; Freiher von Heddesdorff; Willi Haag; Heribert Kerpen; Weingut Karlsmuhle; Karp-Schreiber; *Immich Batterieberg.***

🍷 **Moselblumchen** [moh-sel-bloom-chen] (*Mosel*, Germany) *Mosel-Saar-Ruwer* equivalent to the Rhine's *Liebfraumilch*. With rare exceptions, pretty basic stuff.

Vins de Moselle [van duh moh-zell] (Eastern France) Neighbouring *Alsace*; once full of vines and generally dull wine. There are now a mere 70 hectares planted.

🍷 **Lenz Moser** [lents moh-zur] (Austria) Big producer with a range including crisp dry whites and luscious dessert wines. Best efforts come from the Klosterkeller Siegenfdorf.

☿ **Moss Wood** (*Margaret River*, Australia) Pioneer producer of *Pinot Noir*, *Cabernet* and *Semillon*. The wines have long cellaring potential and have a very French feel to them. The *Semillon* is reliably good in both its oaked and unoaked form; the *Chardonnay* is big and forward and the *Pinot Noir* variable, rarely living up to the promise of the early 1980s.
☆☆☆☆ **1995 Cabernet Sauvignon Reserve £££**

☿ **La Motte Estate** [la mot] (*Franschhoek*, South Africa) Best known for top *Shiraz*.

☿ **JP Moueix** [mwex] (*Bordeaux*, France) Top-class *négoçiant*/producer, Christian *Moueix* specialises in *Pomerol* and *St. Emilion* and is responsible for *Pétrus*, *La Fleur-Pétrus*, *Bel Air*, Richotey and *Dominus* in California. (Do not confuse with any other Moueix's).

☿ **Moulin Touchais** [moo-lan too-shay] (*Loire*, France) Producer of intensely honeyed, long-lasting, sweet white from *Coteaux du Layon*.

☿ **Moulin-à-Vent** [moo-lan-na-von] (*Burgundy*, France) One of the ten *Beaujolais Crus* – big and rich at its best and, like *Morgon*, can benefit from a few years' ageing. 85 88 89 90 91 93 94 95 96 97 *Duboeuf; Degrange; Paul Janin; la Tour du Bief; Charvet; Janodet; Lapierre; Ch. du Moulin-à-Vent.*

☿ **Ch. Moulin-à-Vent** [moo-lan-na-von] (*Moulis Cru Bourgeois*, *Bordeaux*, France) Leading *Moulis* property. 82 83 85 86 89 90 94

☿ **Ch. du Moulin-à-Vent** [moo-lan-na-von] (*Burgundy*, France) Reliable producer of *Moulin-à-Vent*. 85 88 89 90 91 93 94 95 96 97

☿ **Moulis** [moo-lees] (*Bordeaux*, France) Red wine village of the *Haut-Médoc*; often paired with *Listrac*, but making far more approachable good-value *Crus Bourgeois*. 76 78 79 81 82 83 85 86 88 89 90 94 95 96 **Ch. Anthonic; Chasse-Spleen; Maucaillou; Moulis; Poujeaux.**

Mount Barker (Western Australia) Cooler climate southern region with great *Riesling*, *Verdelho*, impressive *Chardonnay* and restrained *Shiraz*. White: 87 88 90 91 93 94 95 Red: 80 82 83 85 86 87 88 90 91 92 93 94 95 96 97 *Plantagenet; Goundrey; Howard Park; Wignalls.*

☿ **Mount Horrocks** (*Clare Valley*, Australia) Inventive producer that has made a speciality out of reviving an old method of winemaking called 'Cordon Cut', which concentrates the flavour of the juice by cutting the canes some time before picking the grapes. ☆☆☆☆ **1996 Watervale Cordon Cut Riesling £££**

☿ **Mount Hurtle** (*McLaren Vale*, South Australia) See *Geoff Merrill*.

☿ **Mount Langi Ghiran** [lan-gee gee-ran] (*Victoria*, Australia) A maker of excellent cool-climate *Riesling*, peppery *Shiraz* and very good *Cabernet*. ☆☆☆☆☆ **1996 Shiraz, Grampians £££**

☿ **Mount Mary** (*Yarra Valley*, Australia) Dr Middleton makes *Pinot Noir* and *Chardonnay* that are astonishingly and unpredictably *Burgundy*-like in the best and worst sense of the term. The *clarety* Quintet blend is more reliable.

Mount Veeder (*Napa Valley*, California) Convincing hillside *appellation* producing impressive reds. Red: 84 85 86 87 90 91 92 93 95 White: 85 90 91 92 95 96 *Mount Veeder Winery; Ch. Potelle; Hess Collection; Mayacamas.*

☿ **Mountadam** (*Eden Valley*, Australia) Son of *David Wynn*; Adam makes classy Burgundian *Chardonnay* and *Pinot Noir* (both still and sparkling) and an impressive blend called 'The Red'. Also worth seeking out are the *Eden Ridge* organic wines and the fruity *David Wynn* range, especially the unoaked *Chardonnay*. ☆☆☆☆ **1996 Mountadam Chardonnay £££**

❦**Mourvèdre** [mor-veh-dr] (*Rhône*, France) Floral-spicy *Rhône* grape usually found in blends. Increasingly popular in France and California where, as in Australia, it is called *Mataro*. **Jade Mountain; Penfolds; Ridge.**

Mousse [mooss] The bubbles in *Champagne* and sparkling wines.

Mousseux [moo-sur] (France) Sparkling wine – generally cheap and unremarkable.

🍷 **Mouton-Cadet** [moo-ton ka-day] (*Bordeaux*, France) A brilliant commercial invention by Philippe de Rothschild who used it to profit handsomely from the name of *Mouton-Rothschild*, with which it has no discernible connection. The recently introduced 'Reserve' is better than the basic and the white less dire than it used to be. None are recommendable.

🍷 **Ch. Mouton-Baronne-Philippe** [moo-ton ba-ron-fee-leep] (*Pauillac 5ème Cru Classé, Bordeaux*, France) See Ch.d'Armailhac.

🍷 **Ch. Mouton-Rothschild** [moo-ton roth-child] (*Pauillac Premier Cru Classé, Bordeaux*, France) The only *château* to be elevated to a first growth from a second, Mouton can have gloriously rich complex flavours of roast coffee and blackcurrant. Current vintages – especially the 1997 – have been eclipsed by *Margaux* and *Latour*. **61 62 66 70 75** 76 78 81 82 83 85 86 88 89 90 91 92 93 94 95 ☆☆☆☆☆ **1990 ££££**

Mudgee [mud-zhee] (*New South Wales*, Australia) Australia's first *appellation* region, a coolish-climate area now being championed by *Rosemount* as well as by *Rothbury*. **Botobolar; Huntington Estate.**

🍷 **Bodegas Muga** [moo-gah] (*Rioja*, Spain) Producer of good old-fashioned *Rioja*s, of which Prado Enea is the best. ☆☆☆ **1991 Rioja Tinto ££**

🍷 **Jacques-Frederic Mugnier** [moo-nee-yay] (*Burgundy*, France) *Chambolle-Musigny* estate that makes long-lived wines from great vineyards, including Bonnes-Mares and *Musigny*. ☆☆☆☆ **1995 Chambolle-Musigny £££**

🍷 **Mulderbosch** [mool-duh-bosh] (*Stellenbosch*, South Africa) South Africa's answer to *Cloudy Bay*: exciting *Sauvignon* and *Meursault*-like *Chardonnay*, not to mention a red blend called Faithful Hound. ☆☆☆☆ **1996 Chardonnay ££**

🍷 **Weingut Müller-Catoir** [moo-luh kah-twah] (*Pfalz*, Germany) Great new-wave producer using new-wave grapes as well as *Riesling*. Wines of all styles are impeccable and packed with flavour. Search out powerful Grauburgunder, Rieslaner and *Scheurebe* wines. ☆☆☆☆☆ **1993 Haardter Herrenletten Riesling Spätlese ££**

🍷 **Egon Müller-Scharzhof** [moo-luh shahtz-hof] (*Mosel-Saar-Ruwer*, Germany) Top-class *Saar* producer. ☆☆☆☆ **1996 Scharzhofberger Riesling Spätlese £££**

❦**Müller-Thurgau** [moo-lur-toor-gow] (Germany) Workhorse white grape, a *Riesling* x *Sylvaner* cross – also known as *Rivaner* – making much unremarkable wine in Germany, but yielding some gems for producers like *Müller-Catoir*. Very successful in England.

🍷 **Mumm/Mumm Napa** [murm] (*Champagne*, France/California) Maker of slightly improved Cordon Rouge *Champagne* and far better *Cuvée Napa* from California. ☆☆☆☆ **1989 Cordon Rouge Vintage £££**

🍷 **Réné Muré** [moo-ray] (*Alsace*, France) Producer of full-bodied wines, especially from the Clos St. Landelin vineyard. ☆☆☆☆ **1994 Riesling Vorbourg, Clos St. Landelin ££**

Murfatlar [moor-fat-lah] (Romania) Major vineyard and research area that is having increasing success with *Chardonnay*.

🍷 **Murphy-Goode** (*Alexander Valley*, California) Excellent *Chardonnays*. Classy producer of quite Burgundian style whites which sell at – for California – affordable prices.

Murray River Valley (Australia) The area ranging between *Victoria* and *New South Wales* producing much of the Antipodes' cheapest wine – a great deal of which is to be found in UK retailers' own-label bottles.

☖ **Bodegas Marqués de Murrieta** [mar-kays day moo-ree-eh-tah] (*Rioja*, Spain) Until recently the best old-style *oaky* white (sold as Castillo Ygay), though recent efforts have been slightly disappointing. The red, at its best, is one of the most long-lived elegant *Riojas* – look out for the old Castillo Ygays from the 1960s with their distinctive old-style labels. ☆☆☆☆ **1989 Ygay Gran Reserva £££**

☖ **Murrietta's Well** (*Livermore*, California) Blends of *Zinfandel* and *Cabernet, Merlot* are rare, but the berryish 1992 proprietary red sold by *Wente* under this name proves that it's an experiment more producers should try.

Murrumbidgee [muh-rum-bid-zhee] (*New South Wales*, Australia) Area formerly known for bulk dessert wines, now improving irrigation and vinification techniques to make good table wines and some stunning *botrytis*-affected sweet wines. *De Bortoli; Kingston Estate; Lindemans; Cranswick Estate.*

☖ **Ch. Musar** [moo-sahr] (Ghazir, Lebanon) *Serge Hochar* makes a different red every year, varying the blend of *Cabernet, Cinsault* and *Syrah*. The style veers wildly between *Bordeaux*, the *Rhône* and Italy, but there's never a risk of becoming bored. Good vintages easily keep for a decade. The *Chardonnay*-based whites are less than dazzling, though. **86** 88 89 91

☙**Muscadelle** [mus-kah-del] Spicy ingredient in white *Bordeaux*, aka *Tokay* in Australia.

☖ **Muscadet des Coteaux de la Loire / Côtes de Grand Lieu / de Sèvre et Maine** [moos-kah-day day koh-toh dur lah lwar / koht dur gron lyur / dur say-vr' eh mayn] (*Loire*, France) Emphatically non-aromatic wines made from the *Melon de Bourgogne*. Worthwhile examples are briefly matured and bottled on their dead yeasts or *lees* ('*sur lie*'). The recently created Côtes de Grand Lieu is worth looking for, as can be the rare Coteaux de la Loire. Sèvre et Maine is less reliable. 94 95 96 *Dom. de Chasseloir; Pierre Luneau; Sauvion; Chéreau-Carré; Metaireau; Bossard; Marquis de Goulaine; Guindon.*

☙**Muscat** [mus-kat] Generic name for a species of white grape (aka *Moscato* in Italy) of which there are a number of different sub-species.

☙**Muscat à Petits Grains** [moos-kah ah puh-tee gran] Aka *Frontignan*, the best variety of Muscat and the grape responsible for *Muscat de Beaumes de Venise, Muscat de Rivesaltes, Asti Spumante, Muscat of Samos, Rutherglen* Muscats and dry *Alsace* Muscats.

☙**Muscat of Alexandria** [moos-kah] Grape responsible for *Moscatel de Setúbal, Moscatel de Valencia* and sweet South Australians. Also known as *Lexia*, and in South Africa it satisfies the sweet tooth of much of the Afrikaner population as *Hanepoot*.

☙**Muscat Ottonel** [moos-kah ot-oh-NEL] Muscat variety grown in Middle and Eastern Europe.

☖ **Musigny** [moo-zee-nyee] (*Burgundy*, France) Potentially wonderful *Grand Cru* from which *Chambolle-Musigny* takes its name. 76 79 82 83 86 87 **88 89 90** 91 92 93 94 95 *De Vogüé; Mugnier; Groffier; Prieur.*

☖ **Dom. Mussy** [moos-see] (*Burgundy*, France) Top-class tiny *Pommard* estate with concentrated wines from that village, *Beaune* and Volnay. ☆☆☆☆ **1992 Beaune Les Montrevenots £££**
Must Unfermented grape juice.
MW See *Master of Wine*.

N

Nackenheim [nahk-ehn-hime] (*Rheinhessen*, Germany) Village in the *Nierstein bereich*, sadly best known for its debased *grosslage*, Gütes Domtal. QbA/Kab/Spät: **85 86 88 89 90** 91 92 93 94 95 96 Aus/Beeren/Tba: **83 85** 88 89 90 91 92 93 94 95 96 *Gunderloch; Heinrich Seip; Kürfurstenhof.*

Nahe [nah-huh] (Germany) *Anbaugebiet* producing wines which can combine delicate flavour with full body. QbA/Kab/Spät: **85** 86 **88 89 90** 91 92 93 94 95 Aus/Beeren/Tba: **83 85** 88 89 90 91 92 93 94 95 96. *Kruger-Rumpf; Schlossgut Diel; Hermann Donnhoff; Hehner Kiltz.*

♀ Ch. Nairac [nay-rak] (*Barsac 2ème Cru Classé*, Bordeaux, France) Delicious, lush, long-lasting wine sometimes lacking a little complexity. 73 75 76 80 81 82 **83** 85 86 88 89 90 91 92 95 96 97 ☆☆☆☆ **1990 ££££**

♂ Nalle (*Sonoma*, California) Great *Dry Creek* producer of some of California's (and thus the world's) greatest *Zinfandel*.

Naoussa [nah-oosa] (Greece) Region producing dry red wines, often from the Xynomavro grape. *Boutari.*

Napa [na-pa] (California) Named after the American-Indian word for 'plenty', this is a region with plentiful wines ranging from ordinary to sublime. Too many are hyped; none is cheap and the region as a whole is far too varied in altitude and conditions to make sense as a single *appellation*. In the future, the more credible among the 20 or so smaller *appellations* within Napa, such as *Carneros, Stag's Leap, Howell Mountain* and *Mt. Veeder* will gain greater prominence – as will nearby regions like *Sonoma*. Red: 84 **85** 86 87 **90 91** 92 93 94 95 96 White: **85 90 91** 92 95 96 *Atlas Peak; Beaulieu; Beringer; Cain; Cakebread; Caymus; Chimney Rock; Clos du Val; Crichton Hall; Cuvaison; Diamond Creek; Dom. Chandon; Duckhorn; Dunn; Flora Springs; Franciscan; Frog's Leap; Heitz; Hess Collection; Ch. Montelena; Monteviña; Mumm; Newton; Niebaum Coppola; Opus One; Ch. Potelle; Phelps; Schramsberg; Screaming Eagle; Shafer; Stag's Leap; Sterling; Turley.*

♂ Napa Ridge (California) Highly successful brand, most of whose pleasant commercial wines are made with juice from grapes grown outside *Napa*. (In fact, European laws against this kind of confusion have led exports to be relabelled as 'Coastal Ridge').

♂ Henry Natter [on-ree na-tehr] (*Loire*, France) Reliable producer of *Sancerre* at the Ch. de Montigny.

♂ Nautilus Estate [naw-tih-luhs] (*Marlborough*, New Zealand) *Yalumba's* New Zealand offshoot. Great fizz and *Sauvignon*. ☆☆☆☆☆ **1997 Marlborough Sauvignon Blanc ££**

♂ Navajas [na-VA-khas] (*Rioja*, Spain) Small producer making increasingly impressive reds and *oaky* whites worth keeping. ☆☆☆☆ **1995 Tinto Crianza ££**

♂ Navarra [na-VAH-rah] (Spain) Northern *DO*, traditionally renowned for rosés and heavy reds but now producing wines to rival those from neighbouring *Rioja*, where prices are often higher. Look for innovative *Cabernet Sauvignon* and *Tempranillo* blends. 81 82 **83 85** 87 89 90 91 92 94 95 96 *Ochoa; Guelbenzu; Senorio de Sarria; Chivite; Nekeas; Palacio de la Vega.*

☙**Nebbiolo** [neh-bee-oh-loh] (*Piedmont*, Italy) Grape of *Piedmont*, producing wines with tarry, cherryish, spicy flavours that are slow to mature but become richly complex – epitomised by *Barolo* and *Barbaresco*. Quality and style vary enormously depending on soil. Aka *Spanna*.

♈ **Nederburg** [neh-dur-burg] (*Paarl*, South Africa) Huge commercial producer. The Edelkeur *late harvest* wines are the gems of the cellar. Sadly, the best wines are only sold at the annual Nederburg Auction.

♈ **Neethlingshof Estate** [neet-lihngs-hof] (*Stellenbosch*, South Africa) *Late harvest* wines are impressive. Others need work.

Négociant [nay-goh-see-yon] (France) (Eléveur) Merchant who buys, matures and bottles wine.

Négociant-manipulant (NM) [ma-nih-pyoo-lon] (*Champagne*, France) Buyer and blender of wines for *Champagne*, identifiable by the NM number which is mandatory on the label.

☙**Negroamaro** [nay-groh-ah-mah-roh] (*Puglia*, Italy) A Puglian grape whose name means 'bitter-black' and produces fascinating spicy-gamey reds. Found in *Salice Salentino* and *Copertino*.

♈ **Bodegas Nekeas** [nek-ay-as] (*Navarra*, Spain) Top-class French-style *Merlot* and *Chardonnay*. ☆☆☆ **1996 Barrel Fermented Chardonnay ££**

Nelson (New Zealand) Small region, a glorious bus-ride to the North-West of *Marlborough*. *Neudorf* and *Seifried/ Redwood Valley* are the stars. White: **89 91** 94 96 Red: 87 89 90 **91 92** 94 95

♈ **Nemea** [nur-may-yah] (Peloponnese, Greece) Improving cool(ish) climate region for reds made from Agiorgitiko. *Tsantalis; Boutari.*

♈ **Ch. La Nerthe** [nurf] (*Rhône*, France) One of the most exciting estates in *Châteauneuf-du-Pape* producing rich wines with seductive dark fruit. ☆☆☆☆ **1994 Cuvée Les Cadettes £££**

♈ **Ch. Nenin** [nay-nan] (*Pomerol*, *Bordeaux*, France) A *château* to watch since its recent purchase by Michel Delon of *Ch. Léoville-Las-Cases*.

Neuchâtel [nur-sha-tel] (Switzerland) Lakeside region. Together with Les Trois Lacs a source of good red and rosé, *Pinot Noir* and *Chasselas* and *Chardonnay* whites. *Ch. d'Auvernier; Porret.*

♈ **Neudorf** [noy-dorf] (*Nelson*, New Zealand) Pioneering small-scale producer of beautifully made *Chardonnay, Semillon, Sauvignon, Riesling* and *Pinot Noir*. ☆☆☆☆☆ **1997 Moutere Sauvignon £££**

Neusiedlersee [noy-zeed-lur-zay] (Austria) *Burgenland* region on the Hungarian border. Great *late harvest* and improving whites and reds. *Willi Opitz;* Tschida; Fieler-Artinger.

Nevers [nur-vehr] (France) Subtlest oak – from a forest in *Burgundy*.

New South Wales (Australia) Major wine-producing state which is home to the famous *Hunter Valley*, along with the *Cowra, Mudgee, Orange* and *Murrumbidgee* regions. White: **85 86 87 88** 90 **91** 94 95 96 97 98 Red: **82** 83 **85 86 87 88** 90 91 93 94 95 96 97 98

New York State (US) See *Finger Lakes* and *Long Island*.

New Zealand Superstar nation with proven *Sauvignon Blanc* and *Chardonnay* and increasingly successful reds. See *Marlborough, Martinborough, Hawkes Bay, Gisborne, Auckland*. White: **89 91** 94 96 97 Red: **87 89** 90 **91 92** 94 95 96 97

Newton Vineyards (*Napa Valley*, California) High-altitude vineyards with top-class *Chardonnay, Merlot* and *Cabernet*, now being made with help from *Michel Rolland*.

Ngatarawa [na-TA-ra-wah] (*Hawke's Bay*, New Zealand) Small superstar winery with impressive reds and even better *Chardonnays* and *late harvest* whites. ☆☆☆☆ 1997 Stables Oak-Aged Sauvignon £££

Niagara (*Ontario*, Canada) Area close to the Falls and to Lakes Ontario and Erie where the *Vidal* is used to make good *Icewine*. The *Chardonnnay, Riesling* and – though less successfully – red varieties such as *Pinot Noir* and *Merlot* are now being used too. *Ch. des Charmes; Reif; Inniskillin.*

Nicholson River (*Gippsland*, Australia) The temperamental *Gippsland* climate ensures that this estate has a frustratingly small production, however its efforts have been repaid over and over by stunning *Chardonnays*. ☆☆☆☆ 1993 Chardonnay £££

Niebaum-Coppola [nee-bowm coh-po-la] (*Napa Valley*, California) You've seen the movie. Now taste the wine. The 'Dracula' and 'Godfather' director's estate now includes the appropriately Gothic *Inglenook* winery, has some of the oldest vines about and makes intensely concentrated *Cabernets* to suit the patient. ☆☆☆☆ 1994 Rubicon Napa Valley £££

Niederhausen Schlossböckelheim [nee-dur-how sen shlos-bok-ehl-hime] (*Nahe*, Germany) State-owned estate producing highly concentrated *Riesling* from great vineyards.

Dom. Michel Niellon [nee-el-lon] (*Burgundy*, France) Estate ranking consistently in the top five white *Burgundy* producers and making highly concentrated wines. ☆☆☆☆ 1993 Chassagne-Montrachet Vergers £££

Niepoort [nee-poort] (*Douro*, Portugal) Small independent *port* house making subtle *vintage* and particularly impressive *colheita tawnies*. A name to watch. ☆☆☆☆ 1994 Vintage Port £££

Nierstein [neer-stine] (*Rheinhessen*, Germany) Village and (with *Piesport*) *bereich* best known in the UK. Some fine wines, obscured by the notoriety of the reliably dull Niersteiner Gütes Domtal. QbA/Kab/Spät: 85 86 **88 89** 90 91 92 93 94 95 Aus/Beeren/Tba 83 85 88 89 90 91 92 93 94 95 96 *Balbach; Gunderloch.*

Weingut Nikolaihof [nih-koh-li-hof] (*Niederösterreich*, Austria) One of the producers of some of the best *Grüner Veltliners* and *Rieslings* in Austria. ☆☆☆☆ 1994 Riesling Federspiel Trocken ££

Nipozzano [nip-ots-zano] (*Tuscany*, Italy) *See Frescobaldi.*

Nitra [neet-ra] (Slovakia) Promising hilly region, especially for *Pinots Blanc, Gris* and *Noir.*

Nobilo [nob-ih-loh] (Huapai, New Zealand) Family-owned firm making richly tasty and oaky (Dixon Vineyard) *Chardonnay* from *Gisborne, 'Icon'* wines from *Marlborough* (including a good *Gewurztraminer*) and a pleasant commercial off-dry *White Cloud* blend.
Noble rot Popular term for *botrytis cinerea.*

Normans (*McLaren Vale*, Australia) Fast improving *Cabernet* and *Shiraz* specialist. ☆☆☆☆☆ 1996 White Label South Eastern Australian Cabernet Sauvignon £££

North-East Victoria (Australia) The region is split between rich *Liqueur Muscat* producers of *Rutherglen* and Glenrowan and the cooler climate viticulture region as seen used by wineries such as *Brown Bros* and *Giaconda*. Grapes range from *Cabernet*, *Riesling*, *Chardonnay* to *Muscat*. White: 86 87 88 90 91 92 94 95 96 Red: 80 82 84 85 86 87 88 90 91 92 94 95 96 *Morris; Giaconda; Chambers; Baileys; Brown Bros.*

�‍❡ **Bodega Norton** [naw-ton] (Argentina) One of Argentina's most recommendable producers, producing a wide range of *varietal* wines. The 'Privada' wines are the cream of the crop. ☆☆☆☆ **1996 Privada Red ££**

☍ **Ch. Notton** [not-ton] (*Margaux*, *Bordeaux*, France) The *second label* of *Ch. Brane-Cantenac*.

Nouveau [noo-voh] New wine, most popularly used of *Beaujolais*.

☍ **Quinta do Noval** (*Douro*, Portugal) Fine and potentially finer estate. The ultra-rare Nacional *vintage ports* are the jewel in the crown, made from ungrafted vines. Also of note are great *colheita tawny ports*. ☆☆☆☆ **1994 Vintage Port £££**

☍ **Albet i Noya** [al-bet-ee-noy-ya] (Spain) Innovative producer with red and white traditional and imported varieties. A future Spanish superstar? ☆☆☆ **1993 Col Leccio Macabeu ££**

☍ **Nuits-St.-Georges** [noo-wee san zhawzh] (*Burgundy*, France) *Commune* producing the most *claret*-like of red *Burgundies*, properly tough and lean when young but glorious with age. Whites are good but ultra-rare. Red 78 79 **80** 82 83 **85** 86 87 **88 89 90** 91 92 93 94 95 96 *Dom. de l'Arlot; Daniel Rion; Jean Grivot; Alain Michelot; Robert Chevillon; Henri Gouges; Faiveley.*

☍ **Nuragus di Cagliari** [noo-rah-goos dee ka-lee-yah-ree] (*Sardinia*, Italy) Good-value, tangy, floral wine from the Nuragus grape.

NV Non-vintage, meaning a blend of wines from different years.

O

☍ **Oakville Ranch** (*Napa Valley*, California) Potentially one of the Napa's most exciting red wine producers, but wines have so far been a little too tough. ☆☆☆☆ **1994 Merlot Napa Valley £££**

Oaky Flavour imparted by oak casks which will vary depending on the source of the oak (American is more obviously sweet than French). Woody is usually less complimentary.

☍ **Bodegas Ochoa** [och-OH-wah] (*Navarra*, Spain) New-wave producer of creamy, fruitily fresh *Cabernet*, *Tempranillo* and *Viura*. ☆☆☆☆ **1990 Navarra Tinto Reserva ££**

Ockfen [ok-fehn] (*Mosel-Saar-Ruwer*, Germany) Village producing some of the best, steeliest wines of the *Saar-Ruwer bereich,* especially *Rieslings* from the *Bockstein* vineyard. QbA/Kab/Spät: **85** 86 **88 89 90** 91 92 93 94 95 Aus/Beeren/Tba: **83 85** 88 89 90 91 92 93 94 95 ☆☆☆ **1996 Ockfener Bockstein Riesling, Reichsgraf von Kesselstadt ££**

Oechsle [urk-slur] (Germany) Scale used to indicate the sugar levels in grapes or wine.

Oenology/ist The science of wine/one who advises winemakers.

Oeste [wes-teh] (Portugal) Western region in which a growing number of fresh, light, commercial wines are being made, of which the most successful has undoubtedly been *Arruda.Red:* **80 85 88 90 91 92 93** 94 95 96

Oestrich [ur-strihckh] (*Rheingau*, Germany) Source of good *Riesling*. QbA/Kab/Spät: **85** 86 **88 89 90** 91 92 93 94 95 96 97 Aus/Beeren/Tba **85** 88 89 90 91 92 93 94 95 96 97 *Wegeler Deinhard; Balthazar Ress.*

🍷 **Michel Ogier** [ogee-yay] (*Rhône*, France) Excellent *Côte Rôtie* producer, making less muscular wines than most of his neighbours.
☆☆☆☆ **1991 Côte Rôtie ££**

Oïdium [oh-id-ee-yum] Fungal grape infection, shrivelling them and turning them grey.

🍷 **Ojai Vineyard** [Oh-High] (*Santa Barbara*, California) The specialities here are a *Sauvignon-Semillon* blend and – more interestingly – a *Rhône*-like *Syrah*. ☆☆☆☆ **1995 Syrah Bien Nacido Vineyard £££**

Okanagan (*British Columbia*, Canada) Principal wine growing region in the west of Canada. Despite frosts, *Pinot Noir* can produce good wine here. **Mission Hill.**

🍷 **Bodegas Olarra** [oh-lah-rah] (*Rioja*, Spain) Unexceptional producer whose whites are reliably and pleasantly adequate.

🍇 **Olasz Rizling** [oh-lash-riz-ling] (Hungary) Local term for the inferior *Welschriesling*.

🍷 **Ch. Olivier** [oh-liv-ee-yay] (*Pessac-Léognan Cru Classé, Bordeaux*, France) An under-performer which has yet to join the *Graves* revolution. Red: 82 83 85 86 88 89 90 91 92 93 94 95 96. White: 90 92 93 94 96

Oloroso [ol-oh-roh-soh] (*Jerez*, Spain) Style of full-bodied *sherry*, that is either dry or semi-sweet.

🍷 **Oltrepò Pavese** [ohl-tray-poh pa-vay-say] (*Lombardy*, Italy) *Lombardy DOC* made from local grapes including the characterfully spicy red Gutturnio and white Ortrugo. Fugazza is the big name. ☆☆☆☆☆ **1995 Vinocurore La Botte no. 18 Selezzione Cabanon ££**

🍷 **Omar Khayyam (Champagne India)** [oh-mah-ki-yam] (Maharashtra, India) *Champagne*-method wine which, when drunk young, has more than novelty value. The producer's cheeky name, '*Champagne* India', is a source of considerable annoyance to the Champenois, but they, in the shape of *Piper Heidsieck*, were happy enough to sell the Indians their expertise. Besides, *Moët* and *Mumm* still shamelessly sell their South American wines as 'Champaña' and 'Champanha'.

Ontario (Canada) The best wine region in Canada, with over 80 per cent of Canada's wine being produced here. Look out for bottles with *VQA* stickers which guarantee quality and provenance.

🍷 **Willi Opitz** [oh-pitz] (*Neusiedlersee*, Austria) Odd-ball pet food-manufacturer-turned-producer of a magical mystery tour of *late harvest* and straw-dried wines, including an extraordinary *botrytis* red briefly labelled – to the discomfort of some Californians – 'Opitz One'. Ever the salesman, Opitz even released a soothing CD of his wines fermenting in cask, presumably allowing fans to decide whether or not they reckon them to be 'sound'. ☆☆☆☆☆ **1995 Gewürztraminer Trockenbeerenauslese £££**

Oppenheim [op-en-hime] (*Rheinhessen*, Germany) Village in *Nierstein bereich* best known – unfairly – for unexciting wines from the Krottenbrunnen. Elsewhere produces soft wines with concentrated flavour. QbA/Kab/Spät: **85** 86 **88 89 90** 91 92 93 94 95 96 97 Aus/Beeren/Tba: **83 85** 88 89 90 91 92 93 94 95 96 97

🍷 **Opus One** (*Napa Valley*, California) Highly successful co-production between *Mouton-Rothschild* and *Robert Mondavi*. Classy and very *claret*-like blackcurranty wine that sells at an appropriately classy claret-like price. The winery, which was excavated into land to the side of the main road through *Napa*, has been described as the world's most expensive hole in the ground following the problems the builders encountered when they unexpectedly struck water there. ☆☆☆☆☆ **1993 ££££**

Orange (*New South Wales*, Australia) Recently developed coolish region which, with *Cowra*, is likely to eclipse the *Hunter Valley* as a major quality wine region of this state. For a taste of things to come, try the classy Orange *Chardonnay* made by Philip Shaw of *Rosemount* from vineyards of which he is the proud co-owner. White: 88 90 **91** 94 95 96 97 ☆☆☆☆ **1994 Rosemount Orange Vineyard Chardonnay ££**

🍷**Orange Muscat** Another highly eccentric member of the *Muscat* family, best known for dessert wines in California by *Quady* and in Australia for the delicious *Brown Brothers Late Harvest* Orange Muscat and *Flora*.

Oregon (US) Fashionable cool-climate state whose bearded, be-sandled winemakers have been known to grow marijuana as keenly as their speciality, *Pinot Noir*. The *Chardonnay*s are even less successful, thanks to the planting of a late-ripening *clone* as recommended by experts from California. Red: 85 88 **89** 90 91 92 94 95 White: **85 88 89 90 91 92 94** 95 *Drouhin; Argyle; Ponzi; Amity;* Adelsheim; *Rex Hill; Eyrie.*

🍷 **Oriachovitza** [oh-ree-ak-hoh-vit-sah] (Bulgaria) Major source of reliable *Cabernet Sauvignon* and *Merlot*.

🍷 **Orlando** (*South Australia*) Huge French-owned (Pernod-Ricard) producer of the world-beating and surprisingly reliable *Jacob's Creek* wines. The RF range is good but the harder-to-find Gramps and Flaxmans wines are more exciting, as are Jacaranda Ridge and the 'Saints' series.

Orléanais [aw-lay-yo-nay] (*Loire*, France) A vineyard area around Orléans in the Central Vineyards region of the *Loire,* specialising in unusual white blends of *Chardonnay* and *Pinot Gris,* and reds of *Pinot Noir* and *Cabernet Franc.* White: **86 88 89 90** 94 95 96 97 Red: **85** 86 **88 89 90** 95 96 97

🍷 **L' Ormarins Estate** [aw-mur-rins] (*Franschhoek*, South Africa) Should-do-better – only the *Shiraz* and the 'Optima' *Bordeaux* blend impress.

🍷 **Ch. Les Ormes-de-Pez** [awm dur-pay] (*St. Estèphe Cru Bourgeois, Bordeaux*, France) Often underrated stable-mate of *Lynch-Bages* and made with similar skill. 75 78 79 **81 82 83** 85 86 88 89 90 92 93 94 95

🍷 **Tenuta dell'Ornellaia** [teh-noo-tah del-aw-nel-li-ya] (*Tuscany*, Italy) *Bordeaux*-blend *Super-Tuscan* from the brother of *Piero Antinori*. This is serious wine that is worth maturing. ☆☆☆☆ **1993 Ornellaia ££££**

🍷**Ortega** [aw-tay-gah] Recently developed variety, and grown in Germany and England, though rarely to tasty advantage. *Biddenden* makes a good one, however, as does *Denbies*, which uses it to produce *late harvest* wine.

🍷 **Orvieto** [ohr-vee-yet-toh] (*Umbria*, Italy) White Umbrian *DOC* responsible for a quantity of dull wine. Orvieto *Classico* is better. Look out for *Secco* if you like your white wine dry; *Amabile* if you have a sweet tooth. *Antinori;* Bigi; Covio Cardetto; Palazzone.

🍷 **Osbourne** [os-sbaw-nay] (*Jerez*, Spain) Producer of a good range of *sherries* including a brilliant *Pedro Ximenez*.

🍷 **Dom. Ostertag** [os-tur-tahg] (*Alsace*, France) Poet and philosopher André Ostertag presides over this superb *Alsace domaine*. **1995 Riesling Moenchberg Vieilles Vignes £££**

Oxidation The effect (usually detrimental, occasionally – as in *sherry* – intentional) of oxygen on wine.

Oxidative The opposite to *reductive*. Certain wines – most reds, and whites like *Chardonnay* – benefit from limited exposure to oxygen during their fermentation and maturation, such as barrel ageing.

🍷 **Oyster Bay** (*Marlborough*, New Zealand) See entry for *Delegats*. ☆☆☆ **1997 Sauvignon Blanc ££**

P

Paarl [pahl] (South Africa) Warm region in which *Backsberg* and *Boschendal* make a wide range of appealing wines. Hotter and drier than neighbouring *Stellenbosch*. Red: **82 84** 86 **87** 89 **91 92** 93 94 95 White: **87 91** 92 93 94 95 *Charles Back/Fairview; KWV; Backsberg; Glen Carlou; Villiera; Plaisir de Merle.*

☰ **Pacherenc du Vic-Bilh** [pa-shur-renk doo vik beel] (*South-West*, France) Rare dry or fairly sweet white wine made from the *Petit* and *Gros Manseng*. A speciality of *Madiran*. ☆☆☆☆☆ **1995 Brumaire, Alain Brumont ££**

Padthaway [pad-thah-way] (South Australia) Vineyard area just north of *Coonawarra* specialising in *Chardonnay* and *Sauvignon*, though reds work well here too. White: **90 91 94** 95 96 Red: 86 **87** 88 **90 91** 94 95 96 *Penfolds; Lindemans; Hardys;* Browns of Padthaway.

☰ **Pagadebit di Romagna** [pah-gah-deh-bit dee roh-man-ya] (*Emilia-Romagna*, Italy) Dry, sweet and fizzy whites from the Pagadebit grape.

☰ **Pahlmeyer** (*Napa Valley*, California) One of California's most interesting winemakers, producing Burgundian *Chardonnay* and a complex *Bordeaux*-blend red. ☆☆☆☆ **1993 Not Filtered Chardonnay £££**

☰ **Ch. Pajzos** [pah-zhohs] (*Tokaji*, Hungary) Serious French-owned producer of new-wave *Tokay*. ☆☆☆☆ **1993 Tokay Aszú 5 Puttonyos £££**

☰ **Bodegas Palacio** [pa-las-see-yoh] (*Rioja*, Spain) Underrated *bodega* with stylish fruit-driven reds and distinctively oaky whites, Also helped by wine guru *Michel Rolland*. ☆☆☆☆ **1995 Cosme Palacio Rioja Red ££**
   Palate Nebulous, not to say ambiguous, term describing the aparatus used for tasting (ie, the tongue) as well as the skill of the taster ('he has a good palate').

Palatinate [pa-lah-tih-nayt] (Germany) Obsolete term for the *Pfalz*. QbA/Kab/Spät: **89 90** 92 **93** 94 95 Aus/Beeren/Tba: **89 90 91 92** 93 94

☰ **Palazzo Altesi** [pah-lat-see-yoh al-tay-see] (*Tuscany*, Italy) Oaky pure *Sangiovese* Super-Tuscan by Altesino.

☰ **Palette** [pa-let] (*Provence*, France) *AC* rosé and creamy white, well liked by holidaymakers in St. Tropez who are so used to extortionate prices for cups of coffee that they don't notice paying more for a pink wine than for a serious. The white, which can be very perfumed, is better value.

☰ **Palliser Estate** [pa-lih-sur] (*Martinborough*, New Zealand) Source of classy *Sauvignon Blanc* and *Chardonnay* from *Martinborough*. ☆☆☆☆☆ **1997 Martinborough Sauvignon Blanc ££**

☰ **Ch. Palmer** [pahl-mur] (*Margaux 3ème Cru Classé*, *Bordeaux*, France) The success story of the late Peter Sichel who died in 1998, this third growth *Margaux* stands alongside the best of the *Médoc* and often outclasses its more highly ranked neighbours. Wonderfully perfumed. **61 66 70 71 75 76 78 79** 80 82 **83** 84 85 86 87 **88 89** 90 91 92 93 94 95 96

☰ **Palo Cortado** [pah-loh kaw-tah doh] (*Jerez*, Spain) Rare *sherry* pitched between *amontillado* and *oloroso*. ☆☆☆☆ **Valdespino del Carascal ££**

🍇 **Palomino** [pa-loh-mee-noh] (*Jerez*, Spain) White grape responsible for virtually all fine *sherries* – and almost invariably dull white wine, when unfortified. Also widely grown in South Africa.

Ch. Pape-Clément [pap klay-mon] (*Pessac-Léognan Cru Classé,* *Bordeaux,* France) Great source of rich reds since the mid 1980s and, more recently, small quantities of delicious peach-oaky white. Red: 70 **75** 82 83 85 **86** 88 89 90 92 93 94 95 96 97

Parducci [pah-doo-chee] (*Mendocino,* California) Steady producer whose *Petite Sirah* is a terrific bargain. ☆☆☆☆ **1995 Petite Sirah £££**

Parellada [pa-ray-yah-dah] (*Catalonia,* Spain) Essentially dull grape used for *cava.* At its best in *Torres'* Viña Sol, but more thanks to winemaking than to any innate quality.

Dom. Parent [pa-ron] (*Burgundy,* France) *Pommard*-based grower/ *négociant,* which includes Thomas Jefferson among its former clients. Wines are quite old-fashioned too, but attractively so in their fruit-packed way. ☆☆☆☆ **1995 Beaune Epenottes £££**

Dom. Alain Paret [pa-ray] (*Rhône,* France) Producer of a great *St. Joseph* and *Condrieu,* in partnership with one of the world's best-known winemakers. (Though, to be fair, Gérard Dépardieu does owe his fame to the cinema rather than his efforts among the vines.) ☆☆☆☆ **1997 le Cinquet ££££**

Parker Estate (*Coonawarra,* Australia) A small producer sharing its name with the US guru, and calling its red 'First Growth'. Marks for cheek and good wine. ☆☆☆☆ **1994 Coonawarra First Growth ££**

Pasado/Pasada [pa-sah-doh/dah] (Spain) Term applied to old or fine *fino* and *amontillado sherries.* Worth seeking out.

CJ Pask [pask] (*Hawke's Bay,* New Zealand) *Cabernet* pioneer with excellent *Chardonnay* and *Sauvignon.* One of New Zealand's very best. ☆☆☆☆ **1996 Hawke's Bay Chardonnay Reserve £££**

Paso Robles [pa-soh roh-blays] (*San Luis Obispo,* California) Warmish long-established region, good for *Zinfandel* (especially *Ridge*), *Rhône* and Italian varieties. Plus increasingly successful *Chardonnay*s and *Pinots.* Red: **85** 86 87 **90 91** 92 93 95 White: **85 90 91** 92 95 96

Pasqua [pas-kwah] (*Veneto,* Italy) Producer of fairly priced reliable wines. ☆☆☆ **1992 Valpolicella Vigneti Casterni £**

Passetoutgrains [pas-stoo-gran] (*Burgundy,* France) Wine supposedly made from two-thirds *Gamay,* one third *Pinot Noir* – though few producers respect these proportions. Once the Burgundians' daily red – until they decided to sell it and drink cheaper wine from other regions.

Passing Clouds (*Bendigo,* Australia) 'We get clouds, but it never rains ...' Despite a fairly hideous label, this is one of Australia's most serious red blends. Worth keeping. ☆☆☆☆ **1992 Ben's Shiraz-Cabernet £££**

Passito [pa-see-toh] (Italy) Sweet raisiny wine, usually made from sun-dried *Erbaluce* grapes in Italy. This technique is now used in Australia by *Primo Estate.*

Ch. Patache d'Aux [pa-tash-doh] (*Médoc Cru Bourgeois, Bordeaux,* France) Traditional, toughish stuff. 83 85 88 89 90 93 95 ☆☆☆ **1993 £££**

Frederico Paternina [pa-tur-nee-na] (*Rioja,* Spain) Ernest Hemingway's favourite *bodega* – which is probably the only reason to buy its wine nowadays. ☆☆☆ **1995 Banda Azul Rioja Tinto ££**

Luis Pato [lweesh-pah-toh] (*Bairrada,* Portugal) One of Portugal's rare superstar winemakers, proving, amongst other things, that the *Baga* grape can make first-class spicy, berryish red wines. ☆☆☆ **1995 Quinta do Riberinho ££**

Patriarche [pa-tree-arsh] (*Burgundy,* France) Huge merchant whose name is not a watchword for great *Burgundy.* The *Ch. de Meursault domaine,* however, produces good *Meursault, Bourgogne* Blanc, *Volnay* and *Beaune.* Has a particular interest in the Marché du Vin in *Beaune,* a show-piece excuse to taste and make your own mind up about the various nuances of the taste of *Burgundy.*

Patz & Hall (*Napa Valley,* California) The maker of delicious, unashamedly full-flavoured *Chardonnays.* ☆☆☆☆ **1995 Mount Veeder Chardonnay £££**

� **Pauillac** [poh-yak] (*Bordeaux*, France) One of the four famous 'communes' of the *Médoc*, Pauillac is the home of Châteaux *Latour, Lafite* and *Mouton-Rothschild*, as well as the two *Pichons* and *Lynch-Bages*. The epitome of full-flavoured blackcurranty *Bordeaux*; very classy (and pricy) wine. 70 75 76 **78** 79 **82** 83 **85 86** 88 89 90 94 95 96 97

☒ **Clos de Pauililles** [poh-leey] (*Languedoc-Roussillon*, France) Top class producer of *Banyuls* and of the little-known *appellation* of *Collioure*. ☆☆☆☆ 1996 Collioure Rosé £££

☒ **Neil Paulett** [paw-let] (South Australia) Small, top-flight *Clare Valley Riesling* producer. ☆☆☆☆ 1995 Polish Hill River Riesling ££

☒ **Dr Pauly-Bergweiler** [bur-gwi-lur] (*Mosel-Saar-Ruwer*, Germany) Ultra-modern winery with good modern *Riesling*. ☆☆☆☆ 1995 Beerenauslese Mosel-Saar-Ruwer Bernkasteler Lay ££

☒ **Ch. Pavie** [pa-vee] (*St-Emilion Premier Grand Cru Classé, Bordeaux*, France) Classy, impeccably made, plummily rich but complex *St. Emilion* wines. 70 78 **79** 81 **82 83** 85 **86** 87 **88 89 90** 91 93 94 95 96 ☆☆☆☆☆ 1990 ££££

☒ **Ch. Pavie-Decesse** [pa-vee dur-ses] (*St. Emilion Grand Cru Classé, Bordeaux*, France) Neighbour to *Ch. Pavie*, but a shade less impressive. 82 83 85 86 88 89 90 92 94 95 96

☒ **Ch. Pavie-Macquin** [pa-vee ma-kah'] (*St.Emilion Grand Cru Classé*, Bordeaux) Returned to form since the late 1980s – and the producer of a startlingly good 1993.

☒ **Le Pavillon Blanc de Ch. Margaux** [pa-vee-yon blon] (*Bordeaux*, France) The (rare) *Sauvignon*-dominated white wine of *Ch. Margaux* which still acts as the yardstick for the growing number of *Médoc* white wines. 85 86 89 **90 91** 92 95 96 97 ☆☆☆☆ 1993 Pavillon Blanc ££££

☒ **Ca' del Pazzo** [kah-del-pat-soh] (*Tuscany*, Italy) Ultra-classy oaky *Super-Tuscan* with loads of ripe fruit and oak.

Pécharmant [pay-shar-mon] (*South-West,* France) In the *Bergerac* area, producing light, *Bordeaux*-like reds. Worth trying.

🍇 **Pedro Ximénez (PX)** [peh-droh khee-MEH-nes] (*Jerez*, Spain) White grape, dried in the sun to create a sweet curranty wine, which is used in the blending of the sweeter *sherry* styles, and in its own right by *Osbourne*, and by *Gonzalez Byass* for its brilliant Noe. Also produces a very unusual wine at *De Bortoli* in Australia. ☆☆☆☆ La Sacristía de Romate Pedro Ximénez £££

☒ **Viña Pedrosa** [veen-ya pay-droh-sah] (*Ribera del Duero*, Spain) Modern wine showing what the *Tempranillo* can do when blended with the classic *Bordelais* varieties. The Spanish equivalent of a *Super-Tuscan*.

☒ **Clos Pegase** [kloh-pay-gas] (*Napa Valley*, California) Showcase winery with improving but historically generally overpraised wines. ☆☆☆ 1992 Merlot Napa Valley £££

☒ **Dom. Henry Pellé** [on-ree pel-lay] (*Loire*, France) Reliable producer of fruitier-than-usual *Menetou-Salon*. ☆☆☆☆ 1996 Menetou-Salon £££

☒ **Pelorus** [pe-law-rus] (*Marlborough*, New Zealand) Showy, big, buttery, yeasty, almost Champagnois-style New Zealand fizz from *Cloudy Bay* – the top exponents, according to some, for quality *Sauvignon Blanc* in this part of the world. ☆☆☆☆ 1992 £££

Pelure d'Oignon [pur-loor don-yon] (France) 'Onion skin': orangey-brown tint of some rosé – including ones that have lost their freshness.

Pemberton (Western Australia) Up-and-coming cooler climate region for more restrained styles of *Chardonnay* and *Pinot Noir;* one to watch out for in the future.

Penedés [peh-neh-dehs] (*Catalonia*, Spain) Largest *DOC* of *Catalonia* with varying altitudes, climates and styles ranging from *cava* to still wines pioneered by *Torres* and others, though some not as successfully. The use of noble *varietals* such as *Cabernet Sauvignon*, *Merlot* and *Chardonnay* allows a far more French expression of winemaking without losing intrinsic Spanish character. Belatedly beginning to live up to some of its early promise. White: 91 94 95 Red: **85 87** 88 89 90 **91** 93 94 95 96 *Torres; Jean Leon; Freixenet; Puig i Roca; Albet i Noya; Juve y Camps; Cavas Hill.*

🍷 **Penfolds** (*South Australia*) The world's biggest premium wine company with a high quality from Bin 2 to *Grange*. Previously a red wine specialist but now becoming a rapidly skilful producer of still white wines, and classy sparklers. See *Wynns*, *Seaview*, *Rouge Homme*, *Lindemans*, *Tullochs*, *Leo Buring*, *Seppelt*, and now James Halliday's *Coldstream Hills* and *Devil's Lair* in the *Margaret River*. ☆☆☆☆ **1994 Bin 28 Kalimna Shiraz ££;** ☆☆☆☆☆ **1994 Bin 707 Cabernet Sauvignon £££**

🍷 **Penley Estate** (*Coonawarra*, Australia) High-quality *Coonawarra* estate with rich *Chardonnay* and very blackcurranty *Cabernet*. ☆☆☆☆ **1994 Shiraz-Cabernet Sauvignon £££**

🍷 **Comte Peraldi** [peh-ral-dee] (*Corsica*, France) High-class *Corsican* wine producer, now also making good wine in Romania. ☆☆☆☆ **1993 Dom. Comte Peraldi, Ajaccio ££**

🍷 **Le Pergole Torte** [pur-goh-leh taw-teh] (*Tuscany*, Italy) Long-established pure *Sangiovese*, oaky *Super-Tuscan*. ☆☆☆☆☆ **1994 Montevertine ££**

🍇**Periquita** [peh-ree-kee-tah] (Portugal) Spicy, tobaccooey grape – and the wine *JM da Fonseca* makes from it.
Perlé/Perlant [pehr-lay/lon] (France) Lightly sparkling.
Perlwein [pehrl-vine] (Germany) Sparkling wine.

Pernand-Vergelesses [pehr-non vehr-zhur-less] (*Burgundy*, France) *Commune* producing rather jammy reds but fine whites, including some *Côte d'Or* best buys. White: **85 86 87 88** 89 **90 92** 95 96 Red: 78 83 **85** 87 **88 89 90** 92 95 96 *Jadot; Pavelot; Rapet; Dom. Rollin; Dubreuil-Fontaine; Laleure-Piot; Chandon de Briailles.*

🍷 **Père Anselme** [pehr on-selm] (*Rhône*, France) Resolutely ordinary *Châteauneuf-du-Pape* presented in a recognisably dust-covered mis-shapen bottle.

🍷 **Pére Caboche** [pehr kah-bosh] (*Rhône*, France) Pleasant, commercial *Châteauneuf-du-Pape* that is best drunk young. The 'Vieilles Vignes' *cuvée* is the one to buy. ☆☆☆ **1995 Vieilles Vignes £££**

🍷 **André Perret** (*Rhône*, France) Producer of notable *Condrieu* and decent *St. Joseph.*

🍷 **Joseph Perrier** [payh-ree-yay] (*Champagne*, France) Family-run producer whose long-lasting elegant *Champagne*s have a heavy *Pinot Noir* influence. ☆☆☆☆ **1989 Cuvée Royale Brut ££££**

🍷 **Perrier-Jouët** [payh-ree-yay zhoo-way] (*Champagne*, France) Sadly under-performing *Champagne* house which, like *Mumm*, curiously enough belongs to Canadian distillers, Seagram. Sidestep the non-vintage for the genuinely worthwhile – and brilliantly packaged – Belle Epoque prestige fizz. ☆☆☆☆ **1989 Belle Epoque ££££**

🍷 **Pesquera** [peh-SKEH-ra] (*Ribera del Duero*, Spain) Robert Parker dubbed this the *Ch. Pétrus* of Spain. Well, maybe. I'd say it's a top-class *Tempranillo* often equal to *Vega Sicilia* and the best of *Rioja*. ☆☆☆☆ **1993 Tinto ££**

Pessac-Léognan [peh-sak LAY-on-yon] (*Bordeaux*, France) *Graves commune* containing most of the finest châteaux. *Ch. Fieuzal, Domaine de Chevalier, La Louvière, Haut Brion, Smith Haut Laffite.*

♈ **Petaluma** [peh-ta-loo-ma] (*Adelaide Hills*, Australia) High-tech creation of *Brian Croser* that has become the role model for other producers in the New World who are interested in combining innovative winemaking with the fruit of individually characterful vineyards. Classy *Chardonnays* from Piccadilly in the *Adelaide Hills*, *Clare Rieslings* (particularly good *late harvest*) and *Coonawarra* reds. ☆☆☆☆ 1995 **Sharefarmers Red £££**

Pétillant [pur-tee-yon] Lightly sparkling.

♈ **Petit Chablis** [pur-tee shab-lee] (*Burgundy*, France) (Theoretically) less fine than plain *Chablis* – though plenty of vineyards that were previously designated as Petit Chablis can now produce wines sold as *Chablis*. Often poor value. 90 92 94 95 96 *La Chablisienne.*

Petit Château [pur-tee sha-toh] (*Bordeaux*, France) Loose term for minor property.

🍇 **Petit Verdot** [pur-tee vehr-doh] (*Bordeaux*, France) Spicy *tannic* variety used in small proportions in red *Bordeaux*, California (rarely) and now Italy and Spain. *Marquès de Griñon.*

♈ **Ch. Petit Village** [pur-tee vee-lahzh] (*Pomerol*, *Bordeaux*, France) Classy, intense, blackcurranty-plummy *Pomerol* now under the same ownership as *Ch. Pichon-Longueville.* Worth keeping. 75 78 79 81 **82** 83 85 86 87 88 89 90 92 93 94 95 96 ☆☆☆☆ **1989 ££££**

🍇 **Petite Sirah** [peh-TEET sih-RAH] Red grape grown in California and Mexico and as *Durif* in the *Midi* and Australia. Nothing to do with the *Syrah* but can produce lovely spicy red. *LA CETTO; Ridge; Fetzer; Morris; Parducci; Turley.*

Petrolly A not unpleasant overtone often found in mature *Riesling.*

♈ **Ch. Pétrus** [pay-trooss] (*Pomerol*, *Bordeaux*, France) Until recently the priciest of all *clarets* (until *le Pin* came along). Voluptuous *Pomerol* hits the target especially well in the US, and is finding a growing market in the Far East. 61 62 **64** 66 70 **71** 75 76 78 **79** 81 82 83 85 86 88 89 90 92 93 94 95 96 ☆☆☆☆☆ **1989 ££££**

♈ **Pewsey Vale** [pyoo-zee vayl] (*Adelaide Hills*, Australia) Classy cool-climate wines from winery associated with *Yalumba*, *Hill-Smith* and *Heggies.* ☆☆☆☆ **1996 Cabernet Sauvignon ££**

♈ **Ch. de Pez** [dur pez] (*St. Estèphe Cru Bourgeois*, *Bordeaux*, France) Fast-improving *St. Estèphe*, especially since its purchase by *Louis Roederer.* In good vintages, well worth ageing. 78 79 **82** 83 85 86 88 89 90 93 94 95

Pfalz [*Pfaltz*] (Germany) Formerly known as the *Rheinpfalz,* and before that as the *Palatinate.* Warm, southerly *anbaugebiet* noted for riper, spicier *Riesling.* Currently competing with the *Mosel* for the prize of best of Germany's wine regions. QbA/Kab/Spät: 85 86 **88 89 90** 91 92 93 94 95 96 Aus/Beeren/Tba: 83 **85** 88 89 90 91 92 93 94 95 *Kurt Darting; Lingenfelder; Müller-Cattoir.*

♈ **Ch. Phélan-Ségur** [fay-lon say-goor] (*St. Estèphe Cru Bourgeois*, *Bordeaux*, France) A good-value property since the mid-1980s, with ripe well-made wines. Could do better. 75 **82** 85 88 89 90 92 93 94 95

♈ **Joseph Phelps** (*Napa Valley*, California) Pioneer *Napa* user of *Rhône* varieties (*Syrah* and *Viognier*), and a rare source of *late harvest* Riesling. *Cabernet* is a strength. ☆☆☆☆ **1993 Insignia Napa Valley ££££**

♈ **Philipponnat** [fee-lee-poh-nah] (*Champagne*, France) Small producer famous for Clos des Goisses, but also notable for *vintage* and rosé.

Phylloxera Vastatrix [fih-lok-seh-rah] Root-eating louse that wiped out Europe's vines in the 19th century. Foiled by grafting *vinifera* vines onto resistant American *labrusca* rootstock. Pockets of pre-phylloxera and/or ungrafted vines still exist in France (in a *Bollinger* vineyard and on the south coast – the louse hates sand), Portugal (in *Quinta do Noval*'s 'Nacional' vineyard), Australia and Chile. Elsewhere, phylloxera has devastated *Napa Valley* vines planted on insufficiently resistant rootstock.

Piave [pee-yah-vay] (*Veneto*, Italy) *DOC* in *Veneto* region, including reds made from a *Bordeaux*-like mix of grapes.

☱ **Ch. Pibarnon** [pee-bah-non] (*Bandol*, France) Top-class producer of modern *Bandol*. 88 **89** 90 92 93 95 96 ☆☆☆☆☆ 1993 **£££**

☱ **Ch. Pibran** [pee-bron] (*Pauillac Cru Bourgeois*, *Bordeaux*, France) Small but high quality and classically *Pauillac* property. 88 **89** 90 92 94 95 96

Pic St.-Loup [peek-sa'-loo] (*Languedoc-Roussillon*, France) Up-and-coming region within the *Coteaux du Languedoc* for *Rhône*-style reds and whites. **Dom. l'Hortus; Mas Bruguière.**

☱ **Ch. Pichon-Lalande** [pee-shon la-lond] (*Pauillac 2ème Cru Classé*, *Bordeaux*, France) The new name for Pichon-Longueville-Lalande. Famed *super second* and tremendous success story, thanks to top-class winemaking and the immediate appeal of its unusually high *Merlot* content. A great 1996. **61** 62 66 **70 75** 76 **78 79 81 82 83 85** 86 88 89 90 91 92 93 94 95 ☆☆☆☆ **1989 ££££**

☱ **Ch. Pichon-Longueville** [pee-shon long-veel] (*Pauillac 2ème Cru Classé*, *Bordeaux*, France) New name for Pichon-Longueville-Baron. An under-performing second growth *Pauillac* until its purchase by *AXA* in 1988. Now level with, and sometimes ahead of, *Ch. Pichon-Lalande*, once the other half of the estate. Wines are intense and complex. Les Tourelles, the *second label*, is a good value alternative. 86 88 89 90 91 92 93 94 95

♣**Picolit** [pee-koh-leet] (*Friuli*, Italy) Grape used to make both sweet and dry white wine. *Jermann* makes a good one.

Piedmont/Piemonte [pee-yed-mont/pee-yeh-mon-tay] (Italy) Ancient and modern north-western region producing old-fashioned tough *Barolo* and *Barbaresco* and brilliant modern fruit-packed wines. Also makes *Oltrepò Pavese*, *Asti Spumante* and *Dolcetto d'Alba*. See *Nebbiolo*, *Gaja*, *Altare*, *Mascarello*, *Conterno*, *Vajra*, *Bava*. Red: 78 79 82 **85 88** 89 90 93 94 95 96 97 White: 91 92 94 95 96 97

☱ **Pieropan** [pee-yehr-oh-pan] (*Veneto*, Italy) *Soave*'s top producer, which more or less invented single vineyard wines here and is still a great exception to the dull *Soave* rule. ☆☆☆☆ **1996 Vigneto La Rocca ££**

☱ **Pieroth** [pee-roth] Huge company whose salesmen visit customers' homes offering wines that are rarely recommended by this or any other critic.

☱ **Pierro** [pee-yehr-roh] (*Margaret River*, Australia) Small estate producing rich, buttery, *Meursault*-like *Chardonnay*. ☆☆☆☆ **1996 Chardonnay £££**

Piesport [pees-sport] (*Mosel-Saar-Ruwer*, Germany) Produced in the *grosslage Michelsberg*, a region infamous for dull German wine and bought by people who think themselves above *Liebfraumilch*. Try a single vineyard – Gunterslay or Goldtröpchen – for something more memorable. QbA/Kab/Spät: **85** 86 **88 89 90** 91 92 93 94 95 96 Aus/Beeren/Tba: 83 85 88 89 90 91 92 93 94 95 96 *Reichsgraf von Kesselstadt*.

☱ **Pikes** (*Clare Valley, South Australia*) Top-class estate with especially good *Riesling*, *Shiraz* and unusually successful *Sauvignon*. ☆☆☆☆ **1994 Reserve Shiraz ££**

☱ **Jean Pillot** [pee-yoh] (*Burgundy*, France) There are three estates called Pillot in *Chassagne-Montrachet*. This one is the best – and a star producer of red examples of this *appellation*.

☱ **Ch. le Pin** [lur pan] (*Pomerol*, *Bordeaux*, France) Ultra-hyped, tiny, recently formed estate whose – admittedly delicious – wines sell at increasingly silly prices in the US and the Far East. The fore-runner of a string of other similar honey-traps (see *Ch. Valandraud* and *la Mondotte*), and one of the wines that is helping to create a burgeoning trade in forged bottles. 81 82 83 85 86 87 88 89 90 92 93 94 95 ☆☆☆☆☆ **1990 ££££**

� **Pine Ridge** (*Napa Valley*, California) Greatly improved *Stag's Leap* producer that is now also making good reds on *Howell Mountain*.

☘ **Pineau de la Loire** [pee-noh dur la lwah] (*Loire*, France) Local name for the *Chenin Blanc*.

Pineau de Charentes [pee-noh dur sha-ront] (*South-West*, France) Fortified wine produced in the Cognac region.

☘ **Pinot Bianco** [pee-noh-bee-yan-koh] (Italy) Aka *Pinot Blanc*. Found mostly in northern Italy, it is sometimes misleadingly sold as *Chardonnay*.

☘ **Pinot Blanc** [pee-noh blon] Rather like *Chardonnay* without all that fruit, and rarely as classy or complex. Fresh, creamy and adaptable. At its best in *Alsace* (Pinot d'Alsace), the *Alto-Adige* in Italy (as *Pinot Bianco*), and in Germany and Austria (as *Weissburgunder*). In California, a synonym for *Melon de Bourgogne*.

☘ **Pinot Chardonnay** (Australia) Misleading name for *Chardonnay*, still used by Tyrrells. Don't confuse with *Pinot Noir/Chardonnay* fizz blends.

☘ **Pinot Grigio** [pee-noh gree-zhee-yoh] (Italy) *See Pinot Gris*.

☘ **Pinot Gris** [pee-noh gree] (*Alsace*, France) White grape of uncertain origins, making full, rather heady, spicy wine. Best in *Alsace* (also known as *Tokay d'Alsace*), Italy (as *Pinot Grigio*) and Germany (as *Rülander* or *Grauburgunder*). *Zind–Humbrecht; Cave de Turckheim.*

☘ **Pinot Meunier** [pee-noh-mur-nee-yay] (*Champagne*, France) Dark pink-skinned grape. Plays an unsung but major role in *Champagne*. Can also be used to produce a still varietal wine. **Bests;** *Randall Grahm; Bonny Doon; William Wheeler.*

☘ **Pinot Noir** [pee-noh nwahr] Black grape responsible for all red *Burgundy* and in part for white *Champagne*. Also grown in the New World with increasing success in sites whose climate is neither too warm nor too cold. Winemakers need the dedication which might otherwise have destined them for a career in nursing. Buying is like Russian Roulette once you've got a taste for that complex raspberryish flavour, you'll go on pulling the expensive trigger. See *Oregon, Carneros, Yarra, Santa Barbara, Tasmania, Burgundy.*

☘ **Pinotage** [pee-noh-tazh] (South Africa) *Pinot Noir* x *Cinsault* cross with a spicy plummy character, used in South Africa and (now very rarely) New Zealand. Good old examples are brilliant but rare; most taste muddy and rubbery. New winemaking and international demand are making for more exciting wines. **Clos Malverne;** *Kanonkop; Warwick; Simonsig; Saxenberg; Grangehurst.*

☒ **Piper Heidsieck** [pi-pur hide-sehk] (*Champagne*, France) Greatly improved *Champagne,* though the ultra-dry *Brut* Sauvage is an acquired taste and the US Piper Sonoma decidedly undistinguished.

☒ **Piper's Brook Vineyards** (*Tasmania*, Australia) The best-known producer in *Tasmania*, Dr. Andrew Pirie is a pioneering producer of fine *Burgundian Chardonnay, Pinot Noir* and *Pinot Gris*. Ninth Island, the *second label*, includes an excellent unoaked *Chablis*-like *Chardonnay*. ☆☆☆☆ **1997 Riesling £££**

☒ **Pira** [pee-rah] (*Piedmont*, Italy) Greatly improved small *Barolo* estate with top class vineyards and long-lived wines.

☒ **Producteurs Plaimont** [play-mon] (*South-West*, France) Reliable co-operative in *Côtes de St. Mont* producing *Bordeaux*-lookalike reds and whites with some use of local grapes. See also *Pacherenc du Vic-Bilh* and *Madiran*. ☆☆☆ **1996 Côtes de St. Mont £**

☒ **Plaisir de Merle** [play-zeer dur mehrl] (*Paarl*, South Africa) Paul Pontallier of *Ch. Margaux* is helping to make ripe soft reds and New World style whites for *Stellenbosch Farmers' Winery* in this new showcase operation. ☆☆☆☆ **1995 Chardonnay ££**

☒ **Plantagenet** (*Mount Barker*, Western Australia) Good producer of *Chardonnay, Riesling, Cabernet* and lean *Shiraz* in this increasingly successful region in the south-west corner of Australia. ☆☆☆☆ **1997 Omrah Unoaked Chardonnay £££.**

☒ **Poggio Antico** [pod-zhee-yoh an-tee-koh] (*Tuscany*, Italy) Ultra-reliable *Brunello* producer. ☆☆☆☆ **1993 Brunello di Montalcino ££££**

☲ **Pol Roger** [pol rod-zhay] (*Champagne*, France) Consistently fine producer, with an unusually subtle non-vintage that improves with keeping. The Cuvée Winston Churchill (named in honour of one of this wine's most faithful fans) is spectacular, and the *Demi-Sec* is a rare treat. ☆☆☆☆☆ **1990 Vintage ££££**

☲ **Poliziano** [poh-leet-zee-yah-noh] (*Tuscany*, Italy) Apart from a pack-leading *Vino Nobile di Montepulciano*, this is the place to find the delicious Elegia and Le Stanze *Vini da Tavola*. ☆☆☆☆ **1995 Le Stanze ££££**

☲ **Pomerol** [pom-meh-rohl] (*Bordeaux*, France) With *St. Emilion*, the *Bordeaux* for lovers of the *Merlot*, which predominates in its rich, soft, plummy wines. *Ch. Pétrus* and *le Pin* are the big names but wines like *Petit Village* and *Clos René* abound. None are cheap because production is often limited to a few thousand cases (in the *Médoc*, 20–40,000 is more common). Quality is far more consistent than in *St. Emilion*. See *Pétrus*, *Moueix* and individual *châteaux*. 79 81 **82 83 85** 86 **88 89** 90 94 95 96

☲ **Pomino** [poh-mee-noh] (*Tuscany*, Italy) Small *DOC* within *Chianti Rufina;* virtually a monopoly for *Frescobaldi* who make a buttery unwooded white *Pinot Bianco/Chardonnay*, the oaky-rich Il Benefizio and a tasty *Sangiovese/Cabernet*. ☆☆☆ **1994 Pomino Rosso ££**

☲ **Pommard** [pom-mahr] (*Burgundy*, France) Very variable quality *commune,* theoretically with a higher proportion of old vines, making slow-to-mature, then solid and complex reds. 78 **85** 86 87 **88 89 90** 92 93 94 95 *Comte Armand; de Montille; Mussy; Château de Meursault; Dom. de Pousse d'Or.*

☲ **Pommery** [pom-meh-ree] (*Champagne*, France) Returned-to-form big-name with rich full-flavoured style. The top label Louise Pommery white and rosé are tremendous. ☆☆☆☆☆ **1988 Cuvée Louise ££££**

☲ **Pongràcz** [pon-gratz] (South Africa) Brand name for the *Bergkelder's* (excellent) *Cap Classique* sparkling wine. ☆☆☆☆ **Cap Classique ££**

☲ **Dom. Ponsot** [pon-soh] (*Burgundy*, France) Top-class estate noted for *Clos de la Roche, Chambertin* and (rare) white *Morey-St.-Denis*. More affordable is the excellent *Gevrey*. ☆☆☆☆ **1995 Chambertin £££**

☲ **Ch. Pontet-Canet** [pon-tay ka-nay] (*Pauillac 5ème Cru Classé, Bordeaux*, France) Rich, concentrated, up-and-coming *Pauillac* benefitting since the early 1980s from the dedicated ambition of its owners who also have *Lafon-Rochet*. **82** 83 85 **86** 88 89 90 91 92 93 94 95 96 97

☲ **Ponzi** [pon-zee] (*Oregon*, US) The ideal combination: a maker of good *Pinot Noir, Chardonnay* and even better beer. ☆☆☆ **1995 Pinot Noir £££**

☲ **Port** (*Douro*, Portugal) Fortified wine made in the upper *Douro* valley. Comes in several styles; see *Tawny, Ruby, LBV, Vintage, Crusted* and *White port*.

☲ **Viña Porta** [veen-yah por-ta] (*Rapel*, Chile) Dynamic winery that specialises in juicy *Cabernet* and *Merlot*. The *Chardonnay* is good too.

☲ **Ch. Potelle** (*Napa Valley*, California) French-owned winery on *Mount Veeder* that achieved fame when its (stylish) wines were served at the White House. ☆☆☆ **1994 Zinfandel £££**

☲ **Ch. Potensac** [po-ton-sak] (*Médoc Cru Bourgeois, Bordeaux*, France) Under the same ownership as the great *Léoville-Las-Cases*, and offering a more affordable taste of the winemaking that goes into that wine.

Pouilly-Fuissé [poo-yee fwee-say] (*Burgundy*, France) Variable white often sold at vastly inflated prices. Pouilly-Vinzelles, Pouilly-Loché and other *Mâconnais* wines are often better value, though top-class Pouilly-Fuissé from producers like *Ch. Fuissé,* Dom. Noblet, or Dom. Ferret can compete with the best of the *Côte d'Or*. 85 86 87 **88** 89 **90 92** 95 96 *Ch. Fuissé; Barraud; Corsin;* Ferret; Lapierre; Noblet; Philibert.

� Pouilly-Fumé [poo-yee foo-may] (*Loire*, France) Potentially ultra-elegant *Sauvignon Blanc* with classic gooseberry fruit and 'smoky' over-tones derived from flint ('*silex*') sub-soil. Like *Sancerre,* rarely repays cellaring. See *Ladoucette* and *Didier Dagueneau*. 94 95 96 97

� Ch. Poujeaux [poo-joh] (*Moulis Cru Bourgeois*, *Bordeaux*, France) Up-and-coming plummy-blackcurranty wine. 70 75 76 78 **79** 81 **82 83** 85 86 87 88 89 90 91 92 93 94 95 ☆☆☆ **1993 £££**

Pourriture noble [poo-ree-toor nohbl] (France) See *botrytis cinerea* or *noble rot.*

� Dom. de la Pousse d'Or [poos-daw] (*Burgundy*, France) Despite the recent tragic death of founder-winemaker Gérard Potelle, this remains one of the top estates in *Volnay*. (The *Pommard* and *Santenay* wines are good too.) ☆☆☆☆ **1995 Volnay Clos de la Bousse d'Or ££££**

Prädikat [pray-dee-ket] (Germany) As in Qualitätswein mit Prädikat (*QmP*), the (supposedly) higher quality level for German and Austrian wines, indicating a greater degree of natural ripeness.

Precipitation The creation of a harmless deposit, usually of *tartrate* crystals, in white wine, which the Germans romantically call 'diamonds'.

Premier Cru [prur-mee-yay kroo] In *Burgundy*, indicates wines that are better than village level and second only to *Grand Cru*. Some major communes such as *Meursault, Beaune* and *Nuits-St.-Georges* have no *Grand Cru*.

� Premières Côtes de Bordeaux [prur-mee-yay koht dur bohr-doh] (*Bordeaux*, France) Up-and-coming riverside *appellation* for reds and (often less interestingly) sweet whites: Whites: 76 **83** 85 **86** 88 89 90 95 96 *Carsin; Reynon*; Grand-Mouëys.

Prestige Cuvée [koo-vay] (*Champagne*, France) The top wine of a *Champagne* house. Expensive and elaborately packaged. Some, like *Dom Pérignon,* are brilliant; others less so. Other best-known examples include *Veuve Clicquot's* Grand Dame and *Roederer's* Cristal.

� Dom. Jacques Prieur [pree-yur] (*Burgundy*, France) Reliable estate with fine vineyards. Improved since takeover by *Antonin Rodet*.

� Ch. Prieuré-Lichine [pree-yur-ray lih-sheen] (*Margaux 4ème Cru Classé*, *Bordeaux*, France) Improving blackcurranty wine benefitting from input by *Michel Rolland*. One of the only *châteaux* with a helicopter landing pad on its roof. 70 **82 83** 85 86 88 89 90 93 94 95 96

Primeur [pree-mur] (France) New wine, e.g. *Beaujolais* Primeur (the same as *Beaujolais Nouveau*) or, as in *en primeur,* wine which is sold while still in barrel. In the US, known as 'Futures'.

� Primitivo di Mandura [pree-mih-tee-voh dee man-doo-ra] (*Puglia*, Italy) Spicy red made from the Primitivo, another name for the *Zinfandel*.

� Primo Estate [pree-moh] (*South Australia*) Extraordinarily imaginative venture among the fruit farms of the Adelaide Plains. Passion-fruity *Colombard,* sparkling *Shiraz* and *Bordeaux*-blends made *Passito*-style, using grapes partially dried in the sun. The olive oil is good too.

� Priorato [pree-yaw-rah-toh] (*Catalonia*, Spain) Traditionally, hefty alcoholic reds and (rare) whites from *Cariñena* and *Garnacha* grapes grown in a very warm region. New-wave producers are bringing real class now with lighter modern reds. *Clos Mogador; Mas Martinet; Clos i Terrasses.*

Propriétaire (Récoltant) [pro-pree-yeh-tehr ray-kohl-ton] (France) Vineyard owner-manager.

� Prosecco di Conegliano-Valdobbiàdene [proh-sek-koh dee coh-nay-lee-anoh val-doh-bee-yah-day-nay] (*Veneto*, Italy) Soft, slightly earthy, dry and sweet fizz made from the *Prosecco* grape, often served from bottles containing the yeast that made them fizz. Less boisterous than *Asti Spumante*.

Provence [proh-vons] (France) Southern region producing fast improving wine with a number of minor *ACs*. Rosé de Provence should be dry and fruity with a hint of peppery spice. **Ch. Routas.**

🍷 **JJ Prüm** [proom] (*Mosel-Saar-Ruwer*, Germany) Top *Riesling* producer with fine *Wehlener* vineyards. ☆☆☆☆ **1994 Wehlener Sonnenuhr Riesling Spätlese £££**

🍷 **Dom. Michel Prunier** [proo-nee-yay] (*Burgundy*, France) Best estate in *Auxey-Duresses*. ☆☆☆☆ **1995 Premier Cru Clos du Val £££**

🍷 **Alfredo Prunotto** [proo-not-toh] (*Piedmont*, Italy) Good *Barolo* producer recently bought by *Antinori*. ☆☆☆☆ **1993 Barolo Bussia ££**

Puglia [poo-lee-yah] (Italy) Hot region, now making pretty cool wines thanks partly to *flying winemakers* like *Kym Milne*. Also see *Salice Salentino* and *Copertino*.

🍷 **Puiatti** [pwee-yah-tee] (*Friuli-Venezia Giulia*, Italy) Producer of some of Italy's most stylish *Chardonnay, Pinot Bianco, Pinot Grigio* and *Tocai Friulano*. The Archetipi wines are the cream of the crop.

🍷 **Puisseguin St. Emilion** [pwees-gan san tay-mee-lee-yon] (*Bordeaux*, France) Satellite of *St. Emilion* making similar, *Merlot*-dominant wines which are often far better value. **82 83 85** 86 **88 89** 90 94 95 97

🍷 **Puligny-Montrachet** [poo-lee-nee mon-ra-shay] (*Burgundy*, France) Aristocratic white *Côte d'Or commune* that shares the *Montrachet* vineyard with *Chassagne*. Should be complex buttery *Chardonnay* with a touch more elegance than *Meursault*. *Carillon, Sauzet, Ramonet, Drouhin* and *Dom. Leflaive* are all worth their money. **85 86** 87 **88** 89 **90 92** 95 Dom. ***Leflaive*; Carillon; *Sauzet; Ramonet*; Marquis de Laguiche.**

Putto [poot-toh] (Italy) As in *Chianti* Putto: wine from a consortium of growers who use the cherub (putto) as their symbol. Taken more seriously in Italy than it deserves.

Puttonyos [poot-TOH-nyos] (*Tokaji*, Hungary) The measure of sweetness (from 1 to 6) of *Tokaji*. The number indicates the number of puttonyos (baskets) of sweet *aszú* paste that are added to the base wine.

🍷 **Ch. Puygeraud** [Pwee-gay-roh] (*Bordeaux*, France) Perhaps the best property on the *Côtes de Francs*. 85 86 88 **89** 90 93 94 95

🍇 **PX** (*Jerez*, Spain) See *Pedro Ximénez*.

Pyrenees (*Victoria*, Australia) One of the classiest regions in *Victoria*, thanks to the efforts of *Taltarni* and *Dalwhinnie*. White: **91 92 94 95** 96 97 Red: **85 86 87 88 90 91 92** 94 95 96

🍷 **Pyrus** [pi-rus] (Australia) See *Lindemans*. ☆☆☆☆ **1994 Pyrus £££**

Q

QbA (Germany) Qualitätswein bestimmter Anbaugebiet: [kvah-lih-tayts-vine behr-shtihmt-tuhr ahn-bow-geh-beet] Basic quality German wine from one of the 11 *anbaugebiet*, e.g. *Rheinhessen*.

QmP (Germany) Qualitätswein mit Prädikat: [pray-dee-kaht] *QbA* wine (supposedly) with 'special qualities'. The QmP blanket designation is broken into five sweetness rungs, from *Kabinett* to *Trockenbeerenauslese* plus *Eiswein*.

�*ℐ* **Quady** [kway-dee] (*Central Valley*, California) Quirky producer of the wittily named 'Starboard' (hint: serve it in a decanter), the *Orange Muscat* Essencia (great with chocolate), *Black Muscat* Elysium, and Electra, low-alcohol. ☆☆☆☆ **Quady's Starboard Batch 88 ££**

☆ **Quarles Harris** [kwahrls] (*Douro*, Portugal) Underrated *port* producer with a fine 1980 and 1983. ☆☆☆☆ **1983 Vintage Port £££**

☆ **Quarts de Chaume** [kahr dur shohm] (*Loire*, France) Luscious but light sweet wines, uncloying, ageing beautifully, from the *Coteaux du Layon*. The *Dom. des Baumard* is exceptional. Sweet White: 76 83 85 86 88 89 90 94 95 96 **Dom des Baumard; Pierre Soulez.**

☆ **Quilceda Creek** [kwil-see-dah] (*Washington State*, US) Producer of one of the best, most blackcurranty *Cabernets* in the North-West.

☆ **Quincy** [kan-see] (*Loire*, France) Dry *Sauvignon,* lesser-known and sometimes good alternative to *Sancerre* or *Pouilly-Fumé*. **Joseph Mellot.**

Quinta [keen-ta] (Portugal) Vineyard or estate, particularly in the *Douro,* where 'single Quinta' *vintage ports* are increasingly being taken as seriously as the big-name blends. See *Crasto*, *Vesuvio* and *de la Rosa*.

☆ **Guiseppe Quintarelli** [keen-ta-reh-lee] (*Veneto*, Italy) Old-fashioned *Recioto*-maker producing some of the quirkiest, most sublime *Valpolicella*. Try the more affordable Molinara. ☆☆☆☆ **1995 Molinara ££**

☆ **Quivira** (*Sonoma*, California) Great *Dry Creek* producer of intense *Zinfandel* and *Syrah* and a deliciously clever *Rhône*-meets-California blend that includes both.

☆ **Qupé** [kyoo-pay] (*Central Coast*, California) Run by one of the founders of *Au Bon Climat*, this *Santa Barbara* winery produces brilliant *Syrah* and *Rhône*-style whites. ☆☆☆☆ **1996 Syrah £££**

R

☆ **Ch. Rabaud-Promis** [rrah-boh prraw-mee] (*Sauternes Premier Cru Classé*, *Bordeaux*, France) Under-performing until 1986; now making top class wines. 83 85 86 87 88 89 90 95 96 97 ☆☆☆☆☆ **1990 £££**
Racking The drawing off of wine from its *lees* into a clean cask or vat.

☆ **A Rafanelli** [ra-fur-nel-lee] (*Sonoma*, California) One of the few non-*Beaujolais* wineries making a success of *Gamay*; the *Zinfandel* is the jewel in the crown though. ☆☆☆☆ **1995 Zinfandel**

☆ **Olga Raffault** [ra-foh] (*Loire*, France) There are several Raffaults in *Chinon*; this is the best – and the best source of some of the longest-lived examples of this *appellation*. ☆☆☆☆ **1994 Chinon les Barnabés ££**

☆ **Raïmat** [ri-mat] (*Catalonia*, Spain) Innovative winery founded by *Codorniu*, in the dry *Costers del Segre* region, and unusual in being allowed to use irrigation. *Merlot,* a *Cabernet Merlot* blend called Abadia and *Tempranillo* are interesting and *Chardonnay* – both still and sparkling – has been good. ☆☆☆☆ **1991 Merlot ££**
Rainwater (*Madeira*, Portugal) Light dry style of *Madeira* popular in the US. ☆☆☆ **Berry Bros & Rudd's Selected Rainwater ££**

☆ **Ch. Ramage-la-Batisse** [ra-mazh la ba-teess] (*Haut-Médoc Cru Bourgeois*, *Bordeaux*, France) Good *Cru Bourgeois* from St. Laurent, close to *Pauillac*. 82 **83** 85 86 88 89 90 91 92 93 94 95 96

☆ **Ramitello** [ra-mee-tel-loh] (*Molise*, Italy) Spicy-fruity reds and creamy citric whites produced by di Majo Norante in Biferno on the Adriatic coast.

☆ **Adriano Ramos Pinto** [rah-mosh pin-toh] (*Douro*, Portugal) Family-run winery that belongs to *Roederer*. *Colheita* tawnies are a delicious speciality, but the *vintage* wines and *single quintas* are good too.

☎ **Dom. Ramonet** [ra-moh-nay] (*Burgundy*, France) Supreme *Chassagne-Montrachet* estate. Mecca for *Burgundy* lovers who queue to buy top flight wines like *Montrachet*, *Bâtard* and *Bienvenues-Bâtard-Montrachet* and fine complex *Premiers Crus*. Pure class; worth waiting for too. ☆☆☆☆☆ **1995 Bâtard-Montrachet ££££;** ☆☆☆☆ **1994 Chassagne-Montrachet Caillerets ££**

☎ **Castello dei Rampolla** [kas-teh-lohday-ee ram-poh-la] (*Tuscany*, Italy) Good *Chianti*-producer whose wines need time to soften. The berryish Sammarco *Vino da Tavola* is also impressive.

Rancio [ran-see-yoh] Term for the peculiar yet prized *oxidised* flavour of certain fortified wines, particularly in France (e.g. *Banyuls*) and Spain.

Rapel [ra-pel] (*Central Valley*, Chile) Important sub-region of the *Central Valley*, especially for reds. Includes *Colchagua* and *Cachapoal*.

☎ **Rapitalà** [ra-pih-tah-la] (*Sicily*, Italy) Estate producing a fresh peary white wine from a blend of local grapes.

☎ **Kent Rasmussen** (*Carneros*, California) One of California's too-small band of truly inventive winemakers, producing great *Burgundy*-like *Pinot Noir* and *Chardonnay* and Italian-inspired *Sangiovese* and *Dolcetto*. ☆☆☆☆ **1995 Chardonnay £££**

Rasteau [ras-stoh] (*Rhône*, France) Southern village producing peppery reds with rich berry fruit. The fortified *Muscat* can be good too. Red: **82 83 85 88 89 90 95** La Soumade; Bressy-Masson; Rabasse-Charavin.

☎ **Renato Ratti** [rah-tee] (*Piedmont*, Italy) One of the finest oldest producers of *Barolo*. ☆☆☆☆ **1993 Barolo £££**

☎ **Ch. Rauzan-Ségla** [roh-zon say-glah] (*Margaux 2ème Cru Classé, Bordeaux*, France) For a long time an under-performing *Margaux*. Now, since its purchase by Chanel in 1994, one of the best buys in *Bordeaux*. **70 82 83 85 86 88 89 90 91 92 93 94 95 96 97**

☎ **Ch. Rauzan-Gassies** [roh-zon ga-sees] (*Margaux 2ème Cru Classé, Bordeaux*, France) Despite recent improvements, compared to *Rauzan-Ségla* its neighbour, this property is still under-performing magnificently.

☎ **Ravenswood** (*Sonoma Valley*, California) Brilliant *Zinfandel*-maker whose individual vineyard wines are wonderful examples of this variety. The *Merlots* and *Cabernet* are fine too. ☆☆☆☆ **1995 Zinfandel £££**

☎ **Ravenswood** (*South Australia*) Label confusingly adopted by *Hollick* for its top *Coonawarra* reds (no relation to the above entry).

☎ **Raventos i Blanc** [ra-vayn-tos ee blank] (*Catalonia*, Spain) Josep Raventos' ambition is to produce the best fizz in Spain, adding *Chardonnay* to local varieties.

☎ **Ch. Rayas** [rih-yas] (*Rhône*, France) The only chance to taste *Châteauneuf-du-Pape* made solely from the *Grenache*. Pricy but good.

☎ **Raymond** (*Napa Valley*, California) Tastily intense *Cabernets* and *Chardonnays*.

☎ **Ch. Raymond-Lafon** [ray-mon la-fon] (*Sauternes, Bordeaux*, France) Very good small producer whose wines deserve keeping. **75 80 82 83 85 86 89** 90 92 94 95 96 97

☎ **Ch. de Rayne-Vigneau** [rayn VEEN-yoh] (*Sauternes Premier Cru Classé, Bordeaux*, France) *Sauternes* estate, located at *Bommes*, producing a rich complex wine. **76 83 85 86 88 89 90 92 94 95 96 97** ☆☆☆☆ **1990 ££££**

RD (*Champagne*, France) Récemment Dégorgée – a term invented by *Bollinger* to describe their delicious *vintage Champagne*, which has been allowed a longer-than-usual period (as much as fifteen years) on its *lees*. ☆☆☆☆☆ **1985 ££££**

Ignacio Recabarren [ig-na-see-yoh reh-ka-ba-ren] (Chile) Superstar winemaker and *Casablanca* pioneer.

Recioto [ray-chee-yo-toh] (*Veneto*, Italy) Sweet or dry alcoholic wine made from semi-dried, ripe grapes. Usually associated with *Valpolicella* and *Soave*.

Récoltant-manipulant (RM) [ray-kohl-ton ma-nih-poo-lon] (*Champagne*, France) Individual winegrower and blender, identified by mandatory RM number on label.

Récolte [ray-kohlt] (France) Vintage, literally 'harvest'.

�* **Redman** (*South Australia*) Improved *Coonawarra* estate with intense reds. ☆☆☆☆ **1992 Cabernet Sauvignon ££**

☀ **Redwood Valley Estate** (*Nelson*, New Zealand) Specialist in *late harvest* Rieslings. See also *Seifried.*

🍇 **Refosco** [re-fos-koh] [(*Friuli-Venezia Giulia*, Italy) Red grape and its dry and full-bodied *DOC* wine. Benefits from ageing.

☀ **Regaleali** [ray-ga-lay-ah-lee] (*Sicily*, Italy) Ambitious aristocratic estate, using local varieties to produce *Sicily's* most serious wines.
☆☆☆☆ **1993 Rosso del Conte Tasca d'Almerita £££**

Régisseur [rey-jee-sur] (*Bordeaux*, France) In *Bordeaux*, the cellar-master.

☀ **Régnié** [ray-nyay] (*Burgundy*, France) Once sold as *Beaujolais Villages,* Regnié now has to compete with *Chiroubles, Chénas* and the other *crus.* It is mostly like an amateur competing against pros. Fortunately for *Régnié,* those pros often aren't on great form. *Duboeuf* makes a typical example. **85 88 89 90 91 93 94 95 96 97 Duboeuf; Trichard.**

🍇 **Reichensteiner** [rike-en-sti-ner] Recently developed white grape, popular in England (and Wales).

☀ **Reif Estate Winery** [reef] (*Ontario*, Canada) Impressive *icewine* specialist. ☆☆☆☆ **1995 Icewine Riesling ££££**

☀ **Remelluri** [ray-may-yoo-ree] (*Rioja*, Spain) For most modernists, this is the nearest *Rioja* has got to a top-class, small-scale organic estate. Wines are more serious (and *tannic*) than most, but they're fuller in flavour too and they're built to last. ☆☆☆☆ **1995 Rioja ££**

Remuage [reh-moo-wazh] (*Champagne*, France) Part of the *méthode champenoise,* the gradual turning and tilting of bottles so that the yeast deposit collects in the neck ready for *dégorgement.*

Reserva [ray-sehr-vah] (Spain) Indicates the wine has been aged for a number of years specified by the relevant *DO*: usually one year for reds and six months for whites and pinks.

Réserve [rur-surv] (France) Legally meaningless, as in 'Réserve Personelle', but implying a wine selected and given more age.

Residual sugar Term for wines which have retained grape sugar not converted to *alcohol* by yeasts during fermentation. In France 4 grammes per litre is the threshold. In the US, the figure is 5 and many so-called 'dry' white wines contain as much as 10. New Zealand *Sauvignons* are rarely bone dry, but their *acidity* balances and conceals any residual sugar.

☀ **Weingut Balthasar Ress** [bul-ta-zah rress] (*Rheingau*, Germany) Classy producer in *Hattenheim,* blending delicacy with concentration.
☆☆☆☆ **1996 Hattenheimer Riesling Qualitätswein Halbtrocken £££**

Retsina [ret-see-nah] (Greece) Wine made the way the ancient Greeks used to make it – resinating it with pine to keep it from going off. Today, it's an acquired taste for non-holidaying, non-Greeks. Pick the freshest examples you can (not easy when there's no vintage on the bottle).

Reuilly [rur-yee] (*Loire*, France) (Mostly) white *AC* for dry *Sauvignons,* good value, if sometimes rather earthy alternatives to nearby *Sancerre* and *Pouilly-Fumé.* Search out spicy *Pinot* rosé from some of the best producers. White: 96 97 Red: **89 90 95 96** *Henri Beurdin.*

☀ **Rex Hill Vineyards** (*Oregon*, US) Greatly improved *Pinot* specialist.

☀ **Chateau Reynella** [ray-nel-la] (*McLaren Vale*, Australia) *BRL Hardy* subsidiary, mastering both reds and whites. ☆☆☆☆ **1995 Basket-Pressed Cabernet-Merlot ££**

☀ **Ch. Reynon** [ray-non] (*Premier Côtes de Bordeaux*, France) Fine red and especially recommendable white wines from *Denis Dubourdieu.*

Rheingau [rine-gow] (Germany) Should produce the finest *Rieslings* of the 11 *Anbaugebiete*, but sadly hijacked by producers who prefer quantity to quality and the *Charta* campaign for dry wines. There are still great things to be found, however. QbA/Kab/Spät: **85 86 88 89 90** 91 92 93 94 95 96 Aus/Beeren/Tba: **83 85 88** 89 90 91 92 93 94 95 96 97 *Künstler; Balthasar Ress; Domdechant Werner'sches;* HH Eser.

Rheinhessen [rine-hehs-sen] (Germany) Largest of the 11 *anbaugebiete,* now well known for *Liebfraumilch* and *Niersteiner.* Fewer than one vine in 20 is now *Riesling;* throughout the region easier-to-grow varieties and lazy cooperative wineries prevail. Pick and choose to get the good stuff. QbA/Kab/Spät: **85 86 88 89 90** 91 92 93 94 95 96 Aus/Beeren/Tba: **83 85 88** 89 90 91 92 93 94 95 96 *Gunderloch; Balbach.*

Rheinpfalz [rine-fahlts] (Germany) See *Pfalz.*

🖢Rhine Riesling/Rhein Riesling Widely used – though frowned-on by the EU – name for the noble *Riesling* grape.

🍷 Rhône [rohn] (France) Fast-improving, exciting, packed with the newly sexy *Grenache, Syrah* and *Viognier varietal* wines. See *St. Joseph, Crozes-Hermitage, Hermitage, Condrieu, Côtes du Rhône, Châteauneuf-du-Pape, Tavel, Lirac, Gigondas, Ch. Grillet, Beaumes de Venise.* White: **82 85** 87 **88 89 90** 91 94 95 Northern Rhône Red: **76 78 82 83 85 88** 89 90 91 95 96 Southern Rhône Red: **78 82 83 85 88** 89 90 95 96

🍷 Rias Baixas [ree-yahs bi-shahs] (*Galicia,* Spain) The place to find spicy apricoty *Albariño.* **Lagar de Cervera; Santiago Ruiz; Pazo de Barrantes;**

🍷 Ribatejo [ree-bah-tay-joh] (Portugal) *DO* area north of Lisbon where *Peter Bright* is very active these days. The cooperatives are fast learning how to make highly commercial white and red wine, but traditional *Garrafeiras* are worth watching out for too. Red: **85 88 90 91 92 93** 94 95 96

🍷 Ribera del Duero [ree-bay-rah del doo-way-roh] (Spain) This is potentially the region to watch in Spain for good reds (whites are forbidden, despite what might be ideal conditions for them). Unfortunately, despite the established success of *Vega Sicilia* and, more recently, that of producers like *Pesquera, Arroyo* and *Alion,* and despite high-tech 'smart card' technology in the cooperatives to check the quality of the grapes, there is still far too much poor winemaking. 82 **83 85** 87 89 90 91 92 94 95 96 **Pago de Carraovejas; Valduero Reserva;** *Pesquera;* **Balbas; Pedrosa;** *Vega Sicilia.*

🍷 Dom. Richeaume [ree-shohm] (*Provence,* France) One of the leading lights in the new wave of quality-conscious southern French estates, and a dynamic producer of good, earthy, long-lived, organic *Cabernet* and *Syrah.* Sadly, as with many other smaller organic wineries, quality can vary from bottle to bottle. Recommendable, nonetheless. ☆☆☆☆ **1996 Cuvé Columelle Rouge £££**

Richebourg [reesh-boor] (*Burgundy,* France) Top-class *Grand Cru* vineyard just outside *Vosne-Romanée* with a recognisable floral-plummy style. 76 **78** 79 **80** 82 83 **85** 86 87 **88 89 90** 92 93 94 95 96 *Domaine de la Romanée-Conti; Anne Gros; Leroy;* D&D Mugneret; *Grivot; Noëllat.*

☚ **Weingut Max Ferd Richter** [rikh-tur] (*Mosel-Saar-Ruwer*, Germany) Excellent producer of long-lived concentrated-yet-elegant *Mosel Rieslings* from high quality vineyards. The *cuvée* Constantin is the unusually successful dry wine, while at the other end of the scale, the *eisweins* are sublime. ☆☆☆☆☆ **1990 Brauneberger Juffer Riesling Auslese £££**

☚ **John Riddoch** (*South Australia*) Classic *Wynn's Coonawarra* red. One of Australia's best and longest-lasting wines. (Not to be confused with the wines that *Katnook Estate* sells under its own 'Riddoch' label.)

☚ **Ridge Vineyards** (*Santa Cruz*, California) Paul Draper, and Ridge's hilltop *Santa Cruz* and *Sonoma* vineyards, produce some of California's very finest *Zinfandel*, *Cabernet*, *Mataro* and *Chardonnay*. ☆☆☆☆☆ **1993 Monte Bello ££££**

☚ **Riecine** [ree-eh-chee-nay] (*Tuscany*, Italy) Small modern estate with fine *Chianti* and an even more impressive la Gioia *Vino da Tavola*. ☆☆☆☆☆ **1994 La Gioia £££**

🍇 **Riesling** [reez-ling] The noble grape responsible for Germany's finest offerings, ranging from light, floral, everyday wines, to the delights of *botrytis*-affected sweet wines which retain their freshness for decades. Reaching its zenith in the superbly balanced racy wines of the *Mosel*, and the richer offerings from the *Rheingau*, it also performs well in *Alsace*, California, South Africa and Australia. Watch out for the emergence of the *Wachau* region as a leader of the Austrian Riesling pack.

🍇 **Riesling Italico** See *Italian Riesling*, etc.

☚ **Ch. Rieussec** [ree-yur-sek] (*Sauternes Premier Cru Classé*, Bordeaux, France) Fantastically rich and concentrated *Sauternes*, often deep in colour and generally at the head of the pack chasing *d'Yquem*. Now owned by the Rothschilds of *Lafite*. R de Rieussec is the unexceptional dry white wine. **67 71 75** 79 82 **83 85 86** 88 89 90 92 93 94 95 96

Rioja [ree-ok-hah] (Spain) Spain's best-known wine region is split into three parts. The Alta produces the best wines, followed by the Alavesa, while the Baja is by far the largest. Most Riojas are blends made by large *bodegas* using grapes grown in two or three of the regions. Small *Bordeaux*- and *Burgundy*-style estates are rare, thanks to restrictive Spanish rules which require wineries to store unnecessarily large quantities of wine. Things are happening in the vineyards, however, including plantings of 'experimental' *Cabernet* alongside the traditional *Tempranillo* and lesser quality *Garnacha*. Such behaviour breaks all sorts of local rules – as does the irrigation which is also now in evidence – but is already paying off for producers like *Martinez Bujanda*. With luck, this kind of innovative thinking will help the region as a whole to live up to its reputation. Reds: **79 80 81** 82 **83 85 87** 89 90 91 92 94 95 *Remelluri; Campillo; La Rioja Alta; Contino; Riscal; Amezola de la Mora; Baron de Ley; Martinez Bujanda; Marqués de Griñon; Palacio; Murrieta; Breton; Ardanza.*

☚ **La Rioja Alta** [ree-ok-hah ahl-ta] (*Rioja*, Spain) Of all the big companies in *Rioja*, this is the name to remember. Its Viña Ardanza, Reserva 904 and (rarely produced) Reserva 890 are all among the most reliable and recommendable wines in the region. ☆☆☆ **1990 Viña Ardanza Reserva £££**

☚ **Dom. Daniel Rion** [ree-yon] (*Burgundy*, France) Patrice Rion, head of this family estate, produces impeccably made *Nuits-St.-Georges* and *Vosne-Romanées*. ☆☆☆☆ **1995 Vosne-Romanée les Chaumes £££**

Ripasso [ree-pas-soh] (*Veneto*, Italy) Method whereby newly made *Valpolicella* is partially refermented in vessels recently vacated by *Recioto* and *Amarone*. *Ripasso* wines made in this way are richer, alcoholic and raisiny. Increases the *alcohol* and *body* of the wine. *Tedeschi; Quintarelli; Masi.*

☚ **Marqués de Riscal** [ris-KAHL] (*Rioja*, Spain) Historic *Rioja* name now back on form thanks to more modern winemaking for both reds and whites. The Baron de Chirel is the recently launched top wine.

Riserva [ree-ZEHR-vah] (Italy) *DOC* wines aged for a specified number of years – often an unwelcome term on labels of wines like *Bardolino*, which are usually far better drunk young.

🍇 **Rivaner** [rih-VAH-nur] (Germany) The name used for *Müller-Thurgau* (a cross between *Riesling* and *Sylvaner*) in parts of Germany and *Luxembourg*.

🍷 **Rivera** [ree-vay-ra] (*Puglia*, Italy) One of the new wave of producers who are turning the southern region of *Puglia* into a source of interesting wines. The red Riserva il Falcone is the star wine here.

Riverina [rih-vur-ee-na] (*New South Wales*, Australia) Irrigated *New South Wales* region which produces basic-to-good wine, much of which ends up in '*South-East Australian*' blends. *Late harvest Semillon*s can, however, be surprisingly spectacular. ***Cranswick Estate.***

Riverland (*South Australia*) Generic name for major irrigated wine-growing regions. Also referred to as MIA (Murrumbidgee Irrigation Area).

🍷 **Rivesaltes** [reev-zalt] (*Languedoc-Roussillon*, France) Fortified dessert wine of both colours. The white made from the *Muscat* is lighter and more lemony than *Beaumes de Venise*, while the *Grenache* red is like liquid Christmas pudding and ages wonderfully. ***Cazes; Ch. de Jau; Força Réal.***

Riviera Ligure di Ponente [reev-ee-yeh-ra lee-goo-ray dee poh-nen-tay] (*Liguria*, Italy) Little-known north-western region, close to Genoa, where local grapes like the *Vermentino* produce light aromatic reds and whites.

🍷 **Ch. de la Rivière** [rih-vee-yehr] (*Fronsac, Bordeaux*, France) Picture-book *Fronsac* property producing instantly accessible, *Merlot*-dominant red wines. Not the classiest of fare, but a lot more fun to drink than many a duller *St. Emilion* or more 'serious' (and pricier) wine from the *Médoc*. 82 83 **85 88** 89 90 94 95 96

Robertson (South Africa) Warm area where new-wave *Chardonnay*s and *Sauvignon*s are grabbing the spotlight from the *Muscat*s that used to be the region's pride. ***Robertson Winery; Graham Beck; Springfield.***

🍷 **Robertson's Well** (*South Australia*) One of *Mildara's* more reliable commercial labels.

🍷 **Rocca delle Macie** [ro-ka del leh mah-chee-yay] (*Tuscany*, Italy) Reliable if unspectacular *Chianti* producer.

🍷 **La Roche aux Moines** [rosh oh mwahn] *See Nicolas Joly.*

🍷 **Joe Rochioli** [roh-kee-yoh-lee] (*Sonoma*, California) Brilliant *Russian River Pinot Noir* producer. ☆☆☆☆☆ **1994 Pinot Noir £££**

🍷 **Rockford** (*Barossa Valley*, Australia) Robert, 'Rocky' O'Callaghan makes a great intense *Barossa Shiraz* using 100-year-old vines and 50-year-old equipment. There's a mouthfilling *Semillon*, a wonderful Black *Shiraz* fizz and a magical *Alicante Bouschet* rosé. Only to be found at the winery. ☆☆☆☆ **1992 Basket Press Shiraz, Barossa Valley £££**

🍷 **Antonin Rodet** [on-toh-nan roh-day] (*Burgundy*, France) Good *Mercurey*-based *négociant*, which has also improved the wines of the *Jacques Prieur* domaine in *Meursault*. ***Ch. de Chamiery; de Rully.***

🍷 **Louis Roederer** [roh-dur-rehr] (*Champagne*, France) Family-owned, and still one of the most reliable *Champagne* houses. No longer involved with the *Jansz* sparkling wine in *Tasmania* but making good fizz – sold as 'Quartet' – at the Roederer Estate in *Mendocino*, California. Roederer's Cristal remains a most deliciously 'wine-like' Champagne. ☆☆☆☆☆ **1998 Cristal ££££;** ☆☆☆☆ **Roederer Estate l'Hermitage ££££**

Michel Rolland [ROH-lon] Based in *Pomerol, St. Emilion*, and now increasingly international guru-oenologist, whose taste for ripe fruit flavours is influencing wines from Ch. *Ausone* to Argentina and beyond.

☎ **Rolly-Gassmann** [rroh-lee gas-sman] (*Alsace*, France) Fine producer of subtle, long-lasting wines which are sometimes slightly marred by an excess of *sulphur dioxide*.

☎ **Dom. de la Romanée-Conti** [rroh-ma-nay kon-tee] (*Burgundy*, France) Aka 'DRC'. Small *Grand Cru* estate. The jewel in the crown is the Romanée-Conti vineyard itself, though *La Tâche* runs it a close second. Both can be extraordinary, ultra-concentrated spicy wine, as can the *Romanée-St.-Vivant*. The *Richebourg*, *Echézeaux* and *Grands Echézeaux* and *Montrachet* are comparable to those produced by other estates – and sold by them for less kingly ransoms. ☆☆☆☆☆ 1994 La Tâche ££££

Romania Traditional source of sweet reds and whites, now developing drier styles from classic European varieties. *Flying winemakers* are helping, as is the owner of the *Comte Peraldi* estate in *Corsica*, but progress is slow. Note that Romania's well-praised *Pinot Noirs* may be made from a different variety which has been mistaken for the Pinot.

🌢**Romarantin** [roh-ma-ron-tan] (*Loire*, France) Interesting limey grape found in obscure white blends in the *Loire*. See *Cheverny*.

Romerlay [rroh-mehr-lay] (*Mosel*, Germany) One of the *grosslagen* in the *Ruwer* river valley. QbA/Kab/Spät: 85 86 **88 89 90** 91 92 93 94 95 96 97 Aus/Beeren/Tba **83 85** 88 89 90 91 92 93 94 95 96 97

☎ **Rongopai** [ron-goh-pi] (Te Kauwhata, New Zealand) Estate in a region of the North Island pioneered by *Cooks*, but which has fallen out of favour with that company and with other producers. The speciality here is *botrytis* wines, but the dry *Sauvignons* are good too.

☎ **La Rosa** (Chile) One of the fastest-growing wineries in Chile, with new vineyards and great winemaking from *Ignacio Recabarren*. Las Palmeras is a *second label*.

☎ **Quinta de la Rosa** (*Douro*, Portugal) Recently established estate producing excellent *port* and exemplary dry red wine, under guidance from David Baverstock, Australian-born former winemaker at *Dow's* and now filling a similar role at the nearby *Quinta do Crasto*. ☆☆☆☆ 1994 Vintage Port £££

Rosato (Italy) Rosé.

☎ **Rosé d'Anjou** [roh-zay don-joo] (*Loire*, France) Widely exported, usually dull semi-sweet pink from the *Malbec*, *Groslot* and *Cabernet Franc*.

☎ **Rosé de Riceys** [roh-zay dur ree-say] (*Champagne*, France) Rare and occasionally delicious still rosé from the *Pinot Noir*. Pricy.

☎ **Rosemount Estate** (*Hunter Valley*, Australia) Ultra-dynamic company which introduced the world to *oaky Hunter Chardonnay* with its Show Reserve. Reliably good-value blends from other areas have followed, including impressive *Syrahs* and *Chardonnays* from the newly developed region of *Orange* and *Mountain Blue* from *Mudgee*. Not the Rolls Royce of Aussie wines; more the BMW. ☆☆☆☆☆ 1994 Balmoral Syrah £££

☎ **Rosenblum** (*Alameda*, California) Terrific characterful *Zinfandels* from a wide variety of individual vineyards in *Napa*, *Sonoma*, *Contra Costa* and *Paso Robles*. There are also some great multi-regional Californian blends.

☎ **Dom. Rossignol-Trapet** [ros-seen-yol tra-pay] (*Burgundy*, France) Once old-fashioned, now more recommendable estate in *Gevrey-Chambertin*. ☆☆☆☆ 1993 Latricières-Chambertin ££££

☎ **Rosso Conero** [ros-doh kon-neh-roh] (*Marches*, Italy) Big *Montepulciano* and *Sangiovese* red, with a rich, herby flavour. Good value characterful stuff. ☆☆☆☆ 1995 Agontano Riserva, Gioacchino Garofoli £££

�})℻ **Rosso di Montalcino** [ros-soh dee mon-tal-chee-noh] (*Tuscany*, Italy)
DO for lighter, earlier-drinking versions of the more famous *Brunello di Montalcino*. Often better – and better value – than that wine. 82 85 88 90 91 93 94 95 96 97 *Altesino; Caparzo*; Fattoria dei Barbi.

☙ **René Rostaing** [ros-tang] (*Rhône*, France) Producer of serious northern
Rhône reds, including a rather more affordable alternative to *Guigal's* la Landonne. ☆☆☆☆ 1995 Côte Rôtie la Landonne ££££

☙ **Rothbury Estate** (*Hunter Valley*, Australia) Founded by *Len Evans*,
Svengali of the Australian wine industry and now – via *Mildara* – a subsidiary of Fosters, this is a great source of *Shiraz*, *Semillon* and *Chardonnay* from the *Hunter Valley*. There are also wines from nearby *Cowra* and first class *Sauvignon* from the bit of the estate that surfaces in *Marlborough*, New Zealand. ☆☆☆☆ 1996 Brokenback Chardonnay ££

☙ **Joseph Roty** [roh-tee] (*Burgundy*, France) Superstar producer of a range
of intensely concentrated but unsubtle wines in *Gevrey-Chambertin*. ☆☆☆☆ 1993 Mazis Chambertin ££££

☙ **Rouge Homme** (*Coonawarra*, Australia) Founded by the linguistically
talented *Mr Redman*, but now part of the huge *Penfolds* empire. This is increasingly one of the most reliable producers in *Coonawarra*. Reds are still more successful than whites, however. ☆☆☆☆ 1994 Rouge Homme Coonawarra Cabernet £££

☙ **Dom. Guy Roulot** [roo-loh] (*Burgundy*, France) One of the greatest
domaines in *Meursault*. ☆☆☆ 1993 Meursault les Vireuils ££££

☙ **Georges Roumier** [roo-me-yay] (*Burgundy*, France) Blue-chip winery
with great quality at every level, from village *Chambolle-Musigny* to the *Grand Cru*, Bonnes Mares and (more rarely seen) white *Corton-Charlemagne*. ☆☆☆☆ 1995 Chambolle-Musigny les Amoureuses ££££

☙ **Round Hill** (*Napa*, California) A name to remember for anyone
looking for Californian bargains. Large-production, inexpensive *Merlots* and *Chardonnays* that outclass many a pricier offering from smart boutique wineries.

🍷 **Roussanne** [roos-sahn] (*Rhône*, France) With the *Marsanne*, one of the
key white grapes of the northern *Rhône*. Producers argue over their relative merits.

☙ **Armand Rousseau** [roos-soh] (*Burgundy*, France) *Gevrey-Chambertin*
estate on top form with a range of *Premiers* and *Grands Crus*. Well-made, long-lasting wines. ☆☆☆☆ 1995 Charmes-Chambertin ££££

Roussillon [roos-see-yon] (*Languedoc-Roussillon*, France) Vibrant
up-and-coming region, redefining traditional varieties, especially *Muscat*.

☙ **Ch. Routas** [roo-tahs] (*Provence*, France) Impressive little producer of
intense reds and whites in the Coteaux Varois. 1995 Rouvier Coteaux Varois £££

☙ **Royal Oporto Wine Co.** (*Douro*, Portugal) Occasionally (very occasionally) successful, large producer.

☙ **The Royal Tokaji Wine Co.** (*Tokaji*, Hungary) Recently-founded
company helping to drag *Tokaji* into the late 20th century. ☆☆☆☆ 1991 Royal Tokaji Aszú 5 Puttonyos £££

☙ **Rubesco di Torgiano** [roo-bes-koh dee taw-jee-yah-noh] (*Umbria*,
Italy) Modern red *DOCG*; more or less the exclusive creation of *Lungarotti*. ☆☆☆ 1986 Rubesco Riserva £££

Ruby (*Douro*, Portugal) Cheapest, basic *port*; young, blended, sweetly fruity.

🍷 **Ruby Cabernet** [roo-bee k-behr-nay] (California) A *Cabernet Sauvignon*
and *Carignan* cross producing unsubtly fruity wines in California, Australia and South Africa.

🍷 **Ruche** [roo-kay] (*Piedmont*, Italy) Raspberryish red grape from northern
Italy producing early-drinking wines. Best from *Bava*.

Rüdesheim [rroo-des-hime] (*Rheingau*, Germany) Tourist town producing powerful *Rieslings*. QbA/Kab/Spät: **85** 86 **88 89 90** 91 92 93 94 95 96 Aus/Beeren/Tba **83 85** 88 89 90 91 92 93 94 95 96 97 ***Georg Breuer.***

🍷 **Rueda** [roo-way-dah] (Spain) *DO* in north-west Spain for clean, dry whites from the local *Verdejo*. Progress is being led most particularly by the *Lurtons*, *Marqués de Riscal* and *Marqués de Griñon*.

🍷 **Ruffino** [roof-fee-noh] (*Tuscany*, Italy) Big *Chianti* producer with impressive top-of-the-range wines, including the reliable Cabreo *Vino da Tavola*. 85 88 90 91 93 94 ☆☆☆☆☆ **1993 Ducale Riserva £££**

Rufina [roo-fee-na] (*Tuscany*, Italy) A sub-region within *Chianti*, producing supposedly classier wine. **78 79** 81 **82 85 88 90** 94 95 97

🍷 **Ruinart** [roo-wee-nahr] (*Champagne*, France) High-quality sister to *Moët & Chandon*, with a superlative *Blanc de Blancs*. ☆☆☆☆☆ **1990 R. de Ruinart ££££**

🍇 **Rülander** [roo-len-dur] (Germany) German name for *Pinot Gris*.

🍷 **Rully** [roo-yee] (*Burgundy*, France) *Côte Chalonnaise commune* producing rich white and a red that's been called the 'poor man's' *Volnay*. See *Antonin Rodet, Jadot* and *Olivier Leflaive*. Red: **78** 80 **85** 86 87 88 89 90 92 95 White: 84 **85 86** 87 **88** 89 **90 92** 95 ***Faiveley; Jadot; Olivier Leflaive; Antonin Rodet.***

Ruppertsberg [roo-purt-sbehrg] (*Pfalz*, Germany) Top-ranking village with a number of excellent vineyards making vigorous fruity *Riesling*. QbA/Kab/Spät: **85** 86 **88 89 90** 91 92 93 94 95 96 Aus/Beeren/Tba: **83 85** 88 89 90 91 92 93 94 95 96 97 **Bürklin-Wolf; Kimich; Werlé.**

Russe [rooss] (Bulgaria) Danube town best known in Britain for its reliable red blends but vaunted in *Bulgaria* as a source of modern whites.

Russian River Valley (California) Cult cool-climate area to the north of *Sonoma* and west of *Napa*. Ideal for apples and good fizz, as is proven by the excellent *Iron Horse*, which also makes impressive table wines. Great *Pinot Noir* country. Red: 84 **85** 86 87 **90 91 92** 93 95 96 White: **85 90 91** 92 95 96 ***Dehlinger; de Loach; Iron Horse; Kistler; Martinelli; Rochioli; Sonoma-Cutrer; Joseph Swann; Marimar Torres; Williams Selyem.***

Rust [roost] (*Burgenland*, Austria) Wine centre of *Burgenland*, famous for Ruster *Ausbruch* sweet white wine.

🍷 **Rust-en-Vrede** (*Stellenbosch*, South Africa) Well regarded producer but could improve, in my opinion. ☆☆☆ **1994 Tinta Barocca ££**

🍷 **Rustenberg** (*Stellenbosch*, South Africa) New winemaking brooms are sweeping through this well-regarded estate. The post 1996 wines look promising – including the lower-priced Brampton efforts.

Rutherford (California) *Napa* region in which some producers believe sufficiently to propose it – and its geological 'bench' – as an *appellation*. Red: **85** 86 87 **90 91** 92 93 95 96 White: **90 91** 92 95 96

Rutherglen (*Victoria*, Australia) Hot area on the *Murray River* pioneered by gold miners. Today noted for rich *Muscat* and *Tokay* dessert and *port*-style wines, incredibly tough reds and *Chardonnays* which are used by cool-region winemakers to demonstrate why *port* and light dry whites cannot be successful in the same climate. **Chambers; Morris; All Saints; Campbells.**

Ruwer [roo-vur] (*Mosel-Saar-Ruwer*, Germany) *Mosel* tributary alongside which is to be found the *Romerlay grosslage*, and includes Kasel, *Eitelsbach* and the great *Maximin Grunhaus* estate. QbA/Kab/Spät: **85 86 88 89 90** 92 93 94 95 96 97 Aus/Beeren/Tba: 83 **85** 88 89 90 92 93 94 95 96 97

Hugh Ryman [ri-man] *Flying winemaker* whose team turns grapes into wine under contract in *Bordeaux, Burgundy*, southern France, Spain, Germany, Moldova, Chile, California, South Africa and Hungary. The give-away sign of a Ryman wine is the initials HDR at the foot of the label. Now though, more wines carry Ryman's own brands: Santara, Kirkwood, Richemont, Rafael Estate. ☆☆☆☆ **1995 Santara Carbonell Cabernet ££**

�*ī* **Rymill** [ri-mil] (*South Australia*) One of several *Coonawarra* wineries to mention *Riddoch* on its label (in its Riddoch Run). Rymill at least has the legitimacy of a family link to *John Riddoch*, the region's founder. The *Shiraz* and *Cabernet* are first class. ☆☆☆☆ **1995 Cabernet Sauvignon £££**

S

Saale-Unstrut [zah-luhr oon-strurt] (Germany) Remember East Germany? Well, this is where poor wines used to be made there in the bad old days. Today good ones are being produced, by producers like Lützkendorf.

Saar [zahr] (*Mosel-Saar-Ruwer*, Germany) The other *Mosel* tributary associated with lean slatey *Riesling*. Villages include *Ayl, Ockfen,* Saarburg, Serrig and *Wiltingen*. QbA/Kab/Spät: **85 88 89 90** 91 92 93 94 95 96 97 Aus/Beeren/Tba: **83 85** 88 89 90 91 92 93 94 95 96 97

Sablet (*Rhône*, France) Good *Côtes du Rhône* village. Red: **78** 81 **82 83 85 88** 89 90 95 96

�*ī* **St. Amour** [san ta-moor] (*Burgundy*, France) One of the eleven *Beaujolais Crus* – usually light and fruity. **88 89** 90 **91** 93 94 95 96 97 **Billards; Patissier; Revillon; la Cave Lamartine; *Duboeuf*.**

�*ī* **St. Aubin** [san toh-ban] (*Burgundy*, France) Underrated *Côte d'Or* village for (jammily rustic) reds and rich, nutty, rather classier white; affordable alternatives to *Meursault*. White: 79 84 **85 86** 87 **88** 89 **90 92** 95 Red: 78 80 83 **85** 86 87 **88 89 90** 92 95 *Marc Colin;* **Roux Père et Fils;** *Gérard Thomas; Olivier Leflaive.*

�*ī* **St. Chinian** [san shee-nee-yon] (*South-West*, France) Neighbour of *Faugères* in the *Coteaux du Languedoc*, producing mid-weight wines from *Carignan* and other *Rhône* grapes. **Ch. Babeau; Ch. Quartironi de Sars; Mas Champart; Mas de la Tour; Maurel Fonsalade.**

✗ **St. Clement** (*Napa Valley*, California) Japanese-owned winery whose best wine is the Oroppas red blend. Just in case you were wondering, the name isn't a native American word, but that of the owner's name spelled backwards.

✗ **St.Emilion** [san tay-mee-lee-yon] (*Bordeaux*, France) Large *commune* with very varied soils and wines. At best, sublime *Merlot*-dominated *claret*; at worst dull, earthy and fruitless. 170 or so '*Grand Cru*' St. Emilions are produced in better-sited vineyards and have to undergo a tasting every vintage to be able to use these words on their labels. (Too few fail.) *Grand Cru Classé* refers to 68 *châteaux*, of which two – *Ausone* and *Cheval-Blanc* – are rated as 'Premier *Grands Crus Classés* "A"' and 11 are 'Premiers *Grands Crus Classés* "B"'. These ratings are reviewed every decade. Supposedly 'lesser' satellite neighbours – *Lussac, Puisseguin, St. Georges* etc. – often make better value wine than basic St. Emilion. **70 75** 78 79 81 **82 83 85** 86 **88 89** 90 94 95 96 *Pavie; Angelus; Ausone; Canon; Figeac; Cheval Blanc; Troplong Mondot.*

✗ **St.Estèphe** [san teh-stef] (*Bordeaux*, France) Northernmost *Médoc commune* with clay soil and wines which can be a shade more rustic than those of neighbouring *Pauillac* and *St. Julien*, but which are often longer-lived and more structured than some of the juicily easy to drink *St. Emilions* and *Pomerols* that tend to win approval from critics. 70 75 76 **78 82** 83 **85** 86 **88 89** 90 91 92 93 94 95 96 *Calon Segur; Cos d'Estournel; Montrose; Phelan-Ségur; Lafon-Rochet; de Pez; Marbuzet; Haut-Marbuzet; Ormes de Pez.*

✗ **St.Francis** (*Sonoma*, California) Innovative winery with great *Zinfandels*, and Reserve *Chardonnays* and *Cabernets*. The first Californian to introduce artificial corks in a laudable effort to protect wine drinkers from faulty bottles. ☆☆☆☆ **1994 Pagani Vineyard Reserve Zinfandel £££**

✗ **St. Georges-St.Emilion** [san jorrzh san tay-mee-lee-yon] (*Bordeaux*, France) Satellite of *St. Emilion* with good *Merlot*-dominant reds, often better value than *St. Emilion* itself. **82 83 85** 86 **88 89** 90 94 95 96 **Ch. St. Georges; Maquin St. Georges.**

✗ **St. Hallett** (*Barossa Valley*, Australia) Superstar *Barossa* winery specialising in wines from old ('old block') *Shiraz* vines. Whites are improving too. ☆☆☆☆ **1996 Faith Shiraz £££**

✗ **St. Hubert's** (*Victoria*, Australia) Improving (since its purchase by *Rothbury*) but now, following a further purchase, part of the Fosters' empire. For the moment at least, pioneering *Yarra* winery with ultra-fruity *Cabernet* and mouthfilling whites. ☆☆☆☆ **1996 Sauvignon Blanc ££**

✗ **Chateau St. Jean** [jeen] (*Sonoma*, California) Named after the founder's wife; now Japanese-owned and a source of good single-vineyard *Chardonnays*, late harvest *Rieslings* and *Bordeaux*-style reds. ☆☆☆☆ **1992 Cabernet Sauvignon Sonoma County Cinq Cépages £££**

✗ **St. Joseph** [san joh-sef] (*Rhône*, France) Potentially vigorous, fruity *Syrah* from the northern *Rhône*. Whites range from flabby to fragrant *Marsannes*. Red: **76 78 82 83 85** 88 89 90 91 95 96 *St.-Désirat; Grippat; Coursodon; Cuilleron; Chave; Gaillard; Graillot; Gripa; Trollo; du Chênes; Gacho-Pascal; Dom. de Fauturie.*

✗ **St. Julien** [san-joo-lee-yen] (*Bordeaux*, France) Aristocratic *Médoc commune* producing classic rich wines, full of cedar and deep ripe fruit. 70 75 76 **78** 79 81 **82** 83 **85 86** 88 89 90 94 95 96 *Léoville-Barton; Léoville-Las-Cases; Ducru-Beaucaillou; Beychevelle; Branaire.*

🍇**St. Laurent** [sant loh-rent] (Austria) *Pinot Noir*-like berryish red grape, mastered, in particular, by *Umathum*.

🍷 **St. Nicolas de Bourgueil** [san nee-koh-lah duh boor-goyl] (*Loire*, France) Lightly fruity *Cabernet Franc*; needs a warm year to ripen its raspberry fruit, but then can last for up to a decade. Lighter than *Bourgueil*. Red: 85 86 **88 89** 90 92 93 95 96 *Jamet*; Mabileau; Vallée.

🍷 **St. Péray** [san pay-reh] (*Rhône*, France) *AC* near Lyon for full-bodied, still white and *méthode champenoise* sparkling wine, at risk from encroaching housing. *Auguste Clape; Alain Voge; Jean Lionnet*.

🍷 **Ch. St. Pierre** [san pee-yehr] (*St. Julien 4ème Cru Classé*, *Bordeaux*, France) Reliable *St. Julien* under the same ownership as *Ch. Gloria*.

🍷 **St. Romain** [san roh-man] (*Burgundy*, France) *Hautes Côtes de Beaune* village producing undervalued fine whites and rustic reds. White: 87 **88** 89 **90** 92 93 94 95 Red: 83 **85** 86 87 **88** 89 90 92 95 **Alain Gras; Thevenin-Monthelie; *Jaffelin*.**

🍷 **St. Véran** [san vay-ron] (*Burgundy*, France) Once sold as *Beaujolais* Blanc; affordable alternative to *Pouilly-Fuissé*; better than most *Mâconnais* whites. Ch. Fuissé is worth keeping an eye out for. White: 89 **90 91 92** 93 94 95 **Dom des Deux Roches; *Corsin*; Luquet; Pacquet; *Duboeuf*.**

🍷 **Ste. Croix-du-Mont** [sant crwah doo mon] (*Bordeaux*, France) Never as luscious, rich and complex as the better efforts of its neighbour *Sauternes* – but often a far more worthwhile buy than wines unashamedly sold under that name. Sweet White: 86 87 **88 90** 92 93 94 95

🍷 **Saintsbury** (*Carneros*, California) Superstar *Carneros* producer of unfiltered *Chardonnay* and – more specially – *Pinot Noir*. The slogan: '*Beaune* in the USA' refers to the winery's Burgundian aspirations! The Reserve *Pinot* is a world-beater, while the easy-going Garnet is the good *second label*. ☆☆☆☆ **1994 Carneros Pinot Noir £££**

Sakar [sa-kah] (Bulgaria) Long-time source of much of the best *Cabernet Sauvignon* to come from *Bulgaria*.

🍷 **Castello della Sala** [kas-tel-loh del-la sah-lah] (*Umbria*, Italy) *Antinori's* over-priced but sound *Chardonnay, Sauvignon*. Also good *Sauvignon*/Procanico blend. ☆☆☆☆☆ **1996 Sauvignon della Sala ££**

🍷 **Salice Salentino** [sa-lee-chay sah-len-tee-noh] (*Puglia*, Italy) Spicy intense red made from the characterful *Negroamaro*. Great value, especially when mature. **Candido; Taurino; Vallone.**

🍷 **Salon le Mesnil** [sah-lon lur may-neel] (*Champagne*, France) Small traditional subsidiary of *Laurent Perrier* with cult following for pure long-lived *Chardonnay* fizz.

🍷 **Saltram** [sawl-tram] (*South Australia*) Much improved since its purchase by *Rothbury*. Now part of *Mildara*. Good, fairly priced *Barossa* reds and whites and top-flight '*ports*'. ☆☆☆☆ **1995 Mamre Brook Shiraz £££**

🍷 **Samos** [sah-mos] (Greece) Aegean island producing sweet, fragrant, golden *Muscat* once called 'the wine of the Gods'.

Cellier des Samsons [sel-yay day som-son] (*Burgundy*, France) Source of better-than-average *Beaujolais*.

San Luis Obispo [san loo-wis oh-bis-poh] (California) Californian region gaining a reputation for *Chardonnay* and *Pinot Noir*. Try *Edna Valley*. Red: 84 **85** 86 87 **90 91** 92 93 95 96 White: **85 90 91** 92 95 96

Viña San Pedro [veen-ya san-pay-droh] (*Curico*, Chile) Huge *Curico* firm whose wines are quietly improving thanks to the efforts of consultant *Jacques Lurton*. ☆☆☆☆ **1995 Cabernet Sauvignon Special Reserve ££**

Sancerre [son-sehr] (*Loire*, France) At its best, the epitome of elegant, steely dry *Sauvignon*; at its worst, over-sulphured, fruitless, dry wine. Reds and rosés, though well regarded and highly priced by French restaurants, are generally little better than quaffable *Pinot Noir*. **90** 94 95 96 **Jean-Max Roger; Bourgeois; Pierre Dézat; Crochet; Vacheron; Natter; Mellot; Vincent Pinard; Vatan.**

Sandeman (Spain/Portugal) North American-owned, generally under-performing but occasionally dazzling *port* and *sherry* producer. Port: **55** 57 58 **60 62 63** 65 66 67 68 **70** 72 75 80 94 ☆☆☆☆☆ **Royal Corregidor Rare Old Oloroso Sherry ££££**

Sanford Winery (*Santa Barbara*, California) *Santa Barbara* superstar producer of *Chardonnay* and especially distinctive, slightly horseradishy *Pinot Noir*. ☆☆☆☆ **1994 Pinot Noir £££**

Sangiovese [san-jee-yoh vay-seh] (Italy) The tobaccoey, herby-flavoured red grape of *Chianti* and *Montepulciano*, now being used increasingly in *Vino da Tavola* and – though rarely impressively – in California. **Atlas Peak; Antinori; Isole e Olena; Bonny Doon.**

Santa Barbara (California) Successful southern, cool-climate region for *Pinot Noir* and *Chardonnay*. See *Au Bon Climat* and *Sanford*, *Qupé* and Ojai. Red: 84 **85** 86 87 **90 91** 92 93 95 96 White: **85 90 91** 92 95 96

Viña Santa Carolina [ka-roh-lee-na] (Chile) Greatly improved producer, thanks to *Ignacio Recabarren* and vineyards in *Casablanca*. Still some way to go. Good reds. ☆☆☆☆ **1997 Maipo Chardonnay-Semillon £££**

Santa Cruz Mountains [krooz] (California) Exciting region to the south of San Francisco. See *Ridge* and *Bonny Doon*. Red: 84 **85** 86 87 **90 91** 92 93 95 96 White: **85 90 91** 92 95 96

Santa Emiliana (*Aconcagua*, Chile) Large producer with good Andes Peak offerings from *Casablanca*, and wines from the new southern region of Mulchen. ☆☆☆☆ **1997 Andes Peak Casablanca Chardonnay ££**

Santa Rita [ree-ta] (*Maipo*, Chile) Back on track after a slightly bumpy patch. The Casa Real is not only Chile's best red; it is also truly world class. ☆☆☆☆☆ **1995 Casa Real £££**

Santenay [sont-nay] (*Burgundy*, France) Southern *Côte d'Or* village, producing pretty whites and good, though occasionally rather rustic, reds. Look for *Girardin* and *Pousse d'Or*. White: 85 86 87 **88** 89 **90 92** 95 Red: 76 78 79 **80** 82 83 **85** 86 87 **88** 89 **90** 92 95 *Girardin; Colin; Pousse d'Or; Bernard Morey.*

Caves São João [sow-jwow] (*Bairrada*, Portugal) Small company which produces high-quality *Bairrada*.

Sardinia (Italy) Traditionally the source of powerful reds (try *Santadi*) and whites, increasingly interesting *DOC* fortified wines, and new-wave modern reds to match the best *Super Tuscans*. **Sella e Mosca.**

☖ **Sarget de Gruaud-Larose** [sahr-jay dur groowoh lah-rohs] (*St. Julien*, *Bordeaux*, France) *Second label of Ch. Gruaud-Larose.*

☖ **Sassicaia** [sas-see-ki-ya] (*Tuscany*, Italy) World-class *Cabernet*-based *Super Tuscan* with more of an Italian than a *claret* taste. No longer a mere *Vino da Tavola* since the *DOC* Bolgheri was introduced in 1994.

☖ **Saumur** [soh-moor] (*Loire*, France) Heartland of variable *Chenin*-based fizz and still white, and the potentially more interesting *Saumur-Champigny*. Red: 83 **85** 86 **88 89 90 95** 96 White: 83 **85** 86 **88 89 90** 94 95 96 Sweet White: **76** 83 **85** 86 **88 89** 90 94 95 **Langlois-Château; Cave des Vignerons de Saumur; Vatan; Villeneuve.**

☖ **Saumur-Champigny** [soh-moor shom-pee-nyee] (*Loire*, France) Crisp *Cabernet Franc* red; like *Beaujolais*, best served slightly chilled. Good examples are worth cellaring. **85** 86 **88 89 90** 95 96 **Ch. du Hureau; Targé; Vatan; Filliatreau; Villeneuve; Foucault;** *Bouvet-Ladubay.*

☖ **Sauternes** [soh-turn] (*Bordeaux*, France) Rich honeyed dessert wines from *Sauvignon* and *Sémillon* (and possibly *Muscadelle*) blends. Should be affected by *botrytis* but the climate does not always allow this. That's one explanation for disappointing Sauternes; the other is careless wine-making, and, in particular, a tendency to be heavy-handed with *sulphur dioxide*. 78 79 80 81 82 83 **85** 86 **88 89 90** 91 92 95 *Barsac; Yquem; Rieussec; Climens; Suduiraut; Bastor-Lamontagne.*

🍇 **Sauvignon Blanc** [SOH-vin-yon-BLON] 'Grassy', 'catty', 'asparagussy', 'gooseberryish' grape grown the world over, but rarely really loved, so often blended, oaked or made sweet. In France at home in the *Loire* and *Bordeaux*. New Zealand gets it right – especially in *Marlborough*. In Australia, *Knappstein, Cullens, Stafford Ridge, Amberley* and *Shaw & Smith* are right on target. *Mondavi's* oaked *Fumé Blanc* and *Kendall Jackson's* sweet versions are successful but *Monteviña, Quivira, Dry Creek, Simi* and – in blends with the *Semillon* – *Guenoc* and *Carmenet* are the stars. Chile is making better versions every year, despite starting out with a lesser variety. See *Caliterra, Canepa, Villiard.* In South Africa, see *Thelema, Mulderbosch* and *Neil Ellis.*

Sauvignon de St. Bris [SOH-vin-yon-dur san BREE] (*Burgundy*, France) *Burgundy's* only *VDQS.* An affordable and often worthwhile alternative to *Sancerre*, produced in vineyards near *Chablis.* 95 96 97 *Brocard; Moreau.*

☖ **Etienne Sauzet** [SOH-zay] (*Burgundy*, France) First-rank estate whose white wines are almost unfindable outside collectors' cellars and Michelin-starred restaurants. ☆☆☆☆ **1995 Montrachet ££££**

🍇 **Savagnin** [sa-van-yan] (*Jura*, France) No relation of the *Sauvignon*; a white *Jura* variety used for *Vin Jaune* and blended with *Chardonnay* for *Arbois.* Also, confusingly, the Swiss name for the *Gewürztraminer.*

☖ **Savennières** [sa-ven-yehr] (*Loire*, France) Fine, if sometimes aggressively dry *Chenin Blanc* whites. Very long-lived. **86 88 89 90** 94 95 96 **Soulez; d'Epiré; Baumard;** *Coulée de Serrant; La Roche aux Moines.*

☖ **Savigny-lès-Beaune** [sa-veen-yee lay bohn] (*Burgundy*, France) Distinctive whites (sometimes made from *Pinot Blanc*) and raspberry reds. At their best can compare with *Beaune.* White: 79 **85** 86 87 **88** 89 **90** 92 95 96 Red: 78 80 83 **85** 86 87 **88 89 90** 92 95 96 *Simon Bize; Chandon de Briailles; Ecard; Girardin; Pavelot; Tollot-Beaut.*

Savoie [sav-wah] (Eastern France) Mountainous region near Geneva producing crisp floral whites such as Abymes, *Apremont, Seyssel* and *Crépy.*

♆ **Saxenburg** (*Stellenbosch*, South Africa) A *Cape* winery to interest anyone who prefers rich, ripely flavoursome wines to some of the mean fare on offer in South Africa.

♆ **Scavino** [ska-vee-noh] (*Piedmont*, Italy) Terrific new-wave, juicy reds, including single-vineyard *Barolos, Barberas* and *Dolcettos.* ☆☆☆☆ 1993 Barolo Canubi £££

♆ **Scharffenberger** [shah-fen-bur-gur] (*Mendocino*, California) Pommery-owned, independently-run producer of top-class, top-value fizz. ☆☆☆☆ Scharffenberger Brut £££

Scharzhofberg [shahts-hof-behrg] (*Mosel-Saar-Ruwer*, Germany) Top-class *Saar* vineyard, producing great *Riesling.* QbA/Kab/Spät: 85 86 **88 89 90** 91 92 93 94 95 96 97 Aus/Beeren/Tba: 83 **85 88 89** 90 91 92 93 94 95 96 97 *Reichsgraf von Kesselstadt.*

Schaumwein [showm-vine] (Germany) Low-priced sparkling wine.

❦**Scheurebe** [shoy-ray-bur] (Germany) *Riesling* x *Sylvaner* cross, grown in Germany and in England. Tastes deliciously and recognisably like pink grapefruit. In Austria, where it is used to make brilliant sweet wines, they sometimes call it Samling 88. *Lingenfelder; Alois Kracher.*

❦**Schiava** [skee yah-vah] (*Alto-Adige*, Italy) Grape used in *Lago di Caldaro* to make light reds.

Schilfwein [shilf-vine] (Austria) Luscious 'reed wine' – Austrian *vin de paille* pioneered by *Willi Opitz.*

Schloss [shloss] (Germany) Literally 'castle', vineyard or estate.

Schloss Böckelheim [shloss boh-kell-hime] (*Nahe*, Germany) Varied southern part of the *Nahe*. Wines from the Kupfergrübe vineyard and the State Wine Domaine are worth buying. QbA/Kab/Spät: 85 86 **88 89 90** 91 92 93 94 95 96 97 Aus/Beeren/Tba: 83 **85 88 89** 90 91 92 93 94 95 96 97

♆ **Schloss Reinhartshausen** [shloss rine-harts-how-zehn] (*Rheingau*, Germany) Innovative estate successful with *Pinot Blanc* and *Chardonnay* (the latter introduced following a suggestion by *Robert Mondavi*). The *Rieslings* are good too. QbA/Kab/Spät: **85 88 89 90** 91 92 93 94 95 96 97 Aus/Beeren/Tba: **83 85 88 89** 90 91 92 93 94 95 96 97

♆ **Schloss Saarstein** [shloss sahr-stine] (*Mosel-Saar-Ruwer*, Germany) High-quality *Riesling* specialist in Serrig. QbA/Kab/Spät: 85 86 **88 89 90** 91 92 93 94 95 96 Aus/Beeren/Tba: **83 85 88** 89 90 91 92 93 94 95 96 ☆☆☆☆ 1996 Serriger Saarsteiner Riesling Spätlese £££

♆ **Schloss Vollrads** [shloss fol-rahts] (*Rheingau*, Germany) Long-time under-performing *Charta* pioneer and devout believer in German dry wines. Following the death of the man behind it – Graf Matuschka-Greiffenclau – things may change.

Schlossbockelheim [shloss bok-el-hime] (*Nahe*, Germany) Village which gives its name to a large *Nahe bereich,* producing elegant *Riesling.* QbA/Kab/Spät: 85 86 **88 89 90** 91 92 93 94 95 96 Aus/Beeren/Tba: 83 **85 88** 89 90 91 92 93 94 95 97 Staatsweingut Niederhausen.

♆ **Schlossgut Diel** [deel] (*Nahe*, Germany) Armin Diel is both wine writer and winemaker. Co-author of the excellent 1998 Gault Millau German Wine Guide, his Dorsheimer Goldloch wines are worth seeking out.

♆ **Dom. Schlumberger** [shloom-behr-jay] (*Alsace*, France) Great, quite sizeable estate whose subtle top level wines can often rival those of the somewhat more showy *Zind Humbrecht.* ☆☆☆☆ 1993 Riesling Kitterlé £££

🍷 **Schramsberg** [shram-sberg] (*Napa Valley*, California) The winery that single-handedly put Californian fizz on the quality trail. Wines used to be too big for their boots, possibly because too many of the grapes were from warm vineyards in *Napa*. The J Schram is aimed at *Dom Pérignon* and gets pretty close to the target. ☆☆☆☆ **1990 J Schram ££££**

🍷 **Scotchman's Hill** (*Victoria*, Australia) *Pinot Noir* specialist in *Geelong*. *Sauvignons* and *Chardonnays* have been less exciting.

🍷 **Screaming Eagle** (*Napa Valley*, California) Miniscule winery the size of many people's living room, and producing around 200 cases of intense *Cabernet* since 1992. The owners are avowedly trying to make California's greatest wine. Sadly most people will only ever read about it.

🍷 **Seaview** (*South Australia*) *Penfolds* brand for (excellent) fizz and (less frequently) *McLaren Vale* red table wines. Look out for the Edwards & Chaffey label too. ☆☆☆☆ **1995 Pinot Noir/Chardonnay £££**

🍷 **Sebastiani** [seh-bas-tee-yan-nee] (*Sonoma Valley*, California) The main activity here lies in producing inexpensive, unexceptional wine from *Central Valley* grapes. Higher grade *Sonoma* wines are more interesting. The *Zinfandel* is the strongest suit.

Sec/secco/seco [se-koh] (France/Italy/Spain) Dry.

Second label (*Bordeaux*, France) Wine from a producer's (generally a *Bordeaux Château*) lesser vineyards, younger vines and/or lesser *cuvées* of wine. Especially worth buying in good vintages. See *Les Forts de Latour.*

🍷 **Segura Viudas** [say-goo-rah vee-yoo-dass] (*Catalonia*, Spain) The quality end of the *Freixenet* giant. One of the better examples of traditional *cava*. ☆☆☆ **Cava Reserva £££**

🍷 **Seifried Estate** [see-freed] (*Nelson*, New Zealand) Also known as *Redwood Valley Estate*. Hermann Seifried makes superb *Riesling* especially *late harvest* style, and very creditable *Sauvignon* and *Chardonnay,* in the up-and-coming region of *Nelson*.

Sekt [zekt] (Germany) Very basic sparkling wine – best won in rifle booths at carnivals. Watch out for anything that does not state that it is made from *Riesling* – other grape varieties almost invariably make highly unpleasant wines. Only the prefix 'Deutscher' guarantees German origin.

🍷 **Selaks** [see-lax] (*Auckland*, New Zealand) Large successful company in Kumeu best known for the piercingly fruity *Sauvignon* first made by a young man called Kevin Judd, who went on to produce *Cloudy Bay!*

🍷 **Weingut Selbach-Oster** [zel-bahkh os-tehr] (*Mosel-Saar-Ruwer*, Germany) Archetypal *Mosel Riesling*.

Sélection de Grains Nobles (SGN) [say-lek-see-yon day gran nohbl] (*Alsace*, France) Equivalent to German *Beerenauslese*; rich, sweet *botrytised* wine from specially selected grapes.

🍷 **Sella e Mosca** [seh-la eh mos-kah] (*Sardinia*, Italy) Dynamic firm with a good *Cabernet* called Villamarina, the rich *Anghelu Ruju* and traditional *Cannonau*. ☆☆☆☆ **1992 Tanca Farra ££**

🍷 **Fattoria Selvapiana** [fah-taw-ree-ya sel-va-pee-yah-nah] (*Tuscany*, Italy) Benchmark *Chianti Rufina*, excellent *vin santo,* and olive oil. ☆☆☆☆ **1994 Chianti Rufina Riserva £££**

🍇 **Sémillon** [in France: say-mee-yon; in Australia: seh-mil-lon and even seh-mih-lee-yon] Peachy grape generally blended with *Sauvignon* to make sweet and dry *Bordeaux*, and vinified separately in Australia, where it is also sometimes blended with *Chardonnay*. Rarely as successful in other New World countries where many versions taste more like *Sauvignon*. ***Carmenet; Geyser Peak; Rothbury, McWilliams; Xanadu.***

🍷 **Seña** [sen-ya] (Chile) Red wine produced by *Mondavi* and *Caliterra*. A Mercedes of a wine: well put together but emphatically unexciting.

🍷 **Seppelt** (*South Australia*) *Penfolds* subsidiary and pioneer of the *Great Western* region where it makes rich still and sparkling *Shiraz*. Other Seppelt fizzes are recommendable too, though the once-fine Salinger seems to have lost its way recently. ☆☆☆☆ **1993 Chalambar Shiraz £££**

🍷 **Serasin** [seh-ra-sin] (*Marlborough*, New Zealand) New venture launched by a British movie cameraman. Impeccable vineyards and really impressive *Chardonnay, Sauvignon* and a promising *Pinot Noir*.

Servir frais (France) Serve chilled.

☲ **Setúbal** [shtoo-bal] (Portugal) *DOC* on the *Setúbal Peninsula*.

Setúbal Peninsula (Portugal) Home of the *Setúbal DOC*, but now equally notable for the rise of two new wine regions, Arrabida and Palmela, where *JM Fonseca Succs* and *JP Vinhos* are making some excellent wines from local and international grape varieties. The lusciously rich *Moscatel de Setúbal*, however, is still the star of the show.

☲ **Seyssel** [say-sehl] (*Savoie*, France) *AC* region near Geneva producing light white wines that are usually enjoyed in après-ski mood when no-one is overly concerned about value for money. *Varichon et Clerc.*

🍇**Seyval Blanc** [aay-vahl blon] *Hybrid* grape – a cross between French and US vines – unpopular with EU authorities but successful in eastern US, Canada and England, especially at *Breaky Bottom*.

☲ **Shafer** [shay-fur] (*Napa Valley*, California) Top *Cabernet* producer in the *Stag's Leap* district, and maker of some increasingly classy *Chardonnay* and *Merlot* from *Carneros*. ☆☆☆☆ **1995 Cabernet Sauvignon Stag's Leap District £££**

☲ **Shaw & Smith** (*Adelaide Hills*, Australia) Recently founded winery producing one of Australia's best *Sauvignons* and a pair of increasingly Burgundian *Chardonnays* that demonstrate how good wines from this variety can taste with and without oak. ☆☆☆☆ **1996 Sauvignon Blanc £££**

☲ *Sherry* (*Jerez*, Spain) The fortified wine made in the area surrounding *Jerez*. Wines made elsewhere – Australia, England, South Africa, etc.– may now no longer use the name. See also *Almacenista; Fino; Amontillado; Manzanilla; Cream Sherry. Barbadillo; Lustau; Gonzalez Byass; Hidalgo.*

🍇**Shiraz** [shee-raz] (Australia, South Africa) The *Syrah* grape in Australia and South Africa, taking its name from its supposed birthplace in Iran. South African versions are, incidentally, as different in style (lighter and generally greener) from the Australians, as the Aussies are from the (less ripe and *oaky*) efforts of the *Rhône. Wolf Blass; Penfolds; Henschke; Rothbury; St. Hallett; Rockford; Plantagenet; Saxenburg.*

Sicily (Italy) Historically best known for *Marsala* and sturdy 'southern' table wine. Now, however, there is an array of other unusual fortified wines and a fast-growing range of new-wave reds and whites, many of which are made from grapes grown nowhere else on earth. *Corvo; de Bartoli; Regaleali; Terre di Ginestra.*

☲ **Sieur d'Arques** [see-uhr dark] (*Languedoc-Roussillon*, France) High-tech cooperative in *Limoux* that ought to serve as a role model to its neighbours. Good *Blanquette de Limoux* fizz and truly impressive *Chardonnays* sold under the Toques et Clochers label.

☲ **Siglo** [seeg-loh] (*Rioja*, Spain) Good brand of modern red (traditionally sold in a hessian 'sack') and old-fashioned whites.

☲ **Signorello** (*Napa Valley*, California) Small winery making Burgundian *Chardonnay* with lots of yeasty richness, *Bordeaux*-style *Semillon* and *Sauvignon* as well as *Cabernets* that are both blackcurranty and stylish.

Silex [see-lex] (France) Term describing flinty soil, used by *Didier Dagueneau* for his oak-fermented *Pouilly-Fumé*.

☲ **Silver Oak Cellars** (*Napa Valley*, California) Specialist *Cabernet* producers favouring fruitily accessible, but still classy, wines which benefit from long ageing in (American oak) barrels and bottle before release. Look out for older vintages of the single-vineyard Bonny's Vineyard wines, the last of which was made in 1991. ☆☆☆☆☆ **1993 Cabernet Sauvignon Alexander Valley ££££**

☨ **Silverado** [sil-veh-rah-doh] (*Napa Valley*, California) Reliable *Cabernet*, *Chardonnay* and now *Sangiovese* winery that belongs to Walt Disney's widow. ☆☆☆☆ **1996 Art Cuvée Chardonnay £££**

☨ **Simi Winery** [see-mee] (*Sonoma Valley*, California) *Moët & Chandon* subsidiary run by the thoughtful Zelma Long and making complex, long-lived Burgundian *Chardonnay,* archetypical *Sauvignon* and lovely blackcurranty *Alexander Valley Cabernet.*

☨ **Bert Simon** (*Mosel-Saar-Ruwer*, Germany) Newish estate in the *Saar* river valley with super-soft *Rieslings* and unusually elegant *Weissburgunder.*

☨ **Simonsig Estate** [see-mon-sikh] (*Stellenbosch*, South Africa) A big estate with a very impressive commercial range, and the occasional gem – try the *Shiraz, Cabernet, Pinotage* and Kaapse Vonkel sparkler. ☆☆☆ **1995 Cabernet Sauvignon ££**

Sin Crianza [sin cree-an-tha] (Spain) Not aged in wood.

☨ **Ch. Siran** [see-ron] (*Margaux Cru Bourgeois, Bordeaux*, France) Beautiful *château* outperforming its classification and producing increasingly impressive and generally very fairly priced wines. 70 **75 78** 81 **82** 83 85 86 88 89 90 93 94 95 96

☨ **Skalli-Fortant de France** *See Fortant de France.*

☨ **Skillogalee** [skil-log-gah-lee] (*Clare Valley*, Australia) Well-respected *Clare* producer, specialising in *Riesling*, but also showing his skill with reds. ☆☆☆☆ **1996 Shiraz, Clare Valley ££**

Skin contact The longer the skins of black grapes are left in with the juice after the grapes have been crushed, the greater the *tannin* and the deeper the colour. Some non-aromatic white varieties (*Chardonnay* and *Semillon* in particular) can also benefit from extended skin contact (usually between six and twenty-four hours) to increase flavour.

Sliven [slee-ven] Bulgarian region offering good value, simple reds and better-than-average whites.

Slovakia Up-and-coming source of wines from grapes little seen elsewhere, such as the Muscatty Irsay Oliver.

Slovenia Former Yugoslavian region in which *Laski Rizling* is king. Other grapes show greater promise.

☨ **Smith Woodhouse** (*Douro*, Portugal) Part of the same empire as *Dow's, Graham's* and *Warre's* but often overlooked. *Vintage ports* can be good, as is the house speciality *Traditional Late-Bottled Vintage Port*. 60 **63 66** 70 75 **77 85** 94 ☆☆☆☆ **1984 Traditional Late Bottled Vintage Port £££**

☨ **Ch. Smith-Haut-Lafitte** [oh-lah-feet] (*Pessac-Léognan Cru Classé, Bordeaux*, France) Rejuvenated property, flying high since its purchase by a former French sportsman and his wife. Increasingly classy reds and (specially) pure *Sauvignon* whites. Grape pips from the estate are also used to make an anti-ageing skin cream called Caudalie that is reportedly used by Isabelle Adjani. Red: **82** 85 86 **89 90** 91 92 93 94 95 White: 92 93 94 95 96 ☆☆☆☆ **1995 ££££**

☨ **Smithbrook** (*Western Australia*) Pinot Noir specialist in the new southerly region of *Pemberton*.

☨ **Soave** [swah-veh] (*Veneto*, Italy) Mostly dull stuff, but Soave *Classico* is better; single vineyard versions are best. Sweet *Recioto* di Soave is delicious. *Pieropan* is almost uniformly excellent. **Anselmi; Masi; Pieropan.**

☨ **Ch. Sociando-Mallet** [soh-see-yon-doh ma-lay] (*Haut-Médoc Cru Bourgeois, Bordeaux*, France) A *Cru Bourgeois* whose oaked, fruity red wines are way above its status. **82** 83 **85 86** 88 **89 90** 91 92 93 94 95 96

♆ **Sogrape** [soh-grap] (Portugal) While outsiders often credit Australians *Peter Bright* and David Baverstock with helping to revolutionise the Portuguese wine industry, it is this huge company that is making the big changes. Having invented *Mateus* Rosé half a century ago, it is now leading the way in modernising the wines of *Dão*, *Douro* and *Bairrada*, bringing out flavours these once-dull wines never seemed to possess. *Sogrape* also owns the *port* house of *Ferreira* and is thus also responsible for *Barca Velha*, Portugal's top red table wine. The *Penfolds* of Portugal.
☆☆☆☆☆ **1995 Sogrape Douro Reserve ££**

♆ **Solaia** [soh-li-yah] (*Tuscany*, Italy) Yet another *Antinori* Super Tuscan. A phenomenal blend of *Cabernets Sauvignon* and *Franc*, with a little *Sangiovese*. Italy's top red? ☆☆☆☆☆ **1993 Solaia, Antinori ££££**

Solera [soh-leh-rah] (*Jerez*, Spain) Ageing system involving older wine being continually 'refreshed' by slightly younger wine of the same style.

♆ **Bodegas Felix Solís** [fay-leex soh-lees] (*Valdepeñas*, Spain) By far the biggest, most go-ahead winery in *Valdepeñas*.

Somontano [soh-mon-tah-noh] (Spain) *DO* region in the foothills of the Pyrénées in Aragon, now experimenting with international grape varieties. **COVISA; Viñas Del Vero; Enate; Pirineus.**

Sonnenuhr [soh-neh-noor] (*Mosel*, Germany) Vineyard site in the famous village of *Wehlen*. See *Dr Loosen*. QbA/Kab/Spät: **85** 86 **88 89 90** 91 92 93 94 95 96 97 Aus/Beeren/Tba: **83 85** 88 89 90 91 92 93 94 95 96 97

Sonoma Valley [so-NOH-ma] (California) Despite the *Napa* hype, this lesser-known region not only contains some of the state's top wineries, it is also home to *E&J Gallo's* super-premium vineyard and the *Dry Creek* area where some of California's best *Zinfandels* are to be found. The region is sub-divided into the *Sonoma*, *Alexander* and *Russian River Valleys* and *Dry Creek*. Red: **85** 86 87 **90 91** 92 93 95 96 White: **90 91** 92 95 96 *Simi; Clos du Bois; Iron Horse; Matanzas Creek; Sonoma-Cutrer; Jordan; Laurel Glen; Kistler; Duxoup; Ravenswood; Kenwood; Quivira; Dry Creek; Gundlach Bundschu; Adler Fels; Arrowood; Carmenet; Marimar Torres; Peter Michael; E&J Gallo.*

♆ **Sonoma-Cutrer** [soh-noh-ma koo-trehr] (*Sonoma Valley*, California) Producer of world-class *Chardonnay* from specified single vineyards, whose wine can rival the best *Puligny-Montrachet*. The 'Les Pierres' is the pick of the litter.

♆ **Marc Sorrel** [sor-rel] (*Rhône*, France) *Hermitage* producer who is – unusually – as successful in white as red. The 'le Gréal' single-vineyard red is the wine to buy, though the 'les Roccoules' white ages well.

♆ **Pierre Soulez** [soo-layz] (*Loire*, France) Producer of *Savennières* from several vineyards. The Clos du Papillon and Roche-aux-Moines *late harvest* wines are the ones to buy.

South Africa The wine revolution is as dramatic here as the ones affecting the rest of South African society. Charles Back of *Fairview* is both helping to launch the first black-owned vineyard and winery, and helping to persuade traditionalists to make fresh, ripe-tasting wines rather than the tired, greenly-acidic fare that was once so prized here. Quality is still patchy, but there are better producers leading the way towards producing characterful wine that apes neither France nor Australia. Elsewhere, look for inexpensive, simple dry and off-dry *Chenins*, lovely *late harvest* and fortified wines and surprisingly good *Pinotages*; otherwise very patchy. Red: 86 87 89 **91 92** 93 94 95 96 White: 92 93 94 95 96 97 *Fairview; Kanonkop; Mulderbosch; Jordan; Grangehurst; Saxenburg; Plaisir de Merle; Vergelegen; Thelema.*

South Australia Home of almost all the biggest wine companies, and still producing over 50 per cent of Australia's wine. The *Barossa Valley* is one of the country's oldest wine producing regions, but like its neighbours *Clare* and *McLaren Vale*, faces competition from cooler areas like the *Adelaide Hills*, *Padthaway* and *Coonawarra*. White: **87** 88 **90 91 94** 95 96 97 Red: **82 84 85 86 87** 88 **90 91** 94 95 96

South-East Australia A cleverly meaningless regional description which helps the Australians get round some of Europe's pettier *appellation*-focused rules. Technically, it covers around 85 per cent of Australia's vineyards.

South-West France An unofficial umbrella term covering the areas between *Bordeaux* and the *Pyrénées*, *Bergerac*, *Madiran*, *Cahors*, *Jurançon* and the *Vins de Pays de Côtes de Gascogne*.

� **Ch. Souverain** [soo-vrayn] (*Sonoma*, California) Good value winery making big, rich, fruit-packed *Chardonnays*, *Merlots*, *Cabernets* and *Zinfandels*.

🍇**Spanna** [spah-nah] (*Piedmont*, Italy) The *Piedmont*ese name for the *Nebbiolo* grape and the more humble wines made from it.

☸ **Pierre Sparr** (*Alsace*, France) Big producer offering a rare chance to taste traditional *Chasselas*. ☆☆☆ **1994 Chasselas Vieilles Vignes ££**

Spätlese [shpayt-lay-zeh] (Germany) Second step in the *QmP* scale, *late harvested* grapes making wine a notch drier than *Auslese*.

☸ **Spottswoode** (*Napa Valley*, California) Excellent small producer of complex *Cabernet* and unusually good *Sauvignon Blanc*. Deserves greater recognition. ☆☆☆☆☆ **1992 Cabernet Sauvignon Napa Valley £££**

☸ **Spring Mountain** (*Napa Valley*, California) Revived old winery with great vineyards and classy berryish *Cabernet*.

Spritz/ig [shprit-zig] Slight sparkle or fizz. Also *pétillance*.

Spumante [spoo-man-tay] (Italy) Sparkling.

Staatsweingut [staht-svine-goot] (Germany) A state-owned wine estate such as Staatsweinguter Eltville (*Rheingau*), a major cellar in *Eltville*.

☸ **Stafford Ridge** (*Adelaide Hills*, Australia) Fine *Chardonnay* and especially *Sauvignon* from *Lenswood* by the former chief winemaker of *Hardys*. ☆☆☆☆ **1996 Lenswood Sauvignon ££**

Stag's Leap District (*Napa Valley*, California) A long-established hillside region, specialising in blackcurranty *Cabernet Sauvignon*. Red: 84 **85** 86 87 **90 91** 92 93 95 96 *Shafer; Clos du Val; Stag's Leap.*

☸ **Stag's Leap Wine Cellars** (*Napa Valley*, California) Pioneering supporter of the *Stag's Leap appellation*, and one of finest wineries in California. The best wines are the Faye Vineyard, SLV and Cask 23 *Cabernets*. ☆☆☆☆☆ **1993 SLV-FAYE Cabernet Sauvignon £££**

Stalky or stemmy Flavour of the stem rather than of the juice.

☸ **Stanton & Killeen** (*Rutherglen*, Australia) Reliable producer of *Liqueur Muscat*. ☆☆☆☆☆ **Rutherglen Liqueur Muscat ££**

☸ **Steele** (*Lake County*, California) The former winemaker of *Kendall Jackson* and a master when it comes to producing fruitily crowd-pleasing *Chardonnays* from various regions. Lovers of more complex wines, however, may be more excited by the *Zinfandels*. ☆☆☆☆ **1994 Zinfandel £££**

Steely Refers to young wine with evident *acidity*. A compliment when paid to *Chablis* and dry *Sauvignons*.

🍇**Steen** [steen] (South Africa) Local name for (and possibly odd *clone* of) *Chenin Blanc*. Widely planted (over 30 per cent of the vineyard area). The best come from *Boschendal* and *Fairview*.

Stellenbosch [stel-len-bosh] (South Africa) Centre of the *Cape* wine industry, and climatically and topographically diverse region that, like the *Napa Valley*, is taken far too seriously as a regional *appellation*. Hillside sub-regions like Helderberg make more sense. Red: 82 84 86 **87** 89 **91 92** 93 94 95 96 97 White: **87 91** 92 93 94 95 96 97 *Meerlust; Rustenberg; Thelema; Mulderbosch; Kanonkop; Bergkelder; Delheim;* Hartenburg; *Warwick; Neil Ellis; Stellenzicht.*

☱ **Stellenbosch Farmers' Winery** (*Stellenbosch*, South Africa) South Africa's biggest producer; wines include Sable View, Libertas, *Nederburg* and, now, *Plaisir de Merle.*

☱ **Stellenryck** [stel-len-rik] (South Africa) The *Bergkelder's* top red and white. Well thought of in South Africa. Looks less impressive overseas.

☱ **Stellenzicht Vineyards** [stel-len-zikht] (*Stellenbosch*, South Africa) The baby sister estate of *Neethlingshof*; a much more attractive proposition with an impressive *Sauvignon* and a *Shiraz* good enough to beat *Penfolds Grange* in a blind tasting. ☆☆☆☆ **1994 Shiraz £££**

☱ **Sterling Vineyards** (*Napa Valley*, California) Founded by Peter Newton (now at *Newton* vineyards) and once the plaything of Coca-Cola, this showcase estate now belongs to Canadian liquor giant Seagram. Among the current successes are the Reserve *Cabernet*, *Pinot Noir* and fairly priced Redwood Trail wines. ☆☆☆☆ **1994 Cabernet Sauvignon ££**

☱ **Weingut Georg Stiegelmar** [stee-gel-mahr] (*Burgenland*, Austria) Producer of pricy, highly acclaimed, dry whites from *Chardonnay* and *Pinot Blanc*, *late harvest* wines and some particularly good reds from *Pinot Noir* and *St. Laurent*. ☆☆☆☆☆ **1995 Juris Trockenbeerenauslese £££**

☱ **Stoneleigh** (*Marlborough*, New Zealand) Reliable *Marlborough* label used by *Cooks/Corbans*. ☆☆☆☆ **1997 Sauvignon Blanc ££**

☱ **Stonestreet** (*Sonoma*, California) Highly commercial wines from the *Kendall-Jackson* stable.

☱ **Stony Hill** (*Napa Valley*, California) Unfashionable old winery with the guts to produce long-lived complex *Chardonnay* that tastes like unoaked *Grand Cru Chablis*, rather than follow the herd in aping buttery-rich *Meursault*. Individual wine for individualist wine drinkers.

☱ **Stoniers** [stoh-nee-yurs] (*Mornington Peninsula*, Australia) Small *Mornington* winery, successful with impressive *Pinot Noir*, *Chardonnay* and *Merlot*. (Previously known as Stoniers-Merrick.) ☆☆☆☆ **1995 Reserve Chardonnay ££**

☱ **Storybook Mountain** (*Napa Valley*, California) Source of great *Zinfandels* that taste good young but are built for the long haul. The *Howell Mountain* bottlings take the longest to develop. ☆☆☆☆ **1992 Zinfandel £££**

☱ **Stratford** (California) British-born Tony Cartledge sells highly commercial blends under this and the Cartledge & Brown labels.

Structure The 'structural' components of a wine include *tannin, acidity* and *alcohol*. They provide the skeleton or backbone that supports the 'flesh' of the fruit. A young wine with good structure should age well.

☱ **Ch. de Suduiraut** [soo-dee-roh] (*Sauternes Premier Cru Classé*, *Bordeaux*, France) Producing greater things since its purchase by French insurance giant, *AXA*. Top wines: 'Cuvée Madame', 'Crème de Tête'. 75 **76** 78 **79** 81 **82 83** 85 86 88 89 90 94 96 97 ☆☆☆☆ **1990 ££££**

Suhindol [soo-win-dol] (Bulgaria) One of *Bulgaria's* best-known regions, the source of widely available, fairly-priced *Cabernet Sauvignon*.

Sulfites US labelling requirement alerting those suffering from an (extremely rare) allergy to the presence of *sulphur dioxide*. Curiously, no such requirement is made of cans of baked beans and dried apricots, which contain twice as much of the chemical.

Sulphur dioxide/SO₂ Antiseptic routinely used by food packagers and winemakers to protect their produce from bacteria and *oxidation*.

☎ **Super Second** (*Bordeaux*, France) A small gang of *Médoc* second growths: *Pichon-Lalande, Pichon-Longueville, Léoville-Las-Cases, Ducru-Beaucaillou, Cos d'Estournel*; whose wines are thought to rival – and cost nearly as much as – the first growths. Other over-performers include: *Rauzan-Segla* and *Léoville-Barton, Lynch-Bages, Palmer, La Lagune, Montrose.*

Super Tuscan (Italy) New-wave *Vino da Tavola* (usually red) wines, pioneered by producers like *Antinori*, which stand outside traditional *DOC* rules. Generally *Bordeaux*-style blends or *Sangiovese* or a mixture of both.

Supérieur/Superiore [soo-pay-ree-ur/soo-pay-ree-ohr-ray] (France/Italy) Often relatively meaningless in terms of discernible quality. Denotes wine (well or badly) made from riper grapes.

Sur lie [soor-lee] (France) The ageing 'on its *lees*' – or dead yeasts – most commonly associated with *Muscadet*, but now being used by pioneering producers to make other fresher, richer and sometimes slightly sparkling wines in southern France.

Süssreserve [soos-sreh-zurv] (Germany) Unfermented grape juice used to bolster sweetness and fruit in German and English wines.

☎ **Sutter Home Winery** (*Napa Valley*, California) Home of robust red *Zinfandel* in the 1970s, and responsible for the invention of successful sweet 'white' (or, as the non-colour-blind might say, pink) *Zinfandel*. *Amador County Zinfandels* are still good, but rarely exceptional.

☎ **Joseph Swan** (*Sonoma*, California) Small Burgundian-scale winery whose enthusiastic winemaker, Rod Berglund, produces great single-vineyard, often attractively quirky, *Pinot Noir* and *Zinfandel*.

Swan Valley (*Western Australia*) Well-established, hot vineyard area: good for fortified wines, and a source of fruit for *Houghton*'s successful *HWB*. *Houghton* also produces cooler-climate wines in the microclimate of *Moondah Brook*.

☎ **Swanson** [swon-son] (*Napa Valley*, California) Top-flight innovative producer of *Cabernet, Chardonnay, Sangiovese, Syrah* and *late harvest Semillon.* ☆☆☆☆☆ **1992 Syrah £££**

Switzerland Produces mostly enjoyable but expensive light, floral wines mostly for early drinking. See *Dôle, Fendant, Chablais*. Also the only country to use screw caps for much of its wine, thus facilitating recycling and avoiding the problems of faulty corks. Clever people the Swiss...

🍇 **Sylvaner/Silvaner** [sihl-vah-nur] Relatively non-aromatic white grape, originally from *Austria* but adopted by other European areas, particularly *Alsace* and *Franken*. Elsewhere, wines are often dry and earthy, though there are some promising efforts with it in South Africa.

🍇 **Syrah** [see-rah] (*Rhône*, France) The red *Rhône* grape, an exotic mix of ripe fruit and spicy, smoky, gamey, leathery flavours. Skilfully adopted by Australia, where it is called *Shiraz* and in southern France for *Vin de Pays d'Oc*. Increasingly popular in California, thanks to '*Rhône* Rangers' like *Bonny Doon* and *Phelps*. See *Qupé, Marqués de Griñon* in Spain and *Isole e Olena* in Italy, plus *Côte Rôtie, Hermitage, Shiraz*.

T

☎ **La Tâche** [la tash] (*Burgundy*, France) Wine from the La Tâche vineyard, exclusively owned by the *Dom. de la Romanée Conti*. Frequently as good as the rarer and more expensive 'La Romanée Conti'. ☆☆☆☆☆ **1994 ££££**

Tafelwein [tah-fel-vine] (Germany) Table wine. Only prefix 'Deutscher' guarantees German origin.

Ch. Tahbilk [tah-bilk] (*Victoria*, Australia) Old-fashioned winemaking in the *Goulbourn Valley*. Great long-lived *Shiraz* from 130-year-old vines, surprisingly good *Chardonnay* and lemony *Marsanne* which needs a decade. The second wine is Dalfarras. ☆☆☆☆ **1995 Marsanne ££**

Cave de Tain L'Hermitage (*Rhône*, France) Reliable cooperative for *Crozes-Hermitage* and *Hermitage*. ☆☆☆ **1993 Crozes-Hermitage ££**

Taittinger [tat-tan-jehr] (*Champagne*, France) Producer of reliable non-vintage, and fine Comtes de *Champagne Blanc de Blancs* and Rosé. ☆☆☆☆ **Taittinger Brut 1990 ££££**

Ch. Talbot [tal-boh] (*St. Julien 4ème Cru Classé, Bordeaux*, France) Reliable, if sometimes slightly jammy, wine. Connétable Talbot is the *second label*. 75 **78** 79 81 **82 83** 84 85 86 88 89 90 92 93 94 95

Talley (*San Luis Obispo*, California) Serious small producer of elegant *Chardonnay* and *Pinot Noir* that lasts.

Taltarni [tal-tahr-nee] (*Victoria*, Australia) Run by Dominique Portet whose brother Bernard runs *Clos du Val*. European-style *Shiraz Cabernets* are the stars from this beautiful *Pyrenees* vineyard, though the *Fumé Blanc* and Clover Hill sparkling wine from *Tasmania* are impressive too.

Tank Method See *cuve close*.

Tannat [ta-na] (France) Rustic French grape variety, traditionally widely used in the blend of *Cahors* and in South America, principally *Uruguay*.

Tannic See *Tannin*.

Tannin *Astringent* component of red wine which comes from the skins, pips and stalks and helps the wine to age.

Tardy & Ange [tahr-dee ay onzh] (*Rhône*, France) Partnership producing classy *Crozes-Hermitage* at the Dom. de Entrefaux.

Tarragona [ta-ra-GO-nah] (*Catalonia*, Spain) *DO* region south of *Penedés* and home to many cooperatives. Contains the better quality *Terra Alta*.

Tarrango [ta-RAN-goh] (Australia) Juicy grape pioneered in a *Beaujolais* style by *Brown Brothers*. ☆☆☆☆ **1997 Tarrango Brown Brothers £**

Tarrawarra [ta-ra-wa-ra] (*Yarra Valley*, Australia) Increasingly successful *Pinot* pioneer in the cool-climate region of the *Yarra Valley*. *Second label* is Tunnel Hill. ☆☆☆☆ **1995 Reserve Pinot Noir, Yarra Valley ££££**

Tarry Red wines from hot countries often have an aroma and flavour reminiscent of tar. The *Syrah* and *Nebbiolo* exhibit this characteristic.

Tartaric Type of acid found in grapes. Also the form in which acid is added to wine in hot countries whose legislation allows this.

Tartrates [tar-trayts] Harmless white crystals often deposited by white wines in the bottle. In Germany, these are called 'diamonds'.

Tasmania (Australia) Cool-climate island, showing potential for sparkling wine, *Chardonnay, Riesling, Pinot Noir* and even (somewhat herbaceous) *Cabernet Sauvignon*. Questions remain, however, over which are the best parts of the island for growing vines. White: **92 94 95** 96 Red: **90 91 92** 94 95 96 *Heemskerk; Moorilla; Piper's Brook; Freycinet.*

Tastevin [tat-van] The silver *Burgundy* tasting-cup used as an insignia by vinous brotherhoods (*confréries*), as a badge of office by sommeliers and as ashtrays by the author. The *Chevaliers de Tastevin* organise annual tastings, awarding a mock-medieval Tastevinage label to the best wines. *Chevaliers de Tastevin* attend banquets, often wearing similarly mock-medieval clothes.

Taurasi [tow-rah-see] (*Campania*, Italy) Big old-fashioned *Aglianico*. Needs years to soften and develop a burnt, cherry taste. *Mastroberardino.*

Tavel [ta-vehl] (*Rhône*, France) Dry rosé. Often very disappointing. Seek out young versions and avoid the bronze colour revered by traditionalists. **Dom du Prieuré; Ch. d'Aquéria; Dom. de la Mordorée.**

Tawny (*Douro*, Portugal) In theory, pale browny-red *port* that acquires its mature appearance and nutty flavour from long ageing in oak casks. *Port* houses, however, legally produce 'tawny' by mixing basic *ruby* with *white port* and skipping the tiresome business of barrel-ageing altogether. The real stuff comes with an indication of age, such as 10 or 20-year-old, but even these figures are approximate. A 10-year-old malt whisky has, by law, to be a decade old; a 10-year-old *port* only has to 'taste as though it is that old'. *Port* shippers incidentally get terribly aerated if anyone ever describes a non-Portuguese fortified wine (such as an Australian, genuinely wood-aged tawny) as '*port*-style' or even '*port*-like'. I love real tawny *port* (and good *port*-style tawnies, from elsewhere!) – and heartily recommend them to anyone who gets a hangover from *vintage port*. *Colheita ports* are tawnies of a specific vintage. (Also derided by most traditionalist *port* shippers). ***Noval; Taylor's; Graham's; Cockburn's; Dow's; Niepoort; Ramos Pinto; Calem.***

🍷 **Taylor (Fladgate & Yeatman)** (*Douro*, Portugal) With *Dow's*, one of the 'first growths' of the *Douro*. Outstanding *vintage port*, 'modern' *Late Bottled Vintage*. Also owns *Fonseca* and *Guimaraens*, and produces the excellent *Quinta de Vargellas* Single-*Quinta port*. **55 60 63 66 70** 75 **77** 83 85 92 94 ☆☆☆☆☆ **20 Year Old Tawny £££**

🍷 **Te Mata** [tay mah-tah] (*Hawke's Bay*, New Zealand) Pioneer John Buck proves what *New Zealand* can do with *Chardonnay* (in the Elston Vineyard) and pioneered reds with his Coleraine and (lighter) Awatea. ☆☆☆☆☆ **1996 Elston Chardonnay £££**

🍷 **Fratelli Tedeschi** [tay-dehs-kee] (*Veneto*, Italy) Reliable producer of rich and concentrated *Valpolicellas* and good *Soaves*. The *Amarones* are particularly impressive. ☆☆☆☆ **1995 Amarone Classico Monte Olmi £££**

🍷 **Dom. Tempier** [tom-pee-yay] (*Provence*, France) *Provence* superstar estate, producing single-vineyard red and rosé *Bandols* that support the claim that the *Mourvèdre* (from which they are largely made) ages well. Curiously, in recent years, the rosé seems to be more reliable than the red.

🍇 **Tempranillo** [tem-prah-nee-yoh] (Spain) The red grape of *Rioja* – and just about everywhere else in Spain, thanks to the way in which its strawberry fruit suits the vanilla/oak flavours of barrel-ageing. In *Navarra*, it is called *Cencibel*; in *Ribera del Duero*, Tinto Fino; in the *Penedés*, *Ull de Llebre;* in *Toro*, Tinto de Toro; and in Portugal – where it is used for *port* – it's known as *Tinto Roriz*. So far, though, it is rarely grown outside Spain.

Tenuta [teh-noo-tah] (Italy) Estate or vineyard.

🍷 **Terlano/Terlaner** [tehr-lah-noh/tehr-lah-nur] (*Trentino-Alto-Adige*, Italy) Northern Italian village and its wine: usually fresh, crisp and carrying the name of the grape from which it was made.

🍇 **Teroldego Rotaliano** [teh-ROL-deh-goh roh-tah-lee-AH-noh] (*Trentino-Alto-Adige*, Italy) Dry reds, quite full-bodied, with lean, slightly bitter berry flavours which make them better accompaniments to food. **Foradori.**

Terra Alta [tay ruh al-ta] (*Catalonia*, Spain) Small *DO* within the much larger *Tarragona DO*, producing wines of higher quality due to the difficult climate and resulting low yields. **Pedro Rovira.**

🍷 **Terra Noble** [teh-rah noh-blay] (*Maule*, Chile) Small winery focusing on making *Bordeaux*-style *Merlot* and *Loire*-style *Sauvignon*.

Terras Sado [teh-rash SAH-doh] (*Setúbal*, Portugal) Up-and-coming region close to Lisbon for new-wave red table wines.

🍇 **Terret** [tehr-ret] (France) Suddenly fashionable, herby, grassy white grape. Possibly best in blends, but a welcome new arrival on the scene. *Jacques Lurton* is a particularly keen – and successful – user.

🍷 **Ch. du Tertre** [doo tehr-tr] (*Margaux 5ème Cru Classé*, *Bordeaux*, France) Recently restored to former glory by the owners of *Calon Ségur*. **70 79 82 83** 85 86 88 89 90 91 92 93 94 95 96 ☆☆☆☆ **1990 ££££**

♀ **Ch. Tertre-Rôteboeuf** [Tehr-tr roht-burf] (*St. Emilion Grand Cru Classé*, *Bordeaux*, France) Good, rich, concentrated if sometimes atypical, crowd-pleasing wines. 85 86 87 **88** 89 90 91 93 **94** 95 96
Tête de Cuvée [teht dur coo-vay] (France) An old expression still used by traditionalists to describe their finest wine.

♀ **Thames Valley Vineyard** (Reading, England) England's most reliable and dynamic winery – and consultancy – thanks to Australian expertise.

♀ **Weingut Dr H Thanisch** [tah-nish] (*Mosel-Saar-Ruwer*, Germany) Once highly illustrious producer, now under-performing woefully, which is especially unfortunate since Thanisch is co-owner of the great *Bernkasteler* Doktor, one of the finest vineyards in Germany.

♀ **Thelema Mountain Vineyards** [thur-lee-ma] (*Stellenbosch*, South Africa) One of the very best wineries in South Africa, thanks to Gyles Webb's skill and to stunning hillside vineyards. *Chardonnay* and *Sauvignon* are the stars, though Webb is coming to terms with his reds too.

♀ **Ch. Thieuley** [tee-yur-lay] (*Entre-Deux-Mers*, *Bordeaux*, France) Reliable property forging the way for concentrated *Sauvignon*-based, well-oaked whites, and silky affordable reds. White: **92** 93 94 95 96
☆☆☆☆ **1996 Cuvée Francis Courselle ££**

♀ **Gérard Thomas** [toh-mah] (*Burgundy*, France) A small *St. Aubin* *domaine* producing exemplary, fairly priced whites and (as is frequently the case in this *commune*) generally rather less impressive reds. ☆☆☆☆ **1992 St. Aubin 1er Cru La Chatenière £££**

♀ **Paul Thomas** (*Washington State*, US) Good *Chardonnay*, *Semillon* and *Cabernet-Merlot* reds, plus pleasant commercial *Chenin Blanc*.

♀ **Three Choirs Vineyard** (Gloucestershire, England) Named for the three cathedrals of Gloucester, Hereford and Worcester, this is one of England's most reliable estates. Try the wines that are being served on British Airways, and the annual 'New Release' *Nouveau*.

♀ **Tiefenbrunner** [TEE-fen-broon-nehr] (*Trentino-Alto-Adige*, Italy) Consistent producer of fair-to-good *varietal* whites, most particularly *Chardonnay* and *Gewurztraminer*.

♀ **Tignanello** [teen-yah-neh-loh] (*Tuscany*, Italy) *Antinori's* 80 per cent *Sangiovese*, 20 per cent *Cabernet Super Tuscan* is one of Italy's original superstars. Should last for a decade. 82 83 **85** 88 **90** 93 **94** 95
☆☆☆☆ **1993 ££££**

♀ **Tinta Roriz** [teen-tah roh-reesh] (Portugal) *See Tempranillo*

♀ **Tio Pepe** [tee-yoh peh-peh] (*Jerez*, Spain) Ultra-reliable *fino sherry* from *Gonzalez Byass*. ☆☆☆☆ **££**

♀ **Tocai** [toh-kay] (Italy) Lightly herby Venetian white grape, confusingly unrelated to others of similar name. Drink young.

♀ **Tokaji** [toh-ka-yee] (Hungary) Not to be confused with Australian *liqueur Tokay*, Tocai Friulano or *Tokay d'Alsace*, *Tokaji Aszú* is a dessert wine made in a specific region of Eastern *Hungary* (and a tiny corner of *Slovakia*) by adding measured amounts (*puttonyos*) of *eszencia* (a paste made from individually-picked, over-ripe and/or *botrytis*-affected grapes) to dry wine made from the local *Furmint* and *Hárslevelu* grapes. Sweetness levels, which depend on the amount of *eszencia* added, range from one to six *puttonyos*, anything beyond which is labelled *Aszú Eszencia*. This last is often confused with the pure syrup which is sold – at vast prices – as *Eszencia*. The heavy investment has raised quality, international interest, and local controversy over the way *Tokaji* is supposed to taste. Traditionalists like it *oxidised* like *sherry*. The newcomers and some locals disagree. *Royal Tokaji Wine Co*; *Disznókö*; *Ch. Megyer*; *Pajzos*.

Tokay [*in France*: to-kay; *in Australia*: toh-ki] Various different regions have used Tokay as a local name for other grape varieties. In Australia it is the name of a fortified wine from *Rutherglen* made from the *Muscadelle*; in *Alsace*, it is *Pinot Gris*; while the Italian *Tocai* is quite unrelated. Hungary's Tokay – now helpfully renamed *Tokaji* – is largely made from the *Furmint*.

🍷**Tokay d'Alsace** [toh-ki dal-sas] (*Alsace*, France) See *Pinot Gris*.

🍷 **Tollana** [to-lah-nah] (*South Australia*) Yet another *Penfolds* brand – and a frequent source of good-value wine.

🍷 **Dom. Tollot-Beaut** [to-loh-boh] (*Burgundy*, France) Wonderful *Burgundy* domaine in *Chorey-lès-Beaune*, with top-class *Corton* vineyards and a mastery over modern techniques and new oak. Wines have lots of rich fruit flavour. ☆☆☆☆ **1995 Chorey-lès-Beaune £££**

🍷 **Torcolato** [taw-ko-lah-toh] (*Veneto*, Italy) See *Maculan*.

🍷 **Torgiano** [taw-jee-yah-noh] (*Umbria*, Italy) Zone in *Umbria* and modern red wine made famous by *Lungarotti*. See *Rubesco*.

🍷 **Toro** [TO-roh] (Spain) Up-and-coming region on the *Douro*, close to Portugal, producing richly intense red wines such as Farina's *Collegiata* from the *Tempranillo*, confusingly known here as the Tinto de Toro.

🍷 **Torre de Gall** [to-ray day-gahl] (*Catalonia*, Spain) *Moët & Chandon's* Spanish fizz. About as good as you can get using traditional *cava* varieties. ☆☆☆☆ **££**

🍷 **Torres** [TO-rehs] (*Catalonia*, Spain) *Miguel Torres* revolutionised Spain's wine industry with reliable wines like Viña Sol, Gran Sangre de Toro, Esmeralda and Gran Coronas, before moving on to perform the same trick in Chile. Today, while these wines face heavier competition, efforts at the top end of the scale, like the *Milmanda Chardonnay*, Fransola *Sauvignon Blanc* and Mas Borras (the new name for the old 'Black Label' *Cabernet Sauvignon*) still look good. ☆☆☆☆☆ **1995 Milmanda £££**

🍷 **Marimar Torres** [TO-rehs] (*Sonoma*, California) *Miguel Torres'* sister is using the same wine-making techniques as her brother and is producing some of the most impressive *Pinot Noir* and *Chardonnay* from a spectacular little vineyard in *Russian River*. ☆☆☆☆ **1995 Chardonnay £££**

🍷 **Miguel Torres** [TO-rehs] (*Curico*, Chile) For a while, Torres' Chilean efforts seemed not be living up to its early promise. More recent wines, including the Santa Digna *Cabernet* and especially the new Manso de Velasco, are back on form. ☆☆☆☆☆ **1995 Manso de Velasco £££**

🍷**Torrontes** [to-ron-TEHS] (Argentina) Promisingly aromatic grape variety related to the *Muscat*, now rarely seen in Spain, but highly successful in *Argentina*. *Etchart* is a star producer. Smells as though it is going to taste sweet even when the wine is bone dry.

Toscana [tos-KAH-nah] (Italy) See *Tuscany*.

🍷 **Ch. la Tour Blanche** [lah toor blonsh] (*Sauternes Premier Cru Classé*, *Bordeaux*, France) Since the late 1980s, one of the finest, longest-lasting *Sauternes*. Also a well-run wine school. 86 88 89 90 92 94 95 96

🍷 **Ch. la Tour-Carnet** [lah toor kahr-nay] (*Haut-Médoc 4ème Cru Classé*, *Bordeaux*, France) Picturesque but *Cru Bourgeois*-level fourth growth. 82 83 85 86 88 **89 90** 91 92 93 94 95 96

🍷 **Ch. la Tour-de-By** [lah toor dur bee] (*Médoc Cru Bourgeois*, *Bordeaux*, France) Reliable, especially in ripe years. 85 86 88 89 90 91 94 95 96

🍷 **Ch. Tour-du-Haut-Moulin** [toor doo oh moo-lan] (*Haut-Médoc Cru Bourgeois*, *Bordeaux*, France) An under-appreciated producer of what often can be *Cru Classé* quality wine. 82 83 85 86 88 89 90 92 94 95 96

🍷 **Ch. la Tour-Martillac** [lah toor mah-tee-yak] (*Graves Cru Classé*, *Bordeaux*, France) Recently revolutionised organic *Pessac-Léognan* estate with juicy reds and fine whites. 82 83 85 86 88 89 90 91 **92** 93 94 95 96

🍷 **Touraine** [too-rayn] (*Loire*, France) Area encompassing the ACs *Chinon*, *Vouvray* and *Bourgueil*. Also an increasing source of quaffable *varietal* wines – *Sauvignon*, *Gamay* de Touraine, etc. White: 95 96 97 Red: **88 89 90** 95 96 97 Oisly & Thésée; Briare; Charmoise.

🍷 **Les Tourelles de Longueville** [lay too-rel dur long-ur-veel] (*Pauillac*, *Bordeaux*, France) The *second label* of *Pichon-Longueville*.

🍇 **Touriga (Nacional/Francesa)** [too-ree-ga nah-see-yoh-nahl/fran-say-sa] (Portugal) Red *port* grape, also (though rarely) seen in the New World.

Traditional Generally meaningless term, except in sparkling wines where the 'méthode traditionelle' is the new way to say '*méthode champenoise*' and in Portugal where 'Traditional *Late Bottled Vintage*' refers to *port* that unlike non-traditional LBV, hasn't been filtered.

🍇 **Traminer** [tra-mee-nur; *in Australia*: trah-MEE-nah] A less aromatic variant of the *Gewürztraminer* grape widely grown in Eastern Europe and Italy, although the term is confusingly also used as a pronouncable, alternative name for the latter grape – particularly in Australia.

Transfer Method A way of making sparkling wine, involving a second fermentation in the bottle, but unlike the *méthode champenoise* in that the wine is separated from the *lees* by pumping it out of the bottle into a pressurised tank for clarification before returning it to another bottle.

🍷 **Bodegas Trapiche** [tra-pee-chay] (Argentina) Big go-ahead producer with noteworthy barrel-fermented *Chardonnay* and *Cabernet/Malbec*.

Tras-os-Montes [tras-ohsh-montsh] (*Douro*, Portugal) Wine region of the *Upper Douro*, right up at Spanish border and source of *Barca Velha*.

🍇 **Trebbiano** [treh-bee-YAH-noh] (Italy) Ubiquitous white grape in Italy. Less vaunted in France, where it is called *Ugni Blanc*.

🍷 **Trebbiano d'Abruzzo** [treh-bee-YAH-noh dab-ROOT-zoh] (*Abruzzo*, Italy) A *DOC* region where they grow a clone of *Trebbiano*, confusingly called Trebbiano di Toscana, and use it to make unexceptional dry whites.

🍷 **Trefethen** [treh-feh-then] (*Napa Valley*, California) Pioneering estate whose *Chardonnay* and *Cabernet* now taste oddly old-fashioned. The Eshcol wines, though cheaper, are curiously often a better buy.

Trentino [trehn-TEE-noh] (Italy) Northern *DOC* in Italy. *Trentino* specialities include crunchy red *Marzemino*, nutty white Nosiola and excellent *Vin Santo*. Winemaking here often suffers from over-production, but less greedy winemakers can offer lovely, soft, easy-drinking wines. **Ferrari; Càvit; Roberto Zeni; Vallarom; Foradori.**

Trentino-Alto-Adige [trehn-tee-noh al-toh ah-dee-jay] (Italy) Northern region confusingly combining the two *DOC* areas *Trentino* and *Alto-Adige*.

🍷 **Dom. de Trévallon** [treh-vah-lon] (*Provence*, France) Superstar long-lived blend of *Cabernet Sauvignon* and *Syrah* that – until 1994 – was sold under the *Les Baux de Provence appellation* but has now (because of crazily restrictive rules) been demoted to *Vin de Pays des Bouches du Rhône*. Needless to say, there is no shortage of sensible wine drinkers who care more about the contents of the bottle than the legally sanctioned words on the label. ☆☆☆☆ **1995 £££**

🍷 **Ch. du Trignon** [treen-yon] (*Rhône*, France) Big estate, producing reliable *Gigondas* as well as *Côtes du Rhône* from *Rasteau* and *Sablet*.

🍷 **Dom. Frédéric-Emile Trimbach** [tram-bahkh] (*Alsace*, France) Distinguished grower and merchant with subtle complex wines. Top *cuvées* are the Frédéric Emile, Clos St.-Hune, and Seigneurs de Ribeaupierre. ☆☆☆☆☆ **1990 Riesling Alsace Cuvée Frédéric Emile £££**

Trittenheim [trit-ten-hime] (*Mosel-Saar-Ruwer*, Germany) Village whose vineyards are said to have been the first in Germany planted with *Riesling*, making honeyed wine. QbA/Kab/Spät: **85 88 89 90** 91 92 93 94 95 96 97 Aus/Beeren/Tba: **83 85 88 89 90 91 92 93 94 95 97**

Trocken [trok-ken] (Germany) Dry, often aggressively so. Avoid Trocken *Kabinett* from such northern areas as the *Mosel, Rheingau* and *Rheinhessen*. QbA (*chaptalised*) and *Spätlese* Trocken wines (made, by definition, from riper grapes) are better. See also *Halbtrocken*.

Trockenbeerenauslese [trok-ken-beh-ren-ows-lay-zeh] (Austria/ Germany) Fifth rung of the *QmP* ladder, wine from selected dried grapes which are usually *botrytis*-affected and full of concentrated natural sugar. Only made in the best years, rare and expensive, though less so in Austria than Germany.

🌿**Trollinger** [trroh-ling-gur] (Germany) The German name for the Black Hamburg grape, used in *Württemburg* to make light red wines.

Tronçais [tron-say] (France) Forest producing some of the best oak for wine barrels.

🍷 **Ch. Tronquoy-Lalande** [trron-kwah-lah-lond] (*St. Estèphe Cru Bourgeois, Bordeaux*, France) Traditional wines to buy in ripe years. 79 82 83 85 86 88 **89** 90 93 94 95 96 ☆☆☆☆ **1990 £££**

🍷 **Ch. Troplong-Mondot** [trroh-lon mondoh] (*St. Emilion Grand Cru Classé, Bordeaux*, France) Brilliantly-sited, top-class property whose wines now sell for top-class prices. **82** 83 **85** 86 88 89 90 91 92 93 94 95 96

🍷 **Ch. Trotanoy** [trrot-teh-nwah] (*Pomerol, Bordeaux*, France) Never less than fine and back on especially roaring form since the beginning of the 1990s to compete with *Pétrus*. Some may, however, prefer the lighter style of some of the 1980s. **61** 64 **67 70 71 75** 76 78 79 81 **82** 83 85 86 **88 89** 90 93 94 95 96 ☆☆☆☆ **1994 ££££**

🍷 **Ch. Trottevieille** [trrott-vee-yay] (*St. Emilion Premier Grand Cru, Bordeaux*, France) Improving but still middle-grade property. 79 81 **82** 83 85 86 88 89 90 91 92 93 94 95 ☆☆☆☆ **1989 ££££**

🌿**Trousseau** [troh-soh] (Eastern France) Grape variety found in *Arbois*.

🍷 **Tsantalis** [tsan-tah-lis] (*Nemea*, Greece) Increasingly impressive producer, redefining traditional varieties.

Tulbagh [tool-bakh] (South Africa) Coolish valley north of *Paarl* where Nicky Krone of Twee Jongegezellen makes aromatic whites and impressive fizz. White: **87 91** 92 93 94 **95** 96 97

🍷**Tulloch** [tul-lurk] (*Hunter Valley*, Australia) Under-performing backwater of the *Penfolds* empire.

Tunisia [too-nee-shuh] Best known for dessert *Muscat* wines.

🍷 **Cave Vinicole de Turckheim** [turk-hime] (*Alsace*, France) Cooperative whose top wines can often rival those of some the region's best estates. ☆☆☆☆ **1994 Pinot-Gris Brand £££**

Turkey Now making clean dry white, but still drowning in *oxidised* red.

🍷 **Turkey Flat** (*South Australia*) Tiny *Barossa Shiraz* and *Grenache* maker. ☆☆☆☆☆ **1994 Grenache Noir, Barossa Valley £££**

🍷 **Turley Cellars** (*Napa Valley*, California) Helen Turley – winemaker here and consultant at several other wineries – has been anointed by guru Robert Parker as the nearest thing to a winemaking goddess. Her intense but not overblown *Petite Sirahs* and *Zinfandels*, including small quantities from very old vines, deserve the praise.

Tuscany (Italy) Major region, the famous home of *Chianti* and reds such as *Brunello di Montalcino* and the new wave of *Super Tuscan Vini da Tavola*. Red: 78 79 81 **82 85 88 90** 94 95 97

🍷 **Tyrrell's** (*Hunter Valley*, Australia) *Chardonnay* (sold as *Pinot Chardonnay*) pioneer, and producer of old-fashioned *Shiraz* and *Semillon* and even older-fashioned *Pinot Noir*, which tastes like old-fashioned *Burgundy*. ☆☆☆☆ **1999 Vat 9 Private Bin Shiraz £££**

U

❦ **Ugni Blanc** [oo-nee blon] (France) Undistinguished white grape whose neutrality makes it ideal for distillation into Cognac and Armagnac. It needs modern winemaking to produce a wine with flavour. Curiously in Italy, where it is known as the *Trebbiano*, it takes on a mantle of (spurious) nobility. For reasonable examples try *Vin de Pays des Côtes de Gascogne*.

❦ **Ull de Llebre** [ool dur yay-bray] (Spain) Literally 'hare's eye'. See *Tempranillo*.

Ullage Space between surface of wine and top of cask or, in a bottle, the cork. The wider the gap, the greater the danger of *oxidation*. Older wines almost always have some degree of ullage; the less the better.

🍷 **Umani Ronchi** [oo-MAH-nee RON-kee] (*Marches*, Italy) Innovative producer whose wines like the extraordinary new Pelago prove that *Tuscany* is not the only exciting region in Italy. ☆☆☆☆☆ **1994 Pelago £££**

🍷 **Umathum** [oo-ma-toom] (*Neusiedlersee*, Austria) Producer of unusually good red wines including a brilliant *St. Laurent*.

Umbria [uhm-bree-ah] (Italy) Central wine region, best known for white *Orvieto* and *Torgiano,* but also producing the excellent red *Rubesco*.

🍷 **Viña Undurraga** [oon-dur-rah-ga] (*Central Valley*, Chile) Improved family-owned estate with a range of single *varietal* wines.

Unfiltered Filtering a wine can remove flavour – as can *fining* it with egg white or *bentonite*. Most winemakers traditionally argue that both practices are necessary if the finished wine is going to be crystal-clear and free from bacteria that could turn it to vinegar. Many quality-conscious new-wave winemakers, however, are now cutting back on *fining* and filtering and some are even making a point of not doing either.

Uruguay Surprising new source of improving *Cabernet Sauvignon* and *Tannat*. **Castel Pujol; Juanico.**

Urzig [oort-zig] (*Mosel-Saar-Ruwer*, Germany) Village on the *Mosel* with steeply sloping vineyards and some of the very best producers, including *Monchof* and *Dr. Loosen*. QbA/Kab/Spät: **85 86 88 89 90** 91 92 93 94 95 Aus/Beeren/Tba: **83 85** 88 89 90 91 92 93 94 95 97

🍷 **Utiel-Requena** [oo-tee-yel reh-kay-nah] (*Valencia*, Spain) *DO* of *Valencia,* producing heavy red and good fresh rosé from the Bobal grape.

V

🍷 **Dom. Vacheron** [va-shur-ron] (*Loire*, France) Reliable, if unspectacular, producer of *Sancerre* – including a better-than-average red.

🍷 **Vacqueyras** [va-kay-ras] (*Rhône*, France) *Côtes du Rhône* village producing fine, full-bodied, peppery reds which can compete with (pricier) *Gigondas* and other more famous southern *Rhône* wines. Red: **85 88 89 90 95 Jaboulet Aîné; Vidal-Fleury; Ch. des Tours; Dom. de Mont Vac; Cazaux; Fourmone; Montmirail; Cave de Vacqueyras.**

♈ Aldo Vajra [vi-rah] (*Piedmont*, Italy) Producer of serious reds, including rich complex *Barolo* and the deliciously different gamey Freisa delle Langhe.

Val d'Aosta [val-day-yos-tah] (Italy) Small, spectacularly beautiful area between *Piedmont* and the French/Swiss border. Great for tourism; less so for wine-lovers.

♈ Vignerons du Val d'Orbieu [val-dor-byur] (*Languedoc-Roussillon*, France) Would-be innovative association of over 200 cooperatives and growers. Apart from the excellent Cuvée Mythique, however, too many wines – including the Laperouse co-production with *Penfolds* – leave plenty of scope for improvement. ☆☆☆☆ **1995 Cuvée Mythique ££**

Valais [va-lay] (Switzerland) Vineyard area on the upper *Rhône*, making good *Fendant* (*Chasselas*) which surmounts the usual innate dullness of that grape. There are also some reasonable – in all but price – light reds.

♈ Ch. Valandraud [va-lon-droh] (*St. Emilion*, *Bordeaux*, France) An instant superstar launched in 1991 as competition for *le Pin*. Production is tiny (of *Pomerol* proportions) and the price astronomical. Values have quintupled following demand from the US and Far East.

♈ Valdeorras [bahl-day-ohr-ras] (*Galicia*, Spain) A barren and mountainous *DO* in *Galicia* beginning to exploit the *Cabernet Franc*-like local grape Mencia and the indigenous white Godello.

♈ Valdepeñas [bahl-deh-pay-nyass] (*La Mancha*, Spain) *La Mancha DO* striving to refine its rather hefty strong reds and whites. Progress is being made, particularly with reds. *Los Llanos; Felix Solis*.

♈ Valdespino [bahl-deh-spee-noh] (*Jerez*, Spain) Old-fashioned *sherry* company that uses wooden casks to ferment most of its wines. Makes a classic *fino* Innocente and an excellent *Pedro Ximénez*.

♈ Valdevieso [val-deh-vee-yay-soh] (*Curico*, Chile) Dynamic winery with good commercial wines, high quality *Chardonnay* and *Pinot Noir* and an award-winning blend of grapes, regions and years called Caballo Loco. A name to watch.

♈ Valençay [va-lon-say] (*Loire*, France) *AC* within *Touraine*, near *Cheverny*, making comparable whites: light and clean, if rather sharp. **85 86 88 89 90** 94 95 96 97

♈ Valencia [bah-LEN-thee-yah] (Spain) Produces quite alcoholic red wines from the Monastrell and also deliciously sweet grapey *Moscatel de Valencia*.

♈ Vallet Frères [va-lay frehr] (*Burgundy*, France) Good, small, traditional – not to say old-fashioned– merchant, also known as Pierre Bourrée and based in *Gevrey-Chambertin*. ☆☆☆☆ **1989 Gevrey-Chambertin les Cazetiers £££**

♈ Valpolicella [val-poh-lee-cheh-lah] (*Veneto*, Italy) Over-commercialised, light, red wine which should – with rare exceptions – be drunk young to catch its interestingly bitter-cherryish flavour. Bottles labelled *Classico* are better; best are *Ripasso* versions, made by refermenting the wine on the *lees* of an earlier vat. For a different experience, buy *Amarone* or *Recioto*. **81 82 85 86 88 90 91** 93 94 95 *Masi; Allegrini; Boscaini; Tedeschi*; Le Ragose; *Serego Alighieri; Guerrieri-Rizzardi; Quintarelli*; Forno.

Valréas [val-ray-yas] (*Rhône*, France) Peppery, inexpensive red wine from a *Côtes du Rhône* village. 78 81 **82 83 85 88** 89 90 95

Valtellina [vat-teh-lee-na] (*Lombardy*, Italy) Red *DOC* mostly from the *Nebbiolo* grape, of variable quality. Improves with age. The raisiny Sfursat, made from dried grapes, is more interesting.

Varichon et Clerc [va-ree-shon ay klayr] (*Savoie*, France) Fair quality, sparkling wines.

Varietal A wine made from and named after one or more grape variety, e.g. California *Chardonnay*. The French authorities are trying to outlaw such references from the labels of most of their *appellation contrôlée* wines. '*Shiraz*' has so far escaped this edict because it is considered a foreign word.

Viña Los Vascos [los vas-kos] (*Colchagua Valley*, Chile) Estate belonging to Eric de *Rothschild* of *Ch. Lafite*, and shamelessly sold with a *Lafite*-like label. The *Cabernet* Reserve is passable but the standard *Cabernet* is uninspiring and the white disappointing, not to say downright poor.

Vasse Felix [vas-fee-liks] (*Margaret River*, Australia) Very classy *Margaret River* winery belonging to the widow of millionaire Rupert Holmes à Court, specialising in juicy, high-quality *Cabernet* and *Shiraz*. ☆☆☆☆ **1996 Cabernet Merlot ££**

Vaucluse [voh-klooz] (*Rhône*, France) *Côtes du Rhône* region with good *Vin de Pays* and peppery reds and rosés from villages such as *Vaucluse*.

Vaud [voh] (Switzerland) Swiss wine area on the shores of Lake Geneva, famous for unusually tangy *Chasselas*.

Vaudésir [voh-day-zeer] (*Burgundy*, France) Possibly the best of the seven *Chablis Grands Crus*.

Vavasour [va-va-soor] (*Marlborough*, New Zealand) Pioneers of the Awatere Valley sub-region of *Marlborough*, hitting high standards with *Bordeaux*-style reds, powerful *Sauvignons* and impressive *Chardonnays*. Dashwood is the *second label*. ☆☆☆☆ **1997 Sauvignon Blanc ££**

VDP (Germany) Association of high quality producers. Look for the eagle.

VDQS (France) *Vin Délimité de Qualité Supérieur*. Official, neither-fish-nor-fowl, designation for wines better than *Vin de Pays* but not fine enough for an *AC*. Enjoying a strange half-life (amid constant rumours of its imminent abolition), this includes such oddities as *Sauvignon de St. Bris*.

Vecchio [veh-kee-yoh] (Italy) Old.

Vecchio Samperi [veh-kee-yoh sam-peh-ree] (*Sicily*, Italy) Best *Marsala* estate, belonging to *De Bartoli*. Although not *DOC*, a dry aperitif similar to an *amontillado sherry*.

Vega Sicilia [bay-gah sih-sih-lyah] (*Ribera del Duero*, Spain) Spain's top wine is a long (10 years) barrel-matured, eccentric *Tempranillo-Bordeaux* blend called Unico sold for extravagant prices. For a cheaper, slightly fresher taste of the Vega Sicilia-style, try the supposedly lesser Valbuena. Alternatively, check out the wines from the new offshoot *bodega Alion*. 60 61 62 64 66 67 69 **70** 72 74 75 76 79 80 82 83 ☆☆☆☆☆ **1990 Valbuena ££££**

Vegetal Often used of *Sauvignon Blanc*, like 'grassy'. Can be complimentary – though not in California or Australia, where it is held to mean 'unripe'.

Caves Velhas [kah-vash-vay-yash] (Portugal) Large traditional merchants who blend wine from all over the country to sell under their own label. Almost single-handedly saved the *Bucelas DO* from extinction. Wines are good, but rarely outstanding.

Velho/velhas [vay-yoh/vay-yas] (Portugal) Old, as of red wine.

Velletri [veh-leh-tree] (Italy) Town in the Alban hills (*Colli Albani*), producing mainly *Trebbiano* and *Malvasia*-based whites, similar to *Frascati*.

🍇**Veltliner** See *Grüner Veltliner.*
Vendange [Von-donzh] (France) Harvest or vintage.
Vendange tardive [von-donzh tahr-deev] (France) Particularly in *Alsace*, wine from *late harvested* grapes, usually lusciously sweet.
Vendemmia/Vendimia [ven-DEH-mee-yah/ven-DEE-mee-yah] (Italy, Spain) Harvest or vintage.
🍷 **Venegazzú** [veh-neh-GAHT-zoo] (*Veneto*, Italy) Good, quite understated *claret*-like *Vino da Tavola* from the *Cabernet Sauvignon*; a sort of 'Super-Veneto' to compete with those *Super Tuscans*. Needs five years. Look out, too, for the rather pricier – and better – black label.

Veneto [veh-neh-toh] (Italy) North-eastern wine region, the home of *Soave*, *Valpolicella* and *Bardolino*.

🍷 **Veramonte** [vay-rah-mon-tay] (*Casablanca*, Chile) New venture by Agustin Huneeus, winemaker of *Franciscan Vineyards* in *California*, already producing impressive reds.
🍇**Verdejo** [vehr-de-khoh] (Spain) Interestingly herby white grape; confusingly not the *Verdelho* of *Madeira* and Australia, but the variety used for new-wave *Rueda*.
🍇**Verdelho** [*in Madeira*: vehr-deh-yoh; *in Australia*: vur-DEL-loh] (Madeira/Australia) White grape used for fortified *Madeira* and *white port* and for limey, dry, table wine in Australia. ☆☆☆ **1997 Capel Vale ££**
🍇**Verdicchio** [vehr-dee-kee-yoh] (*Marches*, Italy) Spicy white grape seen in a number of *DOCs* in its own right, the best of which is *Verdicchio dei Castelli di Jesi*. In *Umbria* this grape is a major component of *Orvieto*.

🍷 **Verdicchio dei Castelli di Jesi** [vehr-dee-kee-yoh day-ee kas-tay-lee dee yay-zee] (*Marches*, Italy) Light, clean and crisp wines to drink with seafood. **Garofoli;** *Umani Ronchi;* Monacesca; Bucci.

🍇**Verduzzo** [vehr-doot-soh] (*Friuli-Venezia Giulia*, Italy) White grape making a dry and a fine *amabile*-style wine in the *Colli Orientale*.
🍷 **Vergelegen** [vehr-kur-lek-hen] (Somerset West, South Africa) Hi-tech winery initially hampered by indifferent bought-in grapes but well run by winemaker Martin Meinert, who has now left to plough his own furrow.
🍇**Vermentino** [vayr-men-tee-noh] (*Liguria*, Italy) The spicy, dry white grape of the Adriatic and, increasingly, in southern French *Vin de Table*.
🍇**Vernaccia** [vayr-naht-chah] (*Tuscany*, Italy) White grape making the Tuscan *DOCG* Vernaccia di San Gimignano (where it's helped by a dash of *Chardonnay*) and *Sardinian* Vernaccia di Oristano. At best with a distinct nut 'n' spice flavour.
🍷 **Georges Vernay** [vayr-nay] (*Rhône*, France) The great master of *Condrieu* who can do things with *Viognier* that few seem able to match. ☆☆☆☆☆ **1996 Condrieu ££££**
🍷 **Quinta do Vesuvio** [veh-soo-vee-yoh] (*Douro*, Portugal) Single *quinta port* from the family that owns *Dow's*, *Graham's*, *Warre's*, etc.
🍷 **Veuve Clicquot-Ponsardin** [vurv klee-koh pon-sahr-dan] (Champagne, France) The distinctive orange label is back on form after a few years of producing a rather green, non-vintage *Brut*. The *prestige cuvée* is called Grand Dame after the famous Widow Clicquot and the *Demi-Sec* is a worthwhile buy. ☆☆☆☆☆ **1989 Vintage £££**
🍷 **Via Gra'** [vee-yah GRAH] (*Piedmont*, Italy) Richard Small uses seedless grapes and *Pinot Blanc* to make organic wines with bite and a creamy – if not particularly long – finish. A favourite with actor Jim Carrey, it apparently goes down well with other celebrities. One of Italy's most thrusting performers. Can he keep it up? ☆☆☆☆ **Spumante Molte-Volte £££**

Victoria (Australia) Huge variety of wines from the *Liqueur Muscats* of *Rutherglen* to the peppery *Shirazes* of *Bendigo* and the elegant *Chardonnays* and *Pinot Noirs* of the *Yarra Valley*.

Vidal [vee-dahl] (*Hawke's Bay*, New Zealand) One of New Zealand's top four red wine producers. Associated with *Villa Maria* and *Esk Valley*. *Chardonnays* are the strongest suit. ☆☆☆☆ **1997 Chardonnay £££**

Vidal [VI-dal] (Canada) A *hybrid* and highly frost-resistant variety looked down on by European authorities but widely and successfully grown in *Canada* for spicily exotic *icewine*. ***Iniskillin;*** **Rief Estate.**

J. Vidal-Fleury [vee-dahl flur-ree] (*Rhône*, France) Grower and shipper that belongs to *Guigal* and shares that firm's attitude towards quality. ☆☆☆☆ **1991 Côtes du Rhône Villages ££**

VIDE [vee-day] (Italy) Marketing syndicate supposedly denoting finer estate wines. Look for VIDE stickers on labels.

Vieilles Vignes [vee-yay veeñ] (France) Wine (supposedly) made from a producer's oldest vines. (In reality, while real vine maturity begins at 25 Vieilles Vignes can mean anything between 15 and 90 years of age.)

Vieux Château Certan [vee-yur-cha-toh-sehr-tan] (*Pomerol*, *Bordeaux*, France) Ultra-classy, small *Pomerol* property, known as 'VCC' to its fans, producing reliable, concentrated, complex wine. 78 79 81 **82 83** 85 86 88 89 90 92 93 94 95 ☆☆☆☆ **1994 ££££**

Dom. du Vieux-Télégraphe [vee-yor tay-lay-grahf] (*Rhône*, France) Modern *Châteauneuf-du-Pape* domaine which does not always live up to expectations. ☆☆☆☆ **1995 Châteauneuf-du-Pape £££**

Ch. Vignelaure [veen-yah-lawrr] (*Provence*, France) Founded by a refugee from *Bordeaux* in an attempt to show that top-quality wines could be made elsewhere. Went through a very dull patch but now back on form following its purchase by David O'Brien, son of Vincent the Irish racehorse trainer. Produces good examples of *Coteaux d'Aix en Provence* red and rosé.

Vignoble [veen-yohbl] (France) Vineyard; vineyard area.

Villa Maria (*Auckland*, New Zealand) One of New Zealand's biggest producers, and one which is unusual in coming close to hitting the target with its reds as well as its whites. *Riesling* is a particular success.

Villa Mount Eden [vihl-luh mownt ee-dn] (*Napa Valley*, California) Under the ownership of Ch. Ste. Michelle and back on form after a dull patch. Wines, from *Mendocino, Santa Barbara, Napa* and *Carneros* are generally impressive as is the *Pinot Blanc*. ☆☆☆☆ **1994 Zinfandel ££**

Villa Sachsen [za-shehn] (*Rheinhessen*, Germany) Estate with good-rather-than-great, low-yielding vineyards in *Bingen*.

Villages (France) The suffix 'villages' e.g. *Côtes du Rhône* or *Mâcon* generally – like *Classico* in Italy – indicates a slightly superior wine from a smaller delimited area encompassing certain village vineyards.

Villany [vee-lah-nyee] (Hungary) Warm area of Hungary with a promising future for soft young drinking reds.

Villard [vee-yarr] (Chile) Improving wines from French-born Thierry Villard, especially *Chardonnays* from *Casablanca*.

Ch. Villemaurine [veel-maw-reen] (*St. Emilion Grand Cru Classé*, *Bordeaux*, France) Often hard wines which are not helped by heavy-handedness with oak. **82** 83 **85** 86 88 **89** 90 92 94 96

Villiera Estate [vil-lee-yeh-rah] (*Paarl*, South Africa) Reliable range of affordable sparkling and still wines from the go-ahead Grier family. The *Sauvignons* and Cru Monro red are the wines to buy. ☆☆☆☆ **1997 Bush Vine Sauvignon Blanc ££**

Vin de Corse [van dur kaws] (*Corsica*, France) *Appellation* within *Corsica*. **Peraldi; *Skalli.***

Vin de garde [van dur gahrd] (France) Wine to keep.

♟ Vin de l'Orléanais [van dur low-lay-yon-nay] (*Loire*, France) Small *VDQS* in the Central Vineyards of the *Loire*. See *Orléanais*.

Vin de Paille [van dur piy] (*Jura*, France) Now quite rare regional speciality; sweet golden wine from grapes dried on straw mats.

Vin de Pays [van dur pay-yee] (France) Lowest/broadest geographical designation. In theory, these are simple country wines with certain regional characteristics. In fact, the producers of some of France's most exciting wines − such as *Dom. de Trévallon* and *Mas de Daumas Gassac* − prefer this designation and the freedom it offers from the restrictions imposed on *appellation contrôlée* wines. See *Côtes de Gascogne* and *Vin de Pays d'Oc*.

♟ Vin de Pays de l'Hérault [dur lay-roh] (*Midi*, France) Huge vine-growing region, producing some 20 per cent of France's wine, nearly all *Vin de Pays* or *VDQS*, of which *Coteaux du Languedoc* is the best known. Also the home of the extraordinary *Mas de Daumas Gassac*.

♟ Vin de Pays de l'Ile de Beauté [dur leel dur boh-tay] (*Corsica*, France) Picturesque name for wines that are improving thanks to outsiders such as *Laroche*. Often better than this island's *appellation* wines.

♟ Vin de Pays des Côtes de Gascogne [day koht dur gas-koyñ] (South-West, France) The region of the Three Musketeers − and a town called Condom − was once only known for Armagnac. Today, people like *Yves Grassa* and the *Plaimont* cooperative are producing good, fresh, floral whites and light reds. Competition is now increasingly tough, however, from the warmer vineyards of *Languedoc-Roussillon*.

♟ Vin de Pays du Gard [doo gahrr] (*Midi*, France) Huge area with one fair *VDQS*, *Costières du Gard*.

♟ Vin de Pays du Jardin de la France [doo jar-dan dur-lah-fronss] (*Loire*, France) Marketing device to describe some 50 million bottles of *Vins de Pays* from the *Loire*.

Vin de table [van dur tahbl] (France) Table wine from no particular area.

♟ Vin de Thouarsais [twar-say] (*Loire*, France) *VDQS* for a soft light red from the *Cabernet Franc*; whites from the *Chenin Blanc*.

♟ Vin de Tursan [toor-san] (South-West, France) *VDQS* whose big country reds are now beginning to be seen outside France.

Vin doux naturel [doo nah-too-rrel] (France) Fortified − so not really 'naturel' at all − dessert wines, particularly the sweet, liquorous *Muscats* of the south, such as *Muscat de Beaumes de Venise*, *Mireval* and *Rivesaltes*.

♟ Vin du Bugey [boo-jay] (*Savoie*, France) Formerly thin astringent whites of little merit, but becoming rather trendy in France as a source of fresh crisp *Chardonnay*.

Vin Gris [van gree] (France) Chiefly from *Alsace* and the *Jura*, pale rosé from red grapes pressed after crushing or following a few hours of *skin contact*.

Vin Jaune [van john] (Jura, France) Golden-coloured *Arbois* speciality; slightly *oxidised* − like *fino sherry*. See *Ch. Chalon*.

Vin ordinaire (France) A simple local wine, usually served in carafes.

Vin Santo [vin sahn-toh] (Italy) Powerful, highly traditional white dessert wine made from bunches of grapes hung to dry in airy barns for up to six years, especially in *Tuscany* and *Trentino*. Often very ordinary, but at its best, competes head-on with top-quality medium *sherry*. Best drunk with sweet almond ('Cantuccine') biscuits. *Isole e Olena; Avignonesi; Felsina Berardenga; Poliziano; Badia a Coltibuono; Selvapiana.*

Vin vert [van vehrr] (*Midi*, France) Light, refreshing, acidic white wine, found in *Roussillon*.

Vina de Mesa [vee-nah day may-sah] (Spain) Spanish for house wine.

🍷 **Vinho Verde** [vee-noh vehrr-day] (Portugal) Young, literally 'green' wine, confusingly red or pale white often tinged with green. At worst, dull and sweet (especially when over-aged; vintages being rarely printed on labels). At best delicious, refreshing and slightly fizzy.

🍷 **Vinícola Navarra** [vee-NEE-koh-lah na-VAH-rah] (*Navarra*, Spain) Ultra-modern winemaking and newly-planted vineyards beginning to come on stream. Owned by *Bodegas y Bebida.*

Vinifera [vih-nih-feh-ra] Properly *Vitis vinifera*: the species name for all European vines.

Vino da Tavola [VEE-noh dah TAH-voh-lah] (Italy) Table wine, but the *DOC* quality designation net is so riddled with holes that producers of many superb – and pricy – wines have contented themselves with this 'modest' *appellation*. Efforts to herd these quality wines into a new *IGT* – *Vin de Pays*-style – designation are being hampered by the fact that, this being Italy, no one knows precisely how new rules will be implemented.

Vino de la Tierra [bee-noh day la tyay rah] (Spain) New Spanish wine designation similar to the French *Vin de Pays* and worth looking out for if you like interesting, affordable, regional wines.

🍷 **Vino Nobile di Montepulciano** [vee-noh NOH-bee-lay dee mon-tay-POOL-chee-AH-noh] (*Tuscany*, Italy) *Chianti* in long trousers; potentially truly noble (though not often), and made from the same grapes. Can age well to produce a traditional full red. Rosso di Montepulciano is the lighter, more accessible version. The *Montepulciano* of the title is the *Tuscan* town, not the grape variety. 78 79 81 **82 85 88 90** 94 95 96 *Avignonesi.*

Vino novello [vee-noh noh-vay-loh] (Italy) New wine; equivalent to French *nouveau*.

Vintage Year of production.

Vintage Champagne (*Champagne*, France) Wine from a single 'declared' year.

Vintage Character (port) (*Douro*, Portugal) Supposedly inexpensive alternative to *vintage*, but really up-market *ruby* made by blending various years' wines.

Vintage (port) (*Douro*, Portugal) Produced only in 'declared' years, aged in wood then in the bottle for many years. In 'off' years, *port* houses release wines from their top estates as single *quinta ports*. This style of *port* must be decanted, as it throws a sediment.

🍷 **Viognier** [vee-YON-nee-yay] (*Rhône*, France) Infuriating white variety which, at its best, produces floral peachy wines that startle with their intensity and originality. Once limited to the *Rhône* – Condrieu and *Ch. Grillet* – but now increasingly planted in southern France, California and Australia. *Andre Perret; Georges Vernay.*

Viré [vee-ray] (*Burgundy*, France) Village of *Mâcon* famous for whites. **88** 89 **90 92** 95 96 97

🍷 **Virgin Hills** [*Victoria*, Australia] A single red blend that is unusually lean in style for Australia and repays keeping. ☆☆☆☆ **1992 £££**

Dom. Virginie [veer-jee-nee] (*Midi*, France) Dynamic estate whose Australian winemaker is performing *Vin de Pays d'Oc* wonders with local grapes such as the *Marsanne* and *Viognier*.

Viticulteur (-Propriétaire) (France) Vine grower/vineyard owner.

Viura [vee-yoo-ra] (Spain) Dull white grape of the *Rioja* region and elsewhere, now being used to greater effect.

Viu Manent [vee-oo ma-nayn] (Chile) A rising star producing quality premium varietals. ☆☆☆☆ **1997 Malbec ££**

Dom. Michel Voarick [vwah-rik] (*Burgundy*, France) Slow-maturing old-fashioned wines that avoid the use of new oak. The *Corton-Charlemagne* is particularly spectacular.

Dom. Vocoret [vok-ko-ray] (*Burgundy*, France) Classy *Chablis* producer known for making wines that age well. ☆☆☆☆☆ **1995 Chablis Blanchot £££**

Roberto Voerzio [vwayrt-zee-yoh] (*Piedmont*, Italy) One of the new-wave producers of juicy spicy reds, including a first-rate *Barolo*. ☆☆☆☆ **1996 Dolcetto D'Alba Piavino £££**

Alain Voge [vohzh] (*Rhône*, France) Traditional *Cornas* producer who also makes good *St. Péray*.

De Vogüé [dur voh-gway] (*Burgundy*, France) Extraordinary *Chambolle-Musigny* estate whose ultra-concentrated red wines last – and deserve to be kept – for ages. Not cheap, but nor are many of life's true luxuries. ☆☆☆☆☆ **1995 Musigny Grand Cru ££££**

Volatile acidity (VA) Vinegary character found in wines which have been spoiled by bacteria – and also in subtler, and more acceptable measure in many Italian reds.

Volnay [vohl-nay] (*Burgundy*, France) Red wine village in the *Côte de Beaune* (the Caillerets vineyard, now a *Premier Cru*, was once ranked equal to *le Chambertin*). This is the home of fascinating, plummy, violety reds. 78 80 83 85 86 87 **88 89 90** 92 95 96 *Francois Buffet; Dom de Montille; Pousse d'Or; Lafarge; d'Angerville; Lafon; Ampeau.*

Castello di Volpaia [vol-pi-yah] (*Tuscany*, Italy) High-quality *Chianti* estate with *Super Tuscan* Coltassala. ☆☆☆☆ **1991 Coltassala ££££**

Vosne-Romanée [vohn roh-ma-nay] (*Burgundy*, France) *Côte de Nuits* red wine village with *Romanée-Conti* among its many grand names, and many other potentially gorgeous, plummy, rich wines, from a variety of different producers. 78 79 80 82 83 **85** 86 87 **88 89 90** 92 95 96 *Jayer; Hudelot-Noëllat; Jean Gros; Méo-Camuzet; Dom. de la Romanée-Conti; Anne Gros; Rion; Mongeard-Mugneret; Leroy.*

Voss (*Sonoma*, California) Californian venture by *Yalumba*, producing lovely intense *Zinfandel*.

Vougeot [voo-joh] (*Burgundy*, France) *Côte de Nuits commune* comprising the famous *Grand Cru Clos de Vougeot* and a great number of growers of varying skill. Red: 78 79 80 82 83 **85 88 89 90** 92 95 96 *Drouhin; Leroy; Anne Gros;* Chopin-Groffier; *Bertagna; Rion;* Ch. de la Tour.

Vouvray [voov-ray] (*Loire*, France) White wines from the *Chenin Blanc*, ranging from clean dry whites and refreshing sparklers to *Demi-Secs* and honeyed, long-lived, sweet *Moelleux* wines. Often spoiled by massive doses of *sulphur dioxide*. Sweet White: **76** 83 **85** 86 **88 89** 90 94 95 White: 83 **85** 86 **88 89 90** 94 95 96 *Huët; Champalou; Dom. des Aubuisières;* Pichot; Clos de Nouys; Foreau.

VQA (Canada) Acronym for Vintners Quality Alliance, a group of Canadian producers with a self-styled quality designation.

Vriesenhof [free-zen-hof] (*Stellenbosch*, South Africa) Tough, occasionally classic reds and so-so *Chardonnay*. ☆☆☆ **1995 Kallista Red ££**

W

Wachau [vak-kow] (Austria) Major wine region producing some superlative *Riesling* from steep terraced vineyards. **Alzinger; Jamek; Pichler; Hirtzberger; Nikolaihof; Prager; *Freie Weingärtner Wachau.***

Freie Weingärtner Wachau [fri vine-gahrt-nur vak-kow] (*Wachau*, Austria) Impressive cooperative with specially reliable *Grüner Veltliner.* Competes on level terms with some of Austria's best small estates.

Wachenheim [vahkh-en-hime] (*Pfalz*, Germany) Superior *Mittelhaardt* village which should produce full, rich, unctuous *Riesling.* QbA/Kab/Spät: **85** 86 **88 89 90** 91 92 93 94 95 96 Aus/Beeren/Tba: **83 85** 88 89 90 91 92 93 94 95 96 97 ***Bürklin-Wolf; Biffar.***

Waiheke Island (*Auckland*, New Zealand) Tiny island off Auckland where holiday cottages compete for space with vineyards. Land – and the resulting wines – are pricy, but this microclimate does produce some of New Zealand's best reds. ***Goldwater Estate;* Stonyridge; Te Motu.**

Waipara Springs [wi-pah-rah] (*Canterbury*, New Zealand) Tiny producer offering the opportunity to taste wines from this southern region at their best. ☆☆☆ **1995 Chardonnay ££**

Wairau River [wi-row] (*Marlborough*, New Zealand) Classic Kiwi *Chardonnays* and *Sauvignons* with piercing fruit character. ☆☆☆☆ **1996 Sauvignon Blanc ££**

Walker Bay (South Africa) Promising southerly region for *Pinot Noir* and *Chardonnay.* Established vineyards include *Hamilton Russell* and *Bouchard-Finlayson.*

Warre's [waw] (*Douro*, Portugal) Oldest of the big seven *port* houses and a stablemate to *Dow's*, *Graham's* and *Smith Woodhouse.* Traditional *port* which is both rather sweeter and more *tannic* than most. The old-fashioned *Late-Bottled Vintage* is particularly worth seeking out too. 55 58 60 **63 66** 70 75 77 85 94 ☆☆☆☆☆ **Warre's Warrior £££**

Warwick Estate [wo-rik] (*Stellenbosch*, South Africa) Source of some of South Africa's best reds, including a good *Bordeaux*-blend called Trilogy. The *Cabernet Franc* grows extremely well here.

Washington State (US) Underrated (especially in the US) state whose dusty irrigated vineyards produce top class *Riesling*, *Sauvignon* and *Merlot*. Red: 85 88 **89** 91 92 94 95 White: **90 91 92 94** 95 ***Leonetti Cellars; Woodward Canyon; Hogue; Paul Thomas; l'Ecole 41;* Ch. Ste. Michelle; *Kiona; Quilceda Creek.***

Jimmy Watson Trophy (*Victoria*, Australia) Coveted trophy given annually for the best young red at the Melbourne Wine Show. Critics complain that the wine is still in barrel (and thus subject to further evolution); winners celebrate the million dollars-worth of sales the trophy can bring. *Mildara's Jamieson's Run* was a notable winner.

Geheimrat J Wegeler Deinhard [vayg-lur-dine-hard] (*Rheingau*, Germany) Producers with estates all over Germany, including a slice of the great Bernkasteler Doktor vineyard; they have also taken the innovative step of simplifying many of their labels and introducing generic examples of Germany's major wine regions. ☆☆☆☆ **1994 Winkeler Hasensprung Auslese £££**

Wehlen [VAY-lehn] (*Mosel-Saar-Ruwer*, Germany) *Mittelmosel* village making fresh, sweet, honeyed wines; look for the *Sonnenuhr* vineyard. QbA/Kab/Spät: 85 86 **88 89 90** 91 92 93 94 95 Aus/Beeren/Tba: **83 85** 88 89 90 91 92 93 94 95 96 *Dr Loosen; JJ Prum; Wegeler Deinhard; Richter; Selbach-Oster.*

☘ **Weingut Dr Robert Weil** [vile] (*Rheingau*, Germany) Suntory-owned winery with stunning *late harvest* wines. ☆☆☆☆☆ **1996 Rheingau Riesling Halbtrocken £££**

☘ **Dom. Weinbach** [vine-bahkh] (*Alsace*, France) Laurence Faller's regularly turns out wonderful concentrated but subtle wines.
☆☆☆☆☆ **1996 Gewurztraminer Altenbourg Cuvée Laurence ££££**

☘ **Bodegas y Cavas de Weinert** [vine-nurt] (Argentina) Excellent *Cabernet Sauvignon* specialist, whose soft ripe wines last extraordinarily well. ☆☆☆☆ **1994 Weinert Merlot ££**

Weingut [vine-goot] (Germany) Wine estate.

Weinkellerei [vine-keh-lur-ri] (Germany) Cellar or winery.

🌿**Weissburgunder** [vi-sbur-goon-dur] (Germany/Austria) The *Pinot Blanc* in Germany and Austria. Relatively rare, so often made with care.

🌿**Welschriesling** [velsh-rreez-ling] Aka *Riesling Italico, Lutomer, Olasz, Laski Rizling.* Dull grape, unrelated to the Rhine Riesling, but with many synonyms. Comes into its own when affected by *botrytis.*

☘ **Weltevrede Estate** [fel-tur-fray-dur] (*Robertson*, South Africa) Pioneer of the *Robertson* area, successful with *Gewurztraminer* and fortified *Muscadel.* ☆☆☆ **1992 Thistle Hill Cabernet Sauvignon ££**

☘ **Wendouree** [*Clare*, Australia] Small winery with a cult following for its often *Malbec*-influenced reds. Wines are hard to find outside Australia but well worth seeking out. ☆☆☆☆ **1992 Cabernet Malbec £££**

☘ **Wente Brothers** [*Livermore*, California] Improving family company which despite – or perhaps because of – such distracting enterprises as producing cigars and joint ventures in Mexico, Israel and Eastern Europe, is still trailing behind firms like *Fetzer. Murrieta's Well* is the strongest card in the Wente pack. ☆☆☆☆ **1995 Estate Grown Chardonnay ££**

☘ **Domdechant Werner'sches Weingut** [dom-dekh-ahnt vayr-nehr-ches vine-goot] (*Rheingau*, Germany) Excellent vineyard sites at *Hochheim* and *Riesling* grapes produce a number of traditional wines that age beautifully.

Western Australia Varied state whose climate ranges from the baking *Swan Valley* to the far cooler *Mount Barker, Margaret River and Pemberton* growing areas. *Cape Mentelle; Capel Vale; Cullens; Houghton Wines; Leeuwin Estate; Pierro; Vasse Felix.*

☘ **De Wetshof Estate** [vets-hof] (*Robertson*, South Africa) *Chardonnay* pioneer Danie de Wet makes up to seven different styles of wine for different markets.

☘ **William Wheeler Winery** (*Sonoma*, California) Inventive producer whose Quintet brings together such diverse grapes as the *Pinot Meunier*, the *Pinot Noir*, the *Grenache* and the *Cabernet Sauvignon.* ☆☆☆☆☆ **1993 Wheeler Quintet ££**

☘ **White Cloud** (New Zealand) Commercial white made by *Nobilo.*

White port (*Douro*, Portugal) An increasingly popular semi-dry aperitif, though it's very hard to say why when vermouth is far fresher and considerably cheaper. *Port* producers tend to drink it with tonic water and ice, which shows what they think of it. *Churchill's* make the one worthwhile version. ☆☆☆☆ **Churchill's White Port ££**

☘ **Whitehall Lane** (*Napa Valley*, California) Impressive *Merlots* and *Cabernets.* ☆☆☆☆☆ **1994 Cabernet Sauvignon Napa Valley Morisoli Vineyard.**

☘ **Wild Horse** (*San Luis Obispo*, California) *Chardonnays, Pinot Blancs* and *Pinot Noirs* are all good, but the perfumed *Malvasia Bianca* is the star.

Wild yeast Fermentation in most European wines is traditionally kicked off by the natural yeasts that live on the skins of the grapes. In the New World, cultured yeasts are now generally preferred because of their predictability. A growing number of New World reactionaries like *Franciscan Winery* and *Frog's Leap*, however, are proving that the European way can make for greater complexity of flavour.

☈ **Wildekrans** [fil-dur-krunss] (Bot River, South Africa) Pioneer of the Bot River area, with a light lemony *Chardonnay*, piercing *Sauvignon* and extraordinary smokey-bacon-and-strawberry *Pinotage*.

Willamette Valley [wil-AM-et] (*Oregon*, US) The heart of *Oregon's Pinot Noir* vineyards.

☈ **Williams Selyem** [sel-yem] (*Sonoma*, California) Recently dissolved, eccentric partnership producing world class Burgundian-style *Chardonnay* and *Pinot Noir*.

Wiltingen [vihl-ting-gehn] (*Mosel-Saar-Ruwer*, Germany) Distinguished *Saar* village, making elegant slatey wines. Well-known for the *Scharzhofberg* vineyard. QbA/Kab/Spät: 85 86 **88 89 90** 91 92 93 94 95 Aus/Beeren/Tba: **83 85** 88 89 90 91 92 93 94 95 96

☈ **Wing Canyon** (*Mount Veeder*, California) Small hillside *Cabernet Sauvignon* specialist with vineyards high in the hills of *Mount Veeder*. Great, intense, blackcurranty wines. ☆☆☆☆ **1994 Cabernet Sauvignon ££££**

Winkel [vin-kel] (*Rheingau*, Germany) Village with a reputation for complex delicious wine, housing *Schloss Vollrads* estate. QbA/Kab/Spät: **85** 86 **88 89 90** 91 92 93 94 95 Aus/Beeren/Tba **83 85** 88 89 90 91 92 93 94 95 96

Winzerverein/Winzergenossenschaft [vint-zur-veh-RINE/vint-zur-geh-NOSH-en-shaft] (Germany) Cooperative.

☈ **Wirra Wirra Vineyards** (*McLaren Vale*, Australia) Reliable producer making first-class *Riesling* and *Cabernet* which, in best vintages, is sold as The Angelus. ☆☆☆☆☆ **1996 The Angelus Cabernet ££**

☈ **Wolff-Metternich** [volf met-tur-nikh] (*Baden*, Germany) Good rich *Riesling* from the granite slopes of *Baden*.

☈ **Woodward Canyon** (*Washington State*, US) Small producer of characterful but subtle *Chardonnay* and *Bordeaux*-style reds that compete with the best of California. *Semillons* are pretty impressive too. ☆☆☆☆ **1994 Cabernet Sauvignon £££**

☈ **Wootton** (Somerset, England) Successful vineyard, noted for its *Schönberger* but more recently entering the commercial arena in a very un-English way with the highly marketable 'Trinity' blend of wines from three separate sources.

Württemburg [voo-thm-burg] (Germany) *Anbaugebiet* surrounding the Neckar area, producing more red than any other German region.

☈ **Wyndham Estate** (*Hunter Valley*, Australia) Ultra-commercial winery which now belongs to Pernod-Ricard. Quite what that firm's French customers would think of these jammy blockbusters is anybody's guess; they're certainly not like anything they'll have seen out of France. ☆☆☆☆ **1997 Bin 777 Semillon-Chardonnay ££**

☈ **Wynns** (*Coonawarra*, Australia) Well-established subsidiary of *Penfolds*, based in *Coonawarra* and producer there of two wines with a cult following: the *John Riddoch Cabernet* and the Michael *Shiraz*, both of which are only produced in good vintages and so tend to sell fast. There is also a big buttery *Chardonnay* and a pleasant commercial *Riesling*. ☆☆☆☆☆ **1994 John Riddoch Cabernet £££**

X

☗ **Ch. Xanadu** [za-na-doo] (*Margaret River*, Australia) The reputation here was built on *Semillon*, but the *Cabernet* is good too. ☆☆☆☆☆
1993 Semillon £££

Xarel-lo [sha-REHL-loh] (*Catalonia*, Spain) Fairly basic grape exclusive to *Catalonia*. Used for *Cava*; best in the hands of *Jaume Serra*.

Y

☗ **"Y" d'Yquem** [ee-grek dee-kem] (*Bordeaux*, France) Hideously expensive dry wine of *Ch. d'Yquem* which, like other such efforts by *Sauternes châteaux,* is of greater academic than hedonistic interest.

Yakima Valley [YAK-ih-mah] (*Washington State*, US) Principal region of *Washington State*. Good for *Merlot*, *Riesling* and *Sauvignon*. Red: 85 88 **89** 91 92 94 **95** White: **90 91 92 94** 95 96 *Columbia Crest, Columbia Winery,* Ch. Ste. Michelle.

☗ **Ch. Yaldara Lakewood** [yal-DAH-ra] (*Barossa Valley*, Australia) Big *Barossa* producer with a creditable, if uncharacteristic, ultra-ripe *Merlot*.

☗ **Yalumba** [ya-LUM-ba] (*Barossa Valley*, Australia) Associated with *Hill-Smith* and producer of good value reds and whites under the Oxford Landing label; more serious reds and dry and sweet whites, fortified wines (including *Rutherglen Muscat*) and some of Australia's most appealing fizz, including *Angas Brut* and the brilliant Cuvée One *Pinot Noir-Chardonnay*. Now also making wine in California under the *Voss* label. ☆☆☆☆ **1997 Botrytis Semillon-Sauvignon Blanc £££**

Yarra Valley [ya-ra] (*Victoria*, Australia) Historic wine district whose 'boutiques' make top-class *Burgundy*-like *Pinot Noir* and *Chardonnay* (*Coldstream Hills* and *Tarrawarra*); but has also produced stylish *Bordeaux*-style reds and, at *Yarra Yering*, a brilliant *Shiraz*. White: **90 91 92 94 95** 96 97 Red: 85 86 87 88 **90** 91 **92** 94 **95** 96 97

☗ **Yarra Yering** [ya-ra yeh-ring] (*Yarra Valley*, Australia) Bailey Carrodus proves that the *Yarra Valley* is not just *Pinot Noir* country by producing a complex *Cabernet* blend, including a little *Petit Verdot* (Dry Red No.1) and a *Shiraz* (Dry Red No.2) in which he puts a bit of *Viognier*. Underhill is the *second label*. ☆☆☆☆ **1994 Underhill ££**

Yecla [yay-kla] (Spain) *DO* region of Spain near *Valencia* producing alcoholic reds.

☗ **Yellowglen** (*South Australia*) Producer of uninspiring basic fizz, and some really fine top-end fare, including the 'Y' which looks oddly reminiscent of a sparkling wine called 'J' from *Jordan* in California.

☗ **Yonder Hill** (*Stellenbosch*, South Africa) New winery making waves with well-oaked reds. ☆☆☆☆ **1993 Merlot ££**

Yonne [yon] (*Burgundy*, France) Northern *Burgundy* département in which *Chablis* is to be found.

🍷 **Ch. d'Yquem** [dee-kem] (*Sauternes Premier Cru Supérieur*, *Bordeaux*, France) Sublime *Sauternes*. The grape pickers are sent out several times to select the best grapes. Not produced every year and not, it seems, particularly profitable, even at the horrendous prices it commands. Currently the subject of a prolonged legal tussle between its manager and part-owner Comte Alexandre de Lur Saluces and members of his family, who want to sell out to the giant Louis-Vuitton Moët Hennessy group which, in turn, wants to sell the wine through their duty-free shops in the Far East. Such is the wine world in 1998. **62 67 71** 73 **75 76** 77 78 79 **80 81 82** 83 84 85 86 87 88 89 90 ☆☆☆☆☆ **1989 £££££**

Z

🍷 **Zaca Mesa** [za-ka may-sa] (*Santa Barbara*, California) Fast-improving winery with a focus on spicy *Rhône* varietals. ☆☆☆☆☆ **1993 Syrah Santa Barbara County £££**

🍷 **ZD** [zee-dee] (*Napa Valley*, California) If you like big, fuity-rich California *Chardonnay*, made the way it used to be before everyone started to copy *Burgundy*, this is the place to come. The *Cabernets* are pretty juicy too.

Zell [tzell] (*Mosel-Saar-Ruwer*, Germany) *Bereich* of lower *Mosel* and village, making pleasant, flowery *Riesling*. Famous for the *Schwarze Katz* (black cat) *grosslage*. QbA/Kab/Spät: **85 88 89 90** 91 92 93 94 95 96 Aus/Beeren/Tba: **83 85** 88 89 90 91 92 93 94 95 96 97

🍷 **Zenato** [zay-NAH-toh] (*Veneto*, Italy) Successful producer of modern *Valpolicella* (particularly *Amarone*), *Soave* and *Lugana*. ☆☆☆☆ **1988 Amarone Classico della Valpolicella £££**

Zentralkellerei [tzen-trahl-keh-lur-ri] (Germany) Massive central cellars for groups of cooperatives in six of the *anbaugebiet* – the *Mosel-Saar-Ruwer* Zentralkellerei is Europe's largest cooperative.

Zibibbo [zee-BEE-boh] (*Sicily*, Italy) Good light *Muscat* for easy summer drinking.

Zimbabwe The industry here started during the days of sanctions and involved growing grapes in ex-tobacco fields. Now the quality is slowly improving to a level of international adequacy.

🍷 **Dom. Zind-Humbrecht** [zind-hoom-brekht] (*Alsace*, France) Extraordinarily consistent producer of highly perfumed, ultra-concentrated, single-vineyard wines and good *varietals* that have won a shelf-ful of awards from the *International Wine Challenge* and helped to draw *Alsace* to the attention of a new generation of wine drinkers. ☆☆☆☆ **1996 Pinot Gris £££**

🍇 **Zinfandel** [zin-fan-del] (California) Versatile red grape, producing everything from dark, jammy, leathery reds, to pale pink, spicy 'blush' wines, and even a little fortified wine that bears comparison with *port*. The finest exponents are undoubtedly *Ridge*. Also grown by *Cape Mentelle* in Australia, and *Blauwklippen* in South Africa.

🍷 **Don Zoilo** [don zoy-loh] (*Jerez*, Spain) Classy *sherry* producer. ☆☆☆☆ **Don Zoilo Oloroso ££**

🍷 **Zonin** [zoh-neen] (*Veneto*, Italy) Dynamic company producing good wines in the *Veneto*, *Piedmont* and *Tuscany*.

🍇 **Zweigelt** [zvi-gelt] (Austria) Distinctive berryish red wine grape, more or less restricted to Austria and Hungary.

UK
MERCHANTS

3D Wines ☆☆☆☆
Holly Lodge, High Street, Swineshead, Lincolnshire, PE20 3LH. ☏ 01205 820 745. FAX 01205 821 042.
E-mail: info.3dwines@btinternet.com
Website: www. btinternet.com/~info.
3dwines By the case only, credit cards, delivery, tastings, mail order only.
A club specialising in Burgundy, Loire and Champagne, with an outlet near Calais.

W.M. Addison Ltd. ☆☆☆☆
The Warehouse, Village Farm, Lilleshall, Newport, Shropshire, TF10 9HB. ☏ 01952 670 200. FAX 01952 677 309. Credit cards, delivery, *en primeur*, cellarage, glass hire/loan, tastings.
Good Australian and traditional French wines.

Adnams Wine Merchants
☆☆☆☆☆ The Crown, High Street, Southwold, Suffolk, IP18 6DP. ☏ 01502 727 220/2. FAX 01502 727 223. E-mail: wines@adnams.co.uk
Credit cards, delivery, tastings, *en primeur*, cellarage, glass hire, mail order case only.
Arguably Britain's best merchant, with an eclectic, stylish list. Especially good at the New World and France.

Allez Vins! ☆☆☆
PO Box 1019, Long Itchington, Rugby, Warwickshire, CV23 8ZU. ☏+FAX 01926 811 969. E-mail: av@ bigfoot.com Credit cards, by the case only, tastings, delivery, glass loan, mail order only.
Go-ahead family company specialising in French wines from small producers.

The Antique Wine Co. of Great Britain ☆☆☆☆
The Old Stables, Thorpe Constantine, Staffs, B79 0LH. ☏ 01827 830 707. FAX 01827 830 539.
E-mail: celebrate@antiquewine.co.uk
Mail order only, credit cards, delivery, cellarage, *en primeur*.
Specialists in anniversary wines.

John Armit Wines Ltd. ☆☆☆☆☆
5 Royalty Studios, 105 Lancaster Road, London, W11 1QF. ☏ 0171 727 6846. FAX 0171 727 7133. E-mail: info@armit.co.uk Website: www.armit.co.uk By the case only, credit cards, delivery, tastings, *en primeur*, cellarage, mail order only.
A stylish list – fine clarets, Domaine Burgundies and some great Italians.

Arriba Kettle ☆☆☆☆
Buckle Street, Honeybourne, Evesham, Worcs, WR11 5QB. ☏ 01386 833 024. FAX 01386 833 541. Mail order only, by the case only, glass hire/loan, delivery.
Small scale operation, broadening its focus from Spain to France.

Asda Stores Plc. ☆☆☆☆
Asda House, Southbank, Great Wilson Street, Leeds, LS11 5AD. ☏ 01132 435 435. FAX 01132 417 766. Credit cards, tastings, glass hire/loan.
Dynamic supermarket chain with wines presented by price and style rather than country.

Australian Wine Club ☆☆☆☆☆
Freepost WC5500, Slough, Berks, SL3 9BH. ☏ 01753 594 925.
Order line: 0800 856 2004.
FAX 01753 591 369. E-mail: sales@austwine.demon.co.uk
Website: www.australian-wine.co.uk
Mail order only, by the case only, *en primeur*, credit cards, delivery.
Rare wines many Australian wine collectors would give their eye-teeth for. Great weekend tastings.

Averys of Bristol Ltd. ☆☆☆☆
Orchard House, Southfield Road, Nailsea, Bristol, BS48 1JN. ☏ 01275 811 100. FAX 01275 811 101. Credit cards, delivery, tastings, *en primeur*, cellarage, glass hire/loan.
Traditionalist with great Bordeaux, Burgundy, Italian and US wines.

B.H. Wines ☆☆☆☆☆
Boustead Hill House, Boustead Hill, Burgh-By-Sands, Carlisle, Cumbria, CA5 6AA. ☏+FAX 01228 576 711.
By the case only, delivery, tastings, glass hire/loan.
Small award-winning company with good wines across-the-board.

Ballantynes of Cowbridge ☆☆☆☆
3 Westgate, Cowbridge, Vale of Glamorgan, CF71 7A2. ☏ 01446 774 840. FAX 01446 775 253. E-mail: ballantynes@btinternet.com Website: www.ballantynes.co.uk
Credit cards, delivery, tastings, *en primeur*, cellarage, glass loan.
Characterful efforts from France (particularly Alsace), Italy and Spain. Also good fortified wines and spirits.

Balls Brothers Ltd. ☆☆☆☆
313 Cambridge Heath Road,
London, E2 9LQ. **C** 0171 739 6466.
FAX 0171 729 0258. E-mail: asiegel@
ballsbrothers.co.uk Credit cards, delivery,
en primeur, tastings, glass hire.
*Wine bar chain with an emphasis on
traditional French wines in general –
particularly claret.*

Adam Bancroft Associates ☆☆☆☆
The Mansion House, 57 South
Lambeth Road, Vauxhall, London,
SW8 1RJ. **C** 0171 793 1902. **FAX**
0171 793 1897. Mail order only, by the case
only, credit cards, tastings, delivery, glass,
cellarage.
*Serious supporter of French and
Italian wines, along with some
very desirable rarities from Western
Australia.*

Georges Barbier of London
☆☆☆☆ 267 Lee High Road, London,
SE12 8RU. **C** 0181 852 5801.
FAX 0181 463 0398. By the case only,
delivery, *en primeur*, cellarage.
*Unusual wines from Spain and
Uruguay, as well as good Burgundy
and old Armagnacs.*

Barrels & Bottles ☆☆☆☆
1 Walker Street, Wicker Arches,
Sheffield, S3 8GZ. **C** 0114 276
9666. **FAX** 0114 279 9182. E-mail:
jmh6868@aol.com Website:
www.members.aol.com/jmh6868
Credit cards, delivery, tastings, *en primeur*,
cellarage, glass hire/loan.
*German specialist. Sister establish-
ment of The Wine Schoppen.*

Bennetts Wines ☆☆☆☆☆
High Street, Chipping Campden,
Glos, GL55 6AG. **C**+**FAX** 01386 840
392. Credit cards, delivery, tastings, *en primeur*,
glass loan.
*Top-class enthusiastic merchant with
classic French wines and some great
examples from the New World.*

Berkmann Wine Cellars ☆☆☆☆☆
12 Brewery Road, London, N7 9NH.
C 0171 609 4711. **FAX** 0171 607 0018.
E-mail: postmaster@berkmann.co.uk
Credit cards, glass hire/loan, delivery.
*Restaurant suppliers with a focus on
France (especially Burgundy), plus
some good Italian, Spanish and South
American wines.*

Berry Bros. & Rudd ☆☆☆☆☆
3 St. James's Street, London, SW1A
1EG. **C** 0171 396 9600. Order **C**
0171 396 9669. **FAX** 0171 396 9611.
E-mail: orders@berry-bros.co.uk
Web Site: http://www.berry-bros.co.uk
Credit cards, delivery, *en primeur*, cellarage, tastings,
glass hire/loan.
*Rejuvenated firm with great French,
and increasingly good New World
wines. Also worth visiting at
Heathrow – or on the Internet.*

Bibendum Wine Limited ☆☆☆☆☆
113 Regents Park Road, London,
NW1 8UR. **C** 0171 916 7706.
FAX 0171 916 7705. E-mail: sales@
bibendum-wine.co.uk Website: www.
bibendum-wine.co.uk By the case only,
credit cards, delivery, tastings, glass loan,
en primeur, cellarage.
*Innovative across the board. Excellent
Burgundies, Rhônes, Australians and
Californians. Great tastings.*

Booths of Stockport ☆☆☆☆
62 Heaton Moor Road, Heaton Moor,
Stockport, SK4 4ND. **C**+**FAX** 0161
432 3309. E-mail: johnbooth4@
compuserve Credit cards, delivery, tastings,
glass hire/loan.
*Well-chosen examples from Iberia,
Australia and Chile.*

Booths Supermarkets ☆☆☆☆☆
4–6 Fishergate, Preston, PR1 3LJ.
C 01772 251 701. **FAX** 01772 255 642.
E-mail: 101475,1546@compuserve.com
Credit cards, glass hire/loan, tastings.
*One of Britain's best supermarkets.
Particularly good on the New World.*

Bordeaux Direct ☆☆☆☆
New Aquitaine House, Exeter Way,
Theale, Reading, Berkshire, RG7 4Pl.
C 0118 903 0903. **FAX** 0118 903 1073.
E-mail: orders@bordeaux-direct.co.uk
Mail order, credit cards, delivery, tastings,
en primeur, cellarage, glass hire/loan.
*French country wines, newsletters
and an excellent tasting festival.*

Bordeaux Index Ltd. ☆☆☆☆☆
4th Floor, Eagle Court, 6/7 St. John's
Lane, London, EC1M 4BH.
C 0171 250 1982/608 1706.
FAX 0171 608 1707. E-mail: zk85@
dial.pipex.com Mail order only,
by the case only, delivery, *en primeur*.
French fine wines.

The Bottleneck ☆☆☆
7 & 9 Charlotte Street, Broadstairs,
Kent, CT10 1LR. **C**+**FAX** 01843 861
095. Credit cards, delivery, tastings, glass
hire/loan.
*Reliable local merchant with a good
range of New World wines.*

Bottoms Up ☆☆☆☆
Sefton House, 42 Church Road,
Welwyn Garden City, Herts, AL8 6PJ.
C 01707 385 000. **FAX** 01707 385
004. Credit cards, delivery, tastings, glass
hire/loan.
*Friendliest part of the Thresher
empire. If you find a case cheaper
elsewhere within seven days, they will
refund the difference and give you an
extra bottle of the same wine.*

The Burgundy Shuttle Ltd.
☆☆☆☆ 13 Mandeville Courtyard,
142 Battersea Park Road, London,
SW11 4NB. **C** 0171 498 0755.
FAX 0171 498 0724. By the case only, credit
cards, en primeur, cellarage, glass loan, delivery.
*As the name suggests, an excellent
Burgundy specialist.*

The Butlers Wine Cellar ☆☆☆☆
247 Queens Park Road, Brighton,
East Sussex, BN2 2XJ.
C 01273 698 724. **FAX** 01273 622
761. Credit cards, delivery, tastings, glass
hire/loan.
*Great odd bottles of Bordeaux,
Burgundy, port and Italian wine in
particular.*

Anthony Byrne Fine Wines Ltd.
☆☆☆☆☆ Ramsey Business Park,
Stocking Fen Road, Ramsey,
Huntingdon, Cambs, PE17 1UR.
C 01487 814 555. **FAX** 01487 814
962. By the case only, delivery, en primeur,
cellarage.
*A major supplier to top restaurants,
with particularly impressive wines
from Alsace and Burgundy.*

Cape Province Wines ☆☆☆
77 Laleham Road, Staines,
Middlesex, TW18 2EA. **C** 01784
451 860. **FAX** 01784 469 267. E-mail:
capewines@msn.com Website:
www.wine.co.za/CapeWinesUK.
Credit cards, mail order, delivery.
*The best place to browse through a
representative range of hard-to-find
modern South African wines.*

Cave Cru Classé Ltd. ☆☆☆☆
Unit 13, The Leathermarket, Weston
Street, London, SE1 3ER. **C** 0171
378 8579. **FAX** 0171 378 8544. E-mail:
enquiry@ccc.co.uk Website:
www.cave-cru-classe.com By the case only,
credit cards, delivery, en primeur.
*Specialists in top vintages of top-of-
the-range wines from Bordeaux and
Burgundy.*

Cellars Direct Wine Club
See Waverley Direct.

The Celtic Vintner ☆☆☆☆
Star Trading Estate, Ponthir Road,
Caerleon, Newport, Gwent, NP6
1PQ. **C** 01633 430 055. **FAX** 01633
430 154. By the case only, credit cards,
delivery, glass hire/loan.
*Award-winning merchant whose wide
range is particularly strong on
Australia and South America.*

Charterhouse Wine Emporium
☆☆☆☆ 86 Goding Street, London,
SE11 5AW. **C** 0171 587 1302.
FAX 0171 589 0982. Credit cards,
by the case only, delivery, en primeur, glass loan.
*Well-chosen wines, particularly from
Australia, Chile and Italy.*

Chateaux Wines ☆☆☆
Paddock House, Upper Tockington
Road, Tockington, Bristol, BS12 4LQ.
C+**FAX** 01454 613 959. Website:
www.btinternet.com/~chateauxwines
By the case only, credit cards, mail order, delivery,
en primeur, cellarage, tastings.
A selection of French wines.

Brian Coad Fine Wines ☆☆☆☆
66 Cole Lane, Stowford Park,
Ivybridge, Devon, PL21 0PN.
C 01752 896 545. **FAX** 01752 691
160. By the case only, delivery, tastings,
glass loan.
*A quietly impressive list of wines
from the Loire, Burgundy and
Bordeaux.*

Cockburns of Leith ☆☆☆☆
The Wine Emporium, 7 Devon Place,
Edinburgh, Scotland EH12 5HJ. **C**
0131 346 1113. **FAX** 0131 313 2607.
Credit cards, delivery, tastings, en primeur, glass
loan, cellarage.
*A merchant to suit the more
conservative Scottish palate: reliable
rather than exciting wines.*

Connolly's Ltd. ☆☆☆☆
Arch 13, 220 Livery Street,
Birmingham, B3 IEU. **C** 0121 236
9269. FAX 0121 233 2339. E-mail:
connowine@aol.com Credit cards, delivery,
tastings, *en primeur*, glass hire/loan.
*Mostly French wines; excellent service
and regular tastings.*

CWS Retail (Co-op) ☆☆☆
New Century House, PO Box 53,
Manchester, M60 4ES. **C** 0800 317
827. FAX 0161 827 5117. Website:
www.co-op.co.uk Credit cards, tastings.
Can be an unexpected source of bargains.

Corkscrew Wines ☆☆☆☆
Arch No. 5, Viaduct Estate, Carlisle,
CA2 5BN. **C**+FAX 01228 43033.
Credit cards, delivery, tastings, *en primeur*,
glass loan.
*Excellent small merchant, covering
the New World and France.*

Corney and Barrow Ltd. ☆☆☆☆
12 Helmet Row, London, EC1V 3QJ.
C 0171 251 4051. FAX 0171 608
1373. E-mail: andrew.gordon@
corbar.co.uk Website: www.corbar1.
demon.co.uk Credit cards, mail order,
delivery, *en primeur*, cellarage, glass hire/loan,
tastings.
*Fine wine specialists, focusing on
Bordeaux and Burgundy.*

Craven's ☆☆☆☆
15 Craven Road, Paddington,
London, W2 3BP.
C 0171 723 0252. FAX 0171 262 5823.
Credit cards, delivery, tastings, *en primeur*,
glass hire/loan.
A small firm specialising in France.

Croque-en-Bouche ☆☆☆☆☆
221 Wells Road, Malvern Wells,
Worcester, WR14 4HF.
C+FAX 01684 565 612. E-mail:
croque@globalnet.co.uk By the case only,
credit cards, delivery, tastings, cellarage.
*Restaurant-cum-wine merchant, with
an extraordinarily encyclopaedic range.*

Rodney Densem Wines ☆☆☆☆
4 Pillory Street, Nantwich, Cheshire,
CW5 7JW. **C** 01270 212 200.
Retail: 01270 626 767. FAX 01270 212
300. Credit cards, delivery, tastings,
en primeur, cellarage, glass loan.
*Focuses neatly on France grand and
humble. Good range of half-bottles.*

Direct Wine Shipments
☆☆☆☆☆ 5/7 Corporation Square,
Belfast, N. Ireland, BT1 3AJ.
C 01232 243 906/ 238 700.
FAX 01232 240 202. E-mail: enquiry@
directwine.com Website:
www.directwine.co.uk Credit cards, delivery,
tastings, *en primeur*, cellarage, glass hire/loan.
*One of the best merchants in the UK,
with good en primeur, plus unusual
wines from the Old and New Worlds
(especially South America).*

Domaine Direct ☆☆☆☆☆
10 Hardwick Street, London,
EC1R 4RB. **C** 0171 837 1142.
FAX 0171 837 8605. By the case only,
credit cards, delivery, cellarage, tastings, *en primeur*.
*A Burgundian heaven in which to find
wines from the best growers.*

Drinks Cabin ☆☆☆
Sefton House, 42 Church Road,
Welwyn Garden City, Herts, AL8 6PJ.
C 01707 385 000. FAX 01707 385
004. Credit cards, delivery, glass hire/loan.
*Part of the Thresher empire selling
lower-priced, larger-volume offerings.*

Eckington Wines ☆☆☆☆
2 Ravencar Road, Eckington,
Sheffield, S21 4JZ. **C**+FAX 01246
433 213. By the case only, delivery, tastings,
glass loan.
*A fine range of big-name Australians
heads a strong list.*

Edencroft Fine Wines ☆☆☆
8-10 Hospital Street, Nantwich,
Cheshire, CW5 5RJ. **C**+FAX 01270
625 302. E-mail: Edencroftfinewines@
btinternet.com Website: http://www.
btinternet.com/~Edencroftfinewines/
index.htm Credit cards, *en primeur*, delivery,
tastings, glass hire.
*A small enterprising range,
specialising in Australian wines.*

El Vino Co. Ltd. ☆☆☆
Vintage House, 1-2 Hare Place,
Fleet Street, London, EC4Y 1BJ.
C 0171 353 5384. FAX 0171 936
2367. E-mail:graham.mitchell@
btinternet.com Website:www.elvino.
co.uk Credit cards, delivery, tastings,
en primeur, cellarage, glass hire.
*Ultra-traditional merchant with four
'tasting-houses' in the City and a huge
range of largely traditional wines,
especially French, sold by the bottle.*

Ben Ellis Wines ☆☆☆☆
The Brockham Wine Cellars,
Wheelers Lane, Brockham, Surrey,
RH3 3HJ. ☎ 01737 842 160. FAX
01737 843 210. By the case only,
credit cards, delivery, tastings, *en primeur*,
cellarage, glass loan.
*An extensive range, principally
focused on the New World and Italy.*

Farr Vintners ☆☆☆☆☆
19-21 Sussex Street, Pimlico,
London, SW1V 4RR. ☎ 0171
821 2000. FAX 0171 821 2020.
By the case only, *en primeur*.
*Fine and rare galore. Known to
collectors and* en primeur *buyers
throughout the world.*

Ferrers Le Mesurier ☆☆☆
'Turnsloe', North Street, Titchmarsh,
Kettering, Northants, NN14 3DH.
☎+FAX 01832 732 660. By the case only,
delivery, cellarage, *en primeur.*
*A short French-biased list with some
really appealing, unusual wines.*

Fine & Rare Wines Ltd. ☆☆☆☆☆
Pall Mall Deposit, 124-128 Barlby
Road, London, W10 6BL.
☎ 0181 960 1995. FAX 0181 960
1911. E-mail: wine@frw.co.uk
Website: www.frw.co.uk Mail order,
credit cards, delivery, *en primeur.*
Wide-ranging serious wines.

Fine Wines Limerick ☆☆☆
Vintage House, 48 Roches Street,
Limerick, Ireland ☎ (00 353) 61 417
784. FAX (00 353) 61 417 276.
E-mail: finewine@indigo.ie Website:
http://www.websters. Credit cards, glass
loan, delivery, cellarage, tastings, *en primeur.*
Specialists in Bordeaux and Chile.

Fine Wines of New Zealand
☆☆☆ PO Box 476, London, NW5
2NZ. ☎ 0171 482 0093/0171 916
8166. FAX 0171 267 8400. E-mail:
margaret.harvey@btinternet.com
Website: www.fwnz.co.uk By the case only,
mail order, tastings, credit cards, delivery.
The name says it all.

Irma Fingal-Rock ☆☆☆
64 Monnow Street, Monmouth,
NP5 3EN. ☎+FAX 01600 712 372.
E-mail: irmafingal-rock@msn.com
Credit cards, delivery, tastings, glass loan/hire.
Good Burgundy and Welsh (!) wines.

Le Fleming Wines ☆☆☆☆
9 Longcroft Avenue, Harpenden, Herts,
AL5 2RB. ☎+FAX 01582 760 125.
By the case only, delivery, *en primeur*, tastings,
glass hire/loan, wine club.
One-woman band with great wines.

Forth Wines Ltd. ☆☆☆☆
Crawford Place, Milnathort, Kinross-
shire, Scotland KY13 7XF. ☎ 01577
863 668. FAX 01577 865 296. Mail order,
by the case only, credit cards, cellarage, delivery,
en primeur.
*Wines from first rate producers in
France and the New World.*

Fortnum & Mason Plc. ☆☆☆☆☆
181 Piccadilly, London, W1A 1ER.
☎ 0171 734 8040. FAX 0171 437
3278. E-mail: info@fortnumandmason.
co.uk Website: www.fortnumandmason.
co.uk Credit cards, delivery, tastings,
en primeur, cellarage.
*Ultra-smart store with some
unexpectedly affordable wines.*

Four Walls Wine Co. ☆☆☆☆☆
1 High Street, Chilgrove,
Nr Chichester, W. Sussex, PO18
9HX. ☎ 01243 535 360. FAX 01243
535 418. E-mail: fourwallswine@
compuserve.com Credit cards, delivery,
en primeur, tastings, cellarage, glass hire/loan.
*Extraordinary list of blue-chip claret,
Burgundies, Germans and Loires.*

Friarwood ☆☆☆☆
26 New Kings Road, London, SW6
4ST. ☎ 0171 736 2628. FAX 0171 731
0411. E-mail: sales@friarwood.com
Website: www.friarwood.com Credit cards,
delivery, tastings, cellarage, glass hire/loan.
Bordeaux and Burgundy specialist.

Fuller's ☆☆☆☆☆
The Griffin Brewery, Chiswick Lane
South, London, W4 2QB. ☎ 0181 996
2000. FAX 0181 996 2087. E-mail:
fullers@demon.co.uk Website:
www.fullers.co.uk Credit cards, delivery,
tastings, *en primeur*, glass hire/loan.
*Award-winning high street
merchant with a great range.*

Gallery Wines ☆☆☆
The Gomshall Gallery, Station Road,
Gomshall, Surrey, GU5 9LB.
☎ 01483 203 795. FAX 01483 203
282. Credit cards, delivery, glass loan.
French wines from small domaines.

Gauntleys of Nottingham

☆☆☆☆☆ 4 High Street, Exchange Arcade, Nottingham, NG1 2ET. ☏ 0115 9110 555/6. FAX 0115 911 0557. Credit cards, mail order, delivery, tastings, *en primeur*.

A tobacconist with a great range of French wines – especially Alsace, the Rhône and Loire. Also Spanish wines and Cuban cigars!

The General Wine Company

☆☆☆ 25 Station Road, Liphook, Hampshire, GU30 7DW. ☏ 01428 722 201. FAX 01428 724 037. Credit cards, delivery, tastings, glass hire/loan.

Covers the field reliably rather than innovatively. Good Champagnes.

William Glasson Fine Wines

☆☆☆☆ North End Way, Hampstead, London, NW3 7HA. ☏ 0181 458 4174. Order Line: 0845 603 1155. FAX 0181 201 9168. Mail order only, by the case only, credit cards, delivery, *en primeur*.

New merchant with a good across-the-board range. France and Spain are particular strengths.

Goedhuis & Co. ☆☆☆☆☆

6 Rudolf Place, Miles Street, London, SW8 IRP. ☏ 0171 793 7900. FAX 0171 793 7170. E-mail: goedhuis@ btinternet.com By the case only, delivery, *en primeur*, cellarage, glass hire/loan.

A source of serious classic French wines – en primeur Bordeaux and Burgundy, and an inventive build-a-cellar scheme.

Gordon & MacPhail ☆☆☆☆

58–60 South Street, Elgin, Moray, Scotland, IV30 1JY. ☏ 01343 545 110. FAX 01343 540 155. E-mail: mail@ gordonandmacphail.com Website: www.gordonandmacphail.com Credit cards, delivery, tastings, glass hire/loan.

Brilliant malt whisky from your birth year, French country wines and good examples from the New World.

The Great Northern Wine Co.

☆☆☆☆ Unit 5, Granary Wharf, The Canal Basin, Leeds, LS1 4BR. ☏ 0113 246 1200. FAX 0113 246 1209. E-mail: gnw.leeds@onyxnet.co.uk Credit cards, delivery, *en primeur*, glass loan, tastings.

One of the best merchants between Edinburgh and Watford, in particular for wines from South America.

The Great Western Wine Co.

☆☆☆☆ Wells Road, Bath, BA2 3AD. ☏ 01225 446 009. FAX 01225 442 139. E-mail: post@greatwesternwine. co.uk Website:www.greatwesternwine. co.uk By the case only, credit cards, delivery, tastings, cellarage, free glass loan, *en primeur*.

Good Burgundies and French country wines. Plenty of half bottles too.

The Greek Wine Centre ☆☆☆☆

48 Underdale Road, Shrewsbury, Shrops, SY2 5DT. ☏ 01743 364 636. FAX 01743 367 960. E-mail: greekwines.uk@clara.net Website: http://home.clara.net/greekwines. uk/home.htm Delivery, tastings.

Exciting new-wave wines from Greece.

Peter Green ☆☆☆☆☆

37 A/B Warrender Park Road, Edinburgh, Scotland, EH9 1HJ. ☏+FAX 0131 229 5925. Credit cards, mail order, delivery, tastings, glass loan, *en primeur*.

Top class wines from Germany, Italy and Australia.

H. & H. Fine Wine Ltd. ☆☆☆☆

29 Roman Way Business Park, London Road, Godmanchester, Huntingdon, Cambs, PE18 8LN. ☏ 01480 411 599. FAX 01480 411 833. Credit cards, delivery, cellarage, *en primeur*.

Thorough French and Australian specialists.

Hall Batson & Co. ☆☆☆☆

168 Wroxham Road, Norwich, Norfolk, NR7 8DE. ☏ 01603 415 115. FAX 01603 484 096. E-mail: hbwine@paston.co.uk Website: www.therepertoire.com Mail order, by case only, credit cards, delivery, glass loan, tastings, *en primeur*.

A broad range that's particularly strong on France, Italy and Australia.

Handford-Holland Park ☆☆☆☆

12 Portland Road, London, W11 4LA. ☏ 0171 221 9614. FAX 0171 221 9613. E-mail: james.handford@virgin.net Website: freespace.virgin.net/james.handford Credit cards, delivery, tastings, *en primeur*, cellarage, glass hire/loan.

Great place to buy and learn about wine, especially from France, Australia and the US.

Roger Harris Wines ☆☆☆☆
Loke Farm, Weston Longville, Norfolk, NR9 5LG. ☏ 01603 880 171. FAX 01603 880 291. E-mail: rhwine.co.uk Mail order only, by the case only, credit cards, delivery. *The best of Beaujolais.*

Harrods ☆☆☆☆
87-135 Brompton Road, Knightsbridge, London, SW1X 7XL. ☏ 0171 730 1234. FAX 0171 581 0490. Credit cards, delivery, cellarage, en primeur, tastings. *High-class Knightsbridge one-stop shop – hot on Bordeaux, Burgundy, Champagne and whisky.*

Harvey Nichols & Co. Ltd.
☆☆☆☆ 109-125 Knightsbridge, London, SW1X 7RJ. ☏ 0171 235 5000 ext 2348. FAX 0171 235 5020. Credit cards, delivery, tastings. *Even higher class than Harrods, with a great collection of old and new classics.*

John Harvey & Sons ☆☆☆☆
12 Denmark Street, Bristol, BS1 5DQ. ☏ 0117 927 5010. FAX 0117 927 5001. Credit cards, mail order, delivery, tastings, en primeur, glass hire/loan. *A broadly-based range of generally traditional wines.*

The Haslemere Cellar ☆☆☆
Rear of 2 Lower Street, Haslemere, Surrey, GU27 2NX. ☏+FAX 01428 645 081. Credit cards, delivery, tastings, en primeur, cellarage, glass loan. *Skilfully chosen French wines.*

Haynes Hanson & Clark ☆☆☆☆
25 Eccleston Street, London, SW1W 9NP. ☏ 0171 259 0102. FAX 0171 259 0103. Credit cards, delivery, tastings, en primeur, glass loan. *France is the area of focus here, and Burgundy the particular strength.*

Hedley Wright & Co Ltd.
☆☆☆☆ Twyford Business Centre, London Road, Bishops Stortford, Herts, CM23 3YT. ☏ 01279 506 512. FAX 01279 657 462. By the case only, credit cards, free delivery, tastings, en primeur, cellarage, glass hire/loan.
A good country merchant offering classy Chileans and stars from the Old World.

Charles Hennings Vintners Ltd.
☆☆☆ London House, Lower Street, Pulborough, Sussex, RH20 2BW. ☏ 01798 872 485. FAX 01798 873 163. Delivery, cellarage, glass loan. *A highly recommendable mixture of traditional wines from Europe, and interesting offerings from the New World.*

Heyman Barwell Jones Ltd.
☆☆☆☆ 130 Ebury Street, London, SW1W 9QQ. ☏ 0171 881 0050. FAX 0171 730 0575. Mail order only, credit cards, delivery, tastings, en primeur, glass hire/loan, cellarage, wine club. *A very good range from all the corners of the globe, with some particularly delicious bottles from Burgundy.*

High Breck Vintners ☆☆☆
Bentworth House, Bentworth, Nr Alton, Hamps, GU34 5RB. ☏ 01420 562 218. FAX 01420 563 827. Mail order only, by the case only, delivery, en primeur, cellarage, glass loan. *Well-established traditional country wine merchant with a well-chosen range of French classic and regional wines.*

Hoults Wine Merchants ☆☆☆
10 Viaduct Street, Huddersfield, HD1 6AJ. ☏ 01484 510 700. FAX 01484 510 712. Credit cards, delivery, glass hire/loan. *Bargain specialists with shops in Leeds and Huddersfield.*

Jeroboams ☆☆☆ 6 Pont Street
London, SW1X 9EL. ☏ 0171 235 1612. FAX 0171 235 7246. Credit cards, delivery, en primeur, delivery, glass loan. *A very smart collection of London shops whose Belgravia branch has everything you need for a brilliant cheese and wine party. The others concentrate on clarets and Burgundies.*

The Hugh Johnson Collection
☆☆☆ 68 St. James's Street, London, SW1A 1PH. ☏ 0171 491 4912. FAX 0171 493 0602. Credit cards, delivery, tastings. *A small yet growing personal selection of bottles from the author of all those best-selling wine books. Also a good place to buy vinous accessories.*

S.H. Jones & Co. ☆☆☆☆
27 High Street, Banbury, Oxon,
OX16 8EW. **℄** 01295 251 179.
FAX 01295 272 352. Credit cards, delivery,
tastings, *en primeur*, cellarage, glass hire/loan.
French and Spanish wines and
excellent malt whiskies.

Justerini & Brooks Ltd. ☆☆☆☆☆
61 St. James's Street, London,
SW1A 1LZ. **℄** 0171 493 8721.
FAX 0171 499 4653. Credit cards, delivery,
en primeur, cellarage, glass hire.
One of Britain's best merchants, in
London and Edinburgh, with a bible-
like list of enticing wines from around
the globe. Brilliant Burgundies.

King & Barnes Ltd. (The
Brewery Shop) ☆☆☆☆
16 Bishopric, Horsham, W. Sussex,
RH12 1QP. **℄** 01403 270 870.
FAX 01403 270 570. E-mail: king.
barnes@btinternet.com Website:
http://www.king&barnes.co.uk
Credit cards, delivery, tastings, glass loan.
Sussex brewer/wine merchant. Good
and fairly priced range, particularly
New Zealand, South Africa and Spain.

Lay & Wheeler ☆☆☆☆☆
Gosbecks Park, Gosbecks Road,
Colchester, Essex, CO2 9JT.
℄ 01206 764 446. **FAX** 01206 560
002. Website: www.layandwheeler.co.uk
Credit cards, delivery, tastings, *en primeur*,
cellarage, glass hire/free loan.
An impeccable range, knowledgeable
staff and a brilliant web site. Still one
of the best regional and mail-order
sources of Old and New World classics.

Laymont & Shaw Ltd. ☆☆☆☆
The Old Chapel, Millpool, Truro,
Cornwall, TR1 1EX. **℄** 01872 270
545. **FAX** 01872 223 005. Mail order,
by the case only, delivery, tastings, glass hire.
An Iberian wine-lover's paradise. This
is the right place to watch the quiet
revolution in the Spanish vineyards.

Laytons Wine Merchants
☆☆☆☆ 20 Midland Road, London,
NW1 2AD. **℄** 0171 388 4567.
FAX 0171 383 7419. E-mail: sales@
laytons.co.uk Website: www.laytons.
co.uk Credit cards, delivery, *en primeur*,
cellarage, glass loan, tastings.
Great own-label fizz and wines from
France, Spain, Germany and Italy.

Lea & Sandeman ☆☆☆☆☆
301 Fulham Road, London, SW10
9QH. **℄** 0171 376 4767.
FAX 0171 351 0275. E-mail: barnes@
l-sandemann. netkonect.co.uk
Credit cards, delivery, *en primeur*, cellarage,
tastings, glass hire/loan.
First class merchant with branches in
Chelsea, Kensington and Barnes.
Well-chosen wines across the board,
but particularly from Burgundy and
Italy.

Lloyd Taylor Wines ☆☆☆
Bute House, Arran Road, Perth,
Scotland, PH1 3DZ. **℄** 01738 447
878. **FAX** 01738 447 979. By the case only,
credit cards, delivery, tastings, glass loan,
en primeur.
One of Scotland's best traditional
merchants.

O.W. Loeb & Co. Ltd. ☆☆☆☆
82 Southwark Bridge Road, London,
SE1 0AS. **℄** 0171 928 7750.
FAX 0171 928 1855. Mail order, delivery,
en primeur, credit cards, tastings, cellarage.
A short list of some of the superstars
of Burgundy, Germany and Alsace.
Bordeaux is also worth a look.

Longford Wines ☆☆☆☆
Great North Barn, Hamsey, Lewes,
E. Sussex, BN8 5TB. **℄** 01273
480 761. **FAX** 01273 480 861. Email:
longwine@aol.com By the case only,
mail order, delivery, *en primeur*, glass hire/loan,
credit cards, cellarage.
Recommended French and German
specialists.

Magnum Fine Wines ☆☆☆☆
43 Pall Mall, London, SW1Y 5JG.
℄ 0171 839 5732. **FAX** 0171 321
0848. E-mail: wine@magnum.
u-net.com By the case only, credit cards,
delivery, *en primeur*, tastings, wine club.
Impressive selection of French fine
wines – especially Bordeaux – at a
price.

Majestic Wine Warehouses Ltd.
☆☆☆☆ Odhams Trading Estate,
St. Albans Road, Watford, Herts,
WD2 5RE. **℄** 01923 298 200.
FAX 01923 819 105. By the case only, credit
cards, delivery, tastings, *en primeur*, glass loan.
A very good range of interesting wines,
supplemented by bargain price one-off
purchases. Great staff.

Marks & Spencer ☆☆☆☆
Michael House, Baker Street,
London, W1A 1DN. **(** 0171 268
8084. **FAX** 0171 268 2674.
M&S chargecard and switch.
*Enterprising chain with a limited but
reliable range. The New World –
Chile and New Zealand especially –
is a particular strength.*

Martinez Fine Wines ☆☆☆☆
36 The Grove, Ilkley, W. Yorks,
LS29 9EE. **(** + **FAX** 01422 320022.
Website: martinez-online.com
By the case only, delivery, tastings, *en primeur*,
cellarage, glass hire/loan.
*Shops in Halifax and Harrogate with
enterprisingly chosen wines from
around the world.*

F. & E. May Ltd. ☆☆☆☆
27 Brownlow Mews, Bloomsbury,
London, WC1N 2LA. **(** 0171 405
6249. **FAX** 0171 404 4472.
By the case only, credit cards, cellarage,
glass loan, delivery, tastings, *en primeur*.
*Lovers of serious classic wines from
Germany look no further; also good
offerings from Alsace, Bordeaux and
Champagne.*

Mayor Sworder ☆☆☆☆
7 Aberdeen Road, Croydon, CR0
1EQ. **(** 0181 686 1155. **FAX** 0181
686 2017. By the case only, credit cards,
delivery, *en primeur*, cellarage, tastings,
glass loan.
*Classy Old World list and some
unusual New World offerings. Very
good service.*

Mitchells Wine Merchants
☆☆☆☆ 354 Meadowhead, Sheffield,
S. Yorkshire, S8 7UJ. **(** 0114 274
5587. **FAX** 0114 274 8481. Credit cards,
delivery, tastings, *en primeur*, cellarage,
glass loan.
*Straight-talking characterful wines –
from both the Old and New World
Great whisky.*

Montrachet ☆☆☆☆
59 Kennington Road, Waterloo,
London, SE1 7PZ. **(** 0171 928
1990. **FAX** 0171 928 3415. Credit cards,
mail order only, by the case only, delivery,
tastings, *en primeur*.
*Excellent French domaines with a
strong bias towards claret and
Domaine Burgundies.*

Moreno Wine Ltd. ☆☆☆☆
2 Norfolk Place, London, W2 1QN.
(0171 706 3055. **FAX** 0171 724
3813. E-mail: moreno-wines@
moreno-wines.co.uk Credit cards,
mail order, glass hire/loan, cellarage, tastings,
delivery, wine club.
*Spanish and South American
specialist with a club that runs great
tutored tastings.*

Morris & Verdin Ltd. ☆☆☆☆☆
10 The Leathermarket, Weston
Street, London, SE1 3ER. **(** 0171
357 8866. **FAX** 0171 357 8877. E-mail:
100072.263@compuserve.com
By the case only, delivery, tastings, *en primeur*,
cellarage, glass hire/loan.
*Brilliant Burgundies and 'new classic'
Californians like Bonny Doon, Jade
Mountain and Ridge. Germany is a
new enthusiasm.*

Wm. Morrison Supermarkets Plc.
☆☆☆ Hillmore House, Thornton
Road, Bradford, W. Yorks,
BD8 9AX. **(** 01924 870 000.
FAX 01924 875 300. Credit cards, tastings,
glass hire/loan.
Great-value mid-price wines.

Nadder Wines Ltd. ☆☆☆☆
2 Netherhampton Road, Harnham,
Salisbury, Wilts, SP2 8HE. **(** 01722
325 418. **FAX** 01722 421 617.
By the case only, delivery, tastings, *en primeur*,
glass loan.
*A laudable range of serious wines
from all of France's major regions and
the New World.*

New Fine Wines ☆☆☆
114 Birckfield Road, Northampton,
NN1 4RH. **(** 01747 853 443.
FAX 01604 459 954. E-mail:
info@newfinewines.co.uk Website:
www.newfinewines.co.uk Mail order,
by the case only, credit cards, delivery, tastings.
*Living up to their name: specialists
in well-selected wines from South
America and Australia.*

New London Wine ☆☆☆☆
1e Broughton Street, London SW8
3QJ. **(** 0171 622 3000. **FAX** 0171 622
2220. By the case only, delivery,
glass loan, *en primeur*.
*Bordeaux provides the focus here –
en primeur and maturely ready
to drink.*

James Nicholson ☆☆☆☆
27a Killyleagh Street, Crossgar, Co.
Down, Northern Ireland, BT30 9DQ.
📞 01396 830 091. FAX 01396 830
028. Credit cards (no Amex, Diners), mail order,
delivery, cellarage, tastings, *en primeur*,
wine club, glass loan.
Impressive merchant with particularly good Burgundy and US wines.

Nickolls and Perks Ltd. ☆☆☆☆
37 High Street, Stourbridge, West
Midlands, DY8 1TA. 📞 01384 394
518/377 211. FAX 01384 440 786.
Credit cards, mail order, delivery, tastings,
en primeur, cellarage, glass hire/loan.
Some excellent Champagnes as well as old classics from Bordeaux. Big in en primeur.

Nicolas UK Ltd. ☆☆☆☆
157 Great Portland Street, London,
W1N 5FB. 📞 0171 436 9338.
FAX 0171 637 1691. Credit cards, delivery,
tastings, glass hire/loan, *en primeur*.
Reliable range from little-known French regional wines to top flight clarets.

Noble Rot Wine Warehouses Ltd.
☆☆☆☆ 18 Market Street,
Bromsgrove, Worcs, B61 8DA.
📞 01527 575 606. FAX 01527 833
133. Credit cards, delivery, tastings,
glass hire/ loan, wine club.
Majestic-like warehouse emporium, offering an energetic, well-priced list. Now launching a wine club.

The Nobody Inn ☆☆☆☆☆
Doddiscombsleigh, Nr Exeter,
Devon, EX6 7PS. 📞 01647 252 394.
FAX 01647 252 978. E-mail: inn.nobody
@virgin.net Mail order, credit cards, delivery,
tastings, glass loan.
Country pub with the best wine list imaginable – including top and lesser-known regions and producers. The range of malts is brilliant too.

Oddbins ☆☆☆☆☆
31–33 Weir Road, Wimbledon,
London, SW19 8UG. 📞 0181 944
4400. FAX 0181 944 4411. Credit cards,
en primeur, delivery, tastings, glass loan.
Simply the best. A great, ever-changing range, fair prices, helpful wine-mad staff. Who could ask for more? (Those asking for more fine wines should try Oddbins Fine Wine shops.)

Pallant Wines Ltd. ☆☆☆☆
17 High Street, Arundel, W. Sussex,
BN18 9AD. 📞 01903 882 288. FAX
01903 882 801. Credit cards, delivery, tastings, glass hire/loan.
Top-class wines from France and Italy. Malts and Madeiras are good too.

Partridges of Sloane Street ☆☆☆
132-134 Sloane Street, Chelsea,
London, SW1X 9AT. 📞 0171 730
0651. FAX 0171 730 7104. E-mail:
partridges@partridges.co.uk Website:
htpp://www.partridges.co.uk Credit cards,
delivery, tastings, glass hire/free loan.
Upmarket grocers whose wines are usually premium brands.

The Pavilion Wine Co. ☆☆☆
Finsbury Circus Gardens, Finsbury
Circus, London, EC2M 7AB.
📞 0171 628 8224. FAX 0171 628
6205. By the case only, credit cards, delivery,
en primeur, cellarage.
Mail order firm specialising in French country wines from smaller producers.

Thos. Peatling ☆☆☆☆
Westgate House, Westgate Street,
Bury St Edmunds, Suffolk, IP33
1QS. 📞 01284 714 285. FAX 01284
714 483. Credit cards, cellarage, delivery, glass
loan, tastings.
Bordeaux specialists. Also stocks over fifty malt whiskies.

Philglas & Swiggot ☆☆☆☆
21 Northcote Road, Battersea,
London, SW11 1NG. 📞 0171 924
4494. FAX 0171 642 1308. E-mail:
philglas@mcmail.com Credit cards,
delivery, glass loan.
Antipodean specialists par excellence.

Christopher Piper Wines Ltd.
☆☆☆☆ 1 Silver Street, Ottery
St. Mary, Devon, EX11 1DB.
📞 01404 814 139. FAX 01404 812
100. Credit cards, mail order, delivery, tastings,
en primeur, cellarage, glass hire/loan.
A solid list with especially good Burgundies and Australians.

Terry Platt Wine Merchant
☆☆☆☆☆ Ferndale Road, Llandudno
Junction, Conwy, Wales, LL31 9NT.
📞 01492 592 971. FAX 01492 592
196. Credit cards, delivery, tastings, cellarage,
glass hire/loan.
A very skilfully selected set of wines.

Le Pont de la Tour ☆☆☆☆☆

The Butlers Wharf Building,
36d Shad Thames, Butlers Wharf,
London, SE1 2YE. ▐ 0171 403
2403. FAX 0171 403 0267. Credit cards,
delivery, glass hire/loan.
*Part of Conran empire. Meticulous
coverage of classic and new regions.*

Portland Wine Company ☆☆☆

152a Ashley Road, Hale, Cheshire,
WA15 9SA. ▐ 0161 962 8752.
FAX 0161 905 1291. E-mail:
portwineco@adl.com Website:
www.portlandwine.co.uk Credit cards,
en primeur, tastings, cellarage, delivery, glass loan.
*A broad range with particularly
choice wines from the New World.*

Quellyn-Roberts Ltd. ☆☆☆☆☆

21 Watergate Street, Chester,
Cheshire, CH1 2LB. ▐ 01244 310
455. FAX 01244 346 704. Credit cards,
cellarage, tastings, delivery, glass hire/loan.
*An enterprising range of South
African wines, ports and Madeiras.*

R.S. Wines ☆☆☆

Avonleigh Parklands Road, Bower
Ashton, Bristol, BS3 2JW. ▐ 0117
963 1780. FAX 0117 953 3797.
By the case only, delivery, cellarage, tastings,
en primeur, glass hire/loan.
Good New and Old World wines.

Raeburn Fine Wines ☆☆☆☆☆

21/23 Comely Bank Road,
Edinburgh, EH4 1DS. ▐ 0131 343
1159. FAX 0131 332 5166. E-mail:
tmahmud@netcomuk.co.uk Credit cards,
delivery, tastings, en primeur, glass loan.
*Merchant with a cult following among
wine lovers on both sides of the border.*

Rare Wine Cellar ☆☆☆

Unit 17, Pall Mall Deposit, 124-128
Barlby Road, London W10 6BL. ▐
0181 964 2240. FAX 0181 964 3177.
E-mail: wine@rarewine.co.uk Website:
www.rarewine.co.uk Mail order only,
credit cards, delivery, en primeur.
See Fine and Rare Wines Ltd.

Reid Wines (1992) Ltd. ☆☆☆☆☆

The Mill, Marsh Lane, Hallatrow,
Bristol, BS39 6EB. ▐ 01761 452
645. FAX 01761 453 642. Mail order only,
credit cards, delivery, tastings, glass loan.
*Eccentric merchant with a witty list
brimming with classic and rare wines.*

La Réserve ☆☆☆☆☆

56 Walton Street, London, SW3 1RB.
▐ 0171 589 2020. FAX 0171 581
0250. E-mail: reynier@lareserve.
netkonect.co.uk Credit cards, delivery,
tastings, en primeur, cellarage, glass loan.
*Top flight wines from Burgundy, Spain
and the US. Also great malts.*

Howard Ripley ☆☆☆☆☆

35 Eversley Crescent, London,
N21 1EL. ▐ 0181 360 8904.
FAX 0181 351 6564. By the case only,
mail order, delivery, tastings, en primeur,
glass loan.
*Burgundy-loving dentist-turned-
specialist wine merchant par
excellence. Nothing but Domaine
Burgundy at its best.*

Roberson Wine Merchant ☆☆☆☆

348 Kensington High Street, London,
W14 8NS. ▐ 0171 371 2121.
FAX 0171 371 4010. E-mail:
wines@roberson.co.uk Website:
www.roberson.co.uk Credit cards, delivery,
tastings, en primeur, cellarage, glass loan.
*An eclectic shop with an appropriate-
ly eclectic range of good young and
mature wines from all over the world.*

The Rogers Wine Co. ☆☆☆

Rectory Cottage, 20 Lower Street,
Sproughton, Ipswich, Suffolk, IP8
3AA. ▐+FAX 01473 748 464.
By the case only, delivery, en primeur, tastings,
glass hire/loan.
*South America and France –
especially Alsace and Loire –
provide the focus here.*

Safeway Stores Plc. ☆☆☆☆

Safeway House, 6 Millington Road,
Hayes, Middlesex, UB3 4AY. ▐ 0181
848 8744. FAX 0181 970 3609/756
2910. Credit cards, glass loan.
*Quietly innovative chain, with good
value wines across the board.*

J. Sainsbury Plc. ☆☆☆☆

Stamford House, Stamford Street,
London, SE1 9LL. ▐ 0171 695
6000. FAX 0171 695 7610. Website:
www.j/sainsbury.co.uk Credit cards,
glass loan.
*Regaining its strength after a dull
patch, Sainsbury is now competing on
much more level terms with Waitrose,
Tesco and Safeway. Innovative ideas
include printing recipes on wine labels.*

Sandiway Wine Company
☆☆☆☆☆ Chester Road, Sandiway, Cheshire, CW8 2NH. ☎ 01606 882 101. FAX 01606 888 407. Credit cards, delivery, tastings, glass loan.
Wacky merchants with fairly priced wines from good producers, in particular in Italy and Australia.

Scatchard Ltd. ☆☆☆
Scatchard Building, 38 Vernon Street, Liverpool, L2 2AY. ☎ 0151 236 6468. FAX 0151 236 7003. Credit cards, delivery, tastings, glass loan.
Spain is the specialist subject, alongside Alsace, sherries and whiskies.

Sebastopol Wines ☆☆☆☆
Sebastopol Barn, London Road, Blewbury, Oxon, OX11 9HB. ☎ 01235 850 471. FAX 01235 850 776. By the case only, credit cards, en primeur, delivery, glass loan.
A fair range of Burgundies, Italians, Bordeaux and Rhônes.

Seckford Wines Ltd. ☆☆☆
2 Betts Avenue, Martlesham Heath, Ipswich, IP5 3RH. ☎ 01473 626 072. FAX 01473 626 004. E-mail: seckford@btinternet.com By the case only, credit cards, delivery, tastings, en primeur, cellarage, glass loan.
Good-value clarets, Germans and Chileans. Great new cellarage.

Selfridges Ltd. ☆☆☆☆☆
400 Oxford Street, London, W1A 1AB. ☎ 0171 318 3730. FAX 0171 491 1880. Credit cards, delivery, tastings, cellarage, glass hire/loan.
A surprisingly fairly priced and highly comprehensive range of wine.

Shaws of Beaumaris ☆☆☆☆
17 Castle Street, Beaumaris, Isle of Anglesey, LL58 8AP. ☎+FAX 01248 810 328. Credit cards, delivery, tastings, glass loan.
A decent broad range of wines.

Edward Sheldon Ltd. ☆☆☆☆
New Street, Shipston on Stour, Warks, CV36 4EN. ☎ 01608 661 409 /661 639 /662 210. FAX 01608 663 166. E-mail:FineWine@Edward. Sheldon.Tel Me.com Credit cards, delivery, tastings, en primeur, cellarage, glass loan.
Claret and Burgundies are the strong point. Good, regular tastings.

Smedley Vintners ☆☆☆☆☆
Rectory Cottage, Lilley, Luton, LU2 8LU. ☎ 01462 768 214. FAX 01462 768 332. By the case only, credit cards, delivery, en primeur, cellarage, tastings, glass hire/loan.
One of Britain's best and friendliest small independent merchants. Particularly good Italian wines.

Somerfield Stores Ltd. ☆☆☆
Somerfield House, Whitchurch Lane, Bristol, BS14 OTJ. ☎ 01179 359 359. FAX 01179 780 629. Credit cards, delivery.
Keenly priced wines, some rather more recommendable than others.

Sommelier Wine Co. Ltd.
☆☆☆☆ 23 St. George's Esplanade, St. Peter Port, Guernsey, Channel Islands, GY1 2BG. ☎ 01481 721 677. FAX 01481 716 818. Credit cards, delivery, cellarage, tastings, glass loan.
Impeccably chosen New World and Italian wines in particular – all gloriously VAT free.

South African Wine Centre Ltd.
☆☆☆☆ 206 Haverstock Hill, Belsize Park, London NW3 2AG. ☎ 0171 431 9090. FAX 0171 431 2360. E-mail: sawc@swig.co.uk Credit cards, delivery, tastings, glass loan/hire.
Precisely what the name would lead you to expect.

Spar (UK) Ltd. ☆☆☆
32–40 Headstone Drive, Harrow, Middlesex, HA3 5QT. ☎ 0181 863 5511. FAX 0181 863 0603. Credit cards.
Good in parts.

Frank E. Stainton Wines ☆☆☆
3 Berry's Yard, Finkle Street, Kendal, Cumbria, LA9 4AB. ☎ 01539 731 886. FAX 01539 730 396. Credit cards, delivery, tastings, en primeur, glass hire.
Particularly good Rieslings, decent Southern French wines, New World and half bottles.

John Stephenson & Sons ☆☆☆
Darwil House, Bradley Hall Road, Nelson, Lancashire, BB9 8HF. ☎ 01282 614 618. FAX 01282 601 161. Credit cards, delivery, glass hire/loan.
You have to pick and choose here but the best wines certainly do repay your efforts.

Stevens Garnier Wine Merchants

☆☆☆☆ 47 West Way, Botley, Oxford, OX2 0JF. ☎ 01865 263 303. FAX 01865 791 315. Credit cards, delivery, glass loan, tastings.

An interesting range from the Loire, Burgundy, Portugal and South America, benefitting from this firm's separate activity as an importer-wholesaler.

Stewarts World of Wine ☆☆☆

224 Castlereagh Road, Belfast, N. Ireland, BT5 5HZ. ☎ 01232 704 434. FAX 01232 799 008. Credit cards, delivery, tastings, glass hire/loan.

Now a subsidiary of Tesco, so the range is likely to change. Hitherto a good place to buy South African and other great wines from the New World.

Stratford's Wine Shippers

☆☆☆☆ High St, Cookham-on-Thames, Berks, SL6 9SQ. ☎ 01628 810 606. FAX 01628 810 605. Credit cards, delivery, tastings, glass loan.

An admirable set of wines from South America, Australia – and England.

The Sunday Times Wine Club

☆☆☆☆ New Aquitaine House, Exeter Way, Theale, Reading, Berks, RG7 4Pl. ☎ 0118 903 0903. FAX 0118 903 1073. E-mail: orders@wine-club.co.uk Credit cards, delivery, tastings, *en primeur*, cellarage, glass hire/loan.

See Bordeaux Direct.

SWIG Wine Merchants ☆☆☆☆

206 Haverstock Hill, London NW3 2AG. ☎ 0171 431 4412. FAX 0171 431 2360. E-mail: imbibe@swig.co.uk Credit cards, delivery, tastings, glass hire/loan.

A laudably innovative range plus a sprinkling of fine and rare. The wedding list service is good too.

T. & W. Wines ☆☆☆☆☆

51 King Street, Thetford, Norfolk, IP24 2AU. ☎ 01842 765 646. FAX 01842 766 407. Mail order, credit cards, delivery, tastings, *en primeur*, cellarage, glass loan.

Covering the whole of France in depth (with particularly mouth-watering Burgundies), California and Austria. Ports and sherries are also a strength – as are half-bottles.

Tanners Wines Ltd. ☆☆☆☆

26 Wyle Cop, Shrewsbury, Shropshire, SY1 1XD. ☎ 01743 234 500/234 455. FAX 01743 234 501. E-mail: sales@tanners-wines.co.uk Credit cards, delivery, tastings, *en primeur*, glass hire/loan.

Friendly country chain with particular strengths in France and Germany.

Tesco Stores Ltd. ☆☆☆☆

Delamare Road, Cheshunt, Herts, EN8 9SL. ☎ 01992 632 222. FAX 01992 658 225. Website: www.tesco.co.uk Credit cards, tastings, glass loan.

Right at the front of the pack these days, with all sorts of bright initiatives and good value offers.

Thresher Wine Shop ☆☆☆☆

Sefton House, 42 Church Rd, Welwyn Garden City, Herts, AL8 6PJ. ☎ 01707 385 000. FAX 01707 385 004. Mail order, credit cards, delivery, tastings, glass loan.

Reasonably well-chosen across-the-board selection, offering the unique 'Wine Buyer's Guarantee' – if you don't like the wine for any reason you can exchange it.

Trout Wines ☆☆☆☆

The Trout, Nether Wallop, Stockbridge, Hants, SO20 8EW. ☎+FAX 01264 781 472. Credit cards, delivery, tastings, glass loan.

A short but fun and affordable list. Also a source of hard-to-find wines.

Turville Valley Wines ☆☆☆☆☆

The Firs, Potter Row, Great Missenden, Bucks, HP16 9LT. ☎ 01494 868 818. FAX 01494 868 832. E-mail: twv wine@aol.com Mail order only, by the case only, delivery, *en primeur*, cellarage.

Bordeaux from 1942–1995, and Burgundy from as far back as 1919. Get the picture?

The Ubiquitous Chip Ltd. ☆☆☆☆☆

12 Ashton Lane, Glasgow, G12 8SJ. ☎ 0141 334 5007. FAX 0141 337 1302. Credit cards, delivery, tastings, cellarage, glass hire/loan.

Glasgow's top merchant, with stars from Bordeaux and Burgundy, plus well-chosen Armagnacs, Cognacs, whiskies and vodkas.

Unwins Wine Merchants ☆☆☆
Birchwood House, Victoria Road,
Dartford, Kent, DA1 5AJ.
📞 01322 272 711. FAX 01322 294
469. Website: www.unwins.co.uk
Credit cards, delivery, tastings, glass hire/loan.
*Fast-improving home counties chain
whose most individual wines for some
reason seem to come from Portugal.*

Valvona & Crolla Ltd. ☆☆☆☆
19 Elm Row, Edinburgh, EH7 4AA.
📞 0131 556 6066. FAX 0131 556
1668. E-mail: sales@valvonacrolla.
co.uk Credit cards, delivery, tastings, glass loan.
*A stunning Italian specialist. Take
part in one of the monthly tutored
tastings or eat and drink at the
restaurant above the shop.*

The Victoria Wine Co. ☆☆☆
Dukes Court, Duke Street, Woking,
Surrey, GU21 5XL. 📞 01483 715
066. FAX 01487 712 007. Website:
www.victoria wine.co.uk Credit cards,
local delivery, glass loan, *en primeur*
*More innovative in recent years
(with a new Martha's Vineyard experimental wine shop) V.W. still hides
good wines in dull-looking shops.
Victoria Wine Cellars are better.*

La Vigneronne ☆☆☆☆
105 Old Brompton Road, London,
SW7 3LE. 📞 0171 589 6113.
FAX 0171 581 2983. Credit cards, delivery,
tastings, *en primeur.*
*Fantastic wines from France, in par-
ticular old Bordeaux and Burgundy.*

Village Wines ☆☆☆
6 Mill Row, High Street, Bexley,
Kent, DA5 1LA. 📞+FAX 01322 558
772. By the case only, credit cards, delivery,
en primeur, glass loan.
*Italy and France are the strongest
suits from a firm begun by a group of
enthusiasts.*

Villeneuve Wines Ltd. ☆☆☆☆
One Venlaw Court, Peebles, Scotland
EH45 8AE. 📞 01721 722 500.
FAX 01721 729 922. E-mail:
villeneuve@wines.scotborders.co.uk
Cellarage, tastings, delivery, credit cards,
glass loan.
*With a new shop in Edinburgh, these
friendly merchants have a good range
and are particularly hot on wines
from Italy and Spain.*

Vin du Van Wine Merchants
☆☆☆☆ Colthups, The Street,
Appledore, Kent, TN26 2BX.
📞 01233 758 727. FAX 01233 758 389.
Mail order, by the case only,
delivery, credit cards, glass loan.
*Extraordinary list with tempting
wines from Australia and
New Zealand.*

Vintage Roots Ltd. ☆☆☆☆
Farley Farms, Bridge Farm, Reading
Road, Arborfield, RG2 9HT. 📞 0118
976 1999. FAX 0118 976 1998. E-mail:
roots@ptop.demon.co.uk By the case only,
mail order only, credit cards, delivery, tastings,
glass hire/loan.
*A wide range of good wines – every
bottle of which is 100 per cent
certified organic.*

Vintage Wines Ltd. ☆☆☆☆
116-118 Derby Road, Nottingham,
NG1 5FB. 📞 0115 947 6565.
FAX 0115 950 5276. By the case only,
credit cards, cellarage, *en primeur*, delivery,
tastings, glass hire/loan.
*France, Germany and Australia are
explored in some depth by this one-off
merchants.*

The Vintry ☆☆☆
Park Farm, Milland, Liphook,
Hampshire, GU30 7JT. 📞 01428
741 389. FAX 01428 741 368.
By the case only, delivery, glass loan.
*Six individual outlets, offering a
good general selection, including
British-made French wines such as
Ch. Méaume.*

Waitrose Wine Direct ☆☆☆☆
Freepost, London, SW19 3YY.
📞+FAX 0800 188 888. Freephone:
0800 188 881. Mail order only, by the case
only, credit cards, delivery, *en primeur*, cellarage.
*Mail order division of Waitrose (once
known as Findlater Mackie Todd),
and showing particular expertise in
the traditional regions of Europe.*

Waitrose Ltd. ☆☆☆☆
Southern Industrial Area, Bracknell,
Berkshire, RG12 8YA. 📞 01344 424
680. FAX 01344 825 255. Credit cards.
en primeur, glass loan, cellarage, delivery,
tastings.
*Traditional wines are always to the
fore, but there are plenty of
innovative bottles to look out for.*

Waterloo Wine Company
☆☆☆☆ 61 Lant Street, London, SE1
1QN. **C** 0171 403 7967. **FAX** 0171
357 6976. Credit cards, delivery, tastings,
glass hire/loan.
*Emphasis on French wines, especially
the Midi. Otherwise New Zealand is
the key area of strength.*

Waters of Coventry ☆☆☆
Collins Road, Heathcote, Warwick,
CV34 6TE. **C** 01926 888 889. **FAX**
01926 887 416. E-mail: rob.caldicott@
dial.pipex.com Credit cards, delivery,
en primeur.
*An eclectic list. Top class Rhônes and
Burgundies, Spanish wines and good
offerings from the New World.*

Waverley Direct ☆☆☆☆
Nest Road, Gateshead, NE10 0ES.
C 0191 495 5000. **FAX** 0191 438
6261. E-mail: customer.enquiries@
waverley-direct.co.uk Mail order only,
credit cards, delivery, tastings, en primeur.
*Bordeaux, Burgundy and the New
World in abundance.*

Weavers of Nottingham ☆☆☆
1 Castle Gate, Nottingham, NE1
7AQ. **C** 0115 958 0922. **FAX** 0115
950 8076. Credit cards, delivery, tastings,
en primeur, glass hire/loan.
*A plethora of malts, some well-chosen
French country wines and wines from
Bordeaux, Chile and Australia.*

Whitebridge Wines ☆☆☆
Unit 21, Whitebridge Estate, Stone,
Staffs, ST15 8LQ. **C** 01785 817 229.
FAX 01785 811 185. Mail order only,
by the case only, delivery.
*Unadventurous but solid range from
France, Spain and the New World.*

Whiteside's of Clitheroe ☆☆☆☆
Shawbridge Street, Clitheroe, Lancs,
BB7 INA. **C** 01200 422 281. **FAX**
01200 427 129. Credit cards, glass loan,
delivery, tastings.
Good source of French country wines.

Whittalls Wines ☆☆☆
Darlaston Road, Walsall,
West Midlands, WS2 9SQ.
C 01922 636 161. **FAX** 01922 636
167. By the case only, delivery, tastings,
glass hire/loan, en primeur, cellarage.
*Good all-rounder Midlands wine
warehouse.*

Wilkinson Vintners Ltd. ☆☆☆☆
Unit 1, Bickerton House, 25/27
Bickerton Road, London, N19 5JT.
C 0171 272 1982. **FAX** 0171 263 2643.
Mail order only, by the case only, delivery,
en primeur.
*Competitively priced cru classé
clarets and vintage ports.*

The Wine Bureau ☆☆☆☆
58 Tower Street, Harrogate, N. Yorks,
HG1 1HS. **C** 01423 527 772.
FAX 01423 566 330. E-mail:
winebureau@psilink.co.uk Website:
http://www.winebureau.co.uk Mail order,
credit cards, delivery, tastings, en primeur,
cellarage, glass loan.
*Interesting finds from both the New
and Old Worlds.*

Wine Cellar ☆☆☆☆
PO Box 476, Loushers Lane,
Warrington, Cheshire, WA4 6RR.
C 01925 444 555. **FAX** 01925 415 474.
Website: http://www.winecellar.co.uk
Credit cards, delivery, en primeur,
glass hire/loan.
*Steaming ahead following a manage-
ment buy-out, this is an innovative
chain, some of whose shops include
cafés. They also have a zappy, interac-
tive internet site.*

The Wine Cellar ☆☆☆☆
10 Station Parade, Sanderstead Road,
South Croydon, Surrey, CR2 OPH.
C 0181 657 6936. **FAX** 0181 657 9391.
Credit cards, delivery, tastings,
en primeur, cellarage, glass hire/loan.
*This independent single outlet offers a
commendable selection, including
fine German wines.*

The Wine Press ☆☆☆☆
Grange Lane, Lye, Stourbridge,
DY9 7HH. **C** 01384 892 941.
FAX 01384 422 913. Credit cards, delivery,
tastings, en primeur, glass loan.
*Burgundy is very well represented
here, along with Champagne and
whisky.*

Wine Rack ☆☆☆☆
Sefton House, 42 Church Rd,
Welwyn Garden City, Herts, AL8 6PJ.
C 01707 385 000. **FAX** 01707 385 004.
Credit cards, delivery, tastings, glass hire/loan.
*The up-market face of Thresher with
a good range, friendly staff and some
great wines.*

Wine Raks (Scotland) Ltd.

☆☆☆☆ 21 Springfield Rd, Aberdeen, AB15 7RJ. ☎ 01224 311 460. FAX 01224 312 186. Credit cards, delivery, tastings, *en primeur*, glass hire/loan.
A good little merchant with old Bordeaux and an interesting collection of Italian wines.

The Wine Schoppen Ltd. ☆☆☆☆

3 Oak Street, Heeley, Sheffield, S8 9UB. ☎ 0114 255 3301. FAX 0114 255 1010. E-mail: jmh6868@aol.com Credit cards, delivery, tastings, cellarage, glass hire/loan.
A vast list which has moved beyond its previous focus on top German wines. Great tastings are a regular feature, and specialist beers are recommendable.

The Wine Society ☆☆☆☆☆

Gunnels Wood Road, Stevenage, Hertfordshire, SG1 2BG. ☎ 01438 741 177. FAX 01438 761 167. E-mail: winesociety@dial.pipex.com Mail order, credit cards, delivery, tastings, glass hire/loan, *en primeur*, cellarage.
Great mail order merchant offering French classics and good South American wines.

The Wine Treasury Ltd. ☆☆☆☆

69-71 Bondway, London, SW8 1SQ. ☎ 0171 793 9999. FAX 0171 793 8080. E-mail:syndicate@winetreasury. demon.co.uk Mail order only, by the case only, credit cards, delivery, tastings, wine club.
The place to look for French classics and Californian wines that are impossible to find elsewhere.

Wine World ☆☆☆

'Owlet', Templepan Lane, Chandlers Cross, Rickmansworth, Herts, WD3 4NH. ☎+FAX 01923 264 718. Mobile: 0410 405 874.Email:lilyaneweston@ connect-2co.uk By the case only, cellarage, delivery, tastings, glass hire/loan.
A limited but good quality range whose greatest strengths are to be found in wines from France and Chile.

The Winery ☆☆☆

4 Clifton Road, Maida Vale, London, W9 1SS. ☎ 0171 286 6475. FAX 0171 286 2733. Credit cards, delivery, tastings, glass hire/loan.
Good Italian and Californian wines and Burgundies.

Woodhouse Wines ☆☆☆

The Brewery, Blandford St. Mary, Dorset, DT11 9LS. ☎ 01258 452 141. FAX 01258 450 147. Credit cards, delivery, tastings, glass hire/loan.
French country wines and some interesting bin ends.

The Wright Wine Co. ☆☆☆

The Old Smithy, Raikes Road, Skipton, N. Yorks, BD23 1NP. ☎ 01756 700 886. FAX 01756 798 580. Credit cards, delivery, cellarage, glass loan/hire.
Great wines from South America, Spain and Australia. Halves galore.

Wrightson & Company ☆☆☆☆

Manfield Grange, Manfield, Darlington, N. Yorks, DL2 2RE. ☎ 01325 374 134. FAX 01325 374 135. E-mail: ed.wrightson.wine@ onyxnet.co.uk By the case only, mail order, credit cards, delivery, tastings, *en primeur*, cellarage, glass hire/loan.
Elegant list with good tasting notes.

Peter Wylie Fine Wines ☆☆☆☆☆

Plymtree Manor, Plymtree, Devon, EX5 4NW. ☎ 01884 277 555. FAX 01884 277 557. E-mail: peter@ wylie-fine-wines.demon.co.uk Mail order only, delivery, *en primeur*, cellarage.
Treasure trove of rare and fine wines.

Yapp Brothers Ltd. ☆☆☆☆☆

The Old Brewery, Mere, Wiltshire, BA12 6DY. ☎ 01747 860 423. FAX 01747 860 929. Credit cards, delivery, tastings, cellarage, glass loan.
Britain's most faithful – and best – Loire and Rhône specialists.

York Wines ☆☆☆

Wellington House, Sheriff Hutton, York, YO60 6QY. ☎ 01347 878 716. FAX 01347 878 546. Credit cards, delivery, *en primeur*, tastings, cellarage, glass hire/loan.
Traditional merchant with tasty wines from France, Italy and Chile.

Noel Young Wines ☆☆☆☆☆

56 High Street, Trumpington, Cambridge, CB2 2LS. ☎ 01223 844 744/566 744. FAX 01223 844 736. E-mail: noel.young@dial.pipex.com Website: www.nywines.co.uk Credit cards, *en primeur*, delivery, tastings, glass hire/loan.
Good broad range, tastings. Brilliant Austrian wines.

WHERE TO BUY

The following section has been included to help you find almost everything – short of a congenial companion – that you are likely to need to enjoy wine. If you are looking for a wine from a specific region, or perhaps glasses, corkscrews, courses, holidays, auctioneers, cellars or wine books, this is the place.

WINE SPECIALISTS

THE AMERICAS
NORTH AMERICA
The Antique Wine Co. (see Page 252)
Adnams (see Page 252)
Averys of Bristol (see Page 252)
Bennetts Wines (see Page 253)
Bibendum (see Page 253)
Booths (see Page 253)
The Bottleneck (see Page 254)
Corkscrew Wines (see Page 255)
Ben Ellis Wines (see Page 256)
Gordon and MacPhail (see Page 257)
The Great Northern Wine Co.
  (see Page 257)
Handford-Holland Park
  (see Page 257)
Charles Hennings (see Page 258)
King & Barnes (see Page 259)
Lay & Wheeler (see Page 259)
Morris & Verdin (see Page 260)
Nadder Wines (see Page 260)
New Fine Wines (see Page 260)
Oddbins (see Page 261)
Terry Platt (see Page 261)
R.S. Wines (see Page 262)
Raeburn (see Page 262)
Sommelier Wine Co. (see Page 263)
Frank E. Stainton Wines
  (see Page 263)
Stevens Garnier (see Page 264)
Stewarts World of Wine
  (see Page 264)
Stratford's Wine Shippers
  (see Page 264)
T.&W. Wines (see Page 264)
Waverley Direct (see Page 266)
The Wine Treasury (see Page 267)

SOUTH AMERICA
Georges Barbier of London
  (see Page 253)
Booths of Stockport (see Page 253)
The Bottleneck (see Page 254)
Charterhouse Wine Emporium
  (see Page 254)
Ben Ellis Wines (see Page 256)
Fine Wines of Limerick
  (see Page 256)
Forth Wines (see Page 256)
Hedley Wright (see Page 258)

Moreno Wine Importers
  (see Page 260)
Stevens Garnier (see Page 264)
The Wine Society (see Page 267)
The Wright Wine Co. (see Page 267)

AUSTRALIA
Adnams (see Page 252)
Australian Wine Club (see Page 252)
Adam Bancroft (see Page 253)
Bennetts (see Page 253)
Booths of Stockport (see Page 253)
Charterhouse Wine Emporium
  (see Page 254)
Direct Wine Shipments
  (see Page 255)
Eckington Wines (see Page 255)
Edencroft Fine Wines (see Page 255)
Great Northern Wine Co
  (see Page 257)
Peter Green (see Page 257)
H.& H. Fine Wines
  (see Page 257)
Hall Batson & Co.(see Page 257)
Jeroboams (see Page 258)
Mitchells (see Page 260)
Philglas & Swiggott (see Page 261)
Christopher Piper (see Page 261)
Portland Wine Co. (see Page 262)
R.S. Wines (see Page 262)
Sandiway Wine Co.
  (see Page 263)
Vin du Van (see Page 265)
Vintage Wines (see Page 265)

AUSTRIA
Forth Wines (see Page 256)
T.&W. Wines (see Page 264)
Noel Young Wines (see Page 267)

EASTERN EUROPE
Wines of Westhorpe
  (See Page 267)
The Royal Tokaji Wine Co.
  C *0171 495 3010.*

ENGLAND
Smedley Vintners (see Page 263)
Stratfords Wine Shippers
  (see Page 264)

FRANCE

ALSACE

Ballantynes of Cowbridge
(see Page 252)
Anthony Byrne (see Page 254)
Gauntleys of Nottingham
(see Page 257)
Haslemere Cellar (see Page 258)
O.W. Loeb (see Page 259)
Scatchard Wines(see Page 263)
Tanners Wines (see Page 264)
Wine Rack (see Page 266)
The Wine Society (see Page 267)

BEAUJOLAIS

Adam Bancroft (see Page 252)
Roger Harris (see Page 258)

BORDEAUX

The Antique Wine Co.
(see Page 252)
John Armit (see Page 252)
Averys of Bristol (see Page 252)
Balls Brothers (see Page 253)
Berry Bros. & Rudd (see Page 253)
Bibendum (see Page 253)
Bordeaux Index (see Page 253)
The Butlers Wine Cellar
(see Page 254)
Anthony Byrne (see Page 254)
Cave Cru Classé Ltd. (see Page 254)
Brian Coad (see Page 254)
Corney and Barrow (see Page 255)
Direct Wine Shipments (see Page 255)
Farr Vintners (see Page 256)
Fortnum & Mason (see Page 256)
Four Walls Wine Co.(see Page 256)
Gallery Wines (see Page 256)
Goedhuis & Co. (see Page 257)
Harrods (see Page 258)
Harvey Nichols (see Page 258)
Justerini & Brooks (see Page 259)
Lay & Wheeler (see Page 259)
O.W. Loeb (see Page 259)
Magnum (see Page 259)
F. & E. May (see Page 260)
Montrachet (see Page 260)
New London Wines (see Page 260)
Nickolls & Perks (see Page 261)
Nicolas (see Page 261)
Oddbins Fine Wines (see Page 261)
Thos. Peatling (see Page 261)
Le Pont de la Tour (see Page 262)
Reid Wines (see Page 262)
Roberson (see Page 262)
Edward Sheldon (see Page 263)
Smedley Vintners (see Page 263)
Tanners Wines (see Page 264)
Turville Valley (see Page 264)
The Ubiquitous Chip (see Page 264)
Waverley Direct (see Page 266)
Wilkinson Vintners (see Page 266)

The Wine Society (see Page 267)
Peter Wylie (see Page 267)

BURGUNDY

3D Wines (see Page 252)
The Antique Wine Co. (see Page 252)
John Armit Wines (see Page 252)
Averys of Bristol (see Page 252)
Adam Bancroft (see Page 253)
Georges Barbier (see Page 253)
Bibendum (see Page 253)
The Burgundy Shuttle (see Page 254)
The Butlers Wine Cellar
(see Page 254)
Anthony Byrne (see Page 254)
Cave Cru Classé (see Page 254)
Brian Coad (see Page 254)
Corney and Barrow (see Page 255)
Domaine Direct (see Page 255)
Farr Vintners (see Page 256)
Fortnum & Mason (see Page 256)
Four Walls Wine Co. (see Page 256)
Goedhuis & Co. (see Page 257)
Harrods (see Page 258)
Harvey Nichols (see Page 258)
Haynes Hanson & Clark
(see Page 258)
Jeroboams (see Page 258)
Lay & Wheeler (see Page 259)
Lea & Sandeman (see Page 259)
O.W. Loeb (see Page 259)
Montrachet (see Page 260)
Morris & Verdin (see Page 260)
James Nicholson (see Page 261)
Oddbins Fine Wines (see Page 261)
Christopher Piper (see Page 261)
Le Pont de la Tour (see Page 262)
Raeburn Fine Wines (see Page 262)
La Réserve (see Page 262)
Howard Ripley (see Page 262)
Stevens Garnier (see Page 264)
T.&W. Wines (see Page 264)
Turville Valley (see Page 264)
The Ubiquitous Chip (see Page 264)
La Vigneronne (see Page 265)
Waverley Direct (see Page 266)
The Wine Press (see Page 266)

CHAMPAGNE

3D Wines (see Page 252)
Farr Vintners (see Page 256)
Fortnum & Mason (see Page 256)
The General Wine Co. (see Page 257)
Harrods (see Page 258)
Majestic Wines(see Page 260)
Oddbins (see Page 261)

COUNTRY WINES

Allez Vins! (see Page 252)
Bordeaux Direct (see Page 253)
The Great Western Wine Co.
(see Page 257)
Nadder Wines (see Page 260)

Nicolas (see Page 261)
The Pavilion Wine Co. (see Page 261)
Smedley Vintners (see Page 263)
Whiteside's of Clitheroe
  (see Page 266)
Yapp Brothers (see Page 267)
LOIRE
Brian Coad (see Page 254)
Four Walls Wine Co. (see Page 256)
Handford-Holland Park
  (see Page 257)
Yapp Brothers (see Page 267)
RHONE
Bibendum (see Page 253)
Croque-en-Bouche (see Page 255)
Farr Vintners (see Page 256)
Gauntleys of Nottingham
  (see Page 257)
Waters of Coventry (see Page 266)
Yapp Brothers (see Page 267)

GERMANY
Adnams (see Page 252)
Four Walls Wine Co. (see Page 256)
Justerini & Brooks (see Page 259)
Laytons Wine Merchants
  (see Page 259)
O.W. Loeb (see Page 259)
Longford Wines (see Page 259)
Majestic (see Page 259)
F.&E. May (see Page 260)
Tanners (see Page 264)
The Wine Schoppen (see Page 267)

ITALY
John Armit (see Page 252)
Averys of Bristol (see Page 252)
Berkmann Wine Cellars
  (see Page 253)
Peter Green (see Page 257)
Hall Batson (see Page 257)
Laytons Wine Merchants
  (see Page 259)
Valvona & Crolla (see Page 265)

NEW ZEALAND
Fine Wines of New Zealand
  (see Page 256)
Vin du Van (see Page 265)
Waterloo Wine Co. (see Page 266)

PORTUGAL
D.&F. Wines 🅲 *0181 838 4399.*
Moreno Wine Importers
  (see Page 260)
Raeburn Fine Wines (see Page 262)

SOUTH AFRICA
Cape Province (see Page 254)

King & Barnes (see Page 259)
South African Wine Centre
  (see Page 263)

SPAIN
Arriba Kettle (see Page 252)
Georges Barbier (see Page 253)
S. H. Jones (see Page 259)
Laymont & Shaw (see Page 259)
Mitchells (see Page 260)
Moreno Wine Importers (see Page 260)
La Réserve (see Page 262)
Scatchard (see Page 263)
Waters of Coventry (see Page 266)

FORTIFIED WINES
PORT & MADEIRA
Ballantynes of Cowbridge
  (see Page 252)
Farr Vintners (see Page 256)
Fortnum & Mason (see Page 256)
Moreno Wine Importers
  (see Page 260)
Pallant Wines (see Page 261)
Thos. Peatling (see Page 261)
Quellyn-Roberts (see Page 262)
Reid Wines (see Page 262)
T.&W. Wines (see Page 264)
Turville Valley (see Page 264)
Peter Wylie (see Page 267)
SHERRY
Ballantynes of Cowbridge
  (see Page 252)
El Vino (see Page 255)
Fortnum & Mason (see Page 256)
Laymont & Shaw (see Page 259)
Lea & Sandeman (see Page 259)
Martinez (see Page 260)
Moreno Wine Importers
  (see Page 260)
Scatchard (see Page 263)
Reid Wines (see Page 262)

SPECIALITY BEERS
Adnams (see Page 252)
Fullers (see Page 256)
King & Barnes (see Page 259)
Majestic Wines (see Page 259)
Mitchells (see Page 260)
Oddbins (see Page 261)
Unwins (see Page 265)
Wine Cellar (see Page 266)
The Wine Schoppen (see Page 267)

SPIRITS
ARMAGNAC & COGNAC
Georges Barbier (see Page 253)
Justerini & Brooks (see Page 259)
Nicolas (see Page 261)
The Ubiquitous Chip (see Page 264)

WHISKY
  Berry Bros. & Rudd (see Page 253)
  Harrods (see Page 258)
  Charles Hennings (see Page 258)
  S.H. Jones (see Page 259)
  The Nobody Inn (see Page 261)
  Oddbins (see Page 261)
  Pallant Wines (see Page 261)
  La Réserve (see Page 262)
  The Ubiquitous Chip (see Page 264)

FINE AND RARE WINES
  John Armit (see Page 252)
  Bennetts (see Page 253)
  Berry Bros. & Rudd (see Page 253)
  Bibendum (see Page 253)
  Bordeaux Index (see Page 253)
  Anthony Byrne (see Page 254)
  Cave Cru Classé (see Page 254)
  Corney and Barrow (see Page 255)
  Farr Vintners (see Page 256)

  Fine and Rare Wines (see Page 256)
  Fortnum & Mason (see Page 256)
  Four Walls Wine Co. (see Page 256)
  Goedhuis & Co. (see Page 257)
  Harrods (see Page 258)
  Harvey Nichols (see Page 258)
  Lay & Wheeler (see Page 259)
  Nickolls & Perks (see Page 261)
  Nicolas (see Page 261)
  Oddbins Fine Wines (see Page 261)
  Thos. Peatling (see Page 261)
  Raeburn Fine Wines (see Page 262)
  Rare Wine Cellar (see Page 262)
  Reid Wines (see Page 262)
  La Réserve (see Page 262)
  Roberson (see Page 262)
  T.&W. Wines (see Page 264)
  Tanners Wines (see Page 264)
  Turville Valley (see Page 264)
  Peter Wylie (see Page 267)
  Noel Young Wines (see Page 267)

AUCTIONEERS

Bigwood Auctioneers ☎ 01789 269 415. ℻ 01789 294 168.
Christie's ☎ 0171 581 7611. ℻ 0171 321 3321.
Website: www.christies.com
Lacy Scott ☎ 01284 763 531. ℻ 01284 704 713.
Lithgow ☎ 01642 710 158.

℻ 01642 712 641. E-mail: lithgow. auctions@onyxnet.co.uk
Phillip's ☎ 01865 723 524. ℻ 01865 791 064.
Sotheby's ☎ 0171 293 6423. ℻ 0171 293 5961.
J. Straker Chadwick & Sons ☎ 01873 852 624. ℻ 01873 857 311.

LEARNING ABOUT WINE

WINE COURSES
Association of Wine Educators/ Grape to Glass Workshops ☎+℻ 0171 995 2277.
Challenge Educational Services ☎ 01273 220 261. ℻ 01273 220 376. E-mail: enquiries@ challengeuk.com
Christie's ☎ 0171 581 3933. ℻ 0171 589 0383.
Ecole du Vin, Château Loudenne ☎ 01279 626 801. ℻ 01279 633 769.
German Wine Academy ☎ 0171 331 8800. ℻ 0171 331 1991.
Justerini & Brooks ☎ 0131 226 4202. ℻ 0131 225 2351. E-mail: od04@ dial.pipex.com
Kensington & Chelsea College ☎ 0171 573 5333. ℻ 0181 960 2693. Website: http://www.kcc.ac.uk
Leicestershire Wine School ☎ 0116 254 2702. ℻ 0116 254 2702.
Leith's ☎ 0171 229 0177. ℻ 0171 937 5257. E-mail: info@leiths.com

Maurice Mason ☎+℻ 0181 841 8732.
North West Wine and Spirit Assoc. ☎+℻ 01244 678 624.
Notts, Arnold & Carlton College ☎ 0115 952 0052. ℻ 0115 953 1230.
Plumpton College ☎ 01273 890 454. ℻ 01273 890 071. E-mail: staff@ plumpton.ac.uk
Scala School ☎+℻ 0171 281 3040.
Sotheby's ☎ 0171 408 5051. ℻ 0171 293 5961.
Vinform ☎ 0181 876 0110.
Wensum Lodge ☎ 01603 666 021. ℻ 01603 765 633.
West Suffolk College ☎ 01284 701 301. ℻ 01284 750 561. E-mail: info@westsuffolk.ac.uk
Wine & Spirit Education Trust ☎ 0171 236 3551. ℻ 0171 329 8712.
Wine Education Service ☎ 0181 886 0304.
Wine Wise ☎ 0171 254 9734.

Wine Holidays

Allez France & Great Escapes
📞 01903 748 100/
748 138. 📠 01903 745 044.

Arblaster & Clarke Wine Tours
📞 01730 893 344. 📠 01730
892 888.

Backroads 📞 01425 655 022.
📠 01425 655 177. E-mail: country-
lane@dial.pipex.com

The Cape Vine 📞 01604 648 768.
📠 01604 644 013. E-mail:
capevine@aol.com

DER Travel 📞 0171 290 1111.
📠 0171 629 7442.

Edwin Doran Travel 📞 0181 288
1000. 📠 0181 288 2955.

Francophiles Discover France 📞
0117 962 1975. 📠 0117 962 2642.

In the French Alps with Wink Lorch
📞 01494 677 728. 📠 07070
714 507.

Grenadier Travel 📞 01206 549 585.
📠 01206 561 337. E-mail:
james@grenadier.demon.co.uk

HGP Wine Tours 📞 01803 299 292.
📠 01803 292 008.

KD River Cruises Europe 📞 01372
742 033. 📠 01372 724 871.

Millers House Hotel 📞 01969 622
630. 📠 01969 623 570. E-mail:
hotel@millershouse.demon.co.uk

Moswin Tours 📞 0116 271 4982.
📠 0116 271 6016.

Page & Moy 📞 0116 250 7000.
📠 0116 254 9949.

Ski Gourmet and Winetrails 📞
01306 712 111. 📠 01306 713 504.

Ski Morgins 📞 01746 783 005.
📠 01746 783 005.

Sunday Times Wine Club Tours 📞
01730 895 353. 📠 01730 892 888.

Tanglewood Wine Tours 📞 01932
348 720. 📠 01932 350 861.

Travel Club of Upminster 📞 01708
227 260. 📠 01708 229 678.

UK Vineyards Assoc. 📞 01728 638
080. 📠 01728 638 442.

Wessex Continental Travel 📞+📠
01752 846 880.

**Wine Journeys Alternative Travel
Group** 📞 01865 315 678.
📠 01865 315 697/8/9.

Wine Accessories

GLASSES

Bibendum (Riedel range)
(see Page 253)

Conran Shop (Riedel range)
📞 0171 589 7401.
📠 0171 823 7015.

Dartington Crystal 📞 01805 626 262.
📠 01805 626 267.

Roberson (see Page 262)

Schott UK 📞 01785 223 688.

The Wine Glass Company
📞 01785 223 522.

CORKSCREWS

Screwpull (The Kitchenware
Merchants) 📞 01264 353 912.
📠 01264 356 396.

STORAGE

Abacus 📞 0181 991 9717.
📠 0181 991 9611.

Consort Wine Care Systems
📞 01635 33993. 📠 01635 41733.

Euro-cave 📞 0181 200 1266.
📠 0181 200 1792.

Smith & Taylor 📞 0171 627 5070.
📠 0171 622 8235.

Sowesco 📞 01935 826 333.
📠 01935 826 310.

Vin-Garde (Storage Cabinets) Ltd
📞+📠 01926 811 376.

WINE RACKS

A.&W. Moore 📞 0115 944 1434.
📠 0115 932 0735.

R.T.A Wine Racks 📞 01328 829 666.
📠 01328 829 667.

Spiral Cellars 📞 01372 279 166.
📠 01372 273 482.

The Wine Rack Company
📞+📠 01243 543 253.

A Million Cellars 📞+📠 0115 9728
559.

ANTIQUES

Bacchus Gallery 📞 01798 342 844.
📠 01798 342 634.

GENERAL WINE ACCESSORIES

Birchgrove Products Ltd. 📞 01483
533 400. 📠 01483 533 700.

The Hugh Johnson Collection
📞 0171 491 4912. 📠 0171 493
0602.

WINE PRESERVATION

Winesaver 📞 0131 266 1488.
📠 0131 226 1499.

CHILLING DEVICES

Chilla ☎ 0181 891 6464. FAX 0181 891 0464.
Vacu Products ☎ 01299 250 480. FAX 01299 251 599.
Coolbags & Boxes UK ☎ 0118 9333 331. FAX 0118 9333 579.

BOOKS

Richard Stanford ☎ 0171 836 1321.
Adnams (see Page 252)
Bibendum
(see Page 253)
Cooking The Books ☎+FAX 01633 400 150.

WINE CLUBS

Alston Wine Club ☎ 01434 381 338.
Amersham ☎ 01494 771 983.
Association of Wine Cellarmen ☎ 0181 871 3092.
Chandlers Cross ☎ 01923 264 718.
Charlemagne ☎ 0181 423 6338.
Cirencester ☎ 01285 641 126.
Confrèrie Internationale de St. Vincent ☎ 0113 267 9258. FAX 0113 228 9307. E-mail: asmalley@mcmail.com
Cornwall ☎ 01872 273 856.
Decant & Taste ☎ 01507 605 758.
Eastbourne ☎ 01323 725 528.
Garforth ☎ 0113 266 6322.
Goring & Streatley ☎ 01491 873 620.
Guild of Sommeliers ☎ 0161 928 0852.
Harrogate Medical ☎ 01423 503 129. FAX 01423 561 820.
Herefordshire ☎ 01432 275 656.
Hextable Wine Club ☎ 01732 823 345.
Hollingworth ☎ 01706 374 765. E-mail: peter-l@msn.com
Ightham Wine Club ☎ 01732 885 557.
Institute of Wines & Spirits ☎+FAX 01324 554 162.
International Wine and Food Society ☎ 0171 495 4191. FAX 0171 495 4172. E-mail: IWandFS@aol.com
L' Académie du Vin ☎ 01803 299 292. FAX 01803 292 008. E-mail: hgpwine@aol.com

Lay & Wheeler ☎ 01206 764 446. FAX 01206 560 002. Website: www.layandwheeler.co.uk
Leicester Evington ☎ 0116 231 4760. FAX 0116 287 5371.
Leicester Grand Union ☎ 0116 287 1662.
Lincoln Wine Society ☎+FAX 01522 680388.
London ☎ 0181 349 2260.
Maidenhead ☎ 01628 25577.
Manchester ☎ 01706 824 283.
Moreno ☎ 0171 286 0678.
Myster Wine Club ☎ 01633 893 485.
North Hampshire ☎ 01256 473 503.
Tanglewood Wine Society ☎ 01932 348 720. FAX 01932 350 861.
Preston ☎ 01772 254 251. FAX 01772 203 858.
Rochester ☎ 01634 848 345.
Scottish ☎ 01368 864 004.
Sittingbourne ☎ 01795 478 818.
West Hampstead ☎ 0171 794 3926.
Windsor and Eton ☎ 01753 790 188. FAX 01753 790 189. E-mail: sails@etonvintners.co.uk
Wine and Dine ☎ 0181 673 4439. FAX 0181 675 5543.
Wine Collectors' ☎ 01306 742 164.
Wine Schoppen ☎ 0114 255 3301. FAX 0114 255 1010.
Winetasters ☎ 01753 889 702.
York ☎+FAX 01904 691 628.

CROSS-CHANNEL SHOPPING

EastEnders Bulk Beer Warehouse
14 rue Gustave Courbet, 62100 Calais. ☎ (33) 3 21 34 53 33. FAX 3 21 97 61 22.
Normandy Wine Warehouse
71 avenue Carnot, 50100 Cherbourg. ☎ (33) 2 33 43 39 79. FAX 2 33 43 22 69.
Le Tastevin 9 rue Val, 35400 St.-Malo. ☎ (33) 2 99 82 46 56. FAX 2 99 81 09 69
Tesco Vin Plus Espace 122, Boulevard du Kent, Cité Europe, 62231

Coquelles. ☎ (33) 3 21 46 02 70. FAX 3 21 46 02 79.
Victoria Wine Unit 139, Cité Europe, rue de Douvres, 62231 Coquelles. ☎+FAX (33) 3 21 82 07 32.
The Wine Society 1 rue de la Paroisse, 62140 Hesdin. ☎ (33) 3 21 86 52 07. FAX 3 21 86 52 13.
The Wine & Beer Company
rue de Judee, Zone Industrielle Marcel Doret, 62100 Calais ☎ (33) 3 21 97 63 00. FAX 3 21 97 70 15.

INDEX

An index that can be used as a supplement to the A–Z (page 92)

C

D

H

I

O

N

P

Q

R

T

Y

Z

WINE ON THE WEB

If you enjoy
The Sunday Telegraph Good Wine Guide
visit Robert Joseph's
Good Wine Guide
site on the World Wide Web
at
http://www.goodwineguide.com
for news, competitions,
an electronic Wine Atlas, comment and links to over
200 wineries and merchants throughout the world.

Visit
http://www.wineschool.com
http://www.robertjoseph.com
for daily interactive food and wine updates
and
http://www.dk.com
for details of other Dorling Kindersley titles.